A LITERARY
HISTORY OF ROME

From the Origins to the Close of the Golden Age

A LITERARY HISTORY OF ROME

*From the Origins to the Close
of the Golden Age*

By

J. WIGHT DUFF

Edited by A. M. DUFF

BARNES & NOBLE INC.

NEW YORK

VXORI AMANTISSIMAE
LIBRORVM MEORVM
CVRIOSAE ADIVTRICI
HOC OPVS
D.D.D.

NOTE TO CORRECTED REPRINT

ALTHOUGH this reprint is mainly photographic, I have been able, thanks to the co-operation of the printer, to make a number of alterations in the text, and also to enlarge the bibliography, remedying omissions in the 1953 edition and including some works which have appeared since that edition went to press. In making corrections and in improving the bibliography I have had invaluable help from Professor G. B. A. Fletcher, of King's College (Newcastle-upon-Tyne) in the University of Durham, to whom I am very glad to record my gratitude.

A.M.D.

ABERYSTWYTH, 1959

PREFACE TO THIRD EDITION

FOR many years my father's two volumes on the literary history
of Rome have been out of print. It has been decided, to my great
pleasure, to re-issue the first volume, which carried the literary
history down to the close of the Golden Age; and it is hoped that a new
edition of the Silver Age volume will follow.

It has seemed best to reprint almost exactly as my father wrote; this
means that much of the bibliographical matter in the footnotes will
appear somewhat outdated to present-day scholars. I have therefore
compiled as an appendix a supplementary bibliography which may be
used along with my father's bibliographical footnotes.

I am very grateful to many friends whom I have consulted, and in
particular to my mother and Mr. Alun Hudson-Williams, Lecturer in
Classics at Aberystwyth, both of whom helped with the checking of the
proofs and with valuable advice. Moreover, I am glad to record the
help given by the printer's reader, and particularly that given by Mr.
Conan Nicholas who in addition to ordinary services amplified and
improved the index.

A.M.D.

UNIVERSITY COLLEGE OF WALES
ABERYSTWYTH, 1953

PREFACE TO FIRST EDITION

THIS volume endeavours to present a connected account of Latin literature in its earliest phases and in its best period. Some preliminary attention has been paid to the descent of the Romans, their language, and character. For the patient research wherewith scholars have brought together the often mutilated fragments of archaic Latin, literary history lies under a great debt. These are profoundly instructive as germs of later productions. In this work, by a sketch of tribal origins, of primitive simplicity in Roman life, of prominent features in national affairs, and of changes in social or intellectual conditions, the suggestion intended to be conveyed is that of a development towards complexity parallel to the development out of the old rude monuments of the language into the finish of Cicero or Virgil. Literary advance has been exemplified by noting new modes of thought, new fashions in composition, and the attainment of new suppleness in expression and new effects in metrical harmony.

Throughout, one of the aims has been to insist upon the permanence of the Roman type despite every novelty and despite the inrush of Greek influences. Hellenism notwithstanding, the civilisation of Rome —principles, aspirations, aesthetics—remained Roman. The Roman borrowed in a Roman way. Not merely passive and impressionable, his masculine vigour strongly controlled and moulded foreign material. The national aspects of the literature have, therefore, been emphasised.

In estimating literary movements and figures, English, French, German, and occasionally Italian authorities have been consulted. Aid obtained from these and from classical periodicals has been acknowledged in the notes. I am particularly conscious of obligations to the 1900 English edition of Teuffel's *History of Roman Literature*, which remains a great quarry of reference, though not always of inspiring criticism. M. Pichon's *Histoire de la littérature latine* has been frequently suggestive. Though it is impossible, and indeed would be undesirable, to divest the memory of critical judgements with which one has long been familiar, yet the book is not a compilation from other histories of Roman literature. The method has been, besides examining modern results, to weigh ancient evidence, and to record impressions made by an independent reading of each classic concerned. In the survey of eminent writers, then, the original sources touching their careers have been indicated, with the hope of stimulating interest in the foundations of our knowledge about ancient authors and books. Citations in the footnotes will, if the reader choose, enable him to test these foundations. To know where fact or theory comes from, to verify how far statements are authentic and how far constructed on guesswork, is obviously essential for the student. But this may have its fascination for the general reader too. A just conception of an author's genius and of the influences operative upon it involves inquiry into his exact date and the order of his writings, and only by reviewing the salient circumstances determining the genesis of great works can literature be shown to reflect not simply the creative mind, but also the communal spirit. Biography, therefore, has been employed to set a man of letters in his environment and to recreate such contemporary conditions as directed his choice of theme or mode of treatment. Similarly, the array of his forerunners and models is designed to suggest literary heredity; for here one deals with factors which, while they cannot explain individual genius, still contributed to make that genius what it was artistically. It is an author's historical significance which is gauged by chronicling his total literary output—lost works included—and by relating him to predecessors, to his own times, and in some degree to successors. But alongside of this historical significance, with its points of racial and literary evolution, the aesthetic significance of the artist claims appreciation. Here, with historical methods must be combined a humanistic attitude which essays through sympathy and taste to divine some portion of the mysterious beauty inherent in a masterpiece.

To support literary criticisms, illustrative passages have been introduced. In great measure, Latin has been relegated to notes and English translations given in the text, so as to render it more continuously readable for those who know little Latin. For these versions into English prose and a variety of metres I am myself responsible. Except a few published in magazines, they have been written for this work. They gave pleasure to compose: they will, I trust, give some pleasure to read.

A brief bibliography, chiefly of modern texts and reference works, and not intended to be exhaustive, is among the notes to each author. The rule in spelling Latin words has been to let the ancients spell in their own way. Classical quotations have *u*, not *v*; and *V*, not *U*. Thus, if cited as Latin, *Seruius* appears; but, if used in the course of an English sentence, no good purpose is served by giving anything but the usual form, 'Servius.' On similar lines, in quoting a scholar of the eighteenth century, his spelling is left untouched, and the *v* purposely retained, as well as his *Virgilius* for *Vergilius*.

The Cicero chapter had the signal advantage of being read by Dr. J. S. Reid, Fellow and Tutor of Gonville and Caius College and Professor of Ancient History in the University of Cambridge. I am much indebted to his kindness for several important modifications. I have to thank Professor R. S. Conway, of the University of Manchester, for discussing matters regarding Italic peoples, and Dr. W. M. Lindsay, Fellow of Jesus College, Oxford, and Professor of Humanity in St. Andrews University, for answering questions regarding his theory of Saturnian verse.

I am, further, very grateful to my wife, who wrote out the complete MS. of my book and gave constant help in proof-reading; to Mr. Basil Anderton, B.A., Public Librarian of Newcastle-upon-Tyne, who read the whole MS. and made many useful suggestions; and to other friends who, like Mr. Harry Anderson and Mr. Malcolm Quin, rendered assistance at different stages of what has been enjoyable though arduous work.

J.W.D.

NEWCASTLE UPON TYNE
31 *March* 1909

PREFACE TO SECOND EDITION

THE favourable reception accorded in this country and in America to *A Literary History of Rome* (*To the Close of the Golden Age*) has made a second edition necessary. In issuing it, with a few slight corrections, I feel impelled to express gratification at the extent to which critical opinion in journals and reviews of standing has signified approval of certain central aims of the book, namely, to indicate the relations of Latin literature with its environment in the national life and to insist on its essential and continuous Roman character. It has been an encouragement to observe that this conception has impressed competent judges as sound, and that the treatment of it has interested the general reader. An acceptable feature has evidently been the free employment of quotation from original sources; for by means of extracts in the text and references in the footnotes the great writers have been cited very largely in their own words to illustrate their particular qualities and significance. In this way readers have been furnished with some such first-hand material as might give point to the aesthetic criticism of literary masterpieces. The use of none but my own translations has secured some justification in the kind welcome given to the renderings in prose and verse.

Many reviewers have been good enough to express a wish that the history of the literature should be continued by me on similiar lines; and it is my intention, as far as the near future may provide the requisite leisure, to pursue my studies in the Latin of 'The Silver Age.'

J.W.D.

NEWCASTLE UPON TYNE

CONTENTS*

* More detailed analyses are given in the body of the book at the begining of
each chapter.

CONTENTS

Introduction

Chapter I

A FOREWORD ON ENVIRONMENT

Literature and Environment – The idea of Rome – Factors which
shaped Rome and the Romans – Nature, Descent, Family, State,
Religion.

THE history of Roman literature, like the history of Rome itself,
is an ever-widening circle. The city-state by the Tiber had, in
many generations, wrought itself through the stage of kingship
into the strongest republic, first of Latium and then of Italy, and had
grappled in deadly conflict with Carthaginian and with Greek, before
literature, in a true aesthetic sense, was evolved. It is natural, therefore,
as it is traditional, to date the beginning of the literature from the time of
Livius Andronicus, about 240 B.C., when Rome had already entered into
relations with the Mediterranean world, and was on the eve of rapid
expansion towards West and East. But the origins lie deeper. Roman
literature, as the written expression of the national genius, cannot be
understood independently of the circumstances and races which determined the growth and the character of the people. Magnetically drawing
writers and inspiration from every quarter of the known world, Rome,
although profoundly influenced by them, possessed through a process
of vital reaction the inalienable faculty of fixing her own impress upon
one and all. The prevailing tendency of thought and ambition was
centripetal, as in France it has been towards Paris. In a literary history
of Rome, contact with many provinces of the world geographical and
intellectual is of high significance; but the cardinal subject, first and
last, is Rome and the Romans.

This very idea of Rome — even though our concern here be with pagan
Rome mainly — is an idea so composite that one is inevitably thrown
back upon its elements. Which were the factors that moulded the
national character, and were therefore, in the ultimate resort, what may
be called the feeders of the literature? It is impossible to lose sight of —
though no history, and least of all a literary history, can hope exhaustively to discuss — the determining facts of existence which constituted
the Roman environment. Among the myriad factors of environment
which act upon and develop a people — proportionately more complex
than those which act upon its individuals — there are some which refuse

3

to be overlooked. External nature, descent, family life, religion, the state, with all their implications, may broadly summarise these. Under the head of nature, there is the factor of land, whether it be the ancestral home with its physical advantages and disadvantages for military, commercial, and colonial expansion, or new territory invaded and conquered; there is, too, the factor of immediate neighbourhood to other Italian tribes and peoples, who, whether in peace or war, modified the national ways of thought and the national mode of expressing thought in language. Under the head of descent, there are semi-biological questions of blood-inheritance and kinship. Under family life come the workings of domestic discipline and custom as well as traditional lore, partly in the form of historical legends, partly in the form of sacred usage. Under religion come observances and beliefs of permanent moment in shaping character. Under the state may be grouped the multitudinous and intricate traces graven on the Roman temperament by the long record of struggles within and without the city, its laws, its contact with foreign and distant peoples, notably with the Greeks, and its development of an imperial idea which was at once a political institution and an inspiring consecration.

Thus, in brief, the land, the city, the Latin people, and the other inhabitants of the peninsula, their languages, the general course of military, constitutional, economic, social, domestic, and religious development, together form a background which, though its details fall within the province of ethnologist or philologist or historian, must still broadly be kept in view for a discriminating estimate of the literature. The character produced in the people and the stage of civilisation attained by the social organism from age to age are essential to the appreciation of the greater authors. The more distinctly these varied factors are remembered, the better will they be seen to receive in poetry and prose an illustration and expression as definite as they do in other products of the Roman mind. Their variety does not detract from the fundamental unity of the idea of Rome. Determining germs of character, endowed with all the potentiality of imperial success, were present in the pastoral folk who settled on the Palatine Hill, just as the basic structure of the language was, notwithstanding copious literary experiments, innovations, and refinements, essentially what the mouths of the primitive herds and tillers of Latium had made it.

Chapter II

THE ORIGINS, GEOGRAPHICAL AND TRIBAL

Rome: Situation of the city – The land of Italy – Aspects of geography and climate – A country of contrasts – Variety of peoples in Italy – The complex heredity of the Latin people and of Latin literature – Etruscans and their enigma – The Italic tribes: Umbrians, Oscans, Sabellians, and Latins – Problems touching their relationship – Their kinship, enmity, and gradual progress towards union – The racial blends in Rome – Was there a non-Aryan strain?

A S IN Roman political history, so in Roman literature, geographical and ethnological considerations form the proper introduction. The central position of Rome and Latium in Italy and the central position of Italy among the peninsulas of the Mediterranean fitted Latin to be a world-language and a world-literature, just as they fitted Rome to be a world-power. The configuration of Italy, with its comparatively harbourless coast on the Adriatic and with its wide plains left between the Apennine range and the Tuscan sea, concentrated the earlier chapters of Roman expansion on the West and South. As a consequence, Hellenic civilisation acted on Rome for generations through the Greek settlements in Southern Italy and Sicily before contact with Greece itself became easy. The situation of Rome[1] on the Tiber[2] destined her to be the emporium[3] for the towns of the plain-country of Latium; and

---

[1] *Roma* is perhaps 'stream-town,' the town by the *rumon*, the old name of the Tiber (Servius ad *Aen.* viii. 90), from the Ind.-Eur. root *sreu-*, flow: *cf.* Gk. ῥέ(F)ω, ῥεῦμα, Irish *sruaim*, stream, O.H.G. *stroum*. See W. M. Lindsay, *Latin Language*, 1894, p. 307. But Lindsay later regarded *Roma* as an Etruscan word: see his Introd., p. x, to G. Dennis's *Cities and Cemeteries of Etruria*, 1907.

[2] *Tiberis* may mean 'mountain-stream.' H. Nissen interprets it as 'Bergstrom,' and compares *Tibur* and (since Latin *b* = Oscan *f*) *Tifernus* (mons, amnis), *Tifernum*, *Tifata*. Varro, *L.L.*, v. 29, declares it a non-Latin word. Another old name of the river was *Albula* (*Italische Landeskunde*, Bd. I., 1883, p. 308).

[3] This favourable situation, which Ihne rather disparages, cannot be better summarised than in the words which Livy (V. liv. 4) puts into the mouth of Camillus when that leader is urging the Romans not to desert Rome for Veii: 'Non sine causa dei hominesque hunc urbi condendae locum elegerunt, saluberrimos colles, flumen opportunum, quo ex mediterraneis locis fruges deuehantur, quo maritimi commeatus accipiantur, mare uicinum ad commoditates nec expositum nimia propinquitate ad pericula classium externarum,

5

the natural outlets by river and sea in this case also looked westwards. But if the back of the peninsula is turned upon the East — and Eastern influences consequently came slowly upon her — Italy faces Spain, as it were 'El Dorado' coveted by both Rome and Carthage, while her toe points to Africa and almost touches Sicily with its once varied population of native Sicels, Phoenicians, and Greeks.

The great mountain barrier of the Alps, to the north of what we call the plains of Lombardy, formed rather an apparent than a real protection to ancient Italy[1] against invasion from Central Europe. The Alps are more easily climbed from their northern sides; and this geographical fact encouraged the successive inroads of races who made up the motley population of Italy in antiquity. The mountains which form so distinctive a feature of the peninsula from north to south were not found impassable. They did not prevent intercourse between different tribes. They were a boon to the land, because they tempered the 'anguish of the solstice' with their breezes, made pasture-grounds for flocks, offered sites for villages and towns safe from the malaria of swampy plains, and granted seasonable refuge to the 'tired denizen' of Rome, eager, like Horace, to escape from the dust, din, pestilence, and sweltering heat of the capital. They also proved a means of developing hardy breeds of Italic stock, in contrast to the enervated inhabitants of many of the Greek settlements, whose enterprise succumbed before the temptations of prosperity and the half-tropical summer of the South. Italy[2] has always been a land of contrasts, with climatic conditions ranging from intense heat to intense cold; with soil rich in corn, oil, wine, and pasture, so that perforce agriculture bulked largely in its life and its literature; but also with fever-haunted marshes and gaunt, barren mountain ranges. Its inhabitants were highlanders of hardy frugality and, at the other extreme, urban voluptuaries, forgetful, and usually disdainful, of old-fashioned country ways (*prisci mores* and *rusti-*

regionum Italiae medium. Ad incrementum urbis natum unice esse locum, argumento est ipsa magnitudo urbis.' This mention of the 'very healthy hills' of Rome implies by contrast the recognition of the danger of malaria in low-lying and swampy districts. It is significant that Fever was personified. The goddess Febris had three temples in Rome.

[1] The original 'uetus Italia' ('ox-land,' *cf. uitulus*) meant only a small south-western portion of the peninsula, from Paestum, about fifty miles south of Naples, to near Metapontum, on the Gulf of Tarentum. Early in the third century B.C. 'Italia' had officially extended north to the Apennines, with the river Rubicon on the east and the Macra on the west as boundaries. It was not till the days of Augustus that 'Italia' included the basin of the Po and was bounded by the Alps.

[2] H. Nissen, in his *Italische Landeskunde*, Bd. I., 1883, deals with seas, mountains, rivers, volcanic districts of Italy, with the general features of its climate and vegetation, as well as its peoples. A shorter treatment is given by J. Jung (I. Müller's *Handbuch d. Klass Alt.*, III. iii. 1), ed. 2, 1897, pp. 3–70. See also E. A. Freeman, *Historical Geog. of Europe*, ed. 3, by J. B. Bury, 1903, ch. iii (esp. pp. 43 *sqq.* for the peoples).

citas),[1] in which, however, some of the best thinkers and statesmen of Rome saw the political asset of moral worth.

Corresponding to this variety of physical characteristics, there was in the peninsula a striking medley of peoples, among which four stocks are prominent — Kelts in the north, Greeks on the southern and the south-western seaboard, Etruscans to the north-west of Latium, and in central and southern Italy a variety of Italic peoples, Umbrian, Oscan, Latin, and Sabellian. An aboriginal stratum is represented by scattered traces of the Iberian stock — certainly non-Aryan — which peopled Spain; by the Ligurian mountaineers round the Gulf of Genua (Genoa), who used to be pronounced a non-Aryan people of Basque affinity; and by the Iapygians, who may have come from Illyricum, rather, perhaps, round than across the Adriatic, and been driven by later comers to their remote southern heel of the land.

Relics of the Stone Age or of an early Mediterranean race,[2] or, again, of a period contemporary with the 'Mycenaean' in Greece, have been comparatively less important in Italy, and, in any case, are too remote from literature to concern us here. The case of Italy is not that of Greece where even 'the braves who lived before Agamemnon' have left echoes of their fame in Homer, and where the roots of the earliest literature must be found in the civilisation of the second millennium B.C. The fabulous connexion of Rome with Troy, which in its treatment by Virgil became one of the finest ornaments of Roman literature, throws no real light on this prehistoric darkness. Before we know the relation of the early strata of the population to the later Italian and Roman civilisation, before, indeed, we fully know who Latins and Romans were, and in what order among the Italic tribes they came into Italy, much evidence has yet to be accumulated. Linguistic connexion does not settle racial connexion. Racial connexion must be established in the last resort by the evidence of archaeology, and of ethnology aided by the investigations of the anatomist and craniologist.

The Romans were, it is now generally admitted, of mixed blood. In them met different Aryan strains, perhaps even non-Aryan elements. The ancient tradition that their Ramnes, Tities, and Luceres stood for three stocks — Latin, Sabine, and Etruscan — represents a truth. Even Mommsen's high authority has failed to convince scholars that the Romans were so free from alien admixture as he would have it. A strong

[1] Pliny (*Ep.*, I. xiv. 4), though himself a good example of *urbanitas*, uses *rusticitas* in a good sense, not as mere clownishness. He admires Brixia for being in a district of Italy which keeps the old simplicity of life ('multum adhuc uerecundiae, frugalitatis atque etiam rusticitatis antiquae retinet ac seruat').

[2] The Neolithic culture of the Terremare represented by lake-dwellings in the plains of the Po, but discovered in Latium and Campania as well, is to be assigned to the aboriginal 'Ligurian' race, who were conquered by Siculan and Umbrian invaders from across the Alps. It is right, however, to add that some authorities consider the Ligurians to have been the Aryan vanguard, and the pile-dwellers to have been 'Itali.'

Sabine blend is the only explanation of many early stories of conflict and alliance,[1] just as Etruscan predominance in Rome itself is the only explanation of the legends about the Tarquin kings.[2] It is when the composite descent of the Latin people is realised that the need is felt for further help from philology, anthropology, and archaeology in the solution of problems important in their bearing on the institutions, folklore, and literature. The action of heredity upon the Roman character, and upon the language too, involves questions of baffling complexity. Many popular customs, characteristics, and beliefs must prove less inscrutable when knowledge can separate them, according to their origin, into borrowings from abroad, direct inheritances from the past, or more subtle atavistic tendencies. Questions such as these arise naturally: How much was Etruscan in Rome? What does Etruscan mean? Where did the Etruscans come from? How far did Etruscan blood leaven Rome as Etruscan thought and art did? How much of Rome was Sabine? Is Sabine virtually the same in race and speech as Latin? Which were the first of the Italic tribes to settle in the peninsula? And what is the relation of Roman and Latin to them? What effect was wrought on the Roman by his kinsmen the Samnites, or his more distant kinsmen the Kelts?

Supposing these and other queries regarding racial traits could receive final answer, and supposing on the linguistic side we knew more exactly the parts played among the old languages of Central Italy by dialects like Oscan and Umbrian, we should still have, from the standpoint of literature, to confront fresh problems. Roman literature, from what in an aesthetic sense may be called its real birth, in the third century B.C., was largely the work of men who, though they wrote at Rome, were not Romans. There was in the literature, as among the people, much that was exotic. Andronicus was a Greek; Plautus an Umbrian; Ennius a Calabrian, who averred that he possessed three souls corresponding to his three languages — Oscan, Greek, and Latin. Terence was African. Caecilius, holder of the premier place in the drama between Plautus and Terence, was a manumitted Insubrian Gaul. In Virgil certain traits were possibly Keltic,[3] while Livy's

---

[1] *E.g.*, the relations of Romulus and the Sabine king, Titus Tatius. Of the Rape of the Sabine women, Greenidge remarks that in its least significance it 'reveals the fact of the close tie of intermarriage between Rome and a non-Latin community' (*Roman Public Life*, p. 290). The presence of Sabine families in Rome like the Titurii partly accounts for the variations of view regarding Tarpeia, who in some accounts is a traitress, in others a heroine. See Ettore Pais, *Ancient Legends of Roman History*, trans. by M. E. Cosenza, 1906, chap. v.

[2] Ettore Pais discusses this, *op. cit.*, chap. vii.

[3] To mention the 'Keltic note' is to incense some critics who believe this element to have been exaggerated by many writers since Matthew Arnold published his lectures on *The Study of Celtic Literature*. It may even be that the Keltic proportion of the people of France has been overstated, and yet it is not altogether fanciful in Pichon to recognise certain qualities of his own country in Roman writers. 'Les Gaulois Cisalpins ont déjà bien des traits de l'esprit

'Patavinity' was also partly of the North. It is prophetic of the cosmopolitan character of Roman literature that from the outset its history points the inquirer beyond Rome itself and Latium to the effect produced on the Roman nature by Umbrian and Oscan, Carthaginian and Greek, and by the Roman nature on them. Later, with the Empire, the literature became less purely a literature of the capital or of Italy. Spain gave birth to the Senecas, Lucan, Columella, Quintilian, and Martial in classical times; Transalpine Gaul and Africa, like other provinces, developed their own centres of learning and their own writers, both Pagan and Christian. Ausonius and St. Paulinus were Gauls; Apuleius, Tertullian, Arnobius, and St. Augustine were Africans. After Nero's death, as Tacitus remarked, men discovered the secret that emperors could be made elsewhere than at Rome.[1] It soon followed that Roman literature could also be written elsewhere, though the imperial city never ceased to exercise her potent spell.

Of the peoples in Italy, those with whom Rome was most concerned for many generations, and who must engage our attention briefly, were the Etruscans and the various Italic tribes. The Etruscans are the standing riddle of Italian ethnology. There is, however, now something like general agreement that neither the race nor the language belonged to the Indo-European family. A thick-set, fleshy race, they were manifestly alien among the slender Italians. Their inscriptions, written in an adaptation of the Greek alphabet, can be read, and at least partially understood. But their *provenance* is a mystery.[2] By ethnologists they have been brought from Central Europe, and especially from the Rhaetian Alps; they have been brought from the East, and especially, in accordance with ancient tradition recorded both by Herodotus and Tacitus, from Lydia;[3] they have been classed as Mongolian; they have been brought from the South ultimately, as 'Pelasgians,' and as a branch of the primitive Mediterranean race of African descent.[4] What-

---

français, la clarté, l'équilibre, la mesure harmonieuse, le naturel, la douceur et la grâce; la simplicité passionnée de Catulle et de Virgile, l'éloquence souple et lumineuse de Tite-Live, l'ingénieuse finesse de Pline le Jeune, nous font reconnaître en eux nos vrais compatriotes' (*Historie de la littérature latine*, ed. 4, 1908, p. 5).

[1] Tac., *Hist.*, I. iv.: 'Euolgato imperii arcano posse principem alibi quam Romae fieri.'

[2] Modern investigators are not so dogmatic as J. W. Donaldson, who dismissed the legend that the Etruscans were Lydians as 'entirely destitute of historical foundation,' and declared that 'unless the Etruscans were old Low Germans of the purest Gothic stock, there is no family of men to whom they could have belonged'! (*Varronianus*, 3rd ed., 1860, p. 18).

[3] The indifference to paternity, which implies descent traced through the mother and a system of female kinship, is regarded by J. G. Frazer as confirming 'the common opinion which modern historians have too lightly set aside that the Etruscans were of Lydian origin' (*Lectures on the Early History of the Kingship*, 1905, p. 248).

[4] 'The Etruscans are western Pelasgians,' says Prof. Sergi, *The Mediterranean Race*, 1901.

ever the origin of this mysterious people, the 'Rasena,' much is clear about their power, their civilisation, and their influence on Rome. They once ruled from the Alps to Campania, and their strength centred in a league of twelve cities, perhaps a model for the Latin League. In the eighth century B.C., their commerce began to rival that of the Phoenicians, and they exploited the mineral wealth of Sardinia, Corsica, and Elba. In the sixth century B.C., they combined with the Carthaginians to ruin the Greek colony at Alalia in Corsica. A long period of power elapsed before they were checked in the south, or crippled and confined by Gauls in the north. Workers in metal, builders of fortress-towns, makers of roads and drains, they left an indelible impress upon Italy. With works of Greek art for models, they often distorted their beauty to a tendency towards the grotesque, the sombre, and sometimes the brutal.[1] Many of their religious notions, much of their ritual, magic, and soothsaying, their divination through the entrails of victims, the insignia of their magistrates, their bloodthirsty amusements, and their dramatic performances, exerted a deep effect upon the younger civilisation of Rome. Something Etruscan has been remarked,[2] perhaps rightly, in the obscurity of Persius. It seems more strained to cite Propertius and Tacitus as typical Etruscans; for Propertius was at most an Umbrian borderer, and the birthplace of Tacitus is too uncertain to form either the basis or the example of a theory.

Of the Italic tribes who inhabited Central Italy, it should be said that their proper grouping among themselves and their relationship to the Latins are matters not yet absolutely settled. Their area may be fairly well mapped out by the places in which their linguistic remains have been discovered. The chief example of Umbrian consists of the Iguvinian or 'Eugubine' bronze tablets, dealing with the ritual of a priestly brotherhood, and found at Iguvium, now Gubbio: and one of the most important of Oscan inscriptions is the *Tabula Bantina*, containing a set of municipal regulations applicable to Bantia, which lies S.E. from Horace's birthplace, Venusia. That Umbrians, Oscans, Sabellians, and Latins were peoples closely akin and that they spoke allied dialects, we know; but the period and the order of their entering Italy are still largely matters of speculation. It has been put forward as a surmise of high probability that about the time of the Dorian immigration into Greece, some ten centuries before the Christian era, many Italic peoples

---

[1] Some relations of Etruscan to Greek art are traced by Jules Martha in *L'Archéologie étrusque et romaine*, esp. ch. iii. Duruy remarks, 'One particular feature of Etruscan manners is, however, in absolute contradiction to the Greek manners. This sensual people loved to heighten pleasure by scenes of death' (*History of Rome*, Eng. trans., Introd. chap. iii).

[2] By Pichon, *op. cit.*, p. 5: 'Les auteurs originaires de l'Étrurie ont quelque chose de plus pénible, de plus tourmenté: ils sont obscurs, comme si la langue et l'esprit de Rome leur étaient moins familiers: Perse et Properce sont du nombre, et si Tacite, comme on l'a souvent cru, était né en Étrurie, il ne ferait pas exception.'

were displaced by the invasion of the Etruscans.[1] But it is more likely
that this displacement was due to the expansion rather than the original
appearance of the Etruscans.[2] The Umbri, traditionally the first of the
Italic stock to settle in Italy, seem to have been dispossessed by the
Etruscans of their wider domains from sea to sea, and when driven
eastwards left many place-names in Etruria to mark their older limits.[3]
The Oscans,[4] in the narrower sense, were a Campanian tribe; but the
term 'Oscan' is broadly used to include Samnite, as by Livy when he
records the fact that in war with the Samnites a Roman consul employed
spies who knew the Oscan tongue.[5] Possibly this implies rather similarity than identity of language; the Oscans may have spread over
Campania, Lucania, and Apulia before the Samnites settled as their
neighbours. The tradition of the Sabine origin of the Samnites is supported by philology and refers them to the Sabellian group, which
includes such tribes as the Paeligni, Marrucini, and Vestini. It has been
doubted whether any great difference existed between Sabines and
Latins. Recent research more than ever seems to prove that Latins and
Romans were essentially the same people as Sabines and Samnites.[6]
The theory that the bearers of ethnic names ending in -ci[7] were earlier
Indo-European inhabitants of Central Italy than the bearers of ethnic
names in -ni (i.e., that Osci, Volsci, Aurunci, etc., preceded Sabini,
Latini, Romani, etc.) imports considerable order and intelligibility
into the confused question of the peopling of Italy by the Italic stocks.
It is for archaeology and ethnology to adduce evidence to prove or dis-
prove that in primitive Latium there were two strata of population, both
Indo-European, but differing in customs and culture—one the Volsci,
pile-dwellers, using bronze and burying their dead; and the second
the Sabini, a race of Keltic affinities, using iron and burning their dead.[8]

[1] See W. Deecke's *Italy*, trans. by H. A. Nesbit, 1904.
[2] 'The ancestors of the Latin, Umbrian, and Oscan tribes found Italy
already occupied by them' (i.e., the Etruscans), says W. M. Lindsay in
Introd. to his ed. of Dennis's *Cities and Cemeteries of Etruria*, 1907. He believes
the immigration of the Etruscans belongs to a far earlier time than that of the
Italic peoples.   [3] R. S. Conway, *Italic Dialects*, 1897, i., p. 395.
[4] *Osci* (older *Opsci*, Gk. 'Οπικοί) came early into contact with Etrurians
and Greeks, and were probably the earliest of the Italic peoples to borrow an
alphabet and write down their language.
[5] Livy X. 20, 'gnarosque Oscae linguae, exploratum quid agatur, mittit.'
[6] 'Essi (i.e., Sabini, Hirpini, Campani, Romani, ed altri) sono, credo io,
essenzialmente un popolo solo. . . . Soltanto gli accidenti della storia fecero i
Sanniti rivali invece che fratelli dei Romani' (R. S. Conway, *I due strati nella
popolazione indo-europea dell' Italia antica*, in *Rivista d'Italia*, August 1903).
[7] In Central Italy tribal names in -no-, *Latini, Sabini, Frentani, Hirpini,*
'seem to belong to the speech of a later stratum of population which everywhere
subdued the bearers, some of whom must have been the authors, of the names in
-co- (*Osci, Volsci, Aurunci, Hernici, Pollusca, Etrusci, Falisci*): cf. *Sidi-ci-ni,
Marru-ci-ni*, where the order of the suffixes is significant' (R. S. Conway, *Ital.
Dial.*, i., Pref. ix).
[8] This is Prof. Conway's contention in the Italian paper already cited.
Similar views were maintained in Prof. Ridgeway's paper *Who were the Romans?*
read before the British Academy, April 24, 1907 (*Athenaeum*, May 4).

The kinship of Latins, Sabellians, and Umbrians was not consciously present to their minds as a force making for amity. Some of Rome's fiercest feuds were with her nearest kin. The rise of Rome from Latin town to mistress of Italy never appears more wonderful than when it is realised that Italy at first contained no principle of union so wide as the Greek pan-hellenic sentiment. Autonomous as the different Greek states were, they had a common national spirit brought home to them by the acknowledged kinship of all Hellenes in contrast with 'barbarians,' by sharing in appeals to the Delphic Oracle, and by the athletic contests at Olympia. The groups of Italian peoples were more isolated. There was a limited community of feeling among the Latins who observed the festival of the Alban Mount; and there was a recognition of the connexion between the Sabines and the other Sabellian tribes in the old legend about the observance of a *uer sacrum* resulting in the despatch of settlers from among the younger tribesmen, some of whom became the Samnites with their ox, some the Picentines with their woodpecker, others the Hirpini with their wolf.[1] But, broadly speaking, the ethnically related Latins, Sabellians, and Umbrians recognised no closer bonds among themselves than they did with other inhabitants of the peninsula—Etruscans, Gauls, Iapygians, and Greeks. It is true that in time 'Rome becomes the great frontier power, the bulwark of the group of blood-related nations against the foreign-speaking Tuscan and the Gaul, whose kinship with herself she had forgotten';[2] and yet she was slow to overcome her exclusiveness. The late admission of the Italian *socii* to Roman citizenship proves the narrowness of conception which prevailed almost to the eve of empire. It was the imperial system, teaching through actual circumstances, which widened the views of the Roman beyond anything which the Greeks had ever imagined in the way of confederate politics.

The primitive Romans and primitive Rome had little in them to suggest their future greatness, literary and imperial. It would have been surprise enough to hear a prophecy that they would outshine even their neighbour Alba. They sprang from Italian folk whose life was mainly agricultural and pastoral. The kernel of the city was the square enclosure of the Palatine Hill, the 'pasture-ground'[3] of the herds and flocks of the pre-historic Roman shepherds. From this primitive *Roma Quadrata* the settlement by the Tiber widened into one of seven elevations—a *septimontium* which anticipated, though it did not equal, the City of the

[1] These animals may be associated with the tribes as totems.
[2] A. H. J. Greenidge, *Roman Public Life*, 1901, p. 290.
[3] *Palatium, Palatinus*, like the shepherds' deity *Pales*, are probably connected with the root in *pasco, pabulum*, etc. But the meaning has been given as 'wandering-place' (*cf. palari*) of the cattle. Much misdirected learning and fancy in deriving the word may be found recorded in *Sex. Pompei Festi De Verborum Significatu quae supersunt cum Pauli Epitome*, ed. W. M. Lindsay, 1913, p. 245.

Seven Hills enclosed within the ramparts of Servius Tullius. It is not certain how far the extension of Rome to the Servian limits implies the blending of *uici* or *pagi* racially distinct and politically independent. Much questioning has arisen as to whether Rome amalgamated varied ethnic elements, Latin, Sabine, and Etruscan,[1] even in the earliest period of her growth. It has already been pointed out that the names of the three primitive tribes, Ramnes, Tities, and Luceres, have been held to argue a mixture of Roman, Sabine, and Etruscan blood. Some would carry the blend of racial types in the Roman community still further back into the mists of primeval history before the coming of men of Indo-European blood. Burial, it is argued, was the custom, not of the Aryan race, but of the indigenous Mediterranean race, from which sprang in time the Roman *plebs*. Their town on the Palatine dates from an epoch effaced by heroic fables, when the valley of the Seven Hills formed a swamp and the Palatine was dotted with huts made of reeds. This view pictures Aryan immigrants who practised cremation finding in Italy an aboriginal people, and would endeavour to trace the 'autochthonous' race of Ausonia in the plebeians and the later Aryan arrivals in the patricians.[2] Even if this hypothesis of a non-Aryan[3] element in the Roman is not accepted, it remains clear that different racial strains met in him, as they have done in so many of the great nationalities in history.

[1] Declaring, as already indicated, that the name 'Rome' is Etruscan, Prof. Lindsay adds, 'It must have been an Etruscan town or village long before Romulus and the Latins appeared on the scene' (Introd. to ed. of Dennis's *Cities and Cemeteries of Etruria*, 1907, p. x).
[2] The 'plébéiens ingenieux et diserts' are thus contrasted with the 'patriciens pleins de courage et de foi' by Anatole France, who gives this theory an interesting dress in *Sur la pierre blanche*.
[3] It will be noted that the theory of *Sur la pierre blanche* brings in a stratum of population which is not part of Prof. Conway's theory in *I due strati nella popolazione indo-europea dell' Italia antica*.

Chapter III

THE LATIN LANGUAGE—
ITS HISTORY AND QUALITIES

The Latin language – Its affinities with Greek, and especially with
Keltic – Sister Italic dialects – Persistence of the dialects – In-
fluence of the dialects on Latin – Main periods of the language –
Cultured diction and the vernacular – Characteristics of plebeian
Latin – Effect of spoken Latin on literature – Developments in the
history of the literary language – Latin after the classical period –
The chief qualities of Latin – Lack of the Greek lightness and
variety – Positive merits – Clumsiness overcome by perseverance –
Roman complaints about the language – The impress of Cicero
and Tertullian upon Latin – Lasting correspondence between
language and people – Horace's attitude to novelties in diction
more liberal than Caesar's – Supreme mastery achieved in the
classical age.

LATIN, at first the language spoken by the Latini, the men of the
plains to the left of the lower reaches of the Tiber, became the
language of a great empire and of a great literature. It did more
than achieve official and literary greatness. Its spoken form became the
parent of the modern languages of Western Europe. Belonging to the
Indo-European or Indo-Germanic family, it has marked affinities with
Greek, and still better marked affinities with the Keltic group, as
represented by the ancient Gaulish, Irish, and Welsh.[1] Apart from a
mass of common roots, striking grammatical forms shared by Latin and
Keltic point to a period when the ancestral forms of the Keltic and of
the Italic tongues must have been spoken in close proximity. Such
similarities are, among verbs, the passive in *-r*;[2] imperfects and futures
in *-bh-* (the Latin *-bam* and *-bo*); among nouns, formations in *-tio*,
tion-is, corresponding to Irish *-tiu*, and certain datives plural in *-bhos*
(Gaulish *matrebo(s)*, Old Irish *mātrib*, Latin *mātribus*, in early poetry
mātribu'). On these and other grounds, a 'Kelto-Italic' period rather

[1] The linguistic relations between Keltic and Latin are discussed in E.
Windisch's chapter on 'Keltische Sprache,' contributed to Gröber's *Grundriss d.
romanischen Philologie*, Bd. I., 1888, pp. 283–312.
[2] P. Giles, points out that Zimmer in Kuhn's *Zeitschrift für vergleichende Sprachforschung*, 30, p. 240, considers this identity of form has another
explanation (see *A Short Manual of Comparative Philology*, ed. 2, 1901, p. 26).

than a 'Graeco-Italic' is likely to have preceded the invasion of the peninsula by the ancestors of the Italic tribes.

The minutiae of the relationship of Latin to the sister Italic dialects, Umbrian, Oscan, and Sabellian, must fall to the province of linguistic study.[1] It is noteworthy that some of the dialects labialise an original guttural sound which remains guttural in Latin (Latin *quis*, Oscan and Umbro-Volscian *pis*), and that a curious parallelism exists not only among Greek dialects but also within the Keltic group, where Welsh often shows *p* against the Irish guttural. Other characteristics in phonology, inflexion, and syntax, which distinguish Latin and Faliscan on the one hand from most of the Italic dialects on the other, do not concern us here. The truth is that, although the study of dialect inscriptions has thrown light on many Latin forms and constructions, the Italic dialects do not play the part in Latin literature which the Hellenic dialects do in Greek. Many of these latter became literary. With the exception of Oscan, there is no evidence that the Italic dialects did so.

Yet two matters deserve passing comment; firstly, the lingering of the dialects in Italy has a bearing on the history of the language, for it shows how slowly Latin won; secondly, the known presence of dialect words in Latin suggests that, had the ancients been closer investigators in this field, and could modern philology obtain fuller data, the influence of the dialects on the language and literature would stand out as really considerable.

Under the first of these heads it is significant that by 240 B.C., at the birth of the artistic literature, Rome had conquered, though she had not successfully attached to herself, the peoples of the peninsula.[2] While she grappled with Hannibal, there were widespread efforts on the part of Italians and Kelts for liberty and against the Romanisation which followed the war with Pyrrhus. After Hannibal's repulse the process of Romanisation again went forward. The evidence of inscriptions best enables one to realise the gradual spread of Latin in Italy. For instance, in the central Oscan area, Larinum,[3] a town of the tribe of the Frentani, had adopted Latin as its official language by 200 B.C., influenced, doubtless, by neighbourhood to the Latin colony founded at Luceria in 314 B.C. In the South Oscan region the *Tabula Bantina*, which may be dated

[1] For a general account of the early languages of Italy, see W. Deecke's chapter on 'Die italischen Sprachen,' contributed to Gröber's *Grundriss d. rom. Phil.*, Bd. I., pp. 335–350.

[2] Of the 'non-Italic' dialects, Etruscan maintained its individuality obstinately. A native Etruscan drama still flourished in the time of Cicero. One representative of it was known to Varro: 'Volnius qui tragoedias Tuscas scripsit' (Varro, *De Ling. Lat.*, v. 55). In the second century of our era Etruscan was still spoken. Gellius implies this in his tale of the man who surprised his hearers with Old Latin words, as much as if he were speaking Tuscan or Gallic (*Noct. Att.*, XI. vii. 4).

[3] R. S. Conway, *Italic Dialects*, i., p. 206.

from 133 to 118 B.C.,[1] shows that the Latin alphabet, if not the Latin language, could be read in Apulia in the second century B.C. Strabo (66 B.C.–21 A.D.) expressly testifies that by his day the Lucanians had become Romans, that is, spoke Latin.[2] But there is the contrasted phenomenon of the persistence of certain dialects. Only gradually did Latin oust them. The victory of the language followed far in the wake of the victory of the state. Even so, it was not an absolutely uniform language which spread over Italy. Needless to say, local peculiarities of sound and idiom frequently prevailed. There were many parts of Italy where Oscan was spoken long after Latin was common in Spain and Southern Gaul. Many of the dialects, for example, Paelignian,[3] spoken in the region to which Ovid belonged, lasted at any rate to the middle of the first century B.C. At Pompeii, where the inhabitants, before they fell under Rome, had been, according to Strabo (V. iv. 8), successively Oscans, Etruscans with Pelasgians, and then Samnites, the old Oscan survived side by side with Latin in the first century B.C.[4] To judge from the ephemeral *graffiti* found on the walls, Oscan lasted right up to the destruction of the town by the eruption of 79 A.D.[5]

The influence of the dialects is an allied matter. The longer their survival, the deeper their influence presumably was. In especial, Oscan, once a literature,[6] the original language of the Atellan plays and of a people in prolonged contact with both Greeks and Romans, is certain to have affected Latin. It is significant that, among the pioneers of Roman literature, Ennius,[7] Pacuvius, and Lucilius were born in Oscan-speaking districts. Such Italic influence upon Latin is better appreciated by the scientific philologist of to-day than by the old Roman scholars themselves. A great amount of the closest philological and epigraphical research has gone to secure the results already reached. The inquiry is mainly for the science of language, but the conclusions are obviously germane to questions in the literature of Rome. Though ancient philologists like Varro, Macrobius, Servius, Festus in his abridgement of Verrius, and Paulus in turn in his abridgement of Festus, do record glosses[8] from such dialects as Oscan, there is great reason to wish for fuller information from antiquity. These matters are more than lin-

---

[1] Conway, *op. cit.*, i., p. 23.   [2] Cited by Conway, *op. cit.*, i., p. 11.
[3] *Ibid.*, i., p. 234.   [4] *Ibid.*, i., p. 55.
[5] C. D. Buck, *Grammar of Oscan and Umbrian*, p. 4; Giles, *Manual Compar. Phil.*, ed. 2, p. 569.
[6] This was Mommsen's view, and is widely accepted; but it has been denied, *e.g.*, M. Schanz, in his *Geschichte der röm. Litt.* (I. Müller's *Handb. d. klass. Alter.*, Bd. VIII), ed. 3, 1907, § 6, referring to Oscan as well as Umbrian, remarks: 'Das politische Übergewicht des römischen Volkes hinderte die Entwicklung jener verwandten Idiome, sie wurden keine Litteratursprachen und gingen schliesslich zu Grund.' *Cf.* ed. 4 (revised by C. Hosius), 1927, § 4.
[7] Not only are there 'Oscisms' in Ennius, but even some of his Greek importations reveal an Oscan form, *e.g.*, *dracuma* from δραχμή, and *lucinus* from λύχνος, F. G. Mohl, *Introd. à la chronol. du lat. vulgaire*, 1899, p. 50.
[8] These will be found collected in Conway's *Italic Dialects*, vol. i.

guistic. It is illuminating to have Macrobius[1] tell us that Punic and Oscan words had once been used in Latin, and that Virgil did not reject non-Latin words (*peregrina uerba*), such as the Gallic *uri* for 'buffaloes' (*Georg.*, ii. 374) and the word almost certainly Oscan[2] which he uses to describe 'crumpled horns' — *camuris hirtae sub cornibus aures* (*Georg.*, iii. 55). Varied flavour is given to a Latin passage if it is recognised to contain words derived from, let us say, one of the '*f*-dialects'[3] of Italy, words like *bufo, rufus, scrofa, tufus, uafer*, or other even commoner words like *caesius, casa, caseus, omasum, rosa*, whose dialectic origin is likely.[4] A proper name, too, gains in signficance if its *provenance* can be discovered; for example, *Caesar*, the ending of which is probably Oscan.[5] *Pompeius* and *Pontius* are Oscan equivalents of the Roman *Quinctius*, a gentile name formed from the ordinal Quintus. *Nero* is Sabine for 'man' or 'manly,' and is cognate with ἀνήρ. To be enabled authoritatively to isolate Umbrian elements in Plautus and Oscan elements in Ennius would possess more than philological value, just as truly as proving the presence of typical Warwickshire words in the text of Shakespeare.

What gives the Italic dialects great significance is the part they played in the formation of the general Latin of Italy. Mohl,[6] in accord with Sittl, strongly contends that the provincial Latin of Italy, *i.e.* the *rusticitas Latina* modified by the words and pronunciation of such tribes as Oscans, Volscians, Hernicans, Paelignians, Marsians, and Picentines, was the almost exclusive source of the vulgar Latin of the Empire, and therefore all-important for understanding the rise of the Romance languages. In this light, linguistic phenomena of the Italic dialects acquire a new attraction. Fresh point is given to Augustus's habit[7] of using the genitive *domos*, when it turns out to be a scrap of Volscian grammar brought by him from his native district of Velitrae.[8] Oscan and Umbrian sounds or idioms become literally alive if they can be traced not merely in the literature, but handed down through spoken Latin to modern languages. Thus, it was probably owing to Northern Italic influence that *ae* became *e* in later Latin. The middle vowels of *quaero* came eventually to be treated like the first vowel of *decem* because dialects like Faliscan and Umbrian identified the two.[9] Similarly, the triumph of certain Italic vocalisms over Latin is seen in the history of the gutturals in vulgar Latin.[10]

[1] Macrob., *Satur.*, VI. iv. 23, 'Necnon et Punicis Oscisque uerbis usi sunt ueteres, quorum imitatione Vergilius peregrina uerba non respuit.'
[2] Conway, *Ital. Dial.*, i., p. 218. [3] *Ibid.*, i., p. 222.
[4] *Ibid.*, i., p. 223. *Rosa* is, however, ultimately from Greek (Aeolic ῥοζά for ῥοδία).
[5] Keller, cited by Conway, *op. cit.*, i., p. 223. [6] Mohl, *op. cit.*, p. 16.
[7] Suet., *Aug.*, lxxxvii. [8] Mohl, *op. cit.*, p. 87.
[9] *Cf.* Umbrian *kvcstur* (Lat. *quaestor*) alongside of *dešen* (Lat. *decem*).
[10] Mohl, *op. cit.*, ch. vi.

The history of Latin may be followed in outline through the main periods of the literature, with this difference, however, that the records of the language go back to a date at least two hundred years before the date generally assigned to the beginning of the literature. These periods are approximately:[1]

(1) *Circiter* 500 B.C.–240 B.C. — the period of the Earliest Latin. This is usually treated as pre-literary and is mainly represented by inscriptions and by legal and ritual remains to be illustrated in a separate chapter. Valuable philologically, the language at this stage is rugged and unwieldy, yet virile and emphatic. The old rustic Latin spoken beside the Tiber in the seventh and sixth centuries B.C. began its gradual spread over Italy, as conquest and military colonisation advanced. This pre-literary Latin, originally nothing more than a *patois,* and not always closely in contact with the regularising language of the metropolis, was especially subject to local influence of idiom, phonology and vocabulary, from the kindred dialects, many elements of which it eventually absorbed.

(2) 240 B.C.–70 B.C. — In the first century of this period, as the Latin of early Epic and early Comedy, of Ennius and Plautus, the literary language had already begun to diverge from the spoken language. Towards the end of the period it passed through its transition towards its epoch of highest finish. The last two generations of the period were marked by activity in political and judicial oratory, which contributed to the advance of prose especially. As to spoken Latin, its struggle for mastery over the Italic dialects had resulted by the time of Hannibal in the formation of certain Latino-Italic varieties in the north and the midlands. In the south this polydialectal Latin, due to fusion with kindred dialects, continued to grow till the days of the Social War. The Social War brought extinction for many of the separate Italic dialects. They left their chief traces in the local varieties of Latin. Thus Varro, who was a Sabine by birth, means apparently by *Sabina lingua* the Latin spoken among the Sabines.

(3) 70 B.C.–14 A.D. — the 'Golden Age' of oratory and of the poets immediately pre-Augustan as well as Augustan. The Latin of literature now underwent its final shaping as an intrument of prose at the hands of Cicero and as an instrument of poetry at the hands of Virgil. The spoken Latin, the resultant of compromise between the old *sermo rusticus* of Latium and the local dialects on the lips of Umbrians, Faliscans, Marsians and others, was now the general language of Italy. Men from the country speaking different dialects entered the Roman service and influenced the Roman tongue. Out of this blend grew the common speech of the imperial times.

[1] It is probably needless to say that there is continuity throughout, and that the dates represent not breaks, but convenient divisions.

(4) 14 A.D.–180 A.D.—the 'Silver Age' of the writers of the Early Empire. Marked by increasing artificiality, and a rhetorical straining after effect, much of the literature stands sharply divided from the vernacular; but the commoner language forces itself into prominence, notably in the pages of Petronius. The vulgar Latin, which had for its base the old provincial Latin of Italy, spread widely over the Empire. Despite its variety, it was a unity, and in some ways made approaches to the literary language under the influence of the official Latin employed for all purposes of administration.

(5) 180 A.D. onwards to the break-up of spoken Latin into the Romance languages. As a literature, this 'Late Latin' finds its typical, though not its only, representatives in Christian writers. They hand it on to be the great medium of medieval learning. Though the literary Latin outlived the spoken Latin by many centuries, the latter died slowly. The decomposition of the vulgar imperial Latin was impossible so long as the Roman Empire remained a powerful unity. In fact, the history of popular Latin is, throughout, the history of the struggle of two opposing tendencies—on the one hand, a centrifugal tendency in the direction of local peculiarities and change; on the other, a centripetal, due to the influence of the written and official Latin, which imposed a certain conventional standard and hindered dissolution. The unity of imperial administration furthered the influence of the classical idiom and postponed the formation of separate Romance languages.[1] Another factor contributing to the partial spread of the more literary Latin in the provinces was the establishment of schools, like those of Gaul.[2] For a period, then, roughly extending from the first to the fourth century A.D., it was a case of the practical disappearance of the indigenous languages of the provinces in favour of a Latin which was broadly one, like the Empire itself. The main exceptions to this conquest of language were to be found in the East, where Greek especially maintained its hold. Finally, the triumphant language itself split up. The troubles of the Empire removed the influences which had made for unity. The provinces were severed and developed different languages.[3]

The cultured diction of the literature and the speech of the common people (*sermo plebeius*) were, of course, both descended from the ancient Latin language.[4] Both were branches from the same stem and

[1] Mohl (*op. cit.*, p. 268) is very emphatic on this. 'Sans le latin classique, les idiomes romans seraient nés cinq ou six siècles plus tôt.'

[2] In Britain the educational policy inaugurated by Agricola (Tac., *Agric.*, xxi.) accounted for considerable culture, though subsequent circumstances effectually prevented the development of a Romance language in the island.

[3] Romance philology teems with questions to be solved only in the light of the spoken usage. *E.g.*, why did Italian keep *loro* from gen. plur. *illoru(m)*, and not keep traces of such genitives plural in the nouns? Because the vulgar Latin used preferably the old gen. plur. in -*um* (Ind.-Eur. -*om*, Sansk. -*sam*) in preference to that in -*orum*, which originally was special to pronouns. *Cf. sestertium*, *Romanom* (inscriptions), etc.

[4] The history and features of both 'Volkssprache' and 'Schriftsprache' are

roots, and the structure of both had been really determined by those who originally spoke the Latin tongue. But the parting[1] came with the dawn of a partially exotic literature under Greek influence. Thereafter they developed in different surroundings. It is all a matter of gradation due to this difference in environment. They continued to diverge, but they also reacted on each other. Learned words filtered down into the speech of the lower orders, making the accents less harsh and the phraseology less uncouth. Plebeian and servile words rose, chiefly through domestic contact, into the parlance of writers. It is reasonable, therefore, to believe that there were other grades[2] of the language more subtly distinguished — the *sermo cotidianus*, or daily speech of the cultured, in which, for instance, the narrative portions of Petronius's novel is written, would be more off-hand than the literary style, but more classic than the *sermo plebeius* of Southern Italy, which Trimalchio and other freedmen in the book are represented as using; more refined, too, than the *sermo rusticus* of outlying districts in Italy. There were, further, the local differences which multiplied as the vulgar Latin spread over the Empire. The settlement of colonists or veterans, the deportation of whole populations, movements of troops, and marriages of soldiers with provincial women, spread and exchanged linguistic elements of the utmost complexity. Not only in the East, but in the coast-towns of Italy, Greek words worked their way into the spoken language, and added to the already large stock of loan-words introduced by writers from the days of Plautus. Even by the time of Cicero, Gallic[3] Latin had noticeable peculiarities. In his speech for the poet Archias, Cicero remarks on an outlandish note of provincialism in the Spanish

---

sketched by W. Meyer in a chapter contributed to Gröber's *Grundriss d. romanischen Philologie*, Bd. I., pp. 351–382. With a due sense of the complexity of the problem, Mohl, *Introd. à la chronologie du latin vulgaire*, ch. vi., recognises four periods of vulgar Latin:

(1) Formation des dialectes latino-italiques.
(2) Constitution du latin général d'Italie.
(3) Unification du latin impérial.
(4) Décomposition du latin vulgaire impérial.

[1] The distinction is essential to the appreciation of Latin style. F. T. Cooper (*Word-Formation in the Roman Sermo Plebeius*, 1895, Introd., pp. xv–xvi) points out that there is no question of two separate languages, but of two kindred dialects, steadily diverging. Objections are made by Bonnet and Sittl. The former (in *Le latin de Gregoire de Tours*, 1890) declines to consider vulgar Latin as a real language apart from Latin strictly so called: 'Le latin vulgaire ainsi compris n'a jamais existé que dans les cerveaux de quelques savants.' The latter says: 'Das Vulgärlatein, mit welchem die Latinisten operieren ist ein Phantasiegebilde.'
[2] See Cooper, *op. cit.*, Introd., p. xx. The danger is that these grades of one language may be viewed as separate entities. Thus between literary and vulgar Latin, Fuchs (*Die roman. Sprachen in ihr. Verhältn. zum Lat.*, pp. 37 *sqq.*) postulates a Volkslatein needlessly; much as Jordan (*Kritische Beitr.*, pp. 73 *sqq.*) fancies a municipal Latin – half official, half popular – between the literary and the rustic.
[3] Cooper, *op. cit.*, Introd., p. xxv.

Latin even at such a centre as Corduba.[1] To take instances nearer Rome, Pollio's reproach of 'Patavinity' against Livy is only less notorious than the reproach of what we may call 'Praenestinity' brought by Lucilius against Vectius, as Quintilian tells us.[2] These charges refer to the use of words or phrases that smacked of the soil to purists of the capital. Hadrian, though born in Rome, made the Senate laugh when he first spoke in it.[3] Septimius Severus never lost his African accent,[4] and had to blush for his own sister's ignorance of Latin.[5] There were, then, copious deviations from standard Latin, even in high places. If we pass to the fourth century A.D., it is not for a moment to be thought that African Latin was identical with that spoken on the Rhine or the Danube. 'The idioms of the separate Roman provinces represent a varying degree of archaism in the order of their dates of conquest.'[6] Broadly, however, what concerns us is that the language of literature and the dialect of popular speech were not the same. Between these the chasm widens markedly, even within the first century of the literature. To be convinced, one need only note how much more Greek Ennius is than Naevius, and how much more polished Terence is than Plautus. The homely phrases and homely accentuation of the earlier dramatist give way before an increase of refined diction and foreign principles of quantity favoured by the literary circle whose centre was the younger Scipio. It was natural that the great comic playwright of the people should keep in touch with the ordinary speech, and be affected not only by everyday turns of expression, but by the everyday pronunciation ready to slur final consonants and shorten unaccented long vowels. It was equally natural that Epic, with elevated traditions based on Greek literature and in the hands of scholarly poets, should incline away from spoken Latin. Ennius, by setting the language to a new verse, the hexameter, displaced the national Saturnian, and was the real begetter of the severance between the speech of the learned and that of burgher and peasant.

Plebeian Latin is important not merely for its influence on the

[1] Cic., *Pro Arch.*, x. § 26: 'Cordubae natis poetis, pingue quiddam sonantibus atque peregrinum.'
[2] Quint., I. v. 56.
[3] Spartian., *Hadr.*, iii.: 'orationem imperatoris (*i.e.* Traiani) . . . agrestius pronuntians.'
[4] Spartian., *Seuer.*, xix.: 'Afrum quiddam usque ad senectutem sonans.'
[5] Spartian., *Seuer.*, xv.: 'uix latine loquens.'
[6] Cooper, *op. cit.*, Introd., p. xxvii. Mohl (*op. cit.*, p. 12) holds with Gröber that, outside Italy, in the provinces first colonised, there were maintained the forms nearest to the old Latin of the Republic. Such Latin, planted as it were in good time, grew strong enough to resist many changes which affected the more unstable language of a crowded metropolis and of Italy in general. But Sittl (*Die lokalen Verschiedenheiten der lat. Sprache*, 1882, p. 43) supports the opposite view that Latin altered more profoundly in the provinces than in Italy. One of several points against Sittl is the fact that under the Empire the inscriptions are more dialectal in Italy – the native soil of the old Italic dialects – than elsewhere (Mohl, *op. cit.*, p. 46).

Romance languages, but because it leaves traces of its presence in all periods of the literature. Its main characteristics were its free invention or adoption of new words and a marked preference for ponderous derivatives and compounds.[1] Nothing is more interesting than its retention of this Indo-European inheritance, which the literary language outgrew—the primitive facility of compounding words. But it had its drawbacks. Long words seemed to be preferred for their length. Prefixes and suffixes were used carelessly, and with a vulgar passion for *sesquipedalia uerba*, as if exaggeration could screen the want of thought. Words in consequence lost their exact force. Frequentatives, whose value was forgotten, were either doubled like *cantitare*, or supplied with a *saepe*, just as diminutives were either doubled like *homullulus* or supplied with pleonastic epithets like *paruus* and *paruolus*. Another feature of plebeian Latin is its unbroken preservation of many archaisms which had dropped out of the literary language. This lowest grade, then, of Latin, spoken by soldiers, traders, and slaves, and corresponding in Rome to the *sermo rusticus* outside the city, was at once conservative in its adherence to old forms and progressive in its readiness to alter and innovate.

The severance between the two styles, it has been remarked, was not absolute. The earlier Roman writers employed diction near enough to the popular to be affected by the plebeian habits of word-formation. They used compounds which the classic literature almost entirely rejected. It is equally natural that spoken Latin should appear in satire, whether of the bitter order of lampoon and invective, or of the easy-tempered order of chatty persiflage. We meet without surprise plebeian elements in Catullus, Horace, Persius, and Juvenal, and in the epigrams of Martial. Writers on technical subjects admit vulgarisms—Vitruvius does, in writing on architecture, Columella on agriculture, Celsus on medicine. Even in the best period the spoken Latin is not without its witness. All was not gold in the Golden Age. Apart from the authors of the *Bellum Africum* and the *Bellum Hispaniense*, which at least possess the merit of being foils to the masterpieces of classical Latin in their own time, there is the distinctly conversational tone and slack usage which Cicero allows himself to adopt in many of his letters. In the next century the folk-speech appears not only in the wall-scribblings of Pompeii which are not literature, but very clearly in Petronius's novel, which is literature.[2] Later still, not a little of the Latin of Apuleius and of Tertullian is due to the way in which people talked their Latin in

---

[1] This is well summarised by Cooper, *op. cit.*, Introd., p. xliii: 'The language was burdened with substantives in -*bulum*, -*mentum* and -*monium*, adjectives in -*arius*, -*icius* and -*osus*; cumbersome archaic suffixes here play a prominent part; compare the abstract substantives in -*ela* and -*tudo*, adjectives in -*bilis*, -*bundus* and -*lentus*, all retained apparently for the sake of their length. Frequentative, inchoative, and desiderative verbs, diminutives and prepositional compounds, are, from the earliest period, freely used in place of the simple word with little or no distinction of meaning.'

[2] As Mohl points out (*op. cit.*), for the study of vulgarisms, since Ullmann,

Africa. Finally, the spoken language has left its most imperishable monuments in the Romance languages. Even in Esperanto, the latest artificial means of intercommunication by language, the living influence of Latin roots is manifest in the greater portion of the vocabulary.

The literary Latin ran a course of its own. Its history, in spite of the occasional influence of the vernacular, was something independent, and is writ large in the works of Roman authors. Cultivated and shaped by Hellenisers, it attained its Golden Age at the end of the Republic and the beginning of the Empire. In the very period when spoken Latin had at length ousted the kindred dialects in Italy, the vigorous plebeian and rustic language is sharply severed from the polished urbanity of writers in the capital. The cadence of sentences and the value of vowel-sounds are studied by Cicero in a manner undreamt of by common employers of the language. The distance between ordinary speech and the art of Virgil, now venturing on some untried effect, now reviving some suggestive archaism, is still more immeasurable. With the Silver Age came a reaction against the classical standard. Trained in rhetoric, learned in literature, an author yearned to say something new, striking, piquant, and worthy of his individuality. Fresh collocations of words and subtle reminiscences of past literature were the characteristics esteemed. So prose borrowed copiously the colour and phraseology of poetry, and poetry was deeply tinged with conceits and erudition. This tendency passed into the archaising movement of the second century A.D., when, with an enthusiasm which sometimes outran discretion, but to which we owe knowledge otherwise unattainable, certain scholars turned to quote and imitate many of the writers before Cicero. The retrogressive fashion which arose in Hadrian's days had its outcome in the writings of Fronto, Gellius, and Apuleius.

The final period in the history of the literary language of Rome is that in which it is best represented by the works of the Christian Fathers. The influence of the vulgar speech and of provincial varieties is evident. It is the eve of the disintegration of Latin into the Romance languages. The transmutation was wrought by the corruption and loss of grammatical endings, the appearance of auxiliary verbs and of articles definite and indefinite, as well as the intrusion of barbarous words. From about the ninth century[1] Latin ceased to be strictly a spoken language. It was replaced by Spanish, French, Italian, Roumanian, and other tongues;

Roman. Forsch. vii., 146 *sq.*, Förster, *Wiener Stud.*, xiv. 278 *sq.*, no one can doubt the high importance of Trimalchio's *conuiuium* in Petronius, and of the *Appendix Probi.*

[1] The transition from Latin to French and the dropping of inflections may be well illustrated by the text of the famous Strasburg oath sworn in 842 A.D. by 'Lodhuvig' (Louis-le-Germanique), and couched in the *Romana Lingua* so as to be understood by the French subjects of his brother Charles ('Pro Deo amur et pro Christian poblo et nostro commun salvament,' etc.). For the full text see C. T. Cruttwell, *Roman Literature*, ed. 7, 1910, p. 22; Donaldson, *Varronianus*, ed. 3, 1860, p. 535; or Bartsch, *Chrestomathie de l'ancien français*, ed. 12, 1927, p. 3.

and of these the nearest representative of the older Latin is, on the whole, Spanish, which traces its descent lineally from the language of the Roman soldiers, colonists, and traders of the second century B.C.[1] But, if no longer spoken, Latin did not become a dead language. The literary language proved its vital power by its diffusion in the Middle Ages as the language of scholars and international statesmen. The theology and philosophy and law of the civilised world were conveyed in it. The Vulgate and rhyming hymns of the Church guaranteed its life. Virtually, with the exception of Ireland from the fourth century to the Carlovingian period, all that Western Europe knew of Greek thought for centuries it knew through Latin books. Long after the revival of Greek studies, learning continued to express itself in Latin, whether it might be Bacon's trumpet-call to scientific observation and inquiry in the *Novum Organum*, or one of the great responses thereto, Newton's *Principia*. The lectures of the medieval Universities were in Latin. In the seventeenth century England had still a Latin State Secretary in the person of Milton; and it was only in the age of Louis XIV that French supplanted Latin as the vehicle of diplomacy. The Peace of Utrecht in 1713 was drawn up in French. For the last two centuries the employment of Latin has been most marked in treatises on questions of scholarship, in commentaries on the classics, and in the services and pronouncements of the Church of Rome. A language which is so preeminently the language of liturgy and ceremonial cannot scientifically be called dead.

The main natural qualities and features of Latin are evident in the remains of the earliest period. It is the language of record and regulation, of epitaph and ritual. Heavy and awkward at first, it possessed virtues equipping it to develop into an ideal language for history and law, for rhetoric and religion. Intrinsically, it was unpoetic, just as the people were inherently unromantic and comparatively unimaginative. The contrast with Greek forces itself upon the mind. Latin is not so rich in purely poetic words. It has not the subtle and supple turns characteristic of the quick-witted and versatile Hellene. It has not the same variety or lightness of endings. It has not the wealth of particles or prepositional usages which import such fine shades of meaning into Greek sentences. Its grammatical forms are less varied; for it lacks the aorist tense, and shows only scanty traces of an optative mood, a middle voice, and a dual number. It has not the Greek facility either in compounding words or in expressing abstractions. As a result, in point of

---

[1] Spanish affords an interesting example of the reaction of the provinces upon Rome. The men of the *Legio VII Galbiana*, brought to the capital by Galba in 69 A.D., were responsible for the first influx of 'Hispanisms' into the speech of Rome. A ceaseless tide of strangers was bringing in other elements of change.

meaning, Latin cannot be expected to exhibit equal niceties. In point of sound, Latin with its heavy terminations, in *-orum* and *-arum*, *-bam* and *-bo*, must appear relatively clumsy. In point of expressing pure speculation, Latin, though distinctly adapted to ethical discussion, could never rival the metaphysical capacity of Greek philosophy.

But the language has undoubted positive merits. Its very heaviness lends it a sonorous solemnity. Well managed, Latin is the best instrument ever devised in the world for clear, emphatic, dignified exposition. Free of a load of particles, it runs all the less danger of becoming prolix. It goes straight to the point. The language is the exact counterpart of the practical character of the people. Therefore it was fitted for Varro's didactic treatises and Lucretius's didactic poetry; for condensing a moral precept of the sort ascribed to Publilius Syrus, for the utterance of a grave eulogium of the dead in the *laudationes funebres*, for formulating a decree by Senate or Emperor or magistrate beyond the possibility of cavil; for Cicero's serious advocacy of a case before a jury or a measure among politicians; for Virgil's impressive declaration of the mission of a great people and the glories of a great empire.

In some ways Latin looks cumbrous, barren, and intractable in the earliest monuments. Even in Plautus, despite the famous saying that if the Muses were to speak Latin it would be in Plautine Latin, there seems scarcely a full promise of the gold of the Augustan Age. The verses of Ennius, as Quintilian[1] remarks with penetration, impress one like fine old trees: they have majesty rather than beauty (*non tantam habent speciem quantam religionem*). But this very majesty is not sustained. Ennius can be greatly impressive in familiar lines like —

> *Moribus antiquis stat res Romana uirisque,*

or —

> *Nec cauponantes bellum sed belligerantes;*

and he attains to noble effects of rhythm and to skilful use of alliteration, of vowel sounds, and of liquid consonants. But his mastery is not sure. He drops into homeliness, and, lower still, into clumsiness, and, lowest of all, into a baldness intolerable in poetry. This material, then, as yet only half pliant, had to be wrought into a finished artistic product by the Roman will. The literary dialect gained flexibility only through persevering experiments made by writers who borrowed Greek idioms and metres, and, in the light of Greek models, shaped their own language. And this shaping by the writers was aided by the moulding of circumstances, for the language expanded as Rome's domains expanded. The contact with other peoples was vivifying. It was a challenge and a stimulus to the men of letters. Latin became a language of imperial dignity, or was made imperial chiefly by Virgil, because his mind and

[1] X. i. 88.

soul were responsive to Rome's imperial destiny. Possessed by a great idea, Virgil rose to his greatest achievement—complete artistic mastery over an obstinate medium.

The Romans themselves recognised certain defects in their language. The poets, drawing comparisons with Greek, realised the heavier movement of Latin. Horace, in a well-known ode, confesses the danger of seeking to soar with Pindar. Lucretius felt the vocabulary of his native Latin too poverty-stricken to do justice to Greek scientific and philosophic terms. His avowal of the *patrii sermonis egestas* is cited with approval by Pliny the Younger.[1] Seneca shares these impressions.[2] No one appreciated the fact better than Cicero. He knew what it was to seek in vain a Latin equivalent for a term in Greek philosophy. Yet he amuses his readers, and perhaps himself, in certain passages[3] where his ambition is ostensibly to contest with the Greeks their pre-eminence in language. Protesting the equality of Latin, he virtually acknowledges the supremacy of Greek. For the moment he is a lawyer holding a national brief. Elsewhere[4] he explicitly owns that Greek is a more copious language. This is his true conviction. Just as Lucretius had not fully succeeded in rendering Latin supple enough to convey gracefully the doctrines of Epicureanism and the transitions from one stage in his argument to another, so Cicero felt its awkwardness when confronted with the task of rendering Greek philosophy. Latin, in fact, during classical times never became an absolutely perfect instrument for the expression of philosophical ideas. This tends to show that the language had not kept pace with the thought of Rome; at least, it could not overtake Greek thought. Certainly, philosophising was never so popular in Rome as it had been in Athens, and Cicero's philosophic works lag far behind Plato's in freshness and vigour. Yet justice demands that credit be given to both Cicero and Seneca for developing in their several ways the clear and logical qualities of Latin. It was greatly owing to them that Latin did in later times prove capable of expressing, with considerable nicety, abstract thought and subtle distinctions. Though it lost in literary grace, the language under the hands of the Christian Fathers and of the eminent schoolmen attained to great power of definition. The new theological writers had to treat of many things remote from the feelings, thought, and diction of classic Rome. When Tertullian, therefore, created ecclesiastical Latin, he created it at the expense of strict Latinity. To obtain a serviceable implement for his purpose, he showed

---

[1] *Epist.*, IV. 18.   [2] *Epist.*, 58.
[3] *De Fin.*, I. iii. 10; *Tusc. Disp.*, III. viii. 16, III. x. 20.
[4] A good example occurs in *Tusc. Disp.*, II. xv. 35. There Cicero remarks that for the two Latin words *labor* and *dolor*, Greek, though a richer language than Latin, has only one term ('Graeci illi, quorum copiosior est lingua quam nostra, uno nomine appellant'). After the criticism 'aliud est enim laborare, aliud dolere,' Cicero patriotically remonstrates with Greece for pluming herself on her abundance of words, 'O uerborum inops interdum, quibus abundare te semper putas, Graecia!'

no regard for classic usage in word-formation[1] or phraseology. He allowed himself what purists denounce as enormities from the vulgar tongue and travesties of correct phraseology, such as *potentator*, *pigrissimus*, *uisualitas*, *nullificamen*, *multinubentia*, *diminoro* for *diminuo*, *inuxorus* for *uxore carens*, *libidinosus gloriae* for *cupidus gloriae*. His free adaptation and inventions of terms had, at any rate, the excuse of being a sign of life. They fitted Latin prose for Christian apologetics. Still, some of the old deficiencies were felt. Jerome long afterwards complained of the inadequacy of Latin to interpret ideas from Greek and Hebrew. He argues[2] that if Cicero met with difficulties in translating from Greek, an allied language, the case of Hebrew was much worse. Yet, maugre difficulties, Latin developed into a cosmopolitan instrument of expression. For a time it bid fair to fulfil its destiny as the universal medium of communication dreamed of by the humanists. The humanists, however, bore their share in defeating their own hopes. By insisting on ultra-classicism and preaching a return to Cicero they shut their eyes to the growth of the language since his day. A Latin with reactionary and highly literary tendencies could not hope to compete against the living force of the modern national languages. Yet among the things that might have been may be imagined a Latin with a place between the Ciceronianism of Erasmus and the monstrous barbarism of the monkish jargon so well satirised in the *Epistolae Obscurorum Virorum*.

Throughout its whole history the language maintained a certain severity, solidity, and dignity reminiscent of the character which marked the people themselves in simpler days. True to a kind of biological law, the Roman nation in ways of thought and speech preserved the marks of early habits. A sensible people with a keen eye for utility, and for having work done, will tolerate only a language that is clear, concise, forcible, and logical. By isolating such qualities in the language one but testifies to the qualities of sound sense, energy, and solidity in the Romans themselves. As we have seen, it was for the *littérateurs* of artistic genius to superimpose refinements by which the sounds of Latin developed unexpected music, and its native dignity rose to positive majesty. The wonder is not that Latin should be less varied than Greek, but that it should have so much variety as it has. Among a people so conservative it was no easy task for men of letters, even at the prompting of art, to introduce bold experiments. Custom and convention ruled in the province of language as the *mos maiorum* ruled in the social sphere. This factor unmistakably hampered adventurous innovators. It was Caesar,[3] daringly unconventional in other

---

[1] For examples of his Latinity see Cooper's *Word-Formation in the Roman Sermo Plebeius* (*passim*), Reisig's *Vorlesungen ü. latein. Sprachwissenschaft*, Bd. I., 1888, p. 65; J. Schmidt, *De latinitate Tertulliani*, Erlangen, 1870; Hauschild, *Die Grundsätze und Mittel der Wortbildung bei Tertullian*, Leipz., 1864.

[2] Hieron. *in Galat.* I., ad i. 11 *sq.*, quoted by Cooper, *op. cit.*, p. xxxiii.

[3] Gellius, *Noct. Att.*, I. x. 4, quotes this from Caesar's first book *De*

ways, who, as if he held literary shipwreck before an author's eyes, laid it down that 'one should avoid an unexampled word as one would a rock.' Horace, himself so well designated as *uerbis felicissime audax*, is more liberal. He contemplates cases arising to justify innovations. One could not tie the language down to what was familiar to the old-fashioned Romans. His advice is, 'Take a licence into your own hands: if you take it within reason, it will be allowed.'[1] He contemplates also variation in the fashions of words. 'Obsolete words,' he says, 'will be revived: words high in favour will become obsolete.' The arbitrament of change he leaves with *usus*, the controller of 'the law and standard of speech.'[2]

It was on principles like Horace's rather than Caesar's that the Latin language made real progress. Upon the stubborn material were forced polish, ornament, new words, new beauties. The end at least was triumph.[3] The great literary effects of Latin are secured by sheer genius after generations of painstaking experiment. The supreme mastery achieved was the work of the classical age. To see Latin at its lightest one must take Catullus and Horace, whose high-water mark only just falls short of the full tide of lyric poetry in Greece. For its most stately rhythm and music one must hear the Ciceronian period, constructed, almost architecturally, of parts admirably fitted and proportioned; or one must divine the pathos and the grandeur of the Virgilian line. For the acme of neatness and brevity, one must read Tacitus with his gift of conveying brilliant pictures and profound reflections in marvellously few brief strokes, or Martial, who, in the shortest epigram, could leave the deepest sting. For the acme of rapidity one must think of the satiric exposures of social abuses and the scathing denunciations of vice which burst from Juvenal in his indignation.

Analogia: 'Habe semper in memoria atque in pectore, ut tanquam scopulum sic fugias inauditum atque insolens uerbum.' Macrobius, *Saturn.*, I. v. 2, quotes it with slight verbal changes, including 'infrequens' for 'inauditum.'

[1] Hor., *A.P.*, 48–51:
> 'Si forte necesse est
> Indiciis monstrare recentibus abdita rerum et
> Fingere cinctutis non exaudita Cethegis,
> Continget dabiturque licentia sumpta pudenter.'

[2] Hor., *A.P.*, 70–72:
> 'Multa renascentur quae iam cecidere, cadentque
> Quae nunc sunt in honore uocabula, si uolet usus,
> Quem penes arbitrium est et ius et norma loquendi.'

[3] 'La langue . . . mérite bien aussi d'être comptée, comme les provinces de l'empire, parmi les conquêtes du génie romain' (Egger, *Latini Sermonis Vetustioris Reliquiae Selectae*, 1843, p. viii).

Chapter IV

THE ROMAN CHARACTER AND RELIGION

National character a continuity – Persistence of the Roman type –
Littérateurs and proletariat – Traits of character – Order a
practical and social quality – Moral qualities – *Grauitas* – Domestic
virtues – Practical common-sense evolved from early rural times –
The practical tempers Roman conservatism – Roman more
practical than Greek or Kelt – The practical in Roman literature –
Practical influence of Rome on later ages – Law preferred to art.
Religion in relation to character: practical features in Roman
religion – The making of gods – Romantic elements borrowed
from Greek literature – Organisation of observances – Domestic
and social elements intertwined – Tolerance – Reasonableness and
dignity of the literature.

A SENTENCE written by Taine in his *Histoire de la littérature
anglaise* to illustrate his method of literary investigation, recognises 'une continuité aussi rigoureuse dans la vie d'un peuple
que dans la vie d'un individu.' A nation, he maintains, has life as the
individual has. A nation has character, spirit, soul. These features,
'visibles dès l'enfance, se développent d'époque en époque, et mani-
festent le même fonds primitif depuis les origines jusqu'au déclin.' This
phenomenon seemed to him true of the Greeks from Homer to the
Byzantine Caesars, of the Germans from the *Nibelungenlied* to Goethe,
of the French from the first *chansons de geste* and the oldest *fabliaux* up
to Béranger and Alfred de Musset. I do not remember that Taine seeks
a parallel in Roman literature. But it seems to me a strong confirmation
of his thesis. If English literature, notwithstanding Latin, French,
Italian and Hellenic influences, can be regarded as radically Teutonic,[1]
it is easier to credit a continuity of spirit in the literature of Rome.
Amid the powerful inrush of Greek influences the persistence of the
Roman type must be affirmed. The Roman was not merely passive and
impressionable. His masculine vigour strongly moulded the foreign
elements. The Roman borrowed in a Roman way. He left his impress on
the Hellenic material. Even a Roman copy of a Greek statue is a Roman

---

[1] Taine's view, ingeniously and vivaciously illustrated in his *Histoire*, has at
least the merit of being an external one. It does not, however, win universal
acceptance. Dr. Courthope, for example, declares that between the poetry
produced in England before the Norman Conquest and the poetry of Chaucer,
'there is no link of connexion' (*A Hist. of Eng. Poetry*, 1895, vol. i., p. 4).

thing.[1] Similarly a Roman elaboration of a Greek play, lyric, legend, is a Roman thing. How truly Roman this literature is cannot be better understood than by noting its invariably close relation to social environment—to movements of progress or reaction, to needs and aspirations, to the fashions, the fancies, and sometimes the follies of an age. Throughout, the Roman mark abides, modified, but never obliterated. This persistence of type is all the more wonderful because no nation has ever owed so much of its literature to outsiders and foreigners. There has been too common a tendency to estimate Hellenism at Rome in such a way as to discount the Roman character and to ignore the extent to which this character, inspiring the principles, tastes, and aims of Rome, pervades its total civilisation. 'The more it changes, the more it is the same thing.' Roman art, and therefore Roman literature, is full of this ineradicable character. An estimate of it must be attempted.

Always hard, it is often dangerous to sum up a people under a few abstract terms. What is essential here is the character displayed in the literature. This literature was so largely divorced from a merely popular appeal, that one might think the common folk hardly fall to be portrayed in a history of Roman literature. Mainly, it looks as if it were only the Roman gentleman and the man in Roman polite society who mattered; for they were the authors. Occasionally, no doubt, the *bourgeoisie* must be remembered. After all, to them Plautus made his appeal in his comedies. They were his audience, though he unfortunately did not describe them. Too few of the fragments of the *togatae* and *tabernariae* are left to show us the common folk who were characters in those plays. We have glimpses in Horace and Juvenal of the lower orders and of slaves. In Petronius, too, the common man who had worked his way up to riches remains the inimitable and charmingly vulgar hero of the 'Banquet.' When all is said, such exceptions and others leave Roman literature the most aristocratic in flavour and authorship of all literatures. The democratic spirit of Athens was absent. Yet Roman literature was no mere plaything of a leisured class. There was no lack of reality. It bore closely on the interests of society and the state. Virgil is remote enough in style and theme from the man of the Roman street, but his work is intimately bound up with the most vital concerns of contemporary Rome. In any case, however elevated the literary works and the literary dialect, there was no essential difference in *ethos* between high and low. The same Roman character—sub-

---

[1] But Roman art is no dull copy of the Hellenistic – it possesses native qualities, and often retains a specially Etruscan realism. Wickhoff has shown that it could secure new effects, among which he notes the 'illusionism' of Augustan and the 'impressionism' of Flavian art. There is nothing in Greek art to rob of their independence the Arch of Titus or the Column of Trajan. A stand against the treatment of Roman art as a phase of Hellenistic art is made by F. Wickhoff, *Roman Art* (Eng. ed.), 1900, and by Mrs. Strong, *Roman Sculpture from Augustus to Constantine*, 1907.

limited it might be—shows among *littérateurs* as among the proletariat. The same character fixed itself even on the stranger who
settled in Rome and contributed to Latin literature.

The Roman character was practical, deliberate, unromantic, industrious, god-fearing to the verge of superstition. These epithets imply the
outstanding qualities. The type was inherited from simple rural times.
It colours all the institutions of Rome. Though they grow complex,
family, society, state, religion, language, literature bear the ancient
stamp. The history of each is the history of sensible and gradual
adaptation of means to ends. Foreign influences acted on each; but each
remained Roman. The prevailing attributes are sound sense and a feeling for order.

Organisation was the soul of Rome. The insistence on order is but
one side of the practical turn. To have a thing done in workmanlike
fashion, the essential need is system. This is a fundamental trait. Under
it come the discipline and the deliberation of the Roman. Order
requires unquestioning obedience, the effacement of the individual, the
impersonal execution of instructions. Order in the state was to the
average Roman mind more likely to result from adherence to tried
principles than from novel experiments. Whether regal city, aristocratic republic, or world-empire, Rome was an incarnation of disciplined will-power. Ordered unity made the strength of the city-state
among the many separate peoples of Italy, and was the secret of Rome's
success. In policy she invariably knew her own mind and held to her
purpose. The systematic subordination of burgher to the commonwealth was the result of an almost Spartan strictness in training. At
every turn the Roman of the early times had encountered rules and
restrictions. The present was constantly in bondage to the past. Precedent in the shape of the *mos maiorum* proved frequently a trammelling
tyranny over the individual. Where the *respublica* was concerned, the
citizen had to be impersonal. Free play for individuality was not deemed
desirable. It might beget selfishness. Environment, therefore, made the
Roman a less original being than the Athenian. The lad who in excess of
bravery fought against his father's orders must, even though he slew the
enemy of Rome, pay the penalty for contumacy. The *Laws of the Twelve
Tables*, learned so scrupulously in the schools, with their commands
and prohibitions, read to us like a glorified system of tribal *tabu*. They
sank deep into the temperament of a Roman, and made him an obedient
and cautious citizen, loyal to the state and to all superior society,
reverential towards rules of conduct or ritual, innocent of questioning
analysis, and chary of initiation.

In this unromantic character the moral qualities mainly developed are
naturally staid and respectable. Largely, at the outset, a pastoral and
agricultural people, the Romans for centuries esteemed the elemental
virtues originally called into play by the struggle with enemies or

nature, by the relationships of domestic and social life, by the need of the protection of the gods. The simple 'manliness' of the tribesman was the trait which gave rise to the term *uirtus*, used by Roman writers in an increasingly complex sense, as society grew heterogeneous. The sense of duty to kinsfolk and to gods was expressed by *pietas*, the quality in Virgil's hero which covers a multitude of what must strike a purely modern taste as unchivalrous blemishes. The greater difficulties of life in early times engendered a serious bearing and sober mien, a somewhat solemn view of things—the famous *grauitas* ingrained in the Roman character and accounting at once for its heaviness and its dignity.

To emphasise *grauitas* with its combined *nuance* of dignity and severity, is not to claim for every Roman that 'portentous gravity' which Addison facetiously ascribed to his mysterious Spectator. We must reckon with the varied Italian temperament—its rebounds into sadness or merriment, its alternate deliberation and impulsiveness, tenderness and cruelty. It is the same in the Italy of to-day. One sees faces with a depth of pathos born of the battle with poverty here or malaria there; one notes light merriment regardless of the passage of time, recalling Sidney's shepherd-boy in *Arcadia* 'piping as though he should never be old.' The literature of such a people will exhibit both the well-weighed word due to deliberate thought and the quick repartee and cutting banter flashed out by a genius for impromptu farce. The *grauitas* of Caesar's *Commentaries*, of Cicero's *Orations*, of Virgil's *Aeneid*, is too obvious to need elaborate mention; but we are not allowed to forget it for long in Roman drama, satire, and lyric—not even in love-poetry, the composition of which to a Roman mind was playing and trifling (*ludere*).

The moral qualities valued were those on which family and state depended for their stability. Recognising the family as the kernel of the state, Roman society and Roman writers set great store by the domestic virtues. Contrasting Rome and Greece in the opening chapter of the *Tusculan Disputations*, Cicero claims that, whatever the originality of Greece, his own compatriots were superior in the conduct of everyday life and of the home, and in affairs of state and law. In war, even greater than their bravery was their trained obedience (*disciplina*). In learning and intellect, he yields the palm to Greece; but in character Rome can hold her own. The traits on which he lays emphasis are thoroughly representative:

> Where among any people has been found a dignity of manners, a firmness, a greatness of soul, uprightness, good faith, or outstanding virtue of every kind, comparable to the qualities of our forefathers?[1]

It was in the domestic circle that the foundations of Roman civic

[1] 'Quae enim tanta grauitas, quae tanta constantia, magnitudo animi, probitas, fides, quae tam excellens in omni genere uirtus in ullis fuit, ut sit cum maioribus nostris comparanda?' Cic., *Tusc. Disp.*, I. i.

virtue were laid. The family was the state in miniature. The unity of the household was really felt. There was intense devotion, in fact, a religious devotion, to the hearth; and intense loyalty to the *paterfamilias* as head. Representative of a line of ancestors, he was regarded as the expounder of the *mos maiorum*. The discipline of the home was in keeping with the discipline of the old burgher army and of the state at large. It inculcated the ideal dignity and self-control. The authority of the father (*patria potestas*), supreme within the household, and derived from patriarchal Aryan days, was a grave moral responsibility. It was enough to sober any right-minded man to realise his power of life and death within the area of the family. His boys, too, had to be trained bodily and mentally to take part in the work of the state. Everything tended to encourage a high sense of duty.

This businesslike disposition in the Romans, this primeval inheritance, survived throughout the ages. A thrifty and frugal rustic folk by origin, they objected to waste of time or substance. The landowner of early days could plough with his slaves,[1] and his wife spin like her women. We come perhaps nearest of all to the matter-of-fact primitive Roman in the writers on agriculture. Cato especially is practical. He sets himself to show[2] how time might be saved in bad weather, when field-work was stopped, by attention to sundry things in the way of cleansing or mending at the farmstead; he shows how slaves should be fed, and certainly not overfed; and by suggested economies and severities betrays part of the mean and unlovely side of the Roman character. To meet the requirements of such farmers as Cato has in view, the early calendars were drawn up in Latin, containing information about the work and the sacrifices suitable to each month. For religion, no less than work, was practical. The portion applicable to May from a calendar of the sort mentioned is a good example:

> The month of May. Thirty-one days. Nones on the seventh. Day has fourteen and a half hours. Night has nine and a half hours. The sun is in Taurus. The month is under Apollo's protection. Corn is weeded. Wool is washed. Young steers are broken in. The vetch of the meadows is cut. The lustration of the crops is made. Sacrifices to Mercury and Flora.[3]

Cato shrewdly advises the farm-bailiff against sacrificial observances at a distance from the farm. That would involve too great an expenditure

---

[1] The most handsome praise at one time in Rome was to be reckoned a good ploughman and a good farmer. 'Virum bonum cum laudabant, ita laudabant: bonum agricolam bonumque colonum. Amplissime laudari existimabatur qui ita laudabatur.' Cato, *De Re Rust.*, Praefat. 2.
[2] Cato, *De Re Rust.*, xxxix.
[3] *Corp. Inscript. Lat.*, vol. vi., 637 – Latin also given in Duruy's *Hist. of Rome* (Eng. tr.), chap. v. The inscription is on a marble cube giving on its four sides the duties and festivals for each month.

C

of time. The serviceable gods should be honoured by the fireside, or at the nearest cross-roads.[1] The absence of sentiment is everywhere conspicuous. Why? Because sentiment is not useful. The hedges and ditches of the *uilla* must be kept in good order: they are barriers to strangers. So much the better, argues Cato; for hospitality is expensive. If a slave fall ill, the rations have been too liberal; therefore reduce them. If a slave grows old or diseased, he must be sold precisely like old oxen or an old cart. The head of an establishment ought to have the faculty of selling rather than buying.[2] Elsewhere[3] Cato lucidly recognises that lending, like Polonius's borrowing, 'dulls the edge of husbandry.'

Outside the field of family, society, and everyday life there are several ways of illustrating this deep-seated, practical ingredient within the Roman mind. It is visible in its power of modifying other traits, in its differentiation of Roman from Greek or Kelt, in its effect upon the course of literature, in its contribution to the influence Rome has exercised upon later ages, in its determination of much of the Roman religion.

Other traits yielded to this overmastering one. Conservatism was ingrained in the Roman, but the practical overcame it. Let a Roman be convinced that a new thing was a good thing and he accepted it. This is clearly stated in the speech which Sallust[4] reports Caesar to have delivered during the debate on the punishment of the Catilinarian conspirators. Remarking that the Romans had taken military inventions from the Samnites and magisterial costume from the Etruscans, 'in fact,' he proceeds, 'anything serviceable noticed among allies or enemies was followed up at Rome with the utmost eagerness—they preferred to copy rather than envy good ideas.'

Face to face with other nations, the Roman betrayed his practical nature by contrast. He instinctively distrusted the versatility of the Greek as something hazardous; his steadiness was amazed at the mutability of the Kelt. Strictly practical, he could not appreciate the many-sidedness which Greeks so often acquired as the fruit of an inborn endowment of curiosity. The Roman was cautious where the Greek took risks. The Greek was more adventurous, whether in dealings with his fellow-men or in literary creation. This is the clue to his originality. It is the spirit which leads to great and often sudden progress in history

---

[1] Cato, *De Re Rust.*, v., 'Rem diuinam nisi compitalibus, in compito aut in foco, ne faciat.'

[2] Cato, *De Re Rust.*, ii., 'Cum serui aegrotarint, cibaria tanta dari non oportuisse. . . . Vendat boues uetulos . . . plostrum uetus, ferramenta uetera, seruom senem, seruom morbosum . . . Patrem familias uendacem non emacem esse oportet.'

[3] Cato, *De Re Rust.*, v.

[4] Sallust, *Catilina*, ch. li. 38, 'postremo quod ubique apud socios aut hostis idoneum uidebatur cum summo studio domi exsequebantur, imitari quam inuidere bonis malebant.'

and to great achievements in literature. It is also the spirit which leads to great disasters. Ultimately it is the same reckless *abandon* in the Athenian temperament which rendered possible the wild expedition to Sicily and the extravagant burlesque in parts of Aristophanes's comedies. Roman history has its disasters, but they do not come of quixotic dreams bewitching the nation or of chimerical ambition overleaping itself. So there is nothing in Roman history to parallel the Sicilian catastrophe; just as there is nothing in Roman literature to parallel the most laughable situations in plays like *The Knights, The Frogs*, or *The Birds*. So deliberately, as a rule, did the Roman official mind move that a temptation presents itself to think of the Romans as rather having empire thrust upon them. Yet, of course, their own efforts achieved it, only it was in that careful, practical manner which ensures success by foreseeing, recognising, and using opportunities. The advice of Augustus in favour of imperial consolidation rather than aggrandisement was scarcely needed by such of his successors as were normally minded. It was different with Pericles's advice dissuading the Athenian democracy from schemes of adventure: the success of their maritime empire had already turned the heads of many of those variable Greeks. They lost sight of the practical policy.

Though still nearer kinsmen of the Romans, the Kelts also serve as a foil to this practical bent. When Caesar pauses in his *Commentaries*[1] to touch on the indefatigable curiosity of the Gauls, their ceaseless questioning of travellers, their desire for novelties, their inability to hold to one line of policy, their general fickleness, he draws a picture which forms an antithesis to Roman doggedness and perseverance. In spite of the notoriously vexed question regarding the precise proportion of Keltic blood in Gaul, we may feel sure that certain traits of Gallic character emphasised by Caesar were essentially Keltic. We may feel equally sure that no stronger contrast to the practical spirit of Rome can be found than the dreamy, mystical, unconventional element in Keltic legend, folklore, and poetry treasured by workers in the modern Irish literary movement.

The practical largely determines the course and themes of Roman literature. The businesslike Roman character explains why Latin literary works have a more intimate bearing on contemporary circumstances than Greek literary works have. So far as causes can be assigned for literary achievement, the causes are more surely traceable in the case of Latin writers. Genius is not to be accounted for. But there is a sense in which Virgil is more explicable than Homer; Plautus and the Roman dramatists, serious or comic, than Aeschylus and Aristophanes; Catullus and Horace than Alcaeus and Sappho. Some of the best Greek literature rose divinely from individual inspiration. It shone forth with

[1] *De Bell. Gall.*, IV. v. 2.

a radiance miraculous, because unborrowed, in the fresh youth of
European literature. Most Roman writers answered some definite
demand of their day. They seem less instinct with subtly incalculable
forces. Before their experiments comes not merely the suggestion of a
want to be met, but also, as a stimulating model, the successful achievement of the Greeks. This is apt to make Roman literature appear by
comparison unoriginal.

From the same root springs the prominence of didactic prose and
poetry at Rome. In no literature do we find such ability to raise the
utile to the level of the *dulce*[1]—the work with a serviceable aim into a
work of art. It is true that many Latin books belong to the 'literature of
knowledge' rather than to the 'literature of power.' There are hand-
books on agriculture, on architecture, on camp-measurement. There is a
massive *corpus* of treatises on grammar; and though these latter, at least,
are enlivened by priceless quotations from ancient writers throwing light
on the history of literature, yet they do not themselves constitute
literature. On the other hand, much that had a definitely useful end to
serve, much that was avowedly meant to teach, became literature.
Lucretius in the *De Rerum Natura*, Virgil in the *Georgics*, and, to a less
extent, Horace in the *Ars Poetica*, elevated didactic into poetry. Cicero,
Seneca, and Quintilian showed how Latin prose could instruct and yet
be beautiful.

The truth is that a Roman's attitude towards knowledge was affected
by his practical outlook. There was far less desire in Rome than in
Athens to know for the sake of knowing. There was none of the boundless and insatiable Hellenic curiosity. This limited the Roman horizon.
A typical Roman would not have sympathised with Plato's distinction in
the *Republic* between an ideal arithmetic and that arithmetic of the baser
sort which is learned for the purposes of trading (τοῦ καπηλεύειν ἕνεκα).
Knowledge, to be worth knowing, must be turned to account. Purely
speculative philosophy could never have flourished at Rome. There
never was a 'mob of gentlemen' in Rome such as there was at Athens
to love inquiry for its own sake. A Roman gentleman might maintain
a Greek philosopher, but the latter was expected to make his philosophy
practical, to advise his patron in cases of difficulty, and to be the keeper
of his conscience. Moral philosophy did appeal to a Roman, for it had a
bearing on conduct. Horace clearly grasps the deadening effect of the
narrow preference for things which paid. It is a cumbersome and disquieting folly, he feels, to act on the maxim, 'My countrymen, money is
the first thing to be sought for; goodness comes second to cash.'[2] This
lust of filthy lucre Horace attacks not only for sapping virtue and

---

[1] Horace, *A.P.*, 343, 'Omne tulit punctum qui miscuit utile dulci.'
[2] Horace, *Epist.*, I. i. 53:

'O ciues, ciues, quaerenda pecunia primum est,
Virtus post nummos.'

banishing contentment from the mind, but for its ruinous effect on *belles lettres*. As a man of letters he insists on the incompatibility of temperament between money-making and poetry. A few lines in the *Ars Poetica* flash the light upon a class of Roman schoolboys. The master is examining orally in arithmetic—easy subtraction and addition. Correct answers delight him—and why? Because the boy will grow up able to look after his property (*rem poteris seruare tuam*). It is hard for literature to thrive in such an atmosphere. Horace's objection is not to the teaching of arithmetic as such, but to the grossly utilitarian spirit in education, defeating the objects aimed at in the best 'Grammar' schools, namely, to give in mathematics, music, astronomy, mythology, and other subjects a training which should enable and stimulate the pupil to understand literature.[1] The want of the ideal in Roman education depresses Horace, and his comment is a question:

> Ah! when this copper-rust, this greed for slavish saving, has once dyed the soul, do we expect poems can be composed worth embalming with cedar oil, or worth preserving in smooth cypress case?[2]

No more fertile, no more solid way of summarily reviewing the character of a nation is to be found than by isolating the ideas and principles which it has caused to live in later ages of civilisation. The strongest elements of a nation's character constitute the permanent portion in that nation's contribution to the future. With her artistic passions Greece has bequeathed chiefly ideas of beauty. With her practical tendencies Rome has bequeathed chiefly ideas of order. Patristic study illustrates the persistence of the passion for order in a new sphere. Bequeathed to the Catholic Church as an heirloom from the past, the supremacy of regulation is traceable from the sub-apostolic age onwards—from the epistles of Clement of Rome to the writings of Cardinal Newman. Broadly, Rome stands out as the great ancient example of an organised constitution, of codified enactments, of method in working an army and governing an empire. So quite apart from the survival of a portion of her religious and methodical spirit in the Church of Rome, apart from the entrance, through the language, of her literary spirit into the memory and imagination of the Middle Ages, apart, too, from the literally magical associations of the name of Virgil and the play of his style upon the *Divina Commedia* of Dante, Rome has impressed the world deeply through her mastery of the principles and application of law. Rome had the merits and the defects of being systematic. The same quality that taught her, and, through her, later civilisations, how

---

[1] G. Boissier indicates the large circle of human knowledge logically comprised by the Roman education under 'grammar' in its best and widest sense (*La fin du paganisme*, ed. 4, 1903, i., ch. i).

[2] Horace, *A.P.*, 330:

> 'An, haec animos aerugo et cura peculi
> Cum semel imbuerit, speramus carmina fingi
> Posse linenda cedro, et leui seruanda cupresso?'

to rule the peoples of the earth diminished her chances of being romantic. The same quality that taught her how to pass on a subject like
rhetoric in handy form, fit for use in law-court or public meeting,
diminished her feeling for art and her contribution to the world's
poetry. It is the old contrast so well described by Virgil:

> More deftly some will mould the bronze to breathe,
> I grant; from marble draw the looks of life;
> Plead cases better; and with compass map
> The heavenly paths, and name the rising stars.
> Roman, take thought, with Empire rule the World!
> These be thine arts—to set the law of peace,
> To spare the vanquished, and to quell the proud.[1]

It was primarily as governors of the world, not as artists, that the
Romans realised their destiny. Before their dominions extended, there
was no natural taste for art. The Curii and Fabricii were content with a
rude statue of the garden-god. The art of painting was so exceptional
that the Fabius who adorned the walls of the temple of Salus bequeathed
in consequence 'Pictor' as a family name.[2] Though the Roman attained
considerable skill in painting, more particularly as an art capable of
beautifying the houses of the well-to-do, the lack of fostering patronage
was a discouragement. Cicero observes pointedly that if Fabius's power
of painting had been considered a credit to him, there would have been
more great artists in Rome.[3] In the plastic arts, Romans were chiefly
copiers or employers of Greek skill. To most of them there was little to
envy in the fame of a Phidias. The very fact that craft in fashioning
marble or bronze so eminently belonged to the Greeks, whom they had
conquered, tended to make it seem unworthy of Roman hands. If in
sculpture they did depart from the imitation of Greek subjects, it was
usually to represent some actual person, some historical event, some bit
of realism, some instructive allegory. So later ages admire chiefly among
the works of Roman hands, not their sculpture, though sculpture too
had its Augustan triumphs, but those solid creations which reflect the
national spirit—their basilicae, amphitheatres, aqueducts, and roads.
In handiwork the Romans were greater engineers than artists.

In yet another field it is instructive to study the domination of the
practical. Much of Roman religion was determined by it. Religion in

---

[1] *Aen.*, vi. 847 *sqq.*:
> 'Excudent alii spirantia mollius aera,
> Credo equidem, uiuos ducent de marmore uoltus;
> Orabunt causas melius, caelique meatus
> Describent radio, et surgentia sidera dicent.
> Tu regere imperio populos, Romane, memento;
> Hae tibi erunt artes, pacisque imponere morem,
> Parcere subiectis et debellare superbos.'

[2] Plin., *Nat. Hist.*, xxxv. 19.
[3] *Tusc. Disp.*, I, ii.

turn enters so largely into the literature as to prove its prominent part
in the environment of the author and his circle. It is impossible to read
Livy without being constantly reminded of the stress the Roman laid
upon prodigy and atonement, upon the attitude of the gods, and the due
observance of ritual by men. It is impossible to understand Virgil if the
deeply religious basis of the *Aeneid* is overlooked. The practical aspect
of the religion confronts one everywhere—in its origins, its development, its application to home and state, its elaboration, and its tolerance
of new cults.

In its beginnings, the religion of the Romans was practical rather than
spiritual. Its roots strike far back into primeval and savage magic.
Wrapt up with a mass of primitive beliefs in the powers of nature,
spirit-worship, tree-worship, dreams, divination and sorcery, it strove to
solve the riddle of the universe in the best interests of man. In the
comparative simplicity and childishness of its rural origin, it made a
strong contrast to the piebald crowd of inconsistent notions and superstitions which had appeared in Rome by the first century of the Christian era. The old Latin theogony was built up after the pattern of the
early family and the pastoral life. Lacking the instinctive idealism by
which Greeks refined their anthropomorphic gods, the Latin farmers
thought of their gods under the concept most intelligible to them, of a
heavenly family, wherein Jove was *paterfamilias* and Juno his dame.
Originally many of the deities were powers of nature, like Jupiter, god
of the sky, Janus (Dianus), god of sunlight, Diana, his feminine counterpart, goddess of the moon; but the plain matter-of-fact Latin seems to
have, wherever possible, made his gods over again in order to correlate
them with his everyday life, and so render them more present aids in
time of trouble. He distributed among the gods special spheres and
functions, great or small, to preside over; he made them useful, even if
he limited and vulgarised them. It is characteristic that these gods with
definite functions often remained vague in form and in name. Generations passed during which the Latin gods had no images and no temples.
The worshipper sometimes knew no more than that he addressed a
spirit of power, a *numen*, of whose very name and sex he might be
ignorant; and so the crude animism of primitive days survives in prayers
or dedications to a deity 'whether god or goddess' (*siue deo siue deae*).
All at the bidding of commonsense, as progress multiplied needs, the
Latin pantheon grew into a well-ordered society of gods interested in the
life and work of man and state. The twelve great gods (*Di Consentes*),
six male and six female, formed a heavenly council.[1] But these were for
the high concerns of life.[2] With what resembles an eye to the main

[1] Their names are arranged in two lines of Ennius:
'Iuno, Vesta, Minerua, Ceres, Diana, Venus, Mars,
Mercurius, Ioui', Neptunus, Volcanus, Apollo.'
(*Annales*, ll. 426–7, in L. Müller's *Q. Ennius*, 1884)
[2] Varro (*De Re Rust.*, I. i. 4) illustrates the Roman adaptation of gods to

chance, as if this celestial senate might not deign to listen to trivial petitions, the Latins created a group of lesser divinities with restricted powers, relieving the supreme gods of responsibility in minor affairs. It was not enough to inherit deities of time-honoured Aryan descent; they were sometimes assigned new duties; they were still oftener assigned new colleagues. Thus, alongside of genuine household deities like Vesta (the primeval fire-goddess at the hearth), the Lares (the ancestral spirits of the home[1]) and the Penates (presiding over the store-closet), there appeared in domestic guise such a nature-god as Janus, originally the Day-spring. As a god of beginnings, he was set by the door (*ianua*); and three assistant porters were found for him — Cardea or Carda, for hinge (*cardo*); Forculus for leaves (*fores*); Limentinus for threshold (*limen*). In this thoroughly prosaic manner, religious conceptions were shaped by the work of the carpenter.

Then for rural needs there were Tellus, deity of earth, Ceres of crops, Ops of plenty, Saturnus of seed, Pales of pastures, Epona of horse-breeding, and even Sterculius or Stercutius of the manure-heap, with a host of others representing the bounty and beauty of earth, woods, and seasons — Liber and Libera, Faunus, Silvanus, Vertumnus, Flora, Pomona. Hercules, it has been argued, may have been a farmyard divinity, the spirit of the enclosure (*herctum*).[2] If so, he is as truly Latin as Heracles is Greek. It is significant that his altar was near the cattle-market. Rivers and springs were believed to have their guardian spirits, who were not so much creations of poetic fancy as guarantors of abundance of water. Juturna is a fair representative.[3] Anatole France, in *Sur la pierre blanche*, writes engagingly about the romantic possi-bilities of her story; how, gifted by Jupiter with immortality, Juturna could not die, as she fain would, along with her beloved brother Turnus, when Aeneas slew him, and how she threw herself into the Tiber. There is certainly a fascinating ring about the legend of this living and plaintive Rutulian nymph in the depths of the stream, of

---

circumstances. Beginning his treatise on agriculture, he feels that the appro-priate invocation is not one to the Muses in the manner of Homer and Ennius, nor even to all the *Di Consentes* 'whose gilded images stand all about the forum,' but to the farmer's special guides, whom he names in six pairs: Jove and Tellus, Sol and Luna, Ceres and Liber, Robigus and Flora, Minerva and Venus, Lympha and Bonus Eventus. They are the personifications of Heaven and Earth, Sun and Moon, Corn and Wine, Mildew and Blossom, Skill and Fertility (respectively the olive-goddess and the garden-goddess), Moisture and Good Success. It is a serviceable, orderly, and unromantic list.

[1] The other theory of the Lares is that they are originally agricultural – the spirits of the family fields.
[2] See F. Granger, *The Worship of the Romans*, 1895, p. 128. Others con-sider him and his worship importations from Greece.
[3] The well and altar of Juturna have been excavated close under the Palatine hillside and hard by the Temple of Castor. A brief account of the *Fons Juturnae* is given in E. Burton-Brown's *Recent Excavations in the Roman Forum*, 1898–1904, ch. ii.

whom the villagers might fancy they caught glimpses under the moonlit waters. Anatole France says the Romans did not develop the idea along the lines of romance: the heroine of such misfortunes was not left to her poetic melancholy; she had a serious occupation entrusted to her—the Romans gave her charge of their wells. 'Ils en firent,' he remarks, 'une déesse municipale.' Is it certain, however, that Juturna was a romantic creation spoiled? Possibly the romance came later than the notion of the goddess of wells. The strange beauty of the story is just as likely to be due to Virgil's poetic sympathy. Fairness, of course, must concede to the Romans considerable native gifts in myth-making; but, as a rule, it was the more romantic Greek mythology that threw a certain glamour and literary charm over the workaday theology of Latium.

Similar protectors for childhood were credited with interest in weaning an infant, in stimulating it to drink, eat, sleep, grow: they presided over its cradle and its first essays in speech.[1] To Tertullian's and Augustine's quotations[2] from Varro's *Antiquitates Rerum Diuinarum* we owe much of our knowledge of this wealth of practical invention which created divine powers like Potina, Educa, Cunina, Ossipaga, Statanus or Statilinus,[3] Cuba, Adeona, Fabulinus. For other ages likewise, and other acts of life within and without the home, there were divinities; so too for the self all through life there was the indwelling *genius*, scrupulously honoured and indulged by the Roman, especially on anniversaries of his birth. Evil powers, too, had to be reckoned with—a spirit of blight (*Robigus*) or a spirit of malaria (*Febris*). The hostile spirits of the dead had to be averted at the *Lemuria* every May: but there is little resembling devil-worship or demon-worship in Latium. Here sound sense revolted from the monsters of ignorance and fear figured by Etruscan imagination in the sepulchral chambers at Corneto and elsewhere. Here the god-making was workmanlike. The Latin would trust or dread only gods whom he might understand through effects which they could produce or prevent. And this type of religious sentiment is still largely unaltered in Italy. It is an admirable instance of continuity from Roman times. Peasants nowadays expect from the Madonna and the saints the same sort of blessings as their far-off predecessors expected from gods and genii. There are saints for the vineyard, for cereals, for cattle, for bodily ailments. Heaven is re-peopled with an army of helpful beings. Out of Jewish monotheism has arisen

[1] Even the unborn child was under the guardianship of Alemona, Nona, and Decima, whose functions apparently would be resigned to the powers presiding over birth, Partula and Lucina (Tertullian, *De Anima*, xxxvii).

[2] Tertullian, *Ad Nationes*, II. xi.; *De Anima*, xxxvii and xxxix. Augustine, *De Ciuit. Dei*, IV. viii., xi. and xxi.; VI, ix.; VII. xxiii. In VI. ix. Augustine especially attacks the absurd multiplication of heathen divinities. He asks, for example, with regard to the marriage-gods, 'Quid impletur cubiculum turba numinum, quando et paranymphi inde discedunt?'

[3] 'Statilinum et Statanum praesides puerilitatis deos apud Nonium ex Varrone legimus,' Aug., *De Ciuit. Dei*, IV. xxi.

a new polytheism.[1] Rustics exact miracles from their holy protectors, and cover them with foul-mouthed invective if the miracles fail.[2]

The same shrewd character appears in the forms of worship. The early observances had the practical aim of winning the favour or averting the anger of a god. Sacrifice and prayers had not the moral quality attached to them in later times. The right ritual, the right victims, the right formula, the right epithet of a deity, became all-important. Appeals were made after the nature of incantations. Prayer was a magical expedient. Hence the value of the *indigitamenta*, or lists containing names of spirits in charge of the acts and risks of human life. Generations of experience made the Romans past-masters in the organisation of religion. All is orderly in the instructions for prayer and sacrifice, in the traditional lore (*disciplina*) of the augurs, in the duties assigned to pontiffs and flamens and vestals. The religious guilds (*collegia*) with their archives are as completely systematised as the boards of magistrates.

Roman religion was eminently practical, too, in the moral effects aimed at. It was a guarantee for sound social virtue. The gods required from men the kind of duties on which the fabric of the family and the community depended. They were just such simple virtues as the *pater-familias* or tribal chieftain would inculcate: obedience; reverence for father and forefathers, for the elders of the state, for the laws; bravery; good faith; decency; diligence. Nothing illustrates this better than the Roman tendency to deify abstractions. As time went on, temples were built and sacrifices offered to Virtus, Honos, Fides, Pudor, Pavor, Fama, Concordia, Spes, Pax, and similar concepts. About all this there was no lustre of romance.[3] But this *prisca uirtus* was the stuff which made Roman literature what it was and which made Rome mistress of the world. One of the greatest forces in Roman life was the feeling that religion was a serious concern, with elements of domestic, social, and national value inextricably intertwined.[4] The *pietas* of the home, the unity of the clan or *gens*, and patriotism in the state, received each its sanction from a ritual which could be shared. No day could pass in a

[1] The more ignorant Italian rustic does not feel it enough to have recourse to God and the Virgin Mary. A hierarchy of saints is required to serve various emergencies. This was well illustrated in April 1906, when the eruption of Vesuvius was at its worst. Crowds of terrified peasants put their trust in statues of San Giuseppe and Sant' Antonio. In case of disaster, prayers were often exchanged for curses.
[2] This commercial rather than spiritual attitude between god and worshipper is in keeping with the legal nature of the Roman mind. The notion of a contract as applied to religion is illustrated in *The Religion of Ancient Rome*, by C. Bailey, 1907, pp. 18–22.
[3] 'Among the ancient Gentile cults there is none so respectable, none so prosaic, as the Roman.' C. Bigg, *The Church's Task under the Empire*, 1905.
[4] Domestic observances and deities often had public analogues. The state had – corresponding to deities of the home – its Vesta, its 'Lares Praestites,' and its 'Penates Publici' (perhaps identified with the Dioscuri, Castor and Pollux).

Roman home without reminders of the divine. The gods had their portion of the daily food. An omen might at any moment alter human plans. Though mainly formal and but scantily spiritual, Roman religion, by an unfailing testimony to the nearness of the Unseen, affected character profoundly.

Composite from early times, and never unified into anything like a creed, Roman religion became an intricate patchwork added to from age to age. In particular, it was profoundly modified by the Greek mythology. Yet, long before Greek influence operated, the indigenous religion was an amalgam of ancient worships descended from different peoples. There were Latin gods and Sabine gods. There were gods perhaps belonging to non-Aryan natives conquered by the Italic invaders. That the Temple of Jupiter Optimus Maximus on the Capitoline, the religious centre of Rome, should be shared with Juno and Minerva may find an explanation in the mingling of the worship of different stocks. The god Terminus, whose chapel was within the same holy precincts, may have been a stone deity of the aborigines. In time, Etruria and Greece made their great contributions to Roman religion. Rome was on the whole tolerant. Literary men were drawn to the poetic mythology of Greece. Their beliefs were eclectic. They drew freely from new religious systems. No bigot, the ordinary Roman was usually content to let Judaism, the Isis-cult, the Mithra-cult, extend side by side with traditional observances. There was no one national religion for the great Empire with its motley population of courtiers and proletariat, Greek and Scythian, bond and free. The one thing that approached to state-religion — Caesar-worship — was only formally imperial. The authorities demanded outward conformity to it from citizens professing the most varied systems of belief. This spirit of tolerance was another illustration of the practical. If old religious usages were found wanting, why not try new? In any case, why unnecessarily run the risk of offending foreign gods? It was also another proof of the parallelism between domestic and civic religion that, just as an individual resorted to fresh magical rites if ordinary means failed, so the state resorted to new forms when, in days of disaster, the ordinary observances failed. Hence the welcome accorded at different periods to the Sibylline books and to novel practices from Etruria, Greece, Egypt, and the East. The persecutions for which Rome was responsible were not caused by bigotry. The hostility to the early Christians was due mainly to two aspects of Roman religion already emphasised — its relationship with the state and its practical nature. Pliny's famous letter[1] to Trajan shows that to the official mind the offence of the Christians was not their creed or their practices, but their apparently disloyal refusal to join in the public sacrifices. The average practical Roman would also be prejudiced against a religion so visionary as Christianity. While its aloofness from political

[1] Pliny, *Epist.*, X. xcvi.

concerns would strike him as bad citizenship, the more ideal aspects of the Christian faith would be beyond his ken. He could not appreciate its self-sacrificing altruism, its resignation to heavenly appointment, its disdain of earthly happiness, any more than he could imagine the more abiding *Ciuitas Dei* towards which the Christian believed his journey lay.

The national character, examined here from several standpoints, inspires all Roman work. What is was in family, in state, in religion, it was in feats of engineering and in written compositions. Serious, practical, dignified, it engraved itself upon the literature, which exhibits the same ultimate qualities as a Roman law, a Roman road, a Roman triumphal arch, an aqueduct across the Campagna, the Pont du Gard near Nîmes, the Wall from Tyne to Solway. There is the same solidity, the same steadfast purpose, the same gift of execution. The undeviating line of a Roman *uallum* or aqueduct is no more typical of fixity of purpose than the straightforward enumeration of a magistrate's *cursus honorum* in an inscription, than Roman victories won by tenacious perseverance despite of failure, or than the definite aim, often a strong didactic aim, which characterises so much of the best that was written in Latin. The literature, like all the products of Roman skill, has a reasonableness and dignity which command the reverence of the ages.

Part I

The Earlier Literature
of the Republic

FROM THE ORIGINS TO 70 B.C.

THE EARLIEST LATIN

THE remnants of Latin belonging to the first five centuries of the city are not primarily interesting as literature. It is unfair and narrow to declare absolutely that there was no literature before the middle of the third century B.C.; but the actual monuments possess a value in which the linguistic, the epigraphic, the historic and the social elements outweigh the purely literary. The remains are not beautiful in thought or form; but they have an importance in literary history by way of contrast with and preparation for what was to follow. They mark the stage of Latin style reached up to the period when authors, acting under the stimulus of Greece, raised its power of expression, and secured for it, by manifold experiment, a suppleness and grace far beyond the apparent promise of the origins.

It is not enough, however, to regard the archaic fragments merely as specimens of the language in the making; or to adduce them as proving how essential to the birth and growth of ideas of beauty at Rome was her contact with foreign influence. Justice must also be done to their historic aspect. Everything written at Rome, whether on stone, metal, or more perishable material, bears the impress of environment; and these fragments are indexes to certain social, practical, and religious features of Roman life. The early monuments are simple, rough, solemn, practical, like the folk of the city-state, who, during centuries of political struggle inside Rome and continuous warfare throughout the length and breadth of Italy, had scant time left them for art.

What, in spite of absorbing national preoccupations, the early Romans did principally achieve was the regulation of worship by ritual and liturgy, the commemoration of the past in song, and recreation for the passing hour in mumming and rude banter. Were it possible to obtain more examples of those old songs and dramas, it is very probable that the ordinary estimate of the Latin genius would be heightened.[1] On the lowest estimate, that genius must be credited with the production of elements capable of high artistic development after Greek models became available. Less imaginative than the Greek, the Roman runs the risk of being allowed no imagination at all. It may be said at once that the vital and enthralling stories of early Roman history cannot all be referred to Greek inventiveness. The Roman could at least create a legend. He had the gift of adaptation too. As the horizon of Rome widened in Italy and beyond Italy, with the responsibility of controlling new nations, there set in a tendency towards the complex, the aesthetic, and finally the luxurious, which was destined more and more to influence thought and habits, language and literature. This was merely a continuance of the principle by which the Roman adapted himself to contemporary needs. The simple life so feasible in primitive days was impossible and impracticable for conquerors of the world. There is no break in the annals of Latin literature, any more than there is a break in the Roman character. 'The Latin literature breathes, from first to last, the sense of a continually developing national life.'[2]

As might be expected, the monuments of the first five centuries entirely illustrate practical aims. They may be grouped according to their objects. Some of them served the uses of religion—either as litanies (*axamenta*) in Saturnian measure like the chants of the Salian priests or the Arval brotherhood, or as the archives of priestly colleges containing lists of divine names and directions for worship (*indigitamenta*). Some, in the shape of rude dramas, served uses which in primitive society are uniformly associated with religion—those of festivity and merrymaking. Some, again, served as records of the past, and, whether official or private, whether annals kept by *pontifices* or tales chiefly intended to satisfy family pride by the glorification of ancestors,

---

[1] 'To speak of the early Italians as having no original gift for literary creation is wholly misleading; as if the imaginative impulse could be implanted where it did not exist, or the gift of the Muses be borrowed like money.' H. Nettleship, 'The Earliest Italian Lit.', in *Journal of Philol.*, vol. xi., reprinted in *Lects. and Essays*, 1885, p. 46.

[2] H. Nettleship, 'Earliest Italian Lit.', in *Lects. and Essays*, p. 46.

formed foundations, but not always very sound foundations, for later history. The uses of government were served by laws, treaties, and other official documents, just as the uses of politics soon called into prominence the power of effective public speaking, and so advanced the language in the direction of oratory. Uses social and domestic[1] were served by proverbs and pithy scraps of worldly wisdom, no less than by such tangible objects as mirrors, or the famous brooch (*fibula*) from Praeneste, which by the inscriptions upon them have added much to our knowledge of archaic Latin.

Though our concern is not with the phonetic and inflexional peculiarities[2] of archaic Latin, nor with the evolution of the Latin alphabet and system of writing,[3] some review of the main examples of the language prior to the classical period is imperative. A difficulty confronts us at the outset. Few of the surviving pieces of archaic Latin—if we except inscriptions—can claim to be perfect specimens of the language at the period from which they come. A process of modernisation, age after age, has often altered the original form almost beyond recognition. Just as the old Northumbrian literature of England was transformed by West-Saxon scribes, so monuments like the *Twelve Tables*, originating in the fifth century B.C., are known to us under the shape given them in later generations. Genuine archaic grammatical forms survive alongside of novel accretions; and—to increase the confusion—the sham antique has sometimes been foisted into the text by archaising scribes of a subsequent period. The student of the early literature and language also labours under the same disadvantage as the student of the early history—the scarcity of written documents before the Gallic capture and devastation of Rome in 390 B.C. Livy virtually throws doubt on the authenticity of the sources of his own first five books by emphasising the remoteness of their times and the wide destruction of archives, private and public, in the conflagration.[4] But the destruction, though widespread, was not total. Roman history claims that the Capitol with its archives escaped the Gauls. Besides, in recent years, archaeology has unearthed monuments of the language from still earlier times.

Of the Latin of the kingly period there is no accredited representative. The fragments of the so-called *leges regiae*, known to us chiefly from Festus, descend from formulae of high antiquity, originally in

[1] Vessels bearing such inscriptions as *Lauernai pocolom* (*Lauernae poculum*) were not domestic, but sacred temple utensils; see F. D. Allen, *Remnants of Early Latin*, 1897, pp. 16–17.
[2] For a convenient summary of these see F. D. Allen, *op. cit.*, pp. 5–12. *Cf.* W. M. Lindsay, *Handbk. of Latin Inscripts.*, 1897, pp. 1–13.
[3] For a sketch of the history and morphology of the Latin alphabet (with bibliography) see J. C. Egbert, *Introd. to the Study of Lat. Inscripts.*, 1896, pp. 17–71, and R. Cagnat, *Cours d'épigraphie latine*, 2me. ed., 1890, pp. 1–34.
[4] Livy, VI. i.: '. . . etiamsi quae (*sc.* litterae) in commentariis pontificum aliisque publicis priuatisque erant monumentis incensa urbe pleraeque interiere.'

verse-form (*carmen*), but modernised in time. Their collected form (*ius Papirianum*) is of uncertain date. So with the *Twelve Tables*,[1] as already noted: had they remained unaltered, they would have been inestimable specimens of the Latin of the fifth century B.C. How much of the *Carmen Aruale*, and how much of the Salian fragments are genuine archaic Latin, how much corrupt, it is impossible to decide. What is commonly reckoned the oldest Latin inscription is that on the Praenestine *fibula*, a brooch found at Palestrina. It is usually ascribed to the fifth century B.C.[2] It runs, in a very ancient style of writing, from right to left:

Mánios med fhéfhaked Númasioi,

i.e., *Manius me fecit Numerio*, 'Manius made me for Numerius.' Linguistically it is most instructive. At this period, the strong stress accent would fall on the first syllable of each word, but the vowel-weakening in syllables following the accent has not set in. So we have *Manios*, not yet *Manius*; *fhefhaked*, not yet *fefeked* (a reduplicated form older than *fecit*); and *Numasioi*, not yet *Numesioi*, which in classical Latin had its intervocalic *s* changed to *r* — *Numerio*. The accusative *med* has the *-d* typical of the ablative in archaic Latin. The sound *f* is conveyed by FH, that is, the Greek digamma with the sign for *h*.

What is regarded by a body of expert opinion as the oldest official Latin document known is an inscription on four sides and one of the bevelled edges of a broken pillar found in 1899 at the north-west corner of the Forum Romanum. It is usually judged to be older — perhaps a century older — than the Gallic invasion of 390 B.C., but not so old as the Praenestine *fibula*. Among the few words left entire, or nearly so, upon the stele are *sacros* (*sacer*), *regei* (*regi*), *kalatorem* (*calatorem*). *iouxmenta* (?*iumenta*),[3] and *iouestod* (possibly an old ablative corresponding to *iusto*). The occurrence of *regei*, accepted as a dative rather than as an infinitive, is taken by some to apply to a political king,[4] by others to the *rex sacrorum*, whose magisterial office continued at Rome till the period of the Samnite Wars.[5] The latter view would regard the inscription as in some sense religious.[6]

[1] A good critical text is that by R. Schöll (Leipzig), 1866.
[2] *C.I.L.*, xiv. 4123. F. Stolz gives it as 'aus dem sechsten vorchristlichen Jahrhundert' in his *Latein. Grammatik* (I. Müller's *Handbuch d. klass. Altertumswissenschaft*, II. 2) ed. 3, 1900, § 2.
[3] Mommsen in *Hermes*, xxxviii,. 1903, pp. 151–153, declines to accept *iouxmenta* as the older form of *iumenta*. 'Diese Annahme ist unzulässig . . . *Iumentum* heisst nicht Jochthier sondern Hülfsthier.' He derives it from *iuuare*.
[4] Mommsen, in the article cited, has no doubt about it. He concludes 'dass die *iouxmenta* des Cippus ebenso dunkel sind wie alle übrigen in demselben enthaltenen Wörter. Eine Ausnahme dürfte höchstens *regei* machen, wodurch, wie ich mit Thurneysen glaube, die Inschrift in die Königszeit hinaufgerückt wird.' *Cf.* R. Thurneysen in *Rhein. Mus.*, lv., p. 484. Professor Ettore Pais scouts the idea that the cippus can be so old as the fifth cent. – far less the regal period. He argues it bears on ceremonies in honour of the god of the dead, Soranus (*Ancient Legends of Roman Hist.*, 1906, ch. ii).
[5] E. Pais, *op. cit.*, p. 282.
[6] For references to the literature discussing the inscription, see E. Pais,

A passing allusion may be made to another of the most ancient monuments of the language, the inscription on the 'Duenos bowl.' The triple earthen vase found in 1880 on the Quirinal is known by this name because its difficult and much disputed legend contains the words *Duenos med feced (Benus me fecit).*[1]

Belonging to a later period is the Latin of the oldest coins, dating from about 350 B.C.

As an example of Latin presumably older than the Second Punic War may be cited a dedicatory inscription found at Tusculum:

M. Fourio C. f. tribunos militare de praidad Maurte dedet,

i.e., M. Furius Gai filius tribunus militaris de praeda Marti dedit, marking that frequent disappearance of final *-s* which plays a considerable part in the scansion of early writers like Plautus.

To much the same period may be referred the well-known epitaphs of the Scipios in Saturnian verse, though it cannot be maintained that they date in each case from the decease of the man commemorated. For instance, the following epitaphs of the Scipio who was consul in 259 B.C. and fought in the first Punic War, are older than those of his father who was consul in 298 B.C.:

   (a) *L. Cornelio L. f. Scipio aidiles cosol cesor,*[2]
   (b) *Honc oino ploirume cosentiont R[omai] (?Romane)*
      Duonoro optumo fuise uiro
      Luciom Scipione. Filios Barbati
      Consol censor aidilis hic fuet a [pud uos]:
      Hec cepit Corsica Aleriaque urbe;
      Dedet Tempestatebus aide meretod.[3]

Less archaic in its forms (*e.g.,* nominatives in *-us*) is the epitaph of his father:

---

op. cit., p. 280, and P. Giles, *Short Manual of Compar. Philol.,* 1901, p. 579. Among its linguistic peculiarities should be noted *esed (erit),* as showing intervocalic *s* not yet rhotacised, and the unaccented *e* of *-ed* not yet weakened to *i.* In addition to Comparetti's large facsimile (*Iscrizione arcaica del foro romano,* 1900), smaller and more easily accessible ones are given by Giles, *op. cit.,* facing p. 579, and Pais, *op. cit.,* p. 16. A facsimile is also given as Tafel I. in F. Steffens's *Latein. Palaeographie,* Abteil. I., ed. 2, 1907, with mention of leading literature on subject in Italian and German. The date there assigned is sixth or fifth cent. B.C.

[1] The extensive and rather inconclusive literature on its inscription and purpose is referred to by Egbert, *Introd. to Study of Lat. Inscripts.,* p. 346. He gives a facsimile on p. 16. *Cf.* Lindsay, *Handbk. of Lat. Inscripts.,* pp. 19–23.
[2] *I.e.,* in Classical Latin: *L. Cornelius Luci filius Scipio aedilis consul censor. C.I.L.,* i., 31; Allen, *op. cit.,* p. 23; Lindsay, *op. cit.,* p. 39.
[3] *I.e.,*   '*Hunc unum plurimi consentiunt Romae*
      Bonorum optimum fuisse uirum
      Lucium Scipionem. Filius Barbati,
      Consul, censor, aedilis hic fuit apud uos:
      Hic cepit Corsicam Aleriamque urbem:
      Dedit Tempestatibus aedem merito.'
     C.I.L., i., 32; Allen, *op. cit.,* p. 23; Lindsay, *op. cit.,* p. 39.

> *Cornelius Lucius Scipio Barbatus*
> *Gnaiuod patre prognatus, fortis uir sapiensque,*
> *Quoius forma uirtutei parisuma fuit,*
> *Consol censor aidilis quei fuit apud uos;*
> *Taurasia Cisauna Samnio cepit,*
> *Subigit omne Loucanam opsidesque abdoucit.*[1]

The inscription on the *Columna Rostrata* erected in the Forum to C. Duilius in honour of his victorious sea-fight against the Carthaginians in 260 B.C. is in prose, and may be a modernised copy of the original or possibly a composition after the antique by some ingenious antiquary under the Emperor Claudius.

Approaching the subject of archaic Latin from a literary standpoint, we may review it under the heads of Poetry and Prose. To what extent did a native poetry exist? The actual remains are notoriously slight; the Romans possessed limited imagination. Can it be claimed that they possessed any poetry before the infiltration of Hellenism? Poetry, it will be allowed, came slowly to them. They were not a stock to breed inspired singers in the youth of their nation. The earliest versifiers must have felt heart-searchings in tentative essays at metrical composition; and listeners probably felt equal heart-searchings in accepting them. It would go hard with verses that possessed no demonstrable utility and had their only justification in an author's love of beauty and impulse to sing. The uncompromising words of M. Porcius Cato ring like a death-knell to poetry in its infancy:

> *Poeticae artis honos non erat: si quis ei re studebat aut sese ad conuiuia adplicabat, crassator (?grassator) uocabatur.*[2]

Thus the staid Roman would reckon the poet to be the peer of the man of riotous living, and his sportive lays only so much misspent ingenuity, if not downright roguery. The term 'grassator' which is almost certainly the right reading, dubs him a vagabond and footpad, a harbinger of François Villon. The Bohemian would not have readily found toleration in pre-Hellenic Rome. The attitude is of a piece with the inborn prejudice against every occupation not directly useful. Singing, dancing,

---

[1] *I.e.*
　　　　　'*Cornelius Lucius Scipio Barbatus*
　　　　　Gnaeo patre prognatus, fortis uir sapiensque,
　　　　　Cuius forma uirtuti parissima fuit,
　　　　　Consul, censor, aedilis qui fuit apud uos;
　　　　　Taurasiam, Cisaunam, Samnium cepit
　　　　　Subigit omnem Lucanam opsidesque abducit.'
　　　　　C.I.L., i., 30; Allen, *op. cit.*, p. 22; Lindsay, *op. cit.*, p. 41.

[2] From Cato's book inscribed *Carmen de moribus* apud Gell., *Noct. Att.*, XI. ii. 5; also cited in E. Bährens, *Frag. Poet. Rom.*, 1886, p. 57. The reading 'in ea re ludebat' probably arose from mistaking the dative 're' for the ablative; *cf.* L. Müller, *Q. Ennius*, 1884, p. 24.

acting were all *artes leuiores*.[1] It was only in Greece that such pursuits could be considered honourable.[2]

Yet there is a danger that these deficiencies may blind one to the existence, prior to the direct action of Hellenism, of a native literature in touch with the development of national life. Without the idealism, inspiration, and glamour of Greek poetry, there were Latin verses responding to social needs. The mere joy in life might never make a Roman sing;[3] but his heart could throb in sympathy with great deeds done by great men, and in admiration of firmness in facing danger. Occasions for songs were afforded by the death of a member of some family which had deserved well of the state, or by the banquets which at once honoured the gods and gladdened men. In the former case the *nenia*, or funeral dirge, developed; in the latter the heroic lay. In both the basis was professedly historical. In other songs the gods were solemnly invoked for material aid or present protection. Imagination was not free to soar. But, if there was no fine frenzy and no Sapphic rapture, it was something even to exaggerate ancestral prowess and to invent new ancestors performing unheard-of exploits. It was something to picture the nearness of the divine to human life. It was also something to initiate a drama in which merry quip and banter were more conspicuous than plot.

The not uncommon refusal to recognise any native literary power in the un-Hellenised Roman is partly due to a reaction against the adventurous extravagance of Niebuhr's theory. He averred that Rome had once possessed, but lost, a massive body of popular epic, whereof the songs once customary at banquets and the legends adorning the earlier books of Livy were distant echoes. All that was really beautiful in Roman story arose, he held, out of complete epics covering the period from Romulus to the battle of Regillus. Niebuhr's theory of a vanished *épopée*, warmly welcomed at first in many parts of Europe, especially by scholars interested in primitive popular poetry, responsible, too, for inspiring Macaulay's *Lays of Ancient Rome*, has long ago been exploded. It received a lively refutation at the hands of Taine,[4] and, indeed, is incredible in the absence of a single surviving fragment or single ancient mention of such epic creation. But certain of Niebuhr's con-

[1] See illustrative quotations in W. S. Teuffel, *Hist. Rom. Lit.*, §1; *e.g.*, the younger Africanus quoted by Macrobius, 'eunt in ludum histrionum, discunt cantare, quae maiores nostri ingenuis probro ducier uoluerunt.'
[2] Tac., *Dial.*, x. 5, 'Si in Graecia natus esses, ubi ludicras quoque artes exercere honestum est.'
[3] Quintilian, taking the Salian hymn to date from Numa's reign, argues that there was at least some interest in music among the early and warlike Romans: 'Veterum quoque Romanorum epulis fides ac tibias adhibere moris fuit. Versus quoque Saliorum habent carmen. Quae cum omnia sint a Numa rege instituta, faciunt manifestum, ne illis quidem, qui rudes ac bellicosi uidentur, curam musices, quantum illa recipiebat aetas, defuisse' (Quint., I. x. 20).
[4] *Essai sur Tite Live*, I. iii., § 2, 'Selon la coutume des novateurs, il pousse la vérité jusqu'à l'erreur.'

tentions are of permanent value. In addition to reiterating the scepticism of De Beaufort in the eighteenth century as to the trustworthiness of what passed for the early history of Rome, Niebuhr had the merit of emphasising the distinct testimony borne by ancient writers to the Roman habit of circulating heroic ballads. 'If passages,' he argued,'like that of Cicero's,[1] in which he states from Cato that "among the ancient Romans it was the custom at banquets for the praises of great men to be sung to the flute," have no authority, I really do not know what have any.'[2] Yet one may fully admit such authority without conceding that it logically implies the existence of what Niebuhr calls 'complete and true epic poems.' Stories like those of Coriolanus, of Curtius, and of the Horatii were not necessarily, as alleged, the subjects of previous epic treatment. The 'verses' so easily detected in Livy's text by Niebuhr were less evident to his critics. Niebuhr, in short, confounded poetic material with poetic achievement.

The products, then, of early Latin imagination, supported by positive evidence, may be summed up as including the themes, religious and secular, expressed in the Saturnian measure common to most Italic tribes; the *Satura*; the Fescennine plays; and, later, under Campanian influence, the Atellan plays.

The *Versus Saturnius*, a metrical scheme of primeval origin, received its name of 'Saturnian' from subsequent poets, acquainted with Greek models, in order to refer it to a mythical past, the golden age of Saturn. The grammarian Marius Victorinus,[3] writing in the fourth century of our era, says it was called *Saturnius* or *Faunius* to denote it as native to Italy. Varro[4] records the tradition that the 'fauns' of the woods used to foretell events in Saturnian lines.[5] Ennius, proud of the Parnassian

---

[1] Cic., *Tusc.*, IV. ii., 'Grauissimus auctor in Originibus dixit Cato, morem apud maiores hunc epularum fuisse, ut deinceps, qui accubarent, canerent ad tibiam clarorum uirorum laudes atque uirtutes.' Cf. Cic., *Brutus*, ch. xix, 75, 'Utinam exstarent illa carmina quae multis saeculis ante suam aetatem in epulis esse cantitata a singulis conuiuis de clarorum uirorum laudibus in Originibus scriptum reliquit Cato.' Varro (quoted by Nonius Marcellus, p. 76, *assa uoce pro sola*), 'In conuiuiis pueri modesti ut cantarent carmina antiqua in quibus laudes erant maiorum, et assa uoce et cum tibicine' (*i.e.*, with or without accompaniment on the flute). Valerius Maximus, II. i. 10, 'Maiores natu in conuiuiis ad tibias egregia superiorum opera carmine comprehensa pangebant, quo ad ea imitanda iuuentutem alacriorem redderent. Quid hoc splendidius, quid etiam utilius certamine?'; then in a patriotic outburst he exclaims, 'Quas Athenas, quam scholam, quae alienigena studia huic domesticae praetulerim? Inde oriebantur Camilli, Scipiones, Fabricii, Marcelli, Fabii.'

[2] Niebuhr, *Lectures on the Hist. of Rome*, ed. Schmitz, 1849, vol. ii., p. 13.

[3] H. Keil, *Gramm. Lat.*, vol. vi (1874), p. 138 (*De Saturnio Versu*), 'Prisca apud Latium aetas tanquam Italo et indigenae Saturnio siue Faunio nomen dedit.'

[4] Varro, *Ling. Lat.*, vii. 36, 'Fauni dei Latinorum, ita ut Faunus et Fauna sit; hos uersibus, quos uocant Saturnios, in siluestribus locis traditum est solitos fari futura.'

[5] Nettleship (*Lect. and Essays*, p. 52), accepting the root-idea of *faunus* as being 'speech' rather than 'light' or 'favour,' remarks, 'The *fauni*, from being the seers of the early rustic communities, become unreal beings, speaking with

excellence of his Hellenic hexameter, sneered at Naevius's rugged
Saturnians:

> Which whilome sylvan elves and warlocks crooned,
> When no man yet had climbed the Muse's crags,
> Or craved for style.[1]

This association with prehistoric antiquity is in accordance with
modern research. Scholars like Bartsch and Westphal[2] have investigated
the similarity between the early Italian and the early Teutonic ballad
metres. The result is to establish the Saturnian metre as an Indo-
European inheritance, and to suggest that its structure is not quantitative but accentual. Servius seems to have been the only ancient grammarian who had a glimmering of the right idea.[3] The attempts made by
most of the others to explain what is really 'folk's poesy' on the analogy
of Greek metrical principles were as futile as the attempts of the older
school of English critics to appreciate Chaucer's melody without a
scientific knowledge of the final -e. Though Saturnian verse may
eventually, when used by poets familiar with Greek literature, have
been partially affected by Hellenic methods of quantitative scansion, its
primitive and essential form cannot be understood by viewing its
syllables as longs or shorts. It is misleading to introduce in its analysis
any principle of quantity, even to the limited extent to which Nettleship, like Wordsworth[4] before him, applied it—namely, 'the arith-

---

unearthly voices in the recesses of mountain and forest.' Before they were
Graecised into πᾶνες and σάτυροι they might appropriately employ the native
Saturnian.

[1] Quoted Cic., *Brut.*, xviii. 71:

> 'Quos olim Fauni uatesque canebant
> Cum neque Musarum scopulos quisquam superarat,
> Nec dicti studiosus erat.'

I have borrowed the word 'warlocks' from the translation (1904) of H. Joachim's
Rom. Lit.

[2] K. Bartsch, *D. Saturn. Vers u. d. altdeutsche Langzeile*, 1867; R. Westphal,
D. älteste Form d. röm. Poesie, 1852; *cf.* his *Metr. d. Griech.* For the theory of the
revival of this primeval prosody in popular songs of later times, see R. Thurneysen, *Der Saturnier u. s. Verhältniss z. späteren röm. Volksverse*, 1885. For supporters of the quantitative theory, see Teuffel, *Hist. Rom. Lit.*, § 62, 3. L. Müller,
in particular, objects to treating Saturnians on metrical principles other than
those borrowed from Greek: see his *Enni Carminum Reliquiae*, 1884 (*Quaest.
Naeuianae*, pp. xxxii, *sqq.*, 'de Versu Saturnio'), and *D. Saturn. Vers u. s.
Denkmäler*, 1885.

[3] Ad Virg. *Georg.*, II. 385, 'Saturnio metro . . . quod ad rhythmum solum
uulgares componere solebant.'

[4] *Fragments and Specimens of Early Latin*, 1874, pp. 396–397. Wordsworth
regarded the regular scheme of the Saturnian as a double set of three trochees,
preceded by an *anacrusis* or base to start the line. The *anacrusis* and the *thesis*
at the end of each half-line could not be suppressed. Substitutions of two shorts
for one long, and of a long for a short in the *thesis* were freely admitted. With the
admitted licences he arranged the full scheme as:

metical equality of one long syllable to two shorts.'[1] Unaccented
syllables practically did not count. They might be dropped or increased
at pleasure. To say that the metre 'allows the shortening of a long
syllable when unaccented (*dĕuíctis*)' is tantamount to admitting that
'length' is meaningless. So 'length' is. It is a term intruded from later
principles of verse and inapplicable to the Saturnian.

Two rival views about the structure of the line hold the field.
According to the first, the scheme, if *x* denotes any syllable, is:

$$\acute{x}\,x\;\acute{x}\,x\;\acute{x}\,x\,x \mid \acute{x}\,x\;\acute{x}\,x\;\acute{x}\,x$$

i.e., applied to the time-honoured example:

>   *Dabúnt malúm Metélli* | *Naéuió poétae.*

Thus, each hemistich or colon normally contains three[2] accented
syllables, and each ends in an unaccented syllable. The basic principle
being accent, several unaccented syllables, or none at all, may come
between accented syllables. It will be noted that the *ictus* of the metre
corresponds with the natural accent of the word in the first and penul-
timate syllables of the second colon (*Naéuio poétae*), and in the pen-
ultimate syllable of the first (*Metélli*).

According to the other view, the scheme, if *x* denotes any syllable,
is of two chief types:

(a) $\acute{x}\,x\;\acute{x}\,x\;\acute{x}\,x$	$\acute{x}\,x\,x\;\acute{x}\,x\,x$
dábunt málum Metélli	*Naéuio poétae*;
(b) less usual,	
$\acute{x}\,x\;\acute{x}\,x\;\acute{x}\,x$	$\acute{x}\,x\,x\,x\;\acute{x}\,x$
prím(a) incédit Céreris	*Prosérpina púer*;

a variety of the second hemistich of the (*a*) type being $x\,x\,\acute{x}\,x\;\acute{x}\,x$
(*adlocútus súmmi*) and a variety of the second hemistich of the (*b*) type
being $x\,\acute{x}\,x\;\acute{x}\,x$ (*fuísse uírum*). On this hypothesis,[3] the Saturnian
metre, like Romance poetry, reckoned — with permissible variations — a
definite number of syllables to the line, seven to the first hemistich, six
to the second. The first hemistich had three accents, main or secondary;
the second had two. The first syllable of the line was invariably accented.
One observable feature about this plausible view is that it makes the
scansion consistent with the ordinary and natural word-stress. It scans

---

[1] Nettleship, *op. cit.*, p. 56.

[2] It has been argued (Allen, in *Zeitschrift für vergleichende Sprachforschung*,
1879) that these half-lines with three beats are curtailed descendants of lines
which originally had four beats. There may thus be a primeval identity of origin
for the Homeric hexameter and the Saturnian.

[3] W. M. Lindsay, *Lat. Lang.*, 1894, p. 128; *cf.* his contribution to *Amer.
Journ. Philol.*, vol. xiv., 1893. Otto Ribbeck dissents, *Geschichte der röm. Dich-
tung*, 2te Aufl., 1894, i., p. 349, 'Den neueren Theorieen von Westphal bis
Lindsay vermag ich nicht beizustimmen.'

dábunt, not *dabúnt*. Thus, although the theory renders obsolete Macaulay's[1] famous example of a perfect Saturnian:

'The queen was in her parlour | eating bread and honey,'

yet it gets rid of many anomalies in previous explanations and fits scientifically into our knowledge of archaic Latin.

The themes treated in Saturnian verse were mainly religious or heroic or popular. Ancient allusions, as well as the nature of the case, suggest that this verse was fostered at the outset by religion. We have seen that, in the plain Latin mind, a stigma might easily attach to poetry too spontaneous, too unaccountable, too remote from obvious needs. It was different when verse was consecrated to holy uses. The poet was then the priest or seer (*uates*), belonging to a class of depositaries[2] of a sacred literature in which religious songs and prophecies bulked largely. Striking instances of such verses are the *axamenta*, litanies in Saturnian measure, annually chanted by the Salian priests of Mars, as in his month of March they bore his sacred shields round the town. Among the very oldest extant specimens of Latin are a few fragments quoted by grammarians from these *Carmina Saliaria*, which were bequeathed from one generation to another till they became, Quintilian[3] tells us, too old-fashioned to be understood even by the reciting priests. All are very doubtful in text to begin with, and still more doubtful in restoration. In illustration I cite one report[4] of the text of Scaurus and one restoration: *cuine ponas leucesiae praetexere monti quotibet etinei de is cum tonarem (cod. Bernensis).* This has been at least plausibly restored:

> *Cume tonas, Leucesie,* | *prae tet tremonti*
> *Quom tibei cunei* | *dextumum tonaront.*

When thou thunderest, Light-god, before thee they tremble,
Sith thy bolts have thundered on the right.

Another venerable monument is the *Carmen Aruale* inscribed on a

---

[1] In a footnote to the Preface to his *Lays of Ancient Rome*.

[2] Lamarre, *Histoire d. l. littér. latine*, 1901, tome i., p. 49, 'L'ancien sacerdoce italique n'avait point méconnu le pouvoir qu'exercent la musique et la poésie sur l'âme humaine. Il eût été difficile dans l'antiquité d'élever la voix au nom des dieux sans tenter de recourir à un parler plus qu'humain, et de là le langage rhythmique dont se servaient les prêtres devins, les sibylles et les législateurs de la religion.'

[3] *Inst. Orat.*, I. vi. 40, 'Saliorum carmina uix sacerdotibus suis satis intellecta.' Horace implies the same difficulty in grasping their meaning in *Epist.*, II. i. 86–7:

> 'Iam Saliare Numae carmen qui laudat et illud
> Quod mecum ignorat solus uolt scire uideri.'

[4] From M. Ring, *Altlateinische Studien*, 1882, p. 51, where the other fragments are given. For a different version see Bährens, *Frag. Poet. Rom.*, 1886, p. 29. A most serviceable examination of the manifold conjectures, with a reconstructed text, is contained in B. Maurenbrecher's *Carminum Saliarium Reliquiae*, 1894.

tablet among the records belonging to the Arval brotherhood[1] in 218 A.D., and found at Rome in 1778. It is, then, an imperial copy of an ancient prayer deformed through a long process of oral tradition and the blunders of the workman who carved it. The *Fratres Aruales* were a body of twelve whose pre-eminent function was the observance of the agricultural festivals of May. Just as the primitive farmer sought to avert evil by the lustration of his lands, so the Arval brethren, with ceremonial dance (*tripudium*) and the amplest sacrifice of pig, sheep, and ox (*suouetaurilia*), and with holy litanies, performed the solemn lustration of the boundaries of the state.[2] As a state cult it was a replica of the worship conducted by a rustic household in the fields, and the invocation of Mars in this early fragment suggests his primitive connexion with vegetation before the needs of the rural community had created him a protecting power in its conflicts with neighbours. The text of the find is substantially this in rude Saturnians:

> *Enos Lases iuuate* (thrice).
> *Neue lue rue Marmar sins incurrere in pleores.* (thrice)
> *Satur fu, fere Mars: limen sali, sta berber.* (thrice)
> *Semunis alternei aduocapit conctos* (thrice).
> *Enos Marmor iuuato.* (thrice)
> *Triumpe, triumpe, triumpe, triumpe, triumpe!*

and approximately the translation is:

> Help us, ye Lares.
> Let not blight and ruin, O Mars, haste upon the multitude.
> Be satiate, fierce Mars: leap the threshold, stay thy scourge.
> Summon ye[3] in turn all the gods of sowing.
> Help us, O Mars.
> Huzza! Huzza! Huzza! etc.

Of broadly similar type are the old prayers quoted in Cato's *De Re Rustica*, prophecies like that quoted by Livy[4] on the draining of the Alban lake, and forms to be used by heralds in solemnly demanding redress or declaring war. To the borderland where religion most naturally touches popular imagination belong spells and incantations descended from primitive magic. These charms sung to cure maladies and wounds form a parallel in metre and spirit to Anglo-Saxon charms considered efficacious for sudden pains, although in the jargon[5] into

---

[1] The most exhaustive work on the records and worship of the brotherhood is G. Henzen's *Acta Fratrum Arualium*, Berlin, 1874.

[2] The festival of the *Ambarualia* is portrayed with fine imagination in the opening chapter of Pater's *Marius the Epicurean*.

[3] Taking *aduocapit* as = aduocabite (an imperative from future stem). But *aduocapit* may be fut. indic.; then translate 'Each one in turn shall summon the gods of sowing' (*alternei* adverbial locative; *conctos* nom. sing.).   [4] V. xvi.

[5] Not much is to be made of Cato's charm for a sprain:

> 'Huat hanat huat; ista pista sista;
> Domiabo damna ustra.'

Varro's cure for pain in the foot is more intelligible:

> 'Terra pestem teneto: salus hic maneto.'
>   Bährens, *F.P.R.*, p. 34.

which the Latin had degenerated we find no poetic suggestions of folklore and elf-shooting as in the Old English. Popular verses must have
existed early. Saturnians served for lullabies,[1] saws,[2] lampoons, and for
triumphal greetings till displaced by the trochaic tetrameter, which
became a favourite with soldiers in moods of mischief and rejoicing.
Other metres, not quite Saturnian, embodied weather-lore:

> *Hiberno puluere, uerno luto,*
> *Grandia farra, camille, metes.*

A winter of dust and a spring of rain
Mean, my lad, bushels of harvest grain.

Others enshrined utterances by the Merlin of early Latin, the half-
legendary bard Marcius, whose prophecy about Cannae was in circulation at the time of the Hannibalic war, and to whom was attributed a
golden rule of silence:

> *Postremus loquaris, primus taceas.*

The great mass of these popular verses has perished. Perhaps its most
distinct traces were left in the military skits cited by Suetonius, in
which, with a sort of Saturnalian licence, mummers plainly reminded a
victorious general of his failings.

More historical content characterised the dirges chanted by *praeficae*
at funerals, the epitaphs on distinguished men, and the already mentioned heroic lays sung at banquets. Apparently this latter fashion
resembled the usage of the Old English mead-hall, which in Caedmon's
days required, as Bede tells us, that the harp should pass from hand to
hand so that all guests should sing in turn. The significance of this
has been treated in connexion with Niebuhr's theory.

The beginnings of popular drama are to be found in the *Versus
Fescennini*, the *Satura*, and the *Atellana*. The most primitive stage
traceable in the old Italian drama is that of verses of the Fescennine
type—merry impromptu rustic banter, out of which in time dialogue
might be developed. Such outbursts of licence, originating in harvest
and vintage festivals,[3] were fancied to avert the evil eye or envy of the
gods on signal occasions of good fortune. Fescennine verses therefore
remained long in vogue at marriages and triumphs,[4] where there was

---

[1] 'Lalla lalla lalla: i aut dormi aut lacta.' – Bährens, *ibid.*
[2] The later popular poetry naturally is much more considerable. See
Edélestand du Méril, *Poésies populaires latines antérieures au douzième siècle,*
1843, where only a few pages are devoted to pre-Christian poems.
[3] Horace (*Epist.*, II. i. 139–146) connects the Fescennine ribaldry with the
jollity of an Italian harvest-home (*condita post frumenta*): he also emphasises the
elements of repartee:
> 'Fescennina per hunc inuenta licentia morem
> Versibus alternis opprobria rustica fudit.'
[4] Pliny, *N.H.*, XIX. 144, says of Caesar's soldiers at his triumph: 'alternis
quippe uersibus exprobrauere lapsana [*i.e.*, meagre vegetarian diet] se uixisse
apud Dyrrhachium.'

alternate rivalry in singing abusive indecencies with corresponding gestures. The custom of linking jests and gibes to the *carmina triumphalia* was a very ancient one: Livy mentions a case in connexion with the victory celebrated over the Aequi in 456 B.C.[1] When metrical at all, the *Fescennini* seem to have been originally in Saturnians, but those which remain to us, in the shape of soldiers' ribald verses sung at Caesar's Gallic triumph, are in trochaic metre.[2] It is a moot question whether this trochaic was borrowed from Greek example through the medium of the stage and adapted to the Latin accent, or was a development of native Latin metre. One thing is clear—the Fescennine verses and tomfoolery were essentially popular, and never reached the theatre. Livy contrasts the performances of professional actors (*histriones*) with the unpolished and offhand Fescennine verse.[3] The origin of the word *Fescennini* has been much debated. The derivation from the Faliscan town of Fescennium in Etruria, and that from *fascinum*,[4] the symbol of procreative power, are both as old as Festus. Philologically, the connexion with Fescennium is simpler, and it has a parallel in the usually accepted connexion of the Atellan plays with the town of Atella.

The next stage is *Satura*.[5] The most satisfactory derivation of this name, which had so great a career in literature, regards it as equivalent to *satura lanx*, the full platter of first-fruits offered to Ceres and Bacchus.[6] It is therefore essentially a medley, and the name was transferred from the rural basket or dish of various ingredients to a performance

---

[1] Livy, III. xxix, 'epulantesque cum carmine triumphali et sollennibus iocis, comissantium modo, currum secuti sunt.'

[2] *E.g.*, Suet., *Iul.*, li:

'Urbani, seruate uxores, moechum caluom adducimus.'
See also *ibid.*, xlix.

[3] Livy, VII. ii., '(histriones) qui non sicut ante Fescennino uersu similem incompositum temere ac rudem alternis iaciebant.'

[4] H. A. J. Munro, *Criticisms and Elucidations of Catullus*, pp. 76 *sqq.*, supports this. As the base of the adjective *Fescenninus* we may postulate a word *fescennus*, meaning a charmer, one with power to avert a curse or evil. This may be the word glossed by Festus, p. 76 (Lindsay), '*fescemnoe* dicti qui depellere fascinum putabantur.' Ribbeck objects to the derivation from *Fescennium* on the ground that these jesting songs belonged to the primitive elements in the life of the people and were not imported like the Oscan farce (*Geschichte der Röm. Dicht.*, 1894, i., p. 349).

[5] The following may be consulted: H. Nettleship, *The Roman Satura*, 1878, and 'Earliest Ital. Lit.,' in *Lectures and Essays*, 1885; H. de Mirmont, *Études sur l'ancienne poésie latine*, 1903, pp. 349-358.

[6] Practically all the ancient Latin scholars suggest that its original sense is a dish of mixed ingredients, a basket of various fruits, a forced meat of different materials, *e.g.*, Diomedes (Keil, *Gramm. Lat.*, i., 1857, p. 485) in addition to the fanciful derivation from 'the Satyrs' ('quod similiter in hoc carmine ridiculae res pudendaeque dicuntur') gives also the derivation 'satura a lance quae referta uariis multisque primitiis in sacris apud priscos dis inferebatur et a copia ac saturitate rei *satura* uocabatur': *cf.* Isidorus, *Orig.*, XX. ii. 8. Herein it resembles *farce*, lit. 'stuffing' (L. *farcire*) of jests put into comedy. Nettleship prefers not to supply a noun, but to compare nouns formed from feminine adjectives, *e.g.*, *noxia*, a fault; *dira*, a curse; so *satura*, a medley. Mommsen's view that it was the masque of the full men (*saturi*), or revellers, has not been widely accepted.

that was a blend of various materials. As to its original form, it seems to
have been a slightly more developed type of drama than the Fescennine.
The peasants in their impromptus assailed their fellows and added some
homely acting. The *locus classicus* on the history of the early *satura* is
Livy, VII. ii. Livy there tells us that in connexion with religious ceremonies intended to avert a plague, in the consulship of Sulpicius and
Stolo (364 B.C.), Etruscan performers were introduced into Rome to
dance to flute music. Their performances he calls *saturae*, complete
with musical accompaniment (*modis impletae*). He contrasts them with
the old and less regular Fescennine dialogue. Etruria, it will be noted,
made the great contribution of music to the early *satura*. Livy proceeds
to say that 'Livius' (Andronicus) was the first to give up these *saturae*
and venture upon a play with connected plot of the Greek type.[1] We
see, therefore, that Greek influence, embodied in drama of a more
regular type, was destined to drive *satura* off the stage. As a primitive
dramatic performance, then, *satura* may be inferred to have been a
rough and ready piece of mumming resembling, but not identical with,
the Fescennine ribaldries, and to have possessed dialogue but little or
no plot. Plot was impossible with contents so miscellaneous and un-
rehearsed; but a vigorous performance was attainable through the
personation of various characters by the mummers.

The failure to hold the stage was a blessing in disguise. It secured for
satura an unexpected future. When, owing to the paramount influence
of Hellenising poets, it ceased to be acted, it became a literary work with
an imaginary and far more inspiring stage. The *satura* developed into
'satire,' and its stage, widened at first to Roman society, became finally
co-extensive with the world. Roman satire always bore certain marks of
its early miscellaneous and dramatic elements. Developing into a composition in various metres, it later still, as Menippean satire, admitted
prose side by side with verse. From it, says Professor Tyrrell,[2] 'was
developed in one direction Latin Comedy through the Atellan farce
and the mime; in the other, that medley of topics and metres with
which Lucilius lashed the town in those open letters to the public,
which were very similar in scope to the modern weekly press.' It is a
long way from the primitive Italian *saturae* to Horace and Juvenal,
longer still to Dryden and Pope, Scarron and Voltaire; yet it is one continuous road through the realms of mockery, sometimes genial, but
oftener mordant.

The *fabulae Atellanae* were almost certainly Campanian, and named
from the town of Atella, though Mommsen denies this. They probably
did not affect Roman taste till about the third century B.C. Once intro-

---

[1] 'Liuius post aliquot annos qui *ab saturis* ausus est primus argumento
fabulam serere.' *Satura* is in sharp contrast to *fabula*, which implies a connected
plot.
[2] *Latin Poetry*, 1898, p. 217.

duced, they were felt to be so thoroughly congenial that they were acted at Rome enthusiastically by amateurs. Those respectable young men, Livy is careful to inform us, did not suffer the usual political disabilities under which the despised actor laboured in Rome.[1] The pieces were distinguished by the constant exhibition of the conventional characters of a country town, and are comparable with the Italian Pulcinello comedy and the time-honoured Punch and Judy. The stock figures were *Maccus*, the fool; *Pappus*, the greybeard to be tricked like a pantaloon; *Manducus*, the guzzler; *Dossennus*, the hunchback; *Bucco*, fatchaps, an embryonic Falstaff. These were introduced in ludicrous situations, as we may judge from the titles[2] of *Atellanae* in the later and more literary form given them by Pomponius and Novius: *e.g.*, *Maccus Miles*, the Fool as Soldier; *Maccus Virgo*, the Fool as Maid; *Maccus Copo*, the Fool as Mine Host; *Verres Aegrotus*, Verres Sick; *Verres Saluos*, Verres Well Again. Another characteristic seems to have consisted of riddles[3] asked in the play. These *tricae Atellanae* were familiar means of raising a laugh, and are attested by Varro, Suetonius, and Arnobius. The career of this type of popular farce was a chequered one. Raised to a higher artistic level by receiving a fully written plot, the Atellan play became a kind of comic burlesque. It could even be Hellenised enough to become a travesty of the myths; that is what titles like *Ariadne*, *Atalanta*, *Marsya*, *Phoenissae*, *Sisyphus* in the Atellan list must signify. Popular for a period as after-plays, they had a brief renascence in imperial times, but eventually succumbed before the superior attractions of pantomime.

It is a truism in literary history that prose is a product of later development than verse. Peoples sing before they write or speak artistically. If the verse during these early ages reached at Rome no pinnacle in the Palace of Art, it is not to be expected that the prose should attain a lofty degree of finish. Yet the foundations of a great prose were undoubtedly laid in the three departments of history, law, and eloquence. In each case the products sprang from national requirements. Religion in particular was the cradle of prose, as it was of verse. It was for the archives of the priestly colleges that prose books on ritual were composed, with a directory of worship and holy names; it was always with religious formality, and in language largely borrowed from religion, that early treaties such as those recorded[4] with Latin tribes or

---

[1] Livy, VII. ii. 12, 'quod genus ludorum ab Oscis acceptum tenuit iuuentus, nec ab histrionibus pollui passa est; eo institutum manet ut actores Atellanarum nec tribu moueantur,' etc.

[2] For a list of recorded titles of *Atellanae*, see the *index fabularum* in O. Ribbeck, *Comicorum Rom. Frag.* (being vol. ii of his *Scaen. Rom. Poesis Frag.*) ed. 3, 1898.

[3] Quint., VI. iii. 47, 'illa *obscura* (if that is the reading and not *obscena*) quae Atellani e more captant.'

[4] Horace, *Epist.*, II. i. 25, mentions the enthusiast for the ancient inspired style of Latin seen in the *Twelve Tables* (originally *Ten*), the kingly treaties, the priests' books, and time-honoured prophecies:

with the Carthaginian power were concluded; and the early *ius ciuile* coincided with the *ius sacrum*.

The priestly literature included *Libri Pontificum*, *Commentarii Pontificum*, *Fasti*, and *Annales*. Originally forming an advisory body to be consulted by the king on matters of ritual, the *pontifices* became the depositaries of sacred tradition and the authorities charged with organising the whole state religion. They were not mediators between the worshipper and his deity, but interpreters of lore and counsellors in puzzling questions of prayer and atonement. Their influence doubtless moulded the so-called *leges regiae*[1] and *commentarii regum*, as records of precedent and guides of conduct. The pontifical *libri* gave the order of ceremonial, and their *commentarii* contained rulings on disputed or difficult points. Their *fasti* at first meant a list of days on which law might be administered by the praetors. Later, by amplifying the enumeration of holy days and market days with anniversaries of disasters and notes on constellations, the *fasti* developed into a calendar combining sacred, legal, historical, and astronomical information. The brief references to events probably made these records no less dry than our *Anglo-Saxon Chronicle*: in any case their appeal was in early times limited; for the public had no access to them until Cn. Flavius published the calendar of religious festivals in 304 B.C. On the other hand, the *Annales Pontificum* or *Annales Maximi*, as they were styled later to distinguish them from briefer chronicles, were intended to appeal to the public. It was an old custom for the *pontifex maximus* to exhibit annually a white table mentioning names of magistrates, memorable events, and prodigies. This information we owe to Servius, who declares that when collected, as they were by the pontifex Scaevola in 120 B.C., they made eighty books. Although the custom of keeping such records went far back into history, yet the oldest portions were repeatedly destroyed by fire in the *Regia*, the official residence of the *pontifex maximus*.

Early history also received contributions from the civic officials. The *Commentarii Magistratuum* and *Libri Magistratuum* recorded magisterial acts and names. Some of the latter were written on one of the most

---

' Sic fautor ueterum ut tabulas peccare uetantis
Quas bis quinque uiri sanxerunt, *foedera regum*
Vel Gabiis uel cum rigidis aequata Sabinis,
Pontificum libros, annosa uolumina uatum
Dictitet Albano Musas in monte locutas.'

Cf. treaties in republican period *cum Latinis populis* (Livy, ii. 33), *cum Ardeatibus* (Livy, iv. 7), and Polybius's record of the first maritime treaty with Carthage, supposed to date from 509 B.C., and difficult of interpretation for even the best scholars in his time, 2nd cent. B.C. (Polyb., iii. **22**, ὥστε τοὺς συνετωτάτους ἔνια μόλις ἐξ ἐπιστάσεως διευκρινεῖν).

[1] The fragments deal with points like pollution of an altar, burial of a victim of lightning, rewards for captors of spoils. Assault on a father is dealt with in these terms: ' si parentem puer uerberit, ast olle plorassit, puer diuis parentum sacer esto.'

ancient materials, linen: these were the *libri lintei* preserved on the
Capitol in the Temple of the goddess of Memory (*Moneta*). Besides
official documents there were private ones, partly prompted by the desire
to record the past, but chiefly designed in the form of family chronicles
to gratify patrician pride by panegyrics on ancestors. Pedigrees (*stem-
mata*), inscriptions (*tituli*, *elogia*) beneath the ancestral busts, and funeral
eulogies (*laudationes funebres*) may have contained a grain of truth in a
bushel of praise, but they fostered the use of both language and imagination.[1] The love of tracing ancestors into the legendary past was
ingrained in the Roman. It found its ideal utterance in Virgil's elaboration of the descent of the Julian house, and is illustrated in the books
which Atticus wrote on the Junian family, the Marcelli, Fabii and
Aemilii.[2]

In the early stages of law, that wonderful fabric which is one of the
noblest monuments of the Roman mind, far the most prominent place
is held by the *Twelve Tables*. They form the most influential work in
archaic prose. The *Tables* were the issue of half a century of political
struggle following the expulsion of the kings. A position of legal
insecurity and ignorance of the unwritten law of custom jealously kept
in patrician hands, drove the plebeians to demand a definite codification. In 452 B.C. a committee of three is said to have returned from
Greece after studying the laws of Solon.[3] Next year the Decemvirs,
specially appointed to register the laws, began their work, with the
elder Appius Claudius as the mainspring of the undertaking. This
Board of Ten, according to one account, received assistance from the
Greek philosopher Hermodorus of Ephesus, the friend of the celebrated Heracleitus. The Greek influence, however, thus alleged to have
acted on Roman law in the middle of the fifth century B.C., was too
restricted to interfere with the national character of the codification.
The *Ten Tables* of 451 B.C. were increased by two next year, and afterwards graven on bronze and exhibited in public.[4] It is doubtful whether
these originals escaped destruction by the Gauls in 390 B.C., and it is
certain that the existing fragments have undergone much modification.
Those we possess deal with such subjects as court procedure (postponement, compromise and debating of lawsuits, summoning of witnesses,
treatment of debtors), property (its transmission by will or otherwise, its

[1] Livy and Cicero both comment on the untrustworthiness of family
funeral orations. Livy, VIII. xl, 'uitiatam memoriam funebribus laudibus reor.'
Cic., *Brut.*, xvi. 62, 'his laudationibus historia rerum nostrarum est facta
mendosior.'
[2] Corn. Nep., *Att.*, 18. Atticus also wrote verses of a biographical and
laudatory kind to be attached to busts ('ita ut sub singulorum imaginibus facta
magistratusque eorum non amplius quaternis quinisue uersibus descripserit').
[3] Gibbon long ago showed the great improbability of this tale. It is rejected
by authorities like Ihne for good reasons.
[4] Livy, III. lvii, 'leges decemuirales quibus *Tabulis Duodecim* est nomen,
in aes incisas, in publico proposuerunt' (446 B.C.).

protection by the state as in case of an owner's insanity), crimes, rights, damage, relation of patron and client, and disposal of the dead. There are provisions against bewitching crops (*qui fruges excantassit*) and against incantations (*qui malum carmen incantassit*). Another declares the killing of a burglar to be justifiable homicide (*si nox furtum faxsit, si im occisit iure caesus esto*).

The code was not merely of immense social value as a declaration of rights and definition of offences, 'the well of all public and private law,' as Livy says in a famous phase.[1] It was also of the highest educational value. Learned by heart in school till the time of Cicero, it wielded a potent influence on thought and phraseology. There is an interesting discussion on its style recorded by Aulus Gellius in the second century A.D. He introduces into one of his *Attic Nights* Favorinus the philosopher and Sextus Caecilius the lawyer, who, while waiting to pay their respects to the Emperor *in area Palatina*, talk about the *Twelve Tables*. The philosopher declares he perused the *Tables* with no less avidity than he had the ten books of Plato on *Laws*; and when the lawyer praises their elegant brevity, the philosopher quite agrees, with the farther remark that there were also portions either very difficult or very harsh.[2]

The plebeian triumph in forcing the codification was considerably lessened by the continued patrician monopoly of the *legis actiones*. Only patricians knew the rules for applying the laws and the forms of lawsuits. This hardship was remedied in 304 B.C., when Cn. Flavius, actuated by App. Claudius Caecus, a descendant of the noted decemvir, published the forms of pleading (*ius Flauianum*), as we have seen he did the calendar.[3] Henceforth law could not be exclusively under patrician control. Legal knowledge was put within the reach of all when Tiberius Coruncanius, the first plebeian *pontifex maximus*, offered to teach law to any applicant. He was consul in 280, and from him, as the first professor of law in Rome, sprang a school of jurists who founded legal science.

Oratory arose out of state affairs. The power of speaking before a senatorial or a popular audience was necessarily developed and esteemed in a community so keenly political; but it was late before the Romans were masters of culture and taste enough to produce a polished type of eloquence. Their early efforts would be of the direct and forcible kind suggested by the homely fable of *The Belly and the Members* related by Menenius Agrippa for the edification of the plebeians who seceded to the Mons Sacer.[4] If we accept the tradition of Roman literary criticism, we must refer the first artistic Latin prose to the time of the Pyrrhic war.[5]

---

[1] III. xxxiv, 'fons omnis publici priuatique iuris.''
[2] *Noct. Att.*, XX. i. 4, 'eleganti atque absoluta breuitate uerborum scriptae . . . quaedam obscurissima aut durissima.'
[3] Livy, IX. xlvi.   [4] Livy, II. xxxii.
[5] Isidor., *Orig.*, I. xxxviii. 2, 'apud Romanos Appius Caecus aduersus Pyrrhum solutam orationem primus exercuit; iam exhinc ceteri prosae eloquentiam condiderunt.'

D

Appius Claudius Caecus, censor of 312 B.C., consul in 307 B.C. and again a decade later, was a broad-minded reformer so versatile of genius and vigorous of action that he well deserved his ancient epithet of 'the hundred-handed' (*centimanus*). On land-laws and finance, aqueducts and roads, jurisprudence and grammar, even on poetry,[1] he left his mark; but perhaps his memory was kept fresh not more by his Appian Way than by the stand he made before his fellow senators in 280 B.C., when, old and blind, seventeen years after his second consulship, he delivered his famous speech against granting terms of peace to King Pyrrhus of Epirus so long as that monarch remained on Italian soil. We can hardly judge of this speech from the Greek summary given by Plutarch;[2] for Plutarch's version seems to owe at least as much to that historian's knowledge of Greek affairs as to any copy of the Latin speech to which he might have had access. The surviving Roman testimonies, however, show that Appius was regarded as representative of a powerful but obsolete fashion of speaking. Cicero, with the speech still extant,[3] considered it rude compared with the oratory of Marcus Porcius Cato (234–149 B.C.). Tacitus, commenting on changes in oratorical style, and passing strictures on cranks who invariably upheld the old-fashioned, is prepared to meet with people who would admire Appius in preference to Cato.[4] Seneca writes of faddists for whom the style of the Gracchan age (second century B.C.) was too polished and fresh—they had to go right back to Appius and Coruncanius.[5]

The influence of this earlier literature upon the later must justify the attention drawn to it. The main survivals may be briefly noted. The Saturnian metre still had a career; we shall be struck with the acceptance of the old metre by Livius and Naevius, who were both acquainted with Greek models. The composition of a long Italian epic like Naevius's *Punic War* in Saturnians was a straight testimony to the author's belief in the power of appeal inherent in the national verse. The persistence of alliteration, an entirely un-Greek artifice, but one which the Saturnian metre shares with the ancient ballads chanted by the Teutonic *scôp*, is another proof of vitality. Not merely earlier poets like Naevius thus 'hunt the letter,' but the device is taken over into the hexameter by

---

[1] His *carmina* were of a sententious cast, such as 'Every man is the fashioner of his own fortune' ('*Appius ait fabrum esse suae quemque fortunae,*' Pseudo-Sallust *ad Caes. de Rep.,* I. i. 2), and 'Forget your woes in the face of a friend' ('*Amicum cum uides, obliuiscere miserias,*' a Saturnian quoted by Priscian, see Bährens, *Frag. Poet. Rom.* p. 36).
[2] *Life of Pyrrhus,* ch. xix.
[3] Cic., *De Senect.,* xvi, 'Ipsius Appi exstat oratio.'
[4] Tac., *Dial.,* xviii, 'Num dubitamus inuentos qui prae Catone Appium Claudium magis mirarentur?'
[5] Sen., *Ep.,* 114: 'Multi ex alieno saeculo petunt uerba; *Duodecim Tabulas* loquuntur; Gracchus illis et Crassus et Curio nimis culti et recentes sunt; ad Appium usque et ad Coruncanium redeunt.' This quotation is most interesting as showing the influence exercised by the archaic period on certain readers of the first century A.D.

Ennius, and, in imitation of him, employed by Virgil with Swinburnian deftness. There are Fescennine echoes in popular trochaics, as we have seen, and in wedding songs from Catullus down to Claudian. The native drama, indeed, might have had a great life before it, but it was strangled in infancy by the dread of outspoken criticism felt among the nobility:[1] there was no chance for an Aristophanes in Rome. Yet the Fescennine masque was not barren. It was the lineal ancestor of Latin Comedy, of pastoral amoebean verses like those in Virgil's *Eclogues,* and of some elements in satire. The old *satura* itself, which the discerning criticism of Quintilian[2] marked out as genuinely Roman, handed on to later literature certain of its dramatic features and its *olla podrida* of material. Finally, so far as drama is concerned, the Atellan farce bequeathed, especially to the literary satire of subsequent times, that habit of mocking provincial oddities which crops out in Horace when he chuckles over the airs given himself by a petty magistrate at Fundi, and in Juvenal when he pictures the ragged aedile who has to smash up short weights and measures in deadly dull Ulubrae.[3] As for the prose of the period, its influence was deepest in the province of law, owing to the prominent part played by the *Twelve Tables* in the educational system.

This native literature, then, is often cumbersome, and as yet lacks the highest distinction of style and grace, but is no less often solemn and dignified—it is always masculine. However powerful and brilliant the incoming Hellenic influence, these pre-Hellenic products of Rome must not be disdained as feeble and disconnected with the literature that was to follow. Impotence cannot create, and this early work had issue. It contained the germs of later success. Genius cannot be borrowed: it can be modified and developed. Above all, it can borrow, and make the loan its own. That was the case with Rome.

[1] *E.g.,* 'Dabunt malum Metelli Naeuio poetae.'
[2] *Inst. Orat.,* X. i. 93, 'Satura quidem tota nostra est.'
[3] Hor., *Sat.,* I. v. 34; Juv. x. 101-2.

Chapter II

THE INVASION OF HELLENISM

The period from 240 to 70 B.C. – External history – Internal politics – Social conditions – Wealth and luxury – Degeneracy alongside of refinement – Traits which defied Hellenism – Sketch of contact with Greek colonies – Contact with the Greek mother-country – Spoils and art collections – Books – The Greek invaders – Causes of opposition – Dangerous versatility and unsettling theories – Variations in Roman attitude towards Hellenism – The victor vanquished – Positive contributions to Roman thought – Literary education under Greek auspices – Crates from Pergamum – Greek rhetoric – Greek philosophy – Polybius and Scipio Aemilianus – Carneades and his colleagues – Cato's vain protest in the cause of morals – Welcome to poets like Archias – Greek foundation of the later 'Trivium' – Cicero's early training as a type.
Outline of the period from a literary standpoint – National movements in the literature – Chief Hellenic aspects.

FROM the end of the first Punic War (241 B.C.) to the first consulship of Pompey (70 B.C.), one hundred and seventy years elapsed. For Rome they constituted a period of manifold change in external relations, in internal politics, in social conditions, in intellectual and artistic progress. Every aspect of change told upon the native genius, but none so powerfully for literary development as the intellectual movements. The national rise into a world-power, the democratic inroad upon the ancient primacy of the senate, the increase of wealth and luxury, brought scores of new responsibilities and problems. These all stimulated the Roman mind; but it was Hellenism which fertilised it.

When this period of less than six generations opens, Rome has in Sicily gained her first province outside Italy; before it closes, she has added Sardinia and Corsica, the Spains, Gaul in part, Illyricum, Macedonia, Achaea, and, in the official sense, Africa and Asia. She has established a protectorate over Egypt; she is on the eve of definitely organising the East. When the period opens, she could not count on the loyalty of all the subject tribes even in Italy: when it closes, the Italian allies have at last wrung from her the privilege of citizenship. Already Rome stands for civilisation in repelling the barbarians on her Macedonian frontier and in checking, by means of Marius's military genius in Gaul, Germanic hordes of the wild type destined ultimately to overwhelm the Empire. Rome's success during this period makes a climax in the history of the world. For centuries to come, peoples widely differing in blood, civilisation, and language were to own the suzerainty of one national will and one code of law. The imperial system was present, in fact though not yet in name.

Internally, the development of politics during a century and three-quarters was no less marked. Though the commons had their legislative power affirmed as early as 449 B.C., and in theory fully established in 287 B.C. under the Hortensian law, yet their authority was overshadowed by the senate, especially during the hundred years of rapidly added foreign conquests from 240. Until past the middle of the second century B.C., circumstances played into senatorial hands. The senate was inevitably predominant, as the body controlling foreign policy, provincial administration, and finance. The close oligarchic ring, it must be allowed, had done great things. It possessed noble traditions of dignity, bravery, and caution. To Cineas, the envoy of King Pyrrhus, it not unnaturally appeared to be 'an assembly of kings.' The change, however, came as the pressure of foreign imbroglios slackened and as home problems craved attention. Among the middle class (*equites*), a strong group of capitalists had thriven on the monopolies secured to them without risk of rivalry, thanks to the aristocratic disdain for trade. State competition in corn, on the other hand, was ruining the Italian peasant farmers, already reduced in numbers owing to the growth of estates (*latifundia*) worked by wealthy owners of slave-gangs or turned into extensive pastures.[1] It was a revival of the old grievance of the fourth century — the excessive holdings in public land possessed by privileged occupiers. Economic discontent prompted the agrarian agitation of the Gracchi brothers, and their campaigns for reform involved a challenge to the position of the senate. But the question became a burning one in other ways. There were growing complaints of oppressed and misgoverned provincials against their extortionate governors, who were often little other than licensed senatorial plunderers whom senatorial juries would not convict.[2] Things were worse still when the war in North Africa against Jugurtha was grossly mismanaged by scions of noble houses actually in the king's pay. It was Marius, a man risen from the ranks, a democratic nominee appointed to supreme command by the popular assembly in defiance of the senate, who brought the war to an end in 105 B.C. Even more than the revelations before the commission which sat to inquire into the military scandals connected with the African campaigns, it was this assumption by the people of control over the army that accentuated the incompetence of the senate. A new epoch of revolution had dawned. The republic was moribund. All the problems

---

[1] Most historians do not now give such a high place to state-competition among the causes of the decline of Italian agriculture in the second century B.C. Cf. H. Last in *Camb. Anc. Hist.*, IX., 1932, pp. 2 ff. – Ed.

[2] Senatorial juries were replaced by equestrian juries in 122 B.C. – Ed.

out of which the imperial *régime* sprang were pressing for settlement. Individualism was the mark of the great politician and the sign of coming monarchy. Sulla's dictatorship was the last attempt to buttress by main force the power of the senate at the expense of the middle class and of the commons with their tribunes. Though his impress on law was permanent, ten years saw his political work undone; and with the overthrow of Sulla's constitution by Pompey and Crassus, in 70 B.C., the days of senatorial ascendancy were numbered. Politics here chiefly interest us for the effect produced on literature. Amid such strenuousness of public life may be discovered the real explanation of increased attention to history and of growth in Roman oratory.

Social environment altered more during a few generations after the defeat of Hannibal than during the five preceding centuries. Foreign imports, comforts, luxuries, tastes, ideas, and beliefs had henceforth to be set in a Roman framework. The Roman became more adventurous in thought as in action. The great wars disclosed realms of intellect and beauty undreamed of hitherto. The common burgher, tempted by prospects of Eastern plunder, could become a half-professional soldier; the moneyed middle-class descried openings for lucrative speculation abroad; members of the oligarchy could, as governors, rifle provinces of gold and art treasures, or, at their choice, master the domains of Greek philosophy. There could be no stagnation in such times. Even though a sense of national security after the final overthrow of Macedon and Carthage might have naturally lulled Roman minds into inaction, any such danger—quite apart from the harassing troubles of protracted guerilla in Spain and risings of armed slaves in Sicily and nearer home—was obviated by vexing problems of internal politics touching land-laws, franchise for the Italians, and other reforms, political, economic, and social. The education drawn from turmoil is as valuable as that drawn from imported ideas, and more vitally affects the national character. But the foreign factors in this period are more obvious, and are certainly not merely superficial. In the social changes it is to be noted that, while non-Greek influences were at work, the Greek influences were very marked: in matters of intellect, formal education, and literature, the Greek influences were decidedly predominant.

The most concrete social feature of the times is the heightened standard of living due to the ubiquitous inpouring of wealth. Unmistakable signs are the rise in prices and rents, greater complexity in architecture of houses, more elaborate furnishings, multiplication of silver-plate and table delicacies, and increase of slaves.[1] Amid the

---

[1] 'Prices were forced up to an incredible degree. An amphora of Falernian wine cost 100 denarii, a jar of Pontic salt-fish 400; a young Roman would often give a talent for a favourite, and boys who ranked in the highest class for beauty of face and elegance of form fetched even a higher price than this (Polyb., xxxi. 25; Diodor., xxxvii. 3). Few could have been inclined to contradict Cato

evidence for extravagant purchase of town and country residences, Oriental purples, effeminately soft materials of dress, ornaments of unfamiliar name, music-girls, dancing-girls, and numberless other ministrants to the most varied demands of caprice and pleasure, it is very easy to overstate the bad effect on Roman morals. The growth of luxury was undeniable. Others besides the stern censor Cato recognised it. The authorities repeatedly took alarm, and to check the danger recourse was had sometimes to excessive rating for articles of value, sometimes to sumptuary laws.[1] Enactments restricting the fowl at dinner to the domestic hen and the wines to native growths proved futile in their quest of a uniform simplicity, because they ignored the extremes of wealth and poverty now existing in the community. There were other ominous signs. Bribery and corruption were rife at elections in the second century as soon as Eastern riches became available. Plautus is acquainted with some law of *ambitus*[2] — probably an early one in the long series devised to secure the purity of the electorate. A sure drift towards degeneracy had set in by the first century before our era. If the common people had not actually become the rabble with the two sole aims which Juvenal sums up as *panem et circenses*, it was perilously easy to be fed and amused in the midst of cheap or free corn-distributions, multiplied festivals, and organised games.

But it is totally misleading to dismiss the age as one of unqualified degeneracy. The moody complaints of Sallust and Livy regarding moral decay in their own or in immediately preceding times must be considerably discounted as due to their exaggerated diagnosis of ailments in the body politic and their roseate painting of a vanished era of simple goodness. Signs of outward prosperity do not necessarily argue deterioration in morals. They are not to be condemned wholesale as pernicious. Some of them, indeed, argue national activity and elevation of taste. The truth is that, with the loss of pristine simplicity, two tendencies set in and worked side by side for centuries — one in the direction of refinement, culture, and literary creation; the other in the direction of vulgar enjoyment, effeminacy, and, it might be, vice. So it is quite intelligible why the period should have in men like Cato its opponents of Hellenism as a suspected agent of weakness and cor-

when he said in the senate-house that Rome was the only city in the world where a jar of preserved fish from the Black Sea cost more than a yoke of oxen, and a boy-favourite fetched a higher price than a yeoman's farm,' A. H. J. Greenidge, *A Hist. of Rome during later Repub. and Early Principate*, vol. i., 1904, p. 18. The general characteristics of a great part of this period are admirably illustrated, *op. cit.*, pp. 1–100.

[1] For legislation regulating gold ornaments, numbers of guests at entertainments, expense of banquets, and even the viands and drinks, see Greenidge, *op. cit.*, pp. 27–29.

[2] *Amph.* (prol.), 73–74:
   'Sirempse legem . . .
   Quasi magistratum sibi alteriue ambiuerit.'

ruption, but also in Scipio and his circle convinced champions of the new cosmopolitan culture.

Before illustrating the effects of Hellenism, which so many Roman patriots regarded as a peril from the East, it is well to note that though in some phases it acted on the national genius at once, the perfect fusion of the best of Greece with the best of Rome belongs rather to a later age than that under discussion. In many phases the action of Hellenism was necessarily slow—for example, it could not promptly turn Romans into philosophers or artists. And there were whole tracts of the Roman temperament which, as we should expect, never yielded to the more humane and refined influence of Greece. Both in the manners of Roman governors and in the amusements of the people, there was an ingrained hardness and barbarity of nature. Nothing could eclipse the cynical Machiavellianism of Rome's final brutality towards ruined Carthage; her refusal to either try or release the thousand *détenus* from Achaea summoned by the senate to Italy in 167 B.C.; her decision against the claim of Demetrius to the crown of Syria, because it suited her designs to favour his cousin, a boy of nine; or her arrangement between the quarrelling royal brothers in Egypt according to the dictates of sheer selfishness.[1] Nothing in Greek history is for cruelty comparable to the Roman manner of throwing upon the market slaves who were prisoners of war, or still more shamefully obtained by piratic kidnappers. It was only by degrees that the iron rigour of the lords of the world, for the most part contemptuous of educated and uneducated slaves alike, changed to intelligent, if not always sympathetic, despotism. The periodic revolts of slaves and the defection, in Sulla's time, of Greek states, Athens included, were so many protests against the overbearing and relentless Roman rule. Then, the popular spectacles were inherently coarse. It would have been well if Rome had been more fully Hellenised in this trait, so as to imitate the graceful athletics and contests in finer arts which marked the Greek games. The mortal combats of gladiatorial pairs at a funeral had originally a sacrificial meaning, but such displays were preserved and extended from a lust for bloodshed long after their religious significance was lost. A typical occurrence interrupted the musical exhibition attempted at a triumph of 167 B.C. The general forced the flutists to play the accompaniment for a sham fight between two sections of the chorus.[2] The public 'hunting' (*uenatio*) of wild beasts, dating from the display of lions and panthers by M. Fulvius in 186, after the Aetolian War, continued this savage craving. It is a trait which we shall find producing a detrimental effect on the drama. Roman society was never permeated with culture comparably with the

---

[1] These are instances reprobated by Polybius, enthusiastic admirer of the Romans though he is: see Polyb., xxx. 32; xxxi. 2 and 10.

[2] Polyb., xxx. 22. L. Müller (*Q. Ennius, Eine Einleitung, u.s.w.*, pp, 37–40) criticises the story severely. He insists that, as Greeks, Polybius, Strabo and Dionysius often fail to appreciate Italian manners and taste.

Athenian society which enjoyed the tragedies and comedies of the fifth
century B.C. Yet it looks as if, at any rate in the time of Plautus, there
was a widespread interest in plays and an audience of Elizabethan
intelligence to appreciate his Greek tags and puns. For an interval,
Rome seems to have caught a general enthusiasm for plays on Greek
lines. Apparently the novelty wore off and this phase of Hellenism lost
its hold on the populace. Low pantomimic exhibitions, and the gladiator
or wild beast

> Butchered to make a Roman holiday,

ousted from favour the more psychological actor, in spite of the greater
proportion of festivals devoted to *ludi scenici*.[1] With the superior polish
of Terence, artistic drama diverts its appeal to higher circles.

When Greek influence began to operate on Rome, it is impossible
exactly to determine. Italy and Sicily had their Greek colonies soon
after the traditional date for the foundation of Rome. There may have
been slight infiltrations of Greek influence in the regal period through
Etruria — the Tarquins were, it is recorded by Livy, of Corinthian
descent. Consultations of the Delphic oracle date back, in legend at
least, to the time of the kings. It is fanciful to picture Rome quickened
by the theories emanating from Pythagoras and his brotherhood in
Italy, and more than doubtful whether she was awakened to such
interest in Greek law as would prompt the alleged despatch of commissioners to study the Solonian code at Athens in the fifth century
B.C. Commerce must have occasioned the earliest important dealings
with Greek-speaking peoples. The intercourse which sailors and traders
from Rome had with the settlements of Magna Graecia was fraught with
great issues. There was much to learn from those highly civilised states.
The borrowing of the alphabet from the Aeolic colonists at Cumae is a
familiar fact.[2] The conquest of Greek states in Campania, South Italy
and Sicily made further steps in the same direction. Greek surnames and
customs became familiar. The keepers of the Sibylline books were of
necessity acquainted with Greek, and the influx of slaves and freedmen
spread some knowledge of the language even among the humbler
orders.

The first contact between Romans and the Greeks of the mother-
country dates from 332 B.C., when Alexander of Epirus, the uncle of
Alexander the Great, crossed to help his kinsmen of Tarentum against
the Samnites. These early relations with Epirus are marked for all time
by the Latin word for the Hellenes. After a tribal name (Γραικοί) in

---

[1] See Teuffel, *Hist. Rom. Lit.*, § 91, 21.
[2] The discussion of the adoption of the Greek alphabet, and its subsequent
modifications must be relegated to the science of language (*e.g.*, Giles, *Manual of
Compar. Philol.*; Lindsay, *Lat. Lang.*). The Greek form of letters in early
Roman inscriptions has been handled by Ettore Pais, *op. cit.*, ch. ii. (on excavations).

Epirus, the Romans called them 'Greeks' (*Graeci*). Diplomacy, as well as trade, came to realise the necessity of knowing the language. At Tarentum in 282 B.C., the Roman representative, Postumius, could make a Greek speech. Cineas, sent by Pyrrhus to treat with the senate a year later, does not seem to have needed an interpreter.[1] The defeat of his royal master was both a revelation of the unsuspected rise of a new fighting power in the shape of the republic, and a proof that the entire Hellenic civilisation in Italy must acknowledge the Roman sway. It is significant that the fall of Tarentum in 272 brought to Rome in the person of Andronicus her first literary interpreter of Greek drama and epic. The first Punic War (264–241) widened the area of contact; for the Greek cities of Sicily, with their opulent and artistic civilisation, ranged themselves on the side of Rome against Carthage. Relations with the Greeks of the mother-country grew still closer when in her first Illyrian War (229 B.C.), Rome put herself forward as a champion of the Greeks. She thereby initiated that pro-Hellenic policy which so favourably impressed the anti-Macedonian feeling among the Hellenes, when, in 196, with imposing ceremony, Flamininus proclaimed Greece free. Thus at the time when Plautus was producing his dramas, Rome liberated the Greeks, and, half a century before she politically enslaved their country, had herself fallen captive to the attractions of their literature.

From the end of the third century B.C. Hellenism is an abidingly strong factor in Roman civilisation. Its strength may be illustrated by the impetus it gave to collections of art and books, and by its contributions to Roman thought through teachers, both bond and free. It was with signal ability and sometimes golden-mouthed eloquence that these teachers fascinated their hearers, as they introduced them to the literature, oratory, and philosophic systems of Greece.

Hellenism acted on Rome with marked effect through a long series of public spoils and private art collections from Greek cities in Italy, Sicily, and the East. It might be argued that many of the spoils brought to Rome and paraded in triumph from the days of Pyrrhus onwards had presumably no more lasting effect on the proletariat than the exhibition of trophies won in Zululand or the Soudan could have had on a London crowd. But the veriest mob does not lack imagination. They must have felt, as spectators of a pageant, some vague stirrings dimly conscious of Rome's strength and the greatness of her oversea dominions. And it must be remembered that masterpieces did not depend on a passing procession for their chance of proving impressive: set up in public places, they were a constant provocative to admiration. At all events, for the better trained their presence was full of meaning and stimulus. It is worth while observing how continuous was the stream of beauty. In 212 B.C. Marcellus brought from Syracuse to deck his triumph the

---

[1] Plut., *Pyrrh.*, 14 and 18.

choicest statues and pictures of that renowned artistic centre. In 211 the
punitive denudation of recaptured Capua augmented the store of the
beautiful, though to a less extent than the rifling of Tarentum in 209 by
Q. Fabius. From Tarentum came Lysippus's colossal Herakles to the
Capitol.[1] Similar acquisitions attended the victories of Flamininus
in 197 over Philip V. of Macedon—which meant that the harrying
of the East had begun—of M. Fulvius over Aetolia in 189, of Mummius
over Corinth in 146.[2] And not only enemies were robbed. Roman
officials could force friendly cities, like Chalcis in 170, to yield their toll
of artistic treasures. The art collections of travelled officials often consisted of booty seized in some vandal foray upon the rightful owners
and shipped to Rome with far less compunction and reverence than
accompanied the Elgin marbles to the British Museum. Much of all this
was a craze of semi-intelligent cupidity. One does not claim that Rome
was trained in a day. Polybius[3] saw Roman legionaries in Corinth
playing at draughts on the Dionysus of Aristides; and there was a tell-
tale clause inserted by Mummius in his contract with his carriers
stipulating that any works of art damaged should be replaced by others
equally good! The Romans had still something to learn about masterpieces in 133, when the royal treasures of Pergamum fell by doubtful
right into their hands. But by this time they were in touch with many
parts of Greece and were not impervious to her best influences. To
take a good example, any visitor to Delos since the excavations of
Homolle can realise its share in educating the Roman in the East.
Already the Graeco-Roman civilisation had begun.

In time the less sensuous influence of Greek books was felt. The
fashion grew of collecting manuscripts as well as curios. When Aemilius
Paulus brought back from Macedon in 167 B.C. the volumes which had
belonged to King Perseus, he formed the first private library in Rome.[4]
The event fittingly coincided with the victory which Polybius judged to
mark the decisive establishment of Roman supremacy.[5] Book-collecting
at the point of the sword continued thenceforth. Sulla, who himself
wrote twenty-eight books of memoirs, aided the advancement of learning by seizing the library of Apellicon, the Peripatetic philosopher of
Teos. It was a collection reputed to have included the original manu-

[1] See J. P. Mahaffy, *Greek World under Roman Sway*, 1890, p. 105.
[2] Sulla amassed similar collections. The cargo of marbles and bronzes
discovered by sponge-divers off Cerigotto in 1901, and now housed in the
National Museum at Athens, may have belonged to one of his ships which
foundered on the way to Rome, containing, according to Lucian (*Zeuxis*, iii),the
original picture of a woman-centaur. From this cargo was recovered the fascinating bronze so suggestive of the marble Hermes by Praxiteles at Olympia
(*Journ. Hellen. Studies*, vol. xxi., 1901, p. 205; vol. xxiii, 1903, p. 217).
[3] Polyb., xxxix. 2.
[4] Plut., *Aem. Paul.*, 28; Isid., *Orig.*, VI. v. 1: 'Romam primus librorum
copiam aduexit Aemilius Paulus.'
[5] Polyb., iii. 4, ἡ αὔξησις καὶ προκοπὴ τῆς Ῥωμαίων δυναστείας ἐτετελείωτο.

scripts of Aristotle and Theophrastus.[1] Like Sulla, another Eastern conqueror, Lucullus, furthered Hellenic influence by transporting the
great collection of the kings of Pontus.[2] His palatial library, surrounded
by cool avenues, became a literary centre, drawing to it the learned of
Rome. There Lucullus might advocate the claims of the Old Academy
and hear Cicero defend the New. The learning among the nobles at the
close of this period may be gauged from the case of Lucullus. Greek was
at his command as freely as Latin. It was reported that he once drew
lots to decide whether a contemplated history should be in verse or
prose, in Latin or Greek.

So far we have mainly considered products of Greek skill seized
bodily and brought to Rome. Now we have to consider the living
Greeks who became residents of the city. Some were slaves of varying
degrees of culture and morality; others were free men, *protégés* befriended by travelled Romans for their talent; some were jesters and
musicians; others professors of rhetoric and lecturers on literature and
philosophy; others representatives of states on some diplomatic mission;
others exiles or virtual hostages, among whom might be a keen observer
and historian like Polybius. The coming of the Hellenes may with
propriety be termed an invasion, not simply because thus through
literature and art Greece won a deathless revenge for her fall under
Roman power, but because there was strong hostility to overcome.
There is no better proof of the power of the movement than its triumph
over opposition by men of undoubted, if narrow, patriotism. Many
reasons made such opposition natural. The master-passions in the best
Greeks, their love of beauty, their love of imagining for the sake of
imagining, their quest of the new for the sake of the new, of knowledge
for the sake of knowledge, were foreign to the Roman genius. For a time
they were unwelcome, because little understood. Conservatism of spirit
made the Roman initially reluctant to accept Greek influence, and, after
its acceptance, made him less supple in manipulating it and less free
to take independent departures. The Greek attitude towards convention
might be described as respectful, but never slavish. The Hellene readily
ventured on variations which observed a tasteful mean between the
traditional and the original. With the Greek artist as with the Greek
thinker and politician, established usage counted for less than with the
Roman. Consequently the eminent individualities of Greece out-

---

[1] Dr. Mahaffy accepts this story from Strabo, XIII. i. 54 (*Gk. World under
Roman Sway*, 1890, p. 99); *cf.* Plut., *Sulla*, 26.
[2] Plut., *Luc.*, 42 (καὶ ὅλως ἑστία καὶ πρυτανεῖον Ἑλληνικὸν ὁ οἶκος ἦν αὐτοῦ
τοῖς ἀφικνουμένοις εἰς Ῥώμην); Isid., *Orig.*, *loc. cit.* 'Lucullus allowed free
access to his books. Here we get the germ of the public library. The first that
was genuinely public belongs to the close of the republican era. It was founded
by Asinius Pollio in the Atrium Libertatis on the Aventine. (Plin., *N.H.*, vii.
115; Isid., VI. v).' Greenidge, *op. cit.*, p. 22.

number the eminent individualities of Rome: they attract and fascinate by reason of their deviations from the normal, which give them a greater freshness than anything attainable by sticklers for the *mos maiorum*.[1] This national difference, which must have been instinctively felt by most Romans, was accentuated when the representatives of a decadent and effete Hellenism showed their versatility, not in the higher walks of the pure reason, but in entertaining trivialities, voluptuous refinements, or in courses of actual vice. Foreign slaves, who became so common a feature of the household, could teach the Greek classics, but often undesirable smartness and duplicity as well. If one pictures the cunning slave of Plautus with a literary veneer, one sees the dangerous type to which Cato the Censor justifiably refused to entrust the education of the home. It was with reason that Cato urged the value of training by parents in preference to slaves, and the necessity of writing on Roman subjects in Latin rather than in Greek. But his opposition to everything Hellenic was too bigoted and uncompromising. He sought to stem the tide in vain; he ended by being caught in it. Cato's last years were largely occupied in the study of Greek. Neither censor nor senate could clog the wheels of change.

But it was not only the instinctively felt contrasts of character which prejudged Greeks in Roman eyes. Historical circumstances combined to cast suspicion on them. Philhellenes at Rome had not always seemed the best citizens. Scipio Africanus the elder, victor of the second Punic War, to his adventurous and partly mystical cast of character added Greek tastes which exposed him to the dislike of the older generation. Contact with Polybius and Panaetius might be fairly suspected as responsible for the dangerously broad views held in politics by Scipio Aemilianus. To constitutional minds the Gracchi were not certificates in favour of Greek tuition. How much of the radicalism of Tiberius Gracchus did he inherit through his mother from the Scipionic unconventionality, how much from the political theories of Blossius of Cumae? In a later generation the support given in Asia and Europe to Mithradates also damaged the credit of the Greeks; they were denounced as ungrateful and disloyal. Indeed, there were at all periods recurrences of the old Catonic distrust of aliens endowed with so many facile, cozening, flattering, and seductive ways.

The attitude towards Hellenism, in consequence of this distrust, is a varying one. Philosophers are at one time welcome, at another banished; they are popular in one circle, detested in another. Greek cults are

---

[1] This contrast is well expressed by S. H. Butcher in *Harvard Lectures on Greek Subjects*, 1904, p. 156: 'In the history of Rome the man is often sunk in the Roman; his features are in low relief; we are led to forget the individual in the type. In Greece great personalities with an ineffaceable stamp of their own are far more numerous – men not only great in the things which they accomplished, but interesting in themselves, in endowments of mind and force of character, in the union of many outwardly discordant gifts – idiosyncrasies, it may be, but the idiosyncrasies of genius.'

accepted, as in the case of the *Ludi Apollinares* of 212 B.C. and the worship of Cybele of 205, or they are denounced as orgiastic and licentious and put down by decree of the senate, as the *Bacchanalia* were all over Italy in 186.[1] When in 181 B.C. two chests were unearthed, the one inscribed as the coffin of King Numa, the other containing his books — seven in Latin on pontifical law, seven in Greek on wisdom — the books were burned at the instigation of the praetor as subversive of orthodox ritual.[2] Nor were Greek teachers tolerated indiscriminately. In 173 B.C. two Epicureans, Alcaeus and Philiscus, were ordered out of Rome.[3] In 155 old Cato was hotly impatient that the philosophic envoys of Athens, instead of staying to lecture, should be sent incontinently away. This happened some six years after an order for the expulsion of Greek rhetors and philosophers had been promulgated (161 B.C.). The edict of 92 B.C. is not a case in point. It banished Latin pedants who imitated Greek professors, and it thereby stamped the teaching of Greek rhetoric by Greeks as the genuine article. Granted that Greeks were naturalised as citizens, that Greek philosophy became acclimatised by the Tiber, and that the sincerest tribute of imitation was freely paid in literary and artistic circles, still the Roman never lost sight of certain national defects in the Greek character. It was not merely that a Cato might utter tirades against Greek corruption or a Juvenal nearly three centuries later represent the disgusted Umbricius as unable to tolerate existence in a Rome hoodwinked by the charlatanry of the 'starveling Greek' (*Graeculus esuriens*). Even a Hellenist like Cicero is not blinded with the glamour. With all his respect for the authority of the Greeks in art and letters, fully conceding that they have noble natures among them, he still despises them, taken all in all, for their dishonesty and indolence.[4]

Stress has been laid on this resistance to Hellenism, because in con-

---

[1] Livy's narrative in XXXIX. viii–xix is supplemented by the text of the *senatus consultum* preserved in one of the most precious early Latin inscriptions (*C.I.L*, i. 196; Wordsworth, *Fragts. and Specs.*, pp. 172–3; Lindsay, *Hdbk. Lat. Inscrns.*, pp. 60–67).

[2] Livy, XL. xxix. This looks like a trick by enthusiastic Hellenisers to supply bogus proof of Greek influence in Numa's time. Perhaps the books were, as Mahaffy suggests, 'hidden away underground when the searching and bloody inquiry of the year 186 was going on' (*Gk. World under Roman Sway*, p. 66).

[3] Athenaeus (XII. lxviii) mentions L. Postumius as consul. This *might* also mean 155 B.C., but for several reasons the occurrence is less likely at the time of the famous and popular visit of the three Athenian scholarchs to Rome.

[4] Cicero, *In Verr.*, II. ii. 7, praising Sicily for its solid work, worth, and frugality, pays it the compliment of saying its inhabitants have nothing in them like the rest of the Greeks – no laziness, no luxury. Defending Flaccus (*Pro Fl.*, 9–12), he grants the Greeks talent in letters, in teaching the arts, in grace of conversation, acuteness, eloquence; but declares they have never observed strictness and truth in giving evidence (*testimoniorum religionem et fidem*); and so leads up to his terrible indictment of them as a people *quibus iusiurandum iocus est, testimonium ludus, existimatio uestra tenebrae, laus merces gratia gratulatio proposita est omnis in impudenti mendacio*. These examples are selected from

trast with the efforts to combat it its positive contribution to Roman
thought shows the greater. The unquestioned debt of Roman literature
to Greece has run some risk of being exaggerated. Horace's inevitably
quoted lines —

> *Graecia capta ferum uictorem cepit et artes*
> *Intulit agresti Latio,*

have been paraphrased as if, being true, they were the whole truth.
There has been a tendency to look on Greek literature — 'the captive
that captured her rude conqueror' — as something instantaneously and
irresistibly imposed upon a semi-barbarous and wholly unliterary
people,[1] and the opposition of a Cato to Hellenic influences has seemed
to give some colour to this view. But it is truer to maintain that the
acceptance of Greek culture was the gradual working of the national
will. The Roman spirit never was quenched: it was unquenchable.
Rome evolved herself. She rose to the conception that with the extension of her domain eastwards she was grown to be a world-power, and
so must embrace world-ideas. In Greek a ready-made instrument of
cosmopolitan appeal lay to hand. Rome grasped it and used it. So doing,
she was active, not passive. So doing, she best realised her destiny of
being infinitely more than a city-state on the Tiber or the mistress of
Italy. While, therefore, Greece acts almost everywhere upon her, Rome
reacts. The most Hellenic of Roman literature is Greek with a difference as vast as that which distinguishes a Greek statue from its Roman
copy.

It is when definitely considered in its action upon Roman thought —
as the moulder of philosophy, oratory, education, and literature — that
the potency of Hellenism is best appreciated. Greece, despite political
overthrow, effectual in the elegant elasticity and fruitful inspiration of
her finest culture, mastered the inner life of her conquerors. It was the
penalty attaching to the narrower system that its physical force and
moral firmness had to yield to intellectual and emotional superiority.
The interaction of the two spirits in literature is writ large upon all the
periods. In this chapter it must suffice to illustrate the early contribution
made by Hellenism to philosophy, oratory, and education at Rome. The
threads are inter-woven. The whole fabric is education. Public lecturers
on philosophy and rhetoric, and *savants* discoursing in the train of

---

Mahaffy's chapter on the 'Hellenism of Cicero' in *Gk. World under Roman Sway*.
Polybius, recognising the failings of his countrymen, remarks that a Roman official would on his bare word of honour administer huge amounts of money, while
for a single talent in Greece the letters were sealed and twenty witnesses needed,
and after all everybody cheated! (Polyb., vi. 56).

[1] H. Joachim, *Roman Lit.*, Eng. ed., 1904, Introd., says of Latin literature,
'Its only Latin matter is its language'; and later, 'The history of Latin literature
is merely the history of Greek influence upon Rome.' To my mind this wholly
ignores the genius of the people and their environment.

grandees, were no whit less educators than the domestic tutors in charge of the more formal training. The resident teacher was an expert linguist, often an expert philosopher. A great intellectual advance was involved in the appearance of *grammatici*. The rise of this class meant something like a secondary education added to the primary or elementary education of the *litteratores*, who taught writing in Latin and ciphering. The *grammatici* taught writing and speaking in Greek, as well as a fuller study of the Latin language. The great educational difficulty in the third century was the scarcity of literary texts. The study of the *Twelve Tables* of the law was useful rather than aesthetic. The study of rough old Saturnian verses was neither very useful nor very aesthetic. To meet a new demand Livius Andronicus translated the *Odyssey* in Latin Saturnians. This was typical of the method of the earliest grammarians. We know from Suetonius that it consisted in interpreting Greek writers and lecturing on some Latin composition of their own.[1] When Suetonius mentions Crates of Mallos as the introducer of 'Grammar' into Rome, he uses the word in a broad sense. Crates was head of the great library of Pergamum, and stood for breadth of study in contrast to the meticulous linguistic inquiries of the Alexandrians. Coming to Rome as an envoy from King Attalus about 165 B.C., he chanced to break his leg. The result of his detention was a series of successful lectures on Greek literature. These must have reinforced the Hellenic influence of the poet Ennius, who had died some four years before.

Alongside of this literary education there grew up a system of still higher learning—somewhat parallel to modern University studies. As Rome entered into world-politics her civil servants had to be better trained. Hence a demand for rhetoric and philosophy. The beginnings of the movement cannot be dated; but we have seen that by 173 B.C. Epicureanism had made itself obnoxious enough to necessitate the expulsion of two of its representatives. The *philosophi et rhetores* banished by resolution of the senate in 161 were probably Greeks who used Latin as the medium of their teaching. The fashion grew in favour of attending lectures by Greek professors. Romans with ambition modelled their oratorical exercises on Lysias, Hyperides, or Demosthenes. Even Cato's manual on the art of speaking, intended for his son, was based on careful scrutiny of Demosthenes and Thucydides. The Gracchi brothers pursued rhetoric under Greek teachers. The whole evidence shows that a 'study of the principles and methods of Greek rhetoric had become common among the upper classes at Rome by the middle of the second century B.C. . . . This was of great service in developing the power and flexibility of the Latin language.'[2] Greek

[1] Suet., *De Gramm.*, i, 'antiquissimi doctorum. . . . nihil amplius quam Graecos interpretabantur, aut si quid ipsi Latine composuissent praelegebant.'
[2] A. S. Wilkins, *Roman Education*, 1905, p. 27.

precedent is more or less marked throughout the series of orators—
Crassus, Antonius, Cotta, Hortensius, and Cicero. And even though
Crassus and Antonius, the leading orators in the generation before
Cicero, are careful, with a rather resentful patriotism, to minimise their
debt to the Greeks,[1] yet the acknowledged mastery of the Greek
teachers was amply proved when in 92 B.C. Crassus himself, as censor,
suppressed establishments where rhetoric was taught through Latin, on
the ground that they were 'schools of impudence.'

Philosophy in time also appealed to the thinking Roman, less as an
intellectual luxury or academic accomplishment than as a guide to
conduct and happiness. Interest in Greek thought was stimulated by the
presence in Italy for some sixteen years of the thousand Achaean
patriots deported in 167 B.C. Separated from motives of prudence and
interned in country towns as well as in Rome, they exerted a wide
influence. The most famous among them was Polybius, who records his
intimacy with Scipio Aemilianus. In one of his early interviews with
Scipio, then a youth of eighteen, Polybius says he found him rather
despondent over his supposed lack of enough ability to make him a
credit to his family. The advice which Polybius gives is significant.[2] He
points out that a sound education is easily obtainable from the many
learned Greeks finding their way to Rome at the time. With the
advantage of the royal library of Macedon, which Scipio's own father,
Paulus, had brought home from the East, and under the influence of
Polybius, the young man developed strong Hellenic sympathies. His
household in later life became the philosophic and literary centre of
Rome.

In 155 B.C. three learned deputies of Athens produced a powerful
movement in the direction of Greek philosophy. Desirous to obtain
remission of a fine imposed by arbitration upon her for violation of the
lands of Oropus, Athens chose as her spokesmen in a bad case the
presidents of her three chief philosophic schools—Critolaus the Peripatetic, Diogenes the Stoic, and Carneades the Academic. At their
first audience with the senate C. Acilius acted as interpreter. A delay in
the decision gave a chance of inviting the envoys to hold public lectures,
which they did. Not so advanced in years as his colleagues, Carneades
proved the most vigorous and attractive professor of the trio. To understand the situation one must remember the usage then prevailing at
Athens of appointing as scholarchs venerable professors drawn from
widely severed parts of the Hellenic world. By this second century
Pyrrhonism had weakened the dogmatism of all the schools of philosophy, except perhaps the Stoic. Carneades, of the New Academy, was

---

[1] See Cic., *De Oratore*, i. 45, for Crassus, who visited Athens on his way
home from his quaestorship; and i. 82, for Antonius, whom Cicero represents as
using the words 'egomet, qui sero ac leuiter Graecas litteras attigissem.'
[2] Polyb., xxxi. 24.

an able representative of what we might call applied scepticism. For the absolute tenets refuted by his polemics he substituted a system of probability to be the criterion in matters of intellect and ethics. The best of all the schools should be combined into a satisfying synthesis. This eclecticism, applied to morals, was exactly calculated to appeal powerfully to Roman common sense during the visit of Carneades to the city. The guidance in life offered by his doctrines was judged to be of value, and from his day eclectic thought invariably had warm supporters among those at Rome who were repelled by the more vulgar developments of Epicureanism and by the extravagance of Stoic paradoxes.

In the opinion of some, however, the brilliance of Carneades placed in jeopardy the traditional sobriety of Roman thought and conduct. Cato advocated immediate settlement of the envoys' case and their summary dismissal from Rome. But he was recognised as an extremist and alarmist. In truth, he may have been reasonably afraid of Epicurean teaching and scornfully mindful of its banished pundits; but there was no Epicurean among the diplomatic trio, and it was unfair to include all Greek philosophy in one condemnation. Suspicions directed against the best Greek philosophy were not well grounded. It was ennobling, not lowering. More idealism in the Roman and a freer receptivity to the less mundane portions of Greek speculation might have saved many from the seductions of merely material comfort and gross voluptuousness. It was not the citizen attracted by the ethereal aspects of Hellenism, but the less philosophic Roman, who now ran most risk of sinking into luxury and vice. Cato's protest, too, came out of due season. How could Roman morals suffer from philosophic disquisitions when for a generation and a half the community had seen staged in their theatre the depravities and rascalities borrowed from the comedies of Menander? It was vain to fight facts. Though the Roman might despise the Greeks as politically and morally inferior, he could not, without forfeiting his claim to be educated, seriously challenge their supremacy in literature, philosophy, and art. To an increasing extent Roman magnates regarded it as correct form to secure the attendance at home, and often abroad, of a Greek philosopher. Thus Scipio Aemilianus retained Panaetius of Rhodes as the mouthpiece of latter-day Stoicism; Lucullus, the Academic Antiochus; and Pompey, Theophanes of Mytilene. Marius was an exception to prove the rule. He was the only great general of the first century B.C. who was clownishly ignorant of Greek culture.[1]

Not only did philosophers find in the establishments of Roman nobles homes of leisured retreat where deferential attention replaced the wordy wrangles of Athens, but poets too were welcome. Archias of Antioch is typical of the literary Greek encouraged by the great about

---

[1] Sallust, *Iug.*, 85: 'Neque litteras Graecas didici: parum placebat eas discere, quippe quae ad uirtutem doctoribus nihil profuerant.'

100 B.C. Loaded with the honours of citizenship by Hellenic muni-
cipalities in South Italy, he had the *entrée* into the best Roman society.
The reasons are not far to seek. Partly it was the fascination of the
superb and the *spirituel* in Greek literature, partly a clear conception of
its uses. Romans of birth knew well that the unrivalled form of Greek
literature set the examplar for the record of great deeds in prose or verse,
just as acquaintance with Greek oratory could be turned to practical
account in a political or legal career. And so Archias wrote poetry for
Marius—little as *he* knew of Greek—on his Cimbric successes, and for
Lucullus on his Mithradatic campaign.

The great progress in education between the second and the first
century B.C. is well marked by the contrast drawn by Mommsen[1]
between Cato's list of departments of culture and Varro's in his
Disciplinarum Libri ix. Cato includes oratory, agriculture, law, war,
medicine. Varro's nine subjects were grammar, dialectic, rhetoric,
geometry, arithmetic, astronomy, music, medicine, architecture. As
Mommsen points out, war, law, agriculture, had become professional
studies. The first three on Varro's list were the three which received
earliest development in Rome, and correspond to the 'Trivium,' or
elementary course, of the Middle Ages. The next four on his list
correspond to the 'Quadrivium,' or more advanced course followed
from the time of Martianus Capella onwards. By the end of our period,
then, Greek, as both vehicle and model for instruction in grammar,
dialectic, and rhetoric, had an absolutely established place in Roman
education. It could not lose its value. It was the *lingua franca* of the
East. It was the language of literature, too, in the East, and in part at
Rome. 'Greek is read by the whole world virtually. Latin is confined to
its own narrow limits,' pleaded Cicero[2] in 62 B.C. It was his cue to argue
thus for Archias, but his statement, if exaggerated, is more than a half-
truth.

The first thirty-six years of Cicero's life fall within the period ending
with 70 B.C. His training may be taken as typical of the education then
available.[3] He applied himself in early youth to practice under Roman
orators, and had special opportunities for Greek study when prominent
Athenian refugees flocked to Rome during the Mithradatic troubles.
Philo's academic denial of certainty in human judgement, the Rhodian
Molo's instructions in pleading, the Stoic Diodotus's dialectic, Piso's
exercises in Latin and Greek declamation, bore their share in fitting
Cicero for the Roman bar. He was of mature years and had already
entered on his public career before he travelled in the East and visited
Asia and Greece. In the next generation—that which immediately
follows our period — to judge from the careers of Cicero's son and nephew,

---

[1] *Hist. of Rome*, Eng. ed., 1877, iv. 563.
[2] *Pro Arch.*, ch. x: 'Graeca leguntur in omnibus fere gentibus, Latina
suis finibus, exiguis sane, continentur.'
[3] Cicero gives an educational autobiography in *Brutus*, lxxxix. 304 *sqq.*

it was fashionable for Roman youths to study in Athens at a rather earlier age.

Surveyed from a literary standpoint, the period under review starts with Andronicus's first play from the Greek, staged the year before Ennius was born, while Plautus was still a boy; it extends to the date of Virgil's birth, when Cicero, as a man of thirty-six, secured his place in oratory by the impeachment of Verres. In outline, it is the period within which practically all Roman drama is confined—for literary comedy of the type established by Plautus and refined by Terence now runs its full course, and tragedy, which reached its zenith in Accius, ceases to impress us as a living reality in the lost plays of the Augustan age, whether acted or not, and certainly does not come into touch with the stage in Seneca's frigid studies. It is the period of the pre-Lucretian epic of Naevius and Ennius, and of the new, but very Roman, turn given to satire by Lucilius. In prose, for the most part represented by fragmentary remains, it is a period in which talent greatly develops history, oratory, and law. As landmarks of progress there stand out in the practice of oratory the names of Cato, Scipio Aemilianus and his friend Laelius; next, among the speakers for or against the revolutionary proposals formulated from 133 onwards, C. Gracchus especially; and later, Antonius and Crassus. In the theoretical treatment of oratory, following on two generations of Greek lectures, appears the first Latin manual of rhetoric, often ascribed to one Cornificius. That encyclopaedic learning, in which Latin always was strong, may be said to begin with Cato's *Origines* and *De Re Rustica*. For history, after the inaugural attempts by Fabius Pictor and Cincius Alimentus in Greek, Latin prose is used by Calpurnius Piso, consul in the year of Tiberius Gracchus's tribunate, and by Antipater (*circ.* 120 B.C.), and at a subsequent date by Claudius Quadrigarius, Valerius of Antium, and Sisenna. In the department of law may be cited the *Tripertita* of Sextus Aelius and his brother (*circ.* 200 B.C.), and from the Gracchan period, the services of the Scaevola family, culminating in the eighteen books on jurisprudence written by Q. Mucius Scaevola in the age of Sulla. The labours of Aelius Stilo (*circ.* 100 B.C.) lay the foundations of Latin philology and grammar. In philosophy, new ideas sown by Epicurean, Academic, and Stoic teachers are germinating, before bearing full fruit in Lucretius's poem and Cicero's treatises. Even this brief *précis* shows the very considerable advance in the imaginative and the scientific literature of Rome.

Distinctly national traits mark the literature at several points. The continuance of the old Saturnian verse in Andronicus and in Naevius contrasts with the greater Hellenism of the Ennian hexameter. It is from the history of Rome that Naevius draws his epic subject and many dramatists the plots of their *praetextae*. National feeling, too, pervades

the reaction against the Terentian drama. Refined diction might appeal
to the cultured set of Scipio and Laelius; but it was caviare to the
general. Terence's polish was thrown away on the masses. Something
more obvious and more concrete in drama was wanted to amuse them.
And for reading circles, when Greek adaptations palled, it was Lucilius
who stepped into the breach with his farrago of satiric comment
on contemporary life. Here was something tangible and Roman.
The remote society of Athens had lost its novelty on the stage. Satire,
with its public appeal, went straight home. Equally national was the
vogue of the *fabulae togatae* and *tabernariae* with their comic treatment
of real Roman life, and the elevation of the Italian *Atellana* into literary
form by Pomponius and Novius. The Roman annalists and historians of
the times wrote at first in the Greek language and on Greek lines. Later
they wrote in Latin, with an increasing recognition of the claims of the
native language to record Roman exploits, and an increasing consciousness of the inspiring material which the national story afforded. This
spirit informs the genuinely Roman history of Cato, who, both as
speaker and writer, was a power in the plain early prose. Assertion of
native force is also to be inferred from the speeches of C. Gracchus and
the letters of his mother Cornelia. At the end of the second century B.C.
two giants in oratory appeared in Crassus and Antonius, the familiar
figures of Cicero's *De Oratore*. Their Greek training they characteristic-
ally combine in an independent manner with Roman eloquence.

What, then, are the Hellenic aspects of this literature? The influence
of the Greek classics is most visible in epic and drama. Homer was the
pattern for Ennius in epic, as he was Andronicus's original; Euripides
was the pattern for Ennius in tragedy, as Sophocles was for Accius.
Menander and other playwrights of the New Attic Comedy were the
sources of the *palliatae* of Plautus, Terence, and their fellows. The mark
of Greece is evident in choice of theme and in mode of treatment, in the
imaginative brilliance which illumines the old stories of Latium and
links some of them to the legends of Greece, and in the process by which
new metres, new rules of quantity, and new words contribute to mould
the language into flexibility. The elevation attained in poetry reacts on
prose as a refining agent, and, as happened with Greek in the days of
Gorgias, lends to oratory a grace otherwise inaccessible. In the middle
of the second century B.C., Alexandria, whose poetry in the next
century was to influence Catullus and Virgil, began to influence Rome
through its studies in literary history. This phase of learning appears in
Accius. As regards philosophy, the effect of Academic and Stoic theories
on general thought has been already touched on. Where philosophy
enters farthest into literature at this time is in Ennius, not so much in
the guise of the shallow impiety of Euhemerus, which he handled in
prose, as through the deeper conclusions associated with his own native
South Italy, land of Pythagoras and the Eleatics, or with Sicily, home of

Epicharmus and Empedocles. To Lucilius, not unnaturally, it is the comic side of Greek hair-splitting and the parade of superficial knowledge that afford most amusement. Even in such a Roman preserve as law, it was partly Greek influence which helped to widen the *ius ciuile* into the *ius gentium*. The larger and more international needs of legal administration were practically recognised by the appointment of a *praetor peregrinus* in 242 B.C. to judge cases in which strangers were involved. It may be, too, that the schematic treatment of legal questions by Scaevola owes something to Greek method. But there is no question as to the inspiring force of Greek thought in an exponent like Panaetius. A pupil of Diogenes, he was responsible for certain new phases of Stoic philosophy whose outcome was a body of doctrine widely accepted in the days of the Empire. Panaetius played a great part in Roman thought as an inmate of the household of Scipio Aemilianus. The philosophic centre of the Scipionic circle, he founded a Stoic school numbering among its adherents Laelius, Q. Mucius Scaevola, and Rutilius Rufus. These were men who in intellect and conduct united the best traditions of Rome and Greece.

Chapter III

THE PIONEERS OF ROMAN POETRY

The stimulus of national achievement – L. Livius Andronicus –
His life – A captive tutor – Actor-author – Combination of epic,
dramatic, and lyric skill – The surviving fragments – The Latin
Odyssey – Dramatic   fragments – Tragedies – Comedies – *Carmen
Nelei.*
Cn. Naevius – His life – Tragedies – *Praetextae* – Comedies – Epic
on the *Bellum Punicum* – The legendary in Naevius and Virgil –
Hellenic and Roman elements – Style.
Q. Ennius – Campaigning in Sardinia – Friendships with great
citizens – His career in Rome – Personal traits – His genius for
tragedy – Dramatic qualities – Survival of his plays – His *saturae* –
The scheme of the *Annales* – Parallels to Homer and Klopstock –
Literary qualities – The Ennian hexameter – Poetic feeling –
Literary influence of Ennius – Virgil's debt to him – Fluctuations
in his popularity – His historic position.

THE exaltation of the national victory in the first Punic War
created the aesthetic literature of Rome. With the fresh consciousness of the first great foreign enemy defeated, of a 'fleet
in being,'[1] of territory won outside Italy, came that fulness of life which
at all periods is the condition of the highest artistic production. Rome's
conquests, we have seen, for her meant economic advance. Her progress
in things material was matched by her progress in the things of the
mind. It is always so. The strong peoples of the world have, in the mid-
career of triumph, felt the strongest stimulus towards the pursuit of
literature, science, and art. The history of Roman literature illustrates
the working of forces similar to those which have acted upon the
Assyrians, Greeks, Arabs, Spanish, English, French, and Americans,
and which may at no distant date act upon Japan.[2] Hitherto all had been
toil and conflict—internal and external. But at last a breathing-space
gave leisure for the calls of intellect. The impetuous inrush of Greek
systems and poetry, amenities and depravities, is apt to conceal the
fact that the real stimulus to literature came from national achievement
and national needs. Hence when Porcius Licinus in not very poetic
trochaics says—

[1] Naval development was an inevitable result of the first Punic War, but
Rome had possessed warships since the middle of the fourth century, if not
earlier: see 'Fleets of the First Punic War,' *Journ. Hell. Stud.*, xxvii., Pt. I, 1907.
[2] Written between 1906 and 1909 – Ed.

87

Mid the second Punic warfare did the Muse with pinioned flight
Visit Romulus' rude people, who in battle take delight,[1]

one must add that the Greek Muses came to inspire, not to silence, the
Italian *Camenae*. Roman demands for education and amusement
required that Greek epic and drama should be adapted to suit contemporary wants. The talent that could imitate Greek models in Latin
was henceforth ensured a hearing.

The first man to seize upon the moment was the Tarentine L. Livius
Andronicus (*circ.* 284–204 B.C.).[2] There are considerable difficulties in
his biography. Some time-honoured statements have been pulled to
pieces learnedly, vivaciously, but perhaps too iconoclastically, by
Mirmont, who dismisses as legendary any tie between the Greek captive
and M. Livius Salinator, and any suggestion that Andronicus opened a
school at Rome. Certain undoubted errors are due to Jerome. He gives
the *praenomen* as Titus instead of Lucius; and he refers the fame of the
poet (*clarus habetur*) to the 'year of Abraham' corresponding to 187 B.C.
which is demonstrably too late. Like so much in Jerome's Latin
amplifications of Eusebius's chronicle, this detail is probably borrowed
from Suetonius, who may have repeated a mistake of Accius or Attius.
This mistake—to the effect that Livius was taken at the capture of
Tarentum by Q. Fabius Maximus (209 B.C.) and produced his first
play eleven years later—must have arisen from a confusion between the
two captures of Tarentum. Cicero is at some pains to correct it, and to
Cicero, and thus indirectly to Accius's blunder,[3] we owe the clear and
important statement that Livius was the first to exhibit a play at Rome,
in the five hundred and fourteenth year of the city (240 B.C.).[4]

A few credibly supported details are left which ensure to Andronicus
his place in the history of Roman epic, drama, and lyric. In 272 B.C,
after the fall of Tarentum, he was brought a slave to Rome, and
probably placed, sooner or later,[5] in the establishment of the father of

---

[1]   'Poenico bello secundo Musa pinnato gradu
          Intulit se bellicosam in Romuli gentem feram.'
                              Apud Gell., *N.A.*, XVII. xxi.
The author's name is more probably Licinus than Licinius. Licinus is known as
a *cognomen* of the gens Porcia.
    [2] For the text of the fragments see E. Bährens, *Frag. Poet. Rom.*, 1886;
O. Ribbeck, *Scaen. Rom. Poes. Frag.*, ed. 3, 1897–8; L. Müller, *Der Saturnische
Vers u. seine Denkmäler*, 1885; L. Müller, *L. Andronici et Cn. Naevii Fabularum
Reliquiae*, 1885. For full discussion of both life and fragments see H. de Mir-
mont, *Études sur l'ancienne poésie latine*, 1903, pp. 5–201.
    [3] The attempt to saddle the mistake on Ateius 'Philologus,' on the ground,
among others, that 'Attius' is a false reading in Cicero, was made by Osann in
Analecta critica poesis Romanorum scenicae reliquias illustrantia, 1816. This view
is refuted by Mirmont, *op. cit.*, pp. 19–23.
    [4] Cic., *Brut.*, xviii. 72.
    [5] The evidence does not support the dogmatic statements sometimes made.
The *patronus* who freed Andronicus was almost certainly a Livius; but 'Salinator' as a cognomen is an anachronism before 204 B.C. Cf. Livy, XXIX. xxxvii,
and Mirmont, *op. cit.*, p. 43.

M. Livius Salinator, the conqueror of Hasdrubal. Suetonius, classing
him and Ennius as the oldest teachers of the *semi-Graecus* type, is the
authority who states that he taught privately and publicly in both
languages.[1] The method, as mentioned in the preceding chapter, consisted in interpretation of Greek originals and composition of Latin
comments to be read to pupils. This does not amount to proof that
Andronicus was strictly a schoolmaster; nor need one regard him as
such in order to appreciate his influence on education. The vital facts
are that he translated the *Odyssey* into Latin Saturnians, and that,
whether intended for a class-book or not, his translation became one,
and remained in use up to the time when the schoolboy Horace had
reason to associate the rough old lines with the cane of Orbilius.[2]

Livius had been manumitted and had reached his prime when his
career as actor-author opened.[3] The aediles of 240 had decided to celebrate the *ludi Romani* with more than ordinary *éclat*, in honour of the
close of the first Punic war. As a change from the representations prevalent since stage-plays had been started under Etrurian influence a century and a quarter earlier (364 B.C.), Livius brought out a comedy and a
tragedy adapted from the Greek.[4] Comedy constructed after the Greek
norm was a striking departure from the plotless *saturae* which held the
stage and the improvement in art commended itself to Roman taste. So
the *fabula palliata* began. Tragedy, too, by reason of its seriousness and a
certain idealism never absent from the Greek originals, was in the
Roman theatre of those days an even greater novelty than anything
comic could be.

The ancestor in epic of Virgil, in comedy of Plautus, in tragedy of
Accius, Livius was in lyric the ancestor of Horace. In 207 B.C., before
the battle of the Metaurus, he was charged with the composition of an

---

[1] Suet., *Gramm.*, i: 'antiquissimi doctorum, qui iidem et poetae et semi-
graeci erant – Liuium et Ennium dico, quos utraque lingua domi forisque
docuisse adnotatum est. . . .' Mirmont suggests that *forisque* is apocryphal.
Citing Plutarch (*Quaest. Rom.*, 59, p. 278 D, πρῶτος ἀνέῳξε γραμματοδιδασκαλεῖον
Σπόριος Καρβίλιος, κ.τ.λ.) as evidence that the first regular schoolmaster in Rome
was Sp. Carvilius, freedman of the Carvilius who was the first Roman to
divorce his wife, Mirmont argues that the remark about Livius and Ennius
being the earliest teachers may have been interpolated in Suetonius. And the
motive? Rhetoricians, he contends, would prefer a nobler origin for their craft
than this link with the freedman of a citizen who owed his notoriety to having
introduced a new facility in divorce. The scepticism is ingenious rather than
convincing.

[2] Hor., *Epist.*, II. i. 69–72, 'carmina Liui . . . memini quae plagosum mihi
paruo Orbilium dictare.'

[3] Osann advances the conjecture that he *may* have been grandson of the
actor Andronicos who taught Demosthenes.

[4] Livy, VII. ii. 8, 'Liuius . . . ab saturis ausus est primus argumento
fabulam serere.' The breaking of his voice owing to his strenuous performances
('cum saepius reuocatus uocem obtudisset') had another important effect on
drama. It originated the custom of employing a *cantor* to sing the words of a
canticum by the side of the flute-player, while the actor made the appropriate
gestures (Livy, *loc. cit.*).

original hymn—not to thank the gods for victory, as is sometimes alleged, but to expiate prodigies and entreat aid in the coming campaign. The style of the hymn, according to Livy,[1] was too rough to merit record, though it found favour on the occasion when the twenty-seven maidens chanted it through the streets. It is probably to a later hymn of praise that Festus refers as written by Livius for girls' voices. It brought the composer public honours. His recompense was the establishment of an association of literary men (histriones and scribae), whose headquarters should be the Temple of Minerva on the Aventine, and whose recognised doyen should be Livius himself.[2] The author cannot have enjoyed his honours long; he would be over seventy in 207. Cato's remark[3] that Livius survived to the time of his adolescence, suggests that, as Cato was born in 234, the death of Livius occurred about 204.

The surviving fragments do not amount to a hundred lines. There are the customary difficulties in forming a critical judgment on an author represented by no one passage of length, but mainly by single lines or phrases quoted by grammarians to illustrate obsolete words, usages, and terminations. There is little reason to wonder at Cicero's dismissal of such early attempts as if they corresponded to the ill-shapen xoana of primitive sculpture.[4] His verdict that the plays are not worth a second reading is of a piece with Horace's expressed surprise that any one should think Livius's poems productions falling little short of perfection.[5] Where the ancient views disappoint is in their failure to grasp his historical importance. The outstanding witness to this is his vogue for at least two centuries. Disdained by the cultured, he survived in schools till about the opening of the Christian era. By the second century A.D. he was viewed as a relic of antiquity, valuable only for archaisms. Gellius, recording his find of a copy of the Latin Odyssey in a library at Patras in Greece, has the air of one previously ignorant of the existence of such a work.[6] With the exception of his four quotations, and those of Festus in the same century, we learn nothing more, till the scholars of the fourth century—Charisius, Diomedes, Nonius Marcellus,

---

[1] Livy, XXVII. xxxvii, 'carmen . . . illa tempestate forsitan laudabile rudibus ingeniis, nunc abhorrens et inconditum, si referatur.'

[2] The Collegium Poetarum was a union to protect the interests of dramatists, whose position was in early days none too strong in the community. This home of poets admitted of festive gatherings appreciated by writers who came as strangers to Rome, and, in spite of their talent, felt the burden of poverty. It became an Academy on a small scale, which fostered literature and tended, if but informally, to legislate for language. It thus served art and learning at a time when grammarians had not begun to lecture on Roman authors, and when recitationes by authors had not become an established custom, as afterwards in the Augustan age. (cf. L. Müller, Q. Ennius, pp. 31 sqq.).

[3] Cic., De Senect., xiv. 50, 'uidi Liuium senem, qui . . . usque ad adulescentiam meam prouenit aetate.'

[4] Cic., Brut., xviii. 71, 'Odyssia latina est sic tanquam opus Daedali, et Liuianae fabulae non satis dignae quae iterum legantur.'

[5] Hor., Epist., II. i. 71.

[6] Noct. Att., XVIII. ix. 5.

Servius Honoratus—burrow in his works. In the fifth century the valuable quotations of Priscian were made, and the record closes over a century later in Isidore of Seville.

His selection of the *Odyssey* for translation is a great testimony to the acumen of Livius.[1] Its vigour was marvellously well adapted to appeal to the Rome which first withstood Carthage. Its lively interest as one of the best stories in the world's literature, its variety of scene and incident, its perilous adventures in wonderlands as romantic as any visited by Sindbad in *The Thousand and One Nights*, its exciting contests and domestic pictures set in un-Roman surroundings, and, equalling in fascination, what it draws from witchcraft, folklore, or from mariners' tales of the Far North, make up a whole which might well take the mind by storm, in virtue of novelties hitherto inconceivable at Rome. And with all such novelties there were familiar elements sure to appeal to the Roman—the spectacle of endurance in the face of danger, the love of home, the fear of the gods, the sombre religious associations with the lower world. Odysseus was a hero more after the Roman heart than Achilles, and Virgil shows this in his modelling of Aeneas. Yet the execution of the task fell far behind the pattern. The rugged Saturnian is no peer of the hexameter. Livius, besides, makes blunders of omission and commission. The extant specimens prove that he can positively mistranslate, and that he does not maintain the fidelity of the familiar opening words:

Virum mihi, Camena, ‖ insece uersutum.[2]

The number of fragments whose place is uncertain is the best proof of inexact translation. As an example of loss of the original fulness, take—

Mea puer, quid uerbi ‖ ex tuo ore superat?[3]

The line gives no hint of the Homeric ἕρκος ὀδόντων. Conversely, an over-expanded form of the Greek appears in the lines

Namque nullum plus corpus ‖ macerat humanum
Quamde mare saeuom: uires ‖ cui sunt magnae, topper
Confringent importunae ‖ undae.[4]

[1] The *Iliad* had to wait till Sulla's days, when it found a translator into hexameters in Cn. Matius, the object of much admiration from Gellius for his learning. The exact date of another translation of the *Iliad*, by Ninnius Crassus, is unknown. J. Tolkiehn, *Homer u. d. röm. Poesie*, 1900, pp. 85–8, gives their period as 'etwa im Anfange des ersten vorchristlichen Jahrhunderts.' As the old Italian *saturnius* had by then disappeared from literature, they followed the verse of the original.

[2] *Odyss.*, i. 1, ἄνδρα μοι ἔννεπε, Μοῦσα, πολύτροπον. Livius Romanises Greek deities, Μοῦσα into *Camena*, Μοῖρα into *Morta*, Ποσειδῶν into *Neptunus*, and so forth.

[3] So L. Havet (*De Saturnio Latinorum Versu*, 1880). Bährens reads *supera Fugit*.

[4] *Odyss.*, viii. 138:

οὐ γὰρ ἔγωγέ τί φημι κακώτερον ἄλλο θαλάσσης
ἄνδρα τε συγχεῦαι, εἰ καὶ μάλα καρτερὸς εἴη.

The dramatic fragments exhibit, in Ribbeck's opinion, an advance in style upon his *Odyssey*. Mirmont rejects this as due to the paralogism of comparing the epic fragments with Virgil and the dramatic fragments with authors nearer in time to Livius himself. But surely greater skill in handling language is shown when Livius adapts varied metres from the Greek, and writes now in iambics, now in trochaics, now in sundry lyric measures. Besides, among the tragic extracts there are traces of power in seizing vivid and salient points and expressing them pithily though ruggedly, while the insistent alliteration hammers the point home as in *Beowulf*. For instance, from the *Aegisthus*:

> *Tum autem lasciuom Nerei simum pecus*
> *Ludens ad cantum classem lustratur (? choro)*;

> Around our fleet there frisked with noses snub
> The playful pack of Nereus, music-mad;

or the fast movement in the trochaics of the *Andromeda:*

> *Confluges ubi conuentu campum totum inumigant.*

> When across the flats in fury flow the watery floods amain.

Nine well-attested titles[1] of his tragedies have come down — *Achilles, Aegisthus, Aiax Mastigophoros, Andromeda, Danaë, Equos Troianus, Hermiona, Tereus, Ino.*[2] It is not always possible to trace the Greek original of adaptations of which only a few words survive — there were, for example, several Greek plays entitled *Achilles*, and at least four entitled *Andromeda*; but the evidence suggests that Livius borrowed most from Sophocles. Another prevailing feature is his preference for themes connected with the Trojan cycle or at any rate mentioned in Homer. It is reasonable to believe that his lead prompted Accius to follow him in a *Tereus* and an *Aegisthus*. The latter play has the interest of dramatising the same subject as the *Agamemnon* of Aeschylus. But it has additional interest. Certain resemblances have been noted between the fragments of Livius's *Aegisthus* and the *Agamemnon* of Seneca. They scarcely prove in the imperial writer any admiration for an author so archaic; but Seneca may conceivably have caught a few echoes of the old poet through the intermediate play by Accius. For nearly three centuries — since the *Syntagma Tragoediae Latinae* of the Jesuit father Delrio in 1619 — the imagination of learned editors has played at settling more or less precisely the context, tragic or comic, of these fragments, and even at weaving around them pieces of plot, in the absence of clues from the grammarians who quote them. The subject has gained in interest, but not always in truth, by such endeavours; for the temptation to let the fancy run riot is powerful.

[1] There are six less certain tragedies – *Teucer, Adonis, Antiopa, Helena, Laodamia, Teuthras*: see Mirmont, *op. cit.*, pp. 177–182.
[2] The *Ino*, from which hexameters of the *uersus miurus* type (last foot being iambus instead of spondee) are cited in a vexed passage by Terentianus Maurus, is arguably a poem by Laevius, not Livius: see Mirmont, *op. cit.*, pp. 174–176.

Slight fragments exist of three comedies — *Gladiolus*, from a play of the New Comedy, 'Εγχειρίδιον, perhaps containing a braggart proto-type of the *Miles Gloriosus* of Plautus; *Lydius* or *Ludius*; and *Verpus* or *Virgo*. Possibly there was also the *Centauri*, though the passage on which the supposition is founded may refer to a portion of Laevius's *Erotopaegnia*. It is still more hazardous to believe in a *Numularia* or *Molaria*.

To the age of Livius belongs the *Carmen Nelei*.[1] Its iambic fragments suggest that it was a tragedy. Plausible arguments point to its source in Sophocles's lost *Tyro*. The secret of its attraction for Romans may have lain in the resemblance between the exposure of the child Neleus and that of Romulus.[2] If so, it was a herald of the national play — the *praetexta*.

In Cn. Naevius (*circ.* 270–*circ.* 199) greater independence and originality are recognisable.[3] He may be called home-born, and the native spirit is strong in him. Especially in the historical plays (*fabulae praetextae* or *praetextatae*) invented by him, and in his epic, he proves himself inspired by the greatness of the national life. His truly Latin genius is testified to by the epitaph in Saturnians (according to Gellius, of his own composition[4]) in which he pitches his claims at their highest, as a poet to be mourned by the divine *Camenae*, one after whose passing men 'forgat to speake the Latin tongue at Rome':

> *Immortales mortales si foret fas flere,*
> *Flerent diuae Camenae Naeuiom poetam:*
> *Itaque postquam est Orchi traditus thensauro,*
> *Oblitei sunt Romai loquier lingua Latina.*

When Gellius remarks that this epitaph is 'full of Campanian pride' (*plenum superbiae Campanae*), he does not necessarily mean that Naevius was born in Campania. Campanian vainglory was as proverbial as that of the Castilian or the Gascon in later times. So, too, a display of 'Hielan' pride' is conceivable in one who is no Kelt. Naevius bore a plebeian name common in Rome, and was most likely Roman;[5] other-

---

[1] H. Keil, *Gramm. Lat.*, i. 84. The fragments are preserved by Festus and Charisius. Teuffel (*op. cit.*, i., § 94, 9), in referring the *Carmen* to the time of Andronicus, is more definite than Egger, who thought it a work 'dont le sujet et l'âge ne sauraient être indiqués d'une manière précise' (*Lat. Sermonis Vetustioris Reliq. Selectae*, 1843, p. xiv).

[2] Mirmont, *Études*, etc., 1903, pp. 205–218.

[3] For fragments of *Bell. Pun.*, Bährens, *F.P.R.*; L. Müller, *Enni Carm. Reliq.*; *Accedunt Naeui Belli Poenici Quae Supersunt*, 1884; for dramatic fragments, Ribbeck, *Scaen. Rom. Poes. Frag.*; selections in W. W. Merry, *Fragments of Roman Poetry*, ed. 2, 1898; L. Müller (*op. cit.*, pp. xx–xlvii) discusses contents and versification of *Bell. Pun.*: *cf.* Lamarre, *Hist. d. l. litt. romaine*, vol. i., pp. 208–217.

[4] *Noct. Att.*, I. xxiv. But it may be from Vairo's *Imagines*.

[5] For this view see *Cn. Naeuii poetae Romani uitam descripsit, carminum reliquias collegit*, etc. E. Klussmann, 1843; *De Naeuii poetae uita et scriptis disseruit*, M. J. Berchem, 1861.

wise the aid of the tribunes might not have been available to release
him from the durance vile to which his dramatic outspokenness subjected him. Gellius[1] quotes Varro *de Poetis* to show that Naevius served
in the first Punic War. From the same passage in Gellius we learn that
his first plays were given in 235 B.C. His comic abilities brought him
into trouble; systematic abuse (*assidua maledicentia*) of men in high
place led to his incarceration. Roman aristocratic government had no
tolerance for the political criticism which had animated the Old
Comedy in democratic Athens. So the less caustic Plautus is moved to
refer to the misfortunes of his brother-dramatist:

> I have heard a Roman poet has to pillar head on hand,
> While two pair of fetters guard him all his weary prison hours.[2]

In time, something like an apology or recantation in his plays, *Hariolus*
and *Leo*, written in prison, brought about the intervention of the
tribunes and his liberation.[3] His ambiguous gibe at the house of the
Metelli:

> *Fato Metelli Romai fiunt consules —*

is only less notorious than the menacing retort by the Metellus who was
consul in 206:

> *Dabunt malum Metelli Naeuio poetae.*[4]

Neither prison nor threats could silence him. In the end he was exiled,
and died at Utica. As the siege of that city by Scipio ended only in 202,
Naevius could not have died there in 204, the date deduced by Cicero
from 'ancient commentaries.'[5] Cicero, however, mentions that Varro,
diligentissimus inuestigator antiquitatis, thinks the traditional date of
death an error, and extends Naevius's life. Jerome's date, 'year of
Abraham 1816,' that is, 201 B.C., is therefore nearly right; and some
have conjectured 199.

It is only necessary to give the seven remaining titles of his tragedies
— *Aesiona* (*Hesione*), *Andromache*, *Danaë*, *Equos Troianus*, *Hector
Proficiscens*, *Iphigenia*, *Lycurgus* — to mark the predominating interest in
the Trojan cycle of legend. Of some forty surviving tragic lines the bulk
may be referred to the *Lycurgus*, which is on the lines of the *Bacchae* of
Euripides. To Naevius's talent for pithy expression we owe the preservation by Cicero of thoughts like

> Ill-gotten gain is lost in pain,[6]

[1] *Noct. Att.*, XVII. xxi.
[2] *Mil. Glor.*, 211–12:
> 'Nam os columnatum poetae esse indaudiui barbaro,
> Quoi bini custodes semper totis horis occubant.'
The 'foreign poet' is so called from the Greek standpoint of the play. The
reference is probably contemporary.
[3] Gellius, *N.A.*, III. iii.   [4] Pseud-Ascon. on Cic., *In Verr. act. pr.* 29.
[5] Cic., *Brut.*, xv. 60.
[6] 'Male parta male dilabuntur.' *apud* Cic. *Phil.* ii. 65.

and that on the height of commendation,

> Praise from thee is precious, father; all the people praiseth thee.[1]

His iambic trimeters too evince, with all their quaint diction, a nascent feeling for beauty, as in the *Lycurgus*:

> Ye trusty guardians of the royal life,
> Hie straight into the forest leaf-yclad,
> Where trees by taking thought do grow unsown.[2]

Inward stirrings of individuality and nationality combined to prompt Naevius's excursions into the domain of Roman history in quest of themes for his *Clastidium*, and *Romulus* or *Alimonium Remi et Romuli*. The former dramatised contemporary events. Its hero was the victor of 222 B.C. and winner of the *spolia opima* from the Keltic chieftain Virdumarus. He was the same Marcellus whom—perhaps with reminiscences of Naevius—Virgil, towards the close of the pageant of souls shown to Aeneas, so affectingly introduces as attended by his youthful descendant, once the centre of imperial hopes.[3] On several occasions such a play might appropriately have been acted—at Marcellus's triumph, or at the funeral games in his honour, or at the dedication of the Temple of Virtus in fulfilment of a paternal vow. In any case, the occasion was like the theme—national. What lustre or interest the other *praetexta* on *The Nurture of Remus and Romulus* shed upon the foundation of Rome, the morsels left are insufficient to show. The example thus set in *praetextae* was bequeathed to Ennius and Pacuvius, but enjoyed no great career. Historical dramas, after long desuetude, were resuscitated in the first century A.D., not for acting, but as a literary expression of hostility to the imperial *régime*. Such were the efforts composed in the time of Nero and Vespasian by Curiatius Maternus, familiar to readers of Tacitus's *Dialogus*. One of those later productions is the sole survivor of the *praetextae*. This is *Octavia*, a dramatisation of the death of Nero's wife. Traditionally coupled with Seneca's tragedies, which it resembles in manner, it is on internal evidence of later date.

But it must have been in comedy that Naevius's varied genius most fully expressed itself. A list of thirty-four *palliatae*—or about five comedies to every tragedy—certifies his fertility. Though the fragments amount only to about 130 lines, and though there has been confusion

---

[1] 'Laetus sum laudari me abs te, pater, a laudato uiro,' *apud* Cic. *Ad Fam.* XV. vi. 1.

[2]
> 'Vos qui regalis corporis custodias
> Agitatis, ite actutum in frundiferos locos,
> Ingenio arbusta ubi nata sunt, non obsita.'

The compound epithet *frundifer* had in later Latin a more obsolete ring than 'leaf-bearing' has in English. Some Middle-English word is analogous; perhaps the Chaucerian 'y-corouned' (with leaves).

[3] *Aen.* vi. 854 *sqq.*

with the records of Laevius, Livius, and Novius, there is enough to illustrate that observation of character which, combined with a fondness for mordant innuendos and unwelcome exposures, made his plays amusing to the plebeian and sometimes too spicy for the noble. The vivid picture of a coquette is now generally considered to belong to his *Tarentilla*, or *The Girl from Tarentum*, herself perhaps the very damsel who

> as if playing ball in a ring, skips from one to another, and is all things to all men, with her nods and winks, her caresses and embraces, now a squeeze of the hand or a pressure on the foot, her ring to look at, her lips to blow an inviting kiss, here a song and there the language of signs.[1]

There was no knowing on what seamy side of politics or morals such a command of realism might throw awkward light. It was not pleasant to have a scandalous episode in the life of a Scipio thus antithetically set before the public:

> *Etiam qui res magnas manu saepe gessit gloriose,*
> *Cuius facta uiua nunc uigent, qui apud gentes solus praestat,*
> *Eum suus pater cum pallio ab amica abduxit uno.*

He was equally scathing when he attacked a whole class, say of spendthrift youths, or of those who brought such rapid ruin on the state, 'the crop of new-fangled speakers, silly young fools!'[2] A more positive note, as if from a moral censor, seems to echo in the advice:

> If you would return to virtue, you must shun depravity—
> Fatherland and father follow, more than foreign infamy.[3]

His butts were to be found outside Rome also; for he had jokes at the expense of the favourite fare of provincial towns like Praeneste and Lanuvium. It is a plausible suggestion that the fun of his *Apella* centres in the mockery meted out to an Apulian woman and her lumpish compatriots.[4] Titles like *Testicularia* and *Triphallus* plainly indicate the coarse nature of some of the plots. Other features of his comedies connect themselves with his treatment of his Greek originals. Already in

---

[1] Or is it 'a *billet-doux* from her own hand?' This passage cited by Isid., *Orig.*, I. 25, as from Ennius, is given by Ribbeck and others to the *Tarentilla* (see *Com. Rom. Frag.*):

> '. . . Quasi pila
> In choro ludens datatim dat se et communem facit.
> Alii adnutat, alii adnictat, alium amat, alium tenet.
> Alibi manus est occupata, alii percellit pedem,
> Anulum dat alii spectandum, a labris alium inuocat,
> Cum alio cantat, at tamen alii suo dat digito literas.'

[2] 'Proueniebant oratores noui, stulti adulescentuli.'
[3] 'Primum ad uirtutem ut redeatis, abeatis ab ignauia,
Domi patres patriam ut colatis potius quam peregri probra.'
[4] Berchem, *op. cit.*, pp. 68–69, quoted by Lamarre, *op. cit.*, p. 203.

Naevius, we know from Terence, had begun the process of *contaminatio*, or weaving together of plots from two separate originals.[1] Already, too, we also learn from Terence, the parasite had cringed and the braggadocio swaggered on the Naevian stage, as they had done on the Menandrian and were now about to do on the Plautine.[2]

The dramatic talents of Naevius cannot be said to have obtained absolutely free play. His comic genius was hampered by the indignant opposition of the great families, while his historical plays were eclipsed by the superior attractions of Greek tragedy. Through the epic of his old age[3] he was destined to exert a far more powerful influence on literature. The *Bellum Punicum*, of which less than eighty lines survive, was in the main a narrative in Saturnian verse of the first war between Rome and Carthage, in which the poet had played a part. But it was more than personal and historical: it drew upon legend. Naevius did not plunge *in medias res*.[4] Preferring to hark back to the origins of the hostile cities, and, possibly in consequence of his campaigns, acquainted with the manner in which the Sicilian Timaeus connected Rome and Troy, he was enabled to decorate his poem with myths of heroes and gods. The paramount interest, then, of the first and second books — for the work was arranged into its seven books by Lampadio[5] — is that they provided sketches in the rough of what became polished scenes in Virgil. The influence of the poem on Ennius must have been immediate: it may well have appeared about 204 B.C., when that author first came to Rome.

The connexion of Rome with Troy had become a familiar idea before Naevius wrote. This is implied in the historic instance from the period of the first Punic War, when the Acarnanians appealed to Rome for help on the ground that they had not assisted the Greeks against Troy.[6] While Naevius makes use of this idea, it is by no means likely, though often alleged, that he introduced the episode of Aeneas's visit to Dido's court, which adds so vital a human interest to the *Aeneid*. Apparently both Naevius and Ennius push the foundation of Rome back to a period contemporaneous with that of Carthage, and they make Romulus, the founder of Rome, a grandson of Aeneas.[7] Aeneas, then, must have reached Italy before the foundation of Carthage; and the words of Naevius,

> *Blande et docte perconctat Aenea quo pacto*
> *Troiam urbem liquisset,*

[1] Ter., *Andr.*, prol. 18. Attacked for blending different plots, Terence retorts:
  '. . . quom hunc accusant, Naeuium, Plautum, Ennium
  Accusant.'
For a different view of *contaminatio* see W. Beare in O.C.D. (s.v. *Contaminatio*) and articles there cited.
[2] Ter., *Eun.*, prol. 25, where reference is made to these personages in the *Colax* of Naevius and *Colax* of Plautus.
[3] Cic., *De Sen.*, xiv: 'Quam gaudebat *Bello* suo *Punico* Naeuius! . . . Eos omnes quos commemoraui his studiis flagrantes senes uidimus.'
[4] But see Suppl. Bibl. under Naevius.
[5] Suet., *Gramm.*, ii. [6] Justinus, xxxviii. 1. [7] Servius on *Aen.*, i. 273.

E

in which some have impulsively seen Dido's request that he should, as in Virgil, recount the 'unutterable woe' of the downfall of Troy, may be more appropriately, if less romantically, referred to old King Latinus.

Ample proof of Naevius's employment of legendary episodes and of their influence on Virgil is afforded by the fragments themselves, by comments on Virgil by Servius—or his interpolator—as well as by Macrobius. Embryonic forms of things familiar in the *Aeneid* emerge, such as the flight of Anchises and Aeneas with their wives from blazing Troy, the storm sent by Juno to harass the voyage, Aeneas's words of heartening to his men, the complaints of Venus to Jove, and Jove's promises of a high future for Rome. Naevius secures his rights again in the records of literature when one notes the Servian comment on Aeneas's speech of encouragement in *Aeneid* I as 'entirely taken over' from the *Punic War*[1] and the similar remarks of Macrobius where, discussing the debt of Virgil to his predecessors, he declares the 'whole passage' of the storm and Venus's subsequent complaints to be 'taken' from Naevius.[2] The saturnians could at best make rough material for Virgil's noble lines; yet it is something to be a hod-man when princes build.

There are, of course, Hellenic echoes in Naevius like his Invocation to the Muses, and like the piece which may be a description of figures upon Aeneas's shield modelled on the Homeric Shield of Achilles.[3] But the total effect of a poem in the native metre and on a native theme is Roman. So Roman is he in details that Naevius significantly hastens to explain his Invocation—with a touch of that prosaic prolixity which so easily beset him—that the 'Nine harmonious sisters, daughters of Jove' are they whom 'Greeks name Musae and whom we name Casmenae.' It is doubtful how much actual history he covered before the Punic War begins in his third book. Did he leap straight to the third century from the mythical lore attending the foundation, or did he rapidly recount the story of the city up to the war with Pyrrhus?[4] In any case, for the historical portions Naevius doubtless borrowed in both matter and expression from the *tituli triumphales* set up in the Capitol by victorious generals and composed in Saturnians. For exploits by individuals he could also draw upon oral tradition as well as family memorials in prose or verse.

In the matter of style there is a risk of doing less than justice to

---

[1] *Aen.*, i. 198–207. The comment is 'totus hic locus de Naeuio (? Naeuii primo) belli Punici libro translatus est.'

[2] Macrob., *Saturn.*, VI. ii: 'In principio Aeneidos tempestas describitur et Venus apud Iouem queritur. . . . Hic locus totus sumptus a Naeuio est ex primo libro *Belli Punici*.'

[3] Bährens, *F.P.R.*, p. 46, § 20. L. Müller (*Enni carm. rel.*, p. xxviii) thinks the figures belong to a ship taken at Mylae.

[4] L. Müller maintains that he covered the longer period, for reasons ingeniously argued out (*op. cit.*, pp. xxv–xxvii).

Naevius. Of his diction it is so easy to say that it shares the faults of early Latin poets, creeps oftener than it soars, and mistakes the baldest annalistic for the poetic. No one will say there is poetry in

> *Manius Valerius consul*
> *Partem exerciti in expeditionem*
> *Ducit.*

Yet there are pieces in our own Wordsworth no better than this simple condescension upon such details as 'a section of an army' led out 'for an expedition'! Of his metre, if one approaches his Saturnians from the standpoint of strictly regular verse, it is hardly possible to form anything but a low opinion. There is a passage formerly referred to Atilius Fortunatianus, but now assigned to Caesius Bassus, a contemporary of Nero, in which the writer, recognising the lawless nature of the lines in the *Bellum Punicum*, confesses that he can hardly find a normal example of Saturnians in Naevius.[1] He does eventually quote a few, but it is evident he is judging by the anachronistic standard of Greek measures. There is no more illuminating criticism on Naevius than that put by Cicero in the mouth of Brutus.[2] He likens the charm of the *Bellum Punicum* to a sculpture by Myron. He admirably weighs the relative merits of Ennius and his forerunner—Ennius, of course, was more polished (*sane, ut certe est, perfectior*), but his disdain for Naevius was merely an affectation. Ennius knew he must reckon with Naevius when he left out of his *Annales* the first Punic War, because 'others have versified it' (*scripsere alii rem uersibu'*). 'Yes,' the passage proceeds, 'versified it with clearness, if with less elegance, Ennius, than your own. This cannot fail to be plain to you, for you borrowed, if you will only acknowledge it, many a thing from Naevius; if you don't acknowledge it, I say you pilfered (*surripuisti*)'. Cicero's judicial attitude prepares one for the place occupied by Naevius in the list in which Volcatius Sedigitus with complacent dogmatism awards their order of merit to ten authors of comedy.[3] Therein Naevius is third. Caecilius Statius heads the list, and Plautus makes a good second. Whatever may be said about Naevius's rustic saturnians, he has in Comedy his revenge—Ennius

[1] 'Ut uix inuenerim apud Naeuium quos pro exemplo ponerem,' Keil, *Gramm. Lat.*, vi. 255 *sqq.*

[2] Cic., *Brut.*, xix. 75, 'Illius quem in uatibus et faunis enumerat Ennius *Bellum Punicum* quasi Myronis opus delectat.'

[3] Gellius, *Noct. Att.*, XV. xxiv, quotes the list from Sedigitus's book on the poets:

> 'Caecilio palmam Statio do mimico;
> Plautus secundus facile exsuperat ceteros;
> Dein Naeuius qui feruet pretio in tertiost;
> Si erit quod quarto detur dabitur Licinio.
> Post insequi Licinium facio Atilium;
> In sexto consequetur hos Terentius;
> Turpilius septimum, Trabea octauum optinet;
> Nono loco esse facile facio Luscium;
> Decimum addo causa antiquitatis Ennium.'

is at the bottom! 'I add a tenth,' says Sedigitus, 'because he is old—Ennius.' The honour is explicitly conferred *antiquitatis causa*.

Strict chronology would present Plautus next in order, but the eminence of Quintus Ennius[1] (239–169) in epic suggests his name immediately after that of Naevius. His birth at Rudiae, an old Calabrian town in touch with Hellenism, made him a 'semi-Graecus,' to use the phrase of Suetonius. Ennius claimed to be of royal Messapian lineage.[2] Brundisium, about twenty miles from his birthplace, was a *colonia* before he was born, so that he may have known Latin when quite young. Jerome's erroneous statement that he was born at Tarentum is conceivably due to his education there. For Ennius Tarentum would mean acquaintance with those Greek dramatic performances which were so deeply to mould him. The first twenty years of his life were years of peace, and let the influences of South Italy sink into his soul. He was, indeed, a resultant of many forces, and used to declare that he had three 'hearts,' because he could speak Greek, Oscan, and Latin.[3] Early environment determined certain of his miscellaneous writings in later days; the Neo-Pythagoreanism acceptable in the South directed him to the works of Epicharmus; a touch of the free-thought of Euhemerus came to him from Sicily; and the luxurious tables of the Greek settlements gave him an insight even into gastronomy, and possibly laid the seeds of that gout to which he facetiously ascribed his poetising,[4] and to which in fact he finally succumbed. But though he stood for Hellenic culture and for a liberal criticism subversive of not a few received notions, one of his 'hearts' was Latin. As a centurion in the Roman army in Sardinia he served creditably, if not with all the Homeric prowess ascribed to him in the rhetorical lines of Silius.[5] It was a paradox of circumstances that he should have attracted the attention of the champion of anti-Hellenism, Cato, then quaestor in Sardinia, should have taught him Greek,[6] and should by him have been brought

---

[1] Text: J. Vahlen, *Ennianae Poesis Reliquiae*, ed. 2, 1903; L. Müller, *Q. Enni Carm. Reliq.*, 1884; for *Annales* and *Saturae*, Bährens, *F.P.R.*; Postgate's *Corp. Poet. Lat.*, 1894 (L. Müller's text); for dramatic fragments, Ribbeck, *op. cit.* For literary criticism, Sellar, *Rom. Poets of the Republic*, and L. Müller, *Q. Ennius, Eine Einleitung in d. Stud. d. röm. Poesie*, 1884. The latter work, by an accomplished metrist, inspired by a real enthusiasm for Ennius, forms most instructive reading, and is entertaining in its criticisms on Vahlen and Mommsen. There is an admirable article by Skutsch in Pauly-Wissowa's *Real-Encyclopädie*, v. 2, 1905, pp. 2588–2628.

[2] Serv. in *Aen.*, vii. 691, *Messapus equom domitor*: 'ab hoc Ennius dicit se originem ducere.'

[3] Gell., *N.A.*, XVII. xvii. 1, 'Ennius tria corda habere sese dicebat quod loqui Graece et Osce et Latine sciret.' The Oscan influence on him is indistinguishable. His use of the Oscan official word *meddix* is nothing but a piece of local colour.

[4] Enn., *Sat.*, Lib. 1, 'Numquam poetor, nisi sim podager'; cf. Hor., *Ep.*, I. xix. 7, 'Numquam nisi potus.'

[5] Sil. It., *Pun.*, xii. 393 *sqq.*

[6] Aur. Victor, *De Vir. Illust.*, xlvii, 'M. Porcius Cato . . . ab Ennio Graecis

to Rome in 204. Ennius apparently never ceased to respect Cato; but the time came when Cato jested at Fulvius Nobilior as 'Mobilior' for taking Ennius abroad on his staff during the Aetolian campaign.

Settled on the Aventine, he lived, according to Jerome, in humble style, content with the service of one maidservant. For a livelihood he taught; for literary stimulus, there was the example of Naevius and of Plautus, and there was his neighbourhood to the Temple of Minerva where the guild of poets met. His friendly relations with prominent Romans—Cato, the elder Scipio Africanus, and Fulvius Nobilior—brought him into contact with the very makers of history. Scipio Nasica, the respected custodian of the image of the Phrygian Mother of the Gods, was sufficiently intimate with Ennius to play upon him the practical joke recorded by Cicero with regard to the exchange of calls.[1] Ennius imbibed a sense of the disciplined greatness of Rome, which permeates his works. Hence his best lines possess a dignity drawn from his aristocratic sympathy with the pilotage which steered the republic through the second Punic War—not a mere class sympathy, but a genuine admiration for the moral stamina and noble past of the whole community. His voice is the voice of a soldier-poet inspired by Rome's victory over Hannibal and by her triumphant progress in the East. Under the domination of a great idea, he became, in spite of his Hellenism, more Roman than the Romans. What Sainte-Beuve said of Virgil is true of Ennius—*il avait touché fortement la fibre romaine*.

By the death of Andronicus and the exile of the too democratic Naevius about the very time of Ennius's arrival in Rome, an opening was made for a new dramatist. Even during the Carthaginian peril, the Romans had enjoyed seeing plays; for a victorious people the aediles had to provide increasing amusement. The contribution to Roman civilisation made by Ennius, especially through his tragedies from the Greek, may be handsomely allowed without drawing, as Mommsen does, an exaggerated picture of a previously existent 'barbarism' among the Romans.[2] The actual vogue of such dramas is the best criticism of the

---

literis institutus'; *cf.* Corn. Nep. (? Pseudo-Nep.) *Cato*, 1, '. . . (Sardiniam) ex qua quaestor . . . Q. Ennium poetam deduxerat: quod non minoris existimamus quam quemlibet amplissimum Sardiniensem triumphum.'

[1] Cic., *De Orat.*, II. lxviii. 276. In this well-known story it was Ennius's *ancilla* who told Nasica her master was out. This may have been amplified by Jerome in 'contentus unius ancillae ministerio,' as Vahlen suggests.

[2] L. Müller (*Q. Ennius, u.s.w.*, i. i.) defends the culture of Ennius's time against Mommsen's insistence on its rawness. Roman audiences of the third and second centuries B.C. suffer in comparison with the fantastically ideal opinion commonly held about the taste of Athenian playgoers in the fifth century. The more highly cultured Roman authors of later times often take too low a view of their predecessors. Thus the remarks of Horace have to be qualified by recognising that (1) he speaks as a representative of the most cultured age of Roman society, (2) he judges by the high standard of the most finished Greek models, (3) he has no clear conception either of the historical conditions of early Latin poetry or of its verse-principles: *e.g.*, much of what Horace would dislike in Plautus as mere roughness was a true representation of Latin spoken in the sixth century of the city.

exaggeration. Magistrates would not stage pieces to excite yawns; they
aimed at winning popularity. Nor would Plautus pun on Greek words
for his own edification; he aimed at creating laughter. The dramatic
activity of Ennius is represented by the fragments of twenty tragedies, two comedies, and one *praetexta*, or, as some think, two. His
individuality, though not necessarily his artistic power, was more
marked in his *saturae* and other miscellaneous poems embodying his
observation of men and his philosophical learning. Continued residence
in the city and experience of the national character led him to plan the
Annales, eventually completed in eighteen books of hexameter verse, as
the epic of the growth of Rome. In the year 189, when he accompanied
Fulvius on service against the Aetolians, the poet found materials for
bringing his *Annales* up to date in the fifteenth book. His patron's son,
some years later, secured him full rights of citizenship[1] and an allot-
ment of land. This did not keep him in comfortable circumstances;
perhaps his social nature and many friendships — like that with the comic
poet Caecilius — forbade economy. Cicero, in any case, cites him as
placidly supporting at seventy the two burdens of poverty and years.[2]
In 169 he died of gout.[3] He was actually engaged in literature to the
end; for his *Thyestes* was produced in the year of his death. There is a
pathetic note of weariness in the eighteenth book of the *Annales*, where,
closing his epic career, he likens himself to a gallant steed which, after
winning at Olympia, finds a restful old age.[4] The honour in which he
was held was signalised by a marble statue of the poet placed at the tomb
of the Scipios.[5]

As a man, Ennius is more familiar to us than many later poets whose
works have been better preserved. The wonderful fertility displayed
during the last thirty-five years of his life was united to a social nature
which encouraged self-revelation and self-confidence. The most valuable piece of autobiography lies in his portrait of a trusted confidant of

[1] *Cf*. his own line – 'Nos sumu' Romani qui fuimus ante Rudini' (*Ann.*,
431, Müller).
[2] Cic., *De Senect.*, v. 14.
[3] Cicero's date (*Brut.*, xx. 78) corresponds to 169 B.C.; Jerome's *ann. Abr.*
1849 to 168 ('articulari morbo perit').
[4] Vahlen, however, places the *sicut fortis equus* in Bk. xii, where Ennius
may have paused to summarise the past and comment on his own times.
[5] The two couplets –

'Aspicite, o ciues, senis Enni imagini' formam!
    Hic uestrum panxit maxima facta patrum.'
and –
'Nemo me dacrumis decoret nec funera fletu
    Faxit. Cur? Volito uiuu' per ora uirum,'

sometimes (*e.g.*, by Sellar) quoted continuously as his epitaph, must be separate.
Cic., *Tusc.*, I. xiv. 34, does not quote them as continuous. His 'idemque' implies
the contrary. Besides, the change of person from *hic* to *me* would be extremely
violent. The first couplet was very likely composed for some bust of Ennius.
The second, one would like to believe his own. See Otto Jahn in *Hermes*, vol. ii.,
(1867), art. 'Satura.'

the general Servilius Geminus. The parallel to the footing on which Ennius stood with Fulvius in Aetolia would naturally suggest itself; but we have the explicit testimony of Aelius Stilo, the intimate of Lucilius and teacher of Cicero, that Ennius was describing himself.[1] The friend was of convivial tastes, interested in the business of forum and senate, capable of guarding a secret frankly confided to him—a nature not prompted to baseness through levity or malice—

> a learned, trustworthy, pleasant man, eloquent, satisfied with his own, serene, tactful, speaking men fair in season, courteous, sparing of words; the keeper of much antique buried lore; one whom lapse of time made master of customs old and new, of laws of many ancient gods and men; a man whose wisdom told him when to speak and when to hold his peace.

In the picture we recognise that combined wisdom and learning and that combined respect for self, for others, and for Rome, which formed the basis of Ennius's greatness. His was the type of character that could calmly leave the direction

> Pay me no tears; nor for my passing grieve:
> I linger on the lips of men—and live,[2]

and could also use his elegiacs in tribute to the exalted conqueror Scipio:

> Here is he laid to whom for daring deed
> Nor friend nor foe could render worthy meed,[3]

and in another inscription:

> From farthest East, beyond Maeotic mere,
> Lives none in proven prowess Scipio's peer;
> If 'tis man's fate to heavenly realms to soar,
> For me alone stands open heaven's high door.[4]

It was self-confidence rather than superstition that prompted his application of the Pythagorean transmigration to himself in the avowal that the spirit of Homer, once incarnate in a peacock, and again in the philosopher Pythagoras, had entered his own body. His *Annales* and *Epicharmus* were the literary illustrations of his creed. His broad eclecticism, touched with Epicurean beliefs, and permeated with the critical spirit of a Euripides or a Euhemerus, prompted the free expression of views which, even if uttered only by *dramatis personae*, Cato

---

[1] Gell., *N.A.*, XII. iv, where the passage from the seventh book of the *Annales* is given in full.

[2] 'Nemo me dacrumis decoret,' etc. See p. 102, n. 5.

[3] 'Hic est ille situs cui nemo ciui' neque hostis
    Quiuit pro factis reddere opis pretium.'

[4] 'A sole exoriente supra Maeoti' paludes
    Nemost qui factis aequiparare queat.
  Si fas endo plagas caelestum ascendere cuiquamst,
    Mi soli caeli maxima porta patet.'

would have gladly placed on some *index expurgatorius*, as dangerous solvents of religion and morality. In his tragedy of the *Telamo* one of his personages incisively sums up the ways of gods to men:

> There are gods; granted; but they do not care how man fares; else good men would have a good time, and bad men a bad time, which is not the case.[1]

Equally incisive in the same play is the criticism on the ways of the soothsayer:

> But your superstitious wizards, fortune-tellers unabashed,
> Arrant lunatics or loafers, or with wits by beggary lashed,
> Point the path out to another which themselves they cannot see,
> And for promise of a fortune fix a drachma as the fee.[2]

By which it is plain that this man of the world had the power of observation which goes to make both playwright and satirist.

The dramatic gift of Ennius was essentially tragic. His comedies are represented by insignificant remnants of the *Cupuncula* and the *Pancratiastes*; and his *praetextae* by The Rape of the Sabines.[3] His tragedies are represented by fragments of twenty plays, amounting to about four hundred lines. In tragedy the preference of the age was for Greek themes with moving situations, such as the revenge of Medea, the guilt of the house of Atreus, the sacrifice of Iphigeneia, and other portions of the Trojan cycle, comprising in conflict, danger, and bloodshed the requisite appeals to pity and fear. The nerves of men who had gone through the Hannibalian War were not easily upset. But Ennius did far more than present external spectacles of suffering. He made his audiences feel and think. His ultimate influence was in some degree formal, due to his manipulation of Greek dramatic measures, and especially to his introduction of the hexameter in the *Annales*; but his immediate influence contributed to civilise the nation. It was his to introduce a flood of Greek ideas — the wide humanity and critical attitude of Euripides, so appropriate to a people whose destiny now called them from circumscribed views to a tolerant cosmopolitanism. Of the plays, eight at least recall Euripides — *Andromeda, Hecuba, Iphigenia,*[4] *Medea Exsul, Melanippa, Telephus, Alexander, Andromacha Aechma-*

---

[1] 'Ego deum genus esse semper dixi et dicam caelitum,
Sed eos non curare opinor quid agat humanum genus;
Nam si curent, bene bonis sit, male malis; quod nunc abest.'

[2] 'Sed superstitiosi uates inpudentesque arioli,
Aut inertes aut insani aut quibus egestas imperat,
Qui sibi semitam non sapiunt, alteri monstrant uiam,
Quibus diuitias pollicentur, ab eis drachumam ipsi petunt.'

[3] L. Müller gives reasons for thinking his *Ambracia* a *satura*.

[4] The *Iphigenia* is an example of tragic 'contaminatio'; for its plot was partly from Sophocles, partly from Euripides. A similarly composite play may have been *Hectoris Lytra* which Vahlen takes to represent a trilogy by Aeschylus.

lotis.[1] Such plays raised the problems of life which are in the forefront
of the Euripidean drama—man's relation to deity, man's right to think
for himself, the vicissitudes of fortune, the contrasts of good and evil,
riches and poverty, master and slave. The erotic element, though not a
dominant *motif*, was also a noteworthy step toward verisimilitude.

This borrowing was not incompatible with a certain originality.
Not everything in Ennius is so literally translated as his opening of the
Medea. It was not simply that the Latin rendering must often be more
diffuse than the Greek because much at Rome needed elaboration which
was clear at Athens; a genius like his demanded freer play for its
expression than a mere paraphrase allowed. His own experience,
reflection, imagination must find a place. So poets like Ennius and
Accius added many products of their own invention, just as Naevius
and Plautus had been doing in comedy. The sententious is one phase of
his philosophic mind. In his dramas he follows the spirit of his own
eminently Roman idea—*philosophandum est paucis, nam omnino non
placet*; and so, in brief terms, he would apply wisdom to life:

He whose wisdom cannot help him, gets no good from being wise,[2]

or give the practical test of friendship:

A friend in need is a friend indeed,[3]

or reveal the secret of independent happiness:

He hath freedom whoso beareth clean and constant heart within.[4]

Still more individual is the control which Ennius possesses of a wide
compass in the notes of emotion. The fragments give tantalising
glimpses of his passionate force. They are vignettes of which we should
welcome more—such as the lyric terror of the parricide Alcmaeon
hounded by the Furies; the shamefast sorrows of Cassandra,[5] filled with
pity for the queen and picturing by a weird 'second-sight' her country's
downfall; the woeful complaints of the distressed mother Hecuba; the
sad music of despair in 'captive Andromache':

> *Quid petam praesidi aut exsequar? quoue nunc*
> *Auxilio exsili aut fugae freta sim?*
> *Arce et urbe orba sum. Quo accidam? Quo applicem? . . .*

followed by the fine emotion of her farewell:

> *O pater, O patria, O Priami domus,*
> *Saeptum altisono cardine templum!*

[1] Vahlen argues, however, that Ennius's play cannot have been modelled on
Euripides's *Andromache*.
[2] 'Qui ipse sibi sapiens prodesse nequit nequidquam sapit.'
[3] 'Amicus certus in re incerta cernitur.'
[4] 'Ea libertas est qui pectus purum et firmum gestitat.'
[5] It is on this passage that Cicero passes the criticism, 'O poema tenerum
et moratum atque molle!' (*De Diuin.*, I. xxxi. 66).

Again, we have dialogue admirably contrived to present now vigorous altercation, now a whole background of poetry, as in the scene where Agamemnon asks 'What of the night?'

> *Quid noctis uidetur in altisono*
> *Caeli clipeo?*

and his old henchman replies —

> *Superat temo*
> *Stellas cogens etiam atque etiam*
> *Noctis sublime iter.*

For one of these plays with their warm blood and masculine force, to barter five of Seneca's frigid experiments would be sheer gain.

These tragedies were still produced in the theatre during the Augustan period, and there is evidence that until the time of Nero tragedies of the republic were to be seen on the stage.[1] From the second century A.D. Ennius's plays are not likely to have been acted, unless they were occasionally revived for circles of *dilettanti* in the archaising epoch. The *sententiae* in the plays may have been collected for school use:[2] and it is not impossible that some reappeared among the maxims ascribed to Publilius Syrus.

The *Saturae*, of which Ennius left four books, were miscellaneous enough to include didactic, sportive, and narrative pieces. In the hands of Ennius and Pacuvius *satura* had the primitive sense of *mélange*, and might tell a story or touch on high questions of intellect and morals, or on minor incidents in life, sometimes in reflective soliloquy, sometimes in more dramatic dialogue, sometimes with a caustic criticism anticipative of 'satire' in its later meaning. In *Epicharmus* Ennius, over a century before Lucretius, philosophises on the nature of things. He derives his teaching about the four elements from a poem in trochaic tetrameters, reputed in South Italy to be by the Sicilian Epicharmus, whose plays had proved his Pythagoreanism. In *Euhemerus*, or *Sacra Historia*, Ennius followed the rationalist Euhemerus by referring the origin of gods to the apotheosis of departed chiefs and heroes. Whether this was in prose or verse is a vexed question. It would be easier for Ennius to handle verse than prose at this period; but the echoes of metre which some, like Vahlen, claim to find in the passages where Lactantius[3] cites the *Euhemerus* cannot be detected by others. The *Protrepticus* conveyed counsels of morality. The *Hedyphagetica* were mock-heroic principles of gourmandising, based on hexameters written a century before by Archestratus the Sicilian. Ennius in his facetious

---

[1] See Sen., *Ep.*, lxxx.
[2] This is an inference from Phaedrus, III, *Epilog.*, 33–35:
> 'Ego quondam legi quam puer sententiam,
> *Palam mutire plebeio piaculum est,*
> Dum sanitas constabit, pulchre meminero.'
[3] *Diuin. Instit.*, I. xi, xiii, xiv, xvii, xxii.

enthusiasm for a dainty fish magnifies it into 'virtually the brain of Jove almighty' (*cerebrum Ioui' paene supremi*). The *Sota*, an abbreviated form of the Greek Sotades, presumably copied that writer's indecency. The work existed in the time of Marcus Aurelius, for he acknowledges a loan of the book in a letter to Fronto.[1] In *Scipio* Ennius honours his patron, Africanus Maior. It is more than doubtful whether it should be called a *satura*;[2] but the fragments show its variety of metres, including the trochaic septenarius. At one point Scipio proudly apostrophises Rome — 'Scipio's toils have reared lines of defence for thee,' and his 'witnesses are those broad plains which the Afric land supports, enriched by tilth.' This generous admiration meets with a fair return in the greeting:

> Hail, poet Ennius, who pledgest men
> In verses from thy marrow—filled with flame.[3]

With this group we may class the charming fable of the field-lark, paraphrased by Gellius,[4] to teach that one should not expect friends to do what one can do oneself.

The *Annales*, in eighteen books as finally issued by the poet, were the great fountain of his influence upon posterity. What survive are roughly six hundred lines or partial lines. The total includes a few continuous passages of about twenty lines each. We possess, then, something like a fortieth of the whole. Ennius's aim was to celebrate the glories of Rome from Aeneas to his own days. In subject he was treading to some extent a beaten track; but the great formal contrast to Naevius was the introduction of the hexameter. This contrast Ennius realises when he reaches the first Punic War and remembers that 'others have written of the matter in the verses of the *fauni* and *uates*,' by which, we have seen, he stigmatises the rusticity of the saturnians. Opening with legends about Aeneas and Romulus, he gives his second and third books to the kings, and then traces the fortunes of the republic to the beginning of the third Macedonian War. The struggles with Pyrrhus and with Carthage are made prominent. The scheme is controlled by chronological order, as the title suggests. This annalistic structure is a defect. There is a consequent disproportion between the full treatment of events near or within the author's lifetime, and the more rapid treatment of the distant past. There is a disproportion, too, in spirit between the legendary and the historic. Invocations of the Muse and the intervention of a deity in imitation of Homer cannot restore the earlier tone suitable to myth. If Ennius remains Homeric, he does so in virtue of rapid descriptions and of that energy with which he can make

---

[1] *Epist. ad Front.*, iv. 2 (61, Naber).
[2] Vahlen (*op. cit.*, ed. 2) gave up his contention that the *Scipio* was one of the *Saturae*.
[3] 'Enni poeta, salue, qui mortalibus
  Versus propinas flammeos medullitus.'
[4] Gell., *N.A.*, II. xxix.

his heroes speak. What unity the work possesses lies in its permeation with the idea of greatness gradually achieved by Rome. In this sense it was a *Romaid*.[1]

The epos of Ennius was not of the naïve and unconscious order, if indeed it is intelligible to talk of 'unconscious' epic. Its affinity is not with the *Chanson de Roland* or the *Nibelungenlied*. Here is an author who lays claim to personal inspiration from Homer—or, rather, claims to be an *alter Homerus*. With words—*Visus Homerus adesse poeta*—which find their echo in Virgil,[2] he introduces the vision wherein Homer taught him the lore of birth and death and the immortality of spirit through reincarnation. His ambition, then, rises beyond acclimatising the Greek epic form by wedding Latin to the hexameter—in itself a mighty task—it rises to the conception of being a Roman Homer and of permanently moulding the poetic feeling of the nation. There is, then, point in the parallel with Klopstock, who stands to modern German literature in an analogous position. The comparison is not one of style—and yet on this score, after all has been said regarding the uncouthness of Ennius, the comparison is in favour of the Roman for verbal influence and lively interest—it is rather historical. Klopstock, like Ennius, was the herald of a new era: by his study of Homer and Milton in the *Messias*, he set fresh tendencies a-working.

Consciously as Ennius kept Homer before his mind, the real power behind the *Annales* is genius rather than art. Ovid's antithesis, *ingenio maximus arte rudis*, is more than a half truth. The inborn force and keen outlook of the man matter most of all. Hence comes an undeniable movement of robust life. From his enthusiasm for the great in character and action, some of that greatness passes into his lines. Infinitely more masculine than Silius in his treatment of the Punic Wars, he can compete even with Virgil in characterisation when he writes of the conqueror of the Samnites and of Pyrrhus—Manius Curius:

> Whom no man could o'ercome by steel or gold;[3]

and of Fabius, who proved a match in tactics for Hannibal:

> One man for us by lingering rescued Rome:
> He set our safety higher than renown:
> So more and more the hero's glory shines;[4]

and of the chivalrous disdain of King Pyrrhus for the barter of prisoners:

> I claim no gold: bid me no ransom-price:
> Not hucksterers in war, but warriors,

[1] Keil, *Gramm. Lat.*, 484 – accepting the reading *Romais*.
[2] *Aen.*, ii. 271.
[3] 'Quem nemo ferro potuit superare nec auro.'
[4] 'Unus homo nobis cunctando restituit rem:
Noenum rumores ponebat ante salutem:
Ergo postque magisque uiri nunc gloria claret.'

On steel, not gold, we each must stake our life.
Find we in fight if Lady Fortune wills
That you or I be master. Hear my word
Withal. Since luck of battle spared the men,
Their freedom 'tis my fixed resolve to spare.
Take grant and gift: the mighty gods approve.[1]

Ovid was right: there is much that is rude. There are lapses into dry annalistic detail and that crudity which forces early Latin to sink oftener than rise. One tires of heavy plays on words and alliteration overdone, as in

O Tite tute Tati tibi tanta, tyranne, tulisti!

which is no better than saying

For thyself, O Titus Tatius, thou tholedst those terrible troubles!

One marvels at a bizarre tmesis like the notorious

saxo cere comminuit brum

for *saxo cerebrum comminuit,* and at the curiously lopped words in

diuom domus altisonum cael,

and

repleat te laetificum gau,

and

endo suom do,

the last of which seems a distorted reminiscence of the Homeric Διὸς ποτὶ χαλκοβατὲς δῶ. The Ennian hexameter suffers when tested by the inevitable touchstone of the Virgilian. It can be clumsily spondaic or fantastically dactylic: it can neglect elisions or admit harsh ones; it can overlook the caesura; it can freely employ monosyllabic and polysyllabic endings.[2] These are not unnatural symptoms of infancy in

[1]   'Nec mi aurum posco nec mi pretium dederitis:
Nec cauponantes bellum sed belligerantes,
Ferro non auro uitam cernamus utrique.
Vosne uelit an me regnare era quidue ferat Fors
Virtute experiamur, et hoc simul accipe dictum:
Quorum uirtuti belli fortuna pepercit,
Eorundem libertati me parcere certumst.
Dono ducite doque uolentibu' cum magnis dis.'

[2] The following lines may serve as examples:
(*a*) 'Olli respondit rex Albaï longaï,'
(*b*) 'Poste recumbite uestraque pectora pellite tonsis,'
(*c*) 'Miscent inter sese inimicitiam agitantes,'
(*d*) 'Hos et ego in pugna uici uictusque sum ab isdem,'
(*e*) 'Cui par imber et ignis spiritus et graui' terra,'
(*f*) 'Exim candida se radiis dedit acta foras lux,'
(*g*) 'Olli respondit suauis sonus Egeriaï.'
(*Cf.* endings *belligerantes, sapientipotentes, augurioque, altiuolantum, induperator.*)

the Latin hexameter. The dropping of final -*s* in scansion and the quantity of certain terminations are rather linguistic than artistic phenomena. Ennius's defects were inseparable from his period and task. He had to wrestle with a new metre not easily rendered tractable in an essentially non-dactylic language. He must be judged in relation to his time. To turn to Ennius immediately after reading the fragments of Livius and Naevius is to be conscious of an ease of movement and a literary power which they never attained. Ennius is rugged when contrasted with Virgil; but he has risen above the awkward Latin of his predecessors. And it is not only that the Hellenic tradition has begun to work. One is in the presence of an artist. The eye for beauty is discernible in his fondness for the adjective *pulcher*, in his fresh open-air delight drawn from the trees of the leafy forest (*siluaï frondosaï*), from places where the sweet willows grow (*amoena salicta*), from the azure depths of heaven (*caeli caerula templa*) by night and by day. His flash of golden sunrise with its effective close on a monosyllable —

> *Simul aureus exoritur sol*

is as good as Coleridge's tropical sunset:

> The sun's rim dips; the stars rush out:
> At one stride comes the dark.

Everywhere there is keenness to mark a telling characteristic. Remus shall expiate his insolence with his 'warm blood' (*calido dabi' sanguine poenas*), and it is the 'sweet sound' of the nymph's voice (*suauis sonus Egeriaï*) that falls on King Numa's ears. A blush could not be painted better than in his line — *Et simul erubuit ceu lacte et purpura mixta*. But there is more than colour. The poet's eye sometimes has its 'fine frenzy' in depth of feeling or dramatic situation. An ecstatic hero-worship prompts the outburst of lament over the passing of the king —

> O Romulus, O godlike Romulus,
> How true a warden of thy land the gods
> Created thee! O Sire, Creative Blood
> God-sprung! Thou broughtst us to the realms of light.[1]

And tenderness animates the prophetic dream which Ilia relates in tears to her sister when she wakes affrighted:

> My body hath no vital vigour left.
> Methought a being fair thro' willows sweet
> Haled me by streams and places strange; and then
> Alone, O sister mine, I seemed to stray,

[1]
> 'O Romule, Romule die,
> Qualem te patriae custodem di genuerunt!
> O pater, O genitor, O sanguen dis oriundum!
> Tu produxisti nos intra luminis oras.'

Track my slow path in quest of thee, nor yet
Held thee in heart: I found no footing sure.
Thereat meseemed my father's voice to call:
    'O daughter, thou hast tribulation first
    To bear: the river shall restore thy weal!'
So spake our sire, O sister, and was gone
Nor let me look upon him, though I longed
And oft upheld my hands to heaven's blue vault
In tears, and called him in the tones of love.
At length sleep left me with my pain at heart.'[1]

The far-reaching literary influence of Ennius gives him an importance
out of all proportion to the thousand lines which time has spared. The
new wave of Hellenism in him, his manifold differences from Livius
and Naevius, his contemporary and posthumous reputation, led to his
being regarded as the real father of Roman literature. That he founded
a school, but was himself taught only by the Muses, is the purport of the
epigram of Pompilius.[2]

    Pacui discipulus dicor; porro is fuit Enni,
      Enniu' Musarum; Pompilius clueor.

To Lucretius, Ennius was 'he who first brought down from lovely
Helicon a crown of unfading leaf, destined to brilliant fame throughout
Italian clans of men.'[3] This is true, with the proper limitations. It is not
to be forgotten that Ennius had also Latin predecessors who influenced
him, and that Roman society and history profoundly impressed him.
But two conceptions, at least, are utterly misleading—Niebuhr's, that
Ennius's envious hostility suppressed the old poetry, is based on the
exaggeration of his ballad theory and a misunderstanding of the literary
situation; Mommsen's, that he was anti-national, is based on oblivious-
ness to the spirit animating the *Annales*. On such principles every
literary revolt would be anti-national, and one might as well aver that
Victor Hugo, from the period of his *Hernani*, was no longer French.
    Beyond expressed admiration, the sincerest tribute to Ennius is paid

---

[1]   'Vires uitaque corpu' meum nunc deserit omne.
       Nam me uisus homo pulcher per amoena salicta
       Et ripas raptare locosque nouos. Ita sola
       Postilla, germana soror, errare uidebar
       Tardaque uestigare et quaerere te neque posse
       Corde capessere: semita nulla pedem stabilibat.
       Exim compellare pater me uoce uidetur
       His uerbis: 'O gnata, tibi sunt ante ferendae
       Aerumnae; post ex fluuio fortuna resistet.'
       Haec ecfatu' pater, germana, repente recessit
       Nec sese dedit in conspectum corde cupitus,
       Quanquam multa manus ad caeli caerula templa
       Tendebam lacrumans et blanda uoce uocabam,
       Vix aegro cum corde meo me somnu' reliquit.'
[2] W. Morel, *Frag. Poet. Rom.* p. 42.   [3] Lucr., i. 117 *sqq.*

by the borrowings of great Latin poets. So Lucretius echoes him.[1] The story went that Virgil once said he was gathering gold from Ennius's dungheap (*ex stercore*). The old gold is often marvellously reburnished.[2] Certainly nothing better brings home to one the potency of the Ennian tradition than to meet comments by Servius declaring that here a verse[3] and there a whole passage[4] is from Ennius, or, again, Virgil's fall of Troy from Ennius's destruction of Alba.[5] Nothing is in this way more illuminating than to consult the chapters where Macrobius quotes many parallels in Ennius and Virgil.[6] The examples indicate that Virgil's copious borrowings were not so much in the handling of material as in detailed description. Ovid also, through Lucretius and Virgil, drew from the same well.[7] Yet there were fluctuations in Ennius's popularity. Broadly, no doubt, so commanding was the position of his epic that up to the second century A.D. it was cited as '*Annales*' *par excellence*;[8] and so important was its text that it became the subject of emendation and comment by scholars like Lampadio, Vargunteius, and Gnipho. Varro and Cicero show profound veneration: Cicero with especial affection enjoys quoting 'noster Ennius.' But in their time, along with that taste for Alexandrine poetry of which one feature in Catullus is typical, there came a reaction. Cicero's admiration is an avowed protest against the *cantores Euphorionis* who aped other fashions.[9] The proved debt of the Augustan poets to Ennius makes their

---

[1] *Cf.* Lucr., iii. 1025:
  'Lumina sis oculis etiam bonus Ancu' reliquit,'
and Enn., *Ann.*, 151 (Müller):
  'Postquam lumina sis oculis bonus Ancu' reliquit.'
  [2] *Cf.* Ennius's bold onomatopoeia:
  'At tuba terribili sonitu *taratantara* dixit,'
with *Aen.*, ix. 503:
  'At tuba terribilem sonitum procul aere canoro
  Increpuit,'
and his metaphor:
  'irarum effunde quadrigas,'
softened in *Aen.* xii. 499, to:
  'irarumque omnes effundit habenas.'
The galloping line in *Aen.*, viii. 596:
  'Quadrupedante putrem sonitu quatit ungula campum,'
closely echoes phrases in Ennius. Perhaps the most famous loan of all is the apostrophe to Fabius Cunctator in Ennius's words with the alteration of a word and a letter, *Aen.* vi. 846.
  [3] Serv. in *Aen.* ii. 241, *O patria*, etc., 'uersus Ennianus.' *Cf.* in ii. 274, *ei mihi* – 'Enni uersus.'
  [4] Serv. in *Aen.* viii. 631, 'sane totus hic locus Ennianus est.'
  [5] Serv. in *Aen.* ii. 486, *At domus interior* – 'de Albano excidio translatus est locus.'
  [6] Macrob., *Saturn.*, VI. i. and ii.
  [7] A. Zingerle, *Ovidius u. s. Verhälts. z. d. Vorgängern, u.s.w.*, 1871, ii. pp. 1–11.
  [8] This is illustrated by the story of the ambiguous question, 'Num quid potes de *Sexto Annali*?' told by Quint., VI. iii. 86.
  [9] Cic., *Tusc. Disp.* III. xix: 'O poetam egregium! quanquam ab his cantoribus Euphorionis contemnitur.'

disdain for his inferior polish savour of ingratitude. Propertius has no better epithet for the old poet's wreath than *hirsuta*![1] For Horace it must be said that, though he attacked the old-fashioned, it was more particularly the form it assumed in the affected archaism of his contemporaries who shunned all new paths of poetry. A man of Horace's common sense was not likely to forget that Ennius was an innovator in his own day. So Horace can both quote and parody him:[2] and every one remembers that he illustrates the unmistakable and essential elements of poetic diction (*disiecti membra poetae*) by a forcible quotation from Ennius.[3] In the first century A.D. the praises of Ennius — where he meets with praise — are often forced. He enjoys a certain respect as an ancient — a respect which wins its classic expression in Quintilian's words, 'Let us worship Ennius like groves hallowed by age, in which the great old oaks are not so much beautiful as awe-inspiring.'[4] The real enthusiast of that time was Silius, who warmly eulogised his predecessor. In the second century A.D. Fronto and Gellius represent the reactionary passion for ante-classical writers, among whom Ennius came into his own again. To the archaistic critics of Hadrian's time he appealed as the master of pre-Virgilian epic. Virgil in poetry was too modern for them, as Cicero was in oratory and Sallust in history. Their favourites, therefore, in these three fields were Ennius and Cato and Caelius. Gellius mentions a public reading from the *Annales* in the theatre at Puteoli by an Ennianist; and he is the last of the Romans to mention a MS. of Ennius. After the third century those who quote Ennius, such as Nonius, Charisius, Diomedes, Macrobius, Servius, and Priscian, probably did not use an original text, but at most some anthology composed for scholastic purposes of extracts from Ennius, Lucilius, and other early authors.

The barest summary proves the man's versatility. He had a high, some would say the highest, place in Roman tragedy, and a minor place in comedy. He was the precursor of Lucilius in satire, of Lucretius in didactic, of Virgil in epic. Not only did he mould the hexameter to Latin use, but he was the introducer of the elegiac distich. He left a permanent impress on the language. The very details of orthography and shorthand notes had an interest for him. It may be that his influence on prose and philosophy is made too much of in some quarters;[5] but it is no mistake that as a channel for the questionings of Euripides and the rationalism of Euhemerus, he distilled into the *Zeitgeist* the sweet poison of doubt. Ennius is the greatest figure in the serious thought of Rome before the days of Lucretius and Cicero.

[1] IV. i. 61. [2] Hor., *Sat.*, I. ii. 37-38.
[3] Hor., *Sat.*, I. iv. 62. [4] Quint., X. i. 88.
[5] L. Müller, *Q. Ennius*, p. 5, 'Sein Werk ist es dass in Cäsars Zeit das römische Volk laut aufjubelte, wenn ein Redner sein Satzgebäude mit einem doppelten Trochaeus schloss.'

Chapter IV

THE THEATRE AND THE MASTERS
OF COMEDY

Occasions for drama – The evolution of the theatre – Theatrical
equipment – Actors.
Plautus – Life – Period of the plays – Plautine canons – Prologues – Arguments – His sources – Menander as representative
of the New Comedy – Its typical plots and personages – The
'halves' of Menander – Greek plays drawn on by Plautus – The
Greek element in him – The independent Roman element – Contemporary allusions – Plautus's originality and relation to his
audience – The best plays – *Amphitruo* – *Aulularia* – *Captiui* –
Trinummus – *Menaechmi* – *Rudens* – *Bacchides* – *Miles Gloriosus* –
Mostellaria – *Pseudolus* – The inferior plays – Character-drawing
of women – Types of men – Love – Fun in Plautus – Outlook
on life – Attitude to morality – The defects of his qualities –
Spontaneity and stage-craft coupled with limitation of subjects – Plautus and Shakespeare – Plautine metres in Diverbium
and Canticum – Acts and scenes – Plautine prosody – Plautine
language.
Caecilius Statius – Contemporary authors of *Palliatae*.
Terence – Life – Chronology of plays – Arguments and pro-
logues – His sources – The plots in the light of the titles –
Andria – *Hecyra* – *Heauton Timorumenos* – *Eununchus* – *Phormio* –
Adelphi – Society portrayed – Contrasts with Plautus – Style –
Humour – Prosody and metres – The influence of Terence.
The last of the *Fabula Palliata* – *Fabula Togata* – Titinius, Atta,
Afranius – *Fabula Tabernaria* – Literary *Atellana* – Pomponius and
Novius – The Mime or *Fabula Riciniata*.

DRAMA has almost universally had a religious sanction for its
origin. In Greece, tragedy and comedy sprang twin-born from
the vintage worship of Dionysus. The medieval Mysteries and
Miracle Plays were based on Holy Writ or legends concerning Saints,
and were often acted at the church-door. Similarly at Rome the
earliest dramatic performances were associated with expiation or
thanksgiving, and in the time of Plautus and Terence they were held
near the temple of a god honoured in the festival of the occasion. The
regular state occasions for plays were the *Ludi Megalenses* in April, *Ludi
Apollinares* in July, *Ludi Romani* in September, and *Ludi Plebeii* in
November. These last two festivals had long been associated with

drama before fresh opportunities were afforded by the Games of
Apollo, instituted in 213 B.C., and the Megalensian games, in honour of
Cybele, which became scenic in 194. Of these the *Ludi Romani* spread
over the longest time. The four days of that festival in the third century
B.C. were subsequently doubled. Other opportunities for plays were
triumphs, or funerals, in accord with that spirit which permitted
caricature of a dead man in his own *cortège*. Thus Terence's *Adelphi*
was given at the funeral games of Aemilius Paulus. The Greek practice
of exhibiting several plays in immediate succession was not followed.
At Rome one piece was played a day. It started about noon and occupied nearly three hours. Only after representations became more
elaborate did a play take longer.

Many generations passed from the time of Andronicus before Rome
had a permanent theatre.[1] At first the temporary wooden structures
were restricted to the stage and to the hurdles on the slopes around,
where spectators stood. Seats there were none, unless spectators brought
them. In 154 B.C. a stone theatre under construction was demolished
by decree of the senate, and the people were forbidden to sit at games.[2]
Mummius in 145, after conquering Greece, secured more impressive
staging and the construction of tiers of raised seats (*auditorium, cauea*);
but for ninety years Rome had still only a theatre of wood, rebuilt yearly
on the Greek model. The first stone theatre was that of Pompey in
55 B.C., built out of his Mithradatic spoil. By 13 A.D. there were the two
other permanent theatres of Cornelius Balbus and Marcellus, so that in
all about 50,000 people could be entertained. The semicircular orchestra
used for the chorus in Greek plays was the first portion of the theatre
furnished with seats for senators—early in the second century B.C. In
67 B.C. the Roscian law reserved fourteen rows for the equestrian order.
In the days of Plautus, about 200 B.C., a crowd of jostling, noisy spectators is to be imagined on the slopes above the orchestra; and, as we
shall see, the nature of this turbulent audience in the open air accounts
for the almost desperate efforts to make the plot clear and to bespeak
attention. In the foreground of the stage rose an altar, which might
upon occasion either be a scamp's refuge, as in the amusing close of
Plautus's *Haunted House*, or add to solemn effect in tragedy. The long
narrow Roman stage (*pulpitum*)—in some cases sixty yards in length—
rendered more natural certain favourite stage artifices, such as the safe
aside, the conversation overheard, the frequent failure to see another
character on the stage, or contrariwise, the sighting of one in the distance making a leisurely approach. The length of stage rendered possible

---

[1] For Roman theatre, 'Das Theater' in L. Friedländer's *Darstellungen aus
d. Sittengeschichte*, Bd. ii.; A Mau, *Pompeii*, Eng. tr. F. W. Kelsey (U.S.A.), ed. 2,
1902, ch. xxi; Teuffel, *op. cit.*, § 12, 2, and authorities there cited.
[2] The senate's objections to seats at performances may have been overcome about 150 B.C., as Ritschl thought. The references to *subsellia* in prol.
65 to the *Amphitruo* prove the prologue to be post-Plautine.

also the comic bustling and hustling of slave or parasite. The normal background (*scaena*) in comedy represented the front of two houses with an alley (*angiportus*) between. Occasionally departures from this arrangement may have been made. The interior of a room was probably shown at the end of the *Asinaria*, and the *Rudens* required rocks and a temple. In tragedy the normal scene was the front of a temple or palace. In both tragedy and comedy, convention ruled that the exit to the left of the actor as he faced the audience led to the *forum* or heart of the town, while the exit to his right led to the harbour or to the country. On the right of the actors, therefore, or the left of the spectators, strangers entered 'from abroad.' The curtain (*aulaeum*) was, contrary to modern practice, lowered at the beginning and raised at the close.

The dress of the characters was modelled on the Greek. In comedy the chief personages wore, over their tunics, the *pallium*, rich in material and colour, or shabby, to suit circumstances. Frequently old gentlemen wore white and young gentlemen purple. The parasite in grey was padded excessively to look ridiculous. Soldiers were in military costume with sword and helmet, country-folk in rough attire. Thus Menedemus in Terence's *Heauton Timorumenos* is dressed in hide for his hoeing.[1] Slaves were in sleeveless tunics of some dull colour. Women wore a white or yellow *chiton* with ornamental border; the *himation* might be worn above. The sandal of comedy made a contrast in footwear to the buskin of tragedy. Tragic clothing, being that of gods, heroes, princes, and mythical personages, was more gorgeous and unfamiliar. Masks on the Roman stage were not introduced until after Terence's death; but among the important items of the actor's make-up were wigs—white for the aged, black for the youthful, and red for slaves. Female parts were taken by men until a late date. Primitive simplicity was widely departed from by the days of Horace, when pageants on the stage, with their glittering appeal to the eye, dwarfed the literary effect of the drama.

As to management, the poet originally produced his own play. This grew less easy when poets ceased to be actors. The usage came to be that the manager of a troupe (*dominus gregis*) bought a piece from the composer, and contracted for its performance with the aediles who were to give the show. The manager was usually leading man as well (*actor primarum*). A freedman himself, he was the owner of most of the players, who were slaves liable to punishment for bad acting.[2] The status of the actor was in consequence low; in general, his calling involved a social stigma (*infamia*). An improvement in his position came in the days when Roscius could attract the familiar patronage of the great, secure the intimacy of Sulla, and win glowing terms of admiration from Cicero. This was a genuine tribute to ability. But when the later craze

[1] Varro, *De Re Rust.*, II. xi. 41.
[2] See Mercury's remarks, Plaut., *Amph.*, Prol. 26 *sqq.*

arose for petting clever *pantomimi*, it marked a retrograde movement in things social as well as theatrical.

T. Maccius Plautus (*c.* 254–184 B.C.) comes midway in time between Naevius and Ennius. Confining himself to comedy without the range of experiment common at this period, he developed the lighter side of Naevius's dramatic achievement, as Pacuvius developed the graver side. The influence of Ennius joined with that of Plautus in Caecilius. The traditional account of the life of Plautus is based mainly on brief statements by Cicero, Gellius (who quotes Varro 'and others'), and Jerome. From Festus[1] comes the evidence for his birth at Sarsina, in Umbria. In the traditional account there are picturesque details of his making money by theatrical work (usually thought to have been stage-carpentry or decoration),[2] of his losing the whole of it in foreign trade, and returning to Rome so poor that he had to toil at driving a flour-mill, and eke out his scanty wages by writing plays.[3] There is something undeniably attractive in the spectacle of this struggle with poverty, and of dramas composed in the intervals of severe manual work. But it hardly so very much matters whether we accept such details on the authority of Varro and others, or, after Professor Leo's incisive dissection of biographic reports in ancient literary history, reject them as inventions. No doubt Varro modelled some of his details on those of Greek literary lives. No doubt many incidents in plays were used by

---

[1] P. 275 (Lindsay). He is there called 'Accius' owing to a confusion of 'Maccius' with 'M. Accius.' His name 'Plotus, postea Plautus' was, as Festus says, given to him because he was flat-footed. If the witness of the Ambrosian palimpsest (about fourth cent. A.D.) settles the matter, as most have agreed since Ritschl, then the poet's name was Titus Maccius Plautus. Coming to Rome as Titus 'Flat-foot,' he gained from his connexion with comic acting the further name 'Maccus,' clown, buffoon. 'Maccus uortit barbare,' the MS. reading in *Asin.*, prol. 11, need not be corrected to 'Maccius.' 'Titus Flat-floot the Clown' changed the 'Maccus' to 'Maccius' when he received Roman citizenship (F. Bücheler, *Rhein. Mus.*, xli. 12). For a searching examination of Plautus's name, see F. Leo, *Plautin. Forsch.*, ed. 2, 1912, pp. 81–84.

[2] Gell., *N.A.*, III. iii. 14, 'cum, pecunia omni, quam in operis artificum scaenicorum pepererat, in mercatibus perdita, inops Romam redisset et ob quaerendum uictum ad circumagendas molas quae *trusatiles* appellantur, operam pistori locasset.'

[3] Gell., *loc. cit.*, 'Saturionem et *Addictum* et tertiam quandam, cuius nunc mihi nomen non subpetit, in pistrino eum scripsisse, Varro et plerique alii memoriae tradiderunt.' *Cf.* Jerome's note, 'propter annonae difficultatem ad molas manuarias pistori se locauerat; ibi quotiens ab opere uacaret, scribere fabulas et uendere sollicitus consueuerat' (*v.l.* scribere fabulas solitus ac uendere). Jerome's note is entered against ann. Abr. 1817, *i.e.*, 200 B.C., which he mistakenly gives as the year of Plautus's death. Now 200 B.C. is one of the few certain dates in Plautus's life. It is fixed by the *didascalia* to the *Stichus* as the year when that comedy was played. Either Jerome confused the death with this event; or his authority, chancing upon no later official entry regarding Plautus's plays, may have inferred that he died about this time. It looks as if the death of several early poets was 'presumed' too rashly from the last appearance of their names in the lists of plays presented. *Cf.* discussion on Naevius, Leo, *Plautin. Forsch.*, p. 69.

biographers as if authentic portions of an author's personal experience.[1] Yet even though few of the traditional records are unimpeached, there is left a solid basis for amazement at the greatness of Plautus. It was a mighty achievement for this stranger from the Gallic frontier to master the spirit of the New Greek Comedy, and by adaptations therefrom to erect one of the immortal monuments of the Latin language and literature.[2] No amount of detail could lessen or explain the mystery of genius, to which the plays, rather than disputed items of biography, are the best testimony. One point, however, should be made clear. If Plautus acquired enough of a fortune to engage in trading, it could not have been as a mere stage-workman. When Gellius says this capital was made 'in operis artificum scaenicorum,' he must mean that Plautus was an actor, very likely in Atellan performances.[3] This modicum, then, of light is shed upon his plays. They were the work of a man who had a practical knowledge of stage requirements.

In the chronology of Plautus's life, we find his death in 184 B.C. vouched for by Cicero.[4] The year of composition of those plays which we can date generally falls within his last two decades. The contention which would place the *Menaechmi*[5] earlier than 215 B.C. being more than doubtful, the oldest surviving plays are probably the *Miles* (c. 206 B.C.)[6] and the *Cistellaria* of the period of the Hannibalian War.[7] Even so, one cannot restrict his literary work to some twenty years. According to Cicero, he had, before 197, produced many plays:[8] another passage in Cicero[9] imagines the possibility of his attacking the Scipios, who met their death in 212; and the inference from yet another passage[10] is that

[1] Leo, *op. cit.*, p. 73, sees in Gellius's phrase 'molae trusatiles' an echo from the *Saturio* or the *Addictus* or the third lost play whose name Gellius forgot. The passage in which it occurred gave rise to the myth that Plautus wrote plays 'in pistrino.' This is ingenious enough to deserve to be true. But it is beyond proof. Part of the suggestion might be confirmed in the improbable event of the recovery of the lost plays. Even then, would the negative be proved – that Plautus did *not* work at the mill?

[2] He must have found difficulty in securing literary education early in life. His is one of the many careers which are triumphs over obstacles. How much Greek did he learn formally from masters? How much did he learn for himself along the undefinable path of genius?

[3] Leo, *op. cit.*, pp. 84–85. This gives special significance to Horace's words about him, *Epist.*, II. i. 173:
'Quantus sit Dossennus edacibus in parasitis.'

[4] *Brut.*, xv. 60, 'Plautus P. Claudio, L. Porcio . . . consulibus mortuus est, Catone censore.'

[5] *Men.*, 412, 'nunc Hiero est.'

[6] *Mil. Glo.*, 211, 'os columnatum poetae . . . barbaro,' already explained as an allusion to Naevius. Cf. *supra*, p. 94.

[7] *Cistell.*, 202, 'ut uobis uicti Poeni poenas sufferant,' implying that the second Punic War was still unfinished.

[8] *Brut.*, xviii. 73, '. . . multas (fabulas) docuerant ante hos consules et Plautus et Naeuius.'

[9] Cic., fragm., *De Repub.*, IV. x, apud Augustin., *de Ciuit. Dei.*, II. ix, '. . . si Plautus noster uoluisset aut Naeuius P. et Cn. Scipioni . . . maledicere.'

[10] *De Sen.*, xiv. 50, 'Quam gaudebat *Bello* suo *Punico* Naeuius! quam *Truculento* Plautus! quam *Pseudolo*! . . .'

he was *senex*, that is, at least sixty years old, when he composed his *Pseudolus* of 191 B.C. Years of writing contemporary with the Scipios before 212, and years of vicissitude in theatre and in commerce before his literary career, make up a life which cannot have begun later than 250.

We possess, more or less complete, twenty plays by Plautus.[1] These twenty and the *Vidularia*, of which only fragments survive, may be reasonably identified with the twenty-one which Varro distinguished[2] as genuine by common consent. Seeing that about one hundred and thirty plays[3] claimed to be Plautine, critics at an early period drew up canons. The authors of half a dozen such lists are mentioned by Gellius, who says that, besides the twenty-one *quae Varrionanae uocantur*, Varro referred others to Plautus on the ground of style.[4] We know the names of over thirty in addition to the extant plays.

Plautus wrote not for readers but for the theatre. The long period during which the plays were handed down in acting-copies opened the way to mutilation and interpolation of the text.[5] During the first

[1] Texts: F. Ritschl, revised by G. Löwe, G. Götz, F. Schöll, completed 1894; J. L. Ussing, Copenh., 1875–87; Götz and Schöll (Teubner), 1893–96; F. Leo, 2 vols., 1895–96; W. M. Lindsay, 2 vols. (fragments included), 1903–06. Also, for textual criticism, Ritschl, *Prolegomena de rationibus . . . emendationis Plautinae*, sep. reissue, 1880; W. Studemund, *Apograph of Ambrosian Palimpsest* (discovered by Cardinal Mai, 1815), 1889; W. M. Lindsay, *Codex Turnebi*, 1898; Leo, *Plaut. Forsch. z. Kritik. u Gesch. d. Komödie*, ed. 2, 1912. Plautine emendation is one of the hardest fields to work in Latin. Beyond the equipment – indispensable for all emendation – of palaeographical training, wide reading, sound sense, and critical insight, it demands grasp of the early Latin vocabulary, grammar, syntax, pronunciation, prosody, and metre. The magnitude of the work done upon the text since Ritschl revolutionised Plautine criticism may be gauged by comparing a good pre-Ritschelian text, say that of Gronovius, with a sound recent one. For the history of Plautus's text in antiquity and for a recent theory on the relation of the Ambrosian palimpsest (which contains about a third in bulk of the extant plays) to the 'Palatine' and other MSS., see Leo, *op. cit.*, pp. 1–53. Leo assigns a comparatively late date – that of the archaistic revival of the second century A.D. – to the original edition of twenty-one plays, from which he considers the Ambrosian palimpsest of the fourth or fifth century and the proto-archetype of the other MSS. were copied. The hiatus common in Plautus was characteristic of the archaistic period, and so, according to Leo, appeared in this original edition.

[2] Gell., *N.A.*, III. iii. 3. 'A ceteris segregauit' does not necessarily imply that Varro issued a separate edition, though this is probable. On these *fabulae Varronianae* see Leo, *Plaut. Forsch.*, pp. 18 sqq.

[3] Gell., *N.A.*, III. iii. 10–11. Varro was reduced to the explanation that many 'Plautian' plays (*a Plautio*) were easily confused with 'Plautine' plays (*a Plauto*) – 'quoniam fabulae *Plauti* inscriptae forent.' It is harder to believe in an unknown Plautius than in the great popularity of Plautus which made it fashionable to shelter acting-editions indiscriminately under his name.

[4] Gell., *N.A.*, III. iii. 3, '. . . quasdam item alias probauit adductus filo atque facetia sermonis Plauto congruentia.' Among these Varro must logically have included the lost *Saturio* and *Addictus* (Gell., *N.A.*, III. iii. 14).

[5] Damage done to MSS. has also greatly interfered with the text. The end of the *Aulularia* is lost along with the first part of the *Bacchides*, which followed it; part of the *Stichus* is wanting; and the text in the *Casina* and *Truculentus* is particularly imperfect. The great stroke of luck was the finding of the Ambrosian MS., which opened the path to sagacious restoration in the plays for which it

revival of enthusiasm for Plautus, in the middle of the first century B.C., when interest in the small stock of Terence's highly refined comedies flagged, and actors were pointed back to the larger store of Plautus with his boisterous fun, many changes must have been made. Of these the furnishing of an alternative *dénouement* and the prefixing of some of the prologues are examples. It is thus we get two endings to the *Poenulus*, and thus we have manifestly post-Plautine prologues to the *Captiui*, *Casina*, *Menaechmi*, and *Poenulus*. The prologue,[1] being of the nature of a play-bill, put the audience in possession of facts germane to the plot. As it sometimes mentioned the original of the play, the prologue is of much value in literary history; and from its habit of familiar address to the audience, whether Plautine or post-Plautine, the prologue, like a Greek *parabasis*, throws light on social and theatrical conditions. There is no prologue to the *Bacchides*, *Epidicus*, *Mostellaria*, *Persa*, and *Stichus*. The *Pseudolus* has a late one of two lines. The prologues to the *Asinaria*, *Aulularia*, *Mercator*, *Rudens*, *Trinummus*, and *Truculentus* are probably authentic, or based on those actually composed by Plautus. The *Cistellaria* and *Miles Gloriosus* have virtually deferred prologues, pronounced after the opening scenes.

Acrostic summaries (*argumenta*), in iambic senarii, precede all the plays except the *Bacchides*, the opening of which is lost. These acrostics are believed to belong to the same period as the post-Plautine prologues. They may have been written by the Aurelius (Opilius) mentioned by Gellius[2] as one of several authors of Plautine *indices*. The non-acrostic additional summaries prefixed to five of the plays[3] are later, and show less knowledge of Plautine versification. They may be the work of Sulpicius Apollinaris of Carthage, the grammarian of the second century A.D., who wrote the arguments to Terence and to the books of the *Aeneid*.

Plautus is the great exponent of the Latin comedy based on Greek

---

was available. A typical testimony to its value is *Mil. Glor.*, 54, 'At peditastelli quia erant siui uiuerent' compared with the false Palatine reading, 'At peditas telu quia erant si uiuerent,' or with such vain imaginations as 'At pedites relliquiae,' etc. *Cf.* reading reported by Geppert, *Cas.* 846, 'quasi Luca bos' for 'quasi iocabo.' In addition, the text has gained by brilliantly inspired corrections like Robinson Ellis's 'ne[c] frit quidem,' *Most.* 595, for 'nec erit quidem'; Seyffert's and Bergk's 'ouis (oui),' *Pers.* 174, for 'quis'; Palmer's 'in ius rapiam exules dica' (*i.e.*, ἐξούλης δίκη), *Rud.* 859, for 'in ius rapiam | exsulem'; Palmer's equally attractive 'nitri,' *Truc.* 902, for 'matri'; and Bücheler's 'gramarum habeo dentes plenos,' *Curc.* 318, for Koch's 'lacrumarum,' itself adopted by Löwe, Götz, and Schöll as a vast improvement on 'os amarum' of the *codices*.

[1] It was usually pronounced by an actor specially attired (*ornatu prologi*). He might be a god appearing for the purpose, *e.g.*, the Lar familiaris in *Aulularia*, or Arcturus in *Rudens*. In one case the prologue is spoken by a god who is to take a prominent part in the play, viz., Mercurius in *Amphitruo*.

[2] *N.A.*, III. iii. 1.

[3] *Amph.*, *Aul.*, *Merc.*, *Mil.*, *Pseud.* (each of 15 lines, except that to *Amph.*, which has 10).

life—the *fabula palliata*,[1] whose models were the Athenian comic dramatists of the fourth and third century B.C., especially Diphilus, Demophilus, Philemon,[2] and Menander. The exact relation of Plautus to his sources is indeterminable for want of complete examples of the later or 'New' Greek Comedy of manners. But the main features of that drama are clearly distinguishable. They were drawn, many of the comedies, from contemporary life; inherited, others of them, from the sentimental tragedy of Euripides even more than from transitional plays of Aristophanes like the *Plutus*; and touched, others of them still, with a popular but semi-philosophic interest in character. The Greek fragments attest the thought and finished style of the New Comedy; but the Latin adaptations by Plautus and Terence, overlaid with Roman colour though the former is, give the fullest conception of its plots and general spirit. In contrast with the Old (or Aristophanic) Comedy, it was better constructed, was domestic or social instead of political, and refined instead of violent. Not original in its plots, the comedy of manners depended greatly for effect upon elegance of style. A well-bred, comfortable, worldly-wise spirit prevailed in its handling of incidents or types of character. Without being a slavish copier of actual humanity, Menander held up the mirror to it so as to evoke the admiring epigram ascribed to Aristophanes, the librarian of Alexandria, 'O Life, O Menander, which of you has imitated the other?'

So it is to Menander (342–291 B.C.) rather than to his rival Philemon —in spite of Philemon's dramatic victories over him and in spite of his deep influence on the plots of Plautus—that the mind turns as the outstanding figure of the New Comedy. His gift might be called a family one, for the comic poet Alexis was his uncle. Contemporary with Theophrastus and Epicurus, Menander reflects the psychological sketches of the one, and the other's detestation of unreason and his appreciation of the joy that is in life. The quest of serene pleasures among the luxurious possibilities of his native Athens and an indulgent interest in his fellow-beings combined to yield him materials for a *comédie humaine*. His reflection, 'Thou art a man,' sounds his intensely human note of acquiescence in the limitations of mortality. But it was more than a secret of wisdom held as a philosophic creed: it was a spur towards dramatising. There is nothing cloistered or merely speculative in his criticism:

> Ofttimes it seemeth not so wisely said—
> The counsel 'Know thyself'; it were, methinks,
> More advantageous to know other men.[3]

---

[1] The *pallium*, the typical dress worn in these plays, corresponded to the χλαμύς. The *fabula togata*, similarly named from the dress worn, was comedy dealing with Italian, especially provincial, life.

[2] For plays and characters of Philemon, see Apuleius, *Flor.*, Bk. iii. (*ad init.*).

[3]
> κατὰ πόλλ' ἄρ' ἐστιν οὐ καλῶς εἰρημένον
> τὸ γνῶθι σεαυτόν· χρησιμώτερον γὰρ ἦν
> τὸ γνῶθι τοὺς ἄλλους.

> Menander, fragm. of *Thrasyleon*.

Unluckily, we have not enough evidence either in the fragments of any one play, or in the remarks of ancient writers, to enable us to compare his dramatic power minutely with that of Plautus and Terence.[1] Comparatively seldom have lines survived from him which are the bases of theirs. Broadly, however, there can be no question that Menander was an artist vastly superior to his Roman followers. The loss of his dramas is, therefore, one of the deeply regrettable blanks in ancient literature. Yet even his fragments speak for themselves through their admirable refinement of style, their forcible sagacity, their acquaintance with life. His lines show better form than Plautus can attain. They are more original in thought, too. One can tell that the Sophists had lived and taught. The influence of Euripides also is visible. Euripides had fixed attention upon human problems; he had introduced into the drama the love-*motif* and other cunning devices to touch the heart. This legacy of warm human feeling Menander, among his fellows, inherited. Though there is in him a tacit acceptance of his social surroundings and a calm toleration for evil, which contrasts with the critical attitude of Euripides, and though Diphilus and Philemon are nearer the old Attic vivacity, still Menander is in countless ways full of a novel spirit of quiet daring.

For the most part a love story is dramatised in these pieces. Around the almost inevitable figure of the love-sick and impecunious youth, on whose crossed fortunes the action hangs, but who is usually less of a 'hero' than his slave, there are grouped many characters stereotyped[2] and more or less exaggerated from real life. The lover's mistress is generally a courtesan in the charge of an exorbitant keeper, but sometimes, a young woman of free birth, the tracing of whose parentage forms a

---

[1] The fragments of Menander are collected chiefly from Stobaeus, Athenaeus, and the commentaries of Donatus (grammarian, b. 333 A.D.) on Terence. For example, Donatus on the prologue to Terence's *Andria*, tells how the openings were managed both in Menander's *Andria* and in the *Perinthia*, the other of the two plays patched together by Terence. Donatus sometimes quotes the Greek. In 1898, the longest fragment till then recovered was deciphered from an Egyptian papyrus and first published, as belonging to the Γεωργός by J. Nicole of Geneva, and later in the same year by B. P. Grenfell and A. S. Hunt, after the discovery that its 87 lines formed a continuity. Many lines are badly mutilated; but enough remains to prove that the play had about a dozen characters representative of the New Comedy, including a youth who has wronged a girl, and on whom a distasteful marriage is being forced by his father. The plot in relation to fragments already known from the Γεωργός makes the subject of interesting conjectures by Grenfell and Hunt. (*Le Laboureur de Ménandre, fragments . . . déchiffrés traduits et commentés*, J. Nicole, 1898. Menander's Γεωργός, *A Revised Text of the Geneva Fragment*, Grenfell and Hunt, 1898.) In 1907 M. G. Lefebvre announced his find at Komishagon in Egypt of sixth-century papyri containing over 1,300 lines of Menander, from different parts of at least four different plays. From these and lesser papyri *plus* the old fragments we have about two-thirds of the 'Επιτρέποντες and two-fifths of the Περικειρομένη and smaller portions of other plays. But, better still, a recently discovered papyrus gives us a whole play, the Δύσκολος. See Suppl. Bibl. *re* p.121.

[2] One need not wonder at stereotyped characters and stereotyped plots in the New Comedy, when one realises the number of plays produced. Diphilus is credited with a good 100, Philemon with 97, Menander with 108.

sub-plot and leads with the mechanical aid of tokens (γνωρίσματα, *crepundia*) to the recognition (ἀναγνώρισις) at the close. Abandonment of infants, rearing of foundlings, kidnapping, piracy, and shipwreck give to the entanglement a certain spice of adventure, which, however, loses much of its savour after frequent employment. The fathers are mostly strict and stingy, the slaves mostly knavish, and preternaturally sharp in wilful fraud and imposition when their young masters stand in urgent need of money to advance their amours. Two of the stock humorous characters are the hungry, toadying, but occasionally useful parasite, and the boastful soldier of adventure — the former as old as the Sicilian plays of Epicharmus, the latter a dramatic echo of the wars which followed the break-up of the empire of Alexander the Great. Matrons, frequently shrewish, procurers, sycophants, and moneylenders assist to make up a representation of Athenian life in which the seamy is the prominent side.

However questionable the intrigues, there is also much moralising. Menander is a master of saws. Practised experience is deftly summed up as good advice in an iambic line, terse and restrained, handy for recollection and quotation. His works became model reading-books, partly for their style, partly for their sententiousness; and everyone remembers the apostle's citation of his:

Evil communications corrupt good manners.[1]

The greatness of the dramatist is realised in the familiar epigram of Julius Caesar, who paid Terence the compliment of calling him a 'Menander halved' (*O dimidiate Menander*). Caesar recognises Terence's pure and polished style — he is *puri sermonis amator* — what he misses in him is *uis comica*. This is the half of his genius in which he falls short of the Greek. And Plautus reads like the other half of Menander — he possesses the *uis comica*; but he lacks the finish of Menander and of Terence. Gellius is another witness to the superiority of the originals over Latin adaptation. This time it is Caecilius who is compared with Menander to the disadvantage of the Roman. When read independently, Gellius remarks, Roman plays from Menander, Posidippus, Apollodorus, Alexis, and others, appear to have charm and taste; but side by side with their models, they strike one as absolutely flat and mean.[2] This general remark Gellius supports by a consideration of passages from the *Necklace* (Πλόκιον) of Menander and from the *Plocium* of Caecilius.

The titles of Greek plays drawn on by Plautus are definitely known in some cases from the prologues, in other cases have been reasonably conjectured, and in other cases are unknown. Philemon's Ἔμπορος

---

[1] I *Corinth.* xv. 33. It is a fragment of Menander's brilliant *Thais*:
φθείρουσιν ἤθη χρήσθ᾽ ὁμιλίαι κακαί.

[2] 'Oppido quam iacere atque sordere incipiunt quae Latina sunt,' Gell., *N.A.*, II. xxiii. 3.

was the model for the *Mercator*, his *Φάσμα* for the *Mostellaria*, and his *Θησαυρός* for the *Trinummus*; Demophilus's *'Οναγός* for the *Asinaria*; and Diphilus's *Κληρούμενοι* for the *Casina*. The influence of Diphilus on Plautus was strong; it was certainly a play of his—its name may have been *Πήρα*[1] which was adapted as the *Rudens*; and possibly his *Αἱρησιτείχης*[2] contributed portions to the *Miles*. Menander was the source of the *Stichus* in a play called the *'Αδελφοί*, or perhaps *Φιλάδελφοι*[3]: his *Δὶς 'Εξαπατῶν*[4] was all but certainly the original of the *Bacchides*: his *Καρχηδόνιος*[5] rather less certainly of the *Poenulus*: another of his plays was possibly used for the *Cistellaria*. Of such originals Plautus was no servile translator, but a free manipulator. His range of character and plot, repetitions notwithstanding, is wide. Too wide to be his own invention, it is a range derived from several Greek poets, each of considerable individuality. But over the multiplicity he shed a unifying atmosphere of irrepressible animation and jocularity that was his own. The originality of Plautus was not in plot, but in treatment. The same genial independence in handling, though with varying artistic success attained, marks all his adaptations. The prevailing spontaneity of spirit and dialogue banishes any suggestion that it could come by way of translation or imitation: and so, however one estimates the proportion, the first-hand contribution of his own Italian genius must infinitely outweigh the second-hand material.

Impossible though it is to dogmatise where the Greek ends and the

---

[1] Schöll's conjecture, *Rh. Mus.*, xliii., p. 298. Diphilus's play may have had similar contents to the model used for the fragmentary *Vidularia* – Studemund, *Ueber zwei Parallel-Comoedien des Diphilus* (Verhandln. d. 36ten. Philologenversammlung, p. 33 ff., quoted in Introd. to *Rudens*, ed. E. A. Sonnenschein, 1891). The Greek original of the *Vidularia* was entitled *Σχεδία* (see *Prologus*, fragm.).

[2] Ritschl saw an allusion to this in 'urbicape' applied to the *Miles*, l. 1055. The action was 'contaminated' with the *'Αλαζών* of some Greek dramatist (ll. 86–87). Certainly some other plot is interwoven with the *'Αλαζών*, whether it was Diphilus's *Αἱρησιτείχης* or Menander's *Κόλαξ*, for the deceiving of the slave Sceledrus is dramatically independent of the deceiving of the captain. The implication of the character as borrowed from the Greek is exhaustively treated by O. Ribbeck, *Alazon: Ein Beitrag zur antiken Ethologie* (w. German trans. of *Mil. Glor.*), 1882.

[3] According to the *didascalia* preserved in the Ambrosian MS., 'Graeca Adelphoe Menandru.' This cannot be the same *'Αδελφοί* as was used by Terence for his *Adelphi*. Some, with Ritschl, take the reading to be *Φιλάδελφοι* to avoid believing in a second play by Menander entitled *'Αδελφοί*.

[4] Allusions to this title seem to be made by Plautus in 'me . . . ludos bis factum,' 1090, and 'bis detonsa,' 1128. Besides, the famous line from Menander's *Δὶς 'Εξαπατῶν*,

Ὃν οἱ θεοὶ φιλοῦσιν ἀποθνήσκει νέος

is translated in 816–7:

'Quem di diligunt
Adulescens moritur.'

[5] None of the surviving fragments of Menander's play can be said to resemble closely anything in Plautus's *Poenulus*. Leo discusses its 'contamination' with another Greek original, *Plaut. Forsch.*, pp. 170 *sqq*.

Roman begins in Plautus, the two elements can be frequently distinguished. Beyond his indebtedness for plot and metres, Plautus manifestly owed to Greece the general setting of his plays—scenes, personages, dress, money—and much of the general attitude towards life.[1] All his plays, the mythological *Amphitruo* included, are concerned with some phase of Greek society. When they leave their commonest scene, Athens,[2] it is only to migrate to other spheres of Greek civilisation— Aetolia, Ephesus, Cyrene. The playgoer of Plautus's time would be conscious of a foreign air in the wild revelry and dissolute excesses described or enacted: so to indulge was to 'play the Greek' (*pergraecari*). Equally un-Roman at first must have appeared the scant respect shown for old age and the familiarity and subtlety of slaves. The Romans, in whom the traditions of morality remained strong after the practice had become weak, felt their curiosity stirred by representations of the questionable and reprehensible in Athenian society. So long as faults and foibles, knavery and intrigue, were staged as Greek, and not Roman, they could be held to amuse rather than shock. A certain Pharisaism might have flattered itself that it was comfortable and edifying to behold the effrontery and deceit of which the undisciplined Hellene could be guilty. Many of the reflections and counsels are redolent of the culture and social criticism of Athens. Megaronides' suggested scheme in the *Aulularia* for an improved marriage-system and the concluding precept of the *Mercator* that men of sixty should retire from amours are on Greek lines. Palaestra's exclamations against the gods in the *Rudens* have the Greek ring. The philosophising slave —and the slave is markedly given to proverbial wisdom—has more of Euripides in him than of any other literary ancestor. There are also echoes of the tragic manner, heightening the tone of diction, as in Bromia's awe-struck narration[3] of the epiphany of Jupiter in the hour of Alcmena's travail, or in Pardalisca's pretended terror over the male 'bride's' doings in the *Casina*.[4] In similar style, Pseudolus breaks into mock-heroics[5] which call forth the comment, 'How the hang-dog rants like a tragedian!' (*ut paratragoedat carnufex!*).

On the other hand, a strong Roman flavour is added to everything. The very metres seem transformed in the borrowing; so Latin do they become with alliterations and assonances strange to the Greek. A force absolutely unborrowed appears in the homely native idiom. Plots are laid under contribution only to be freely combined and modified. The

---

[1] See Leo, *op. cit.*, pp. 87–187 (chap. on *Plautus u. seine Originale*). His retention of Greek expressions in their original form (*e.g.*, εὖγε, πάλιν, παῦσαι) or Latinised (*e.g.*, *parasitus*, *gynaeceum*), or turned into grammatical hybrids (*e.g.*, *euscheme* for εὐσχημόνως or εὐσχήμως) is a minor point.

[2] Athens is the scene in twelve of the twenty extant plays.

[3] *Amph.*, 1053 *sqq.*, 'Spes atque opes uitae meae iacent sepultae in pectore.'

[4] *Cas.*, 621 *sqq.*, 'Nulla sum, nulla sum, tota, tota occidi,' etc.

[5] *Pseud.*, 703 *sqq.*, 'Io, te, te, turanne, te, te, ego,' etc.

dominant fact is that Plautus was a man of the people with a real vocation towards comedy. He had, therefore, natural endowments and personal experiences separated *toto caelo* from anything in his originals. He is essentially Italian in keen observation, merry inventiveness, and quick rejoinders. Possessing a share of the native turn for farce, he is not afraid to outstep the limits of a play of the New Comedy. He does not hesitate to insert an incident of Roman life, provided it is laughable enough. Trade, and still more misfortune, had acquainted him with his fellows; and his own contact with humble and middle-class life stood him in good stead. The Italy of his day, far more than Greek reading, taught him how to put flesh and blood upon the boards. So his plays, like Shakespeare's, bristle with lively anachronisms. There is a Roman severity in the punishment of *lora* and *crux* with which slaves are constantly threatened, and a Roman coarseness in the emphasis laid on the pleasures of eating and drinking. Occasionally efforts are made to square the irrepressible Roman allusion with its Greek surroundings. When the parasite in the *Captiui*, not content with swearing by Greek deities to assure Hegio that his son has returned safe, proceeds, 'full of strange oaths,' to Grecize Praeneste, Signia, Frusino,[1] he is asked why he swears by 'barbarian towns.' When Tranio in the *Mostellaria*, with droll impudence, is conducting his old master over the house alleged to be the young scapegrace's latest purchase, he praises the artistic workmanship of the doorposts as beyond the reach of a Roman — 'none of your porridge-eating barbarian craftsmen ever made this.'[2] But for the the most part, the anachronisms are frankly thrown in without fear or apology. The plays, despite Greek setting and characters[3] mostly called by Greek names, teem with Roman customs and institutions. The parasite has his *prouincia* in marketing;[4] the *uilicus* has his *praefectura* in the country;[5] the *comitia* will be held to decide matters of import; and Greek gentlemen fume and fret when detained by the inroads upon their time made by the claims of *clientela*.[6] The most notable plunge into a Roman environment is made in the *Curculio*.[7] The scene is in Epidaurus. The choragus, in an interlude, declares his difficulty in classing Curculio satisfactorily — he is such a quick-witted knave — and so he indicates to the audience in what parts of Rome different types of rascality may be met with, and goes on tour to the *Comitium*, the shrine of *Cloacina*, the *basilica*, the *forum piscarium*, and so forth. After this, it need not surprise us that the Carthaginian Hanno turns expressly to speaking Latin in the Greek city of Calydon,[8] or that the *Lar familiaris* presides over an Athenian home.[9] The residents of distant cities fre-

---

[1] *Capt.*, 882 *sqq.*, 'ναὶ τὰν Πραινέστην . . . ναὶ τὰν Σιγνέαν . . . Quid tu per barbaricas urbis iuras?'
[2] *Most.*, 828, 'Non enim haec pultiphagus opifex opera fecit barbarus'
[3] The titles of Plautus's plays, on the other hand, are chiefly Latin.
[4] *Capt.*, 474.   [5] *Cas.*, 99.   [6] *Cas.*, 566–7; *Men.*, 571 *sqq.*
[7] *Cur.*, 470 *sqq.*   [8] *Poen.*, 1029.   [9] *Aul.*, opening scene.

quent the streets and gates of Rome; they talk as if the local administration were in the hands of praetors, quaestors, aediles, and tresviri, as if the Roman law of debt, Roman processes of emancipation, Roman methods of summoning witnesses, Roman forms of contract held good among them, and as if they understood Roman military strategy, and worshipped Roman divinities like Jupiter Capitolinus and Laverna or the more typically abstract Salus and Opportunitas. The Praenestine is sneered at for his boastfulness, as if he were the ancient Tartarin of Tarascon, for his provincialism in the expression *tammodo* and in using *conia* for *ciconia*.[1] We pass, in fine, through a delightful topsy-turvydom which it seems ungrateful to analyse.[2] Its effect is parallel in its rich confusion to certain medieval paintings of Scripture history.

Plautus admits not only the general atmosphere of Rome, but also references to contemporary history. The expansion of Roman power affects him. The reduction of the Boii, the condign punishment visited upon Campanian states during the second Punic War, the importation of Syrian slaves following the defeat of Antiochus, sundry enactments against gaming and luxury, are made the subject of topical allusions which 'the house' would follow as readily as the Athenian theatre followed the more frequent excursions of Aristophanes into burning questions. The struggle with Carthage is partly accountable for the *Poenulus* and for its Semitic passages. Sometimes Plautus appears to have prevision of the ruling destinies of his country, when he pauses to offer advice on politics, law, and war.[3] And a grim irony of situation must have struck him when he introduced Hellenic characters in an attitude of contempt towards those 'pulse-eating barbarians' who were in his own times victorious over Macedon and on the eve of the annexation of Greece.

His social and historical environment, then, acted as a check upon Plautus's growth into a consistent artist. He would not be fettered by his models. This defiant carelessness is one phase of his originality. It prevents his making an artistic unity out of a couple of plots when he seeks to interweave them. He patches his fable together loosely in his passion for the incidental and his indifference to complete harmony. So he fails to triumph over the difficulties of *contaminatio*, and Horace was justified in his description:

Securus cadat an recto stet fabula talo.[4]

[1] *Bacch.*, frag. 12; *Trin.*, 609; *Truc.*, 691.
[2] For other Roman allusions, see W. Y. Sellar, *Roman Poets of the Rep.*, ed. 3, 1889, p. 174, and the list in Middleton and Mills, *Student's Companion to Latin Authors*, pp. 20–22.
[3] *Cistell.*, 199–202:

    'Seruate uostros socios, ueteres et nouos,
    Augete auxilia uostris iustis legibus,
    Perdite perduellis, parite laudem et lauream,
    Ut uobis uicti Poeni poenas sufferant.'

[4] *Epist.*, II. i. 176. Leo goes so far as to say, 'Alles was in Plautus' Komö-

Plautus relies upon carrying his piece through with the help of ludicrous scenes imperfectly dovetailed, and on the strength of his excellent dialogue.[1] His successes are the successes of the careless artist. Sometimes by his sovereign heedlessness and his unconscious wealth of genius, he captures an effect beyond the reach of pains. The explanation of this Plautine boldness lies in his relation to his times. He had the ability to respond exactly to a demand. The task before him was to interest in scenes of Greek life a Roman audience of limited refinement. To them, bent on amusement at a dramatic festival, it was not by unity of plot, *finesse* of conception, or polish of language, that a playwright could appeal. Intrigue and impostures rendered absolutely patent to the spectators; gross incidents of eating, drinking, and wenching; dialogue piquant with retorts, scolding matches, puns, proverbs, coined words and illustrations from manifold walks in life; rapid changes of metre and music, with gesticulation and dancing, made up a rich and varied compound attractive to both ear and eye. The prologues bring his audience before us — an audience which must be told to keep quiet during the performance, must be bantered into good humour, and must be pointedly instructed in the outlines of the plot. Given such an audience, and given Plautus's need to make a livelihood, one understands why he did not write much of the most elevated or the most elevating poetry, and why he did not aim at artistic unities. Ennius sought to satisfy the national pride in past achievements; Plautus, the national rebound towards relaxation. His aim was the comic effect of the moment. He did not, therefore, dissipate his energy upon epic or tragedy. He knew his *forte*. The impression he produces is not versatility, but, within his limits, amazing exuberance.

However much difference there might be about the wholly unnecessary determination of an exact order of merit among the plays, no two lists would differ essentially concerning the best ten. These are the *Amphitruo, Aulularia, Bacchides, Captiui, Menaechmi, Mostellaria, Miles Gloriosus, Pseudolus, Rudens, Trinummus*. These surely surpass the author's own favourite,[2] the *Epidicus*, the complexity of which strangles interest. Whether because of involved 'contamination' by the poet, or excessive condensation by actors, it is one of the plays which make the least favourable and least permanent impress.

In one sense, the *Amphitruo* stands alone. It is not strictly a *fabula palliata*; it is not a Rhinthonic farce;[3] it has burlesque elements, but it

---

dien der dramatischen Schöpferkraft entsprungen ist, ist nicht sein eigen; die Schritte, die er als Dramatiker versuchte waren Fehlschritte' (*op. cit.*, p. 186).

[1] 'Plautus in sermonibus poscit palmam' was Varro's verdict. *Men. Sat.* 399 (Bücheler).

[2] If one may so interpret *Bacch.* 214-15.

[3] No *Rhinthonica* has survived to show how Roman writers adapted the farcical travesties of tragic themes (ἱλαροτραγῳδίαι) composed by Rhinthon of Tarentum.

is not unqualified burlesque. It is best designated by Plautus's own term, *tragicomoedia*.[1] It contains, alongside of an unseemly intrigue and some screaming farce, features which are among the most serious and touching in Plautus. Jupiter, masquerading as the sham Amphitruo, is an unclean trickster. Mercury, masquerading as the slave Sosia, is a practical joker, who befools and thrashes the real Sosia, and gets his human counterpart into a scrape by pretending to be in liquor and by insulting the real Amphitruo with a douche of water from his own house-top. There is unalloyed fun in Sosia's bewilderment on finding another Sosia as like him 'as milk is like milk.' One does not know whether to marvel more at Roman toleration for such representation of the gods, or at the author's introduction in such surroundings of his sweetest and purest woman. Alcmena's character is apparent in her unaffected grief over parting[2] from her husband, her love of virtue, and conscious freedom from wilful guilt. Her spotless honesty makes the supreme god a charlatan. Irony reaches its height when she swears *per supremi regis regnum*. The character is carefully developed—her vexation at the suggestion of unchastity giving way to the confidence of innocence (*quae non deliquit decet audacem esse*), and her proclamation of the ideal of wifehood:

> What the world doth deem a dowry is not woman's real dower:
> That is pure and modest honour, victor over passion's power,
> Fear of god and love of parent, concord with a kinsman's mood,
> Meekness to her husband, bounty in the ministry of good.[3]

She will leave her home, unless her name is cleared; if her husband will assign her no slave, then, like Godiva, she will go forth waited on by chastity (*comitem mihi Pudicitiam duxero*). This one character is serious. The rest of the play, with its tricks, lies, abuse, even its *dénouement* in thunderbolts and the marvellous twins, is burlesque. The blend then justifies the classification as *tragicomoedia*.

Of the other nine strongest plays the *Aulularia*, *Captiui*, and *Trinummus* succeed owing to their psychologic interest, the *Rudens* is unique in its romantic setting, the *Menaechmi* is a most laughable comedy of errors, and the others depend on clever trickery. The *Aulularia*, or *The Play of the Hidden Pot of Gold*, contains in Euclio one of the renowned misers of literature. The two other great portraits of a miser are French; for neither Ben Jonson's Volpone nor Shakespeare's Shylock loved gold after the typical manner of *L'Avare*. Molière's Harpagon and Balzac's Grandet insistently cross the mind as one reads. The play is lively, from the prologue spoken by the Lar of the miser's ancestral home up

---

[1] *Amph.* 59, 63.   [2] *Amph.*, 635 *sqq.*
[3] *Amph.*, 839:
'Non ego illam mi dotem duco esse quae dos dicitur,
Sed pudicitiam et pudorem et sedatum cupidinem,
Deum metum, parentum amorem, et cognatum concordiam.
Tibi morigera atque ut munifica sim bonis, prosim probis.'

F

to the point where the text abruptly ends. Underneath the exaggeration expected in comedy lies deep psychological truth. Euclio, like the reprobate father in the *Asinaria*, is a specimen of inherited tendencies. His grandfather had amassed a treasure, and had been too suspicious of his own son—Euclio's father—to trust him with the secret. Buried for a generation, it had now been revealed to Euclio, inasmuch as the Lar destined it to be the daughter's marriage-portion. If there is nothing in the *Aulularia* so terrible as the gleam in the dying Grandet's eyes lighting up for the last time at the sight of the silver crucifix, still Euclio is unforgettable. A convincing realism pervades his paroxysms of nervous fury as he bundles his old woman-servant out of the house with threats of scourging, blinding, and the cross; his mortal dread of spies while he assures himself that the precious pot (*aula*) is safe; his rigid instructions to admit no one during his absence; his misreading of friends' politeness; his unallayable distrust of the wealthy Megadorus's proposal for his daughter's hand; his shiver at the sound of the spade digging in the next garden; and his vengeance upon the barndoor rooster scraping the ground too near the crock of gold. Plautus suggests, without dwelling on, the pitiful side. It is comedy, and so we have the caricature of Euclio's stinginess according to the slaves who bring provisions for the wedding luncheon:

> He ties a bag in front at night to avoid losing breath; he grudges to part with his washing-water; he wouldn't give you hunger, if you asked for it; he treasures the parings of his nails![1]

Not the funniest, but the noblest, of Plautus's works is the *Captiui*, or *The Prisoners of War*. Lessing thought it the best play ever staged. Elsewhere in Plautus there is a surfeit of smart deceptions by which extravagance and profligacy are cloaked. But in the *Captiui* the lie is what Plato might call 'a noble remedy' for the desperate situation in which the prisoners find themselves by no fault of their own. The pretence that man is master, and master man, serves as an example of fidelity and self-sacrifice all the more beautiful in that with dramatic irony it produces the hot-headed and merciless punishment by Hegio of his unrecognised son, the slave Tyndarus. Both prologue and epilogue have given us an appreciation of at least the moral value of the *Captiui* by contrasting it with other plays:

> It is not hackneyed or just like the rest;
> It has no filthy lines one must not quote,
> No perjured pander, and no wicked wench,
> Nor captain full of empty vapourings.[2]

---

[1] *Aul.*, 300 *sqq.*
[2] *Capt.*, 55 *sqq.*:
> 'Non pertractate factast neque item ut ceterae,
> Neque spurcidici insunt uersus inmemorabiles:
> Hic neque periurus lenost nec meretrix mala
> Neque miles gloriosus.'

The play is technically *stataria*, not *motoria* or bustling like the *Menaechmi*. The interest is sentimental and centres in the affection between master and slave, and in Hegio, driven into unrelenting cruelty by the way in which the world has used him and his sons. 'No one pities me,' he says bitterly, to excuse his iron resolution.[1]

The *Trinummus*, which might be rendered *Three Didrachms' Worth of a Sharper*, is also dependent on character rather than incident. It possesses fine traits. There is (at the cost of being misrepresented by the gossips) the unswerving loyalty of old Callicles to the trust reposed in him by the absent Charmides—the trust of caring for his son, daughter, and treasure. And if Lysiteles is—for Plautus—oppressively virtuous, there is his genuine friendship with his intemperate young comrade Lesbonicus, whom he pities, helps in straits, defends against censure, and pleads for when his disappointed father returns from abroad. Even Lesbonicus has qualms of conscience and gleams of nobility; he is ashamed to betroth his sister undowered and to trespass on the handsome generosity of his friend—he will rather part with his last field. The sterling fidelity of the slave Stasimus to the old house is a winning feature, which, though it leads him to misjudge Callicles, yet contrasts pleasingly with the rascality of most Plautine servants. It is altogether a play with much human feeling.

In the *Rudens*, or *The Rope*, we breathe an atmosphere of romance and poetry like that of *The Tempest* or *The Winter's Tale*. Considerable beauty of words, lightness of treatment, and the wild scenery, serve to make the piece fascinating. The impression is rather that of some idyll of a rock-bound coast than of a perfectly constructed drama; certainly the later portion drags. It was a brilliant conception which gave the pronouncement of the prologue to the star Arcturus (*splendens stella candida*), the author of the avenging storm sent upon the fugitive slave-dealer. The shipwreck in the angry sea,[2] the dialogue between eye-witnesses to the struggles of survivors in gaining land, the befriending of the two girls by the priestess of Venus, the teeth-chattering[3] of the

Cf. 1029 sqq.:
> 'Spectatores, ad pudicos mores facta haec fabulaat . . .
> Huius modi paucas poetae reperiunt comoedias,
> Ubi boni meliores fiant.'

[1] *Capt.*, 765:
> 'Neminis
> Miserere certum est, quia mei miseret neminem.'

[2] *Rud.*, 167 sqq.:
> 'Non uidisse undas me maiores censeo,' etc.

[3] *Rud.*, 533 sqq.:
> If I only had luck to be a du-duck,
> So that all the wa-water would leave my back dry!
> 'Utinam fortuna nunc anetina ut-uterer,
> Ut, quom exissem ex aqu-aqu-aqua, ar-arerem tamen.'

Cf. 536:
> 'Pol clare crepito dentibus.'

half-drowned Labrax, his attempt to get the girls into his clutches again, the saving from the sea of the chest holding the proofs of Palaestra's birthright, the squabble between fisherman and slave over the rope (*rudens*) of the fishing-net, make a succession of vivid incidents culminating in the restoration of Palaestra to lover and to father.

The *Menaechmi*, or *The Indistinguishable Brothers*, is a triumph of fun beyond challenge. It has uproariously funny situations and remarkably skilful dialogue. Mistaken identity well managed is an unerring provocative of laughter; and Plautus with his long-separated twins, 'as like as water to water or milk to milk,'[1] holds his own with Shakespeare's *Comedy of Errors* all the better because he does not ask us to believe in two pair of 'doubles.'

The *Bacchides*, *Miles Gloriosus*, *Mostellaria* and *Pseudolus* are, with considerable variety of circumstances, alike in their dependence upon lies brazen in audacity, if golden in cleverness. They display the slave in his normal position as monarch of the Plautine stage. He is an artist (*poeta*) in chicanery. When his cozening is perfected he rejoices as a victor at a siege.[2] In a scene of broad farce, when the ball is at his feet, he will make his young master kneel to him or even carry him on his back! The *Bacchides*, which might be entitled *The Gay Sisters of Athens and Samos* or *Two Tricks in a Day*, though at times unsavoury, is effective in intrigue. As a foil to the slave Chrysalus, the resourceful abettor of the young roysterer's flirtation, we find the *paedagogus* Lydus distressed over the moral jeopardy of his charge. A *laudator temporis acti*, Lydus bemoans with no little Roman feeling the decay of the pristine simpler education; but he is made to betray his insufficient power of reading character. The youth whom he holds up as a paragon has been engaged in the risky occupation of tracing the winsome Bacchis of Samos for his absent friend. The result of this work as private detective is his falling under the spell of her sister, Bacchis of Athens. This brings about a quarrel with his friend, who suspects false play, until it is discovered that there are two girls of the same name. The real centre of interest, however, is Chrysalus, and his means of raising money. Hopelessly discredited to all appearance as the fabricator of an elaborate tissue of falsehoods, he restores the fortunes of his admiring young master by a trick which is one of the most ingenious and impudent in the whole of Plautus.[3] In a letter written by the young scapegrace, but dictated by Chrysalus himself, he orders his own arrest by the old father. He then forces the old man's attention by representing the youth to be in imminent danger from a fire-eating officer, and so secures the needed 200 minae. Scoring point after point, he regards

---

[1] *Men.*, 1089: *cf.* Sosia's simile in *Amphitruo*, 601.
[2] The triumph of Chrysalus 'over Troy' is a literary allusion. Tranio in *Most.* settles his metaphorical plan of campaign like an *imperator*, and the details come from experiences of the Hannibalian War.
[3] *Bacch.*, 763 *sqq.*

himself as a second captor of Troy. The appearance of the two hoary-headed lechers as rivals to their sons forms a repulsive close.

The *Miles Gloriosus*, or *The Boastful Recruiting Officer*, dramatises the befooling of a vain captain of the type of Bobadil. He poses as man-killer and lady-killer. The comedy would gain by condensation. At times its iterations become irritatingly wearisome. A sharp *meretrix* like Acroteleutium ('Mistress Fag-end') does not need elaborate schooling in trickery so fussily imparted to her with annoying reminders. The slave's farewells to the boastful captain are overdone—at least they tire one in the reading, though the fun in acting might carry them off. One feels, too, that the captain's vanity and folly are overdrawn.

The plot of the *Mostellaria*, or *The Play of the Haunted House*, is not one of Plautus's complex ones. It consists of a series of ready lies forged by Tranio, who must at all costs keep his old master, on his sudden return, from entering the house where his son is entertaining a party of revellers. Running the most daring risks, and backing invention with invention, Tranio is the mainspring of the 'fable.' His insolent repartees, from safe sanctuary, after all is discovered, are irresistibly amusing.

Of the *Pseudolus*, or *The Slave that was Master of Cunning*, we read in Cicero that it was, with the *Truculentus*, a joy to its author in old age.[1] Pseudolus's outwitting of the slave-dealer Ballio, a loathsome and blustering Roman Legree, means the triumph of a lesser over a greater vice. His song of delight, accompanied with music and gesture, is an instance of the Italian popular element in Plautine comedy, and his drunken dance to celebrate his knavery has in it something Fescennine.

The inferior dramas play variations on the same theme of *fourberies*. The exception is the *Stichus*, a slight piece on *The Happy Return of Master and Man*, which contains no trickery, but is an interesting social document with its opening spectacle of two 'grass-widows' awaiting with resolute fidelity the long-delayed return of their husbands. The play becomes more *bourgeois* in type as it proceeds through the comicalities of 'Master Laughable' (*Gelasimus*), the parasite, and reaches the orgy in which the slaves celebrate their home-coming. For the remaining plays I am content to suggest sub-titles. They are the *Asinaria* (or *How the Sham Steward Got Paid for the Asses*), *Casina* (or *The Male-Bride Drawn by Lot*), *Cistellaria* (*The Play of the Casket* or *How Selenium Found her Parents*), *Curculio* (or *Weevil the Parasite and the Stolen Seal*), *Mercator* (or *A Girl and her Purchasers*), *Persa* (or *The Counterfeit Persian*), *Poenulus* (or *The Little Carthaginian*), and *Truculentus* (or *The Taming of the Churl*).

In reviewing the dramatic qualities of Plautus, it is dangerously easy to overstate his limited psychology and monotony of plot. Admit-

[1] Cic. *De Sen.* 50.

tedly, the smart lies pall and the recurrent personages almost become bores. But it is with Plautine comedy as in a strange country: the faces at first seem much the same, and one marks the differences in time. His brightness of language and haphazard mirth of incident tend to obscure the power he can exhibit in character-drawing: the caricatures blur the good portraits. Those ·who read Plautus oftenest will find least sameness in him. His gallery is extensive. Among the women of the plays, the range is restricted by the social conditions represented. Attachment to a free maiden in the bosom of her family could not run a romantic course as in modern society; there were the bars of semi-oriental seclusion and parental arrangement of marriages. Festive enjoyment was sought elsewhere than at home—in the company of ladies of easy virtue. But even among those engaged in or intended for the calling of the *meretrix* there is a diversity often overlooked. A craving after showy toilette and cosmetics, a want of heart and a lust for money are not uniform features. There is a wide difference between the affectionate courtesan in the *Mostellaria* and Acroteleutium in the *Miles*, who is too knowing to be loving; while the *Truculentus* presents in Phronesium the most repulsive type of all. A separate group is that of girls kidnapped in infancy, and rescued from shame by the timely discovery of their free birth.[1] Of other women, the matrons in the *Asinaria, Casina, Mercator,* and *Menaechmi* are made suspicious shrews—consistently with the mockery of marriage traditional in the New Comedy; and it does not appear whether hen-pecking is the cause or the effect of their husbands' undoubted lapses from virtue. But Plautus by no means confines himself to the scold. The widowed sister of the *Aulularia* holds strong views on the necessary subjection of woman, and is capable of advising her brother sensibly on the momentous concern of matrimony. The noble character of Alcmena has been already discussed, and the *deux jeunes mariées* of the *Stichus* very beautifully reconcile filial obedience with loyalty to their husbands—'Do your duty without repining, even if your absent husband forget his.'[2] The miser's daughter in the *Aulularia* takes no share in the action; but the daughter of the parasite in the *Persa* is a girl of spirit, who loathes the part her father makes her play of a pretended captive, and answers the test-questions with at least a minimum of falsehood. The strongest traits in the women may be set to the account of Plautus's observation of Roman life.

Among men there is still more variety. Round the frequent central character of the consummate trickster revolves a crowd of figures, some natural, some grotesque, and of different shades of morality. There are elderly gentlemen, like Philto in the *Trinummus*, of strict principles and kindly heart; like Callicles, the incarnation of friendship, in the same

---

[1] *E.g.*, Palaestra in *Rudens*, Planesium in *Curculio*, Selenium in *Cistellaria* and the two sisters in *Poenulus*.
[2] *Stichus*, 34–46.

play; like Hegio, a good disposition soured, in the *Captiui*; and there
are old libertines, like those who deserve their exposure in the *Asinaria*
Bacchides, *Casina*, and *Mercator*. There is the genial old bachelor
excellently represented by Periplecomenus in the *Miles*. There are
exemplary young men, like the two husbands in the *Stichus*, and Lysiteles in the *Trinummus*, who goes through his own 'Choice of Hercules,'
and would fain keep his friend straight. This friend, Lesbonicus, is the
type of the reckless spendthrift with some of the lovable frankness of a
Charles Surface. Philolaches in the *Mostellaria* is a fair example of the
roysterer who upon occasion reflects. But the enamoured youth is
outshone by the precursors of the French Scapin. Chrysalus in the
Bacchides, Tranio in the *Mostellaria*, Palaestrio in the *Miles*, Pseudolus
and Epidicus in the plays which bear their name, scheme and lie with
complete *sang-froid* in full vision of the punishment certain to attend
discovery. The Saturnalian liberties taken by the gleeful slaves of the
Asinaria and of the *Stichus* constitute farce, cheap and broad. Sosia of
the *Amphitruo* is a poltroon meant to be jeered at. But not all slaves are
faithless in Plautus, any more than they were in real life. Tyndarus in
the *Captiui*, Messenio in the *Menaechmi*, Grumio in the *Mostellaria*,
Sceledrus in the *Miles*, Stasimus in the *Trinummus*, are trusty servants.
Even the parasites vary. The most active are Curculio, who can further
his patron's amour by robbing his rival of a seal wherewith to falsify a
letter, and Saturio in the *Persa*, who obligingly conducts a sham sale of
his daughter. Frequently the parasite does little beyond enlivening
matters and bringing news—and he knows good news involves a feast.
In the *Menaechmi* the parasite contributes to the merry confusion by
informing against the one brother when piqued by the conduct of his
double. Of several vainglorious officers the one most elaborated is the
Miles, an absurd combination of peacock pride and elephantine heaviness. Of the slave-dealers the most impressive is the brutal Ballio. Of
minor characters no one remains longer in the memory than the doctor
of the *Menaechmi*, whose professional examination of his patient, unjustly suspected of insanity, is excellently rendered.

Love is the mainspring of much of the plotting in Roman comedy.
Like the character of the young people of both sexes, it varies. What
romantic love exists is linked with irregular attachments, though many
of these are on the most matter-of-fact mercenary principles. The unromantic attitude to marriage appears from Lysiteles' farewell to love[1]
—he is henceforth to be a business man and wed his friend's sister!
This model youth delivers a homily to his friend on the dangerous
artillery of love[2] and the madness of putting up at Cupid's inn. Quite

---

[1] *Trin.*, 223–275, *e.g.*, 'Apage te, Amor, tuas res tibi habeto.'
[2] Literally, Plautus likens love to the ball hurled from the engine (*ballista*
in Plautine Latin is the thing thrown) – 'Plautus gebraucht sowohl *ballista* wie
catapulta nur zu Bezeichnung der Geschosse.' Langen, *Beiträge*, p.275). *Trin.*,
668 *sqq.*:

consistently, the friend, little improved by many homilies, is at the close sentenced for his escapades to be married! Wedlock is his punishment—and 'quite enough,' says his father, 'though I *was* angry with you!' The strict Callicles takes a sterner view: 'If for his sins he had to marry a hundred wives it would be too slight a penalty!'[1] In sharp contrast are such lovers as Charinus, broken-hearted over the prospect of losing his sweetheart,[2] and Phaedromus, ecstatic over the meeting and embraces of the enamoured:

> 'Welcome kings to keep their kingdoms, welcome rich men to their pelf,
> Let each man keep fame and glory, hard-fought victories to himself;
> So they grudge me not my darling, let each man keep what's his own.'[3]

The sweethearts of the *Cistellaria* are the pair most romantically in love. With a revulsion against coquetry,[4] Selenium rises above her training and her associates to a constant affection for Alcesimarchus. She is sad and pale, with a heartache (*cordolium*) which she only half understands. *Eho an amare occipere amarum est, opsecro?* she asks—to be told by her more sophisticated friend:

> *Namque ecastor Amor et melle et felle est fecundissimus.*[5]

Her passion is returned, and on the authority of the god Auxilium requited love is declared to be the sweetest.[6] Where *she* is love-sick, the youth is distracted. His state of mind is manifest in the *canticum* where he exclaims against Love as the primeval torturer. His woes on Love's wheel and amid the angry waves of Love are not to be taken too seriously; but they have a wonderfully modern ring:

> Sure 'twas Love first began, in the annals of man, the torturer's art to discover,
> I can tell from my load without stirring abroad—for I am a languishing lover.
>
> > Not the throes of all mankind
> > Equal my distracted mind.

> 'Ita est Amor ballista ut iacitur: nihil sic celere est neque uolat:
> Atque is mores hominum moros et morosos ecficit. . . .
> Insanum [et] malumst in hospitium deuorti ad Cupidinem.'

[1] *Trin.*, 1183–1186; *cf.* the attitude of the two highly respectable old gentlemen to their wives in *Trin.*, 51 *sqq.* They regret to have to say their wives are in good health!

[2] *Merc.*, 851 *sqq.*: 'I will follow the Quest of my Lady to the ends of the earth. River, mountain, ocean shall be no bar: I will fear no gale or wintry weather – endure toil, sunheat, and thirst – rest neither day nor night till I track my Lady-love – or Death.'

[3] *Curc.*, 178 *sqq.*:

> 'Sibi sua habeant regna reges, sibi diuitias diuites,
> Sibi honores, sibi uirtutes, sibi pugnas, sibi proelia;
> Dum mi apstineant inuidere, sibi quisque habeant quod suomst.'

[4] *Cist.*, 83.   [5] *Cist.*, 69.   [6] *Cist.*, 193.

> I strain and I toss
> On a passionate cross:
> Love's goad makes me reel,
> I whirl on Love's wheel,
> In a swoon of despair
> Hurried here, hurried there —
> Torn asunder, I am blind
> With a cloud upon my mind.
>
> Where I am, I am not;
> I am not where I thought;
> Fancies rush to and fro;
> I say yes and say no.
> Mocking Love's hue and cry
> Presses eagerly nigh
> To snatch and to catch
> Or in wiles to outmatch —
> Love with offers seeming kind
> Cheats the wearied lover's mind.
>
> Love disowns his command,
> And commands what he bann'd.
> I am tost on Love's sea:
> It makes shipwreck of me.
> My catastrophe to crown
> Needs but that my barque go down![1]

The fun of Plautus is multitudinous — broadest farce, rollicking jest, extravagant caricature, witty retort, dry humour, or play upon words. The laughter is occasioned, it may be, by situation, as when the true and the false Sosia meet, and it may be by character, as when the braggart Anthemonides relates his Munchausen-like exploit of slaughtering the 'volatic men,'[2] or as when a parasite mourns over the boycotting of his best *bons mots*[3] or chuckles over a perfectly Rabelaisian list of Gargantuan junketings suited to an insatiable appetite.[4] Like the slaves' rueful remembrances or expectations of stripes, and their flouting and jeering, the jokes of the parasites can be overdone; but perhaps no parasite succeeds in being funnier than Gelasimus when, finding his occupation gone, he holds an imaginary auction of himself:[5]

I'm Master Laughable. My father called me that, because I was a droll chap from a tiny little boy (*a pusillo puero ridiculus fui*). . . . I'm an obliging fellow; I can't say 'no' to a dinner. . . . But hospitality's going out of fashion: folk say, 'I'd invite you, only I'm dining out.' So I'll have to follow the Roman style of auction and put myself up for sale! For the benefit of prying persons anxious to know the reasons for an auction, I'll advertise — Selling off — a Parasite, owing to losses

---

[1] *Cist.*, 203 *sqq.*   [2] *Poen.*, 475 *sqq.*
[3] *Capt.*, 461–490, *e.g.*, 'nemo ridet; sciui extemplo rem de compecto geri.'
[4] *Capt.*, 768–780, 901–908.   [5] *Stich.*, 174 *sqq.*

sustained (*damna euenerunt maxuma*), depreciation of property in dinners and death of drinking-parties (*potationes plurumae demortuae*)! ... Great Public Compulsory Clearance Sale without Reserve! (*foras necessumst quidquid habeo uendere*). Attend, please! Huge bargains! (*praeda erit praesentium*). Sale of funny *bons mots*! Come, bid up! Who offers a dinner? Who offers a breakfast? ... Unrivalled stock of Greek unguents (*nemo meliores dabit* ...), nice little compliments, nice little fibs suitable for parasites. ... Going, a Parasite—empty—handy for storing scraps of food in. ...'All must be cleared for what they will fetch!'

Sometimes the fun lies in sarcasm, satire, and parody. Plain ladies are advised to attend temple service before daylight—before Venus awakens, else their ugly faces might frighten the goddess away![1] When the lover, in a transport of admiration, tells his slave to hang himself, for he can never hear such words again as those that fall from his lady's lips, and declares 'She speaks honeyed wine,' the slave plays up to him, 'Oh, simply sweet sponge-cake, sesamum, and poppy....'[2] Sometimes the fun lies in brief phrase—'the deadest man alive,' 'the twinniest of twins,'[3] 'Who's this two-handled jug walking about?'[4] or in puns nearly as ineffective in the Latin as in a translation.[5]

Primarily, Plautus's object was not to lecture but to amuse, and yet there is more than infinite jest and trickery in him. If he was no deep student of human nature and no deep thinker on human destiny, he did not lack feeling for the earnest of life. With his merry laughter went broad sympathies. His own outlook on existence must have coloured the character of some of the slaves whom he paints with zest—a cheerful attitude to what seems a game, a readiness to take one's luck and to rise above untoward events buoyant and resourceful. Mirth is not necessarily stone-blind to sadness: so comedy, while it laughs, may contain as much real criticism of life as tragedy. In comedy the flesh and blood of reality must be obvious; in tragedy it may be obscured by greater conventionality and abstraction. The serious in Plautus easily eludes one in the midst of so much fooling: yet it is there. Take the roysterer's reflections in the *Mostellaria*.[6] Because they are sung, and because many *cantica* are light and airy, like the libretto of a comic opera, they are not to be dismissed as without significance. It is one of the most impressive things in Plautus to hear the prodigal reason with himself in the spirit of FitzGerald's 'Indeed, indeed, repentance oft

[1] *Poen.*, 323.
[2] *Poen.*, 309–325; cf. 365 for parody of lovers' speeches.
[3] *Pers.*, 831, 'geminissumus.'
[4] *Pers.*, 308, 'ansatus' (referring to Sagaristio 'carrying himself with arms akimbo and tricking himself out with fine airs').
[5] E.g., *Capt.*, 860:
  'Non enim es in senticeto, eo non sentis':
  You're not in a quickset hedge, so you've no quick sensation!
[6] *Most.*, 84–156.

I swore' (*recordatu' multum et diu cogitaui*, etc.). He draws the moving picture of his own character as a fair fabric, the ruin of which means bitter agony to the parent who had toiled to build it up. This touches, and not flippantly, one of the deep anxieties in life—the future of children on whom care has been spent. When he proceeds to the first year away from home, and the gradual ruin of a good disposition after the 'storm of idleness' came (*uenit ignauia—ea mi tempestas fuit*) and 'brought the hail and rain' upon the 'House Beautiful,' we realise that 'The Rake's Progress' is being rehearsed by the rake himself. Dramatically, in the next scene, before another plunge into pleasure, the roysterer is still harping on his old idea of the weather-beaten house—it is the rain of Love and Cupid which is deluging his heart (*mihi Amor et Cupido in pectus perpluit meum*).

Despite the plots, there is feeling for the value of morality. True, much shameless deceit is condoned along with much sexual laxity, and only a very rough-and-ready justice is meted out in the plays. Sympathy is with the enamoured youth, and against the procurer and procuress. Yet there is more than the triumph of smaller over greater vice. The Plautine theatre is no carnival of unredeemed profligacy. The worst vices are made repulsive. The morality of Plautus is undeniably better than that of Congreve and Wycherley. Depravity in the aged is derided, and the sanctities of family life are respected. Besides, there are many positive examples of the estimable—self-sacrifice rewarded in the *Captiui*, perfidy overthrown in the *Rudens*, avarice defeated in the *Aulularia*, and a loyalty indifferent to the world's judgment justified in the *Trinummus*. Plautus can draw a good man and a good woman. It is not unintentional that he puts in the mouth of his most maidenly character[1] the thought that a single wall will serve a city, if it is free of the Ten Deadly Sins, which she enumerates. This is 'the righteousness which exalteth a nation.'

Rapid workmanship, the visible sign of his prolific genius, induced his carelessness. As the supreme laughter-raiser of his day, he had the strength to blunder. In the train of his vigour, abundance, merriment, eagerness to entertain the 'groundlings,' came mistakes and defects— loose-jointed plots, episodic patchwork, defiance of verisimilitude,[2] protracted teasings,[3] tantalising postponement of answers to questions,[4] inordinate anachronisms, and his strange mixture of illusion and reality as if he did not deign to lose himself consistently in the action. For he often pauses to address the spectators directly—'Remember, this is

---

[1] *Persa*, 554 *sqq*.
[2] *E.g.*, the marvellous coincidences of the *Menaechmi* or the *Poenulus*.
[3] *E.g.*, the banter between the boy-messenger and the girl-messenger in the *Persa*, 205 *sqq*.
[4] *E.g.*, the bottling up of news in *Stichus*, 333–371. *Cf. Merc.* 134–181, when nearly fifty lines are spent on platitudes and captious rejoinders before the slave explains his meaning in saying 'We're lost.' Similar humour recurs *Merc.*, 885 *sqq*.

what they do in Athens'—or he mischievously allows them peeps
behind the scenes by revealing details of theatrical equipment—'This
is only stage gold, not real money,' or 'We must get the costumes for
our disguised Persian from the *Choragus*.' A quite extraordinary hotch-
potch occurs towards the close of the *Poenulus*.[1] The Carthaginian,
Hanno, is about to realise the dream of his life and recover his long-lost
daughters. His pious prayer to Jupiter, as arbiter of human life, has its
foil in the flippancy of the young coxcomb Agorastocles, who warrants
Jupiter will do all that's expected—'Why, He's under my thumb—He's
afraid of me!' 'Hush, pray,' is the shocked request of the old man,
who is in tears. Even Agorastocles notices this, though he does not
understand the pathos of the situation. *Ne lacruma, patrue*, he remarks,
and then breaks out enthusiastically. 'Kinniest of kinsmen' (*patrue mi
patruissime!*), he hails his elderly relative: 'she's a jolly nice girl, and
how sensible she is' (*est lepida et lauta: ut sapit!*). 'Takes after her
father in being sensible,' is the reply of the father, who, now that he
has travelled the known world over to track his daughters, proceeds, in
violation of human feeling, to have some amusement by teasing them
before he reveals himself! He pretends to summon the girls to court.
But before he elaborates his false charge of theft, Agorastocles counsels
brevity. One moment the players identify themselves with the situation
and are *dramatis personae*; the next, they recall their individuality as
professional actors in the theatre, and are no longer in Calydon, as the
scene requires. 'But soft! methinks I scent the morning air; brief let me
be,' says the ghost in *Hamlet*. 'Be brief,' says Plautus's actor; 'the
audience want a drink!' (*In pauca confer: sitiunt qui sedent.*) So when the
real welcome comes, and the girls embrace their father, we have to re-
focus our glasses before we realise that Plautus no longer has tongue in
cheek. Such sudden juxtapositions leave Plautus exposed, like Thack-
eray, to the charge of being over-sarcastic and cynical. This scene of joy
over recovery of lost ones and the realisation of yearning (*tandem
cupitum contigit*), strikes the dramatist as the very subject for a great
painter: 'O Apelles, O Zeuxis the painter, why did you die too soon to
paint a picture on this theme? for I don't fancy other artists representing scenes like this.' Hanno is full of heartfelt gratitude: he offers
thanksgivings (*di deaeque omnes, uobeis habeo merito magnas gratias*). But
the young man is in a hurry. He reminds Hanno of his betrothal to his
elder daughter. 'Memini,' says the father curtly. The youth does not
forget to add, 'And then there's the dowry you promised!' To this
there is no reply. The whole is a curious blend. But then life is, too.

The Plautine dramatic faults will not stand the strict analysis of
artistic criticism.[2] Yet they generally have the justification of spon-

---

[1] *Poen.*, 1174–1279.
[2] The dramatic weaknesses of Plautus are discussed with great fulness by
P. Langen, *Plautin. Studien*, 1886.

taneity. Repetitions of incident, of character, of joke, flippancy and seriousness, truth to nature and wild travesty, are inevitable, if a playwright takes pretty much the first idea that comes. They are all part of his naturally rich endowment. And they have the further justification of suiting the stage. When the last word has been said by way of censure, it remains to say that Plautus had the true theatrical instinct. He could make his characters 'wear the motley' to excellent purpose, because he could himself act. So, as a master of stagecraft, he plays a whole gamut of comic effects, and manipulates to his liking the elements of comedy, farce, burlesque, operetta, pantomime, and extravaganza. His carelessness, like so much more in him, reminds one of Shakespeare. Plautus, of course, was not 'myriad-minded.' There is ground for charging him with a limited range of subjects. Endless rascality palls, it is urged. In its high colours it suits the stage, but it is not true to life. The plots, it may be said, are no more completely representative than the stories of the *Decamerone* and the trickery of the *fabliaux* are of the whole Middle Ages, or the modern problem play and problem novel are of the whole of contemporary society. Yet it would be a fool's part to expect a mere transcript of actual life in a theatre. More than a photographic copy is wanted, and less than the whole truth is wanted. Menander himself had to be the mirror of life in a sublimated sense. What one desires in Plautus is not less exaggeration, but something more of the diversified life, which existed in the society forming the background of his plays, and something still more daring in the way of anachronism—that is, still more of the Roman. For though not all his youths are immoral, not all his slaves sharpers, and not all his fathers made to be hoodwinked, still there was a wealth of material teeming with comic possibilities from which Plautus never drew.

Without the variegated profusion of the Elizabethans, Plautus possesses no little of their full-blooded vigour. He has a share of the same joy in living and interest in man. The analogy with Shakespeare is not merely fanciful.[1] The constant riddle of genius reappears in both —the mystery of early education, an apprenticeship served rather to life and work than to the schools, an early connexion with players and the stage, a gift of rapid acquisition and adaptation. If as an artist Plautus is not to be spoken of in the same breath, he was akin to him in knowing good stagecraft. Without Shakespeare's discernment of the deep recesses of the human soul, Plautus had much of his exuberance of spirit and language and much of his triumphant recklessness. In freedom he resembles that wild 'forest' to which Johnson likened Shakespeare in contrast with the 'garden' of the correct writer. He cares as little whether Thebes had a harbour[2] as Shakespeare cares whether there

---

[1] See Mommsen, *Hist. of Rome*, Eng. ed., ii. 440 (footnote): Sellar, *Roman Poets of Rep.*, 1889, pp. 161–2.

[2] Plautus gives Thebes a harbour in *Amph.*, 164.

was a coast of Bohemia. Plautus rises but rarely into the poetry which enchants with depth of suggestiveness or beauty of finished art. He has not the woodland sweetness of Shakespeare's songs. Nor has he the joyous *abandon* of Aristophanes's fun, which ranges from the clouds to Hades, jesting with equal effect at obnoxious policies and persons, at demagogue, poet,. philosopher, at men's stupidities and women's rights, and which creates comic extravagances like the 'Thinking-shop' or 'Sky-cuckoo-borough' or the poetical competition before Dionysus. Yet Plautus is a poet in the creative sense. Like his stage-slave, he is a 'maker' of trick and jest,[1] and in his songs he proves his vast command of lyrical melody. His dramatic power receives its best testimony in the revivals of interest in him during Roman times, and in his influence upon European drama since the Renaissance.[2]

Technically, a Plautine comedy—if we do not count the prologue as an integral part—fell into two divisions, *diuerbium* and *canticum*, indicated in some MSS. by DV and C respectively. *Diuerbium* was the spoken portion, that is, dialogue and soliloquy in iambic senarii without musical accompaniment. The spoken portion was roughly about a fourth of the play. The septenarii and octonarii were rendered to a musical accompaniment, in a kind of recitative, and so were intermediate between the spoken lines and the varied musical metres of the *cantica* proper, which were monologues (μονῳδίαι) delivered with gestures to the accompaniment of the flute.

Plautus fits his metres with great skill to changes in idea or feeling. Straightforward narration or calm thought is expressed by the iambic senarius, which in Roman comedy admits many more licences and metrical resolutions than in Greek comedy. Acceleration of feeling is associated with the trochaic septenarius (trochaic tetrameter catalectic, *i.e.*, seven feet and a half), and the iambic septenarius (iambic tetrameter catalectic, *i.e.*, seven feet and a half)—both favourites in Plautus, the former being handled with especial force.[3] Still higher excitement is suggested by lines half a foot longer—the octonarii, either trochaic or iambic (tetrameters acatalectic, *i.e.*, eight full feet).[4]

---

[1] Pseudolus is a *poeta* inventing the non-existent, *Pseud.*, 401.

[2] *E.g.*, a lively play like the *Mostellaria* has had its imitators from Italy to Denmark.

[3] It is the familiar metre of Tennyson's *Locksley Hall*, and suits rapid thought or bustling action. Compare the line of the breathless Pylades in the *Orestes*:

θᾶσσον ἤ μ' ἐχρῆν προβαίνων ἱκόμην δι' ἄστεος

with the spirit of *Poen.* 522–3:

'Liberos homines per urbem modico magi' par est gradu
Ire, seruoli esse duco festinantem currere.'

Men of free birth thro' the city ought with leisured step to go,
But to rush in frantic hurry argues one a slave, I trow.

[4] The metre is sometimes abruptly changed to suit dramatic circumstances. If in a scene written in septenarii or octonarii it is necessary to introduce a

The octonarii may be inventions of Plautus. They are not Greek. Besides these, there is a wealth of long and short lines in the lyrics. The *cantica* present one of the many difficulties concerning Plautus. There is no absolute agreement about the arrangement of lines and the designation of the metres, though a general preference has been shown by editors for the division into lines and cola adopted in the best MSS. In any case, the *cantica* best prove the versatility of Plautus as a metrist. For example, in the *Amphitruo*, 161 *sqq.*, he works in all the lyric metres which he could handle—trochaic octonarii, Ionics *a minore*, sotadeans, anapaests, cretics, bacchiacs. But there remains unsettled the problem of the relation in which the lyric measures of Plautus stand to the Greek dramatic lyrics of the two centuries which followed Euripides. Much more must be known about Hellenistic lyrics before it is possible to assess his originality in the polymetry of his *cantica*.[1]

The divisions into 'Acts' recognised by Horace[2] as normal for the drama was not known to the old Roman comedians. It was of Alexandrian origin, and critics from the time of Donatus have found it difficult of application both to Roman comedies and Greek tragedies. In Plautus's time a play proceeded continuously from the lowering of the curtain at the beginning to its rise at the end, save for short breaks filled generally by simple music from the *tibicen*.[3] The division into 'Scenes' is ancient, and regularly indicated in MSS. of Plautus and Terence. The chorus of the Old Greek Comedy had gradually been dispensed with in the later Greek period, largely owing to expense of equipment. The chorus has disappeared from Roman comedy even to the limited extent of its function in Roman tragedy.[4] But it has left its principal legacies in soliloquies and in passages of reflection.

Plautine prosody is notoriously hard.[5] The scansion of Plautus was

---

passage *extra actionem*, Plautus marks this commonly by altering the metre. Prof. E. A. Sonnenschein points out (*Cl. Rev.*, Dec., 1906) that when a letter is read aloud (*Bacch.*, 997), when an oath is administered (*Rud.*, 1338), when the actor, dropping his dramatic *rôle*, directly addresses the audience (*Amph.*, 1006), such changes mark the situation vividly.

[1] The Alexandrian erotic fragment published by Grenfell in 1896 illustrates the kind of verse on which Plautine *cantica* may have been modelled. Crusius, reviewing the fragment (*Philol.*, lv., pp. 353 *sqq.*) pointed out the similarity. Consistently therewith Leo puts forward the theory that the *cantica* close a long process of lyric evolution which opened in the monodies of Euripides. Leo, *Die plautinischen Cantica u. die hellenistische Lyrik*, 1897, and review by Sonnenschein, *Class. Rev.*, xii. 319 *sq.*

[2] Hor., *A.P.*, 189-190.
'Neue minor neu sit quinto productior actu
Fabula quae posci uolt et spectanda reponi.'

[3] *E.g.*, *Pseud.*, 573-574, 'Exibo, non ero uobis morae; tibicen uos interibi hic delectauerit.'

[4] For the position of chorus in Roman tragedy, as a contribution to the realism of effect, see Otto Jahn in *Herm.*, ii. (1867), pp. 227-229.

[5] To consult on metres and prosody: F. Ritschl, *Proleg.* (for differences from usages in 'classical' poetry); W. Wagner, *Aul.*, ed. 2., Introd.; W. Christ,

less understood in Cicero's days[1] than that of Chaucer was in Johnson's. Nor could it ever be understood on principles of quantity alone. These principles were made binding chiefly through the influence of Ennius in his use of the hexameter, and were only partly operative in Plautus's time; for instance, the law of length by position was not yet definite. In general, the iambics and trochaics of the drama—whether written by Ennius himself, Plautus, Terence, Accius, or Pacuvius—had not the metrical length and value of their syllables fixed invariably. It was left for Catullus and Horace to compose iambic metres with the correctness observed in hexameters. The main characteristics of Plautine prosody include the frequent shortening of long syllables and the weakening or dropping of final -*m* and final -*s*. We scan *bónĭs*, *dómĭ*; the imperatives *cáuĕ*, *áuĕ*, *ténĕ*, *ábĭ*; *ferĕntarium*, *simíllimae*, *ĭnmortalis*, *ĕsse*, *ĕcce*; and before consonants *enĭm*, *parŭm*; *sáluŏs sis*, *ludĭfĭcátŭs sit*. Plautine scansion, though rescued from the pre-Ritschelian welter of confusion, is by no means a settled matter. Authorities are not yet agreed what exact proportion to assign, in iambic senarii and trochaic septenarii, to accent and to quantity.[2] The crucial matter—even more so than the much-debated hiatus—is the law of the 'Brevis Brevians,' the principle by which a short syllable shortens a succeeding syllable, the principle, that is, by which words like *ăue*, *uŏlo*, *uŏluptatem*, may have their second syllable short. Is the phenomenon 'linguistic' or 'metrical'?[3] The most satisfactory explanation is that, like so much in Plautus, it reflected the contemporary pronunciation of conversational Latin. The comic dramatists adhered to the system of colloquial pro-

---

Metrik der Griechen u. Römer, ed. 2, 1879; A. Spengel, *Reformvorschläge z. Metrik d. lyrischen Versarten*, u.s.w., 1882; R. Klotz, *Grundzüge d. altröm. Metrik*, 1890; F. Skutsch, *Forschungen z. lat. Gram. u. Metrik*, Bd. 1 (*Plautinisches u. Romanisches: Studien z. Plaut. Prosodie*), 1892; W. M. Lindsay, *Journal of Philol.*, xxi, No. 42; xxii, No. 43; F. Leo, *Plaut. Forsch.*, 1895 (esp. v, 'Auslautendes *s* und *m*'; vi, 'Hiatus u. Synalöphe bei auslautendem *ae*').

[1] Cic., *Orat.*, lv, 184, 'Comicorum senarii propter similitudinem sermonis sic saepe sunt abiecti, ut non nunquam uix in eis numerus et uersus intellegi possit'; xx. 67, 'apud quos [*i.e.* comicos poetas] nisi quod uersiculi sunt, nihil est aliud cotidiani dissimile sermonis.'

[2] See Sonnenschein's art. in *Cl. Rev.*, April, 1906, discussing Exon's theory of February, 1906.

[3] E. A. Sonnenschein, in *Cl. Rev.*, vii. 132–136, noticing Klotz's *Grundzüge*, deals with the diversity of opinion on this cardinal doctrine of Plautine metre. The various theories fall into two great classes: (*a*) those which explain the shortenings as due to pronunciation out of relation to metre, (*b*) those which throw the burden of explanation upon the metrical ictus. The first class includes those who follow Ritschl in emphasising syncope, synizesis, and loss of final consonants; and those who, like Wagner and Brix, in the main follow Corssen in emphasising the 'Hochton,' or prose accent. The other class is represented by C. F. W. Müller, who argues that shortenings are found only in a certain relation to the *ictus metricus* (*Plautin. Prosodie*, 1869, pp. 83–85). The opposition to the theory held by Corssen and Brix as to the shortening effect of the accent on adjacent syllables is seen in Ussing, who believed a long syllable following a short is shortened by assimilation.

nunciation of words and word-groups, and while imitating the quantitative metres of the Greeks, they endeavoured to keep the metrical
ictus in unison with the natural accentuation of everyday speech. If this
is correct, to read aloud the lines of Plautus with attention to the
metrical beat of the spondees and trochees composing them, is to
obtain a fair idea of how his sentences would sound in the ordinary talk
of his period.[1] One of the many proofs of Bentley's insight was his hint
—it was only a hint in his *schediasma* on Terence's metres—towards the
proper study of Plautine prosody. He discerned that the common prose
accentuation of a word was generally in comedy identical with the ictus
of the verse. The hint was too long overlooked. Popular pronunciation
reduces to order, or at least accounts for, many apparent anomalies.
The word-accent, for instance, prevailed to bar certain metrically
'correct' collocations, *e.g.* ending an iambic senarius with two such
iambic words as *locum dabo*, where the word-accent in each case is on
a different syllable from the metrical accent. Again, conversational
Latin modifies versification, as in the dropping of the final vowel of *-que*
and *-ne*, which Skutsch discovered.[2] On the other hand, regarding the
interaction of the two principles, some lay stress on the cases where the
verse ictus overrides the prose accent.

The language[3] of Plautus, like his prosody, is based on that of
ordinary life. Inflexions,[4] syntax, vocabulary, were in a relatively fluid
stage in his time, so that anomalies[5] are not necessarily blunders by
copyists, but may often be true to the actual condition of the Latin
of the second century B.C. Though one of the great difficulties is to
ascertain in detail how far his text has been modernised, broadly we
have in Plautus the spoken Latin, turned to brilliant account by a
genius who treats it as he did his Greek originals—freely selecting,
rejecting, combining, inventing. Above all, he retains its liveliness. His
style has the verve and colour of life.[6] He can use homely illustrations,
current sayings, plebeian slang and abuse. Under how many titles does
the trickster appear—an 'architect,' a 'carpenter,' a 'generalissimo,' a
'fowler,' a 'poet'! The dupe is 'shorn' like a sheep, 'limed' like a bird;

[1] See W. M. Lindsay, *Cl. Rev.*, vi. 402–404; also his articles, *Jrnl. Phil.*,
1891, maintaining that no syllable was shortened in the metre of dramatists
which was not shortened in the ordinary pronunciation of the time, and that a
naturally long vowel was never shortened by the law of 'Brevis Brevians' except
in a final syllable.

[2] So *nemp(e)* is often the scansion, not *ně(m)pe*, according to the old theory.

[3] For Plautine language see commentaries of J. Brix on *Mil. Glor.*, ed. 4,
1916, and A. O. F. Lorenz on *Pseud.*, 1876 (esp. *Einleitung*). Plautine usages are
examined by P. Langen, *Beiträge z. Krit. u. Erklg. d. Plautus*, 1880.

[4] *E.g.* the question arises how far the old *-d* of the ablative should be
retained in the text.

[5] *E.g.* variations of verb-forms in Plautus are collected by A. W. Hodgman,
Classical Quarterly, I. i, April, 1907.

[6] Lamarre, *Hist. litt. lat.*, 1901, says, 'Rien de plus vif et de plus coloré que
son style.'

he is 'polished off,' he has 'words palmed off on him,' or he 'has his nose wiped.' Plautus revels in his supply of words available for a catalogue of rogueries[1] or torrents of invective.[2] He can employ, too, and improve upon, the popular terms of endearment—'meus ocellus, mea rosa, mi anime, mea uoluptas,'[3] or concoct a love-letter bristling with diminutives, 'teneris labellis,' 'molles morsiunculae,' 'oppressiunculae' and the like.[4] His very tautologies prove that he can echo the easy-going popular manner which verges on the garrulous.[5] But he often strikes into novelties of diction, unknown to common parlance— ingenious alliances of words, picturesque phrases, coined words—and into an animated dialogue which is the best talk idealised. Such qualities in him led Cicero to associate Plautus and the Old Attic Comedy with the better kind of comic power which is 'graceful, polished, talented, and witty'[6] (*elegans, urbanum, ingeniosum, facetum*). 'The Muses,' said Stilo, Varro's famous master, 'would employ the language of Plautus, if they wished to speak Latin.'[7] And in plain historical fact, his services to the language were immense. His works were far more than a valuable store of old words and old forms: they were a vital influence on Latin. Yet, his most lasting title to fame is not linguistic. Rather it lies in the virile spontaneity animating his exuberance of expression, his inventiveness in situation and his overflowing mirth. Such are the qualities which make Plautus the greatest dramatic genius of Rome.

Caecilius Statius (*c.* 219–166 B.C.), an Insubrian Gaul,[8] was brought a slave[9] to Rome sometime after the war with his countrymen broke out in 200 B.C. Subsequently freed, he was intimate with Ennius, and, though he had at first a struggle to win the ear of his audiences,[10]

---

[1] *Asin.*, 560–575.
[2] *Persa*, 406 *sqq.*; *Pseud.*, 357–370, a comic scene where the young gentleman and his slave stand on either side of Ballio and yell offensive terms at him.
[3] *Asin.*, 664. [4] *Pseud.*, 62 *sqq.*
[5] P. Langen, *Plautin. Stud.*, 1886, subjects Plautus, play by play, to dissection for his tautologies as well as contradictions, improbabilities, and dramatic weaknesses. Passages like *Mostell.*, 85 *sqq.*, 'Recordatu' multum et diu cogitaui Argumentaque in pectus multa institui Ego, atque in meo corde, si est quod mihi cor, Eam rem uolutaui . . .' prove how much he would gain by condensation artistically. But they also resemble the prodigal richness of nature.
[6] Cic., *De Off.*, i. 104. In the same strain Gellius calls Plautus 'homo linguae atque elegantiae in uerbis Latinae princeps,' *N.A.*, VI (VII). xvii. 4; and 'linguae Latinae decus,' *N.A.*, XVIII. viii. 6.
[7] Quint., X. i. 99, 'In comoedia maxime claudicamus, licet Varro Musas, Aelii Stilonis sententia, Plautino dicat sermone locuturas fuisse, si Latine loqui uellent.'
[8] Hieron, *Euseb. Chron.*, ann. Abr. 1838 (=179 B.C.), gives the date of his fame (*comoediarum scriptor clarus habetur*). Jerome's words there, 'mortuus est anno post mortem *Enni*,' are usually read with the addition of *tertio* (Ritschl) or *quarto* (Dziatzko) to end Caecilius's life in the year of Terence's *Andria* (166 B.C.)
[9] 'Statius' is his servile name. Gell., *N.A.*, IV. xx. 13.
[10] L. Ambivius Turpio, the actor-manager, speaking Prol. ii. to Terence's *Hecyra*, declares:
'In eis quas primum Caecili didici nouas,
Partim sum earum exactus, partim uix steti.'

became the leading comic dramatist of his day and the recognised adviser of the aediles regarding new plays. The pretty anecdote[1] of young Terence reading his first play, the *Andria*, to him, and gradually riveting the attention of his senior, is illuminating, even if apocryphal. Of his *palliatae* some forty titles and some three hundred lines survive. The identity of sixteen of his titles with Menander's, his preference for Greek titles in contrast to the habit of Naevius and Plautus, and signs of closer artistic pains, mark him as representative of the transition to the more Hellenic comedy of Terence. His fragments prove his retention of the standard characters, slaves, parasites, the *demi-monde*. He may have displayed individuality in their treatment. At any rate, a mordant cynicism, which one can detect, shows how lively he could be, as in his two marvels—the father so generous that he need not be cheated and the courtesan so loving that she can refuse money; or, again, in his only too realistic elaboration of the stock attacks upon the *morosa uxor*. The husband's complaint that his wife kisses him on his home-coming draws from the candid friend the two-edged rejoinder: 'It's all right about her kiss: she means it as an emetic for what you've been drinking outside!' (*Nil peccat de sauio: ut deuomas uolt quod foris potaueris*). Criticisms upon him vary. Sedigitus's list[2] exalts him to the primacy in comedy. (*Caecilio palmam Statio do mimico*); Horace[3] admires his *grauitas*; Varro[4] says his *forte* lies in his plots (*in argumentis poscit palmam*); Cicero thinks his Latinity bad.[5] The most memorable and the fullest piece of ancient criticism upon him is the chapter[6] in which Gellius arrays parallel passages of Menander's Πλόκιον and Caecilius's adaptation, and on count after count pronounces in favour of the Greek. In Gellius's eyes, the two differ in value as Diomedes's armour from Glaucus's. Caecilius is inferior in charm of incident and expression (*uenustatem rerum atque uerborum*), in distinction, point, and wit (*quae Menander praeclare et apposite et facete scripsit*), in the grace of simple truth to ordinary life (*illud Menandri de uita hominum media sumptum, simplex et uerum et delectabile*), and in wealth of varied emotion (*hi omnes motus eius affectionesque animi*). Read alone, he struck Gellius as not at all dull and uninteresting, but not to be compared with his model.[7]

Contemporary authors of *palliatae*[8] were Trabea; Atilius, composer

---

[1] It is told in Suet., *Vita Terenti*.   [2] *Cf. supra*, p. 99
[3] *Ep.* II. i. 59.   [4] *Men. Sat.* 399 (Bücheler).
[5] *Ad Att.*, VII. iii. 10. Yet Cicero finds Caecilius useful in court to exemplify the relations of a father and sons (*Pro Rosc. Amer.*, xvi. 46). Referring to Caecilius, he urges that dramatic poets mean spectators to see 'our manners sketched and the image of our daily life represented under the guise of fiction' (*ut effictos nostros mores in alienis personis expressamque imaginem nostrae uitae cotidianae uideremus*).   [6] *N.A.*, II. xxiii.
[7] Certain verses Gellius considers 'mutilated copies of Menander and a patchwork of tragic bombast' (*trunca quaedam ex Menandro dicentis et consarcientis uerba tragici tumoris*); *N.A.*, II. xxiii. 21.
[8] For their scanty fragments, see O. Ribbeck, *Com. Rom. Frag.*, ed. 3, 1898.

of a *Misogynos*, called by Cicero 'durissimus poeta' and probably[1] the same Atilius who translated Sophocles's *Electra*; Aquilius, who should be credited with the *Boeotia*, although Varro insisted it was Plautine;[2] Licinius Imbrex (? Tegula), who wrote a *Neaera*; and the Luscius Lanuvinus (not Lavinius), the 'maliuolus uetus poeta' on whom Terence retorts in all his prologues except that to the *Hecyra*. Terence turns the tables on the spiteful critic of his plot-weaving with the declaration that Luscius spoiled Menander's Φάσμα in the borrowing and made a legal 'howler' when copying the Θησαυρός.[3]

It was the achievement of the young African, P. Terentius Afer (*c.* 195?–159 B.C.), to put upon Roman comedy the highest Hellenic polish. For his career our fullest source of knowledge is the interesting *Life of Terence* excerpted from Suetonius's work *De Poetis* and luckily preserved by Donatus in his commentary upon Terence. Suetonius is at pains to quote his authorities—some of them more than once— Fenestella, Nepos, Porcius, Volcatius, Varro, C. Memmius, Santra, Q. Cosconius, Afranius, Cicero, and Caesar. Besides Donatus's brief addendum there are Jerome's notes based on Suetonius, Terence's own prologues, and the *didascaliae* upon his plays. Neither his race nor the date of his birth can be stated decisively. His birth at Carthage, recorded by Suetonius, does not prove Phoenician blood: his cognomen 'Afer' rather suggests that he belonged to some native tribe conquered by the Carthaginians. Since his whole life falls between the second and the third Punic conflict, his slavery at Rome was certainly not due to capture in war. He may have been a regular purchase from a Carthaginian master or a victim of kidnappers. In any case he was educated by his Roman owner, a senator, Terentius Lucanus, and manumitted. His African origin was conceivably his initial recommendation to Africanus the Younger[4] and through him to Laelius and other members of the Scipionic circle. Their patronage of the talented youth led to aspersions on his character and insinuations that the plays he produced were theirs. His first play, the *Andria*, was performed in 166 B.C. The six which he composed before his departure for Greece in 160 B.C. have all survived. At that date, according to the best texts of

[1] See W. S. Teuffel, *Rom. Lit.*, § 107, 2.

[2] Gell., *N.A.*, III. iii. 4, where the parasite's curses on the invention of sundials are quoted. Once upon a time the stomach had been the best timekeeper (*uenter erat solarium*)!

[3] Donatus ad Ter. *Eun.*, prol. 10, 'Arguit Terentius quod Luscius Lanuuinus contra consuetudinem litigantium defensionem ante accusationem induxerit.'

[4] *I.e.* to that son of L. Aemilius Paullus, who was adopted by the son of Scipio Africanus Maior and became the conqueror of Carthage. He was quite young when Terence was introduced to him, and perhaps the adoption had not yet taken place. Terence was dead before Scipio earned by achievement (Cic. *De Rep.* vi. 11) the name Africanus which he had inherited through his adoptive father. – Ed.

Suetonius,[1] he had not yet entered his twenty-fifth year. This would imply that Terence made his mark with a stage-play of finished style in his eighteenth year: and this is well-nigh incredible. Though he was Scipio's 'contemporary' (*aequalis*), the term may be vaguely used, and there is no need to ascribe to him the same birth-year, 185 B.C. Indeed, there is the evidence of Fenestella and of Santra that he was senior to Scipio and Laelius.[2]

As a dramatist his fortune was made on the afternoon when in humble attire (*contemptiore uestitu*) and unknown to the poets' college he presented himself, by order of the aediles, before Caecilius at dinner to read his first play to him. He had not gone far before the stranger's stool was exchanged for a place at table, and the whole was received enthusiastically after dinner. His fortunes, however, were chequered. If the *Eunuchus* was repeatedly staged and commanded unprecedented earnings, the *Hecyra* was fated to have its audience slip away to the superior allurements of rope-dancing[3] and to fare little better at its next presentation five years later. If his refinement delighted his exalted friends, he had to face carping criticisms of the kind rebutted in his prologues. Indeed, one recorded reason for that journey to Greece from which he never returned was his disgust at the allegation that he published other men's work as his own. The more likely reason reminds one of the quest after Hellenic perfection in which Virgil's life closed. Terence desired to study at first hand the ways of the people who were the subject of his dramas. His death in 159 is wrapped in mystery. Was he lost at sea, as one account ran, homeward bound with a stock of plays adapted from Menander in Menander's own country, or did he die in Arcadia broken-hearted over the lost manuscripts of his latest plays?

The chronology of the plays[4] presents vexed questions. It is import-

[1] 'Post editas comoedias, nondum quintum atque uicesimum ingressus (? egressus) annum,' etc. The number xxxv is much more plausible, though only in interpolated MSS. This would make his birth 195 B.C.

[2] Nepos, quoted by Suetonius, *Vit. Ter.*, records that Terence, Scipio, and Laelius 'aequales omnes fuisse.' Fenestella (*ibid.*) declares of Terence 'utroque maiorem natu fuisse.' Santra (*ibid.*) refutes the rumours about Terence's literary dependence on his patrons by saying that 'if he had needed helpers in composition, he could not have made use of Scipio and Laelius, who were then mere striplings (*adulescentuli*), but rather the learned Sulpicius Gallus. . . . . or Q. Fabius Labeo and M. Popillius, both men of consular rank and poets.'

[3] *Hec.*, prol. i. 4–5:
> 'Ita populus studio stupidus in funambulo
> Animum occuparat.'

[4] Texts: ed. et appar. crit., F. Umpfenbach, 1870; ed. K. Dziatzko, 1884; ed. R. Y. Tyrell, 1902. On classification of Calliopian family of MSS., see also E. M. Pease, *Trans. Amer. Philol. Soc.*, 1887, vol. xviii. For ancient comments, *Donati Commentum Terenti*, etc., 2 vols., rec. P. Wessner, 1902–05. The commentary in its present form is not all from the hand of Donatus: see H. T. Karsten, *Mnemosyne*, xxxii (1904) pp. 209–51 and 287–322, on the chief contributor and four other interpolators after Donatus. For chronology, Lamarre, *Hist. d. l. litt. lat.*, tome 2, p. 27; Ph. Fabia, *Les Prologues de Térence*, 1888.

ant for an appreciation of the prologues. The prologue to the *Hecyra*, for instance, belongs to its complete presentation at the Roman Games of 160 B.C., and not to the original date of production, 165 B.C. Regarding the order of the plays and the occasions of their presentation, there are certain discrepancies, among the *didascaliae* of the best MS., the Codex Bembinus, the *didascaliae* in the Calliopian MSS., and the information in Donatus. These discrepancies are partly due to presentations at different dates.[1] Arranged according to their first performance, the plays are *Andria*, 166 B.C.; *Hecyra*, 165 (interrupted; resuscitated unsuccessfully in 160 for the funeral games of Aemilius Paulus, at which the *Adelphi* was presented, and completely presented later in the year at the Roman Games in September); *Heauton Timorumenos*, 163; *Eunuchus*, 161;[2] *Phormio*, 161; *Adelphi* (*Adelphoe*), 160. The commonest occasion was the Megalensian festival in April.

Metrical arguments (*periochae*, περιοχαί) of twelve iambic senarii were prefixed to the plays by C. Sulpicius Apollinaris of Carthage, the probable author of the non-acrostic summaries of Plautus's plots and a teacher under whom Gellius studied. The prologues have the great value of personal and critical interest. Unlike some of the Plautine prologues, they are genuine utterances by the dramatist. They give information about the Greek source of the play, they request a favourable hearing, they indulge, with one exception, in recriminations against spiteful old Luscius. The one prologue which is not polemic, that to the *Hecyra*, has the interest of revealing certain difficulties besetting artistic comedy. It is in his prologues that Terence answers charges of plagiarism as an artist should:

Nullumst iam dictum quod non sit dictum prius,[3]

—and of 'contaminating' Greek plays by citing the precedent of Naevius, Plautus, and Ennius in their free departures from rigid translation.[4] In answer to the charge that he had resorted to *belles lettres* with insufficient training (*repente ad studium hunc se adplicasse musicum*) and to the recurrent allegation of borrowed plumes (*amicum ingenio fretum haud natura sua*), his appeal is from biased to unbiased judgement.[5] Tact prompted him to repel but faintly the suggestions of his indebtedness to the Scipionic circle. It was, he could urge, his highest glory to please the noble houses whose services were their country's unfailing resource.[6] At most Terence received stimulus and friendly criticism from his cultured coterie, and one may as confidently

---

[1] *E.g.*, *Phormio* was given at Ludi Romani acc. to Calliopian MSS., and at Megalensian Games acc. to Cod. Bemb. and Donatus.

[2] There were certainly two performances of the *Eunuchus*. Most authorities give the first as 161 B.C. and a revival in 146 (Teuffel). Fabia believes in an earlier performance than 161 and dates *Eun.* next after *Andria*.

[3] *Eun.*, prol. 41.   [4] *Andr.*, prol. 15 *sqq.*
[5] *Heaut.*, prol. 22 *sqq.*   [6] *Adelph.*, prol. 15 *sqq.*

deny Scipionic or Laelian authorship of the comedies under his name as one denies a Baconian origin for Shakespeare's plays. Criticasters panting after excitement were sure to find in him 'thinness of dialogue and triviality of style' (*tenui esse oratione et scriptura leui*). They got their answer in his claim that he avoids extravagances and improbabilities.[1] His aim, stated elsewhere,[2] is to compose a drama of the quiet (*stataria*) type. There is in him a fine contempt for cheap and trite means of winning popular applause. Filled with a lively sense of the overpowering seductions of rope-dancing, boxing (*pugilum gloria*), and gladiatorial fights, it is in the higher interests of comedy that he devotes part of the later prologue of the *Hecyra* to an appeal for such support as will hearten the author himself in the teeth of venomous backbiting and encourage the actor-manager in dramatic enterprise.

About his sources there is no doubt. Two of the six plays are based on Apollodorus of Carystus, the *Hecyra* on his Ἑκυρά, the *Phormio* on his Ἐπιδικαζόμενος. The other four are drawn from Menander and, except one, are 'contaminations'—the *Andria* from Ἀνδρία and Περινθία, the *Heauton Timorumenos* from Ἑαυτὸν Τιμωρούμενος,[3] the *Eunuchus* from Εὐνοῦχος and Κόλαξ, the *Adelphi* from Menander's Ἀδελφοί and such part of Diphilus' Συναποθνῄσκοντες as Plautus did not use in his *Commorientes*. His decided preference for Menander's plots brought Terence much of Menander's spirit. It accounts for the chief features of his dramatic qualities.

His plays, then, confront us with the same society as Plautus put on the stage, but the spirit is different. At every turn in criticising Terence the comparison with Plautus is inevitable.[4] But the head and front of the contrast appears on the most cursory survey of Terence's plays. With him the scene is uniformly Athens, and we are seldom tempted to imagine ourselves in Rome. A slight sketch will reveal his dramatic world. *The Lady of Andros* does not herself appear, though the secret love between her and young Pamphilus is the hinge of the action. He

---

[1] *Phorm.*, prol. 6 *sqq.*
[2] *Heaut.*, prol. 35 *sqq.*
> 'Adeste aequo animo, date potestatem mihi
> Statariam agere ut liceat per silentium,
> Ne semper seruos currens, iratus senex,
> Edax parasitus, sycophanta autem impudens,
> Auarus leno adsidue agendi sint mihi
> Clamore summo, cum labore maxumo.'

[3] Terence calls attention to the absence of 'contamination' in the plot; *Heaut.*, prol. 4:
> 'Ex integra Graeca integram comoediam
> Hodie sum acturus.'

It is interesting to note that the model of the 'uncontaminated' *Heaut.* was one of the earliest of Menander's plays. E. Bethe argues that is was an apprentice-piece (*Anfängerstück*), *Herm.*, xxxvii. 278 *sqq.*, 1902.

[4] For his main differences from Plautus, see Lamarre, *op. cit.*, tome ii, 1901, 113 *sqq.*

is in danger of being forced to renounce his *inamorata* and marry at his father's dictation a neighbour's daughter beloved by his friend. The daring tactics suggested by his slave compensate in some degree for the absence of the romantic, and are much more entertaining than the half-expected discovery that the fair Andrian is in reality a daughter of the very neighbour with whose house an alliance was sought. In the *Hecyra*, or *The Innocent Mother-in-Law*, a bride during her husband's absence quits his house, not because of any disagreement with his mother, but because of a mishap in her past, for which, as it turns out, her own husband had been responsible. There is nothing comic in the play, but a good deal of the sentimental. The play might well be entitled *Why the Bride Went Back to her Home*; for that is the puzzle which affects in different ways the bridegroom, his mother, and the fathers of the two parties. The self-sacrificing part played by the courtesan in reuniting the separated pair betokens an unusual, but quite Terentian, tenderness in such a character.

The *Heauton Timorumenos*, or *Self Tormentor*, is a father who imposes penitential hardships on himself out of remorse for the strictness which has driven his son abroad. His elderly neighbour, who preaches at him when the play opens, needs to be reminded of his own theories before the close; for his own son repays his indulgence and encouragement of frank confidences by escapades far more extravagant than those of his self-exiled comrade, whom he is now sheltering on his secret return. The blindness of the old neighbour to his own son's misconduct facilitates the slave's trick which cheats him out of money to serve the young scapegrace. In true Terentian manner, when all comes out the mother's love is pitted against the hot anger of the father. More in the manner of the New Comedy, the profligate must be conventionally settled in life. Forgiveness is conditional on his marriage. Conventionally, too, he accepts the terms, but with a touch of fresh realism demurs to his mother's first suggestion: 'What! that red-haired girl, with cat eyes, blotchy face, and tip-tilted nose? I can't, father!'[1] and he is allowed to pick a more acceptable bride.

In the *Eunuchus*, or *Sham Eunuch*, an Ethiopian slave is being sent by Phaedria to his mistress, Thais. Phaedria's brother disguises himself as the slave to pursue his amour with a girl in Thais's establishment. The girl is traced by her brother, proved to be free-born, and united to her lover. At a parasite's instigation, an inglorious bargain is struck between Phaedria and a soldier for shares in Thais's favours. This makes the least pleasing consummation in Terence, and recalls the final scenes in Plautus's *Asinaria* and *Bacchides*.

The *Phormio*, or *A Parasite's Brains to the Rescue*, dramatises the

[1] *Heaut.*, 1061–2:
'Rufamne illam uirginem,
Caesiam, sparso ore, adunco naso? Non possum, pater.'

help in love rendered to two youths who are cousins. The parasite
Phormio, in collusion with Antipho, one cousin, engineers a legal quirk
by which Antipho receives an order of court to marry a pretty and lonely
mourner with whom he has fallen in love. Cousin Phaedria is desperately fond of a music-girl, but as desperately devoid of means. Phormio's
smartness in getting money and the double life led by Antipho's
uncle, Chremes, secure happiness for the youth. Sympathy is with the
parasite when old Chremes, by endeavouring to maltreat him, brings
about merited exposure in the eyes of his wife.

The title of *Adelphi* is doubly appropriate. It applies to the elderly
brothers, Micio, the good-natured townsman, and Demea, the stern
countryman. It applies also to the young brothers, Demea's sons, the
frankly extravagant rake Aeschinus, and that supposed model Ctesipho.
Psychologically, the play rivets attention. The forbearance of Micio, the
effect of his system of upbringing on character, the blustering reproofs
of his brother, the antithesis in disposition between the youths, prove
how successfully Terence can dispense with external incident. It is
impossible not to like Micio. He is far more gentlemanly than Plautus's
Periplecomenus. His riotous nephew and adopted son, too, has sparks
of shame and gratitude, and honours him as a better man in the sight
of heaven.[1] For the greater part of the play our sympathies are enlisted
for Micio, who can take the ravings of his moralising brother philo-
sophically[2] and talk calmly over the training of Demea's lads.[3] But with
the astonishing *volte-face* made by Demea, Terence seems to change
psychology for something very like extravaganza. It is the drollest thing
in Terence. The countryman suddenly alters his system of life. He
recognises the fresh lessons of facts, age, experience (*res, aetas, usus*).
Strictness does not pay. Laxity does. He contrasts his own unpopularity
with his brother's popularity. He resolves to try geniality. 'If it can be
done by giving presents and honouring people, I'll not be behindhand.'[4]
He begins practising affability on two slaves. Then, in his new *rôle* of
the easy-going father, he tells Aeschinus not to worry over preparations
for his marriage, and recommends he should start without flute-player
or wedding-hymn, and knock down the wall between the houses to
bring the bride in with less trouble! Next, he coolly suggests that Micio
must really marry the bride's mother! She has nobody to look after her.
It is now the turn of the old bachelor to quake. He makes an amusing
struggle for freedom,[5] but—a victim to his easy-going principles—
succumbs and reluctantly agrees to marry. The bride's relative, Hegio,
must, like her mother, have something: so the now irresponsible Demea
makes the offhand proposal that Hegio should have a 'little field' of
Micio's. After arranging all this at Micio's expense, Demea rubs
merrily into him his former remark that the common blemish of old age

---

[1] *Adelph.*, 700–705.   [2] *Ibid.*, 738 *sqq.*   [3] *Ibid.*, 805 *sqq.*
[4] *Ibid.*, 880.   [5] *Ibid.*, 934–45.

is over-attention to money and property: 'we ought to shun this blot' (*hanc maculam nos decet ecfugere*). But Demea's humour is not yet ended. He insists that the slave, Syrus, be freed—he is so sharp at marketing, and at providing questionable company for his young master, that he deserves a good turn, *pour encourager les autres* (*prodesse aequomst: alii meliores erunt*). Syrus having expressed a wish that his wife Phrygia should be freed, Demea of course seconds this heartily. Finally, Demea tells Micio he must produce ready money for his new freedman to start in life. Thus Demea has brought Micio's facile system *ad absurdum*. The last word lies with Demea. 'I have shown,' he says in effect, 'that your reputation as a jolly good fellow[1] is based not on principles of sound justice, but on giving people their own way. Now,' he remarks to the youths, 'if you wish me to restrain you in pursuits the consequences of which you are too young to foresee, I am ready to render that service.' And Aeschinus, the slackly brought up' youth, agrees that his father knows more of what is right and proper (*plus scis quod opus factost*). Thus the whole conclusion has the surprising quality of paradox.

The Terentian characters are more subtle, more refined, more humane than those of Plautus. The same society reappears—more amiable, but less virile.[2] At heart it is no better, but fuller concessions are made to outward appearance. A woman's purity or a child's life may go for little, and a veneer may gloze over excesses, and yet something is gained in the realm of feeling. Youths exhibit increased affection for fathers, slaves increased respect for masters. The prevailing urbanity reflects Terence's own circle, and stamps him the dramatist of the aristocracy, as Plautus was the dramatist of the people. Nothing jars in the considerate politeness of Chremes in the *Andria* when he declines to renew his daughter's engagement to Simo's son. Similar courtesy permeates the interviews of the fathers of the separated pair in the *Hecyra*. Such fathers in general treat their sons rationally, and expect regard and open confidence in return. Micio roundly scolds his adopted son for his misconduct, but he recognises all the time that 'if serious, it is human,' and he wins the young man's real gratitude.[3] A son in Terence does not wish the death of a father who crosses his passion— he may go the length of wishing him three days in bed without serious injury to health. Most Terentian sons are more deferential than Clitipho in the *Heauton Timorumenos*, who does not listen to his father

[1] *Adelph.*, 986, 'quod te isti facilem et festiuom putant.'
[2] Cicero (quoted in Suet., *Vit. Ter.*):

'Tu quoque qui solus lecto sermone, Terenti,
Conuersum expressumque Latina uoce Menandrum
In medium nobis *sedatis motibus* effers,
Quiddam come loquens atque omnia dulcia miscens.'

[3] *Adelph.*, 687 *sqq.* Micio (*Adelph.*, 101 *sqq.*) develops into a system the common indulgence towards youthful excesses on the principle of 'sowing wild oats.' Cf. Phidippus in *Hec.*, 541 *sqq.*

(*surdo narret fabulam*), and jests over his father's indiscreet revelations
in his cups. The relations of master and man have palpably improved.
It is unusual to find in Terence such fierce threats as are hurled at Davos
in the *Andria*. This very Davos, distrusted as much too smart (*mala
mens, malus animus*), is the one who reminds Pamphilus of his duty to
his father.[1] Slaves receive fair treatment. The cynical defiance of torture
is not ridden to death as in Plautus. The soldier lies and boasts more
plausibly. The parasite also is more real. Gnatho of the *Eunuchus* is not
such a grotesque figure as the Plautine gourmandisers, for his studied
flattery and its success are not so very impossible in actual life; while
Phormio has independent brains and deserves his reward. A parallel
refinement in the courtesan has taken place. The most repulsive type
has given place to one capable of genuine feeling, hurt[2] when her affection is doubted, lonely though she has gallants, and devoted to her
foster-sister. Humility in the presence of a matron and the virtue of
self-sacrifice are still nobler traits. Thais in the *Eunuchus* and Bacchis
in the *Hecyra* have touches almost prophetic of *La Dame aux Camélias*.
Broadly, the elemental problem of sex retains too much of the conventional in its treatment to become romantic. Chaerea's passion in the
Eunuchus is abnormally furious for Terence.[3] A more representative
lover is Pamphilus, who reveals his love for Glycerium at the funeral
scene in the *Andria*, and declares that death alone will part him from
his beloved.[4] Here, as elsewhere, Terence practises restraint. Rhap-
sodical passion could not be so consonant with his spirit as the tamer
gallantry of Phaedria in the *Eunuchus*, whose motto that 'It is something to love, even if you're out of the lists'[5] may explain his acquiescence in the claims of his military rival. In such social circumstances,
marriage at the close of a play is frequently a retarded reparation for
an act of brutality.

Terence's polished repression was purchased at the expense of
energy. There is an absence of impetuosity in action, less caricature
among characters, fewer freaks of language, as compared with Plautus.
But the gain in regularity has meant a loss of vigour, colour, daring.
Terence substitutes a minuter psychology and a more pervading
sentimentality for the broad strokes of Plautus, but he is tame in proportion. No one character, no one scene, no one play, stands out with
such pre-eminent distinctness as several in Plautus do, although there is
a pervading sense of finish. It is characteristic that there should be
recurrent *motifs*, and confusingly recurrent names of personages in
different plays.[6] The author did not elaborate in the direction of

[1] *Andr.*, 687 *sqq.*   [2] *E.g.*, Thais, *Eun.*, 129.
[3] *Eun.*, 296, 'O faciem pulchram! deleo omnis dehinc ex animo mulieres.'
[4] *Andr.*, 697, 'Valeant qui inter nos discidium uolunt: hanc nisi mors mi
adimet nemo.'
[5] *Eun.*, 640, 'Certe extrema linea amare haud nil est.'
[6] In four plays of the six, *And.*, *Heaut.*, *Eun.*, *Phorm.*, a girl is discovered

individuality, and his characters are not abiding creations. In other
dramatic qualities and artifices Plautus and Terence differ widely. The
imperfectly constructed plots, the extravagant and irrelevant episodes,
the provoking tautologies, the teasing postponements of a piece of news,
the unfettered anachronisms, have gone, but with them also much of
Plautus's robust strength and rollicking humour. There is no hearty
laughter in Terence. One must pay for better workmanship. The kernel
of the matter lies in Caesar's criticism—Terence lacked the full share of
uis comica. He was an artist; Plautus, an untutored genius.

The style of Terence is the perfection of lightness and clearness. A
foreigner, he wrote Latin with an Attic grace. The purity of his idiom,
remarked by Caesar, had been from the first guaranteed by rumours of
Scipionic authorship. Hitting the mean between the florid and the
simple style, he was for Varro[2] the model of *mediocritas*, as Pacuvius
was of *ubertas* and Lucilius of *gracilitas*. Critics, English and French,
have noted his Addisonian qualities. One might almost parody the
sentence with which Johnson closes his *Life of Addison* and declare—
Whoever wishes to attain a Latin style, familiar but not coarse, and
elegant but not ostentatious, must give his days and nights to the
dramas of Terence. Certainly Terence possesses the merits of the best
English literature of the eighteenth century—'regularity, uniformity,
precision, and balance.'[3] Like the eighteenth century, he eschews the
vulgar and polishes to *finesse* the choice language of aristocratic culture.
Here again the contrast with Plautus is decided. Taste renounces his
common colloquialisms and slang, as it renounces his almost barbaric
exuberance of puns and alliterations.[4] The goal is correctness rather
than variety, refinement rather than originality. As in the eighteenth
century, there is no horror of the commonplace, provided it be rendered in consummate form:

to be free-born. In the same four there is a Chremes, thrice for an old and once
for a young man. Sostrata is given as a matron's name in three plays. Davos and
Syrus are repeated as slaves' names.

[1] Caesar (quoted in Suet., *Vit. Ter.*):

'Tu quoque, tu in summis, o dimidiate Menander,
Poneris et merito, puri sermonis amator,
Lenibus atque utinam scriptis adiuncta foret uis
Comica, ut aequato uirtus polleret honore
Cum Graecis, neue hac despectus parte iaceres.
Unum hoc maceror ac doleo tibi desse, Terenti.'

[2] Gell., *N.A.*, VI. xiv. 6, 'Vera autem et propria huiuscemodi formarum
exempla in Latina lingua M. Varro esse dicit ubertatis Pacuuium, gracilitatis
Lucilium, mediocritatis Terentium.'

[3] Matthew Arnold, Pref. to *Six Chief Lives of the Poets*.

[4] Jingles and alliterations are rare in Terence: *e.g.*,
And., 218:

'Nam inceptiost amentium, haud amantium';
Phorm., 863–4:

'Pone reprendit pallio, resupinat: respicio, rogo
Quam ob rem retineat me.'

What oft was thought, but ne'er so well expressed.

This is the secret of Terence's wealth of phrases eminently quotable for pith, point, or balance. They often give final literary expression to some experience or to shrewd homespun wit: *e.g.*, the inadvisability of mentioning 'benefits forgot' —

> *Istaec commemoratio*
> *Quasi exprobratiost immemori benefici:*

a secret detected —

> *Hinc illae lacrumae:*

the slave who is not good at conundrums —

> *Dauos sum, non Oedipus:*

the 'falling out of faithful friends' —

> *Amantium irae amoris integratiost:*

'the proper study of mankind' —

> *Homo sum: humani nil a me alienum puto:*

unpalatable work —

> *Nullast tam facilis res quin difficilis siet,*
> *Quam inuitus facias:*

'while there's life there's hope' —

> *Modo liceat uiuere, est spes:*

the silent praise of the jealous —

> *Tacent: satis laudant:*

'fortune favours the brave' —

> *Fortis fortuna adiuuat:*

'many men, many minds' —

> *Quot homines, tot sententiae: suos quoique mos:*

the wisdom of taking a hint —

> *Dictum sapienti sat est:*

the malady of years —

> *Senectus ipsast morbus:*

the unexpected which happens —

> *Quam saepe forte temere*
> *Eueniunt quae non audeas optare:*

the value of expectations —

> *Ego spem pretio non emo.*

Much of the definitely proverbial[1] and reflective in Terence came from the Greek, and received a fresh lease of life from the brevity and force of his translation.

The humour of Terence is essentially quiet. He has genial satire for extremes. The too strict brother, who propounds a system of precepts and a 'mirror of morality,' he parodies in the slave's culinary mirror — the bright saucepan to test kitchen-work. The too indulgent brother he ridicules by pushing his system to its utmost bounds. Terence's humour is the outcome of that Menandrian moderation which tempers his whole outlook. He would hold with his own cheerful Micio that life is a game,[2] and the bad in it must be mended with skill — not with passionate invective. If a character has to be laughed at, there is nothing ill-natured, just as there is nothing boisterous, in the laugh. So Ctesipho — the 'Joseph Surface' of Terence — who is content that his brother[3] should be suspected for his sake, is let off lightly. The Terentian humour is seen to advantage in the clever little scene in the *Phormio* designed to[4] satirise the advice of friends — those 'prophets of the past' as Byron calls them. And without possessing Plautus's humour, Terence has the saving grace of being able to jest at his own art. A mock realism of effect is introduced in the *Hecyra* by contrasting the life of his play with the tricks of the stage. 'No need for so much as a whisper,' says Pamphilus, who has the best of reasons for hiding from his father the manner of his getting a young lady's ring, 'we don't want this to happen exactly as in comedies, where everybody knows everything.'[5]

The prosody of Terence, though more 'regular' than that of Plautus, follows the same fundamental principles: that is, the accent of spoken Latin plays a dominant part in regulating scansion.[6] There is a marked decrease in the variety of metres. They are prevailingly iambic (senarian or septenarian) and trochaic (septenarian) to suit less or more animated dialogue. Lyric measures other than trochaic octonarians are rare. The musical accompaniments for the portions sung were provided by 'Flaccus, the slave of Claudius.' It is recorded that

[1] *E.g.*, 'Ne quid nimis,' *And.*, 61; 'nodum in scirpo quaeris,' *And.*, 941; 'aquilae senectus,' *Heaut.*, 521; 'inscitiast aduorsum stimulum calces,' *Phorm.*, 77; 'cantilenam eandem canis,' *Phorm.*, 495; 'auribus teneo lupum,' *Phorm.*, 506.

[2] *Adelph.*, 738, 'Ita uitast hominum quasi quom ludas tesseris.' Micio appends the words to his tranquil acceptance of circumstances which he cannot alter: 'Nunc quom non queo (*sc.* mutare) aequo animo fero.'

[3] *Ibid.*, 261, etc. [4] *Phorm.*, 445 *sqq.*

[5] *Hec.*, 866:

    'Placet non fieri hoc itidem ut in comoediis
    Omnia omnes ubi resciscunt.'

[6] In addition to works cited in connexion with Plautine prosody may be mentioned O. Brugman, *Quemadmodum in iamb. sen. Romani ueteres uerborum accentus cum numeris consociarint*, 1874; O. Podiaski, *Quomodo Terentius in tetr. iamb. et troch. uerborum accentus cum numeris consociauerit*, 1882; and authorities in Teuffel, *op. cit.*, § 111, 7.

four sorts of flutes, differing in length and key, were employed by him.[1]

A drama so consistently Hellenic in manners and style was too subtly artistic to hold the populace. With Terence comedy became aristocratic and gradually withdrew from the theatre.[2] His appeal was to the refinement of his day; and at all times he is best appreciated in the study. His classic purity was a potent influence on literature. It won not panegyrists only but imitators. Cicero is particularly fond of quoting Terence. Horace found in him much that was congenial, and borrowed his phrases freely.[3] To Quintilian he was 'elegantissimus,' and this very elegance made him appear insidiously dangerous in the eyes of those Fathers of the Church who denounced his world of lustful intrigue. Yet it was the nun Hrosvitha who imitated his plays in the tenth century; and in the sixteenth Schoon ('Schonaeus') of Gouda wrote his *Terentius Christianus*, six plays in Terentian style upon subjects drawn from Holy Writ, in which the pagan and the biblical are quaintly blended.[4] The influence of Terence was maintained by being studied and acted in the schools of the Middle Ages; it acted powerfully on Erasmus, Melanchthon, and scholars of their time. The influence was widened by translation into different vernaculars,[5] and from the Renaissance onwards, his plays, by example, contributed to inculcate, especially in France, a regard for the 'unities' of the drama. Indeed, it is in France, the home of the best modern prose and the best modern conversation, that Terence has since the seventeenth century gained his most sympathetic admirers, and most firmly fastened his hold upon literary taste.[6]

With Terence the *palliata* culminated and nearly ended. Its remaining authors, like Juventius and Valerius, are barely more than names; Vatronius barely a name. The one writer of account in this kind was Sextus Turpilius, who died at an advanced age in 103 B.C.[7] Menander's influence persists in him, and apparently suggested six of the thirteen titles known. It is hard to piece together the fragments into a connected story;[8] but there are signs of force and liveliness in him. Certainly his

---

[1] *Tibiae pares, impares, duae dextrae* (both treble), *Sarranae* ('Tyrian'); see the *didascaliae*.

[2] There was a revival of his plays on the stage in the first century B.C.

[3] For exx. see W. Y. Sellar, *Roman Poets of Rep.*, ed. 3, 1889, p. 218.

[4] They are *Naaman, Tobaeus, Nehemias, Saulus, Josephus, Juditha*. Improprieties are eschewed, morality is inculcated; but Jupiter and Juno are still referred to as real powers, and respectable characters swear by Pollux.

[5] The *Andria*, for example, received various English renderings in the fifteenth and sixteenth centuries.

[6] Sellar, *op. cit.*, p. 220, refers to the two 'Nouveaux Lundis' devoted by Sainte-Beuve to Terence. Sainte-Beuve regards Terence as the bond of union between Roman urbanity and the Atticism of the Greeks.

[7] 'Senex admodum Sinuessae moritur,' Hieron. *Euseb. Chron.*, ann. Abr. 1914. For fragments of Turpilius, Juventius, Valerius, see Ribbeck, *op. cit.* For Vatronius see Teuffel, *Hist. Rom. Lit.*, § 114.

[8] It is attempted for fragments of his *Epicleros* (*The Heiress*) and *Leucadia* by W. W. Merry, *Selected Fragts. of Rom. Poetry*, ed. 2, 1898, pp. 108 *sqq.*

burlesque of the story of Sappho in his *Lady of Leucas* (*Leucadia*) had great comic possibilities.

The few later imitations of Greek comedy were little other than literary exercises addressed to select circles.[1] Such *palliatae* as appeared on the stage of the later Republic or of the Empire were old plays revived. After Turpilius, comic dramatists had turned to new lines. Comedy had become too Hellenic for the people. The attempt was therefore made to engross their attention by the *fabula togata*, or comedy of Italian manners, where the scene was laid in Latin towns and the *pallium* was replaced by the *toga*. It was a more national and realistic drama, but certainly no more moral. Country folk, from a Roman point of view, could be made a perennial source of merriment. In the *togatae* it accorded with Roman feeling that slaves were not made wiser than their masters, as they were in the *palliatae*, and that women were more important. In this respect the very titles are suggestive — *The Lady Lawyer*, *The Stepmother*, *The Flute-Girl*, *The Woman of Ulubrae*. Could one such play have survived, it would have been a vastly instructive social document. The first composer of these national comedies was Titinius, who wrote after Terence's death and has bequeathed fifteen titles and less than two hundred lines. Less is left of T. Quintius Atta (d. 77 B.C.), the life of whose plays were prolonged by the fascinating acting of Roscius. Atta was reckoned singularly skilful in portraying female character.[2] The most celebrated master of the *togata* was L. Afranius (b. about 150 B.C.). His enthusiasm for Terence, whom he preferred to all comic writers, and his reputed share in the spirit of Menander[3] (his borrowings from whom he frankly avowed) led him to refine in some degree the *bourgeois* drama of Italian life. The typically Latin titles employed by these writers and the lively tone of the fragments indicate the popular nature of their appeal. Bickering between husband and wife, or between weavers and fullers — a class often made fun of in the *tabernariae* and in the later *Atellanae* of Novius and Pomponius — possessed much of the same rough force as marked the 'Flyting' match of early Scottish poetry. The spectator was no longer transported to Greece. In Titinius's *Setina* (*The Lady of Setia*) he had before him the sayings and doings of a secluded town on the Pomptine Marshes; in Atta's *Aquae Caldae* (*The Hot Springs*) he could watch the frequenters of a watering-place. He could see the Italian holiday-maker

---

[1] *E.g.* in imperial times Vergilius Romanus composed adaptations of the Old Greek Comedy; see Teuffel, *op. cit.*, § 15, 2, 3; § 332, 7.

[2] *Cf.* Fronto ad M. Caes., iv. 3, (Naber, p. 62): 'Partim scriptorum animaduertas particulatim elegantis, Nouium et Pomponium et id genus in uerbis rusticanis et iocularibus ac ridiculariis, Attam in muliebribus, Sisennam in lasciuis, Lucilium in cuiusque artis ac negotii propriis.'

[3] Suet., *Vit. Ter.*, 'Hunc (*sc.* Terentium) Afranius omnibus comicis praefert, scribens in *Compitalibus*: "Terenti numne similem dicent quempiam"'; Hor., *Ep.*, II. i. 57:

Dicitur Afrani toga conuenisse Menandro.'

in Atta's *Aedilicia* (*The Games the Aediles Gave*) or in Afranius's *Compitalia* (*The Feast of the Cross-roads*). The domestic, legal, political customs of his own land were the keynote of *The Divorce, The Letter, The Freed Slave, the Sisters, The Maiden, The Defeated Candidate, The Twin that Lived* (*Vopiscus*), and in fact of the majority of over forty plays by Afranius. In 57 B.C. his *Simulans* (*The Dissembler*) gave rise to a political demonstration, when its emphatic words:

> *Haec, taeterrime,*
> *Sunt postprincipia atque exitus malae uitiosae uitae*

turned the eyes of everybody upon Clodius and drove him from the theatre. Even in the days of the Empire his pieces held their place on the stage.

A slight deviation from the *togata* served to develop the *fabula tabernaria*—the comedy of tradesfolk and their ways. The next novelty in comedy belongs to the time of Sulla and Cicero's youth. This was the artificial *fabula Atellana*—the literary handling of the ancient Oscan farce by Pomponius of Bononia and by Novius.[1] Seventy titles by the former and some forty by the latter prove the vitality of the development. But total salvage of three hundred lines furnishes a scanty notion of the plots. Keeping the stereotyped personages, Maccus, Pappus, Bucco, and Dossennus,[2] the Atellan farce now passed out of the hands of amateurs into those of comedians. Improvisation was replaced by composition and rehearsal, and prose by verse.[3] Better literary form was secured by employing many of the artifices of regular comedy. At the same time, plot, we may be sure, was secondary to fun. Humble life supplied the commonest butts for the mockery of a Latin which was striking in its vigour and rustic homeliness. Rural associations cling to Novius's *Farmer* and *Neatherd*, and to Pomponius's *She-ass, Miller, Slave-Barracks, Fortune Teller* or *Village Barber*. Pomponius's range was wide. Not only did he write *The Campanians* and *The Gauls Beyond the Alps*, but in his *Armorum Iudicium* he burlesqued the story of Ajax, which had been seriously treated by Pacuvius and Accius. These farces of an improved type, partly helped by the Italian movement for the franchise, tickled Roman audiences with their jests and indecencies for a generation; and some of them were resuscitated in the imperial age.

[1] Jerome's date for Pomponius's fame ('clarus habetur') corresponds to 89 B.C. Novius is often mentioned before Pomponius as if a predecessor; but Velleius regards Pomponius as an originator (Vell., II. ix), 'Pomponium, sensibus celebrem, uerbis rudem, et nouitate inuenti a se operis commendabilem.' For the fragments, see Ribbeck (*op. cit.*).

[2] How the changes are rung on the old themes is seen from Novius's titles, *Maccus as Mine Host, Maccus Banished, A Pair of Dossenni*, and Pomponius's *The Twin Macci, Maccus as a Young Lady, Maccus as Soldier, Pappus Turned Farmer*. Both produced a play on *Pappus at the Bottom of the Poll* (*Pappus Praeteritus*).

[3] H. J. G. Patin, *Études sur la poésie latine*, ed. 4, 1900, ii. p. 333.

G

In the next period it was the turn of the *Atellana* to yield to the *Mimus*, which even before the time of Pomponius had been an attraction, especially as an after-play (*exodium*). The mime ($\mu\hat{\iota}\mu os$) was of Greek origin, and was imported into Rome from the cities of the South. When managed with the admirable realism of a Herodas its literary effect was irresistible. But now in Rome, supplanting the higher drama, making a parade of filth and immorality, and inaugurating the performance of female parts by women, the mimes pandered to the vilest proclivities. With much less to recommend them than the gladiatorial shows, they deserved the scathing references of Ovid to their unsavoury jokes and to their continual introduction of a foppish paramour whose disreputable fooling of a husband won the applause of apparently respectable people.[1] The stock characters of the mime were the doltish cuckold, the frail wife, and the *soubrette*, whose wearing of a short mantilla (*ricinium*) led to the classification of the mime as *fabula riciniata*. The mime had a reputable side, which we shall find represented in the time of Caesar by the more serious lines of Laberius and those reflective maxims common to all stages of Roman Comedy and grouped together as the *Sententiae* of Publilius Syrus.[2] Outspoken in so many ways, the mime admitted an undercurrent of political satire. But it contained one fatal element. Lively gesticulation came to play such an increasing part that it eventually suppressed words altogether. The mime turned into *pantomimus* or dumb-show, which is not within the purview of literature. Such was the end of Roman Comedy.

[1] Ovid, *Trist.*, ii. 497 *sqq.*:
   'Quid si scripsissem mimos obscena iocantes,' etc.
[2] For names of other writers of *mimi*, see Teuffel, § 8.

Chapter V

ROMAN TRAGEDY AFTER ENNIUS

Pacuvius – Eccentricities and virtues of style – Accius – Heroism of
spirit and other dramatic qualities – Chorus in Roman Tragedy –
Tragic metres – Tragedies and *praetextae* in relation to the Roman
mind – The passing of tragedy.

M. PACUVIUS (*c.* 220–*c.* 130 B.C.) was the nephew,[1] and in
tragedy the pupil, of Ennius. Born at Brundisium, he
migrated to Rome and was admitted into the circle of
Laelius. Like a Michael Angelo or a Rossetti, he united the gifts of
poetry and painting. His long life almost completes a link between
Ennius and Cicero; for Pacuvius was on friendly terms with his tragic
successor, Accius, whom Cicero could remember meeting. When
Pacuvius was eighty, and Accius thirty, the same aediles secured plays
from both of them.[2] Later, when Pacuvius had retired to Tarentum,
Accius spent a few days with him and read his *Atreus* aloud by request.
Pacuvius criticised it as 'sonorous and elevated, but a trifle harsh and
crude.'[3] The younger poet took the criticism admirably: 'You are right;
and I don't object. . . . It is with genius as with fruits—the harsh and
crude have the promise of mellowing.' Pacuvius is now represented by
over four hundred lines and by the titles of twelve tragedies and of
one *praetexta*. His *saturae* are lost. His single *praetexta*, *Paulus*, was
more likely concerned with the victory of Pydna in 168 B.C. than
with the victim of Cannae.

His debt to Greek originals, on the score of suggestion, is evident
from such titles as *Antiopa* (from Euripides), *Armorum Iudicium* (on
Ajax), *Atalanta*, *Chryses*, *Dulorestes*, *Hermiona*, *Pentheus*, and *Niptra*
(from Sophocles). Doubtless it is his Hellenism to which Horace alludes
in his epithet 'doctus.' Yet his adaptations of plot may have been as free
as his style, which was characterised by a vigorous originality verging
on the eccentric. His awkward pomposities, obscure intricacies, and
ornamental flourishes merited the sneers of Lucilius. His passion for

---

[1] Plin., *N.H.*, XXXV. 19., 'Ennii sorore genitus.' Jerome says wrongly,
'Ennii poetae ex filia nepos' (ad ann. Abr. 1863). Both record his painting.
[2] Cic., *Brut.*, lxiv. 229.
[3] Gell., *N.A.*, XIII. ii, 'sonora . . . et grandia, sed . . . duriora paulum
et acerbiora.'

strange compounds[1] created a diction so full of excrescences that Persius appropriately jested at his 'warty *Antiopa*, her dolorific heart pressed by tribulation.'[2] In the manner of his uncle, Pacuvius puts into the mouths of some of his characters philosophical and even rationalist sentiments, as in his well-known passages on fortune and on soothsayers. Certainly one sees the Roman in the didactic and oratorical ring of several of the fragments, such as

> *Conqueri fortunam aduersam, non lamentari decet:*
> *Id uiri est officium; fletus muliebri ingenio additus.*

It is, too, with some national pride that Cicero[3] praises Pacuvius because his Ulysses in the *Niptra* shows more fortitude under bodily pain than the hero does in Sophocles. A directness and universality in his reflections kept Pacuvius long on the stage. The readiness of an audience to apply his words to contemporary politics may be illustrated by the indignation aroused against the murderers of Caesar when they heard the complaints of Ajax against ingratitude:

> *Men' seruasse ut essent qui me perderent.*[4]

High testimony is borne to his dramatic power by Cicero's explicit description of the feeling which some of his lines demanded from the actor—'his eyes, it seemed to me, glowed out of the mask.'[5] Such lines, he argues, were never composed in a tranquil and phlegmatic mood. To this power of passion and pathos Pacuvius added a power of character-drawing of which the contrast between the blunt Zethus and the contemplative Amphion in the *Antiopa* is a salient example. Such qualities serve to explain the tendency of the Ciceronian age to see in Pacuvius Rome's greatest tragic poet.[6] What impressed Varro[7] was his *ubertas*, a luxuriance, that is to say, likely to involve faults like inflation, and perfectly compatible with shaky Latinity. Cicero seems to note in him a southern provincialism to match the northern provincialism of

---

[1] *E.g.*, 'flexanima,' 'tardigrada,' and the extreme example describing dolphins:
> 'Nerei repandirostrum incuruiceruicum pecus':

Cf. Martial's epigram (XI. xc) addressed to Chrestillus as an insatiate lover of rough old poetry:
> 'Attonitusque legis *terraï frugiferaï*
> Accius et quicquid Pacuuiusque uomunt.'

[2] Pers., i. 77:
> 'Sunt quos Pacuuiusque et uerrucosa moretur
> *Antiopa* aerumnis cor luctificabile fulta.'

[3] *Tusc. Disp.*, II. xxi.

[4] Suet., *Iul.*, 84.

[5] Cic., *De Orat.*, II. xlvi., 'cum ex persona mihi ardere oculi hominis histrionis uiderentur . . . . Quid? Pacuuium putatis in scribendo leni animo ac remisso fuisse?'

[6] Cic., *De Opt. Gen. Or.*, i., 'Itaque licet dicere et Ennium summum epicum poetam et Pacuuium tragicum et Caecilium fortasse comicum.' Velleius, I. xvii., gives Accius the highest place in tragedy.

[7] Cited Gell., *N.A.*, VI. xiv. 6.

Caecilius.[1] At the same time, to Cicero we owe the preservation of the best example of Pacuvius's eye for the angrier aspects of nature when he describes in graphic trochaics, helped by alliteration and assonance, the start for Troy in a storm:

> Happy when their fleet left harbour, they could watch the fish at play,
> They were never weary watching, though they watched the live-long day.
> Meanwhile when it turned to sundown, rough and rougher grew the main,
> Darkness doubled, blinding blackness came with night and clouds of rain,
> Flame flashed out athwart the welkin, thunder made the heavens rock,
> Hail, with plenteous sleet commingled, sudden fell with headlong shock.
> Everywhere the gales broke prison, cruel whirling winds arose,
> And the ocean boiled in fury. . . .[2]

Quintilian regards Pacuvius and his junior Accius as the greatest of the ancient authors of tragedy for dignity of thought, force of language, and impressiveness of characters (*grauitate sententiarum, uerborum pondere, auctoritate personarum*). The lack of elegance (*nitor*) and of finish (*summa manus*) in their works he refers rather to their age than to themselves. Accius, he says, is credited with greater force; Pacuvius with greater learning.[3]

L. Accius[4] (170 B.C.–*c.* 86 B.C.) was born at Pisaurum, on the Keltic side of Umbria. Like Horace, he was of 'libertine' descent. We know of his friendly relations with Pacuvius, and of the patronage extended to him by D. Brutus.[5] When he read his *Atreus* to Pacuvius at Tarentum, Accius was starting for one of those tours in Greece which became so fashionable for Roman authors. Cicero had opportunities of conversing with him on literary topics.[6] To amplify ancient criticism on him, we have some 45 titles—more than from any other tragic writer—and 700 lines. In breadth of interest he recalls Ennius. Besides his tragic plays based on Greek legend, he dramatised in *praetextae* two chapters of

---

[1] *Brut.*, lxxiv. 258, 'Caecilium et Pacuuium male locutos uidemus.'
[2] 'Sic profectione laeti piscium lasciuiam
    Intuentur, nec tuendi capere satietas potest.
    Interea prope iam occidente sole inhorrescit mare,
    Tenebrae conduplicantur, noctisque et nimbum obcaecat nigror,
    Flamma inter nubes coruscat, caelum tonitru contremit,
    Grando mixta imbri largifico subita praecipitans cadit,
    Undique omnes uenti erumpunt, saeui exsistunt turbines,
    Feruit aestu pelagus.'
[3] Quint., X. i. 97, 'doctiorem,' like Horace's 'doctus' (*Ep.*, II. i. 56), must apply to his acquaintance with Greek literature.
[4] MSS. give the dialectic variant Attius less frequently.
[5] Cic., *Arch.*, 27; *Brut.*, 107. D. Brutus Callaicus (*cos.* 138) is meant.
[6] *Brut.*, xxviii. 107.

national history, the self-devotion of Decius Mus in *Decius* or *Aeneadae*, and the overthrow of the kingly dynasty in *Brutus*. From the latter came the line which Cicero proudly declares was applied by the audience to himself and repeatedly encored amid rounds of applause:

Tullius qui libertatem ciuibus stabiliuerat.[1]

Only unsatisfying morsels remain of his *Didascalica*, a sketch of Greek and Roman poetry, in prose and in verses mainly sotadean. The work was on the lines of Aristotle's διδασκαλίαι. Literature was also treated in the trochaic tetrameters of his *Pragmatica*, agriculture in his *Praxidica* (a title to be identified with Persephone), and history after the epic manner of Ennius in his *Annales*. Accius took a scholarly interest in questions of language. On Greek analogy he advocated the spelling 'aggulus' instead of 'angulus.' To indicate long quantity in the vowels *a*, *e*, *u*, he introduced the habit of doubling them—*e.g.*, 'paastor.' But his real greatness was dramatic. Among his prominent plays were *Andromeda*; *Armorum Iudicium*, an independent handling of the legend used by Pacuvius and burlesqued by Pomponius; *Atreus*, containing the sinister words dear to the heart of Caligula, 'oderint dum metuant'; *Eriphyla*, in which Alcmaeon is a sort of ancient Hamlet with a mission of vengeance specially directed against his mother; *Medea* or *Argonautae*, famous for a vivid description of the gigantic Argo; *Meleager*, where the mother's remorse gave scope for pathos; and *Philoctetes*, which seems to have laid under contribution all the three great tragic poets of Greece.

There is much in the fragments to explain the high regard in which Accius was held, and to merit Horace's epithet 'altus' and Ovid's 'animosus.' There is a lofty dignity of style which is the counterpart of the poet's firm outlook upon life. There is insight into sorrow, and the faculty of stirring pity with which all great tragedy is endowed, but there is no surrender to weakness. Again and again comes insistence on the sovereignty of moral courage and the grandeur of triumph over vicissitude. This heroism of the spirit defiant of fate animates the prayer of Ajax for his son which Accius borrowed from Sophocles:

In worth match thou thy sire, outmatch his luck,[2]

and which in turn made one of Virgil's borrowings from Accius. Similar strength pervades such utterances as

---

[1] *Pro Sest.*, lviii. 123, 'Nominatim sum appellatus in *Bruto* . . . Millies revocatum est.'

[2] 'Virtuti sis par, dispar fortunis patris': from Soph. *Ajax*, 551–2. *Cf.* Virgil, *Aen.*, xii. 435–436:

'Disce, puer, uirtutem ex me uerumque laborem,
Fortunam ex aliis.'

For Virgil's refinements on Accius, see Macrob., *Sat.*, VI. i. 58.

> If fortune hath availed to steal my crown
> And wealth, she cannot steal my honesty,[1]

and

> He stirs compassion most whose nobleness
> Ennobles misery.[2]

Forcible delineation of passion appears in the lines:

> Tereus with untamed mood and ruthless heart
> Looked on her, frenzied with his flaming lust —
> A desperate man: then of his madness shapes
> A deed most foul.[3]

The excellence of the speeches in his dramas made Accius a model for speakers. His vogue was over by the time of Tacitus; for the *Dialogus* expects from orators a 'poetical grace, not disfigured with the mouldiness of Accius or Pacuvius, but issuing from the shrine of Horace, Virgil, and Lucan.'[4] So striking were the dramatic repartees of Accius that he was once asked why he did not take up court-practice. His reply was that in his tragedies he could say what he liked; at the bar his opponents would say what he did not like at all. On another side of his genius he is almost a pioneer. He is one of the first Roman authors to have glimpses of the poetry of farm-life and the beauty of the country:

> Mayhap ere Dawn, that heralds blazing beams,
> When yokels drive the new-waked ox afield,
> To cleave with plough the red dew-sprinkled soil,
> And from the yielding tilth to turn the clods.[5]

The lyrics sung by the sailors accompanying Ulysses to Lemnos in Accius's *Philoctetes* are suggestive of the position of the chorus in Roman tragedy.[6] The determining factor is its appearance on the stage, and not in the orchestra as in Greek tragedy. This necessitated a change from its ideal Greek attitude between the spectators and the actively engaged personages. In the earlier Roman tragedy the chorus could come and go, as the Greek chorus seldom did. This lent a reality to its activity. So it might sing a hymn at a religious festival which was being represented, as in Naevius's *Lycurgus* or Pacuvius's *Antiopa*; it

---

[1] 'Nam si a me regnum fortuna atque opes
  Eripere quiuit, at uirtutem non quit.'
[2] 'Nam huius demum miseret, cuius nobilitas miserias
  Nobilitat.'
[3] 'Tereus indomito more atque animo barbaro
  Conspexit in eam amore uecors flammeo
  Depositus: facinus pessimum ex dementia
  Confingit.'
[4] *Dial. de Orat.*, xx.
[5] 'Forte ante Auroram, radiorum ardentum indicem,
  Cum e somno in segetem agrestes cornutos cient,
  Ut rorulentas terras ferro rufulas
  Proscindant, glebasque aruo ex molli exsuscitent.'
[6] Otto Jahn in *Hermes*, 1867, ii. 227–229.

might take part in the dialogue, as the fragments of Ennius, Pacuvius and Accius prove; or it might contribute to realistic effect, as when, in Pacuvius's *Niptra*, the chorus carries in the wounded Ulysses. This intervention at suitable moments in the action distinguishes the earlier chorus from the usage of the later literary tragedy, where the inserted lyrics imply the disappearance of the chorus. They are, in fact, lineally descended from the independent songs (*embolima*), which since the time of Agathon and Euripides had aimed more at entertaining the public between acts than at welding the drama into an artistic whole.

As to tragic metres in general, for dialogue, almost without exception, the iambic trimeter was used: occasionally, to convey notions of display, rejoicing, or rapidity, the trochaic tetrameter catalectic. The *cantica*, sung to the *tibia*, do not attempt to follow the variety and richness of the Greek plays. Anapaests and cretics prevail, varied by tetrameters, iambic and trochaic, and by dactylic lines. Later, for their songs, Pollio, Varius, and their fellows imported fresh measures from Greece. Seneca and Pomponius Secundus borrowed freely from Horace's *Odes*. After Augustus, all the tragic poets make use of anapaestic monometers unlinked by synapheia.

To apportion the greatness of Ennius, Pacuvius, and Accius in tragedy is a problem insoluble, owing to the scanty remains and the conflict among the literary judgements of antiquity. If the three furnish some eighty titles, their tragic fragments together do not much exceed the bulk of a single play. But two facts in the history of tragedy are significant. One is the persistence of the serious drama on the stage despite a popular preference for lighter performances.[1] Beyond question, comedy, satire, and epic were more in accord with the national genius. Yet tragedy lived on, encouraged chiefly by the Roman aristocracy. They found something congenial to the existing order of things in such political thought as tragedy admitted—for the Greek 'tyrannophobia' was shared by the optimates of Rome. They could draw from its grave rhetoric hints for the practical needs of public speaking. Hence it was only with the establishment of empire and the eclipse of the old families and of the old freedom of speech that tragic composition faded into a mere literary exercise. The other fact is the comparative rarity of *praetextae*. We know for certain some ten titles of historical plays after Naevius set the example followed by Ennius, Pacuvius and Accius. Cornelius Balbus wrote a play on Caesar's doings in 49 B.C. Persius as a boy wrote a *praetexta*. The feelings of the imperial age prompted a choice of heroes from the close of republican history, as in the *Cato* and *Domitius* of Curiatius Maternus. This, however, does not hold good of the Flavian *Octavia*, the one *praetexta* preserved, or of the

---

[1] *E.g.*, post-Plautine prol. to *Amph.*, 52:
  ' Quid? contraxistis frontem quia tragoediam
  Dixi futuram hanc? Deu' sum – commutauero.'

Aeneas of Pomponius Secundus in Claudius's time, if indeed it was not more saga than play. Certainly, material was abundant: and there is evidence[1] that historical plays of which there is now no vestige must have occupied the Roman stage. But the total effect was small. Dramatists probably felt, as Horace did, that the Greek myths offered more opportunity for character-drawing than did actual scenes from Roman annals. The result was not unimportant for culture in Rome.[2] Society continued to have held up before it the ideal sorrows of Greek legend. True, they are often imbedded in a Roman didacticism; and thanks to this craving for a direct application to life, the ethereal essence of Greek tragedy has evaporated. The wrestling with mysteries of existence and destiny was too intangible for the Roman mind. Consequently the typically Hellenic dramatists, Aeschylus and Sophocles, are not so much followed as the more cosmopolitan dramatists of the stamp of Euripides. There is a loss of the Hellenic curiosity and romance, but a closer approach to everyday experience.

After Accius there is no name[3] so great in the history of Roman tragedy. His influence was traceable in the tragedies of the orator C. Titius, who, according to Cicero,[4] belonged to about the same period as the orators of his boyhood, Antonius and Crassus. Little more can be done beyond recording the names of Atilius, C. Julius Caesar Strabo, Cassius of Parma, and Santra (not the grammarian). In Cicero's time the acting of Aesopus contributed to a revival of older tragedies, notably those of Pacuvius and Accius. This revival nearly coincided with a fresh return upon the strictly classical Greek dramas as models, resulting for the most part in the composition of book-dramas. The four tragedies written by Q. Cicero in sixteen days can hardly have been anything but literary exercises. On the new dramatic school of the early imperial period Horace's *Ars Poetica* directly bears as a collection of hints for aspirants after dramatic fame. Of Asinius Pollio's work,[5] of

---

[1] *E.g.*, Plaut., *Amph.*, prol. 41 (reference to appearance of 'Virtus,' 'Victoria,' 'Bellona,' in plays); Cic., *ad Fam.*, VII. i. 2; Hor., *Ep.*, II. i. 189–193.

[2] The theatre contributed in some degree to a diffusion of taste and to a feeling for correct Latin. Cicero, *Orat.*, li. 173, testifies to the sensitiveness of an audience regarding pronunciation ('in uersu quidem theatra tota exclamant si fuit una syllaba aut breuior aut longior'). 'They don't understand metrical feet,' he continues, 'but they do know right and wrong by ear.'

[3] For lists of Roman tragedies see Ribbeck, *Trag. Rom. Fragm.*, ed. 3, 1897. The names of about 36 tragic poets are known, and of about 150 tragedies. Roman tragedy with Greek subject matter is termed *crepidata* sc. *fabula* (from *crepida*, κρηπίς, denoting the *cothurnus* or buskin worn by the tragic actor). Lydus, *De Mag.*, I. xl., in this sense distinguishes κρηπιδᾶτα from πραιτεξτᾶτα.

[4] Teuffel, § 141, 7.

[5] Pollio followed the principles of the new poetic school, to judge from Hor., *Sat.*, I. x. 42–43, where he is mentioned with Fundanius, Varius, and Virgil. L. Müller is right in dismissing as an exaggeration the allusion in Tac., *Dial. de Orat.*, xxi, to Pollio as copying the old style of Pacuvius and Accius. Pollio probably contented himself with borrowing a few archaisms from republican tragedy.

Varius's *Thyestes* and Ovid's *Medea* the traces are too few to admit of profitable study. It is possible, as Ribbeck has suggested, that older tragedies like Livius's *Ino* and Ennius's *Athamas* may have been modernised in the first century A.D. What has definitely survived from that century is the group of Seneca's plays in which the stream of Greek tragedy is frozen.

Chapter VI

THE SATIRES OF LUCILIUS AND
MINOR POETRY

C. Lucilius – Life – Relation to his times – The fragments of the
thirty books – Their chronology – Political aspects of his *farrago* –
The personal note and social interest combined – Likeness and
unlikeness to Horace – Crusade against evil – Attitude to philosophy – His interest in literature and language – Influence on
later writers – Horace's criticisms on Lucilius – Horace's debt to
Lucilius – Satire continued by two Varros.
Minor poetry – Ennian tradition in Epic – Didactic verse before
Lucretius – Elegiacs after Ennius – Laevius and Alexandrinism.

THE importance of C. Lucilius (*c.* 180–103 B.C.) is great. He
gave the ancient *satura* its true popular turn and its sting.
He vividly reflected his times. He was a strong individuality.
He was highly admired by many later writers. He had a deep influence
on Horace.

Jerome's date for his birth corresponds to 148 B.C. This is incredible.
Lucilius could not have served as an *eques* in the Numantine War at the
age of fourteen, and Velleius records his service under Scipio.[1] And if
born in 148, he would not have been an old man when he wrote his
satires, as Horace implies he was.[2] The best solution is that Jerome
confused the consuls of 148 with the similarly named consuls of 180
B.C.[3] Lucilius was a native of Suessa Aurunca in Campania. He came of
a family of wealth and standing. At Rome he had the *entrée* into the
circle consisting of the younger Africanus, Laelius and other nobles,
who had befriended Terence and fostered Greek tastes. He settled in
the house built for the hostage-son of Antiochus the Great.[4] Not being
a Roman citizen, Lucilius had no distractions in public life; indeed, in
126 B.C. he had temporarily to quit Rome as a *peregrinus*. But if he took
no actual part in politics, he was in close touch with those who did.

[1] Vell., II. ix.
[2] *Sat.*, II. i. 34.
[3] F. Marx agrees, *C. Lucili Carm. Reliq.*, vol. i, 1904, *Proleg.* p. xxiii.
Jerome, consistently with his error as to the birth, noted his death 'anno
aetatis xlvi.' Munro's suggestion (*Jrnl. Philol.*, vol. viii, 16) that this is a
blunder for 'lxvi' would refer his birth to 168 B.C. This is approved by Sellar,
op. cit., pp. 229–232, and by Wilkins, *Prim. Rom. Lit.*, but is not so satisfactory
an explanation. Marx concludes that he died in 102 or 101 B.C.
[4] Ascon. p. 12, 9 (in Cic., *Pison.* 54); *cf.* Marx, *op. cit.*, *Proleg.* p. xxiv.

About five years junior to his friend Scipio Aemilianus, he remained an interested spectator of the life of the Romans. He was among them 'taking notes.' This gave his work its bearing on social conditions.

His relation to his times indicates the changes setting in. Ennius in his epic had expressed the feelings of the generation which had conquered Carthage and could be content with wedding Greek forms to the national record. Lucilius is permeated with the new ideas of the Gracchan age. Social and political discontent begot criticism of private and public life. Though learned in Greek thought and fond of introducing Greek tags, Lucilius did not go to Greek literature for his materials. He had the life of the capital to draw from. The moderately progressive party of the day saw plentiful reason for dissatisfaction with the luxury and venality of the nobles, their failure to govern properly, their preference of self to state. The unrest finds voice in Lucilius. He is a social critic—frequently a very sharp one.[1]

His thirty books of satire are represented by over 1,300 lines of fragments. For their preservation we are indebted to Nonius mainly. A very few extracts consist of eight or ten lines; most are single lines quoted for some peculiarity, and many of them, what with gaps, miscopying and lack of context, are now 'irrecoverably dark.' Adhesion to the text of the almost irremediably corrupt fragments on the one hand, and emendation without the guidance of context on the other, are equally insecure foundations for a full estimate of Lucilius's meaning and power as an author. Modern attempts to serve the texts and its interpretation[2] are the best proofs of flaws in the wording as well as in our understanding of the fragments, which, humanly speaking, could be made good only by some such stroke of luck as the recovery of a roll of the satires from Herculaneum.

The thirty books fall into three groups: i–xxi, in hexameters; xxii–xxv, in elegiac metre apparently; xxvi–xxx, in varying metres— trochaic septenarii, iambic senarii, and in the last book hexameters again. Internal evidence proves that the numbering does not represent the order of publication.[3] The last five books were the fruits of experi-

---

[1] For sketch of 'La Satire et Lucilius,' see Lamarre, *Hist. d. l. litt. lat.*, vol. ii, chap. x; *cf.* Sellar, *op. cit.*, pp. 222–252.

[2] Text: *C. Lucili Satur. Reliq.*, em. et adnot., L. Müller (acc. Acci et Suei carm. reliq.), 1872; Bährens, *F.P.R.*, 1886, pp. 139–266; *C. Lucilii Carm. Reliq.* F. Marx, vol. i (*Proleg., Carm. Reliq.* etc.), 1904, vol. ii. (*Commentarius*), 1905. Müller is especially useful in his account of Nonius and other authors to whom the rescue of the fragments is due. Marx, in his *Prolegomena* to his first vol. and the learned exegetical commentary of his second, has done most for Lucilius. But owing to his failure to resist the temptation to invent imaginary situations as settings for certain fragments, he is not to be implicitly trusted in his emendations or his explanations. Some of his merits are acknowledged by W. M. Lindsay, reviewing vol. i, *Cl. Rev.*, xix., 271; they are less evident among the strictures of A. E. Housman, 'Luciliana' in *Class. Quarterly*, vol. i, 1907.

[3] It is one of Marx's plausible suggestions that in view of the family connexion between Lucilius and Pompey the Great – Pompey was the son of Lucilius's niece – and in view of interest felt by scholars of the Pompeian circle

mental years of authorship; and the earliest in composition was book xxvi, so that the satirist first tried trochaics, then iambics, and hexameters. Finding the hexameters of book xxx most to his liking, Lucilius retained them in books i–xxi, and thereby made them the regular form for *satura*, to be followed by Horace, Persius, and Juvenal. Unity of idea is not to be looked for in the separate books, any more than in Horace's *Satires*. The *satura* itself, as well as Lucilius's genius, favoured discursive writing. Consistently devoted to his old commander, he found a cue in everyone and everything which ran counter to the Scipionic circle. Lucilius's early attacks on matrimony[1] gain point from the aims of Scipio's rival, Metellus Macedonicus, to encourage marriage when censor in 131 B.C. When Metellus made Lupus 'princeps senatus,' here was another object for invective and another source of merriment for Scipio and Laelius.[2] Political bias also stirred his animosity against Mucius Scaevola,[3] Hostilius Tubulus, the corrupt judge, and Papirius Carbo, the supporter of Tiberius Gracchus, suspected of murdering Scipio. Yet his writings, even during Scipio's life, are not all, in the narrow sense, political. For all their bias, one cannot deny them public spirit, and much is frankly miscellaneous. If there are hits at Metellus in remarks on women, and flattering allusions to Scipio in the echoes of past campaigns

> *Percrepa pugnam Popili, facta Corneli cane,*

there are also introductory comments on his own new racy and chatty style of verse, written not for your savants but for the 'general reader'

> *Nec doctissumis; nam Gaium*
> *Persium haec legere nolo, Iunium Congum uolo,*[4]

and to entertain this average man there are plain thoughts on human life, its brevity and drawbacks, the follies of one's fellows, and the eccentricities of philosophy. The death of Lupus opened the way for book i, which imagines the gods convened to discuss his demise.

---

in his satires, the present unchronological order may be the work of Valerius Cato. His edition would follow the usages of his time, which was to arrange hexameters before elegiacs, and both before iambic or other metres. Horace in the *Ars Poet.* and Quintilian treat metres in this order.

[1] 'Homines ipsi hanc sibi molestiam ultro atque aerumnam offerunt,
    Ducunt uxores, producunt, quibus haec faciant, liberos.'
[2] Hor., *Sat.*, II. i. 67:
> 'laeso doluere Metello
> Famosisque Lupo cooperto uersibus.'
[3] Pers., i. 115:
> 'Secuit Lucilius urbem
> Te Lupe, te Muci, et genuinum fregit in illis.'
The prosecution of Scaevola by Albucius for 'repetundae' was dealt with in Bk. ii by Lucilius.
[4] So Bährens. Marx edits:
> 'Nec doctissimis <*nec scribo indoctis nimis*>. Man<*il*>ium
> Persium <*ue*> haec legere nolo, Iunium Congum uolo.'

Thenceforth the series of hexameter satires was issued from time to time like a caustic periodical, universal in its range, and discovering food for comment in public life and private oddities, personal adventures and national exploits, and in ethics, religion, literature, and grammar. To judge from the meagre remains of the elegiac books,[1] they appear to have been epitaphs and epigrams concerned with Lucilius's slaves.

The true conglomerate nature of the *satura* survives in Lucilius. His metres vary; so do the forms which his thought assumes. Monologue, dialogue, direct homily and epistle to the reader, tirade on vice, report of another's discourse, personal reminiscences of travel, storm, fight, country merrymaking, constitute an astonishing *farrago*. Anecdotes, quotations, jests, and parodies enliven the miscellany. We have observed that his attacks were not always dispassionate attempts at reform. But if political bias made Scipio's enemies of necessity his, and so partly shaped his views for him, yet Lucilius was in most respects an independent voice. The bulk of his political satire was doubtless sincere. He was justified in lashing the unpunished blunders and crimes of the aristocracy and the incompetence of commanders like Mancinus, Manilius, and Popilius Laenas. In his outspokenness he so recalled the Old Attic Comedy that Horace's mistake[2] in calling him an imitator of Eupolis, Cratinus, and Aristophanes is half excusable.

In another way, Lucilius recalls the Old Attic Comedy. As the dramatist in the *parabasis* addressed the spectator directly, Lucilius established familiar relations with his reader. Author, reader, and society were linked together in an unprecedented manner. The autobiographic touches combining the personal and the social proved particularly attractive to Horace, who revealed himself more in his satires and epistles than in his odes. Here was the first author who unlocked his heart with the key of the *satura*. He confided his inmost secrets to his books, as Horace says (*Sat. II.* i. 32–4).

> *Quo fit ut omnis*
> *Votiua pateat ueluti descripta tabella*
> *Vita senis.*

Many of his characteristics resemble Horace's, and may have specially commended him to Horace. There is in him a Horatian independence, preference for leisure, and dislike of regular employment.[3] We see, too, a Horatian commonsense in his attitude to life.[4]

---

[1] No fragment can with certainty be referred to bk. xxiv. The book closing the hexameter series (xxi) is also unrepresented. This does not prove Marx's argument from the silence of grammarians that the book had disappeared from a supposed unique copy before the time of Nonius, any more than the absence of quotation in Varro's *De Ling. Lat.* proves that the *Vidularia* of Plautus had been already lost by Varro's time.   [2] *Sat.*, I. iv, *ad init.*

[3]   'Publicanu' uero ut Asiae fiam scripturarius
      Pro Lucilio, id ego nolo, et uno hoc non muto omnia.'

[4]   'Cum sciam nihil esse in uita proprium mortali datum,
      Iam qua tempestate uiuo χρῆσιν ad me recipio.'

There are, again as in Horace, frank self-revelations, and chatty impressions of his own experiences or his friend's, such as Scipio's mission to the courts of Egypt and Asia, or his own journey to Capua and the Sicilian straits, which Horace took for his model when he related his trip to Brundisium.[1] On the other hand, Lucilius contrasts with Horace as an artist; he is greatly inferior to Horace in workmanship, and, indeed, because he has so little poetry in him, he is inferior to Ennius, Plautus, and Terence. Nor has he Horace's easygoing toleration for the objects of his satire. There is already present more than the germ of Juvenal's fierce indignation. So if Horace, like Chaucer, laughs genially at peccant humanity in its foibles, Lucilius, with the engaging variety and open confidences of a Montaigne, rather anticipates the vehemence of Langland.

Associating with prominent public men and thinkers,[2] sharply observant, too, of his fellows, he honestly felt the value of morality and straight dealing for the state. In a panoply of keen sense and cutting invective he conducted a crusade against evil. Juvenal pictures the drawn sword of his attack, and the blush of his conscience-stricken victim, whose very heart-strings sweat with secret guilt.[3] Under this exaggeration can be recognised the force of Lucilius as a critic of social life. Preserved with anything like completeness, he would have been as useful an index to his times as Horace was to his a century later. Banquets, quarrels of gladiators, the sham grief of hired mourners, gluttons, spendthrifts, and misers fall under his whip. He fixed the names of certain objectionable characters destined to reappear, as if types, in Horace—Nomentanus, Maenius, and 'Pantolabus' ('Grab-all'). Among his vividly satiric sketches are the miser inseparable from his money-bag (*cum bulga cenat, dormit, lauat*), and that whirlpool of gluttony, Gallonius, who never dined well though he could spend a fortune on a huge sturgeon. His censure, too, is pronounced upon all in Rome, of high or low degree (*populusque patresque*), for their eagerness from morning to night, holiday and workday (*festo atque profesto*), to devote themselves to chicanery and underhand dealing in the struggle of life (*pugnare dolose*); and for their desire by polite flatteries and by assuming a virtue even if one had it not (*bonum simulare uirum se*) to entrap fellow-citizens as if they were enemies.

On the theoretical side, his philosophy is sometimes serious, sometimes humorous. He can indulge in a wordy and rambling description

---

[1] Hor., *Sat.*, I. v.
[2] Besides Scipio and Laelius, he had among his friends Albinus, Granius, Aelius Stilo, to whom he dedicated Book i, and the philosopher Clitomachus, who dedicated a book to him (Cic., *Acad.*, II. xxxii. 102).
[3] Juv., I. 165:
> 'Ense uelut stricto quotiens Lucilius ardens
> Infremuit, rubet auditor cui frigida mens est
> Criminibus, tacita sudant praecordia culpa.'

of the social nature of virtue, the salient points being that it consists in attaching true worth to things, in understanding the right, useful, and honourable, in knowing the limits of desire, in rendering due honour to office, in supporting good men and good principles, and

> thereto to hold
> Our highest happiness our country's weal,
> And next our parents'; third and last, our own.[1]

Or, again, he can whimsically apply the Empedoclean doctrine of the four elements to the case of the offender summoned for trial, whose first punishment for contempt is the loss of two of his elements when interdicted from 'fire and water,' and whose final punishment may be the loss of his remaining two — his body, which is earth, and his soul, which is air![2]

Questions of literature and language have their interest for him. He criticises Euripides and his own predecessors in Roman poetry, parodies a line from Ennius,[3] and deals with the spelling of Latin words. Thus, he condemns as needless Accius's device of doubling a vowel to denote length, and he suggests that *puerei* might be the form for the nominative plural and *pueri* for the genitive singular. Preaching what he does not perform, he objects to the interlarding of Latin with Greek words, when he likens the style of Albucius to a mosaic pavement of Grecisms.[4] The nomenclature of criticism he endeavours to improve by suggesting that 'poema' should mean a short poem, like the epigram, distich, or epistle, while 'poesis' should apply to works like the *Iliad* or Ennius's *Annals*.

Lucilius was highly valued by men so different as Cicero, Juvenal, Tacitus, Quintilian, and, notwithstanding many censures, by Horace. Tacitus mentions in the same breath readers who preferred Lucretius to Virgil and readers who preferred Lucilius to Horace.[5] Quintilian mentions admirers so fervent that they preferred Lucilius not merely to other satirists, but to all other poets. Quintilian expressly dissents from this extreme laudation, as he does from certain of Horace's judgements on him. Adopting a middle course, he credits him with the qualities of learning, outspokenness, invective, and wit.[6] The vitality of

[1]   'Commoda praeterea patriaï prima putare,
        Deinde parentum, tertia iam postremaque nostra.'
[2] Bk. xxviii, 784–790. (Marx's ed.)
[3] Ennius's line, 'Sparsis hastis longis campus splendet et horret,' Lucilius carpingly said ought to have run, 'horret et alget,' Serv. ad *Aen.*, xi. 601, where Virgil has made one of his effective reproductions:
                              'Tum late ferreus hastis
          Horret ager.'
[4]   'Quam lepide λέξεις, compostae ut tesserulae omnes
        Arte pauimento atque emblemate uermiculato.'
[5] *Dial. de Or.*, xxiii., 'Versantur ante oculos isti qui Lucilium pro Horatio, et Lucretium pro Vergilio legunt.'
[6] *Inst. Or.*, X. i. 93, 'Nam eruditio in eo mira et libertas atque inde acerbitas et abundantia salis.'

Lucilius is shown in the traces of his influence upon Lucretius, Catullus, and Virgil.[1] It is less surprising to find it in satire—strongly impressed on Horace and still surviving in Persius and Juvenal.

Horace's criticisms upon Lucilius and his debt to Lucilius are subjects intimately wrapped up with a true estimate of both writers. The impression was produced in Horace's own time that, because he criticised him, he was unfair to his predecessor. An examination of his attitude will justify Horace against such a misconception. In three satires[2] Horace occupies himself with Lucilius. He begins with the misleading statement that Lucilius entirely followed the Old Comedy of Greece in attacking the infamous, altering merely the metre.[3] Horace grants that Lucilius is witty and shrewd, but objects that he is harsh and too rapid in composition—too suggestive of marvellous work against time, 'two hundred verses an hour, while the author stands on one foot!' This accounts for the muddy stream of lines (*cum flueret lutulentus*) and the absence of self-criticism. Subsequently comes the valuable remark that satire, such as Horace's own or Lucilius's, contains a prose element: remove the metre and it is 'sermo pedester.' Horace disclaims any intention to be poetic in satire, and Lucilius certainly never is. In the tenth satire of the first book Horace resumes his criticisms—'Yes,' he opens, 'I did say that Lucilius's verses run with an offhand lack of rhythm. Who can deny he is rugged? True, he rubbed the city down smartly (*sale multo urbem defricuit*), but that does not make a poem.' Touching Lucilius's medley of Greek and Latin words (a medley all the more curious in the light of his own satire on the style of Albucius) Horace asks whether Latin is not good enough. The very idea of adding to Greek literature nowadays is 'to carry wood into the forest'! Horace himself had given it up. Coming to his own satires, Horace claims that perhaps he writes better than Varro of Atax, but he is not equal to the inventor of this style, Lucilius. What if he did criticise him? That does not mean he plucks his glorious crown.[4] Is no fault to be found with Homer? Did not Lucilius himself pass strictures on Ennius? One is entitled to ask oneself in reading Lucilius whether he or his subject was to blame for his lack of polish and

---

[1] See Sellar, *op. cit.*, p. 249, for Lucretian imitations. Virgil, as we learn from Macrobius and Servius, owed to Lucilius not only phrases and thoughts, but incidents, *e.g.*, the council of the gods upon the death of Lupus in Lucilius, book i, is made use of by Virgil, Serv. ad *Aen.*, x. 104.

[2] The important passages are Hor., *Sat.*, I. iv. 6–12, 57; x. 1–5, 20–24, 48–71; II. i. 17, 29–34, 62–75.

[3] Nettleship (*Essays*, etc., 2nd ser., p. 34) argues that Horace did not approve of this narrowing of the metre from the old medley of forms in the *satura*. Yet it is significant that Horace himself does not in his satires use anything but the hexameter. Conceivably Horace felt that Lucilius had caught the spirit of invective from the Old Comedy without its versatility, brilliancy, and wit.

[4]   'Neque ego illi detrahere ausim
         Haerentem capiti cum multa laude coronam.'

melody. It may be assumed, thinks Horace, that he would have pruned carefully had he belonged to the Augustan age. Horace returns to the subject in the first satire of his second book. The lawyer Trebatius has advised him to celebrate Octavian's exploits as Lucilius did Scipio's. Horace replies that his *forte* is satire, and nothing so ambitious as epic. He is best pleased to put his thoughts into the style of the old man who so revealed his inner life to his books that one may read it therein as in a picture. But, it is objected, is not satire perilous? Well, Lucilius did not find it so. He first unmasked fair-seeming shams. And surely he did not offend his great friends, Laelius or Scipio? Lucilius—and here Horace does justice to the moral force behind his satires—was the friend of virtue and of virtue's friends. He could withal quietly enjoy the pleasures of society. Horace closes with a glance at the parallel between their positions. He too, though inferior to Lucilius in wealth and genius (*infra Lucili censum ingeniumque*), had known how to live with the great.

Clearly the impression left by the criticisms here paraphrased is that for Lucilius Horace entertained a very deep respect. But his sincerest flattery was paid in his imitations. He modernises his phrases; condenses his old-fashioned prolixity; serves up again details of Lucilius's southern journey in describing his own journey to Brundisium, and retells, as one of his own experiences, the story of a bore who pestered Lucilius.[1] The effusive and unwelcome greeting of the bore refines the Lucilian realism of the person who 'beslobbers, embraces, and devours one with affection' (*commanducatur totum complexu' comestque*). The famous opening words echo the Lucilian fragment *ibat forte* quoted by Nonius, just as Horace's conclusion with his final escape from the tormentor, *sic me seruauit Apollo*, translates the more pedantic Greek of Lucilius, τὸν δ'ἐξήρπαξεν Ἀπόλλων.

What contribution was made to satire by Varro of Atax (82–37 B.C.) is undiscoverable from the brief allusion made to him in Horace.[2] In any case, we know that, unlike Horace, he deserted satire for epic. A more important name is that of M. Terentius Varro (116–27 B.C.), whose Menippean satires fall to be considered with his life in the next period. Equally with Lucilius interested in social phenomena, he is less personal than he, and, albeit the introducer into satire of Greek cynicism, he was also the restorer of the genuine old medley, which adopted or rejected metre at will.

As to minor poetry, the example of Naevius and Ennius in choosing national history for epic treatment was followed by Accius in his *Annales*,

---

[1] To compare great things with small, it is like Max O'Rell's copying, in *L'Ami Macdonald*, of Dean Ramsay's Scottish stories. R.Y. Tyrrell, discussing Horace's debt to Lucilius, *Lectures on Lat. Poetry*, pp. 167–185, remarks that Horace did for Lucilius 'very much what Pope did for the coarse tales of Chaucer.' On the same point, see Sellar, *op. cit.*, pp. 241–242.

[2] *Sat.*, I. x. 46.

THE SATIRES OF LUCILIUS AND MINOR POETRY 179

by Hostius, whose *Bellum Histricum* relates the war of 125 B.C.,[1] and by
A. Furius of Antium.[2] This Ennian tradition in epic carries us into the
next period, through Cicero's early poem on Marius to his *De Consulatu
Suo*. Varro of Atax (whom we shall find reason to connect with the
group of 'Cantores Euphorionis') was the author, not only of a free
version of Alexandrine epic in his *Argonautae*, but also of a poem on
Caesar's operations against the Sequani, in which, as a Gaul, Varro
might take especial interest. The graceful and melodious movement of
his hexameters marks the new skill attained since the early period, *e.g.*,

> The chill North shook the woodland's honour down,

and

> The hounds had ceased to bay, the towns were hushed:
> So all was tranquil — lulled in Night's repose.[3]

Good verses were also written by M. Furius Bibaculus of Cremona in
his epic on Caesar's Gallic War, but he is unluckily best remembered
for his conceit about 'Jove spitting the hoary snow all o'er the wintry
Alps!'[4] The same tradition persists in Varius's poem on Caesar's death.
A different line of epic influence is seen in the translations of the *Iliad*
by the Cn. Matius who introduced scazons into light poetry from the
mimiambi of Herodas, and by Ninnius Crassus, of date unknown. The
idyllic poetry of Sueius[5] in his *Moretum* may be mentioned, if only to
contrast his harsh pedantry in rural themes with the grace of the more
famous 'Virgilian' *Moretum*.

Didactic verse between Ennius and Lucretius is represented by
Accius in his *Didascalica* on dramatic history, and his contemporary Q.
Valerius of Sora, whose lines on the all-powerful fatherhood of Jupiter
are quoted by St. Augustine.[6] Lucilius was the first to handle grammatical subjects in verse. Criticism, which, after Varro, came to be more
usual in prose, found metrical expression about 100 B.C. in Porcius
Licinus, who wrote upon Roman poets in trochaic tetrameters,[7] and in

---

[1] Ennius had narrated the Istrian war of 178 B.C.
[2] A few hexameters of Hostius and Furius are preserved by Macrobius, *Sat.*,
VI. i. 31–34, 44; iii. 5, 6; iv. 10; v. 8. Six more from Furius are defended by
Gellius, XVIII. xi., including:
'Omnia noctescunt tenebris caliginis atrae,'
and
'Increscunt animi, uirescit uulnere uirtus.'
[3] 'Frigidus et siluis Aquilo decussit honorem,'
and
'Desierant latrare canes urbesque silebant:
Omnia noctis erant placida composta quiete.'
[4] 'Iuppiter hibernas cana niue conspuit Alpes,' Porphyr. ad Hor., *Sat.*,
II. v. 40.
[5] Ribbeck thinks he was the same as Seius, a friend of Varro and of Cicero.
[6] *De Ciuit. Dei*, VII. ix and xi.
[7] *E.g.*, his lines already quoted (p. 88) on the late arrival of the Muse in Rome
(Gell., *N.A.*, XVII. xxi), and his bitter verses upon the neglect of Terence by
his exalted friends (Suet., *Vit. Ter.*).

the scholar and antiquary Volcatius Sedigitus, whose *Liber de Poetis* was in iambic senarii. The brief citations from him, including his list, already given, of authors of *palliatae* in order of merit, do not necessarily prove that he restricted his attention to the drama. To the same period may belong the poet—if he is not Volcatius himself after all—who is quoted by Donatus as witness to the younger Scipio's share in composing Terence's plays, and whose mutilated name has been restored variously as Vallegius and Vagellius.[1]

The elegiac epigram, after Ennius, appears in the epitaph on the Scipio who was praetor in 139 B.C.; in Pompiliius's claim—already noted—to be a pupil of Pacuvius; and in certain books of Lucilius. About 100 B.C. Lutatius Catulus and Valerius Aedituus, as well as Porcius Licinus, composed epigrams, chiefly erotic imitations from the Greek. They do not deserve all the praise showered on them by Gellius;[2] for the pentameter of the time, with a tendency towards harsh elisions and conclusions in words of three or more syllables, falls short of its finished form. They do, however, prove a deftness in use of the distich, and make important links in the chain which ends in Ovid.

Up to the time of Cornelius Gallus erotic poetry mainly took the form of epigram. The chief exception was a poet who lived fully a generation[3] before Catullus, and whose very existence used to be doubted, and his name confused with that of Naevius, Livius, and others. This was Laevius (born *c.* 129 B.C.). There is reason to think that he bore the cognomen Melissus, which suggests either Greek origin or Greek tastes. In his *Erotopaegnia* he is the predecessor of Catullus. This consisted of at least six books of love-songs and amatory incidents in widely varying lyric metres. It is not clear whether other titles of his, like *Alcestis*, *Ino*, *Protèsilaodamia*, denote separate works on mythological personages or sub-divisions of the *Erotopaegnia*. His profuse variety in metres was accompanied by a straining after the bizarre in diction, such as 'Aurora of the shamefast hue' (*Auroram pudoricolorem*), or, instead of 'frozen streams,' 'streams with their onyx covering' (*flumina gelu concreta* '*tegmine*' *esse* '*onychino*' *dixit*).[4] At times, in the Rhodian manner, he toyed with words till he could build them into fantastic shapes, such as a wing in his *Phoenix*. Neither Catullus nor Horace mentions Laevius;

---

[1] Donat. in auct. Suet. *Vit. Ter.* Ribbeck and Schanz accept *Vagellius*. One MS. alters *Vallegius* to *Valgius*, which may be rejected. Bücheler suggests *Volcacius*.

[2] Gell., *N.A.*, XIX. ix. 10, referring to verses by the three poets, says, 'quibus mundius, uenustius, limatius, tersius Graecum Latinumue nihil quidquam reperiri puto.'

[3] His jest:

    'Lex Licinia introducitur,
    Lux liquida haedo redditur,'

at the encouragement of the simple life by the Licinian law of 103 would have no point after its repeal in 97.

[4] For many other examples of his style see Gell., *N.A.*, XIX. vii.

perhaps they did not desire to weaken their claim to originality in introducing lyric measures. His significance, however, is out of all proportion to his fragments.[1] He may be reasonably placed in the vanguard of a fresh advance of Greek influence upon Roman literature.[2] Just as Livius Andronicus initiated Rome into Hellenic classicism, so Laevius initiated it into Alexandrinism, and led the way for Catullus and Ovid.

[1] E. Bährens, *F.P.R.*, 1886, pp. 287–293.

[2] See 'Le Poète Laevius,' in H. de Mirmont, *Études sur l'ancienne poés. lat.*, 1903, pp. 221–345. His conclusion is, 'Il semble permis, malgré le peu de fragments qui nous restent des *Erotopaegnia*, de conjecturer dans Laevius le premier initiateur de l'alexandrinisme à Rome.' *Cf.* Teuffel, *op. cit.*, § 150, 4 and 5.

Chapter VII

THE PROGRESS OF PROSE

Roman historians who wrote in Greek: Fabius Pictor, Cincius, Acilius, Albinus – M. Porcius Cato, the father of Latin prose – Early historians who wrote in Latin: Cassius Hemina, Piso Frugi, Sempronius Tuditanus, Junius Gracchanus, Caelius Antipater, Sempronius Asellio – Group at opening of first century B.C.: Claudius Quadrigarius, Valerius Antias, Cornelius Sisenna, Licinius Macer – Autobiographic or contemporary interest seen in Cornelia, Aemilius Scaurus, Rutilius Rufus, Lutatius Catalus, Sulla, Lucullus.

Oratory masters technique more rapidly than history – Three divisions of pre-Ciceronian eloquence – Cato and his contemporaries – The Scipionic circle – The Gracchi, and orators pro-Gracchan and anti-Gracchan – The end of the second century and age of Antonius and Crassus – *Rhetorica ad Herennium.*

Special sciences, learning, and technical knowledge – Philosophy – Scholarship and Aelius Stilo – Agriculture and Cato's treatise – Other works on agriculture – Law in the hands of the Aelii and Scaevolae.

NATIONS, like M. Jourdain, use prose without knowing it. Yet an artistic prose is always of slow growth. It develops with the power to turn consciously upon itself for criticism and analysis. At Rome, native power was originally less evident in history than in oratory, for there were Roman orators before Greek rhetoricians taught the rules. In the historical field, the superiority of Greek authors to the official Latin records determined that the first Romans to attempt connected history in prose should use the Greek language. This was the case with Fabius Pictor in the second Punic War, his younger contemporary L. Cincius Alimentus, and later C. Acilius and Postumius Albinus.[1] Fabius's history of Rome from Aeneas to his own time was of service to Polybius, Dionysius, and Livy. Dionysius though he can censure yet respects Fabius. Polybius is more crotchety in his complaints and may have felt some Scipionic jealousy towards an author too obviously panting after the glory of the Fabian clan. A Latin version, perhaps by a later Fabius, was issued of Fabius's Greek text. As for

[1] For fragments of Roman historians, see H. Peter, *Hist. Rom. Reliq.*, 1906–14. For their value, *Die Röm. Annalistik v. ihr. erst. Anfängen bis auf Valerius Antias*, K. W. Nitsch, 1873.

Cincius Alimentus, he was one of Hannibal's prisoners of war.[1] There
is no evidence to prove Mommsen's idea that his *Annales* were an
Augustan forgery, and nothing serious to damage Dionysius's witness
that Cincius as well as Fabius wrote in Greek.[2] Certain books on
constitutional and military antiquities by a later Cincius have been,
however, erroneously ascribed to Alimentus.[3] Acilius acted as interpreter in the senate for the deputation of Athenian philosophers in 155.
His history was translated into his mother-tongue by one Claudius,
presumably Claudius Quadrigarius. Albinus accentuated his Hellenising enthusiasm by dedicating his work to Ennius. His excessive
Hellenism offended old-fashioned Romans, and his apology for his want
of Greek idiom deserved Cato's retort that no one compelled him to
write Greek.[4]

Contemporary with Acilius and Albinus, M. Porcius Cato (234–
149) was a scathing critic of the weaknesses in Hellenism. His Roman
austerity and shrewdness distinguished him, as 'Cato the Censor,' from
his descendant 'of Utica,' and made him a fitting father of Latin prose.[5]
He was censor in 184, the year of Plautus's death. A soldier and man of
affairs, he remained the unflagging enemy of aristocratic cliques and
Grecian fashions. He wrote much, though he affected to despise letters.
The narrowness of his patriotism must not obscure the versatility of his
genius.[6] He is a landmark in prose, whether we consider history,
oratory, or the special sciences. He gave history a new scope; he was the
first Roman who published speeches on a large scale; he was the
founder of the encyclopaedic method. Here we are concerned with his
contribution at an advanced age to history in the seven books of
Origines. The second and third books on the rise of Italian cities gave
the name to the whole.[7] The first book treated the regal period; the
fourth, the first Punic War; the fifth, the second Punic War; the last two
brought the narrative down to 149. The *Origines*, particularly in the
books on Italian cities, would have been, if extant, a most precious
salvage from antiquity—a prose epic with some of the matter but none
of the poetry of Ennius's *Annales*. The title inevitably but unfairly
suggests the qualifications exacted by a modern standard from an
inquirer into 'origins.' The days of systematic research in anthropology
were not yet. The broad basis of comparative method applied to ethnology, law, custom, folklore, chronology, religion, is not to be looked
for in Cato. He is not a trained philologist nor a trained historian. Yet

[1] Livy, XXI. xxxviii.
[2] Dionys., *Ant.*, I. vi: *cf.* his allusion in I. lxxix.
[3] *De Luciis Cinciis* (w. fragments), M. Hertz, 1842.
[4] Polyb., XXXIX. i. 1–5.
[5] Cic., *Brut.*, xvi. 61. Than Cato Cicero knows of nothing older in prose
except *laudationes* on the dead and Appius's famous speech.
[6] Livy, XXXIX. xl, 'Versatile ingenium sic pariter ad omnia fuit ut natum
ad id unum diceres quodcunque ageret.'
[7] Corn. Nep., *Cato*, iii. 3.

Cato had the originality to depart from the annalistic tradition by going
beyond the Palatine and Capitol to Italy for his unit and by introducing
speeches into his record. Another feature was due to his anti-aristocratic
bias. Suppressing the names of generals, and celebrating with grim
humour Surus, the bravest elephant of the Carthaginian army,[1] he
pointedly showed that history need not be the handmaid of family pride.
There is more left of his oratory than of his history, and more of his
agricultural treatise than of his oratory, whereon to form an opinion
about his style; but throughout there is the same unadorned directness,
leaving the impression of force rather than form.[2]

Cato's choice of Latin as his language and his wider range of historical treatment were followed by L. Cassius Hemina and then by L.
Calpurnius Piso Frugi, who, as consul of 133, strongly opposed
Tiberius Gracchus. Piso's old-fashioned Latin satisfied Gellius in much
the same proportion as it failed to satisfy Cicero.[3] The consul of 129,
C. Sempronius Tuditanus, displayed antiquarian ability in treating the
aborigines of Italy, and, like his contemporary M. Junius, surnamed 'the
Gracchan' to mark his politics, dealt with the constitutional powers of
the magistrates. A more distinguished historian was L. Caelius (or
Coelius) Antipater, who wrote on the second Punic War. He recorded
a story got at first hand from C. Gracchus,[4] and outlived him. A
critical faculty impels him to the investigation of ancient and, if not
Carthaginian, at least Greek sources favourable to the Carthaginians.[5]
Not always temperate in the use of rhetorical artifices and high colour,
and lacking complete polish, he wins from Cicero the modified credit of
having 'roughhewed his work as best he could' (sicut potuit, dolauit),
but also the distinct assertion that he was an improvement upon his
predecessors in point of style (uicit tamen superiores).[6] His juniority
makes it unlikely that he influenced Polybius at all; but he was used by
Livy in his third decad, by Plutarch, and by Dio. If Caelius introduced
rhetoric into history, the introduction of a philosophic basis was the
work of Sempronius Asellio, an officer under Scipio at Numantia in
134 B.C. He attacks the annalistic method of recording deeds and battles

[1] Corn. Nep., Cato, iii. 4, 'Sine nominibus res notauit.' Plin., N.H., VIII.
11: 'Cato, cum imperatorum nomina annalibus detraxerit, eum (elephantum) qui
fortissime proeliatus esset in Punica acie "Surum" tradidit uocatum.'
[2] E.g., the longest piece from the Origines, preserved by Gell., N.A., III.
vii. 1, is a plain but admirably vivid narrative of the way in which 400 Roman
soldiers covered the retreat of comrades in the first Punic War.
[3] Gell., N.A., VII. ix. 1, 'res perquam pure et uenuste narrata a Pisone';
XI. xiv. 1, 'simplicissima suauitate et rei et orationis'; Cic., Brut., xxvii. 106,
'annales sane exiliter scriptos.'
[4] Val. Max., I. vii. 6, re not the Punic War, but Gracchus's ominous dream.
[5] E.g., Cic., De Diuin., I. xxiv. 49, gives the source of Hannibal's dream in
Caelius as Silenus.
[6] Cic., De Or., II. xii. 54, 'Addidit maiorem historiae sonum uocis uir
optimus, Antipater. Ceteri non exornatores rerum, sed tantummodo narratores
fuerunt.'

to the exclusion of motives and causes. Like Polybius, he holds the theory that reasons must be expounded. He has a salutary dread of swamping movements and policy under detailed facts, and explicitly states the difference between telling stories for boys and writing history.[1]

Another group belongs to the opening of the first century B.C. Q. Claudius Quadrigarius struck out a new line by dropping the mythical period. His work of at least twenty-three books began with the Gallic conflagration, so that he could rely more on documents and less on legend. His habit of blending reflections with his narrative resembles Sallust. Concise and antithetical, he had the archaic flavour requisite to commend him to the scholars of the second century A.D. Unequal to Quadrigarius in sobriety, Valerius Antias began his voluminous history with the earliest times, and vitiates it by his passion for overstatement and his partiality for the Valerii. Dionysius, Plutarch, Livy, and the elder Pliny make use of him. With Livy's approach to his own times comes his recognition of the wildness of Valerius's statistics affecting military losses or captives. L. Cornelius Sisenna (119–67 B.C.)—to be distinguished from Sisenna the commentator of Plautus—was principally concerned with the Sullan troubles and the Marsian War. His translation of the coarse Milesian stories of Aristides might suggest that he was more a romancer than a historian. Certainly, he wrote of contemporary themes in a remote style, characterised by obsolete and unusual words.[2] His friend Licinius Macer (died 66 B.C.), the father of the poet Calvus, was both orator and historian.[3] Treating the earliest times from a democratic standpoint, he claimed, as several allusions in the first decad of Livy prove, to have inspected ancient records (*libri lintei*) with industry; but he does not escape the censure of Dionysius for carelessness.

The increasing tendency to take up contemporary history is evident from the number of monographs and autobiographical works composed. The *Letters* of Cornelia, mother of the Gracchi, may be regarded as broadly of the same kind as numerous memoirs by Aemilius Scaurus (162–89), Rutilius Rufus (consul 105), Lutatius Catulus (consul 102). Sulla (138–78), who wrote verses and had a taste for light literature, finished the twenty-second book of *Commentarii Rerum Suarum* two days before his death.[4] His notes were completed by his freedman,

[1] See quotation in Gell., *N.A.*, V. xviii. Likening 'annales' to a 'diarium, quam Graeci ἐφημερίδα uocant,' Asellio proceeds, 'Nobis non modo satis esse uideo, quod factum esset, id pronuntiare, sed etiam quo consilio quaque ratione gesta essent, demonstrare.'
[2] Cic., *Brut.*, lxxiv. 259, touches on the impossibility of preventing Sisenna 'quominus inusitatis uerbis uteretur.' In *Brut.* lxiv. 228, Cicero considers him 'doctus' and 'bene Latine loquens,' but not sufficiently trained as a speaker.
[3] Neither his oratory nor his history commended itself to Cicero's judgement. The former had accuracy but lacked charm (*Brut.*, lxvii. 238); the latter was marred by diffuseness (*De Leg.*, I. ii. 7).
[4] Plut., *Sull.*, 37.

Epicadus.[1] It is hardly remarkable that their value is greatly lessened by anti-Marian bias. Lucullus (c. 118–56), to whom Sulla dedicated his work, had produced in early life a sketch of the Marsian War in Greek, but Lucullus never did justice either in oratory or in history to his talents and culture.

Of all this work it may be said that nothing powerful appeared in Latin historical writing before Sallust and Caesar. Cicero comments on the badness of historical composition up to his time, and the fragments suggest that, with few exceptions, the writers followed the abrupt and unperiodic style of Cato.

In oratory the mastery over technique was a more rapid attainment. Three influences co-operated—the stress of politics, the requirements of legal pleading, and the rules of rhetoric. Native gifts were eventually reinforced by foreign skill. An upholder of Roman taste so staunch as Cato based his speeches on Thucydides and Demosthenes. In time followers were claimed even by that florid 'Asianism' which represented the degenerate and trans-Aegean form of Isocrates's 'Atticism.' The striving after effect, traceable in C. Gracchus's speeches, in Caelius Antipater's narratives, becomes more patent by the period of the *Rhetorica ad Herennium*. Before the time of Cicero it is evident that Greek rhetorical attention to figures of speech, poetical colour and the rhythmical period has not been lost upon the Roman.[2]

It is not easy to convey an adequate idea of the many orators[3] who flourished during five generations before Cicero composed his *Verrines*, and to trace the development from bare rugged vigour to polished art. The names which might be drawn from Cicero's *Brutus* seem legion. Many in themselves are comments on the transitoriness of fame. To learn from Cicero that Curio was considered in his boyhood the high-water mark of eloquence[4] affects one like some antiquated pronouncement on the eternal greatness of the poet Cowley or on the popularity of Pomfret's *Choice*. Broadly, however, there are three periods in pre-Ciceronian oratory—the age of Cato, the age of Laelius and the Gracchi, and the age of Crassus and Antonius. Linking these together, there are certain sets of orators.

We are not in a position to assess the oratorical worth of Cato's contemporaries:[5] Q. Fabius Maximus, the 'Cunctator,' who pro-

---

[1] Suet., *Gramm.*, 12.

[2] For the relation of Latin to Greek prose style see E. Norden, *Die antike Kunstprosa vom vi Jahrhundert v. Chr. bis in die Zeit der Renaissance*, 1898, 2 vols.

[3] For fragments, *Oratorum Rom. Fragmenta ab Appio inde Caeco usque ad Q. Aurelium Symmachum*, H. Meyer, 1837 (2nd ed., 1842).

[4] *Brut.*, xxxii. 122 (where Cicero is speaking of Curio's speech on behalf of Ser. Fulvius), 'nobis quidem pueris haec omnium optuma putabatur.' The Curio referred to was praetor in 121.

[5] Teuffel, § 123.

nounced a funeral eulogium on his son; Q. Caecilius Metellus, consul of
206, who pronounced one on his father; P. Licinius Crassus 'Dives,'
famous in forensic, deliberative, and popular eloquence; Africanus the
elder; Tib. Sempronius, father of the Gracchi; L. Aemilius Paulus,
father of the younger Africanus, and noted for an address to the people
on his own exploits; and a junior contemporary, C. Sulpicius Gallus,
who was an astronomer and enthusiast for Greek literature. In Cato
himself we have more to go upon. Of his 150 speeches known to Cicero,
we have fragments or records of nearly 90. They are the utterances of a
zealous and patriotic moralist, whose ideal orator was the *uir bonus
dicendi peritus*. The pervading earnestness and simplicity are suggestive
of Wyclif's sermons, and spring from Cato's principle of composition —
rem tene, uerba sequentur. Clear as a rule, he is not free from pedantry
and awkwardness. What he signally excels in is vigour. Whether a
passage reflects his own egotism, or denounces luxury and arrogance, or
attacks misgovernment, or argues against a mistaken policy, there is
always strength.[1] It is characteristic of him to lecture the mounted men
at Numantia on the lasting effects of sound work and the swift disappearance of pleasure:

> *Cogitate cum animis uostris, si quid uos per laborem recte feceritis,
> labor ille a uobis cito recedet, bene factum a uobis, dum uiuitis, non
> abscedet. Sed si qua per uoluptatem nequiter feceritis, uoluptas cito
> abibit, nequiter factum illud apud uos semper manebit.*[2]

In a speech on the apportionment of war plunder, he bitterly resents
the indulgence granted to peculation in high places:

> *Fures priuatorum furtorum in neruo atque in compedibus aetatem
> agunt; fures publici in auro atque in purpura.*[3]

When he discusses a magisterial outrage, his indignation rises from
simple statement to passion, and the effect is enhanced by amplification
and redoubled questions almost Ciceronian:

> *Iussit uestimenta detrahi atque flagro caedi: decemuiros Bruttiani
> uerberauere; uidere multi mortales. Quis hanc contumeliam, quis hoc
> imperium, quis hanc seruitutem ferre potest? . . . Ubi societas? Ubi fides
> maiorum? . . . Quantum luctum, quantum gemitum, quid lacrumarum,
> quantum fletum factum audiui?*[4]

The best, as it is the best-known, example of Cato's style is a passage
from his speech against declaring war on the people of Rhodes. This is
one of its paragraphs:

---

[1] This quality made his speeches the subject of study till Hadrian's age.
Gellius, *N.A.*, VI. iii. 53, passes on Cato a criticism that cannot be bettered:
'his speeches might show more distinction and rhythm (*distinctius numerosi-
usque fortassean dici potuerint*), but could not be more forcible and graphic
(*fortius atque uiuidius*).'

[2] Gell., *N.A.*, XVI. i. 4.   [3] *Ibid.*, XI. xviii. 18.

[4] *Ibid.*, X. iii. 17.

Scio solere plerisque hominibus [in] rebus secundis atque prolixis atque prosperis animum excellere, atque superbiam atque ferociam augescere atque crescere. Quo mihi nunc magnae curae est, quod haec res tam secunde processit, ne quid in consulendo aduorsi eueniat, quod nostras secundas res confutet, neue haec laetitia nimis luxuriose eueniat. Aduorsae res edomant, et docent quid opus sit facto. Secundae res laetitia transuorsum trudere solent a recte consulendo atque intellegendo. Quo maiore opere dico suadeoque, uti haec res aliquot dies proferatur, dum ex tanto gaudio in potestatem nostram redeamus.[1]

This, like the paragraphs which follow, is luminous and forcible, but it lacks form and comeliness. There is a want of variety both in expression and in sound. Synonyms are piled on each other to secure emphasis. There is no studied rhythm, and no horror of a jingle at the end of clauses. In respect of art, we are still a long way from Cicero.

Most of the orators in the period just before the Gracchi may be connected with the Scipionic circle.[2] There were the younger Scipio Africanus himself (184–129) and Laelius 'Sapiens,' who composed a funeral oration on the elder Africanus to be pronounced by his nephew. Their speeches were read in Cicero's day, and 'Scipionis oratiunculae' were excerpted by Marcus Aurelius. The best-known piece of Scipio is his horrified account of the decay of morals, illustrated by his visit to a school of music and dancing.[3] In another speech he introduced an effective climax:

Guiltlessness is mother of worth, worth of honours, honours of power, and power of freedom.[4]

Born half a century after Cato, and partial to literature, Scipio displays more distinction and harmony of style. Sulpicius Galba was an ornate and trenchant speaker; but the artificial figures, to which, according to Cicero,[5] he resorted first among Roman orators, did not save his style from a roughness, old-fashioned in comparison with Laelius, Scipio, and Cato himself. Other contemporaries were M. Furius Philus, famed for the literary flavour of his talk, and Q. Metellus Macedonicus, the political adversary of Africanus the younger.

With the age of the Gracchi,[6] popular oratory became more than ever indispensable. Of the two brothers, Tiberius, being milder in disposition than the younger, was a cooler but less effective speaker. Gaius was noted for his loud impetuous delivery and excited gestures. It was said he instructed a slave to sound a flute-note in order to modulate his high tones. His qualities embrace, according to Cicero, energy, dignity, and fulness. His untimely death was a loss to Latin literature,

---

[1] Gell., *N.A.*, VI. iii. 14   [2] Teuffel, *op. cit.*, § 131.
[3] Quoted in Macrob., *Saturn.*, ii. 10.
[4] 'Ex innocentia nascitur dignitas, ex dignitate honor, ex honore imperium, ex imperio libertas.'
[5] *Brut.*, xxi. 82.   [6] Teuffel, *op. cit.*, §§ 135, 136.

for in his sphere he had no rival. His performances, however, missed the finishing touch, so that the promise of his eloquence surpassed his actual achievement.[1] How far advance has been made from Cato's prose in the direction of elaborate subordination of clauses, harmonious period, better collocation of words, fuller cadence, may be inferred from this example:

> Si uellem apud uos uerba facere et a uobis postulare, cum genere summo ortus essem, et cum fratrem propter uos amisissem, nec quisquam de P. Africani et Ti. Gracchi familia nisi ego et puer restaremus, ut pateremini hoc tempore me quiescere, ne a stirpe genus nostrum interiret, et uti aliqua propago generis nostri reliqua esset—haud scio an lubentibus a uobis impetrassem.

From the group of political orators, either pro-Gracchan or anti-Gracchan, whose qualities we know chiefly from Cicero's *Brutus*, may be singled out Papirius Carbo, a vehement supporter of the Gracchi, and C. Scribonius Curio on the same side; and, among opponents, T. Annius, reckoned an invincible debater, C. Fannius, and Aemilius Scaurus, a writer of strange Latin already mentioned as his own biographer.

Before the end of the second century B.C. the prominent speakers[2] included Q. Metellus Numidicus, author of a renowned harangue upon compulsory wedlock; T. Albucius, at whom Lucilius jeered; C. Galba, whose peroration in his own defence was got up by heart in Cicero's boyhood;[3] and C. Titius, the tragedian. A step brings us to the age of the great orators M. Antonius (143–87) and L. Licinius Crassus (140–91), contemporaneous with Cicero's early years, and celebrated by him as chief interlocutors in the *De Oratore*. Cicero's ideal picture, especially of his master Crassus, whom he portrays much after his own image, does not give an exact conception of their qualities. Antonius was the more attractive because more imaginative; Crassus, thanks to legal training and vast experience of cases, was a master of lucid exposition. Antonius had an objection to publishing speeches, for the truly oratorical reason that they lost effect when read; Crassus did not share this objection, but Cicero would have had him write more. What survives marks still further advance, closer attention to rhythmical laws, and arrangement of clauses based on the best Greek usage.[4] Other notable

[1] *Brut.*, xxxiii. 125: 'Damnum illius immaturo interitu res Romanae Latinaeque litterae fecerunt. . . .' 126: 'Eloquentia nescio an habuisset parem neminem. . . . Manus extrema non accessit operibus eius; praeclare incohata multa, perfecta non plane.' See Teuffel, § 135, 4, for criticisms by Plutarch, Tacitus, and Fronto.
[2] A crowd of others belong to the same period, Teuffel, § 141, 6.
[3] *Brut.*, xxxiii. 127: 'Exstat eius peroratio qui epilogus dicitur; qui tanto in honore pueris nobis erat ut eum etiam edisceremus.'
[4] Cicero, *Orator*, lxvi. 223, illustrates, by quoting from Crassus, what he considers a good arrangement of clauses, viz., two brief sentences (κόμματα, *incisa*), a longer sentence (κῶλον, *membrum*), and a completing period (*com-*

speakers of the time were L. Marcius Philippus, a poor third to
Crassus and Antonius;[1] the jurist Q. Scaevola (consul 95 B.C.); Julius
Caesar Strabo, whose tragic tastes engendered in him a new and stagey
sort of pleading; P. Sulpicius Rufus, who modelled his speaking on
Crassus; and C. Aurelius Cotta, who modelled his on Antonius.

The success attained, on the eve of Cicero's appearance, in combining
the Latin spirit with Greek erudition, may be measured from the
Rhetorica ad Herennium. It is a manual of oratory in four books, based
on the Greek system, but avowedly dispensing with useless subtleties
and keeping Roman needs in view.[2] Thus, while the author follows the
technicalities, divisions and subdivisions, figures and forms, of his
sources, he has the merit of producing an original effect by his quotations from Ennius, Plautus, and Pacuvius in the second book, by his
selection for argument of actual dilemmas from Roman history, and by
inventing rhetorical specimens in the last book. Traditionally ascribed
in manuscripts to Cicero and often printed with his works,[3] the *Rhetorica*
is now usually assigned to one Cornificius of the time of Sulla. This is
supported by the facts that Quintilian's citations from the *Rhetorica* of
Cornificius correspond with the text of the *Ad Herennium*, and that
Cicero himself in his juvenile *De Inuentione* borrows portions of it.[4]
The style of the treatise is bald, marred by dull repetitions of similar
forms of expression, and by sentences and paragraphs which have the
merit of a catalogue. Yet it is a milestone on the march of Oratory.

Under the literature of special sciences, learning, and technical
knowledge may be marshalled philosophy, philology, antiquities,
domestic and rural economy, and law. In philosophy the period was one
of absorption. Exalted Romans like Scipio and Laelius 'the Wise'
patronised philosophers and heard them gladly. The Stoics of the
Gracchan age fostered thought as well as social reform. Yet Roman
gentlemen, being for the most part eclectic amateurs haunted by the
suspicion that philosophy was but solemn trifling, wrote little or
nothing. Largely guided by their particular profession, they picked and
chose among the doctrines of the schools. Jurists like Tubero, Rutilius
Rufus, Pompey's uncle Sextus, the Scaevolae and Lucilius Balbus,

---

prehensio). 'Missos faciant patronos, ipsi prodeant' (κόμματα). 'Cur clandestinis
consiliis nos oppugnant?' (κῶλον). 'Cur de perfugis nostris copias comparant
contra nos?' (*comprehensio*). Cicero continues with an example of his own, more
elaborate in arrangement and more effective in rhythm.

[1] Cic., *Brut.*, xlvii. 173: 'Longo interuallo, tamen proxumus.'

[2] I. i. 1: 'Illa quae Graeci scriptores inanis arrogantiae causa sibi assump-
serunt reliquimus. . . . Nos ea quae uidebantur ad rationem dicendi pertinere
sumpsimus.' Bks. I and II handle 'inuentio'; III 'dispositio,' 'pronuntiatio',
'memoria'; IV 'elocutio.'

[3] *E.g.*, at beginning of C. F. A. Nobbe's *Cic. Opera Omina Uno Vol.
Comprehensa*, 1850. Separate critical ed., F. Marx, 1894.

[4] L. Jeep, in opposition to F. Marx, maintains the authorship by Cornificius, *Deutsche Literaturz.*, 1897, p. 492 *sqq*. For authorship and analysis of *Ad
Herennium* see A. S. Wilkins, edn. of Cic. *De Orat.* I., Introd.

liked the rigorous precision of Stoic dialectic. Orators like Cotta, Lucullus, Catulus, and Piso, accustomed to view both sides of a question, found the less rigid theories of the Academy or the Peripatetics more to their taste. Pythagoreanism was about to have among its few adherents the learned Nigidius Figulus, while Epicureanism with its sceptical implications had supporters in Velleius and Albucius, and its earliest literary exponents in Amafinius and Rabirius.

The linguistic and antiquarian learning of the period might be viewed as amassing knowledge from which Varro could draw. Its scholar was L. Aelius 'Stilo,' born at Lanuvium about 150 B.C. Of equestrian rank, and trained in Stoic thought, he showed his greatest enthusiasm in the systematic study of Latin language, literature, and antiquities on historical principles. He interpreted the hymns of the Salii, edited the old Latin poets, and became a dictator on questions of grammar and etymology. Through the stimulus given by him to Varro and to pupils, of whom Cicero was one, he exerted an influence on scholarship which it is not easy to overestimate. Learning was also served not only by Accius and other poets already mentioned, but by teachers of rhetoric like Plotius Gallus. It was served, too, by Ennius, the grammarian, and by critics of literature like the Plautine scholars Aurelius Opilius and Servius Clodius—who was able to recognise a line of Plautus by its ring.[1] Finally it was served by the Ennian scholars Antonius Gnipho (another of Cicero's masters) and Pompilius Andronicus the Syrian.

In the department of technology, as in history and oratory, we meet Cato again. His chief didactic work was an encyclopaedic *Vade-mecum* for his son, and consisted of rules on farming, health, military tactics, morals, and other subjects.[2] A collection of his genuine sayings was made, and led later to spurious imitations in the so-called 'Catonis disticha.' The single work, however, which represents him in bulk is his treatise *De Agri Cultura* or *De Re Rustica*. Most likely originating in notes made for private use, the work has by a process of modernisation largely lost its archaic diction, but happily preserves its archaic spirit. A youth spent on a Sabine farm gave Cato a practical insight into Italian agriculture. The work is, then, the fruit of experience. As a handbook, it is hardly literature; yet, because readable, it somehow makes its claim good. There is the barest minimum of Italian landscape in it; there is no love of beauty, but there are vivid glimpses of the steading, its *uilicus* and the labourers under his charge, of the fruit-trees and crops, the olives and wine, the cattle and their ailments. In the extant form, the absence of systematic order strikes one. If the beginnings are workman-

---

[1] Cic., *Ad Fam.*, IX. xvi. 4. He was Aelius's son-in-law, Teuffel, § 159, 9.
[2] Pliny praises him as 'omnium bonarum artium magister' (*N.H.*, XXV. 4), and Cicero records the exhaustive sweep of his inquiries: 'Nihil in hac ciuitate temporibus illis sciri disciue potuit, quod ille non cum inuestigarit et scierit tum etiam conscripserit' (*De Orat.*, III. xxxiii. 135).

like, in handling land-purchase and the duties of a landholder and his
bailiff, the treatise soon turns to a discursive range over fig-trees and
willows, slaves and live-stock, wine-press (*torcular*) and olive-store,
walls and mortar, oil-mill and oil-vat, planting and manuring of trees,
bedding for cattle, pruning, the lime-kiln, duties for the season (and
especially for spring), grafting, household rations and clothes, tilling,
vessels for oil and wine. Between medicine for cattle and the construction of a threshing-floor are sandwiched recipes for cakes and
cracknel (*spiram uti facias*) and many old-world dainties. Cato proceeds
to give advice on the inroads of the weevil, barrenness in olives, on
dangers to figs, to vines, or to sheep, on the moth that corrupts and
the snake for whose bite sow's dung is the sovereign specific. His
matter-of-fact turn produces a curt parsimony of expression. Take his
list of duties for rainy weather:

> *Cum tempestates pluuiae fuerint, quae opera per imbrem fieri potuerint,*
> *dolia lauari, picari, uillam purgari, frumentum transferri, stercus foras*
> *efferri, sterquilinium fieri, semen purgari, funes sarciri, nouos fieri,*
> *centones, cuculiones, familiam oportuisse sibi sarcire* (sc. *reuoca ad*
> *rationem*).[1]

Of the absentee landlord he briefly disapproves: the owner will have
a finer farm and fewer blunders the oftener he is on the scene: better
work is done before the master's face than behind his back—*frons*
occipitio prior est.[2] Condensation could not go further than in the com-
mandments laid down for the land-steward—a couple of words serve
for some sentences:

> *Haec erunt uilici officia. Disciplina bona utatur. Feriae seruentur.*
> *Alieno manum abstineat. . . . Parasitum ne quem habeat. Haruspicem,*
> *augurem, hariolum, Chaldaeum ne quem consuluisse uelit. . . . Primus*
> *cubitu surgat. Postremus cubitum eat. . . . Opera omnia mature con-*
> *ficias face. Nam res rustica sic est, si unam rem sero feceris, omnia opera*
> *sero facies.*[3]

He is equally matter-of-fact when, for an ox that is ill, he prescribes a
raw egg to be swallowed whole, and next day a chopped leek's head in
wine. The ox must be standing up like the man dosing him. And the
virtue of the medicine apparently depends on an empty stomach in both
patient and administrant.[4] The parsimonious style consorts well with
such a penurious counsel as this to a master: 'Every time a slave is
allowed a new garment, remember to get the old one for patches.' There
is no element in the book which has more human value than its religion,
particularly in recorded prayers of the type used for the land at the
sacrifice of the *suouetaurilia*:

---

[1] *Cap.* ii.   [2] *Cap.* iv.   [3] *Cap.* v.
[4] *Cap.* lxxi.: 'Bosque ipsus et qui dabit sublimiter stet. Ieiunus ieiuno
boui dato.'

Mars pater, te precor quaesoque uti sies uolens propitius mihi domo familiaeque nostrae, quoius rei ergo agrum terram fundumque meum suouetaurilia circumagi iussi. Uti tu morbos uisos inuisosque, uiduertatem (dearth) *uastitudinemque calamitates intemperiasque prohibessis, defendas, auerruncesque, etc.*[1]

So the cares and concerns of the ancient farm rise to view, and one can see the pains taken over the *bouquet* of wine (*odorem deteriorem uti uino demas*), the test for adulteration, the preserving of olives, the treatment of the gouty, the management of dogs, the sacrifice before harvest. What we now have of the book closes with a few homely and miscellaneous paragraphs on cabbages, on chafed skin (*intertrigo*), on the charm to be chanted for a sprain, on the growing of asparagus and the curing of hams! It is all useful, and more thorough system would have made it still more useful but perhaps no more quaint and entertaining. If *le style est l'homme même*, one must not say there is no style; for the book is Cato all over. The short emphatic sentences make a natural staccato where Seneca's staccato is artificial. But one must not demand magic of words or flashes of sentiment. It remained for Virgil to link this very subject and some of Cato's own words to the most finished hexameters ever written.

The treatment of the land was of ancestral moment for Italy. The Carthaginian Mago's system of agriculture was translated by order of the senate, and the husbandry of Cato was followed by the Sasernae, father and son (cited several times in Varro), and by Tremellius Scrofa. Cicero and Atticus were friendly with Scrofa, and he imported elegances of style into the subject of agriculture. He is the leading figure in the opening books of Varro's *De Re Rustica*.

In contradistinction to philosophy, law was sufficiently positive and practical to attract the Roman mind strongly. Jurisprudence therefore made important progress. The two Aelii were the leading jurists of the sixth century of the city. About 200 B.C. the younger brother Sextus Aelius Paetus—he was praised by Ennius and was consul in 198— produced his *Tripertita*. Its three portions were the text of the *Twelve Tables*, their interpretation, and forms of lawsuits. Posterity deemed the work 'the cradle of the law' (*cunabula iuris*). Scipio Nasica, Cato and his son, with others, made smaller contributions. Manius Manilius of the Scipionic circle framed his formulae of purchase, M. Junius Brutus wrote on the civil law, and Ser. Fabius Pictor (confused by Nonius with the annalist) on pontifical law. During the half-century before Sulla the Mucii Scaevolae were the leading family in jurisprudence.[2] P. Mucius Scaevola (consul, 133) possessed the true pontifical interest in law and in official documents. His brother,

---

[1] *Cap.* cxli.
[2] Pompon., *Dig.*, I. ii. 2, 39, 'Post hos (*i.e.* the Catos) fuerunt P. Mucius et Brutus et Manilius, qui fundauerunt ius ciuile.'

known by his adopted name, P. Licinius Crassus Mucianus, was less renowned as a jurist. Quintus Mucius—to be distinguished from his kinsman Quintus 'the Augur,' who shone in legal consultations—was the greatest jurist at the opening of the first century B.C. Consul in 95, an orator of reputation in the age of Antonius and Crassus, and cruelly murdered in the Marian massacres, he was one whose character, like that of the best Roman lawyers, will stand the test of the touchstone of honour. To him was due a methodical system, including wills, inheritance, damages, contract, and procedure. In method and comprehensiveness his work marked an advance. He founded a tradition in civil law, not only through the influence of his writings, but also through his pupils. He instructed Lucilius Balbus and Aquilius Gallus, who in their turn handed on his teaching to Cicero's friend, Sulpicius Rufus, the most illustrious jurisconsult of the classic age. From Sulpicius descended the great legal schools of imperial times, when the Roman code became cosmopolitan. Q. Mucius Scaevola is thus ultimately one of the founders of the jurisprudence of modern Europe.

PARTS II AND III

The Literature of the Golden Age

70 B.C.—14 A.D.

A PROEM TO THE GOLDEN AGE

The Age of Gold and its two periods, Ciceronian and Augustan –
The political aspect – Money-making and morals – Ferment in
literature and art – Survivals of Alexandrinism among the Augustans – Contrast in literary spirit between close of Republic and
beginning of Empire – The age of the great classics.

THE title 'Golden Age' represents a traditional view. It may
have tended in some quarters to foster too narrow a conception
of classical Latin, as if Tacitus might safely be taken for a less
wonderful magician in prose than Cicero, or Juvenal an inferior
satirist to Horace. But the 'Age of Gold' is in itself a picturesque
phrase. And there can be small quarrel with it, when taken to declare
the truth that during the century before the accession of Tiberius—
during the period, that is to say, which includes the names of Lucretius,
Catullus, Cicero, Caesar, Sallust, Virgil, Horace, Ovid, and Livy—
Roman literature attained its zenith for inspiration, quality, and lasting
influence. The phrase, however, must not unclassicise writers of the
Empire with their forceful rhetoric and intense human interest. The
'Silver' Latin often shines with glitter rather than steady light; still, it
is 'Silver.' What must be admitted is, that despite great names like
Tacitus, Juvenal, Quintilian, and Pliny, there is not, in general, the
same lofty afflatus or the same sure artistic achievement. The literature
of the Golden Age, on the other hand, was the output of an epoch
rendered momentous by the final battle-stress of republican politics
and the birth-throes of empire. Widespread vitality in ideas and in
feelings which pulsate in response to national greatness must favour
aesthetic fertility. In the atmosphere of a Periclean democracy, of
Augustus's newly organised empire, of spacious Elizabethan adventure,
or of Louis XIV.'s grand monarchy, literature puts on the very strength
and spirit and colour of the times. The Golden Age itself falls into two
periods—the 'Ciceronian' (or, what would equally well describe its
politics, the 'Caesarian') and the 'Augustan.' The two periods saw
mighty changes in state, society, and letters.

With the close of the generation which had known the Gracchi, a
great historic process had reached fulfilment.[1] Out of the ancient
variety of communities, Latin, Osco-Sabellian, Umbrian, Etruscan, and

---

[1] It is examined in detail by Gugl. Ferrero, *The Greatness and Decline of
Rome* (tr. A. E. Zimmern), 1907, vol. i, 'The Empire Builders.'

Greek, had emerged a new Italy. The admission of the allies to civic rights constituted an Italian nation, in which the uniting overpowered the disuniting forces. Differences in race, politics, and prejudices were less significant than the common civilisation, military power, and trade interests which made Italy one as against the rest of the world. By a remarkable paradox, it was in an era of intestine strife that this unity was confirmed. Through the welter of civil bloodshed and the fluctuations of party rivalry, the one recurrent lesson taught was that no oligarchic cabal could perpetuate the conflict of class with class and rule in its own exclusive interests. A divided Rome became more and more impossible as a governing machine. The oligarchic reaction under Sulla could not but be temporary in face of an industrial democracy. The political ideals suitable for an agricultural aristocracy were hopelessly obsolete. The shackles of senatorial ascendancy were struck off by the help of individuals who grasped the change in circumstances. So the corollary to Italian union was the Roman Empire: a century of great protagonists – the Gracchi, Marius, Pompey, and Caesar – closed in Augustus, and carnage gave way to peace.

Ways of money-making were at the same time multiplied. There was a brisk traffic in slaves, as mere labourers, as skilled mechanics, or as professional grammarians, copyists, and physicians. Incomes could be made from working quarries or mines or clay-pits, from money-lending for the purposes of trade and agriculture, from house-building and house-letting, and from shares in syndicates of *publicani* who farmed taxes or leased public lands. Ever-growing wealth had its invariable concomitant in growing extravagance, debt, and profligacy. The circle of Catullus in the Ciceronian period and that of Ovid in the Augustan period may serve to illustrate the luxury and immorality which Augustus set himself to stem by statesmanship and by a religious revival calculated to stir the old Roman conscience. This religious renascence is, like the consciousness of Italian unity, enshrined in the *Aeneid*. Virgil was seer enough to know how deadly was the poison in social life, and Horace, though no lover of austerity, felt a genuine admiration for the simplicity of old-fashioned morals.

Alongside of commercial expansion and speculative enterprise there was a quickened intellectual movement. To the ferment in politics and society corresponded a ferment in thought and taste. There were proud recollections of the old Latin poets in the quotations of Cicero and the lines of Virgil. There was that keen interest in the encyclopaedic knowledge of Greece to which the writings of Varro and Cicero could appeal, and which was signalised by Caesar's library schemes, by the actual foundation of the first public library at Rome by Pollio in 39, and of the *Bibliotheca Palatina* in 28. There were various currents and eddies in the broad stream of Hellenism – the opposing philosophies of the Academy, the Porch, and the Garden; opposing poetic traditions from

the classic ages of epic, lyric, and tragedy, or from the romantic decadence of Alexandria; opposing tendencies in oratory towards the
chastened Attic manner or towards florid Asianism; and a corresponding clash of tastes according as one admired Phidian sculpture or
the less restrained Hellenistic art. Apart from all imitations of Greek
masterpieces, the Romans responded in the plastic arts to the stimulus
of their own history. The frieze commemorative of the battle of Actium,
fought in 31 B.C., and the *Ara Pacis* of 13 B.C. are typical of the impulse
given to decorative art by the establishment of empire.[1] The growing
interest in the external form of buildings, marked by the *De Architectura* of Vitruvius in 14 B.C., may be summarised in the boast of
Augustus that he found Rome built of bricks and had made it a city of
marble.

Of the literature substantially the best has survived. The crowd of
ephemerals has vanished. In a well-known list of poets by Horace,[2]
Fundanius represents comedy, Pollio tragedy, Varius epic, Virgil
pastorals, and Varro of Atax satires. It is true that of this list only Virgil
is left. Of Propertius's equally well-known list[3] mentioning the same
Varro for his translation from the *Argonautica*, along with Catullus,
Calvus, and Gallus, only Catullus is left. Yet it is doubtful whether we
ought to view these blanks with half as much regret as we do the missing
books of Livy. The inference for literary history to be drawn from
obscure poems which have been rescued under the shadow of a great
name is that their inferior workmanship is typical of the general mass
of production at the time.[4] Linked with Tibullus we have the rather dry
imitations and overstrained verse-technique of Lygdamus, and the love-
letters of Sulpicia, in which some criticism, surely too severe, detects an
awkward management of poetic diction. Among the pseudo-Virgilian
poems the *Culex* does not consistently rise above vulgarisms, and much
in the *Ciris* may be best explained as a survival from the Alexandrine or
'neoteric' fashion of the preceding generation. This brings one to the
distinction so commonly drawn between the poetry of the Ciceronian
and that of the Augustan age. No literary movement had been more
phenomenal than the Alexandrinism which fascinated the circle of
Catullus and shrank before the more unfettered art of Virgil and Horace.
Such a movement does not shrink without leaving its traces. Another
school grows up: third-rate copiers of the old are left high and dry in
the midst of the latest style. These are the survivals who continue to
dress up the obsolete after the march of literature has left it behind.
So we have an Aemilius Macer with the Hellenistic style of his didac-

---

[1] See E. Strong, *Roman Sculpture*, 1907, p. 38 *sqq*. Cf. *Res Gest. Div.
Aug.* (Mon. Ancyr.), ch. xii, text restored with help of the corresponding
Greek, 'Cum ex Hispania Galliaque ... Romam redi(i) ... Aram Pacis Augustae
senatus pro reditu meo consacrari censuit ad Campum Martium.'
[2] Hor., *Sat.*, I. x. 40 *sqq*.   [3] Propert., II. xxxiv. 85.
[4] See F. Leo on *Vergil und die Ciris* in *Hermes*, xxxvii (1902) p. 47 *sqq*.

tics: so we find poetasters like Bavius and Mevius malevolently assailing the poetry of Virgil and Horace, and cutting sorry figures because they fought against the talents to which the future belonged.[1] It was by a natural law that Virgil and Horace should recoil from the romanticism of the 'neoterics.' Without exaggerating their feeling against Alexandrinism into that phantom idea which, Riese complained, has haunted books on Roman literature, one may be permitted to say that Horace's

Simius iste
Nil praeter Caluum et doctus cantare Catullum

can hardly imply less than dislike.[2]

Deeper than any altered trend of fashion is the altered spirit in the Augustan as contrasted with the Ciceronian literature. The Augustans, in a word, reflect imperial ideas. The change is visible even as between the earlier and the later Horace. The pessimism of *Epode* xvi is recanted in the third and fourth books of the *Odes*.[3] Some of the political tranquillity of the Augustan age seemed to pass over into its poetry. It is as if Augustus in tranquillising the world had also tranquillised letters — as if imperial discipline were schooling as well as inspiring authorship. The poetry of the age of Caesar had more freedom, if it showed more inequality. It was an age whose turbulence did not strangle production. Its poetry was nurtured in storm. The man of affairs and the man of blood could find solace in literary pursuits. Cicero wrote philosophy and verse; Caesar wrote on grammar and style. A mob of gentlemen composed. Their lives were usually anything but placid. It is to be expected that there should be a daring in Lucretius or Catullus which is absent from Virgil and Horace.

In the latter we meet a poetry of peace attained. It is significant that the life of the average and only very mildly philosophic citizen of the Augustan era was in practice regulated on Epicurean principles. Under an emperor with considerable Stoicism in his conception of duty, the prevailing attitude in conduct was Horace's easy-going Epicureanism. The same comfortable outlook was the aspiration of Sallust, Messalla, Pollio, and Maecenas. At the same time a host of new ideals had arrived to hearten and inspire a writer like Virgil, whose high thinking was concentrated upon a revived Italy, Rome's mission in the world, peace on earth, and a return of the 'Golden Age' of Saturn.

To these two great periods, the Ciceronian and the Augustan, belong

[1] See Leo, art. in *Hermes* cited in note 4 on p. 199.
[2] E. K. Rand invents with unconvincing ingenuity the analogy of 'a Methodist with pre-Raphaelite leanings. . . . whose acquaintance with English poetry was limited to two of his recently sanctioned hymns, *Crossing the Bar* and *The Recessional*.' To satirise such an one would not show disrespect to Tennyson or Kipling, he submits – 'Catullus and the Augustans' in *Harvard Studies in Class. Philol.*, vol. xvii.
[3] *E.g.* Hor., *Od.*, IV. ii. 37-40.

the greatest poetry, the greatest oratory, and save for Tacitus the greatest history written in Latin. It was an age of scholars and critics; but neither scholarship nor criticism killed creative work. The best creations of the time are classic because they retain an undying ascendancy through their power to illuminate, inspire, ennoble, and console the mind of man. Theirs is that gift of beauty which makes immortal appeal to all ages possessed of culture.

Chapter I

LUCRETIUS, THE POET OF EPICUREANISM

Difficulties in Jerome's account – Cicero's editorship of Lucretius's poems – Memmius, the poet's patron – Relation of Lucretius to his times – Date of the work – Epicureanism – Attitude of Lucretius to Epicurus – Its bearing on Lucretius's originality – Other sources – The books of the *De Rerum Natura* – Lucretius's threefold claim to renown – His science – His philosophy of life and death – The poetic side of his genius – Is there a tendency towards mysticism? – Tenderness – Eye for external nature – Prosaic, dull, and archaic elements – The Lucretian hexameter – Triumphs of expression – The text – Influence on his immediate successors – Lucretius and Virgil.

AN APPROPRIATE obscurity enwraps the life of the masterly poet of the greatest pagan system of quietism. T. Lucretius Carus (*circ.* 99–55 B.C.),[1] standing with Roman independence aloof from the literary Alexandrinism of his day and with Epicurean wisdom avoiding politics, made his appeal in the *De Rerum Natura* to a circle of readers necessarily circumscribed. Hence, though his influence on the greatest poets of Rome was considerable, it is scarcely surprising that there exists only one reference to his works which can be called contemporary. Apart from the little to be inferred from his own poem, almost all our information about his life comes from Jerome's note,[2]

---

[1] Text: C. Lachmann, 1850; notes and translation, H. A. J. Munro, 1891–93 (1st ed. 1864); *Corp. Poet. Lat.*, 1894, J. P. Postgate from Munro's text. Subject-matter: Constant Martha, *Le Poème de Lucrèce*, 1869; W. Y. Sellar, *Roman Poets of the Republic*, ed. 3, 1889; J. Masson, *Lucretius, Epicurean and Poet*, 1907; E. Zeller, *The Stoics, Epicureans, and Sceptics* (Eng. trans., ed. 2, 1880); A. W. Benn, *The Greek Philosophers*, 1882, vol. ii; W. Wallace, *Epicureanism*, 1880.

[2] Hieronym. *Euseb. Chron.* ad ann. Abr. 1922 (=95 B.C.): 'T. Lucretius poeta nascitur, qui postea amatorio poculo in furorem uersus, cum aliquot libros per interualla insaniae conscripsisset, quos postea Cicero emendauit, propria se manu interfecit anno aetatis xliiii' (=52 B.C.).

which reads like an awkward attempt to crush into a nutshell details
once recorded by Suetonius. Every clause in Jerome's entry has been
disputed. It has been plausibly argued that he made Lucretius's birth
and his death each four years too late; and it has been denied that
Lucretius was driven frenzied by a love-philtre, or, though insane, wrote
several books during lucid intervals, or committed suicide, or that his
works were 'emended' by 'Cicero.' According to the *Life of Virgil*
ascribed to Donatus, Lucretius died on the very day in 55 B.C. on which
Virgil assumed the dress of manhood. Though some have taken this for a
fiction symbolic of one side of Virgil's literary ancestry, it receives support from the fact that we find Cicero writing to his brother in February of 54 about their impressions of Lucretius's poems, which they
have been reading. Jerome's words, difficult to accept in their entirety,
cannot be dismissed as absolutely unfounded. True, the well-controlled
reasoning power evinced in the *De Rerum Natura* gives no hint of
insanity. Yet the story of Lucretius's madness, so beautifully handled
by Tennyson, may have a firmer basis than the invention of those, not
necessarily Christians, in whose eyes the poet's 'impious' attack upon
orthodox beliefs might well seem to augur and deserve an evil end. This
at least is clear, that the work comes to a sudden conclusion. A mind
evidently acquainted with the strange shapes of delirium, and capable
of such perfervid concentration on the colossal theme of the universe,
might easily become overwrought; and a breakdown accompanied by a
more than ordinary access of pessimism might beckon a lover of 'death
immortal' towards a sure anodyne in self-destruction. The story of the
love-philtre would be a slight refinement, easily prompted by the contemptuous attitude towards love in the fourth book.[1]

A wide consensus of opinion holds that Lucretius's work was published under the superintendence of Marcus Cicero himself rather than
of his brother Quintus. Editorship did not necessarily imply correc-
tion, rearrangement, or finishing touches. But it was a fitting task for
one whose youthful translation of Aratus had been freely imitated by
Lucretius, and an easy task for one whose Epicurean friend Atticus had
trained copyists at his service. The single express mention of Lucretius
in Cicero, already alluded to, has been much debated and needlessly
emended. Taken in the natural sense of the passage in the MSS., it runs:

The poems of Lucretius are, as you say in your letter, marked by
many flashes of genius, and all the same by much skill; but (more of
this) when you come. I shall think you a hero, if you read through
Sallust's *Empedoclea*; but I shan't think you a human being.[2]

[1] The divergence of opinion regarding Lucretius's death is well illustrated
in Giacomo Giri, *Il Suicidio di T. Lucrezio*, Palermo, 1895, and Ettore Stampini, *Il Suicidio di Lucrezio*, Messina, 1896. The former dismisses philtre and
suicide as legends; the latter defends Jerome's narrative. For a notice of Stampini's opinions, see *Class. Rev.*, 1898, xii, pp. 237–245.
[2] *Ad Quint. Fr.*, II. ix. 3, 'Lucreti poemata, ut scribis, ita sunt: multis

This view of words written four months after the poet's death, and contrasting 'genius' with 'skill,' possesses the interest of linking to the literary movement of the day Cicero's criticism of the work recently put into his hands. Lucretius represented the older line of Latin poetry which reflected the inborn Roman spirit. The newer school, partly inaugurated by Catullus, was enamoured of Alexandrine models, and aped the art of Callimachus and of Euphorion of Chalcis.[1] They were the exponents of refinement in phraseology and versification, as distinguished from the rugged genius of a bygone age. It was therefore a pointed claim for Lucretius when Cicero credited him with the 'genius' of an Ennius and the 'art' of the Alexandrine imitators.[2]

The single contemporary mentioned by Lucretius is the Memmius (*Memmi clara propago*) to whom he dedicates his poem. C. Memmius, praetor in 58, had considerable interest in literature, wrote erotic verses, and took Catullus and Cinna on his staff to Bithynia in the year after his praetorship. Versatile but shallow, he was an untrustworthy politician. His anti-Caesarian stand, which delighted Cicero, was succeeded by a *volte-face* and by sundry underhand dealings. A charge of bribery drove him into exile. His sympathy with Epicureanism must have been of the slightest, for Cicero had to appeal to him to preserve the site of Epicurus's famous gardens at Athens, which had come into his hands by purchase.[3] Altogether, he little deserved Lucretius's glowing compli-

---

luminibus ingeni, multae tamen artis; sed cum ueneris – Virum te putabo, si Sallusti *Empedoclea* legeris, hominem non putabo.' Many editors have insisted on inserting *non* either before *multis* or before *multae*. Munro and Tyrrell find a satisfactory contrast without any such addition. Shuckburgh in his translation of *The Letters of Cicero*, 1899, vol. i, p. 266, takes the contrast to be 'many flashes of genius, yet very technical,' referring to the fine poetical passages in Lucretius as against the mass of philosophical exposition. There is no call for ingeniously far-fetched emendations like Nettleship's (*Journ. Phil.*, 1885): *multae tamen* (or *etiam*) *artis ipse dicam ueneris artium.*

[1] These poets of the latest fashion are called by Cicero νεώτεροι, when he playfully tells Atticus to pass off upon them a spondaic hexameter, tossed into one of his letters (*Ad Att.*, VII. ii. 1). They are disdainfully termed *hi cantores Euphorionis*, when he rapturously praises Ennius in opposition to their neglect of him (*Tusc. Disp.*, III. xix. 45).

[2] Apropos of Cicero's criticism, it is doubtful what weight should attach to new data in a *Life of Lucretius* written early in the sixteenth century by Borgius (Girolamo Borgia). First published by Dr. J. Masson in *Acad.*, No. 1155 (1894), it was subsequently discussed *Journ. of Philol.*, xxxiii, 220 *sqq.* Cf. *Class. Rev.*, x. 323–4; Masson, *Lucretius*, etc., 1907, 38 *sqq.* Masson maintains that it draws material from Suetonius independent of Jerome. This is denied by Fritsche, *Berl. Phil. Woch.*, xv. 541, and by Woltjer, *ibid.*, 317, and *Mnemos.*, 1895, xxiii, 222. The most interesting item is Borgius's report that Cicero advised Lucretius to observe restraint in metaphors, citing as objectionable 'Neptuni lacunas' and 'caeli cauernas.' That the former expression does not occur in our text of Lucretius, and that the latter was used by Cicero himself in his early *Aratea*, do not convincingly prove that the story is a forgery by the humanists.

[3] *Ad Fam.*, XIII. i.

ments,[1] and was presumably little impressed by his exposure of the evils of ambition and sensuality. The serene tone of equality adopted towards Memmius forbids one to believe that the poet was of servile descent, as has been sometimes inferred from the strangeness of 'Carus' as a cognomen of the *gens Lucretia*. It is probable that, like Caesar, Lucretius was a native of Rome.

Lucretius lived through the horrors of the Marian and Sullan massacres and the Catilinarian peril. He saw the first triumvirate followed by the bravado of Caesar's consulship. Yet this gloomy period leaves its impress not in definite allusions—there is only one[2]—but in the sombre colours of the background.[3] He sees decay in the world;[4] he is acquainted with the pomp and circumstance of war;[5] and, sick of the meanness and meaninglessness of ambitious strife, he yearns for an ideal of philosophic calm:

> Naught sweeter than to hold the tranquil realms
> On high, well fortified by sages' lore,
> Whence to look down on others wide astray —
> Lost wanderers questing for the way of life —
> See strife of genius, rivalry of rank,
> See night and day men strain with wondrous toil
> To rise to utmost power and grasp the world.[6]

One feature of the age was restless doubt, acceptance of strange Eastern cults, and a revolt from traditional beliefs and observances. Less than ever could augur meet augur without smiling. Caesar in the Catilinarian debate openly rejected the conception of a future life. Cant was producing the inevitable reaction. The old doctrines were dissolving. Consistently with the times, the darker shadows in the *De Rerum*

---

[1] *E.g.*, I. 26:
> 'Memmiadae nostro, quem tu, dea, tempore in omni
>   Omnibus ornatum uoluisti excellere rebus.'

[2] I. 41–43:
> 'Nam neque nos agere hoc patriai tempore iniquo
>   Possumus aequo animo nec Memmi clara propago
>   Talibus in rebus communi desse saluti.'

[3] 'On se persuade que Lucrèce n'a pas été un spectateur indifférent des guerres civiles, et que son âme a connu toutes les tristesses du désespoir politique,' Martha, *op. cit.*, ed. 7, p. 29.

[4] II. 1150 *sqq.* For the apparently decreasing productiveness of land, Columella sees a truer reason in the mismanagement which trusted agriculture 'to any hangdog of a slave' (*pessimo cuique seruorum uelut carnifici*: *De Re Rust.* Praef. § 3).

[5] II. 40 *sqq.*, and II. 323 *sqq.*

[6] II. 7–13:
> 'Sed nil dulcius est, bene quam munita tenere
> Edita doctrina sapientum templa serena,
> Despicere unde queas alios passimque uidere
> Errare atque uiam palantis quaerere uitae,
> Certare ingenio, contendere nobilitate,
> Noctes atque dies niti praestante labore
> Ad summas emergere opes rerumque potiri.'

Natura reflect the throes which have wrung the author's soul. He has triumphed over intellectual and religious doubts, and has found peace. But the struggle has left scars. Convinced of his duty to liberate men from disquieting superstitions, and especially from the dread of death, he becomes a missioner for the system of Epicurus. This gives Lucretius his fervour. With him Epicureanism is no jaunty *insouciance* of the luxurious upper classes, but an earnest evangel. His free-thought is worthy of the age of Caesar. The first, if we except Ennius, to build a Latin poem on Greek philosophy, he virtually proclaims the failure of conventional thought to satisfy the intellect, and of conventional religion to satisfy the soul. He is an ancient protestant, fiery, not cold, in his disbelief. His work, addressed nominally to Memmius, is in reality addressed to the world and to time. This is the best of reasons why it contains so little trace of current history.

The *De Rerum Natura* consists of six books. The last two betray signs of lacking final revision, and presumably belong to the poet's closing years. No exact chronology of the work is obtainable. In the fourth book an illustration of the theory of colour drawn from the theatre awnings[1] implies a date after 69, and the reference in the sixth book to awnings of canvas[2] must be later than their introduction in 59. The invocation to Venus at the opening of the first book may possibly be one of the latest passages composed by Lucretius.[3]

The theme is the universe, explained on the atomic principles propounded in Greece by Leucippus and Democritus, and from Democritus borrowed by Epicurus to form the physical side of his philosophy. On the ethical side for Epicurus the *summum bonum* was Pleasure, in the form of peace of mind ($\dot{a}\tau a\rho a\xi\acute{\imath}a$), secured by refined enjoyments, the simple life, and an avoidance of excessive passions and of political entanglements. The danger that ignorance might feed superstition prompted him to embody physics in his system. The laws of nature would prove the best antidote to the supernatural. So he wrote one of his many voluminous works—the $\Pi\epsilon\rho\grave{\imath}\ \Phi\acute{\upsilon}\sigma\epsilon\omega s$, in thirty-seven books of prose. This philosophy of the secluded and happy Garden suited the decadent spirit which arose under the Macedonian primacy in Greece. Its fitting counterpart was the comic drama of Menander. Life was to be taken easily. The practical problem was how to get the maximum of sustained pleasure. Happiness rather than truth was the aim. Materialist in basis and discountenancing public duties, it was a philosophy exposed to attack on the grounds of atheism and selfishness. Its adaptability to different temperaments was at once the secret

---

[1] IV. 75–77.   [2] VI. 109–110.

[3] The invocation to Venus may have been suggested by the fact that Memmius was son-in-law to Sulla, who was devoted to the goddess. It would have a special point in the year of Lucretius's death in view of Pompey's dedication of the temple to Venus Victrix when he built the new theatre. See F. Marx. *Neue Jahrb. f. d. klass. Altertum*, III. viii, 1899.

of its success and the reason for the hostility of Christian writers like
Lactantius.[1] The social life of Athens, grown comfort-loving and
moribund, was a different thing from that of Rome, convulsed and
blood-sodden, but big with the potentialities of empire. Yet it was the
system of this very period that Lucretius adopted and expounded with
the confidence of a benefactor of society. The tenth book of Diogenes
Laertius, with its excerpts and letters of Epicurus, the criticisms, moreover, in Cicero, Seneca, Plutarch, Lucian, and others, with the fragments of Epicurus's own and of Epicurean works deciphered among the
papyri rescued at Herculaneum in the eighteenth century, leave no
doubt as to the accuracy of the Lucretian exposition.[2] But it is more
than a truthful presentation. It is the one artistic utterance of Epicureanism.

There is a spiritual ecstasy in the attitude of Lucretius towards
Epicurus. It is as if the poet felt the holiest sacrament in life to be a
reverent communion with the teaching of the great master who had
redeemed mankind from woe and beckoned the soul to a paradise of
unruffled pleasure. At one time Lucretius sees in him heroic manhood
inspired by intellect, at another time a godhead with a revelation to raise
mankind. He extols Epicurus[3] as 'the man of Greece who first dared
lift his mortal eyes to face the monster Superstition lowering with
hideous aspect above prostrate humanity, and who, undeterred by
myth or thunderbolt, first yearned to burst the fast barriers of nature's
gates':

> So vivid force of mind prevailed. He passed
> Far o'er the flaming ramparts of the world,
> And traversed the immeasurable All
> In mind and soul.[4]

The daring was rewarded by a victorious penetration into the mysteries
and laws of the universe. Elsewhere Lucretius proclaims his disciple-
ship:

> I follow thee, thou glory of the Greeks,
> And in thy footprints firmly plant my steps;[5]

---

[1] *Diuin. Instit.*, III. xvii: 'Epicuri disciplina . . . ut ad se multitudinem
contrahat, apposita singulis quibusque moribus loquitur. Desidiosum uetat
literas discere; auarum populari largitione liberat; ignauum prohibet accedere
ad rem publicam, pigrum exercere, timidum militare. Irreligiosus audit deos
nihil curare.'

[2] For other Epicurean documents, such as the Vatican 'Exhortation' and
the Oinoanda inscription summarising the chief tenets of Epicurus, see Masson,
op. cit., pp. 319 *sqq.*

[3] I. 62 *sqq.*

[4] I. 72–74: 'Ergo uiuida uis animi peruicit, et extra
Processit longe flammantia moenia mundi
Atque omne immensum peragrauit mente animoque.'

[5] III. 3–4: 'Te sequor, O Graiae gentis decus, inque tuis nunc
Ficta pedum pono pressis uestigia signis.'

and this not from rivalry but from love (*non ita certandi cupidus quam propter amorem*) — how should the swallow vie with the swan?

> Thou, father, art discoverer of things,
> Enriching us with all a father's lore;
> And, famous master, from thy written page,
> As bees in flowery dells sip every bloom,
> So hold we feast on all thy golden words —
> Golden, most worthy aye of lasting life.[1]

Before Epicurus the terrors of the mind disperse, and to him the divine nature is revealed (*apparet diuum numen*) — a vision of stormless calm and generous light wherein the gods dwell at ease. It is with mingled ecstasy and awe that Lucretius realises this triumphant unveiling of nature.[2] In the fifth book,[3] a rapturous eulogy culminates in a deification of Epicurus. Who could suffice to sing the praises of the founder of a system which brought life out of darkness into light?

> God was he, god, O famous Memmius;[4]

and his gift of the tranquil mind 'transcends the boon of bread and wine.' As a friend of man he outrivals all fabled slayers of monsters. In similar tones the introduction to the sixth book declares that the best gift of Athens to man was Epicurus, who saw that misery of mind yields, not to wealth and honour, but to wisdom, and who taught that to happiness there is but one narrow way.[5] With such enthusiasm, it is natural that Lucretius should overestimate the originality of his master.

How Lucretius first encountered the influence of Epicureanism can only be guessed. There were in the city Greek professors of the system established beyond the risk of the banishment meted out to their predecessors in the second century. The hold obtained is evident from the popular language and design of treatises by writers who are mentioned by Cicero and who were not Greeks — Amafinius, Rabirius, and Catius the Insubrian. Cicero himself in youth had been taken with the tenets of such lecturers, and his circle in later life included many Epicureans besides Atticus and the Cassius who was among Caesar's murderers. The existence of works intended as propaganda for Epicureanism bears on the question of Lucretius's originality. His originality does not hang on any absolute priority as a Latin mouthpiece of the

---

[1] III. 9–13: 'Tu, pater, es rerum inuentor, tu patria nobis
   Suppeditas praecepta, tuisque ex, inclute, chartis,
   Floriferis ut apes in saltibus omnia libant,
   Omnia nos itidem depascimur aurea dicta,
   Aurea, perpetua semper dignissima uita.'
[2] III. 28–30: 'His ibi me rebus quaedam diuina uoluptas
   Percipit atque horror, quod sic natura tua ui
   Tam manifesta patens ex omni parte retecta est.'
[3] V. *ad init.*
[4] V. 8: '... deus ille fuit, deus, inclute Memmi.'
[5] VI. 26–27.

theory. His unrivalled feat was to make Epicureanism epic. He turned philosophy and science into poetry. He made them practical also by applying them to the spiritual nightmares of his times. He gave a Roman cast to Greek material. Thus, with all his worship for his Hellenic guide, he remains one of the line of Ennius in spirit no less than in old-fashioned phrase.

He had other sources. Much of his inspiration was drawn from that extraordinarily brilliant Dorian thinker, Empedocles of Agrigentum, a unique blend of philosopher, poet, mystic, politician, physician and engineer, from whose poem Περὶ Φύσεως less than five hundred hexameters survive. His biological conception of the unity pervading matter and mind, his anticipation of the modern doctrine of natural selection, his poetic translation into terms of 'love' and 'hatred' of the principles of attraction and repulsion, as well as his metre, were adopted by Lucretius. Lucretius's reading in Greek extends beyond philosophers whom he imitates and those whom, like Heraclitus, Anaxagoras, Plato, and the Stoics, he criticises. He borrows from Homer and Euripides, from Thucydides and Hippocrates. He is versed too in the national poetry, as echoes of Naevius, Ennius, Pacuvius, Accius and Lucilius serve to prove. The contemporary verses of Cicero are not lost on him.

Of the six books, two are on the atomic theory, two on psychic processes, two on the evolution of nature and the causes of the most impressive natural phenomena. The two fundamental postulates of atoms and the void are laid down in the opening book, and contrasted with erroneous physical theories. The next book considers more amply the properties of atoms, and modifies their parallel rush by that minute swerve (*exiguum clinamen principiorum*) which wrests the mind from Necessity and explains Freewill.[1] The third is a wonderful book. The theme is the inter-relation of body and soul. Half in the spirit of science, half in the spirit of poetry, Lucretius dives into the very 'soul of the soul.' Nearly thirty reasons are marshalled against the belief in immortality, and the book ends in victory over fear of death or of future punishments. Self-consciousness once broken, death has no sting:

Nil igitur mors est ad nos neque pertinet hilum.

Yet there is no shutting of the eyes to sorrow. What keen poignancy of suffering death brings to the bereaved, Lucretius well knows. Gray's adaptation in his *Elegy* has made doubly familiar the lines:

> 'Soon shall thy home greet thee in joy no more,
> Nor faithful wife nor darling children run
> To snatch first kiss, and stir within thy heart
> Sweet thoughts too deep for words. Thou canst no more

1 'Fatis auolsa uoluntas.' II. 257

Win wealth by working or defend thine own.
The pity of it! One fell hour,' they say,
'Hath robbed thee of thine every prize in life.'[1]

But he does not let pathos daunt him: his comment is that of the philosopher:

Hereat they add not this: 'And now thou art
Beset with yearning for such things no more.'[2]

The envious apostrophe of the heart-sore survivor to the dead lulled to rest and freed from every pang;[3] the analogy of the sleeper recking naught if his sleep be eternal:[4] the restrained rebuke that is in universal nature for the man who dares not die;[5] the denunciation of the only hellish tortures—those of the passions in this life;[6] and the picture of the unceasing but ineffectual endeavour of the victim of *ennui* to escape from self,[7] all present Lucretius, like Keats, as 'half in love with easeful Death.' The attitude towards final dissolution is brave acceptance, not that shrinking which begets in Omar Kkayyam the desperate argument

'While you live
Drink!—for once dead, you never shall return.'

To Lucretius, 'Let us eat and drink, for tomorrow we die' is vapid reasoning: it is as though the dead would miss such things.[8] This question of life and death, the central matter of his speculations and the pivot on which the whole of his earnestness revolves, gives place to a book considerably less poetic. The fourth book is occupied mainly with the senses. The theory of inconceivably fine films emitted from objects (*rerum simulacra*) is used to explain sight. Colour, shadows, refraction, sleep and dreams are discussed before love is reduced to its physiological terms, and sarcastically laid bare in its extravagance and ruinous effects. Much power is exhibited in the fifth book. The evolution of the world, of man and his culture, forms its subject. Most readers will agree that its cosmic portions on the origin of earth, sky, sea, on the heavenly bodies and their motions, are far outshone by its biology and anthropology. It is in the fancy of the fertile motherhood of earth, teeming in a distant past with superabundant production, in glances at extinct

[1] III. 894 *sqq.*:
' " Iam iam non domus accipiet te laeta, neque uxor
Optima nec dulces occurrent oscula nati
Praeripere et tacita pectus dulcedine tangent.
Non poteris factis florentibus esse, tuisque
Praesidium; misero misere" aiunt "omnia ademit
Una dies infesta tibi tot praemia uitae." '
[2] III. 900–901:
' Illud in his rebus non addunt – " Nec tibi earum
Iam desiderium rerum super insidet una." '
[3] III. 904 *sqq.*   [4] III. 919 *sqq.*   [5] III. 931 *sqq.*
[6] III. 978 *sqq.*   [7] III. 1060 *sqq.*   [8] III. 914 *sqq.*

species of monsters eliminated because unfit, in re-creating the hardy
existence of primeval man, in picturing the atmosphere of danger in
which man moved, and in tracing the gradual development of kindliness, language, fire, law, religion, metallurgy, music, and all the arts
of civilisation, that Lucretius shows the marvellous insight of both
thinker and artist. With a union of pessimism and courage, he has
unfolded his argument till he finds all life and matter to be in the same
series of things, and man and the earth infinitesimal portions[1] of a
universe of similar products everlastingly decomposing to recompose in
the infinite drift of atoms. Man, then, is of the same stuff as earth and
stars. Genius is a scintillation of body. Lucretius's very hexameter —
and he is fond of noting the analogy between its component letters and
the atoms — might be defined, in terms applied by a poet[2] to blank
verse, as a 'material emanation of the concrete mystery, matter.' The
sixth book, though it deals with mighty processes in nature, is much less
imposing. From the phenomena of thunder and lightning, clouds, rain-
bows, and the magnet, it proceeds to the theory of disease. It concludes
with a description of the great plague at Athens, imitating and sometimes closely translating, though not without blunders, the account of
Thucydides.[3]

Any estimate of an author must hinge on his aim. In Lucretius this
is clear. Conscious of his difficult subject and his poetic mission, he
bases his claim to remembrance upon three counts:

> How dark my theme, I know within my mind:
> Yet hath high hope of praise with thyrsus keen
> Smitten my heart, and struck into my breast
> Sweet passion for the Muses, stung wherewith,
> In lively thought I traverse pathless haunts
> Pierian, untrodden yet of man.
> I love to visit those untasted springs
> And quaff; I love to cull fresh blooms, and, whence
> The Muses never veiled the brows of man,
> To seek a wreath of honour for my head;
> First, for that lofty is the lore I teach;
> And cramping knots of priestcraft I would loose;
> And eke because of mysteries I sing clear,
> Decking my poems with the Muses' charm.[4]

---

[1] Cf. VI. 649–652.   [2] John Davidson, *Triumph of Mammon*, 1907.
[3] Thuc., II. xlvii–liv. Lucretius was in turn imitated by Virgil, *Georg.*, iii.
478–566; Ovid, *Met.*, vii. 523–613; and by Livy more than once.
[4] I. 922 *sqq.*:

> 'Nec me animi fallit quam sint obscura: sed acri
> Percussit thyrso laudis spes magna meum cor
> Et simul incussit suauem mi in pectus amorem
> Musarum, quo nunc instinctus mente uigenti
> Auia Pieridum peragro loca nullius ante
> Trita solo. Iuuat integros accedere fontis
> Atque haurire, iuuatque nouos decerpere flores

The three pillars of his fame, then, are his scientific system, his attitude to religion, and his poetic power.

If the science of Lucretius could be isolated from its underlying purpose and poetry, his genius would still be assured a place in the history of thought, independent of the history of literature. His lucid and forcible exposition of the Democritean conception of the ultimate constitution of the universe would compel attention, if only for its anticipations of modern speculation. The atomic theory, revived in the seventeenth century by Gassendi, and handed down through Boyle, Newton, and Dalton, is still for scientific thought its basic hypothesis. Even in the light of the flashes of the spinthariscope which mark the off-shooting of helium atoms from radium, it is not more than a modification of nomenclature that is necessary. Chemistry and physics still interpret their phenomena on the assumption that matter consists of discrete particles. To call these particles, as in recent physical speculation 'electrons' or 'nucleons' instead of 'atoms' is merely to find the ultimate entities some grades further down. In many other ways he anticipates modern conclusions. He does so in generalisations like 'the indestructibility of matter' and 'the conservation of energy,' in affirming the equal velocity of bodies falling in a vacuum, in his denial of 'design' in nature, in his recognition of the circulation of sap in plants, in his perception of principles so essentially Darwinian as 'the struggle for existence' and 'the survival of the fittest,' and in his substantial agreement with recent anthropology on the progress of primitive man and the origin of beliefs in the divine. Without Descartes's dualism of body and soul, he resembles Descartes in ascribing no 'secondary qualities' to his fundamental substance. Lucretius interposes no supernatural agents, no metaphysical abstractions, between things and their causes. He is concerned directly with things and their laws. His attitude is essentially that which Comte calls the third and highest in knowledge — the positive and scientific. Broadly, his seeming atheism in theology, his materialism in physics, his sensationalism in psychology, and his hedonistic utilitarianism in ethics make up a whole which is parallel to later systems as a provocative of misrepresentation. He feels bound, indeed, to reassure Memmius against suspicions of his dangerously advanced thought.[1] Such foreshadowings, even where they are not of his own invention, are the more impressive in one who

---

   Insignemque meo capiti petere inde coronam
   Unde prius nulli uelarint tempora musae;
   Primum quod magnis doceo de rebus et artis
   Religionum animum nodis exsoluere pergo,
   Deinde quod obscura de re tam lucida pango
   Carmina, musaeo contingens cuncta lepore.'

[1] I. 80: 'Illud in his rebus uereor, ne forte rearis
   Inpia te rationis inire elementa uiamque
   Indugredi sceleris.'

depended on observation instead of experiment. His lapses are proportionately less surprising. An array of crudities and errors is not far to seek. He denied the existence of the antipodes: he fancied the earth in equilibrium at the centre of the universe; he declared the real size of the sun and other heavenly bodies to be roughly equal to their apparent size; he gravely explained why a lion is afraid of a cock; and, innocent of any conception of brain and nervous system, he took the mind to be a subtle substance accommodated in the breast. His method of argument is frequently loose, especially in his resort to unconvincing analogies, and in his impartial contentment with different explanations of the same phenomenon. His atomic scheme itself has its weaknesses. Though he finely suggests the hidden processes of nature in a line worthy to serve as motto for the minutest research in microbiology:

Corporibus caecis igitur natura gerit res,[1]

yet the words seem to cover a multitude of omissions. No attempt is made to show how atoms, destitute of all content, and, except for shape, of absolutely negative quality, can in combination generate life. Lucretius assumes no protoplasm, no 'mind stuff.' The gap is concealed rather than bridged by terms implying creative powers, such as 'seeds' (*semina*) and 'birth-giving bodies' (*genitalia corpora*), which he imposes upon the atoms.

The truth, however, is that the greatness of Lucretius does not depend on whether his science is impeccable, but on his philosophy of life. It matters much more that he sought to teach man how to defy death than that he approached the solution of the ultimate composition of matter, or that he held a geocentric theory of the universe, or failed to anticipate Kepler's laws of planetary motion. His attitude to religion is the kernel of his thought. It produces the earnestness which is the mainspring of his system and the very breath of his style. Concerned with the ultimate constituents of all animate and inanimate nature; handling, in the supreme confidence of settling for ever, speculations about the divine, about creation, about the soul, about a future existence; embracing high arguments of Miltonic seriousness which involved invasion, if not abolition, of the provinces

'Of providence, foreknowledge, will and fate,'

his theme is scientific and philosophic, and necessarily abstract. Yet it is practical. He spoke of the world to man and for man's good:

> Needs then dispel this dread, this gloom of soul,
> Not by the sunbeams nor clear shafts of day,
> But by the face of nature and its plan.[2]

[1] I. 328.
[2] I. 146–148:

Man should no longer disquiet himself in vain with the fear of gods, of death, of eternal punishment. He should be initiate in a true doctrine of the universe; through his acquiescence in what from the premises must be, despite its faults,[1] the best of all possible worlds, he should attain an Epicurean tranquillity. The poem is the triumphant achievement of an intellect which coped with gigantic problems. And it is great for more than its profundity: it is also brave and humane. Lucretius was a reformer, a liberator from paralysing delusions. His *De Rerum Natura* is not a work of speculation for speculation's sake. It is designed to cure humanity heartsick over the evils of life.[2] His proem is, therefore, fittingly followed by his praise of Epicurus's revolt against religion and the touchingly beautiful picture of Iphigeneia's sacrifice, culminating in the scathing line:

Tantum religio potuit suadere malorum.'[3]

It is an attitude to religion which becomes clearer in the light of periodic panics which unnerved Rome, when overmastering dread of divine anger drove the community into the most superstitious of expiations, and sometimes into ruthless extirpation of rites popularly believed to savour of pollution.

Lucretius claimed to unite clearness and beauty in his verses. But the poetic cannot be restricted to style in any narrow sense. It is too easy to over-accentuate the antithesis between the scientific and the poetic in him, as if his system promised little beyond the merely didactic. It may be urged that he views the universe in no Wordsworthian fashion. He is not oppressed with the mystery of 'all this unintelligible world.' Its burden he can bear, because it is intelligible. He explains it.[4] He deduces it from first principles. He will leave nothing to fear—not gods, nor religion, nor death, nor Hades. Yet it is risky to call even his speculations unpoetic. It is to overlook that dual and inextricably intertwined endowment of philosophic and poetic powers wherein his mind resembles Goethe's. It is to overlook that depth of feeling which makes the dry bones of his science live, and brings poetry into his physics and even into his anti-religion. Why should it be assumed that his subject

---

'Hunc igitur terrorem animi tenebrasque necessest
Non radii solis neque lucida tela diei
Discutiant, sed naturae species ratioque.'

[1] II. 181:
'Tanta stat praedita culpa.'
The blemishes of the world to Lucretius's mind prove the fortuitous concourse of atoms and disprove any divine providence.
[2] In a vivid though homely simile, he likens his exposition to administering medicine to children. His doctrine may be unpalatable; but his poetry is the honey smeared on the rim of the cup: I. 936–950.
[3] I. 101.
[4] 'Lucrèce est sur tous points content de sa doctrine: il n'en désire pas une meilleure.... La tristesse est dans le système.' – Martha, *op. cit.*

is intractable from a poetic standpoint? To compose an epic on the universe is in itself a majestic and poetic idea. There is drama enough if the stage is the illimitable void where atoms have their ceaseless exits and entrances.[1] Lucretius wrote an epic of creation. His poem was not composed, like Caedmon's *Genesis*, in a simple and rugged versification and with unquestioning adherence to a traditional account; it was possessed by a spirit of inquiry into the new and of criticism towards the old, with frequent elaboration and beauty, with a wealth of imagery, and a poet's heart. The very inconsistencies in his science are largely due to the bard within. A strictly scientific naturalism akin to the systematic investigation conducted by physicist or chemist frequently in Lucretius passes over into an ideal naturalism akin to such conceptions as the Providential Reason of the Stoics, or Giordano Bruno's fundamental Cause and Unity magnificent in beauty, or Goethe's Mighty Goddess exacting worship and admiration. This upholder of the fortuitous concourse of atoms lapses into phrases implying purpose and even passion in 'Nature.' More than once she is *rerum natura creatrix*:[2] elsewhere she pilots things, *gubernans*. It is 'jealous' (*inuida*) Nature that keeps her gradual processes of decay unseen.[3] It is Nature acting in a providential way that allows nothing to be torn from the atoms, reserving them as seeds for things (*reseruans semina rebus*).[4] Logically, the Chance of his hypothesis is thrown over in favour of growth according to fixed laws (*per foedera naturai*).[5] It is the poet, not the man of science, who yearns for a guiding principle in *dux uitae dia uoluptas*.[6] It is Nature who reasons with the man afraid to die, telling him, if lucky, to part like a satisfied guest from a banquet, and, if unlucky, to expect no better things in her realm, where, as with Tennyson's Lotus-Eaters, 'all things always are the same' (*eadem sunt omnia semper*).[7] Love and death, which are of the essence of poetry, are also among his themes. They do not wear, it may be said, their lyric or dramatic aspects. Love is made a portion of psychology and physiology, and death a physical change—the loss of a certain amount of heat and breath. Yet here, too, over the coldly scientific investigation, the poet in him rises. Love can be idealised into Venus, and over death defied a rhapsody of triumph can be sung. In a score of ways, fortunately for literature, romance prevails against his rationalism. There is an anti-Lucretius, as Patin reminds us.[8]

So much poetry is there in his science and his anti-religion that at times he verges on mysticism. Perhaps it is too much to say that he was

---

[1] VI. 493-494:
    'Et quasi per magni circum spiracula mundi
    Exitus introitusque elementis redditus exstat.'
[2] I. 629; II. 1117.   [3] I. 321.   [4] I. 614.
[5] II. 302.   [6] II. 172.   [7] III. 931 *sqq.*
[8] 'L'Antilucrèce chez Lucrèce,' in Patin's *Études sur la poésie latine*, i, ch. vii.

groping towards a higher faith. Yet the inconsistencies in his explanation of the universe, when he ascribes personality, guidance, and creative
power to nature, do mark flitting gleams of something behind and higher
than the atoms. With a tribunician vehemence he assails the bondage of
religion; yet he sympathetically and even reverently notes the effect on
worshippers of a procession with the image of the Earth-mother
Cybele, who, Madonna-like

> With silent blessing mutely makes men rich.[1]

He denies the divine origin of things; yet in the very refusal to believe
that so imperfect a world could be god-created he pays implicit homage
to the idea of the divine, and some of his most beautiful lines are devoted
to the Epicurean view of the gods enjoying peace everlasting, far remote
from mortal concerns, exempt from pain and peril, untouched by
favour or by wrath.[2] Little mysticism appears in his attitude to the
myths. It is entirely critical, except where he consciously chooses to
accept their glamour. There is a cool condescension and analytic aloofness in an author who pauses to remark that, should any one prefer to
say 'Neptune' for sea, 'Ceres' for the fruits of the earth, 'Bacchus' for
the juice of a grape, it is to be allowed, provided such person refrains
from sullying his mind with 'foul superstition.'[3] How absolutely
conscious is his attitude to mythology may be seen in his treatment of
the story of Phaethon, which he relates *con amore* as an illustration of the
antipathy between fire and water, and then dismisses as 'severed from
true science.'[4] But he knew the poetic value of the mythological, partly
for ornament, partly for its time-honoured association with learning,
partly to idealise forces in nature. It is in this spirit that he hails the
Venus of his resplendent invocation. The fragrance of spring is around
the goddess. She is the quintessence of the charm, the joy, the growth
in life. Her introduction is at once an embellishment, a reminiscence of
the Aphrodite of Empedocles, and a symbol of the birth-giving power in
nature which defeats the ugliness and tyranny of superstition. This is
the finest effort of his poetic symbolism.

There are other phases of poetry in Lucretius. His tenderness verges
on the Virgilian. There is a human heart behind his free-thinking. His
frenzied hatred of love and of superstition, and his contempt for error
and fear, have in them so little of the Epicurean calm that one
wonders how much pity for man can in other moods possess him. He

---

[1] II. 625: 'Munificat tacita mortalis muta salute.'
[2] II. 646 *sqq.*:
> 'Omnis enim per se diuom natura necessest
> Inmortali aeuo summa cum pace fruatur
> Semota ab nostris rebus seiunctaque longe;
> Nam priuata dolore omni, priuata periclis,
> Ipsa suis pollens opibus, nil indiga nostri,
> Nec bene promeritis capitur neque tangitur ira.'
[3] II. 652 *sqq.*   [4] V. 396 *sqq.*

can be bitter and sardonic towards the cruelty of priests and towards
deceptive doctrine. The vials of his mocking satire are emptied upon
love's follies and upon gods who smite their own temples—do they
throw their thunderbolts, he asks, for practice, to keep their sinews
fit?[1] But he views kindly the natural errors of common men. He has
studied human sorrow, ingorance, and wretchedness. Compassion for
perturbed souls is his chief stimulus. The motive which kindles his
enthusiasm is the salvation of mankind from mental agonies. His lines
on the piteous fate of Iphigeneia, and his whole treatment of death,
show the depth of his feeling. Among similar instances may be cited the
account of the endeavour to prevent Saturn from eating his child, thus

> Dealing the mother's heart a deathless wound;[2]

the picture of the aged yokel despondently shaking his head to find
that the labour of his hands is in vain;[3] and the likening to a mariner,
cast up by the tide, of the newborn babe, naked and helpless, as it wails
prophetically of the troubles in store for it.[4] His sympathy extends to
the brutes. There are few better known passages in Lucretius than that
describing the uncomforted lowing of the cow searching in vain for her
missing calf which has been sacrificed.[5]

Lucretius has also the poet's eye. Keenness of observation gives him
a fertile yield of graphic illustrations. Sometimes it is a point noted
indoors—the turmoil of motes in sunlight streaming through a dark-
ened room,[6] or the sleeping dog barking on the imaginary trail of his
dreams, or the smell of a lamp extinguished, or the escaped *bouquet* of
wine (*Bacchi cum flos euanuit*). But oftener, with the gift of a naturalist,
he draws upon the living creatures of the sea, the gay-plumaged birds,
wild beasts, and pathless jungles. For a sense of the open air pervades
and relieves the heavy doctrine of the atoms. He pictures flocks of
bleating sheep on green pastures, the frolic butting of lambs, grass
jewelled with fresh dew or studded with flowers,[7] the echoing hills,[8] the
serpent casting its slough among the briars,[9] the war-elephants (*boues
Lucae*) trampling on friend and foe, or the same 'snake-handed'

---

[1] VI. 397: 'An tum bracchia consuescunt firmantque lacertos?'
[2] II. 638: 'Aeternumque daret matri sub pectore uolnus.'
[3] II. 1164–1170:
> 'Iamque caput quassans grandis suspirat arator
> Crebrius, incassum manuum cecidisse labores,' etc.
[4] V. 222 *sqq.*:
> 'Tum porro puer, ut saeuis proiectus ab undis
> Nauita, nudus humi iacet,' etc.
[5] II. 352 *sqq.*   [6] II. 114 *sqq.*
[7] II. 319: 'Inuitant herbae gemmantes rore recenti.'
V. 461–462: 'Aurea cum primum gemmantis rore per herbas
> Matutina rubent radiati lumina solis.'
II. 32–33:   'Cum tempestas adridet et anni
Tempora conspergunt uiridantis floribus herbas.'
[8] IV. 572 *sqq.*   [9] IV. 60 *sqq.*

animals fencing India with a rampart of ivory.[1] He has a love of morning and of birds and their notes as unaffected as Chaucer's when he hears 'smale fowles maken melodye.'[2] Loving things as minute as the changing colours on a pigeon's neck,[3] he equally appreciates the mighty forces in nature, the winds with 'forest-rending blasts' (*siluifragis flabris*), the mountain pines tempest-tossed till 'they flashed with flower of flame,'[4] floods beyond the strength of bridges to withstand, the ocean in fury and its white-crested waves (*uertitur in canos candenti marmore fluctus*), cloud-shapes, storms, earthquakes, eruptions. In this comprehensive love of nature Lucretius resembles Whitman. It is not new to compare them in their welcome of death.[5] But the parallel is susceptible of extension. Both rationalist, though Whitman is less systematic; both at times prosaic and careless of form, though Whitman is excessively so; both frankly approaching all processes of life in their naked simplicity; both perhaps seeking, though Whitman more evidently, for some ideal essence behind things, they are in nothing more alike than in their sense of the open and their joy in the free growth that is in nature. Lucretius, it is true, looks on the scheme of things with something of the enjoyment felt by the spectator of a great tragedy. He feels both *horror* and *uoluptas*. But if he has not Whitman's violent dithyrambic raptures over each throb of universal nature, his love is not less real because more restrained.

His mastery of poetic expression is by no means sure. He creeps and soars. The unpoetic is partly inherent in his matter. The search for causes, definitions, and proofs, requires a logical exactitude in statement like his guarded *minus aut magis indupedita*, and prosaic phrases of inference and transition recurring with wearisome insistence, like *quod superest, at nunc, huc accedit, denique, praeterea, etiam atque etiam*, or his argumentative formula *fateare necessest*. A straining after clearness leads to repetitions equally wearisome. Worse still, there are long dreary flats. A case in point is the second book. Opening with the deservedly renowned *Suaue mari magno* on the sovereignty of reason over painful cares and closing in musical pessimism, it contains dull tracts of scientific exposition which make it perhaps the driest of the six. His half-Ennian archaism, too, militates against perfect expression. It is a serious and dignified archaism, like Spenser's in the *Faërie Queene*, and unlike Balzac's excessive and none too correct archaism in the *Contes Drôlatiques*. Yet it gives Lucretius a ruggedness which places

[1] V. 1339; II. 537.
[2] I. 256: 'Frondiferasque nouis auibus canere undique siluas';
II. 144:   'Primum aurora nouo cum spargit lumine terras
            Et uariae uolucres nemora auia peruolitantes
            Aëra per tenerum liquidis loca uocibus opplent.'
[3] II. 801 *sqq.*
[4] I. 900.
[5] For this aspect, see R. Y. Tyrrell, *Latin Poetry*, 1898, p. 72.

him, as an artist in words, at a disadvantage when compared with Virgil.[1]

Besides, his hexameter, though more artistic than that of Ennius, did not reach the finished technique of Virgil. Unlike Virgil in his endings he admits with ready tolerance a polysyllabic heaviness (*principiorum, materiaï*) and a monosyllabic jerkiness (*recens in, simul cum, hoc tamen est ut*). He has not the fine Virgilian feeling for the place of words in relation to the metrical feet. His tendency to begin the third foot with a new word severs the first two feet abruptly from the rest of the line and tells against the rhythmical effect of the caesura.[2] Sometimes the caesura is crushed out.[3] Frequently, in the manner of Cicero and Catullus, ending the fourth foot with a word, he has also a liking for a single word in the fourth foot. He thus loses a metrical pause common in Virgil, who would write *terras quae frugiferentis* for the *quae terras frugiferentis* of Lucretius. There is, too, the deformity of clumsy elisions, and, in general, a certain monotony of structure.

When all has been said, however, on roughnesses and monotonies in Lucretius, his verse remains undeniably strong and majestic. It has slow, solemn movements conveying a sense of sublimity; it has quicker movements conveying feelings of rapidity and force. In beautiful passages like the Introduction, followed by the idyll of the War-god love-sick in the arms of Venus, or like the pageant of the seasons,[4] a sense of harmony comparable to the Virgilian is most obvious. Just as his science yields to fancy, so his precision and roughness yield to melody. His master-strokes depend, as the best literary expression always must do, on a blend of thought and word inseparable without hurt to both. So Lucretius attains a music of his own, and can be the more valued because he is himself and not Virgil. While his greatness must be tested on a larger scale, still even when judged by single lines he will be found to leave an abiding impression. One does not readily forget the 'smiles of calm ocean's crafty harlotry'

Subdola cum ridet placidi pellacia ponti,[5]

the reflection on generations of living creatures quickly changing and handing on the torch to other runners in the race

Et quasi cursores uitai lampada tradunt,[6]

[1] In addition to old forms like *induperator, indugredi*, and an old-fashioned liking for compounds (*frondiferas, fluctifrago, montiuagae*),Lucretius is markedly fond of tmesis: *e.g., disque supatis* (i. 651), *conque globata* (ii. 154), *perque plicatis* (ii. 394), *inque pediri* (iii. 484), *inter enim iectast* (iii. 860). Sometimes he uses a violently inverted tmesis: *e.g., ordia prima=primordia* (iv. 28), and, most astonishing of all, *facit are=arefacit* (vi. 962).

[2] *E.g.* I. 109, 'Religionibus atque minis obsistere uatum.'

[3] *E.g.* II. 1059; *cf.* Munro's note there.

[4] V. 737.

[5] II. 559.

[6] II. 79.

the glimpse of Pan as he plays his pipe

Pinea semiferi capitis uelamina quassans,[1]

the thought of the bitter-sweet of love

Medio de fonte leporum
Surgit amari aliquit quod in ipsis floribus angat,[2]

or the impressive fancy of eerie faces of gloom in a threatening thunder-cloud

Inpendent atrae formidinis ora superne.[3]

Although Quintilian considered him *difficilis*, the chief difficulties associated with Lucretius are not those of meaning; for he is a clear thinker. They are, or rather were, textual. Indeed, the labours of Lachmann removed Lucretius from the class of really difficult authors by ridding the text of the corruptions contracted in its descent from an uncial archetype of the fourth or fifth century. The preservation of Lucretius certainly hung at one time on the slender link of a single MS. No one who has read Munro's Introduction is likely to forget his history of the text. 'By some fatality or other, by its falling into the hands of a Gifanius, Havercamp, Wakefield, instead of those of a Salmasius, Gronovius, Heinsius, Bentley, the criticism of Lucretius remained for centuries where it had been left by Lambinus, nay, even retrograded.' And no one who studies Munro's edition will fail to understand what the services of Lachmann and Munro himself have been.

The *De Rerum Natura* never enjoyed a vogue. But in one transcendent way its influence on literature was powerful. Its thought and language sank deeply into the impressionable soul of Virgil. Sincere admiration for his predecessor inspires Virgil's noted passage

Felix qui potuit rerum cognoscere causas,
Atque metus omnes et inexorabile fatum
Subiecit pedibus strepitumque Acherontis auari,

with its reminiscence of Lucretius's own words on 'the proper study of mankind'

Naturam primum studeat cognoscere rerum.[4]

The borrowings are most evident in the *Georgics*, but from the *Eclogues* onwards, by actual incorporation or vaguer echo of Lucretian phrases, and by reverence for Lucretian speculation,[5] the younger poet renders homage. This is the more wonderful in a genius full of reverence for ideals—religious, political, and social—with which Lucretius could have no sympathy. Certain turns in the episode of Theseus and Ariadne in the *Peleus and Thetis* look as if the spell was felt at once by his con-

[1] IV. 587.   [2] IV. 1134.
[3] VI. 254.   [4] III. 1072: *cf. Georg.*, ii. 490.
[5] *E.g., Eclog.*, vi. 31 *sqq.* In the *Aeneid* Virgil significantly makes the minstrel Iopas at Dido's court sing an epic of creation, and sets Anchises in the Lower World to tell the story of the universe.

temporary Catullus.[1] However this may be, later poets manifestly imitated Lucretius. To Manilius his natural science appealed, and to Horace the sketch of savage man and of the gods at ease.[2] But Horace's smiling and unruffled Epicureanism owed little to the passionate advocacy of the doctrine by Lucretius. To one of so different a temperament as Ovid, who names him twice, he seems both 'sublime' and 'rapid.'[3] Statius has in a neat phrase alluded to the 'soaring frenzy' which he unites with 'learning.'[4]

In antiquity there were those who preferred Lucretius to Virgil.[5] The conflict has raged in modern times. It has been maintained and denied that the great poets of the last age of the Roman Commonwealth, Lucretius and Catullus, were fairly comparable in point of art to their Augustan successors.[6] Mrs. Browning stands for Lucretius in *A Vision of Poets*

> He denied
> Divinely the divine, and died
> Chief poet on the Tiber-side.

Virgil has never lacked champions. Yet to essay the assignment to the very great of their exact grade of honour is labour lost. Let it be enough that both are of the greatest—great in ways so different that to measure their stature becomes an impertinence. It is more satisfying to note that difference of aspect in their work which balks comparison. Virgil encircles the highest national aspirations of his epoch in a halo of beauty and legend. He is essentially spiritual. The past is an inspiration to him. Although his deeper learning could only be appreciated after converse with the great departed of Greece and Alexandria, yet in the *Aeneid*, with its bearing on the newly founded empire, he went straight to the heart of Rome in his own day. There is a sense in which Lucretius is more modern. He goes straight to the mind of the scientific inquirer of to-day and of any age. His strenuous earnestness regarding life and his fresh interest in nature speak directly to all readers. With all his philosophy he is more concrete than Virgil. His broad appeal to humanity is the secret of the perennial attraction towards this Titanic genius, splendidly intrepid in the search after truth, disdainful of all pettiness, preaching apathy with fervour, godlike in his revolt against the gods.

---

[1] Munro collects parallel passages in his note to Lucr. III. 57.

[2] *Cf.* Lucr., V. 1028 *sqq.* and Hor., *Sat.*, I. iii. 99 *sqq.*; Lucr., V. 82 *sqq.* and *Sat.*, I. v. 101 *sqq.*

[3] Ovid, *Am.*, I. xv. 23; *Trist.*, ii. 425.

[4] *Siluae*, II. vii. 76, 'docti furor arduus Lucreti.'

[5] Tac., *Dial.*, xxiii. 2 'isti qui Lucilium pro Horatio et Lucretium pro Vergilio legunt.'

[6] The issue between Munro and Conington was discussed in Conington's lecture on *The Style of Lucretius and Catullus as compared with that of the Augustan Poets*, 1867.

Chapter II

THE ALEXANDRINE MOVEMENT
AND CATULLUS

Motives favouring Alexandrinism – The literature of Alexandria –
Poets who influenced Rome – Alexandrine qualities and their
recurrence – The new school fostered by learning – *Cantores
Euphorionis* – Catullus's early life – The Rome of his day – Catullus
and 'Lesbia' – Closing years – Catullus as metrist – The triumph
of simplicity over artificiality – Truth to nature – Contrast with
Lucretius – Catullus and Horace – Sappho, Shelley, Herrick,
Burns – The Influence of Catullus.

THE age of Caesar was one of political division, intellectual
hesitancy, and moral corruption. Favourable to oratory, it
lacked the positive allegiance to any one prevailing sentiment
capable of fostering the greatest poetry. Its absence of enthusiasm fitted
it to be Alexandrine. Its decadent poetry makes more prominent the
passionate daring of Catullus where he breaks away from its influence.
It shows up in splendid isolation the gigantic intellect of Lucretius,
standing aloof from that pervading Alexandrinism, which, because of its
sparse surviving fragments, and despite its traces in the more learned
portions of Catullus, may be said to have dominated a lost school of
poetry. Many motives favoured the new tendency. The growth of
critical studies had helped, in the judgment of the 'erudite,' to elevate
the older Greek literature to more unapproachable heights, and to
depress the early Latin poetry to depths of barbarous rudeness. The loss
of the ancient Ennian audacity in copying classics of more massive
proportions — an epic or a tragedy — pointed to the more easily imitable
poets of Alexandria. Their precept and example marked the love of
smaller things.[1] They had abandoned long epics for brief mythological
narratives, for epyllia, idylls, elegies, and *tableaux de genre*. Their hesi-
tant elaboration harmonised with a Roman age distracted with turmoil
and intrigue. So Theocritus and Callimachus seemed within a reach
which could not compass Homer or Sophocles.

Early in the third century B.C. a bookish society had grown up at
Alexandria around the Museum and Libraries of the Ptolemies. The
atmosphere was one of erudition. A sense of oppression may very

---

[1] Μέγα βιβλίον μέγα κακόν was a dictum ascribed to Callimachus.

222

credibly have weighed upon men who reflected and commented on the mass of Greek literature before their day. From them the pristine vigour of Homeric or Athenian times was not to be expected. The national sentiment behind the classical Greek literature had been broken up in Egypt by a tide of cosmopolitanism amid a dense and varied population. Despotism warned talent off politics towards personal emotion, rural amenities, or mythological sketches. The feminine influence at court played its part in producing a strain of romantic love.[1] A literature grew up, self-conscious where the older Greek literature had been spontaneous, and cosmopolitan where the older literature had been essentially Hellenic. What potency the era possessed lay in elaboration and criticism, not in creation. So it was that the Alexandrians served themselves heirs to the literature and knowledge of Greece. Their works formed an inventory of the past. The heyday of the Greek commentator had come. Alexandria was renowned for the science of the librarian Eratosthenes, the scholarship of Zenodotus, Aristophanes, and Aristarchus, for a rich yield of merry plays and interludes unhappily lost, for the sevenfold glory of the tragic 'Pleiad' long since eclipsed, and for a poetry combining standard conventions with latter-day preciosity.

Our chief concern is with those poets of Alexandria who acted powerfully upon Roman literature. Although the actual remains of importance are confined to the *Idylls* of Theocritus, the *Alexandra* of Lycophron, the astronomical verses of Aratus, the *Hymns* of Callimachus, and the *Argonautica* of Apollonius, still it must be remembered that many of the lost poets exerted an influence which it is impossible now to gauge. It is reasonable to suppose, for example, that Philetas, the instructor of Theocritus at Alexandria, and one whose amatory elegies Propertius preferred to those of Callimachus, made a deeper impress on Catullus than can be proved from his fragments. Similarly the debt to the epigrams and heroic verses of the later poet Euphorion is but slightly suggested by Cicero's lumping the Alexandrine set at Rome as 'cantores Euphorionis.' Of those whom we can judge, Theocritus (*flor.* 285 B.C.) stands out pre-eminent. In his Sicilian pastorals, classic elegance comes nearest to recapturing poetic inspiration. Not free from artificiality, he is yet the most natural of the Alexandrians. The sights and sounds of the country live for him more vividly than for his greatest Roman imitator, Virgil. His mythology is so little cumbersome that his readers almost forget how unreal such a critical era had made the satyrs and the dryads. His contemporary, Lycophron, earned the title of 'the Obscure' (Σκοτεινός) from his unreadable iambic monologue in which *Alexandra* or *Cassandra* prophesies the

---

[1] 'A Berenice or an Arsinoe, queens or ladies of court, required of a poet that he should flatter and amuse them,' W. R. Hardie, chap. on 'The Vein of Romance,' in *Lectures on Classical Subjects*, 1903.

downfall of Troy. His influence is just traceable in Catullus, and more traceable in a misguided emulation which tempted Cinna to over-elaborate his *Zmyrna*. Aratus, Alexandrian in spirit and partly by residence, represents the short didactic in his astronomical Φαινόμενα. His influence on the *Georgics*, and his fortune or fate to be thrice translated into Latin, by Cicero, Caesar Germanicus, and Festus Avienus, recall if they do not fulfil Ovid's prophecy

Cum sole et luna semper Aratus erit.[1]

In the hymns, epigrams, and elegies of Callimachus there is but a faint streak of romance. There are dainty turns here and there in the epigrams and in *The Bath of Pallas*, and there is enterprise in his search for new stories from the lips of the people; but on the whole learning has ousted imagination. Ovid appropriately says

Quamuis ingenio non ualet, arte ualet.[2]

One but mildly regrets the loss of his *Lock of Berenice*, and that mainly because it would have been interesting for comparison with Catullus's imitation. In his quarrel with Apollonius of Rhodes, once his pupil, afterwards the butt of his *Ibis*,[3] sympathy rather makes for the younger poet. Apollonius at least saw, if he could not rival, the charm of simplicity in the older epics, and Callimachean gibes did not deter him from his venture upon the story of the Argonauts. His treatment of the love of Jason and Medea only just falls short of complete romance. Partly his own Greek, partly the translation by Varro Atacinus, ensured his work a considerable vogue in Rome.

Literature at Alexandria implied erudition often weakened into dulness and obscurity, exclusive precision in style and versification, absence of truth to nature, and corresponding horror of the simple. Mythology had become machinery and love gallantry. But such qualities are not confined to Alexandria. They are inevitably recurrent in all literatures whenever preoccupation with conventional form checks the free play of individual inspiration and pursuit of novelties in expression ousts plain sincerity. There was 'Alexandrinism' among *Les Précieuses* and in the English literature of the eighteenth century. The poets of Alexandria loved art for art's sake; only, they did not love wisely. In Rome, assiduous translation, study of versification, prizing of rarities in phrase, avoidance of long works, and disdain for the old Latin poetry were its marks. Thus arose a poetry often pretty and even brilliant, but as often, in its excesses, shallow and affected. Love of elaboration drove authors back on legends, to rehandle them not in fresh enthusiasm, but with a critical taste and sentimentality, straining after effect by technical skill in metre, novel collocations, and experiments in fancy. It easily passed the thin partitions which divide learning from pedantry and

---

[1] Ovid, *Am.*, I. xv. 16.   [2] Ovid, *Am.*, I. xv. 14.   [3] Imitated by Ovid.

fancy from conceit. The movement may be dated from Laevius's *Erotopaegnia*. It reached its height with the circle of young poets in Catullus's day, and its mark never entirely left Roman literature. Cicero's early verses were under its influence. Virgil, beginning in the 'neoteric' style, learned to combine it with older literary models and patriotic inspiration. Indeed, though Alexandrinism is by no means characteristic of Roman literature at large, this kind of short, polished, and occasionally romantic poetry accounts for part of the changed spirit noticeable on turning from Attic poetry to Propertius and Ovid. Apart from spirit, its legacy to literature consisted in intensified care for form, in fixed ordinances regulating metrical quantity, and in the rescue of the final -*s* which earlier poets had sometimes elided.[1]

Based on the latest Greek fashion, this poetry by the learned for the learned encountered severe criticism.[2] It was flouted as the new-fangled work of *neoterici* and *Cantores Euphorionis*. Among the teachers whose learning fostered this school, the most eminent foreigner was Parthenius. Its most influential 'Italian' master was P. Valerius Cato, one of many scholars from Cisalpine Gaul. He was a true Alexandrine in combining the parts of rhetorician and poet. Very questionably there have been assigned to him from among the pseudo-Virgilian remains two pieces now recognised as separate. These are the *Lydia*, which proves how erudite a lover's complaint may be made, and the *Dirae*,[3] on grievances perhaps inflicted by the Sullan proscriptions. How largely instrumental he was in spreading Alexandrinism is indicated by Bibaculus's lines

> *Cato grammaticus, latina Siren,*
> *Qui solus legit ac facit poetas.*

Ten poets are classed as 'Cantores Euphorionis' by Bährens.[4] The phrase hardly fits Catullus at all.[5] But to the group may be added

---

[1] The sole example of this elision in Catullus is cxvi. 8:
> 'At fixus nostris tu dabi' supplicium.'

[2] Since L. Müller's biography of Horace (1880) too much, some think, has been made of an alleged opposition of Horace and Virgil to the Alexandrine movement as represented by Catullus. There was a reaction among Augustan poets; but Virgil wrote the *Eclogues* under Alexandrine influence, and frequently borrowed from Catullus. See the protest against this 'phantom' idea of opposition, *Acad.*, May 4, 1907, reviewing E. K. Rand's 'Catullus and the Augustans' in *Harvard Studies in Class. Philol.*, vol. xvii, as already mentioned in note 2, p. 200.

[3] See Teuffel, § 200; and the chapter in this book on 'The Minor Poems attributed to Virgil.'

[4] *F.P.R.*, 1886, p. 317 *sqq.*

[5] As used by Cicero, some ten years after Catullus's death, *Tusc. Disp.*, III. xix. 45, it can scarcely include Catullus. But, of course, he was associated with the school. Indeed, one of many attempts to explain Catullus's lines to Cicero (xlix), that by P. H. Damsté (*Mnemos.*, xxx. 4, 1902), argues that Catullus is there boasting that he is a member of the new clique – a *pessimus omnium poeta* in Cicero's eyes. It is, however, too readily assumed that the piece is written in a tone of sneering or ironical thanks. It remains perfectly arguable that its mock modesty is a bit of genial playfulness.

I

Catullus's friend in the North, Caecilius of Novum Comum, who was engaged on a poem about Cybele;[1] and P. Terentius Varro designated as 'Atacinus' from his birth near the river Atax, in Gallia Narbonensis. This is the Varro whom Horace adds to the roll of Latin satirists, and who turned from his historical epic, *Bellum Sequanicum*, to Alexandrine adaptations.[2] His *Argonautae* was a free version of Apollonius, his *Chorographia* was imitated from Alexander of Ephesus, and his *Ephemeris* through its borrowings from Aratus left traces on the *Georgics*. To the credit of his Alexandrinism may be set the graceful movement already noted in some of his hexameters.[3] Of Bährens's ten, represented some of them by a word or a line, it is enough to mention five. M. Furius Bibaculus (previously mentioned, like Varro of Atax, in the sketch of post-Ennian epic) betrays Alexandrine proclivities in his admiration for his compatriot Valerius Cato and in his notorious conceit, already cited, in reference to 'Jove spitting the wintry Alps all o'er with hoary snow.'[4] C. Helvius Cinna, one of whose fragments suggests that he was a northerner, was an intimate of Catullus. He accompanied him to Bithynia;[5] and thence Cinna brought Aratus's *Diosemiae* written on mallow leaves.[6] Probably he was the man murdered, through a mistaken identity rather than for his 'bad verses,' by the Caesarian mob of 44 B.C.[7] His sportive lines, epigrams, and *Propempticon* — a versified guidebook for Pollio's use on a journey to Greece — are not so significant as his mannered poem on the incestuous passion of *Zmyrna*. By the scrupulous polish of nine years[8] he practically anticipated Horace's rule for those about to publish (*nonumque prematur in annum*).[9] The resultant weight of recondite allusion and ornament set the commentators immediately to work on this heavy production. It is one of time's 'little ironies' that only three lines survive, one for each three years of toil. But in its day the poem was a landmark. It made Cinna the *doyen* of his

---

[1] Catull., xxxv:

'Est enim uenuste
Magna Caecilio incohata Mater.'

[2] Varro's erotic pieces are alluded to by Propertius, II. xxxiv. 85.

[3] *E.g.*, 'Frigidus et siluis Aquilo decussit honorem.'

[4] It is one of about a dozen lines left of his *Annales* on Caesar's Gallic War:

'Iuppiter hibernas cana niue conspuit Alpes,'

which is parodied in Hor., *Sat.*, II. v. 41. Horace means Furius in his reference to 'Alpinus' murdering Memnon (*i.e.* by his bombastic epic style in an *Aethiopis*), *Sat.*, I. x. 36. W. A. Heidel argues for the identity of Furius Bibaculus with the Furius of Catullus, xi, xvi, xxiii, xxvi. *Cl. Rev.*, xv. 215.

[5] Catull., x. 30.

[6] W. Morel, *F.P.R.* p. 89. The *Diosemiae* is the latter portion of Aratus's *Phaenomena*.

[7] Suet., *Iul.*, lxxx; Plut., *Brut.*, xx. *Cf.* Shakespeare, *Julius Caesar*, Act III., Sc. iii.

[8] Catull., xcv. 1–2:

'Zmyrna mei Cinnae nonam post denique messem
Quam coepta est nonamque edita post hiemem est.'

[9] Hor., *A.P.*, 388.

circle; for the *Zmyrna* gave the cue to other toy-epics, the *Io* of Calvus, the *Glaucus* of Cornificius, and the *Peleus and Thetis* of Catullus. C. Licinius Calvus (82–47 B.C.), son of the annalist Licinius Macer, was a greater barrister than poet. Cicero pronounces Calvus to have been hypercritical of his own style — too painstaking to secure real force in speech.[1] On the other hand there is Seneca's anecdote about Vatinius interrupting Calvus's impassioned speech for the prosecution with the frank testimony: 'I put it to you, gentlemen of the jury, surely I should not be found guilty just because he is eloquent?'[2] This 'eloquent mannikin' (*salaputtium disertum*)[3] — the epithet is the same as in Seneca's anecdote — Catullus liked well enough to rally freely at times. Catullus's real feelings are best seen in the touching lines of consolation penned on the death of Calvus's wife.[4] Like Catullus he lampooned Caesar, and with Catullus he is coupled by Horace as representative of the latest poetry which was all a certain 'monkey' knew:

> *Nil praeter Caluum et doctus cantare Catullum.*[5]

Finer associations cling round Ovid's words linking him with his brother-poet when he craves a welcome in the 'Elysian vale' for Tibullus newly dead

> Meet thou him, come, thy young brows ivy-wreathed
> Scholar Catullus, and thy Calvus too.[6]

Q. Cornificius was the author of the above-mentioned epyllion *Glaucus*: and Ticidas, of whose *hymenaeus* and epigrams the merest scraps survive, is recorded by Ovid to have written love-poems on Perilla.[7]

C. Valerius Catullus[8] (*circ.* 84–54 B.C.) was born at Verona. There,

[1] Cic., *Brut.*, lxxxii., 283–284, 'nimium tamen inquirens in se,' etc.
[2] Sen., *Contr.*, VII. iv. 6 *sqq.*, 'Caluus qui diu cum Cicerone iniquissimam litem de principatu eloquentiae habuit, usque eo uiolentus actor et concitatus fuit, ut in media eius actione surgeret Vatinius reus et exclamaret: "Rogo uos, iudices, num, si iste disertus est, ideo me damnari oportet?" ' – *Cf.* Tac. *Dial.*, xviii.
[3] Catull., liii.
[4] Catull., xcvi:
> 'Certe non tanto mors inmatura dolori est
> Quintiliae, quantum gaudet amore tuo.'
[5] Hor., *Sat.*, I. x. 19. *Cf. supra*, p. 200.
[6] Ovid, *Am.*, III. ix. 61–62:
> 'Obuius huic uenias hedera iuuenalia cinctus
> Tempora cum Caluo, docte Catulle, tuo.'
[7] Ovid, *Trist.*, ii. 433 *sqq.*
[8] Text: R. Ellis, ed. crit., Proleg., Commentary, ed. 2, 1889; A. Riese, 1884; E. Bährens, 2 vols., 1885; L. Schwabe, 1866, ed. 2, 1886; E. Rostand and E. Benoist (comment., Fr. verse trans.), 2 vols., 1882–1890; S. G. Owen (w. *Peruigilium Veneris*), 1893; J. P. Postgate in *Corp. Poet. Lat.*; F. W. Cornish (expurg. w. prose trans.), 1904.
Translation: Theodore Martin, *Poems of Catullus trans. into Eng. Verse*, ed. 2, 1875.
Other works: L. Schwabe, *Quaestiones Catullianae*, 1862; A. Couat, *Étude*

with peculiar fitness, the rediscovery in the fourteenth century of the one surviving manuscript of his poems led to the renascence of his fame.[1] It is settled that Jerome's note of his death in 57 is wrong. His poems prove that he outlived Caesar's invasion of Britain in 55.[2] He certainly died young, perhaps at thirty, as Jerome says. But it is of small moment whether 87 or 84 was his birth-year. His *praenomen* is generally accepted as 'Gaius,' not 'Quintus,' which inferior transcripts of his poems give.[3] He came of a family of consequence. His father was in a position to show hospitality to Caesar when he was governor of Gaul. Catullus's occasional complaints about his purse, when he declared it to be 'full of cobwebs,'[4] or when he expressed chagrin over meagre returns from his stay in Bithynia,[5] cannot imply more than temporary embarrassment due to extravagance. He was well enough off to hold estates near Tivoli and at Sirmione on the Lago di Garda, to sail home from the East in his own yacht, and to possess a library at Rome.[6] His native Cisalpine Gaul possessed much local culture.[7] It yielded notable scholars and authors to Rome. The North, then, fostered his education and his first essays in verse. His precocity may be inferred from his record of copious love poetry 'in the sweet springtime of his flowery youth.'[8] His reference in his dedicatory poem to trifles which his friend Cornelius Nepos, the historian, used to praise, suggests that his juvenile efforts have entirely perished.[9]

His presence in Rome before 62 cannot be substantiated. Rome, as Catullus first knew it, was a bundle of contradictions. The effects of

---

sur Catulle, 1875, and *La poésie alexandrine*, 1882; G. Lafaye, *Catulle et ses modéles*, 1894; H. A. J. Munro, *Criticisms and Elucidations on Catullus*, ed. 2, 1905; R. Ellis, *Catullus in the Fourteenth Century*, 1905; E. K. Rand, *Catullus and the Augustans* (*Harvard Studies in Class. Philol.*, vol. xvii); J. E. Sandys, *A Hist. of Class. Scholarship*, 1903, ch. viii, on 'The School of Alexandria'; F. Susemihl, *Geschichte d. griech. Litt. in d. Alexandrinerzeit*, 2 vols., 1891-2.

[1] lxii alone has independent MS. authority. It is contained in the 'Thuanean' MS. written about A.D. 900.

[2] See xi. 11 and xxix. In xlv. 21-22, the preference of 'love-lorn Septimius' for his sweetheart Acme rather than for 'all your Syrias and your Britains' implies in addition a reference to the appointment of Crassus to the province of Syria in 55.

[3] Scaliger's reading of 'Quinte' for 'quippe' in the difficult line lxvii. 12 has nothing but ingenuity to recommend it. On the other hand, to accept 'Gaius' from Apuleius and Jerome is to give additional force to x. 29-30 (A. Palmer, *Cl. Rev.*, v. 7).

[4] xiii. 8, 'Plenus sacculus est aranearum.'

[5] x. 6-11.

[6] xxxi, xliv, iv, and lxviii. 35.

[7] Suetonius singles out among great teachers in Gallia Togata, Octavius Teucer, Pescennius Iacchus, and Oppius Chares (*De Gramm.*, iii).

[8] lxviii. 15-17:

> 'Tempore quo primum uestis mihi tradita pura est,
>   Iucundum cum aetas florida uer ageret,
> Multa satis lusi.'

[9] i. 3-4:   'Corneli tibi; namque tu solebas
>   Meas esse aliquid putare nugas.'

Hellenic culture, it is true, had now had time to sink deep; but power in the state implied the bloodstained sword as much as the trained intellect. On the one hand was refinement of manners and broadening of ideas; on the other, faction, anarchy, proscription, and massacre. It was the generation of Curio, Dolabella, and Caelius Rufus, hankering with unquenchable appetite after artistic and sensual enjoyments. Read with becoming discount, Cicero's speeches and Sallust's histories supplement Catullus's poetry as an index of contemporary immorality. This gentleman of Verona had access to the best Roman houses. He made numerous friends in aristocratic and literary society. The world of fashion and licence offered itself to the young genius with his hot Keltic blood: and he had not the self-control to resist its attractions. The giddy round of his life is reflected in the constantly altering atmosphere of his poems. Whispered scandals, nameless vices, the gay girls of Pompey's portico, Caesar's minions, Egnatius, like Dickens's Mr. Carker showing his white teeth in everlasting smiles, the Roman cockney so suitably named Arrius to admit of his superfluous aspirates,[1] doltish husbands with pretty wives, pilfering guests, faithful and faithless friends, make a vivid register of human nature in the great capital. One side of the picture is filled with the *joie de vivre*; and the first smiles of society light up graceful verses sparkling with gaiety as yet undarkened.

But there was a serious side to the picture. This was his infatuation for 'Lesbia,' who can only have been the dangerously fascinating and voluptuous Clodia, wife of Metellus Celer, governor of Cisalpine Gaul in 62. Catullus chose the disguised name as a reminiscence of the Lesbian poetess, Sappho, one of whose odes he adapted and despatched among his first love-missives.[2] He may have come to Rome furnished with letters of introduction from the governor of his province. Anyhow, the *liaison* began during the husband's absence. It was in 61 that Metellus returned and stood for the consulship. The young northerner's admiration made a transient episode in Lesbia's life—she was older and more sophisticated than he. His passion for her stirred the depths of his being. For a time love was his 'whole existence,' not 'a thing apart.' Lesbia, the ruin of his life, proved his passport to fame. For Catullus must always be best remembered for the fervid poems of his love's first dreams, when his affection was returned, and for the 'pageant of his bleeding heart' passing before us in poems of mistrust, disillusion, hopeless yearning, agonising vacillation, and final paroxysms of hatred. What Shelley intended for Byron fits Catullus:

---

[1] lxxxiv. 1-2:

       " 'Chommoda' dicebat si quando 'commoda' uellet
          Dicere, et 'insidias' Arrius 'hinsidias.' "

[2] li. The famous 'Ille mi par esse deo uidetur,' etc., from Sappho's φαίνεταί μοι κῆνος ἴσος θέοισιν, κ.τ.λ.. For Byron's and other versions of Catullus, see J. Wight Duff, *Byron: Selected Poetry*, 1904, pp. 278 and 382.

> Most wretched men
> Are cradled into poetry by wrong:
> They learn in suffering what they teach in song.

'The Medea of the Palatine' was not the worst title which Clodia's evil courses won for her. Her charge of attempted poisoning trumped up against Caelius Rufus, one of her victims who had supplanted Catullus, gave Cicero, as counsel for the defence, the opportunity of arraigning her profligacy in the *Pro Caelio*. Cicero and Caelius united to thrust upon her the nickname of a *Clytaemnestra quadrantaria*; and it is too probable that she had poisoned her husband and sold her favours cheap.[1] Cicero's phrase, Ἥρα βοῶπις, besides its picture of her alluring eyes, contains the awful suggestion of incest.[2] Such was the woman who inspired Catullus—his 'lustrous goddess of the delicate step,' the creak of whose sandal he could remember as she 'set her shining foot on the well-worn threshold,'[3] whose beauty he once thought beyond compare,[4] who had stolen all the graces from all other women,[5] and whom in a transport of infatuation he dares liken to Laodamia.[6] Her shameless infidelities at last awoke him to the truth. In total renouncement lay his only salvation.[7] But a long torment had to be gone through. The poems show us little rifts in the lute, quarrels and reconciliations,[8] indulgences to Lesbia's frailties,[9] appeals to rivals, reproaches passing from the half-playful to the more and more pathetic,[10] and love mastering him in spite of reason:[11]

---

[1] Catullus's words in lviii. 4–5, declaring her a common prostitute, are probably an angry exaggeration.

[2] Her brother Clodius is probably meant in lxxix, 1–2:
> 'Lesbius est pulcher: quid ni? quem Lesbia malit
> Quam te cum tota gente, Catulle, tua.'

[3] lxviii. 70–72:
> 'Quo mea se molli candida diua pede
> Intulit et trito fulgentem in limine plantam
> Innixa arguta constituit solea.'

[4] xliii. 6–8: 'Ten prouincia narrat esse bellam?
> Tecum Lesbia nostra comparatur?
> O saeclum insapiens et infacetum!'

[5] lxxxvi. 5–6:
> ' Lesbia formosa est: quae cum pulcherrima tota est,
> Tum omnibus una omnis surripuit Veneres.'

[6] lxviii. 73 *sqq.*

[7] lxxvi. 13:
> 'Difficile est longum subito deponere amorem,
> Difficile est, uerum hoc qua lubet efficias:
> Una salus haec est, hoc est tibi peruincendum,
> Hoc facias, siue id non pote siue pote.'

[8] cvii: 'Restituis cupido atque insperanti, ipsa refers te
> Nobis. O lucem candidiore nota!'

[9] Catullus speaks as an accommodating lover in lxviii. 135:
> 'Quae tamen etsi uno non est contenta Catullo,
> Rara uerecundae furta feremus erae.'

[10] Note the deepened feeling in lxxii as compared with lxx (on Woman's Vows).

[11] lxxv is in the same tone as lxxxv:

> I hate, yet love: you ask how this may be.
> Who knows? I feel its truth and agony.

The struggle to steel his mind against love gives dramatic force to the intensely moving monologue *Si qua recordanti benefacta priora uoluptas.* His prayer to heaven is 'not for her love, not for her chastity—that is impossible—but for health of soul and deliverance from its foul malady.'[1] Finally the time came when he could send his brief scathing message of farewell—she is welcome to live with her three hundred paramours, loving none truly, but breaking hearts and ruining lives:

> Let her no more, as once, my passion heed—
> My passion which her sin has made to bleed,
> Like flower bruised at margent of a mead
>   By passing ploughshare.[2]

This was written towards the end of his life. Before the embers of passion could so have died, years had to pass and fresh scenes distract his mind.

Partly to disentangle himself, partly to satisfy a scholar's yearning for scenes of Greek civilisation,[3] Catullus, along with Cinna, joined the staff of Memmius, who went abroad as propraetor of Bithynia in 57. Either on the outward[4] or on the homeward journey he visited with pious sorrow the grave of his brother, who had been buried in the Troad. His brother is the one kinsman whom his poems mention, and his memory is enshrined in

> 'That "Ave atque Vale" of the Poet's hopeless woe.'

The year 56 brought more than 'calm of mind, all passion spent' as far as Lesbia was concerned. Catullus had gained 'new acquist of true experience.' Joy in the spring is rapturously expressed in *Iam uer egelidos refert tepores*, where he parts from the delightful society of his

---

'Odi et amo: quare id faciam fortasse requiris.
Nescio, sed fieri sentio et excrucior.'

[1] lxxvi. 23–26.
[2] xi. 15 *sqq.*:

> 'Pauca nuntiate meae puellae
>   Non bona dicta,
> Cum suis uiuat ualeatque moechis,
> Quos simul complexa tenet trecentos,
> Nullum amans uere, sed identidem omnium
>   Ilia rumpens:
> Nec meum respectet, ut ante, amorem,
> Qui illius culpa cecidit uelut prati
> Ultimi flos, praetereunte postquam
>   Tactus aratro est.'

[3] xlvi. 6: 'Ad claras Asiae uolemus urbes.'
[4] The homeward journey is not suggested by the opening of poem ci:
'Multas per gentes et multa per aequora uectus.'
It has been argued that Catullus went on a special Eastern journey to visit his brother's tomb.

comrades in the expectation that their several routes will meet in
Rome.[1] Eastern travel had suggested new subjects. Cinna and he in
Bithynia would find consolation in turning from the society of their
detestable chief, Memmius, to deepen their acquaintance with Alexandrine poetry. The *Attis*, whose tumultuous galliambics suit the orgiastic
cult of Cybele, may be safely said to have owed its inspiration to his
contact with Phrygia. The *Peleus and Thetis*, over which Catullus
probably spent years, must in the episode of Ariadne have drawn
materials from his cruise among 'the isles of Greece.' His return to
northern Italy is celebrated with a dignity of tempered delight in
fourteen scazons which tempt one to render them in sonnet-form:

> Half-islet Sirmio, the gem of all
>   The isles, which god of sea or god of mere
>   Upholds in glassy lake or ocean drear,
> On thee with heart and soul my glances fall.
>
> Scarce can I think me safe when I recall
>   Bithynia's plains afar and see thee near:
>   Ah, what more joyous than the mind to clear
> Of care, and burdens lay aside that gall?
>
> By distant travail worn we win our hearth
>   And on the long-wished couch siesta take:
>   This is the one reward for those who roam.
> Hail, Sirmio, the fair! Greet me with mirth;
>   Be mirthful, Lydian waters of the lake!
>   Laugh out, ye realms of merriment at home![2]

His stay in the North lasted long enough to include fresh intrigues at
Verona. But Catullus was soon in Rome again.[3] To these closing years
belong his attacks on Caesar and on creatures like Mamurra battening
on a general's spoils. In politics his feelings were against the democrats;

[1] xlvi. 9: 'O dulces comitum ualete coetus,' etc.
[2] xxxi: 'Paene insularum, Sirmio, insularumque
           Ocelle, quascumque in liquentibus stagnis
           Marique uasto fert uterque Neptunus;
           Quam te libenter quamque laetus inuiso,
           Vix mi ipse credens Thuniam atque Bithunos
           Liquisse campos et uidere te in tuto:
           O quid solutis est beatius curis?
           Cum mens onus reponit, ac peregrino
           Labore fessi uenimus larem ad nostrum,
           Desideratoque acquiescimus lecto.
           Hoc est quod unum est pro laboribus tantis.
           Salue, o uenusta Sirmio! atque hero gaude;
           Gaudete uosque O Lydiae lacus undae!
           Ridete quicquid est domi cachinnorum!'

In line 13 Scaliger rejects *Lydiae* and scouts the connexion with Etruria as a
dream (*docti colonias Tyrrhenorum nescio quas somniant*). His *ludiae* for 'the
merry dancing waters' is a more attractive suggestion than Munro's *uiuidae*.
Another conjecture is *liquidae*.
[3] This is evident from x.

but likes and dislikes rather than principles swayed him. His circle, beyond the new literary set, included many of Cicero's friends — Hortensius, Manlius Torquatus, and Sestius. Cicero and he could unite in loathing Clodia, Clodius, Piso, and Vatinius. For his foul lampoons on Caesar he eventually apologised and was magnanimously forgiven.[1] Almost to the end, excesses and animosities competed with higher tastes for dominion over him. He had lived fast, and the strain told. There is a sense of numbered days and ebbing life in what may be the last thing he wrote. It is the little piece sent to Cornificius complaining, with Byronic depression and sensitiveness, of illness 'worsening every hour of every day,' and imploring 'some small word of comfort, sadder than Simonides' tears.' It reads like a swan-dirge from his deathbed.[2]

The 116 poems are out of all chronological order. As we have them, they are arranged in three groups — the first, i–lx, short poems of lyric stamp, in hendecasyllabics, pure iambics, scazons, glyconics, with two in the Sapphic stanza; the second, lxi–lxiv, longer poems — two epithalamia (one in a system of four glyconics and a pherecratean, the other in hexameters), the *Attis*, and the *Peleus and Thetis*; third, lxv–cxvi, elegiacs, introduced by the *Coma Berenices* and its *envoi*. Over a third of the whole are in the hendecasyllabic or phalaecian metre.[3] Pre-Catullan specimens are so negligible and his manipulation is so individual that he may be proclaimed its originator. He indulges in a metrical variety of base which Martial, its other great master, does not allow himself. But it is in varied effects that he proves his power. In the same metre he can be gossiping, satiric, sportive as in his address to his book, passionate as in *Viuamus mea Lesbia*, sorrowful as in *Lugete, O Veneres Cupidinesque*. The former suggests English octosyllabics:

> Let's live, my Lesbia, and love.
> Let's value not a whit above
> A penny all that dotards grey
> In tones of condemnation say.
> The sun can set, the sun can rise:
> Once let the brief light quit our eyes,
> And we through endless night must keep
> The couch of one unbroken sleep.
> Give me a thousand kisses — more!
> A hundred yet: add to the score

[1] See esp. xxix: Suet., *Iul.*, lxxiii., 'Catullum . . . satisfacientem eadem die adhibuit cenae hospitioque patris eius sicut consueuerat uti perseuerauit.' *Cf.* Tac., *Ann.*, iv. 34, 'Carmina Bibaculi et Catulli referta contumeliis Caesarum leguntur.'   [2] xxxviii.
[3] For the metres of Catullus see Ellis's ed. (proleg.) and summary in F. P. Simpson's *Select Poems of Catullus*, ed. 2, 1879, App. I. For their origin, see Lafaye, *Catulle et ses modèles*; and Wilamowitz-Möllendorff, *Die Galliamben des Kallimachos u. Catullus*, in *Herm.* 1879, xiv, p. 194.

A second thousand kisses: then
Another hundred, and again
A thousand more, a hundred still.
So many thousands we fulfil,
We must take care to mix the count —
Bad luck to know the right amount —
Lest evil eye impose its spell
When it can all our kisses tell.[1]

The other produces almost the impression of a sonnet:

Mourn all ye Powers of Love and Loveliness!
    Mourn all the world of taste for beauty rare!
Dead is my lady's sparrow — to possess
    Her pet was more than her own eyes to her.
The bird was honey-sweet, and knew his friend
    As well as maiden knows a mother's face;
Nor left her lap, but twittered without end
    To her alone, and hopped from place to place.
Now fares he on the darkling path of gloom
    From which no traveller returns, 'tis said.
Hell-shades that prey on beauty, black your doom,
    That carried my fair sparrow to the dead!
Woe, deed of ill! For thee, poor little bird,
My lady's eyes with tears are red and blurred.[2]

His pure iambi have a pristine dash. In the scazons or choliambics, in which he followed Hipponax and other Greeks, he can be both grave and gay. His light and airy glyconics make true marriage-music, while the rushing galliambics, joined to poetic fancy and strangely suggestive of the frenzied renunciation of manhood by the votaries of Cybele, make the *Attis* unique in Latin, or rather in any literature.[3] The Catullan hexameter resembles the Lucretian in frequent breaks at the end of the fourth foot (the 'bucolic caesura'). But Catullus was more distinctly under later Greek influence than Lucretius was. This accounts for the greater part played in Catullus by spondaic endings and spondaic rhythms. This comes of his Alexandrinism. Both Lucretius and Catullus construct rather separate lines than complete passages. Virgil's cunning *enjambement*, on the other hand, avoided the monotony of closing the sense with the metre. The elegiacs of Catullus were nearer the Greek in freedom. They had not yet taken the stricter Latin form imposed on them by Propertius and especially by Ovid. So in Catullus we do not find the Ovidian avoidance of elision, or the preponderance of dactyls, or the Ovidian habit of closing the thought with the couplet and closing the pentameter with a disyllable.[4]

[1] v.   [2] iii.

[3] Grant Allen, enthusiastic over its poesy, mysticism, Keltic glamour, and associations with tree-worship, declares it to be 'the greatest poem in the Latin language.' Introd. to *The Attis translated into Eng. Verse,* 1892, p. xv.

[4] Statistics of Catullus's pentameter endings: 1 monosyllable, 121 disyllables,

The first reading of Catullus is a revelation in Latin literature. Here is a heart on fire. Here are poems possessed of brevity—the brevity of passion and of youth. They are vital with the glow of love or indignation. Their lightning flashes are to be annotated not from mythology or literature, but from knowledge of mankind. This is the more surprising in Catullus because he had another side. Versed in the poetry of Alexandria, he deserved the coveted epithet 'doctus' conferred by Ovid's melodious and worshipful lines. Quite apart from the use he makes of Homer, Hesiod, Pindar, Sappho, and the tragedians, he owes a large verbal debt to Theocritus, Callimachus, Apollonius, and other late Greek poets. His metrical debts are still more obvious. In subject-matter and structure, Greek influence acts most distinctly on the *Attis*, the *Peleus and Thetis*,[1] and the *Coma Berenices*. As a rule, his learning sits lightly upon him.[2] It provides sweet names, as in his verse

> *Perge linquere Thespiae*
> *Rupis Aonios specus,*
> *Nympha quos super irrigat*
> *Frigerans Aganippe,*[3]

and it lends a copious suggestiveness to the description of the hunt after a friend—a hunt which could not but be fruitless:

> *Non custos si fingar ille Cretum,*
> *Non si Pegaseo ferar uolatu,*
> *Non Ladas ego pinnipesue Perseus,*
> *Non Rhesi niueae citaeque bigae.*[4]

Even in the *Coma Berenices* the artificial notes are usually pleasant, and in the protestation by the lock of its unwillingness to be shorn from the queen's head:

> *Inuita, o regina, tuo de uertice cessi,*

the prettiness half conceals the rhetoric, so that an indulgence is bespoken for the parody of the line which Virgil makes Aeneas utter to Dido's shade.[5] But it is not Catullus's learning which leaves the most lasting impress, makes him the greatest lyric poet of Rome, and enrols him in the company of Burns and Heine. His full strength does not lie in the unparalleled *Attis*, nor in his clever though unsatisfying *Rape of Berenice's Lock*, nor yet in the polished *Marriage of Peleus* with its

---

83 trisyllables, 98 tetrasyllables, 17 pentasyllables, 1 heptasyllable, viz., lxviii. 112:

'Audit falsiparens Amphitryoniades.'

[1] The recovery of portions of Callimachus's *Hecale* has an important bearing on the nature of an epyllion. See account by R. Ellis, *Jrnl. Phil.*, xxiv, No. 47, 1895, and text in *Cl. Rev.* vii. pp. 429–430.
[2] lxviii. 107 *sqq.* shows Catullus at his worst.
[3] lxi. 27 *sqq.*
[4] lv. 14 *sqq.*
[5] lxvi. 39: cf. *Aen.*, vi. 460.

opulence of music and colour. Rather it lies in a handful of short poems, wherein truth to the heart is unmistakable, because the poet has mastered the secret of giving utterance, at once simple and strong, to fervent passion. There is the truest poetry, but the least feigning, when he revels to distraction over Lesbia's kisses in their hundreds and thousands, and touches with inimitable lightness the superstition, never dead, that it is unlucky to count one's blessings. Equal artlessness of spirit marks his grief over the sparrow, lamented because it was her pet, but also because he felt the pitifulness of beauty dead. So with the whole story of his heart — the loving of Lesbia despite the promptings of reason and resentment, the fierce struggle against her fascinations, and the impassioned good-bye. In Catullus there is not the chivalry of love which characterises the troubadours of Provence or the more idealistic treatment of passion in the *Minnelieder* of Germany. Catullus is at once more elemental, sensuous, and frank. So all the Hellenism in him — and it is only in part Alexandrine — is outweighed by that 'simplicité passionnée' which so many of his critics have followed Fénelon in emphasising.

With no less sincerity he feels the inspiration of death. His laments under bereavement, and especially the sobbing music of the *Multas per gentes*, closing with the eternal farewell

Atque in perpetuum, frater, aue atque uale,

are in words that have wrung the heart. They have the accent of truth, and they are poetry. There are the same accents of truth in his tenderness — his boyish glee over a friend's home-coming,[1] the thought of the old mother welcoming her son from abroad,[2] or the child smiling on its father.[3] Sincerity informs his love of nature also — his rapture in spring, his delight in the Italian lake-scenery, his eye for colour and flowers, which becomes an instrument of perfectly unaffected adornment. Thus, tears suggest a familiar Alpine picture:

> As crystal-clear on wind-swept mountain-top
> Forth leaps a runnel from a mossy crag.[4]

The miraculous birth of Diana 'by the Delian olive-tree laid lowly on the ground' signifies

> That on the hills Thou shouldst be Queen
> And Lady of the woodland green,
> Ruling the glade's sequestered scene
> And rivers that resound.[5]

---

[1] ix.   [2] ix. 4.   [3] lxi. 216–220.

[4] lxviii. 57–58: 'Qualis in aerei perlucens uertice montis
> Riuus muscoso prosilit e lapide.'

[5] xxxiv. 9–12: 'Montium domina ut fores
> Siluarumque uirentium
> Saltuumque reconditorum
> Amniumque sonantum.'

The English is from the author's 'Hymn to our Lady of the Crossways,' in *Cl. Rev.*, xxii. 7, 231 (1908).

Maidenly purity is

> As springs in garden close a flower remote,
> Unknown to kine, unbruisèd by the plough,
> Wind-kist, sun-strengthened, nursling of the showers,
> The quest of many a youth and many a maid.[1]

It is to flowers that his similes recur as he thinks of a bride:

> As in some proud-pied garden-bed
> Of wealthy lord a stately bloom
> Of hyacinth uprears its head —
> But thou dost lag: the day makes room.
> Come forth, bride newly-wed.[2]

and later:

> Now mayest thou approach, O groom:
> Her cheeks alight as flowers sweet,
> Thy bride awaits thee in her room,
> Paling like some white marguerite
> Or poppy's yellow bloom.[3]

There is a corresponding naturalness in his language. Even his foul-mouthed abuse — and he can be unspeakably coarse — has only too much truth to the manners of his age. At times, the veritable talk of Rome lives again in colloquial idioms, off-hand turns, fashionable slang, and coaxing endearments.[4] The diminutives, always prevalent in the common tongue, Catullus loved for their own sake and for the sake of his

---

[1] lxii. 39 sqq.:

> 'Ut flos in saeptis secretus nascitur hortis
> Ignotus pecori, nullo contusus aratro,
> Quem mulcent aurae, firmat sol, educat imber:
> Multi illum pueri, multae optauere puellae.'

[2] lxi. 91 sqq.:

> 'Talis in uario solet
> Diuitis domini hortulo
> Stare flos hyacinthinus –
> Sed moraris. Abit dies.
> Prodeas noua nupta.'

[3] lxi. 191 sqq.:

> 'Iam licet uenias, marite:
> Uxor in thalamo tibi est,
> Ore floridulo nitens
> Alba parthenice uelut
> Luteumue papauer.'

[4] E.g., his favourite indefinite expressions: (i. 8) quicquid hoc libelli quale-cunque quidem, (iii. 2) quantum est hominum uenustiorum; familiar expressions: (iii. 13) uobis male sit, (v. 3) unius aestimemus assis; words from the people's mouth: scortillum, lutum, lupanar, conscribillare; fashionable terms of approval or disapproval: bellus, sordidus, dicax, lepidus, illepidus. For further instances, see F. P. Simpson's ed., App. ii. Of some twenty newly-coined words in Catullus (like siluicultrix, nemoriuagus), and of about fifty in Lucretius, based on the old faculty for compounding, hardly any were destined to live in subsequent classics.

metre.[1] Here there is a marked contrast with the artificial Augustan diction, which, to its own great loss, virtually forswore this coinage of the heart.

The contrast with Lucretius inevitably suggests itself. Lucretius represents the serious doubt of the age, Catullus its pleasure-loving sensuality. Lucretius is a poet of retirement; Catullus of society. The one is the reflecting, the other the unreflecting Epicurean. There is a world of difference in their scale. Lucretius produced a single work of vast proportions on one theme which had engrossed his thought for years. The bulk of Catullus consists of short poems which make a moment's feeling eternal in its intensity. His grace and lightness — qualities unborrowed because here Catullus is most himself — are not to be paralleled in the graver poet. Nor does the feeling for form desert him, as it often does Lucretius. But it is not to Catullus one must go for serious and connected thought. Self-reproof is rare in him. There may be a transient weariness of an idle life

Otium, Catulle, tibi molestum est,

or the lament over the degeneracy of the world inserted to close the *Peleus and Thetis.* Catullus's troubles, however, are not those of the world, but those of his own experience. Even there his conscience is clear. He sees nothing to condemn in stolen amours with Lesbia, even during her husband's life-time.[2] In *Si qua recordanti* he can find no offence against honour wherewith to reproach himself; and for his worst indecencies he can allege the excuse

Nam castum esse decet pium poetam
Ipsum, uersiculos nihil necesse est.[3]

This claims unfettered licence to make every heart-throb vocal. It is this dominion of impulse which, on its better side, led Tennyson to call him

'Tenderest of Roman poets nineteen hundred years ago.'

To argue whether the superlative is just would be unprofitable. But, clearly, his tenderness is more restricted than that of Lucretius, who, if he has not Catullus's passion in love, shows more catholic feeling for all the 'natural shocks that flesh is heir to,' and more Virgilian penetration into the sorrow at the heart of things.

Quite as inevitable as the contrast with his contemporary Lucretius is that with the other great lyric poet of Rome. The comparison with Horace formed part of the issue between Conington and Munro in the

---

[1] *E.g.* (nouns) *amiculus, medullula, puellula,* and among many others two which Cicero borrows: (*imula*) *oricilla* and *ocellus*; (adjectives) *aridulus, eruditulus, mollicellus, pallidulus.* S. B. Platner (*Amer. Jrnl. Phil.*, 1895, pp. 186 *sqq.*) shows that there is more diminutive force in the nouns than in the adjectives.

[2] lxviii. 145.   [3] xvi. 5–6.

last century, as mentioned in comparing Lucretius and Virgil. The
arguments by which Conington defended his Augustan and Munro his
pre-Augustan clients it would be idle to restate.[1] Ultimately the
matter narrows itself to personal taste, on which dispute is fruitless.
There must always be those who prefer the more natural qualities of
Catullus and those who prefer the more artificial technique of Horace.
The two are so different in kind that they elude the would-be exact
appraiser. There is nothing in Horace like the wild *abandon* of Catullus's love poems, or the rapidity, colour, pathetic repinings, and
enslaving god-sent frenzy of the *Attis*. There is nothing in Horace to
parallel those portions of Catullus in which others than Macaulay have
found tears.[2] On the other hand, there is nothing in Catullus to equal
the finished structure of the best Horatian odes, and nothing to equal
Horace's sane criticism of life. Nor can there be anything better in their
way than Horace's sketches from human nature on his journey to
Brundisium and during his encounter with the bore on the Via Sacra.
How is it possible, and, after all, what need, to compare the hendecasyllabics of Catullus with the alcaics of Horace? Such poets are incommensurate magnitudes.

The place of Catullus is among the greatest lyric poets of the world —
Mackail says 'the third beside Sappho and Shelley.'[3] I shall not
attempt to number his place precisely: enough that it is high among the
best. For how can finality in such assessments be hoped for? What is
Goethe's place? What is Herrick's? Swinburne's declaration that
Herrick is 'the greatest song-writer — as surely as Shakespeare is the
greatest dramatist — ever born of English race' is as exaggerated in one
direction as, in the other, is Munro's contemptuous allusion to 'the
obsolete cranks and whimsies of the poetaster Herrick.'[4] Avoiding
rhapsodic estimates or the reverse, one notes in Catullus a fervency
recalling Sappho, and elsewhere an aerial lightness rivalling Shelley's
skylark qualities. Traits in him certainly do resemble Herrick. Each is a
prince among songsters. Each unites artificiality and simplicity. Herrick's 'blossoms, birds, and bowers' are present in the Latin poet,
though Alexandrinism left him freer from conceits than the 'metaphysical school' left Herrick.[5] The ancient mythology makes an

---

[1] See Conington's lecture already cited on *The Style of Lucretius and
Catullus*, etc., and 'Catullus and Horace' in H. A. J. Munro's *Criticisms and
Elucidations of Catullus*, ed. 2, 1905, pp. 229 *sqq*.
[2] The first lines of *Miser Catulle*, the lines to Cornificius, and part of *Si qua
recordanti* (viii, xxxviii, lxxvi).
[3] *Latin Lit.*, 1895, p. 54.   [4] *Criticisms and Elucidations*, p. 237.
[5] Herrick in a pomp of poets pledges his health:
    'Then this immensive cup
        Of aromatic wine,
    Catullus, I quaff up
        To that terse muse of thine.'

analogue to Herrick's 'Court of Mab and the fairy King.' Both could write an 'epithalamy' with gusto, and Catullus might subscribe at least the first third of Herrick's couplet

> I write of youth, of love, and have access
> By these to sing of cleanly wantonness.

But the key to Catullus's strength is in qualities wherein he resembles Burns much more. Catullus never becomes so affected and cold as Herrick; nor could he have sympathised with the trend of thought which in the English poet competes with a fresh feeling for meadows and flowers

> I must confess, mine eye and heart
> Dote less on Nature than on Art.

It is not for Alexandrine daintiness that we value Catullus any more than it is for excursions into the pseudo-classic conventionalism of the eighteenth century that we value Burns. The gold in both is depth of passion uttered in simple and unforgettable words.

The *lepidus libellus* of Catullus was a prelude to the Augustan age. Therein he showed himself a follower of Laevius as the introducer of lyric, and the predecessor of Horace, whose claim to have first turned the Aeolian measures into Latin is historically unjustifiable. He also showed himself the predecessor of Virgil in epic; of Gallus, Propertius, Tibullus, and Ovid in elegy; of Martial in epigram and occasional verse. Catullus pointed the way to a more exact prosody and a richer versification. We cannot estimate the debt Gallus owed him; but all the other poets just named imitate him consciously.[1] His lines especially commended themselves to the fastidious ear of Virgil. So his influence lived from the time of the Virgilian *Catalepton*, past Martial, who incessantly borrows from him, up to the days of Dracontius.[2] A long oblivion followed in the Middle Ages. Then, after the rediscovery of his poems, Catullus came into his own again. His influence on many leading Italian humanists of the fourteenth century, and especially on Petrarch, is very striking.[3] The notary of Verona who saved the single precious manuscript must be for ever gratefully honoured by all lovers of poetry.

[1] For a list of imitations, see F. P. Simpson, *Select Poems of Catullus*, pp. xxxviii *sqq.*
[2] B. Barwinski, *De Dracontio Catulli imitatore*: parallels quoted *Rh. Mus.*, xliii. (Dracontius had at least read the *Peleus and Thetis*).
[3] The subject is dealt with by Prof. R. Ellis in *Catullus in the Fourteenth Century*, 1905. For the merits of the greatest editions of Catullus from the fifteenth century, see R. Ellis, *Commentary* (Preface).

Chapter III

VARRO AND LEARNING

M. Terentius Varro of Reate – Life – His chief works – The extant
portions – Aim and influence of *Saturae Menippeae* – Social
criticism and poetry in them – *Antiquitates* – *De Lingua Latina* –
Analogy and Anomaly – Varro as grammarian – *De Re Rustica* –
Italian spirit of the work – A comparison with Cato – The philosophic in Varro and his social services – Some phases of his
influence on literature – Nigidius Figulus and other scholars –
Jurisprudence.

M. TERENTIUS VARRO 'REATINUS' (116–27 B.C.), the
renowned pupil of Aelius Stilo, is the best representative of
Roman encyclopaedic learning.[1] It was to knowledge rather
than to *belles lettres* that Varro's most memorable services were rendered; but in Roman, of all literatures, it is least possible to ignore the
history of knowledge. His appeal, as St. Augustine has it, is to the lover
of facts, as Cicero's is to the lover of words.[2] Through a life stretching
from a generation after the death of old Cato to the establishment of the
Augustan *régime*, Varro displayed, till he was almost a nonagenarian,
a well-nigh incredible diligence – beyond the pitch of the elder Pliny.
His energy in accumulating and disseminating knowledge was a practical anticipation of St. Benedict's counsel against idleness as the enemy
of the soul. Cicero's epithet πολυγραφώτατος[3] is but a mild intimation
of his miraculous fecundity. Quintilian admires him as *uir Romanorum
eruditissimus*;[4] and St. Augustine, a close student of his works, cites
Terentianus's words on his all-round learning, and declares Varro's
reading so wide that we wonder he had time to write anything, and his

---

[1] *De Ling. Lat.*, emend. et annot. K. O. Müller, 1833; A. Spengel, 1885
(based on L. Spengel); (w. Macrobius and Mela), Fr. trans., M. Nisard, 1883.
Menippearum reliq., ed. F. Oehler, 1844; (w. Petronius and *Priapea*, etc.) ed. 4,
Bücheler, 1904. *De Re Rustica*, ed. W. Keil (w. Cato), 1884–1891. *Antiquitates*,
fragments in R. Merkel's ed. of Ovid's *Fasti*, 1841; R. Agahd, 1898. Gramm.
fragments, ed. A. Wilmanns, 1864. Hist. fragments in H. Peter, *Hist. Rom. Reliq.*,
1906–1914. *Cf.* F. W. Ritschl, *Opusc.*, iii., 1877, pp. 419 *sqq.*; G. Boissier,
Étude sur la vie et les ouvrages de M. T. Varron, ed. 2, 1875.
[2] *C. Dei*, VI. ii.: 'doctrina atque sententiis ita refertus ut in omni eru-
ditione . . . studiosum rerum tantum iste doceat quantum studiosum uerborum
Cicero delectat.' Quintilian with equal acumen says that in oratory Varro was
'plus scientiae collaturus quam eloquentiae.'
[3] *Ad Att.*, XIII. xvii. 2.
[4] Quint., X. i. 95.

writings so many that we might well believe scarcely any one could have read him through.[1]

Born at Reate,[2] in the Sabine country, he belonged to the propertied class. His education was completed at Athens under the philosopher Antiochus of Ascalon. Learning did not make Varro a hermit. He was tribune and aedile; he held several military commands, including a lieutenancy under Pompey in the operations of 67 against the pirates; his satires prove how observantly he mixed with his fellows; and his *Agriculture*, he tells us, is based not merely on reading and hearsay but on his own farming. In politics he gave vent to his disfavour for the coalition of Caesar, Pompey, and Crassus by writing his Τρικάρανος.[3] But he was anti-Caesarian without rancour. He served on Caesar's commission of 59 to assign land-allotments to veterans in Campania; and though he acted as a Pompeian officer in Spain during the Civil War, once it became clear that Pompey no longer stood for the state, he made his peace with Caesar. The reconciliation was sealed by his nomination to the charge of the public library designed by the dictator.[4] Himself saved, though his villa and books were not, from Antony's vindictive fury[5] after Caesar's death, he was eventually exempted from the proscription and allowed to spend his closing years in peaceful study at Rome.

No division of contemporary learning was left untouched by Varro. He is quoted by Gellius as saying that by the beginning of his seventy-eighth year he had written seventy 'hebdomads' of books.[6] This for-givable sum of 'seventy times seven' agrees with that in Jerome's list, which, incomplete as it avowedly is, gives thirty-nine — or by an equally probable reckoning forty-eight — different works, consisting of 490 books.[7] The grand total for Varro's whole life has been estimated by Ritschl as seventy-four different works consisting of 620 single volumes. As poet and satirist Varro wrote, besides 150 books of *Saturae Menippeae*, other collections of *saturae* (perhaps without the prose admixture of the *Menippeae*), *poemata*, and *pseudo-tragoediae*, which were probably

---

[1] *C. Dei.*, VI. ii.

[2] Symmachus, *Ep.*, I. ii, calls him 'Reatinus.' Varro often refers to his possessions at Reate in his *De Re Rust.* The authority for the dates of birth and death is Jerome (*Euseb. Chron.*, ad ann. Abr. 1901, *i.e.* 116 B.C., and ad ann. Abr. 1990, *i.e.* 27 B.C.), who calls him 'filosophus et poeta.'

[3] Appian, *B.C.*, II. ix. (60 B.C.), καί τις αὐτῶν 'τήνδε τὴν συμφροσύνην συγγραφεὺς Οὐάρρων ἐνὶ βιβλίῳ περιλαβὼν ἐπέγραψε Τρικάρανcν.

[4] Suet., *Iul.*, xliv.

[5] Cic., *Phil.*, II. xl. 103.

[6] Gell., *N.A.*, III. x. 17, '. . . ad eum diem septuaginta hebdomadas librorum conscripsisse, ex quibus aliquammultos, cum proscriptus esset, direptis bibliothecis suis, non comparuisse.'

[7] Jerome's letter *ad Paulam*, containing the list, was re-discovered at the beginning of a MS. of Origen. If the *Singulares X* of the list are ten different tractates, Jerome's total of separate works is forty-eight. Jerome adds, 'et alia plurima quae enumerare longum est. Vix medium descripsi indicem, et legentibus fastidium est.'

dramatic only in name. As antiquary and historian, in addition to his forty-one books of *Antiquitates Rerum Humanarum et Diuinarum*, he produced his *Annales, Res Vrbanae, De Gente Populi Romani* (on the national pedigree and its relation to other peoples),[1] *De Vita Populi Romani* (a sketch of Roman civilisation suggested by the Βίος Ἑλλάδος of Dicaearchus), and the *Aetia* (an investigation, on the lines of the Αἴτια of Callimachus, into the reasons for Roman customs, which Plutarch used freely for his Αἴτια Ῥωμαϊκά). The *Logistorici* were on the borderland between history and philosophy. They were disquisitions, largely ethical in subject, and some of them dialogues in form, with historical examples, *e.g. Marius de Fortuna* and *Orestes de Insania*. As Heraclides of Pontus and Ariston of Chios had blended peripateticism with mythology, Varro may have desired to blend his discussions with history—to be '*logistoric*' where they were 'mythistoric.' As jurist he composed fifteen books *De Iure Ciuili*; as geographer and meteorologist he wrote *De Ora Maritima, Libri Nauales*,[2] and weather almanacs for sailors and farmers. In the department of literary and linguistic inquiry, from a crowd of works on poets, poetry, rhetoric, grammar, stage equipment, dramatic records, and Plautine criticism, there stand out two. These are his *De Lingua Latina Libri xxv*, and his *Hebdomades* or *Imaginum Libri xv*, a gallery of seven hundred celebrated Greeks and Romans, which has the distinction of being the first illustrated work.[3] The portraits illustrating the prose text were accompanied by brief verse inscriptions.[4] In the field of science, he wrote treatises on agriculture, mathematics, and astronomy. Philosophy he handled both separately and in combination with other subjects when in his nine books of *Disciplinae* he drew up a complete scheme of education in the liberal arts—grammar, logic, rhetoric, geometry, arithmetic, astronomy, music, medicine, and architecture—in the first seven of which one recognises the medieval *trivium* and *quadrivium*.

This record might be made still more formidable by the enumeration of other titles. But it is fruitless to specify exhaustively the number of

[1] The influence of other nations came within Varro's purview. Thus, St. Augustine, who borrowed a good deal from the *De Gente*, mentions his chronological introduction on the small state of Sicyon, 'a quo ille undecunque doctissimus M. Varro scribens de gente populi Romani, uelut antiquo tempore, exorsus est.' (*C. Dei*, XVIII, ii).
[2] These may have included his book on tidal estuaries, mentioned *De Ling. Lat.*, IX. 26.
[3] Pliny praises Varro's ingenuity, *N.H.*, XXXV. 11, 'benignissimo inuento,' etc.; *cf.* Gell., *N.A.*, III. x. 1; xi. 7. A somewhat parallel grouping of the heroes of the Trojan War in Aristotle's Πέπλος makes it likely that Cicero's allusion in 'Πεπλογραφία Varronis,' *Ad Att.*, XVI. xi. 3, is to the *Imagines*.
[4] Bährens, *F.P.R.*, p. 296, assigns to Varro's book the well-known epitaphs on Naevius ('Immortales mortales,' etc.), on Plautus ('Postquam est mortem aptus Plautus,' etc.), on Pacuvius ('Tamenetsi adulescens properas,' etc.), and seven hexameters on the Seven Sages of Greece.

books of collected speeches, letters, and sayings,[1] authentic or not. The
ground must be cleared by concentrating attention on the principal
remains of Varro and on two works, the *Antiquitates* and the *De
Philosophia*, about which Augustine's interest in ancient theology and
philosophy has led him to bequeath especially full information. Of
Varro's voluminous output we naturally know most about the *De Re
Rustica*, whose three books we possess practically complete, and the
De Lingua Latina, of whose twenty-five we possess six. The most
interesting of the fragments consist of about six hundred lines from the
Menippeae, for most of which we are indebted to Nonius's citations. To
these poetic or semi-poetic remains we address ourselves first.

From Quintilian we learn that Varro was the author of an older type
of satire than that of Lucilius—one composed in many sorts of metre
and in prose as well.[2] These are the *Saturae Menippeae*. They were so
entitled by Varro as being based on the Cynic dialogues of Menippus,
the philosopher of Gadara in the third century, whose spirit and figure
are so amusing in his imitator Lucian. Varro's aim was comparable to
Addison's in the *Spectator*—to introduce academic thought to the
average reader.[3] Realising the need of gilding the philosophic pill for
the unlearned, and bent on overcoming the national repugnance to
speculation, he seasoned esoteric truth and logical discussion with
jocularity in his treatment of contemporary society. The outcome was a
mass of 150 books, as motley in theme as in form. The tradition of this
medley passed through Seneca's *Apocolocyntosis* and Petronius's
Satyricon into the pedantic fantasia of Martianus Capella, *De Nuptiis
Philologiae et Mercurii*. Through that educational manual, once a standard, it influenced medieval compositions of the *chantefable* order.
Boethius also represents the tradition when he diversifies the prose of his
De Consolatione Philosophiae with poems in varied metres—like so many
lyric interludes amidst his tragic sorrows. Fully ten centuries later, in
the political *Satyre Menippée* which helped to consummate the victory
of Henry IV over the League, although prose predominates, there still
are inserted pieces of verse to recall the ancient model.

Cicero makes Varro speak of the *Saturae* as old writings of his. Many
doubtless belonged to his early career; but a work so extensive must

---

[1] The *Sententiae* contain much which is not in Varro's manner, but which
has been rashly ascribed to him by his epitomisers.
[2] Quint., X. i. 95, 'alterum illud etiam prius saturae genus, sed non sola
carminum uarietate mixtum condidit Terentius Varro': cf. Cic., *Acad. Post.*, I.
ii. 9, 'ipse uarium et elegans omni fere numero poema fecisti.'
[3] Cic., *Acad. Post.*, I. ii. 8, purports to describe Varro's method and aim:
'In illis ueteribus nostris quae Menippum imitati, non interpretati, quadam
hilaritate conspersimus, multa admixta ex intima philosophia, multa dicta
dialectice; quae quo facilius minus docti intellegerent, iucunditate quadam ad
legendum inuitati,' etc. Cf. *Spect.*, No. 10: 'I have brought philosophy out of
closets and libraries, schools and colleges, to dwell in clubs and assemblies, at
tea-tables and in coffee-houses.'

have spread over a prolonged period. Some are certainly late, such as the *Sexagessis* and the Γεροντοδιδασκαλος. Even in their fragmentary state, one can detect the astounding variety of range on social, ethical, and literary topics.[1] Varro sketches life around him without invective. It is the old racy *satura* revived, with a strong dash of cynicism imported from the Greek. Plebeian expressions jostle learned terms. Dramatic situations and offhand dialogue form the framework to point a moral. The ancient mythology and the 'dog-world of Diogenes'[2] are laid under contribution now for serious and now for comic effect. Two threads of thought run on continuously—one, the absurdity of much Greek philosophising, with which Varro would contrast his own homely lessons; the other, the tightening grip of luxury, with which Varro would contrast the good old days. The very titles are instructive. Many are delightfully quaint—in Latin, in Greek, or in a blend of both: *e.g.*, *Nescis quid uesper serus uehat* (on dinner-parties), *Longe fugit qui suos fugit*, Δὶς παῖδες οἱ γέροντες,[3] Ἄμμον μετρεῖς (on covetousness), *Aborigines* περὶ ἀνθρώπων φύσεως (a study of human civilisation recalling the fifth book of Lucretius, though there is nowhere any sign of his influence on Varro), *Andabatae*[4] (gladiators with closed vizors who here allegorise the blindness of the soul), Ἀνθρωπόπολις (picturing family life as 'Man-town' and satirising extravagance in the married),[5] *Bimarcus* ('The Double Marcus,' *i.e.* Varro holding dialogue with his other self and satirising the ten τρόποι of the Sceptics), *Est Modus Matulae* περὶ μέθης ('A Pot has its Limits'—on drunkenness), *Eumenides*,[6] *Caprinum Proelium* ('The Battle of the Goats'

[1] A lively account of the *Menippeae* is given by Mommsen, *R. Hist.*, Eng. ed., 1877, vol. iv., pp. 594–598. A representative selection, with an attempt to weave each set of fragments into a connected whole, is given by Merry, *Fragts. of Rom. Poetry*, pp. 196–222.

[2] *E.g.*, Κυνίστωρ, Κυνορρήτωρ, Ἱπποκύων and the like.

[3] *Cf.* Aristoph., *Clouds*, 1417.

[4] A. Gercke in *Hermes*, xxviii., 1893.

[5] Wedlock is the purge that cleans a purse out – 'Et Hymenaeus qui primo lauere aluum marsuppio solet.'

[6] This is a vigorous work. At dinner Cynics and Stoics are played off against each other. An adjournment to go the round of the town gives a chance of testing the Stoic proposition that all men are mad. Galliambics introduce a touch of realism as the inquirers visit the temple of Cybele. Townsfolk are seen to be pursued by the Furies, the third of whom is Madness. The narrator tries to help; but is haled before 'Current Thought' (*Existimatio*) and entered on the list of the insane. This registration of the thinker as mad matches the cynicism expressed earlier in the satire by one of the speakers, 'There is no outrageous nightmare of a delirious patient which may not be found in the utterance of some philosopher or other':

'Postremo nemo aegrotus quicquam somniat
Tam infandum, quod non aliquis dicat philosophus.'

Then 'Grey-haired Truth' (*Cana Veritas*) comes as a worshipful monitress to console the thinker who has been misunderstood and evilly entreated by the world. This personification is quite a Roman trait. It also anticipates the spirit of medieval poetry, like the *Roman de la Rose*, *Piers Plowman*, and the Morality plays, where abstractions appear as real and active figures.

—on pleasure), *Cycnus* (on burial), *Manius*[1] ('Old Up-in-the-Morning,'
and how he sets his slaves to work, with scenes from old Roman
farm-life). Others laugh at social lies and foibles, the empty
nothings of a funeral oration or of flirtation with a pretty woman;[2]
or attack profligacy, medical prescriptions, or the changes in Rome
for the worse, as when Varro like a Roman Rip van Winkle
(*Sexagessis*, 'Old-Sixty-Years') wakes up after a slumber of half a
century. It is a favourite theme with Varro, this harping on ancient
plainness. The Γεροντοδιδάσκαλος treats it with a different setting by
bringing together a man of mature years and a type of youthful luxury.
The *Marcipor* (*i.e.*, *Marci puer*, 'Varro's Slave'), probably a piece of
moralising in a Horatian manner, contains a powerful description of a
storm, with which we may illustrate the poetical side of the *saturae*:

> Sudden, about the very noon of night,
> When air, bedecked with distant-glowing fires,
> Revealed the starry ring-dance in the heavens,
> The fleeting clouds with cold and watery veil
> Did hide the golden grottoes of the sky,
> And belched their waters on mankind below.
> Then from the icy pole burst forth the winds,
> Delirious scions of the Northern Wain,
> With tiles and boughs and brooms upon their path.
> But we dejected castaways—like storks,
> The feathers of whose wings the lightning-flash
> Hath scorched—fell stricken from on high to earth.[3]

The *Antiquitates*, published about 47 B.C., formed a system of

[1] Mommsen's sketch (*op. cit.*, p. 598) shows that this *satura* reflected rural morality and religion of that primitive, manly, and independent sort which enabled the peasant, without the intervention of a priestly caste, to pray and sacrifice face to face with the gods.
[2] In *Papiapapae* περὶ ἐγκωμίων, one fragment touches the fulsome eulogy whereby 'some most thievish and rascally citizen, when dead, is made a Scipio of,' another jests at mincing compliments with their affected diminutives:
> 'Oculis suppaetulis nigelli pupuli
> Quantam hilaritatem significantes animuli.'
[3] The lines, pieced together from diverse citations by Nonius, form the best example of Varro's style in iambics. It is difficult to see how the *naufragi* can in this passage be shipwrecked mariners. Merry detects 'a reminiscence of the flight of Menippus to the court of Zeus.'
> 'Repente noctis circiter meridie,
> Cum pictus aër feruidis late ignibus
> Caeli chorean astricen ostenderet,
> Nubes aquali frigido uelo leues
> Caeli cauernas aureas subduxerant,
> Aquam uomentes inferam mortalibus.
> Ventique frigido se ab axe eruperant,
> Phrenetici septentrionum filii,
> Secum ferentes tegulas, ramos, syros.
> At nos caduci naufragi, ut ciconiae,
> Quarum bipennis fulminis plumas uapor
> Perussit, alte maesti in terram cecidimus.'

antiquities divided into twenty-five books on *res humanae* and sixteen on *res diuinae*. The Christian Fathers depended greatly on it for information about Roman life and worship; but the work cannot be shown to have been in use after the time of Priscian, in the early sixth century. In both sections Varro grouped his matter rigidly under the headings of persons, places, times, and things. Of the past he possessed a knowledge in his day unrivalled. But his enormous store of facts and dates constituted the materials of history rather than history itself. In ability to subordinate decisively the less important, to marshal details effectively, to rise to those general views which make history scientific, Varro was deficient. He loses himself in curiosities. The same fault besets his linguistic research. In history he has not the critical sense to examine authorities or analyse a legend. So he is a learned antiquary and chronicler; but he is not a historian. As theologian, Varro pointedly concerns himself not with the mythical religion of the poets, nor with the systematic creeds of the philosopher, but with the religion of the state. This he expounds and commends. At a time when Lucretian speculation sought to cut the ground from under religion, Varro's sympathy with the formal and political aspects of worship served as a counterblast. The insistence on piety as the secret of Roman greatness and the veneration for time-honoured ceremonial, coupled with the dedication to Caesar as Pontifex Maximus, contributed to shape the attitude of Augustus as Emperor towards the state-religion.

Of twenty-five books *De Lingua Latina*, six (v–x) survive with certain gaps and corruptions. Like the much smaller *De Re Rustica*, the work fell into three parts, after the introductory book,[1] Etymology (ii–vii), Inflexion (viii–xiii), and Syntax (xiv–xxv).[2] Thus we possess half the 'etymological' and half the 'inflexional' portion. From the fifth book onwards it was dedicated to Cicero in return for his dedication to Varro of the second edition of the *Academics*, by which he had 'fished' for the long-desired compliment. The date of publication cannot then be later than 43.[3] What with dry subject-matter, pedantic subdivisions repeated *ad nauseam*, and the clumsiness of an unperfected terminology, the *De Lingua Latina* cannot be called exhilarating — unless, indeed, one can find adequate entertainment in the fanciful derivations which

---

[1] *De Ling. Lat.* VII. 110.

[2] It is difficult to believe that so much of the work went on syntax strictly. Questions of style may have been included. K. O. Müller, in his ed. of *De Ling. Lat.*, 1833, p. 1, closes his table of Arguments with the pertinent remark: 'Sed nescio syntaxisne Varroniana tam elaborata et profligata fuerit ut omnes undecim libros ad ultimum usque complere potuerit; an scriptor in inferioribus libris ad usum vocabulorum et orationis ornatum et similia argumenta transgressus sit.'

[3] Much of the composition might be earlier: *e.g.*, the discussion of the name of the month *Quintilis* reads as if it preceded Caesar's reform of the calendar (*De Ling. Lat.*, VI. 34.)

earned the gibes of Quintilian.[1] Even Varro's keen and recurrent sense
of the changes wrought by time on the look of words[2] does not deter
him from rash and superficial explanations. It is only fair, however, to
allow that the work is at times lit up by penetration. Even in etymology
he has good things; *meridies*, for instance, he correctly explains as
medius dies, and notes having seen the old form *medidies* engraved on a
sundial at Praeneste.[3] He has the sagacity to doubt whether *Tiberis* is of
Latin origin.[4] Equally sagacious are his remarks on poets' words and
words still older,[5] and his clear conception of the power which popular
dramatists possess for moulding the language.[6] There is historical
interest in his reference to Greek grammarians and to Aelius, whom he
often cites. Particularly valuable for rare words and usages are the
abundant quotations from old Latin poets. They vivify the seventh book
especially. On occasion he breaks into lively rejoinders worthy of the
author of the *Menippeae*; as when he twits bigoted opponents of new
words with the queries, 'Does one object to new clothes? or new laws?
or to the Greek names of vases which have become the fashion?'[7]

Analogy and anomaly in language are threshed out in books viii–x.
Varro is an analogist. But the strict maintenance of the analogist
position he virtually surrenders in granting the claims of custom (*consuetudo*) to justify anomalies.[8] Really, the common sense of Horace in his
remark on

[1] *E.g.*, V. 21, *terra*, 'quod teritur' backed by the authority of Aelius and by
the spelling with one *r* in the 'Augurum libri'; V. 40, *prata*, 'sine opera parata';
V. 101, *cerui=gerui*, 'quod magna cornua gerunt.' Sometimes he gives alternative derivations, among which he may or may not hit the truth; V. 18–20, for
caelum he on the whole prefers 'cauum' (which he connects with 'chaos'!);
V. 99, for *canis* he offers a choice between 'catus' and 'canere'; V. 101, *apri*,
'ab eo quod in locis asperis, nisi a Graecis quod hi κάπροι'; VI. 9, *uer*, 'quod
tum uirere incipiunt uirgulta ac uertere se tempus anni, nisi quod Iones dicunt
ἦρ uer.'

[2] V. 5, 'Vetustas pauca non deprauat, multa tollit. Quem puerum uidisti
formosum, hunc uides deformem in senecta. Tertium saeculum non uidet eum
hominem quem uidit primum. Quare illa quae iam maioribus nostris ademit
obliuio, fugitiua secuta sedulitas Muti et Bruti retrahere nequit. Non, si non
potuero indagare, eo ero tardior, sed uelocior ideo si quiuero; non mediocres
enim tenebrae in silua ubi haec captanda; neque eo quo peruenire uolumus
semitae tritae; neque non in tramitibus quaedam obiecta quae euntem retinere
possent.'

[3] VI. 4.   [4] V. 29.

[5] V. 9, 'Non enim uidebatur consentaneum quaerere me in eo uerbo quod
finxisset Ennius causam, neglegere quod ante rex Latinus finxisset; quom
poeticis multis uerbis magis delecter quam utar, antiquis magis utar quam
delecter.'

[6] IX. 17.   [7] IX. 20 *sqq.*

[8] *E.g.*, VIII. 26 and 33. On the other hand, he makes a spirited claim to the
right of correcting bad usage in words, IX. 10–15 (*e.g.*, § 11, 'Non sequitur ut
stulte faciant qui pueris in geniculis alligent serperastra, ut eorum deprauata
corrigant crura? Cum uituperandus non sit medicus, qui e longinqua mala
consuetudine aegrum in meliorem traducit, quare reprehendendus sit qui
orationem minus ualentem propter malam consuetudinem traducat in meliorem?') Besides, he maintains that custom and analogy are not necessarily
opposed, IX. 3.

Usus
Quem penes arbitrium est et ius et norma loquendi

may be said to suggest the last word on a subject discussed by Cicero, Caesar, the elder Pliny, Quintilian, and others,[1] sometimes over nicely, but with the useful effect of forcing continuous attention on grammatical forms. Save for this one good fruit, the debate between analogists and anomalists is barren logomachy. The grammatical discussions are occasionally illumined by homely illustrations. These are shrewdly borrowed from the ability of new slaves to 'decline' their comrades' names the moment they hear the nominative; they play upon the dissimilarity between parts of the same residence (*atrium*, *peristylum*, *cubiculum*, *equile*), or upon the unequal size of the couches in a dining-room.[2]

Systematic treatment of the laws of the Latin language, on Greek lines, might have been expected any time after Crates lectured in Rome in the second century. But Crates's method did not mature either in Accius's grammatical reforms or in the handling of the old literature by Lampadio and Vargunteius. Not till it reached the hands of Aelius Stilo in Sulla's time did Latin grammar approach the scientific stage. From him and from Greek authorities Varro drew to such purpose that his work conserved its reputation alongside of famous successors like Ateius and Verrius Flaccus. Varro had certain accurate, if limited, conceptions of the philosophy of language. He appreciated the need of turning back to the very origins, as we have already seen.[3] Without being Stoic,[4] he had imbibed the Stoic care for the value of words, and for the general principles of language. But he also inherited the defects of Greek grammarians—their *penchant* for subtle and often worthless problems, and their haste towards inferences from incomplete investigation of details. Obviously, nothing could be less scientific than his derivations. Yet some indulgence is due to an early worker in an arduous field. Varro's signal triumph is to have helped to make grammar a study worth the notice of men like Cicero, Caesar, Pollio, and Messalla.

When his eightieth year gave warning that he 'must be packing for departure from this life,'[5] Varro addressed himself to treat agriculture in what he meant for a set of Sibylline books on the subject. The scheme is Book I, Agriculture (*de agricultura*), Book II, Cattle (*de re pecuaria*); Book III, Game and Fish Preserves (*de uillaticis pastionibus*). The use of dialogue enhances the literary form. Each book has a different scene,

---

[1] See Sandys, *Hist. Class Scholarship*, ed. 3, 1926, i. pp. 180–181.
[2] VIII. 6; and 29.
[3] V. 9.
[4] Varro's sympathies were with the Old Academy, whose tenets are among those which he is represented as expounding in Cic., *Acad. Post.* K. O. Müller's contention (pref. to ed. of *De Ling. Lat.*) that he was Stoic is untenable.
[5] *De Re Rust.*, I. i. 1, 'Annus enim octogesimus admonet me ut sarcinas colligam antequam proficiscar e uita.'

and is addressed to a different person. Different interlocutors are introduced with such suggestive names as Scrofa, Agrasius, Vaccius. The first book, addressed to Fundania, his wife, contains some pleasant talk on the joys and profits of farming. It considers the situation, equipment, and manning of a villa, and the duties for different seasons. The sudden close is almost too vivid. The *aedituus* whom the speakers await in the temple of Tellus has been murdered, and his freedman arrives in tears to invite the company to the funeral next day. They disperse sorrowfully, 'complaining of the lot of humanity rather than wondering that it had happened at Rome.'[1] The resumed talk of the second book on stock-breeding is less varied in interest. There are, however, typical Varronian hits at the mania for Greek names for parts of a Roman house,[2] at the growth of a luxurious idleness, and the change by which hands that once cultivated the vine are now busy with applause in the theatre. The third book has a realistic setting. The speakers are momentarily expecting the results of an election of aediles, and there are dramatic interruptions, such as the news of a man just caught surreptitiously slipping extra voting-tablets into the box.[3] The subjects handled – game and fish preserves, flower nurseries, plantations, colonnades, tessellated floors, and marble aviaries – form an instructive index to the comfort enjoyed by well-to-do Romans at their country seats.

The Italian spirit of the *De Re Rustica* cannot be missed. Invoking, as the author says, not the Muses but the *Di Consentes*, he strikes a national note which rings through the treatise. The praises of Italy,[4] the admiration for the peasantry as defenders of their land,[5] and the belief in country life as honourable as well as useful, harmonise with a subject-matter which is inevitably drawn from actual life, whether there is under review simple farm work or elaborate game-preserves. The Roman literary backgrounds are in keeping. They are among the many proofs that Varro, though well aware of the formidable array of *savants*[6] before him on this very subject, succeeded in being individual and original in his handling.

One instinctively compares him with Cato. There are many differences. The world had moved since Cato wrote. Varro had wider learning and a wider outlook. His form is more literary; and he is quite as businesslike as Cato, whose sole aim is useful precept. Varro is even

[1] I. lxix. 3, 'de casu humano magis querentes quam admirantes id Romae factum.'

[2] II. *praef.*, 2.

[3] III. v. 18.

[4] I. ii. 3, 'Vos qui multas perambulastis terras, ecquam cultiorem Italia uidistis? . . . Non arboribus consita Italia est ut tota pomarium uideatur?'

[5] III. i.

[6] I. i, he says more than fifty authors – chiefly Greeks – had written on the subject. He quotes from some of the Greeks, besides from Cato, *De Orig.* and *De Re Rust.*, and from Ennius and Pacuvius.

more systematic. He has more kindliness and less parsimony. He has the heart to advocate consideration for hirelings and slaves.[1] In Varro there is less about religion — but then he had treated it so fully elsewhere; less old-world lore, so that one welcomes a few proverbs like *Est homo bulla* and *Romanus sedendo uincit*; less superstition, too, though Agrasius protests, 'I might become bald if I did not have my hair cut when the moon is on the wane!'[2] On the whole, one is conscious of some disappointment that Varro's scholarship has not made a greater advance on Cato. The style[3] seems uncomely, the matter wearisome, and the dialogue ill-managed in comparison with the rhetorical and philosophical discussions composed by Cicero years before. To turn to the *De Oratore* is to realise how relatively inartistic Varro's prose is.

Neither was his philosophy transcendently great. It was shrewd rather than profound. Greek idealism was tempered with the Róman love of the practical. Though Jerome calls him 'philosopher' as well as 'poet,' and though Varro had studied much in Athens, yet a certain limitation on the philosophical side prevents his attainment to a completely unified system.[4] But he made approaches thereto. He coordinated subjects into an educational whole foreshadowing the training of the Middle Ages. In the *De Vita Populi Romani* the suggestion of continuous life of a people from infancy to maturity is a philosophic conception. The ironic exposure of philosophers' extravagances in the *Menippeae* is not the least philosophic thing in him. Both in the *Menippeae* and in the *De Re Rustica* he held penetrating ethical views on the dangers of luxury to society. The weakness was that with his encyclopaedic industry he had not the co-ordinating genius requisite to elevate compilation into inspiring synthesis. Varro was not an Aristotle. His faculty for subdivision constantly obtains dominion over him. In his prose works he can scarcely be said to have his moments so surely as the elder Pliny had. Yet, when all is said, his was a valiant endeavour to keep abreast of all that was worth knowing and to Romanise learning. Helped possibly by collaborators and by slave copyists who have left no sign, he took over and acclimatised much of the intellectual heritage of Athens, Pergamum, and Alexandria. The one animating passion that spurred this polymath to his life of arduous toil was to place at the disposal of his fellows the inexhaustible arsenal of his own knowledge. This is consistent with the sense of social duty exemplified practically in

[1] I. xvii.
[2] For the effect of a waning moon on sheep-shearing and hair-cutting see I. xxxvii.
[3] Varro's prose style strikes one as a strange combination of the simple and the cumbrous.
[4] Cic., *Acad. Post.*, I. 9; Varro is urged to write on philosophy something better than suggestive sketches – 'philosophiam multis locis incohasti, ad impellendum satis, ad edocendum parum.'

his public career and theoretically in the *De Philosophia*.[1] So determined
was he to enlighten his compatriots that even for the *profanum uulgus*
Varro wrote *résumés* of some of his longer works.[2] Varro's fame is fair
recompense for bringing so much knowledge within the common reach.
In the Positivist Calendar Comte has appropriately set him in 'the
month of ancient science' to open the 'week' which leads through
Columella, Vitruvius, Strabo, Frontinus and Plutarch to Pliny the Elder.

The ramifications of his influence are too intricate to follow, but in
the province of literature alone his effect is very noticeable on Virgil and
on criticism. Virgil's imitations of Varro are guaranteed by Servius.
These are but natural. The *Georgics* belong to the decade after the *De Re
Rustica*, and Virgil's poem was rendered possible only by the practical
works of predecessors.[3] But to sound precept Virgil united a winning
grace. The old dry nomenclature is illumined by beauty; with him
agriculture becomes literature. Upon literary history, including criticism, Varro's mark may have been deeper than we can guess, now that
so much of him is lost. It is true that his precise formulation of merits in
a given poet does not promise the most fertile criticism. He had a turn
for labelling literary virtues to match his turn for subdividing scientific
themes. Thus he tells off the palm to Caecilius for invention, to Terence
for character, and to Plautus for dialogue. He might have done worse;
only the method does not take us very far. But it would not be fair to
judge him by fragmentary pronouncements. His services to Plautine
scholarship were really considerable. The *Quaestiones* were valuable
exegetically, and the *De Comoediis Plautinis* established a sound canon
of authority. To possess his works on literature would clear up some
vexed problems. We should learn, for instance, regarding the Roman
satura, whether Diomedes's well-known passage on its nature is borrowed from Varro or from Suetonius;[4] and whether it was a hint, or
more than a hint, in Varro which led Horace to connect the Lucilian
satire with that of the Old Comedy of Eupolis, Cratinus, and Aristophanes.[5] For his services to literature all round, no better summary
can be given than Cicero's polished eulogy. Discerning that Greek
scholarship and science had left Varro in spirit a Roman of the Romans,
Cicero prefaces a concise review of his achievements with the fine
testimony:[6]

[1] The *De Philosophia* is analysed by St. Aug., *C. Dei*, XIX. i–iii; *e.g.*, iii.
ad fin., 'Hanc uitam beatam etiam socialem perhibent esse.' *Cf.* Boissier, *op. cit.*,
p. 314, 'Il n'apprenait pas pour lui seul; il aimait à faire part aux autres de ses
connaissances.'
[2] The three ἐπιτομαί of the *Antiquitates*, *Imagines*, and *De Lingua
Latina* on Jerome's list may not be by Varro's hand; but his method in some
subjects seems to have been to compose (*a*) preliminary studies, (*b*) an exhaustive
work, (*c*) an epitome.
[3] *Georg.*, i. 176, 'Possum multa tibi ueterum praecepta referre.'
[4] See F. Leo in *Hermes*, xxiv., 67.
[5] Hor., *Sat.*, I. iv. 1–6.
[6] *Acad. Post.*, I. iii. 9, 'Nam nos in nostra urbe peregrinantis errantisque

When we felt ourselves foreigners and wanderers—strangers, as it were, in our own Rome—your books may be said to have conducted us home, and enabled us at length to perceive who we Romans were and where we lived.

The figure who, for erudition, ranked next to Varro was the neo-Pythagorean *savant* Nigidius Figulus (98–45), once already alluded to. He was praetor in 58. He treated grammar, augury, and natural science.[1] For grammatical terminology he introduced a few improvements in accuracy.[2] Learning was greatly stimulated by Greeks living in or visiting Rome.[3] No figure was more important than Posidonius, who had been a pupil of Panaetius, and whose travels brought him more than once to the city. As head of the Stoics at Rhodes, he drew thither inquirers like Varro, Cicero, and many young Romans, and, through his gift of combining Platonic and Aristotelian views with his Stoicism, he wielded an incalculable influence on thought.[4] Among scholars at Rome there stands on the threshold of the period Staberius Eros, who taught the children of the Sullan *proscripti* gratuitously,[5] and was the instructor of Brutus and Cassius. The elder Pliny magnifies him into the *conditor grammaticae*.[6] Ateius Praetextatus, a captive from Athens, who assumed, in virtue of his recognised learning, the epithet 'Philologus,' was friendly with Sallust, and afterwards with Asinius Pollio, helping the one with an abstract of materials and the other with rules of style. Santra, presumably non-Italian also, wrote on literary history. Lenaeus, Pompey's learned freedman, who assailed Sallust out of affection for his patron's memory, was one of the professors of the day. Among such should be included Orbilius from Beneventum, Horace's severe master; Epidius, the instructor of Antony, Augustus, and Virgil; and Parthenius of Nicaea, who owed his emancipation to his talent, and also, it was said, had Virgil for his pupil. Some of the work of Cicero and his immediate circle may be appropriately mentioned here. Cicero's own literary criticism is chiefly contained in his writings on oratory and orators. His great friend, T. Pomponius Atticus (109–32) served learning as much

tamquam hospites tui libri quasi domum reduxerunt, ut possemus aliquando qui et ubi essemus agnoscere. Tu aetatem patriae, tu descriptiones temporum, tu sacrorum iura, tu sacerdotum, tu domesticam, tu bellicam disciplinam, tu sedem regionum, locorum, tu omnium diuinarum humanarumque rerum nomina, genera, officia, causas aperuisti, plurimumque poetis nostris omninoque Latinis et litteris luminis et uerbis attulisti.'

[1] Gellius, *N.A.*, IV. ix. 1, declares him 'iuxta Varronem doctissimus.' He more than once quotes him on soothsaying and augury. So does Lydus, *e.g.*, *De Ostent.*, 27, κατὰ τὸν 'Ρωμαῖον Φίγουλον.
[2] Gell. *N.A.* XVII. vii. 5; XIX. xiv. 3.
[3] A list of prominent Greek professors about this period is given in Rostand and Benoist's ed. of Catullus, p. xxxvi.
[4] For the influence of Posidonius see F. Leo, *Die Röm. Lit.* in *Die Kultur d. Gegenwart* (ed. P. Hinneberg), I, Abt. viii, 1907, pp. 360–361.
[5] Suet., *Gramm.*, 13.
[6] Plin., *N.H.*, xxxv. 199.

254 THE LITERATURE OF THE GOLDEN AGE

by his copying and publishing establishment as by his own writings. They were mainly historical—Roman chronology, family records, and in Greek the sketch of Cicero's consulate composed in 60 B.C. Cicero's faithful Tiro, who edited a great part of his letters and speeches, wrote a biography of his master, elaborated a system of shorthand, and a treatise on the Latin language.

The jurisprudence of the Ciceronian age[1] is well represented by Servius Sulpicius Rufus (105–43), who had been taught by C. Aquilius Gallus, a pupil of Scaevola the Pontifex. Rufus, besides having a school of followers in law, was a scholar and orator.[2] His letter of sympathy to Cicero on the death of Tullia, with its noble subjection of the individual woe to sorrow for freedom lost and cities ruined,[3] would alone preserve the fame of him whom Byron in *Childe Harold* called:

> The Roman friend of Rome's least mortal mind,
> The friend of Tully.

---

[1] For other jurists see Teuffel, § 174, §§ 207–208.

[2] Quint., X. i. 116, 'Sulpicius insignem non immerito famam tribus orationibus meruit.'

[3] Cic., *Ad Fam.*, IV. v., 'tot oppidum cadauera proiecta iacent,' echoed in Byron's 'sepulchres of cities.'

Chapter IV

CICERO AND ORATORY

Variety of his literary achievements – Cicero and his times – Education – Bar practice and *Wanderjahre* – His mark made in the *Verrines* – Anti-democratic speeches of his consulate – The Catilinarian plot – How the Triumvirate affected him – Speeches of the period before and after exile – Retirement which produced the *De Oratore* and *De Republica* – Provincial governorship and attitude in the Civil War – Cicero and Caesar – Period of the philosophic masterpieces – What the *Philippics* cost Cicero – Cicero as a man – Cicero as a poet – Cicero as a translator – The great speeches – Characteristics of his oratory – The collection and periods of his letters – Their interest; historical, social, and personal – Style of the letters – Political science in the *De Republica* – Differences from Plato's *Republic* – *De Legibus* – Minor rhetorical treatises – The great rhetorical triad – Cicero as a literary critic – Essays and theology – The four chief works on philosophy – His eclecticism – Imperishable rather than original. The oratory of Hortensius – Attic reaction among younger orators.

A GREAT historical figure, Cicero is, as a literary figure, incomparably greater.[1] About his significance in politics opinions will vary; there can be no question about his services to Latin literature. His work is imposing in bulk, diversity, seriousness, and purity of execution. The author's surpassing receptivity and catholic sympathies found room for so much that is human—for a host of qualities ranging from awe-inspiring solemnity to the softest of emotions, and from vindictive bitterness to exquisite delicacy. His own

[1] Complete text: J. G. Orelli (J. G. Baiter and C. Halm), 1845–63; C. F. A. Nobbe (*Cic. opera omnia uno volumine comprehensa*), ed. 2, 1850, ed. 3, 1869; J. G. Baiter and C. L. Kayser, 11 vols., 1861–69; C. F. W. Müller and others, 1890–96. Correspondence: R. Y. Tyrrell and L. C. Purser, 7 vols., 1885–94, ed. 3, 1904, etc.; tr. E. S. Shuckburgh, 4 vols., 1899–1900; A. Watson, *Select Letters*, 1870 and 1891; tr. G. E. Jeans, ed. 2, 1887; L. Mendelssohn, *M. T. Ciceronis Epist. lib. xvi*, 1893 (valuable *Praefatio*). Poetry: Bährens, *F.P.R.*, 1886, pp. 298–315. Orations: Text, A. C. Clark (Oxford Class. Texts, 1905 ff.); among sep. edns. are A. C. Clark, *Pro Mil.*; W. E. Heitland, *Pro. C. Rabirio*; H. A. Holden, *Pro Sest.*, *Pro Planc.*; J. R. King, *Philippics*, i–xiv; J. E. B. Mayor, *Second Philippic*; W. Peterson, *Pro Cluent.*; J. S. Reid, *Pro Arch.*, *Pro Balbo*, *Pro Mil.*, *Pro Sulla*; E. Thomas, *Verrines* (Paris), 1894; A. S. Wilkins, *In Catil.*, *Pro Leg. Man.* (fuller list in J. B. Mayor's *Guide to Choice of Classical Books*, or Middleton and Mills's *Student's Companion to Latin Authors*). Ancient commentary: *Asconii Orationum Quinque Enarratio*, Kiessling u. Schöll, 1875. Treatises: T. W. Dougan and R. M. Henry, *Tusc.* 1905–34; O.

mobile impressionability goes far towards explaining his varied performance—his unsurpassable eloquence, his unaffected charm as a letter writer, his success in making Greek thought dynamic in the Roman and thereby in the medieval world. His very verses—lacking inspiration doubtless, but undeserving of Juvenal's biting dismissal— are a fair gauge of the technical skill attained by the poets of his youth. Such movements in literature and learning as he took no part in, he was at least in touch with. He scoffed at the poetic apes of Alexandrinism. Catullus, it is fairly certain, he included among the *Cantores Euphorionis*. Yet his admiration for older Latin poetry did not wholly blind him to modern merit. He probably edited, if he did not fully appreciate, Lucretius,[1] and he reverenced the colossal erudition of Varro. But none of his achievements can rival what he did for Latin prose. Therein he was master. By genius and by those infinite pains which may be its concomitant, he raised Latin prose style to a level of universality. Cicero fitted it to be the vehicle of thought for centuries and the basis of expression over a wide area of modern Europe.

His matter is of what may be termed evidential value. Cicero is the supreme index to his age. He is in contact with all its interests. His works, therefore, form a history of his era—of its politics and society as well as its literature and knowledge. On the social aspects of the age nothing could flash light more natural than his letters, or more vivid and occasionally lurid than speeches like the *Verrines*, the *Pro Cluentio*, or the *Pro Caelio*. We see the pride and prejudice of the old Roman houses, the methods of the middle-class capitalists which produced the deserving but usually vulgar *parvenu*, the selfish misgovernment of foreign possessions by the nobles, and their helplessness before the irresistible wave of the new democracy on whose crest Julius Caesar rose to power. We see, in fact, what Cicero himself, despite his extraordinarily clear and keen political vision, could not perhaps fully see— the republic dying amid the ruin of senatorial prestige, the shattering of

Heine, *Tusc.*, ed. 6, 1885; H. A. Holden, *De Off.*, new ed., 1899; M. Kellogg, *Brutus*; J. Martha, *Brutus*; J. B. Mayor, *De Nat. Deor.*, 3 vols.; K. W. Piderit, *Orator*, ed. 2 (Halm), 1876; J. S. Reid, *Academica, De Amic., De Sen., De Fin.,* i and ii; J. E. Sandys, *Orator*; A. S. Wilkins, *De Oratore*, 3 vols.

Life and Times, etc.: G. Boissier, *Cicéron et ses amis*, ed. 10, 1895; Gugl. Ferrero, *The Greatness and Decline of Rome*, Eng. tr. 1907 (vol. i, esp. chaps. xii, xv, xvi; II. ix, xvii); E. Masè-Dari, *M. T. Cicerone e le sue idee sociale ed economiche*, 1901; Mommsen, *Hist. Rome*, 1877, vol. iv; J. L. Strachan-Davidson, *Cicero and the Fall of Roman Republic*, 1895; W. H. D. Suringar, *Ciceronis Commentarii rerum suarum*, etc., 1854; W. Warde Fowler, *Social Life at Rome in the Age of Cicero*, 1909; Th. Zielinski, *Cicero im Wandel der Jahrhunderte*, ed. 2, 1908.

[1] It is not easy absolutely to determine whether Cicero or his brother edited Lucretius. Cicero certainly had the poem in his hands, and was not wholly unappreciative, according to the widely accepted reading in the famous passage 'multis luminibus ingeni, multae tamen artis': see discussion in chapter on Lucretius, pp. 203–204.

Cicero's own political ideals, and the sure coming of empire. The political interest, then, of his career is its coincidence with the fall of the last free state of the ancient world. Its tragic interest is its vain endeavour to preserve the Roman republic. To trace Cicero's life is to follow the main course of public events at Rome for the half century preceding the death of Caesar. If ever burning questions existed, they existed then. The eloquence of Rome's greatest orator and his political speculation came, as it were, refined out of a fiery furnace of political turbulence.

A native of the Volscian country-town of Arpinum, M. Tullius Cicero (106–43 B.C.)[1] came of a well-to-do, but not noble, family, which had taken some part in local government. The son of a Roman knight, he was in the equestrian order until he entered the Senate. He never lost his equestrian sympathies. Another fact had its influence. He was proud of being a fellow-townsman of Marius.[2] Without being democratic and without closing his eyes to the faults of Marius, Cicero from the first detested the arbitrary domination of Marius's aristocratic opponent. This prejudice against the *regnum Sullanum* was strengthened by a training in constitutional law. Sent to Rome young for the customary studies in literature, rhetoric, and philosophy, he received part of his instruction with his brother and his cousins, the sons of Aculeo. Diodotus the Stoic—long an inmate of his home—was his preceptor in logic; and Philo the Academic impressed him with a system which gradually obliterated the once powerful influence upon him of the seductive Epicureanism in the lectures of Phaedrus. In law, Cicero attached himself to the Scaevolae. His education in literature directed him to the Greek classics, and to the old Latin plays and epics, from which he quotes freely. They were the wellspring of much of his dignity of sentiment and fulness of phrase. On them he sought to refine in his juvenile poems. He was in the habit of conversing on literary topics with the old dramatist Accius, and to the Greek poet Archias he acknowledged especial obligations in matters of taste.[3] But his diligence in philosophic and literary pursuits was eclipsed by his marvellous assiduity in rhetoric. He received a powerful stimulus from listening to the great speakers in the forum.[4] The passionate fondness for his profession which he praises in Hortensius[5]

[1] His birthday was January 3rd: *Ad Att.*, XIII, xlii. 3, 'Diem meum scis esse iii Non. Ian.' For his birthplace, Hieron., *Chron. Euseb.*, ann. Abr. 1911.
[2] Cicero was influenced by the family connexion with Marius, whatever it was (Asconius says he was 'arta necessitudine coniunctus' with Marius's father). Cicero's judgements on Marius exemplify his wideness of vision. There is no virtue or fault in him which is not abundantly recognised – the expressions range from 'ille diuinus uir' to 'omnium perfidiosissimus.'
[3] *Brut.*, xxviii. 107; *Pro Arch.*, i. 1.
[4] *Brut.*, lxxxix. 305. A most interesting biographical account of his studies and his rivalry with Hortensius follows down to xciv. 323.
[5] *Brut.*, lxxxviii. 302, 'Ardebat autem cupiditate sic ut in nullo umquam flagrantius studium uiderim.'

K

soon took possession of Cicero. Ambition spurred him to incessant practice in private declamation: 'My devotion was such that I never let a day pass without some exercise in oratory.'[1] What was a return visit to Rome paid by Apollonius Molo of Rhodes in Sulla's dictatorship led to a second course of rhetoric under him.[2] During Eastern travels later, Cicero applied himself once again to Molo's teaching. Effective deportment and gesture he studied under Roscius, the comic actor, and Aesopus, his tragic *confrère*.[3]

In the Social War Cicero saw military service under Pompey's father and under Sulla. But he was no Sullan. One of his earliest speeches,[4] the defence of Roscius of Ameria on a charge of murder, involved him in vigorous opposition to Sulla's powerful freedman Chrysogonus. The *Pro Roscio Amerino* is clever in its apologetic daring. This was in 80 B.C. Partly the uneasy sense of having made a marked man of himself, partly a breakdown in health, partly, too, his insatiate intellectual ambition, suggested to the young advocate of twenty-six the advisability of *Wanderjahre* in the East. He visited Athens, Asia Minor, and Rhodes, engrossed in philosophy and rhetoric wherever possible. At Athens it was like going back to college from the bar. He renewed his study of rhetoric under Demetrius the Syrian. Six months he gave to philosophy under Antiochus, who was Stoicising the Academy.[5] In the province of Asia he held a sort of rhetorical progress in state, attended by the principal orators of the country. At last[6] he reached Rhodes, where to Apollonius Molo's careful pruning of a style grown too luxuriant[7] he added a memorable attendance on Posidonius. It was then that the young orator's miraculous power over the Greek language extorted from his instructor, Apollonius, the envious confession that Cicero possessed the ability to transfer to Rome the only possessions which Greece still retained—learning and eloquence.[8] After two years of absence Cicero returned to Rome with health established[9] and his style restrained. He was in a position to dispute the sovereignty of the forum with the two kings of oratory, Cotta and Hortensius.

His marriage to Terentia brought him a handsome portion, but a

[1] *Brut.*, xc. 309, ' Ita eram deditus ut ab exercitationibus oratoriis nullus dies uacuus esset.'

[2] *Brut.*, lxxxix. 307; xc. 312.

[3] Plut., *Vit. Cic.*, v; *cf. Brut.*, lxxxiv. 290, of Roscius as the perfect actor 'in scena.'

[4] In his first extant speech, *Pro Quinctio*, 81 B.C., he refers to previous efforts at the bar, § 4.

[5] *Brut.*, xci. 315; Plut., *Vit. Cic.*, iv. Some of Cicero's companions are mentioned, *De Fin.*, V. i. 1.

[6] *Brut.*, *loc. cit.*,: 'Post a me Asia tota peragrata est, cum summis quidem oratoribus, quibuscum exercebar ipsis libentius.'

[7] *Brut.*, xci. 316. It was the fault which Cicero himself afterwards recognised in his earlier work: *e.g*, he notes the *iuuenilis redundantia* of *Pro Rosc. Amer.* in *Orator*, xxx. 108.

[8] Plut., *Vit. Cic.*, iv.

[9] His spare frame had alarmed his friends (*Brut.*, xci. 313).

shrewish partner.[1] From this period remains the *Pro Roscio Comoedo*, his pleading for his actor-friend in a suit concerning a share in damages paid for the death of a slave-pupil. In 75 Cicero filled his first administrative post. He was quaestor for Western Sicily. His ability and fairness during a season of dearth won from the provincials opinions so golden that, with the self-confidence of a civil servant of thirty-one, Cicero imagined his name was in every Roman mouth. To his deep mortification he discovered on his way home that he was utterly unknown to the pleasure-seekers at Puteoli.[2] But the Sicilian connexion was to bear fruit. It furnished him with a magnificent opening in oratory. He was retained by the Sicilians to impeach their ex-governor Verres, in 70, for a shameless record of high-handed tyranny and rapacity. The trial was of singular importance as an attack on senatorial misgovernment at a time when Pompey and Crassus had effected a coalition between the equestrian order and the democrats. Against a claimant acting in collusion with Verres, Cicero maintained his own right to prosecute by his *Diuinatio in Q. Caecilium*. In his *Actio Prima in Verrem* his *résumé* of the charges which he proposed to substantiate by witnesses forced the culprit to accept guilt by retiring into exile. The *Actio Secunda* in five parts, though never spoken, was circulated as much for public as for literary reasons.[3] The *Pro Tullio* and *Pro Fonteio*, both mutilated, are respectively for a plaintiff's claim to damages arising out of a farm-dispute and for a defendant charged with oppression in Narbonensian Gaul. The *Pro Caecina* of 69 supported his client's right to an inheritance. Cicero's praetorship in 66 B.C. was momentous. He pronounced his first purely public oration and the finest of his speeches in a criminal court. His career now touched Pompey's. The year before, the Gabinian Bill had assigned to Pompey three years of supreme command over the navy in the Mediterranean and a special jurisdiction over islands and seaboard with a view to the suppression of piracy. Such powers, opposed by the senate, were favoured by the knights, who were losing business through risks at sea and raids on land; by the country-folk of Italy, who found even main roads like the Appian sometimes infested by raiders; and by the populace, who had their corn intercepted, and who objected to a dear loaf or none at all. The interests of Cicero's own equestrian class[4] were bound up with Pompey's success and a pacified East. It was, then, to promote the extension of Pompey's command to Bithynia,

---

[1] Plut., *Vit. Cic.*, xxix.

[2] He tells an amusing anecdote against himself, *Pro Plancio*, xxvi. 64.

[3] It was well that Verres's enormities should be made known. Cicero, whose preference was to act for the defence, desired also to show what he could do as counsel for the prosecution. The current idea was that prosecution was legitimate only in two cases: (1) where the prosecutor was young and had a name to make; (2) where he had a private wrong to avenge. The case of Cicero was the first – it was necessary to win his victory over Hortensius.

[4] Cicero was born of equestrian parentage, but his quaestorship had brought him into the senatorial class. – Ed.

Pontus, and Armenia for the purpose of finally avenging the *pogrom* organised by Mithradates that Cicero delivered the *Pro Lege Manilia* or *De Imperio Cn. Pompei*. His warm panegyric on Pompey's services flowed easily from one who repeatedly felt a glamour in Pompey's personality, and who, notwithstanding intervals of despair, inclined to repose hopes in him which only the defeat of Pharsalia could dispel. Cicero reaped his reward in the support of Pompey's adherents at home when in 64 he stood for the consulate. The other speech of 66 B.C. was the *Pro A. Cluentio Habito*, the defence of an alleged poisoner, and an elaborate attempt to clear the accused from the suspicion of having bribed the jury in a case he had once brought against the supposed victim. The oration marshals with unquestionable ingenuity the most intricate ramifications of domestic relationships and feuds. It is exactly the kind of case regarding which Cicero might boast that he had 'thrown dust in the eyes of the jury.'[1]

In his candidature for the highest magistracy, Cicero was handicapped in the eyes of the nobility. He was a *nouus homo*.[2] Few men without ancestral honours had risen to the consulate during recent generations — the most notorious exception was his townsman Marius.[3] With revolutionary competitors in the field like Catiline, and a widespread ferment of unrest, the moderates among both democrats and senators felt drawn to Cicero. The middle-class in town and country backed him. This secured his election along with C. Antonius, whom he speedily and diplomatically rendered innocuous by yielding the province which had fallen to him by lot.[4] Cicero's loyalty to Pompey — ill requited by that man of tortuous and halting ways — led him to combat the Agrarian Bill brought forward early in 63 by the tribune Servilius Rullus with the connivance of Julius Caesar and others whom Cicero calls *machinatores*. Its proposal of a Board of Ten, empowered to realise all the property of the Roman People outside Italy with a view to land-purchase in Italy and colonisation abroad, and, further, the contemplated annexation of Egypt, were covertly designed to counterbalance Pompey's authority in the East. Of the speeches *Against Rullus*, the first — to the senate — survives in its conclusion: the second and third are addresses to the people (*contiones*). Though Cicero advanced

---

[1] Quintil., *Inst. Or.*, II. xvii. 21: 'Nec Cicero, cum se tenebras offudisse iudicibus in causa Clueti gloriatus est, nihil ipse uidit.'

[2] Cicero's position is well realised in the letter written by his brother to him during his candidature. This *Commentariolum Petitionis* is a manual discussing the means of influencing the three estates of 'senatus,' 'equites,' and 'multitudo.' Marcus Cicero may be said to have returned the compliment five years later in his instructions on a governor's duties sent to Quintus when propraetor of Asia (*Ad Q. F. I.* 1). The *Commentariolum* is accepted as genuine by every editor 'from Valerius Palermus to Bücheler,' as Prof. Tyrell says. Eussner's contention that it is a cento from Cicero's works is dismissed, Tyrell and Purser, *Corresp.*, i. (1904), pp. 116 *sqq.*

[3] Others were T. Didius in 98 and C. Caelius in 94.

[4] *In Pis.*, ii. 5.

ostensibly democratic objections to the measure, he had really at the outset of his consulate crossed the path of the popular leaders. The *Pro C. Rabirio* supported the appeal by an aged anti-democratic knight against his condemnation for slaying Saturninus over thirty-six years before. The trial was a reversion to an antiquated but not abolished procedure. The charge was treason (*perduellio*): the issue was whether the proclamation of the *senatus consultum ultimum* condoned acts of violence done in pursuance thereof. In this strongly pro-senatorial speech Cicero further thwarted the policy of Caesar and the democrats.

A much more serious conflict was brewing—one which made him for the time, and to his endless gratification, leader of the state. It was a position which he fondly fancied he regained on returning from exile in 57. But only once again did he approach it, when, twenty years after his consulate, he strained every oratorical sinew to denounce and ruin Mark Antony. In 63 the weakness in the democratic ranks was the presence of desperadoes with fortunes cursedly dipped, who saw in revolution the sole chance of rehabilitation. To this section the Catilinarian anarchists belonged. The unmasking of their treason, the forcing of Catiline into flight, and the execution of his accomplices, were acts by which Cicero never ceased to boast that he had saved his country. The four speeches *In Catilinam* give rather more than we need to know of Cicero's version, and might be supposed to have exhausted Cicero's magazine of invective until one reads the *In Pisonem* or *The Second Philippic*. The first of the four, on November 8th, was a frontal attack on Catiline in the senate, opening with the impatient *Quousque tandem abutere, Catilina, patientia nostra?* It demanded that he should leave Rome, because the secret service had discovered all. The second, delivered next day before the people, was intended to still popular apprehensions and overawe the conspirators remaining in Rome, now that Catiline had left (*abiit, excessit, euasit, erupit*). Less than a month elapsed, and the conspirators were detected and arrested in treasonable correspondence with the Allobrogian envoys. The third oration is addressed to the people after the senate had discussed the arrest; while the fourth, two days later in the senate, is Cicero's contribution to the debate on the fateful question of the punishment of the prisoners. In the midst of this crisis 'our witty consul,' as Cato dubbed him, found time to defend Murena, his successor-elect, charged with bribery. The *Pro Murena* is a good speech, always remembered for poking fun at the Stoicism of Cato, who was one of the counsel for the prosecution. The worth of Cicero's services during office is manifest—without his exuberant insistence—from the plainer narrative in Sallust's *Catiline*. Unluckily, the plaudits of the nobility made his brain reel. By an irony of circumstances, his *bourgeois* birth impelled him to a snobbish regard for the good opinion of the aristocrats. Vanity prompted incessant jubilation. A growing fondness for display soon tempted him to the purchase of an enormous residence on the Palatine at three and a half million sesterces. The disillusion was to come. He had summarily, under the authority of the senate, put citizens to death. But the right of appeal was an ancient and inalienable prerogative of every Roman, and the democratic party now held that a bulwark of the constitution had been impaired. It was a sinister omen when at the end of his year, as he came to lay down office and proposed to address the people, his mouth was shut by the veto of the tribune Metellus Nepos. It ought to have been still more alarming to note that Metellus was really a political agent-in-advance for Pompey.

For the time all seemed fair. An *entente cordiale* united senators and *equites*. The ideals enshrined in Cicero's watchwords, *concordia ordinum* and *consensus Italiae*, had been, he thought, realised. He felt unconcealed delight in being hailed 'father of the fatherland' by Catulus and Cato. He could flatter himself that he led the optimates. But nothing short of a miracle could keep the senate at the helm. If Sulla's strong arm had availed to guarantee a new lease of power for barely ten years, Cicero's choicest phrases were impotent to save the *ancien régime*. Optimate bigotry and jealousy snubbed Pompey when he returned from his Oriental durbars as a veritable King of Kings. The refusal to ratify formally his organisation of the East drove this soldier of indecisive, reticent, but not dangerous character to make common cause with Caesar and the democrats. Pedantic strictness on the part of senators regarding the state contracts alienated the equestrian order.[1] So the triumvirate of Caesar, Pompey, and Crassus in 60 reduced the senate to a political isolation, which became positive helplessness before the appalling defiance of Caesar's consular acts in 59—'the consulate of Julius and Caesar.'[2] It is credible that Caesar had desired a quattuorvirate—the fourth allied consular to be none other than Cicero himself. The collaboration of a constitutional lawyer so plausible in oratory would have been manifest gain. But here lay the difficulty. Nothing frightened Cicero more than Caesar's disdain for constitutional principles. Consequently, during Caesar's consulship, Cicero's position was one of eclipse. He shared the aristocratic stupefaction at Caesar's arbitrary measures. As he could not refrain from criticism, it became obviously politic that when Caesar was absent in Gaul, Cicero must not be left unmuzzled. An outspoken complaint on the evil times cost Cicero dear. His arch-enemy, Clodius, was promptly made a plebeian,[3] to qualify him for a tribunate which should avenge the execution of the Catilinarians. Caesar, willing to save Cicero from the consequences of illegality, offered him a commissionership to carry out the new agrarian

---

[1] Cicero himself admitted the demands of the *equites* to be outrageous, but he counselled concessions on the ground of dire expediency.
[2] Plut., *Vit. Iul.*, xx; *cf.* Dion Cass., xxxviii. 8.
[3] Suet., *Iul.*, xx.

legislation, or a lieutenancy under himself in Gaul. On his refusal,[1] Caesar decided to allow Clodius—more ochlocrat than democrat—to propose in 58 the bill for the banishment of anyone who had put Roman citizens to death without regard to the right of appeal. The adorable Pompey did not stir a finger to help. This was black treachery from one whose promises to protect Cicero had been direct and explicit. Before the coming storm Cicero bowed, and retired into an exile in Epirus and Macedonia which caused him, as his letters prove, the most poignant mental suffering.

From the period between his consulate and exile we have three speeches. The *Pro Sulla* of 62 defended an alleged accomplice of Catiline, and in the same year the *Pro Archia*—which there is no convincing reason to reject as un-Ciceronian—maintained the poet's legal status of citizenship. It is a charming little effort—all the more charming because it deserts strict relevance and the usage of the law courts to sound the praises of literature. In 59 the *Pro Flacco* rebutted a charge of oppression in Asia. Cicero's recall in 57 marked an increase of sympathy for him and of revulsion against lawless inroads on the constitution. Pompey, too, had his reasons for checking Clodius. The welcome which the returning exile received in the country towns, and from the Roman crowd thronging temple steps to catch sight of him, is glowingly described by himself.[2] It was natural he should again over-estimate his own power and that of the senate, and under-estimate the power which Caesar was building up during a strenuous absence. Cicero's speeches of 57 turned largely on matters arising out of his exile. In *Post Reditum I* he thanked the senate the day after he reached Rome; *Post Reditum II*, if genuine, thanked the people a day later from the *rostra*. The *De Domo Sua* argues the illegality of Clodius's consecration of Cicero's confiscated house. In 56 the *De Haruspicum Responso* replies in the senate to Clodius's declaration before the people that Cicero had offended the gods by restoring his house after it had been consecrated. The *Pro Sestio*, in defence of Sestius, charged with violent conduct during his tribunate, is typical of the orator's habit of introducing his own services, of descanting on his considerate withdrawal into exile to avoid bloodshed, and of attacking enemies like Clodius, Piso, and Gabinius. All the same, it contains passages hardly surpassed elsewhere in Cicero for brilliance.[3] It was followed by the speech *In Vatinium*, an examination into the life of one of Caesar's creatures who had borne witness against Sestius. The *Pro Caelio* threw back on the notorious Clodia her allegations of attempted poisoning. The same year saw the current of his oratory peremptorily diverted. Pom-

---

[1] Cicero was so bitter (he represents Caesar as complaining) that he would not accept even honours from his hand, *Ad Att.*, IX. ii. a, 1 ('ita me sibi fuisse inimicum, ut ne honorem quidem a se accipere uellem').

[2] *Ad Att.*, iv. 1.

[3] *E.g.* the description of the two consuls, *Pro Sest.*, viii. 18.

pey had proved a sorry guardian of the peace against mob-rule, and Cicero's letters contain evidence of Pompey's growing unpopularity. So far from being strengthened, Pompey's position had been much weakened in Caesar's absence. He had coquetted with Cicero since his recall until it suited the purpose of the triumvirs to meet at Luca and renew their compact. This left Cicero politically helpless. Once more his idol had joined an unholy alliance: once more his criticism was silenced. He had given notice of motion in the senate to reopen the question of the legality of Caesar's *lex Campana* of 59. But now his brother Quintus was given to understand that he must keep Marcus straight—that is, submissive to the Three. It must have been with heart-searchings that Cicero in 56 argued in *De Prouinciis Consularibus* that Caesar should be granted a prolongation of the Gallic command. This was a 'recantation'[1] in sharp contrast to his attitude in *De Haruspicum Responso, Pro Sestio* and *In Vatinium*. Then came the *Pro Balbo*, to prove the civic status of one who was a friend of Caesar and Pompey.

In the ensuing period of vacillation there are a few speeches—the incomplete *In Pisonem* of 55, in which no epithets are too abusive as retorts to the ex-governor's angry speech after his recall from Macedonia at Cicero's instigation; *Pro Plancio* of 54, claiming an acquittal on a charge of corrupt electoral combination brought against one who had befriended Cicero in exile; *Pro Scauro*, rebutting an indictment for misgovernment in Sardinia; *Pro Rabirio Postumo*, in defence of a partisan of Caesar charged with extortion; and the *Pro Milone* of 52, in defence of the murderer of Clodius. This last is a skilful elaboration, replacing the actual speech which Cicero, intimidated by the rapscallions of Clodius, and even by Pompey's guards,[2] delivered with so much less than his usual effectiveness that his client was found guilty.[3] When the amended version reached the banished Milo with the author's compliments, he congratulated himself that Cicero had not spoken as he had written—such eloquence would have lost to Milo his dinners on the excellent red mullet of Marseilles! But these were times when Cicero felt happiest in private study and composition. It was one of the two periods when he became pre-eminently a man of letters. Just

---

[1] Mommsen and others have identified the *De Prouinc. Cons.* with the παλινῳδία of *Ad Att.*, IV. v. 1. Prof. J. S. Reid has made out a strong case to show that the παλινῳδία there mentioned could not be an oration at all, *Hermathena*, Vol. XI, p. 298 (1901). *Cf.* T. Rice Holmes, *Roman Rep.*, 1923, ii. 295 *sqq.*

[2] *De Opt. Gen. Orat.*, iv. 10. Cicero refers to the absurdity of expecting that 'with an army stationed in the forum and in all the temples round it,' he could have pleaded for Milo just as in a civil case before a single judge.

[3] The evidence of Plut., *Cic.*, xxxv., and of Ascon., xxxi. ('non ea qua solitus est constantia dixit') does not support the whole of Froude's imaginative picture, *Caesar*, ch. xviii.: 'He stammered, blundered, and *sat down*.' The speech actually delivered for Milo was taken down in shorthand, was published and was extant long after, certainly in the time of Quintilian (J. S. Reid, Introd. to *Pro Mil.*, 1897, p. 22).

as Caesar's final ascendancy thrust Cicero back on philosophy, so to the disillusionment resultant on the Luca conference we owe in rhetoric the three polished books *De Oratore*, and, in political science, the series of Scipionic dialogues, of which the now incomplete works *De Republica* and *De Legibus* form part.

Under recent legislation on provincial government it came to Cicero's turn in 51 to go abroad as proconsul of Cilicia. He was above all things a townsman, and missed Rome with no less sincerity and for better reasons than Ovid did two generations later. He was desperately afraid his office might be prolonged.[1] Yet he honestly put his principles into practice as governor.[2] He had a legacy of faults from his predecessor Appius Claudius to remedy, and he had crushing weights of debt upon the subject communities to alleviate. Though his connexion with the equestrian financiers did not leave him free to adopt drastic measures of fiscal reform, he set his face against exorbitant interest, and, to his credit, he knew how to refuse friends who asked unfair favours.[3] For his capture of a fort during his miniature war among the mountains a *supplicatio* was decreed by the senate. Hopes of a triumph long haunted his mind, and after reaching Italy the withered laurels of victory were still carefully kept on his attendants' staves. Many triumphs had been accorded for less—even to generals who had been 'well thrashed,' as Sallust makes Marius say. He had returned to find his country on the brink of civil war. Caesar's quarrel with the senate regarding his Gallic command was in progress. Pompey had long ago drifted apart from Caesar. Now, too late, the senate began to see Pompey with Cicero's eyes, as its only possible champion. Cicero left Rome as the nobles did, when Caesar crossed the Rubicon. He remained charged with the district round Capua, professedly in Pompey's interest, though he was in correspondence with both sides. His dilemma was protracted. It was further complicated when Pompey took the inevitable step—so much criticised by Cicero—of leaving Italy. Cicero seems to have persuaded himself that he could best help the cause of peace where he was. At times he writes as if there were little to choose between the two sides—whichever might win, he dreaded proscriptions and confiscations. He could not help admiring Caesar's generosity in the first months of success, but he could not help detesting the bloodthirsty vapourings

---

[1] *Ad Att.*, V. xi. 1, where he explains 'Non dici potest quam flagrem desiderio urbis, quam uix harum rerum insulsitatem feram.'
[2] *Ad Att.*, V. xxi. 5, 'Nos enim et nostra sponte bene firmi, et mehercule auctoritate tua inflammati uicimus omnes (hoc tu ita reperies) cum abstinentia, tum iustitia, facilitate, clementia.' He proceeds to say that he and his staff had scrupulously avoided extravagance and unfair commandeering.
[3] In the Salaminian case (*Ad Att.* V. xxi. 10–13; VI. ii. 7–9) he refused to sanction interest at 48%, but lacked the firmness to conclude the transaction at 12% (the legal rate) and therefore left the final settlement open to a successor who would be all too likely to comply with the demands of the Roman usurers. –Ed.

of Pompey's supporters. He shuddered to think what their victory
would mean for Italy. Yet theirs was the patriotic cause, he felt,[1] and
the old affection for Pompey was not dead. Things had gone against
the Pompeians at many points before Cicero embarked for the East,
only to encounter a cool welcome from the optimate officers. He was not
present at the defeat of Pharsalus. Soon after he returned to Brundisium,
and spent almost a year of suspense as to what the conqueror's attitude
would be. At length Caesar returned. With his habitual magnanimity he
met Cicero and effected a reconciliation. He was free to enter Rome.

But his influence in politics was gone. He could turn again to literature and philosophy. He might serve exiled Pompeians by pleading
their cause with the dictator, but no independent line was possible.
This is the period of the three 'Caesarianae' — *Pro Marcello*, offering
extravagant thanks for Caesar's 'inaudita clementia' towards an exiled
Pompeian orator; *Pro Ligario*, on behalf of Ligarius, charged with outrageous violence in prosecuting the African war against Caesar; and
Pro Rege Deiotaro of 45, to disprove an alleged attempt by the tetrarch
of Galatia on Caesar's life some years before. Of these the *Pro Marcello*
is representative. It broke a silence of six years.[2] There is unreserved
praise for Caesar's stupendous career,[3] and his indulgence towards the
defeated;[4] there are statesmanlike words on services which he may yet
render to public tranquillity, justice, credit, and morals;[5] there are
roseate prophecies touching Caesar's immortal fame,[6] and anticipating
with a veracity which the speaker did not realise, the impartial judgment by posterity, 'uninfluenced by affection, self-seeking, hatred, or
prejudice.'[7] But the exquisite language is spoiled by its inherent
hypocrisy. The fulsome compliments and affected solicitude for
Caesar's safety make melancholy reading when confronted with Cicero's
transports over the assassination. It is true that in 45 Cicero drafted a
letter of political advice to Caesar, and it may have hinted at the danger
of too arbitrary government.[8] At any rate, Balbus and Oppius, Caesar's

---

[1] *Ad Fam.*, VII. iii. 2, 'nihil boni praeter causam.'
[2] *Pro Marcello*, i. 1, 'Diuturni silenti quo eram his temporibus usus . . .
finem hodiernus dies attulit.' The date is 46 B.C.
[3] *Ibid.*, ii.   [4] *Ibid.*, vi.
[5] *Ibid.*, viii. 23, 'constituenda iudicia, reuocanda fides, comprimendae
libidines, propaganda suboles.'
[6] *Ibid.*, ix. 28, 'Nec uero haec tua uita ducenda est, quae corpore et spiritu
continetur. Illa, inquam, illa uita est tua, quae uigebit memoria saeculorum
omnium, quam posteritas alet, quam ipsa aeternitas semper tuebitur.'
[7] *Ibid.*, ix. 29, 'Erit inter eos etiam qui nascentur, sicut inter nos fuit,
magna dissensio, cum alii laudibus ad caelum res tuas gestas efferent, alii
fortasse aliquid requirent, idque uel maximum, nisi belli ciuilis incendium
salute patriae restinxeris, ut illud fati fuisse uideatur, hoc consili. Serui igitur
iis etiam iudicibus, qui multis post saeculis de te iudicabunt, et quidem haud
scio an incorruptius quam nos. Nam et sine amore et sine cupiditate et rursus
sine odio et sine inuidia iudicabunt. Id autem etiamsi tunc ad te, ut quidam falso
putant, non pertinebit, nunc certe pertinet esse te talem ut tuas laudes obscura-
tura nulla unquam sit obliuio.'
[8] Strachan-Davidson, *Cicero*, p. 374.

friends to whom the draft was submitted, criticised some points adversely. The letter was never sent. Even if it had been, it is incredible that Cicero could have altered Caesar's iron will, or made him seem to play the king any less in the eyes of republicans. Cicero never under-stood the nature of Caesar's work for Rome.

After thirty years of married life he had divorced Terentia in 46. He blamed her for inattention to his interests. His union with his young ward Publilia was as brief as it was unsuitable. She was divorced because she failed him notably amid his grief over the death of his only daughter, Tullia, in 45. Bereavement redoubled his devotion to philosophy, for which political eclipse had already given him leisure. His energy was untiring. His production in two years would be creditable for a lifetime of literary work. Between 46 and 44 he composed, in rhetoric, two treatises which rank nearly as high as the *De Oratore*, namely, his history of Roman oratory in the *Brutus* and his portraiture of the finished speaker in the *Orator*; the dry catechism of the *Partitiones Oratoriae* belongs to 54, but he now wrote the equally dry exposition of arguments on Aristotelian lines in the *Topica*, and the *De Optimo Genere Oratorum*, which maintains with exemplary brevity the supremacy of Atticism in oratory by way of introduction to his lost translations of the speeches by Demosthenes and Aeschines for and against Ctesiphon. The same fertile years brought into being Cicero's works in philosophy. The *Paradoxa* of 46 is a short handling of six Stoic paradoxes, due partly to the genuine admiration for Cato which underlay the persi-flage of the *Pro Murena*, partly to Cicero's great interest, shown elsewhere, in this side of Stoicism. To 45 belong the *Consolatio*, now in fragments, a record of deaths of the great suggested by the loss of Tullia; the lost *Hortensius*, in praise of philosophy maligned by Hor-tensius; the *De Finibus Bonorum et Malorum*, a masterly summary in five books of the typical theories on the ethical end; an earlier and later edition of the *Academica*; and the *Tusculanae Disputationes* in five books on the essentials that make for happiness. The year 44 yielded the *De Natura Deorum*, in three books, on the schools of theological thought; the essays *De Senectute* and *De Amicitia*, both charming, but the latter especially so, with a gravity almost religious; the two books *De Diuina-tione*,[1] a practical supplement to the more abstract theology of the *De Natura Deorum*; *De Fato*, incomplete at beginning and end; the two lost books *De Gloria*; and, for the exhortation of his unworthy son, the three books *De Officiis*. There are traces of works *De Virtutibus*, *De Auguriis*, and of a translation of Plato's *Timaeus*. The translation of the *Protagoras* may, like that of Xenophon's *Oeconomicus*, belong to Cicero's youth.

After Caesar's murder on the ides of March, 44, Cicero appeared for

[1] The list of his philosophical writings at the beginning of *De Diuin.* II is a valuable source of information.

the last time in the forefront of politics. With an outspokenness
which cost him his life next year, he assailed Antony as an unscrupulous
representative of Caesarism in the fourteen *Philippic Orations*, which
Gellius more appropriately termed 'Antonianae.' Most of them were
delivered in the senate; but the fourth and sixth were addresses to the
people, whilst Cicero's masterpiece in oratory, the 'inspired' second
Philippic, which took up in irreconcilable hate the gauntlet thrown
down by Antony, was composed as if spoken in his presence, but really
circulated as a pamphlet after he had left Rome. Cicero's hopes centred
in young Octavian. At one time it looked as if the future emperor were
to take the constitutional side and keep Antony in check. But trium-
virates were fated to ruin Cicero's hopes. The alliance of Octavian with
Antony and Lepidus placed the Roman senate in the background for
ever. The proscription which sacrificed Cicero to the unforgiving
animosity of Antony was one step nearer the foundation of empire. By
his inhuman exhibition of the mutilated head and hands on the *rostra*,
which Cicero's eloquence had adorned, Antony, as Plutarch quaintly
remarks, exposed rather his own soul than his enemy's face.[1] Time
brought its revenge for the house of Cicero. In 30 B.C., after Antony's
overthrow, Octavian, who had not yielded Antony his victim without a
hard struggle, took Cicero's son to be his colleague in the consulship
and in that year Antony's statues were destroyed.[2] One day, long after,
Augustus came suddenly on one of his grandsons nervously trying
to conceal a book he had been reading. He took it from him. It was a
work by Cicero. The emperor stood a long time perusing it; and the lad
doubtless quaked. At last the book was handed back, with the words:
'An eloquent man, my boy, an eloquent man, and a lover of his
country.'[3]

With richly varied mental endowments, Cicero was a man of equally
varied moods. His aims for both self and country were lofty. It was,
however, chiefly on the side of intellectual ambition—the desire to be a
master of rhetorical utterance—that he showed unswerving determination. His political ambition was in part satisfied by his consulate; then
his hopes of guiding the state on lines which he honestly considered
most sound were dashed by circumstances too strong for him and
resolutions more iron than his. From a high-strung and impressionable
temperament radiated admirable as well as despicable qualities. Affection for son and daughter, responsiveness to friendly advances, warm-
hearted sympathy, were in keeping with that command of pathos by
which he could touch a jury. But the influence of a transient feeling is
dangerous to fixed principle. His vanity made him too susceptible to

[1] Plut., *Cic.*, xlix.
[2] Plut., *Cic.*, *ad fin.*, οὕτω τὸ δαιμόνιον εἰς τὸν Κικέρωνος οἶκον ἐπανήνεγκε τὸ τέλος.
[3] Plut., *Cic.*, xlix. λόγιος ἀνήρ, ὦ παῖ, λόγιος, καὶ φιλόπατρις.

flattery and too morbidly sensitive in the face of criticism to maintain a strong line of independence. The momentary temptation to utter a taunt—and he had a biting tongue[1]—overmastered all prudent consideration of the 'gentle art of making enemies.' The nervousness which he confesses beset him in rising to speak,[2] and which nearly led to a breakdown in the defence of Milo, also beset him when confronted by any step of vital importance. On the threshold of an enterprise Cicero halted and stumbled—seeing two sides to each question, conformably with his practice in law, his Academic doubts, and his timorous nature. The same qualities as made him an effective orator made him an ineffectual statesman. Such emotionalism and pliability were incompatible with the even tenor of a definite policy. Swayed by the impulses of the passing moment, he had the candour to commit to his letters a faithful record of his exultant vanities and pusillanimous despairs. But he was too great an egotist to judge himself and realise his lack of strength. His chronic state of suspended judgment, which was partly philosophic, clashed with a flutter of excited and totally unphilosophic feelings, and made Cicero impossible as a permanent leader. The mighty ones of the world have less emotion and more will. Yet his faults lie on the surface. Insincerities, whinings, and cowardice blot his correspondence. But in justice it must be remembered that famous men have not been given to revealing the inner working of their mind as Cicero did. He is seen in his nakedness; they in their outward covering of glory. Because we know all his weaknesses, it does not follow that he was all weakness. It is the miserable figure he cuts at certain crises which has led his sharpest critics to minimise his whole career. He was much more significant than Drumann or Mommsen allow. He stood for a Party of the Centre. To unite the forces of order, supported by senatorial traditions and equestrian industry, was his cherished aspiration. It must be allowed that even his inability to lead was largely due to moral scruples. He could never have joined Caesar without changing his moral nature, while Caesar's unscrupulousness was congenital. If Cicero misread his times, they were, perhaps, of all times in the world the most complicated for a contemporary to read. He at least realised the danger and the falsehood of extremes. The caustic judgments passed on Cicero's alleged trimming and tergiversation are sagely explained by Boissier's words: 'Il paye la peine de sa modération.'

So remarkable was Cicero's poetry[3] early in life that Plutarch says he was not only first orator, but best poet of his day.[4] This held good until

---

[1] See Plut., *Cic.*, xxv. *sqq.*, for an account of Cicero's repartees.

[2] *Pro Cluent.*, xviii. 51: 'Semper equidem magno cum metu incipio dicere. Quotienscunque dico, totiens mihi uideor in iudicium uenire non ingeni solum sed etiam uirtutis atque offici.'

[3] V. Faguet. *De Poetica M. Tullii Ciceronis facultate.* 1856: V. Clavel, *De M. Tullii Ciceronis Graecorum interprete,* 1868; H. J. G. Patin, *Études sur la poésie latine,* ed. 4, 1900, ii., pp. 414–478; R. Y. Tyrrell, *Latin Poetry,* 1898, pp. 14–19.

[4] Plut., *Cic.*, ii.

Lucretius and Catullus outshone him. Cicero chose mythological, historical, and didactic subjects. One of his boyish efforts was *Pontius Glaucus*, in tetrameters, on the legend of the fisher who became a seagod. *Marius* may belong to his youth. It was a tribute in hexameters by one famous native of Arpinum to another. We owe to Cicero himself[1] the preservation of the passage where Marius, close to the oak which his townsfolk called after him, sees the lucky omen of the eagle defeating the snake. It is a forcible rendering of a familiar passage in the *Iliad*, which Virgil imitated in turn.[2] In still another poem Cicero felt drawn to the works of a native of the Eastern province he was one day to govern. This was Aratus. Aratus's scientific poem was dressed in more flowing but less vigorous lines by Germanicus under Tiberius and by Avienus under Theodosius. The learned father of Statius[3] also translated him, and his greatness in the eyes of Roman poets may be estimated by Ovid's enthusiasm:

> *Cum sole et luna semper Aratus erit.*[4]

From Aratus Cicero translated the *Phaenomena* in youth and the *Prognostica* later.[5] His muse was long silent, until retirement whispered that his consulate, already celebrated in Greek and Latin prose, deserved epic treatment; as he makes Urania say:

> Thy chafing cares relaxing in repose,
> Thou hast devoted rest from calls of state
> To learning and the muses.[6]

The *De Consulatu Suo* was followed after his exile by *De Temporibus Meis*, on his misfortunes. When his brother was serving under Caesar in Britain, Cicero writes that he is contemplating a poem on the island, to be depicted with Quintus's colours and his own brush.[7] He returns to this promising subject, as he considers it, in another letter to his brother, where he sees poetic material in the commander himself. He then asks why Caesar did not like the later part of the poem on his consulate — 'He wrote me that he had read the first book,' says the author; 'about the first part he felt he had never read anything better in Greek.'[8] Afterwards, the projected epic on Caesar lost favour with him. He

[1] *De Diuin.*, I. xlvii. 106.
[2] *Cf.* Hom., *Il.*, xii. 200; Virg., *Aen.*, xi. 751.
[3] Stat., *Sil.*, V. iii. 19 *sqq.*
[4] Ovid, *Amor.*, I. xv. 16, as cited in chapter on 'The Alexandrine Movement and Catullus.'
[5] *N. D. II.* xli. 104; *Ad Att. II.* i. 11. Cicero translated *Phaen.* 1–732 in his youth and the *Prognostica* or *Diosemiae* (=*Phaen.* 733–1154) later.
[6]   'Tu tamen anxiferas curas requiete relaxans,
        Quod patria uacat hic studiis nobisque sacrasti.'
                            – Quoted, *De Diuin.*, I. xiii. 22.
[7] *Ad Q.F.*, II. xiii. 2: 'Mihi date Britanniam, quam pingam coloribus tuis, penicillo meo.'
[8] *Ad Q.F.*, II. xv. 4, 5.

apologises to Quintus for not sending the expected verses: and one of the hindrances mentioned was not unnaturally a want of enthusiasm.[1] Cicero seems to have collected his poetical *jeux d'esprit* in a *iocularis libellus*, and his poetical criticisms in the *Limon* (λειμών) — the 'meadow' from which his lines in praise of Terence's style are culled.

But his poetic gift shows to best advantage when he is a translator — in those passages from Homer and the Greek dramatists with which he embellished his treatises. His iambic trimeters range from impressive dignity in representing Aeschylus to an easier and more Terentian style in representing Euripides. He translated freely, using his originals much as Coleridge did Schiller's *Wallenstein*. Patin says aptly that he weighed rather than counted his words.[2] Nothing in his verse surpasses his adaptation of the fate of Hercules from the *Trachiniae* of Sophocles. Unmistakable force animates the final apostrophe by the agonised hero to his wasting limbs, the touching recollection of mighty labours, and his noble shame at the groans which agony wrings from him:

> Have pity! All the world will wail my pain.
> Fie, that a girlish sob should 'scape his lips
> Whom no man ever saw groan o'er an ill![3]

The carping criticisms of antiquity[4] fastened on the notoriously unlucky lines

O fortunatam natam me consule Romam!

and

Cedant arma togae, concedat laurea laudi.

But it is gross injustice to treat his verse as if it were mainly jingling and bombast. The attacks read as if Cicero were judged by the standard of his own oratory, which overshadowed his poetry, or by that of Virgil,

[1] *Ad Q.F.*, III. iv. 4, 'sed abest etiam ἐνθουσιασμός.'

[2] Patin, *op. cit.*, p. 447: 'Cicéron . . . pesant les mots au lieu de les compter et plus jaloux de conserver l'esprit que la lettre de son modèle, me paraît avoir montré dans ses traductions des tragiques grecs une louable flexibilité.'

[3]
> 'Miserere! gentes nostras flebunt miserias.
> Heu! uirginalem me ore ploratum edere,
> Quem uidit nemo ulli ingemiscentem malo!'
> – Quoted, *Tusc. Disp.*, II. ix. 21.

[4] Sen. rhetor, *Contr.*, iii. (*praef.*), 'Ciceronem eloquentia sua in carminibus destituit.' Sen., *De Ira*, III. xxxvii., 'Cicero, si derideres carmina eius, inimicus esset.' Tac., *Dial.*, xxi. (in reference to conceivable admirers of speeches by Caesar and Brutus): 'Fecerunt enim et carmina et in bibliothecas rettulerunt, non melius quam Cicero, sed felicius, quia illos fecisse pauciores sciunt!' Quint., *Inst. Or.*, XI. i. 24: 'In carminibus utinam (Cicero) pepercisset, quae non desierunt carpere maligni.' Martial (II. lxxxix. 3–4) is as biting as Tacitus:
> 'Carmina quod scribis Musis et Apolline nullo
> Laudari debes: hoc Ciceronis habes.'
Juvenal's gibe (x. 122–124) is the best known of all:
> ' "O fortunatam natam me consule Romam!"
> Antoni gladios potuit contemnere si sic
> Omnia dixisset!'

whose incommensurate superiority owed some debt after all to the poets of the Ciceronian age. There is an old-fashioned ring in Cicero's tragic adaptations which explains why some were for long attributed to Accius. Now this suggests the true view. Cicero is a vivacious and taste-ful intermediary who transmitted to Lucretius[1] and Catullus the ancient Latin versification enhanced in dignity and, still more decidedly, in technique.

Of Cicero's speeches fifty-seven survive. There are fragments of about twenty more, and titles of another thirty. They extend over a period of nearly forty years, and mark a progress from 'Asianism' and the *iuuenilis redundantia* of the *Pro Roscio Amerino* to a more temperate use of the 'grand' and the 'middle' style. In the *Verrines* at thirty-six he found his strength. There are some things in them which he scarcely excelled. He is nowhere more impassioned, more lucid, more damaging in cogent argument, more adroit in his arrangement of facts. Such a digression as that over the legendary associations of Henna[2] introduces an effective note of romance. But Cicero produced finer literature than the *Verrines* — sentences more melodious, and suggestions more ima-ginative. He frequently attained such measure of the poetic as lies in silvery music and in ideals undimmed by practical aims. From 70 to 43 we have a noble pomp of orations, in which stand out, before his exile, the *Pro Lege Manilia*, *Pro Cluentio*, *In Catilinam*, *Pro Murena*, *Pro Archia*; and, after his exile, *Pro Sestio*, *Pro Caelio*, *Pro Plancio*, and *Pro Milone*. But the permanent value of the latter group is impaired by the constant obtrusion of Cicero's consular actions and the searing recollec-tion of outlawry. The failure of the actual speech for Milo seemed an evil omen. The 'Caesarian' speeches, which broke a silence of six years, do not show the orator at his best, though the beauty of language in the *Pro Marcello* cannot be missed. But with the *Philippics* the old power re-emerges almost unabated — those who feel certain that the *Second Philippic* is his masterpiece will say it is enhanced. On any view, the *Philippics*, for massive effect and telling power, if they do not bear the palm alone, can hardly take a second place. For the last time, Cicero is a statesman commanding an audience. The consciousness of this reacts on him. The dramatic interest is greater than that of the *Catilinarians*. There the conclusion was foregone. Here there is a stake, and the duel is to the death — for Cicero or for Antony. After the *First Philippic*, every stroke is aimed at Antony's ruin, and the unforgivable insults could be wiped out only by Cicero's blood. As we read the 'divine' *Philippic* the illusion grows that we are listening to a speech. Artifices pretending that the scene is the senate, and that Antony is within ear-shot as Catiline once was, combine with its white-heat of passion to

---

[1] Munro's conviction that Lucretius studied and imitated Cicero's verse should be remembered.

[2] *In Verr. Act. Sec.*, IV. xlviii. 106–107.

make one forget it was a pamphlet. And so we seem to hear the peroration:

> Return to your senses, I beg you, Mark Antony, in time: consider your ancestry, not your associates. Behave as you will towards me; but be reconciled to your country. Still, these are your concerns. For myself, I shall avow my position. I defended the republic in my youth: I will not desert her in my age. I scorned the swords of Catiline: I will never quail before yours. Nay, I would cheerfully put my body in danger's way if, by my death, the freedom of the state can be realised, so that the anguish of the Roman people may at last bring to the birth its prolonged travail.
>
> If nearly twenty years ago in this very temple I said death could not come untimely to one who had been consul, how much more truly can I say this of an old man! I tell you, my lords, death is now even desirable, after the honours I have gained and the duties I have performed. I have but two desires: the one, that at my death I may leave the Roman people free—than this no greater boon can be bestowed on me by the immortal gods—the other, that every man's lot may be what he deserves of his country.[1]

As with his character, the faults of his oratory lie on the surface. The worst are prolixity and conceit. His personalities[2] and puns[3] would not be tolerated in a modern court—still, this only means that we dislike what met with no objection in ancient times. Taken in the mass, the orations exhibit too little parsimony. There is an exuberance of verbosity which proves an intoxication. Even in a fairly short speech like the *Manilian* there is a redundance of laudation. In others, like the four *Catilinarians*, there is redundance of invective. However useful for carrying Cicero's end as consul, the whole of the four speeches cannot be deemed requisite as art. They are, of course, dominated by the occasions out of which they arose. But it is self-praise which is most wearisome. He keeps too well his promise not to forget his services.[4] His pride over saving Rome—which at times he ascribes to divine guidance as well as to his own energy[5]—induces him to link his glory with Pompey's as a saviour of the Eastern domains.[6] Pompey's failure to respond chagrined but could not silence him. So it is usually on self

---

[1] *Phil.*, II., xlvi, 118, 119: 'Resipisce, quaeso, aliquando,' etc.
[2] In the *In Pisonem* he addresses his opponent as 'belua,' 'carnufex,' 'caenum,' 'furcifer,' 'O tenebrae, O lutum, O sordes.' Only a very long list could exhaust his vocabulary of abuse.
[3] In the *Verrines* he introduces notorious puns, cited or invented: *e.g.*, 'negabant mirandum esse *ius* tam nequam esse *Verrinum*,' *Act. Secund.*, I. xlvi. 121; the eagerness of Verres to make a clean sweep of the province, 'ad *euerrendam* prouinciam,' *Act. Secund.*, II. vii. 19; so again Cicero calls Verres a dragnet, '*euerriculum*,' or a boar wallowing in the mire, 'quem (*sc.* Verrem) in luto uolutatum,' *ibid.*, IV. xxiv. 53. All extant writings on rhetoric show that these were by no means considered blemishes.
[4] *In Cat.*, III. xii. 27–29
[5] *Ibid.*, III. viii–ix. 18–22
[6] *Ibid.*, III. xi. 26

alone—and not on Pompey or the gods—that Cicero harps. His glorious
consulate and sorrowful exile haunt his later oratory irrepressibly. To
an egoist of his stamp the memory of the Catilinarian peril became an
obsession of the mind. As Plutarch tells us, this unending boastfulness
made Cicero unpopular.[1] The impeccable, often magnificent, Latin does
not atone for the odious monotony. Yet it ought to be needless to say
that it is by his merits he must be judged—by the command of moods
which enabled him to range from fiercest indignation to tenderest pity,
the command of words which might often develop a fatal facility, but
which yielded the wealth of effect needed to give Cicero his place beside
Demosthenes[2] among the orators of all time, and the command of those
indispensable virtues which characterise the greatest oratory—clearness,
order, ingenuity of argument, and rhythm. Amazing variety is only
what might be expected from his versatility. His praise was as handsome
as his invective was bitter. He is equally master of the brief sentence—
sometimes in off-hand style—and of the resounding period; of pathos,
innuendo, sarcasm, and banter; of perorations, now angry, now touching, now solemnly religious.

Though Cicero's oratory is literature and has the world for its
audience, still the secret of his success lay partly in his adaptability to
hearers in his own day. He was skilled to play on the feelings. His lava-
tide of passion swept a southern audience along as surely as his tearful
entreaties could move their pity. So it was not by irresistible logic that
he triumphed. Indeed, he often of set purpose blurs the straight issue.
In his forensic pleading his rhetoric descends not seldom into sophistry,
and a cloud of words envelops a weak case.[3] But he can at choice treat
his theme with admirable lucidity, secured by surprising aptness and
fulness of phraseology and by the cumulative effect of a telling arrangement of arguments.[4] Much of his wordiness may be excused, because
it springs from a laudable craving after clearness. It is his luminous

---

[1] Plut., *Cic.*, xxiv.

[2] Cicero's style is the more learned, more ornate, more witty; but in sustained moral earnestness Demosthenes surpasses him. Plutarch's comparison,
following his *Life of Cicero*, makes some points - good so far as they go.

[3] His shrewdness, observation, and learning suggested all sorts of special
pleading and opportunism in reasoning. It may be impressive to introduce an
argument from the doctrine of immortality, *Pro C. Rabir.*, x. 21, *In Cat.*, I.
sub fin., *Pro Arch.*, xi.; but it is also convenient in *Pro Cluent.*, lxi. 171, to argue
on the supposition that there is no future life. How fallaciously and plausibly he
can use the dilemma may be seen in *Pro Cluent.*, xxiii. 64, or in the inquiry 'uter
utri insidias fecerit' on which rests much of the clap-trap in his *Miloniana*. Needless to say, Cicero does not stand alone herein. Sophistry is not absent from
forensic oratory now or ever. Demosthenes teems with it; and ancient treatises
on rhetoric provided series of lessons in sophistry.

[4] Cicero in *Brut.*, xciii. 322, gives an excellent notion of the broad basis and
methods of his oratory. He rests it upon acquaintance with literature ('studuisse
litteris quibus fons perfectae eloquentiae continetur'), philosophy, law, and
history ('memoriam rerum Romanarum'); brief and incisive confutation of an
opponent; skilful appeal to the minds of the judges; transitions from grave to

recital of facts that makes the strength of the *Verrines*, where many plain-told stories of injustice cause the blood to boil without any need of heated vituperation or horrified laments (*O tempora! O mores!*). His vivid narratives and descriptions impress the memory with perfectly dramatic force—the sleuth-hounds of Verres (*canes uenaticos diceres*) doing their foul work of tracking treasure for him; Verres's entertainment of the young Syrian prince with the design of stealing his jewelled candelabrum; the affectionate parting of the Segestans from their beloved statue of Diana carried off by Verres; the brutal crucifixion of Gavius; in the *Pro Cluentio*, the whole account of the bribery of the jury which tried Oppianicus; Strato's burglary and the saw which gave the clue; in the *Pro Caelio*, the profligacies of Clodia and the 'wild oats' of Caelius; in the *Pro Milone*, the affray between Clodians and Milonians on the Appian Road; in the *Philippics*, the scandalous revels of Antony. The Ciceronian clearness is so ubiquitous and apparently easy that there is a risk of overlooking the close application which went to form this style. Nothing proves his hard work better than a perusal of his rhetorical treatises, with their painstaking analysis of the component parts of an oration, of a sentence, of a word. Down to the minutest syllable there is deft adaptation of sound to ear. Behind the grandiose cadences, with the sonorous regularity of inrolling waves, worked definite principles of prose-rhythm. The subtle avoidance of rhythms appropriate to verse is insisted on in the *Orator*, and might take for its motto the obtrusive *esse uideatur* noted by Quintilian. But it is in this century that the law of Ciceronian clause-endings has received its most careful examination and most ingenious statement by Zielinski.[1] Naturally it is when Cicero feels the inspiration of lofty ideas that his music is most effective. As in the *Pro Archia*, the best literature is that which is least relevant in law—the testimony to the consciousness of immortality as a spur to exertion,[2] the adoration of the sacred name of poet,[3] or the praise of letters:

These studies are the food of youth, the charm of age, an ornament in prosperity, in adversity a refuge and solace; a delight at home, and no hindrance in public life; they are our comrades of the night, in foreign lands, amid country scenes.[4]

---

gay; consideration of the issue from a general standpoint; pleasant digressions ('delectandi gratia digredi parumper a causa'); and the faculty of inducing anger or tears.

[1] Th. Zielinski, *Das Clauselgesetz in Ciceros Reden*, 1904.

[2] *Pro Arch.*, xi. 28–30: 'Nulla enim uirtus aliam mercedem,' etc.

[3] *Pro Arch.*, viii. 19: 'Sit igitur, iudices, sanctum apud uos, humanissimos homines, hoc poetae nomen, quod nulla umquam barbaria uiolauit. Saxa et solitudines uoci respondent, bestiae saepe immanes cantu flectuntur atque consistunt: nos instituti rebus optimis non poetarum uoce moueamur?'

[4] *Pro Arch.*, vii. 16: 'Haec studia adulescentiam alunt, senectutem oblectant, secundas res ornant, aduersis perfugium ac solacium praebent, delectant domi, non impediunt foris, pernoctant nobiscum, peregrinantur, rusticantur.'

Such passages and innumerable longer pieces of sustained eloquence attest how Cicero's combined lucidity and plenitude made Latin prose one of the most perfect instruments for the expression of human thought. He handled a noble language with such vivacity, clearness, and music that it became the model of the centuries.

Of the correspondence four collections have come down — two larger, *Epistulae ad Familiares* and *Ad Atticum*, each in sixteen books; and two smaller, *Ad Quintum Fratrem* in three books, and *Ad Brutum* in two. Classical allusions to lost books and letters prove that the extensive *corpus* gradually formed by Cicero's freedman Tiro has, except in the case of the letters to Quintus, suffered considerable mutilation.[1] The letters *Ad Brutum*, most of which are now allowed to be genuine,[2] are very imperfectly represented. The usual view is that Tiro edited those called *Ad Familiares*.[3] The title has no good MS. authority and is inaccurate, because several correspondents were not intimates of Cicero. It is not, however, bad Latin like the alternative *Ad Diuersos*. The letters *Ad Atticum* were prepared for publication, if they were not actually published, by Atticus.[4] A preconcerted plan avoided overlapping between the two collections: only two letters were common to the *Ad Familiares* and *Ad Atticum*. The replies of Atticus were left out, as Tiro's replies were; so that one has the feelings of a bystander who hears the speaker at only one end of a telephone. Cicero had no hand in collecting his letters. On the contrary, it is their pre-eminent charm that no haunting idea of publication fettered their spontaneity. But near the end of his life Cicero alludes to some such project.[5] Of the total number, 774 are by Cicero and 90 by correspondents. They extend over a quarter of a century — from 68 to 43 B.C. The opening years, 68 to 65, are sparsely represented by eleven letters. There is no letter from 64 or from the year of Cicero's consulate — Atticus was then in Rome. The period best represented is the close of his life; for the last nine years there are over six hundred letters.

Despite an enthusiastic commendation by Fronto[6] in the second

---

[1] L. Gurlitt, *De Cic. epistulis earumque pristina collectione*, 1879, denies there ever was any larger collection.

[2] P. Meyer subsequently modified views expressed in *Untersuchung über d. Frage d. Echtheit d. Briefwechsels Cic. ad Brut.* 1881.

[3] But *cf.* B. Nake, *Hist. crit. Ciceronis epistularum*, 1861. It is difficult to accept Nake's belief in the editorship by Atticus. There are good positive reasons supporting Tiro, such as known intention and the insertion of letters sent to him. Besides, Atticus could hardly have passed such a reflection on himself as 'hercle quod timidus ipse est, θορυβοποιεῖ,' *Ad Fam.*, XVI. xxiii. 2.

[4] J. S. Reid pointed out to the author that there is a good deal to show that the letters *Ad Att.* were not accessible to the public for a considerable time.

[5] *Ad Att.*, XVI. v. 5, 'Mearum epistularum nulla est συναγωγή, sed habet Tiro instar septuaginta. Et quidem sunt a te quaedam sumendae. Eas ego oportet perspiciam, corrigam; tum denique edentur.'

[6] Fronto, *Ad M. Antonin.*, II. v. (Naber, p. 107), 'Omnes Ciceronis

century, the letters did not retain the same popularity as Cicero's other works. It was in the fourteenth century at Verona that Petrarch rediscovered those *Ad Atticum*, *Ad Brutum*, and *Ad Q. Fratrem*, with the spurious epistle to Octavian. Before the end of that century the *Ad Familiares* were known again. It is strange that a self-revelation of such historic import and lively interest should ever have lost favour. The topics range from international complications and national questions to petty domestic squabbles and the most intimate confessions. There are political compacts, jealousies in high life, election news, bribery and wire-pulling, judgments on contemporaries, the talk of the town, and literary opinions. It is a memorable experience for a reader to be brought by Cicero into close contact with world-renowned events *quorum pars magna fuit.* We meet as flesh and blood, in letters to or from them, Caesar, Pompey, Mark Antony, Brutus, and Cassius; reverend signiors and flippant youths; the learned, complaisant, astutely neutral Atticus and the brilliant turncoat Curio. Now there is the great letter of consolation from Sulpicius with Cicero's reply, now a note with slang to suit Caelius and Dolabella as types of the *jeunesse dorée.* Public criticism can be seen fermenting among partisan cliques and in the larger sphere of the circus and theatre. A past society lives again in a chat with Pompey, in a call paid by Caesar when a conversation turned largely on literature (φιλόλογα *multa*),[1] in the fops (*barbatuli iuuenes*), in a *menu*, in descriptions of dinner-parties —some of them in questionable company.[2] But the political and social interest pales before that of Cicero's own personality. A human heart is laid bare without extenuation of shortcomings. We see conceit, duplicity, timidity, lacrimose outpourings over an exile bitter as the waters of Marah, petulant faultfinding mixed with self-recrimination;[3] but also patriotism, industry, family affection, and tender consideration for subordinates. It is this interplay of good and bad that makes the letters so intensely human. And there is the dramatic interest of noting a change of tone, on the whole for the better, in later letters, as if Cicero were chastened by his misfortunes.[4]

In style, the contrast between speeches and epistles is much greater than that which distinguishes Johnson's *Rambler* or *Rasselas* from *The Lives of the Poets* at their lightest. The letters themselves exhibit enormous differences of style; but, broadly, the change is towards a freer and more conversational manner. Cicero becomes frequently

---

epistulas legendas censeo, mea sententia uel magis quam omnes eius orationes. Epistulis Ciceronis nihil est perfectius.' Fronto also mentions making elegant extracts from the letters.

[1] *Ad Att.*, XIII. lii. 2.   [2] *Ad Fam.*, IX. xxvi.
[3] Piqued at the attitude of the nobles, he calls himself a 'downright ass' (*asinum germanum*) for not having made common cause with the triumvirate.
[4] R. S. Conway on 'The Inner Experience of Cicero,' *Contemp. Rev.*, June, 1902. Reprinted in *New Studies of a Great Inheritance*, 1921, pp. 1–17.

chatty, colloquial, and even slangy. The stateliness of the orations, is, in the majority of the letters, gone, simply because there is less need for it,[1] and momentary impressions, fancy, pique, nervousness are granted full play. This liberation from the elaborate and from the *arrière pensée* constitutes a mighty relief, for Cicero's vanity itself wearies less when no longer pranked in sonorous periods. The author's varying moods are naïvely reflected. He can write like Horace Walpole at his airiest or Cowper at his gravest. He has some of the coxcombry of the former and something of the tragic personality of the latter. Cicero is not starched by the consciousness of impending publication as Seneca, Pliny, and Madame de Sévigné all were. He shows more freedom than Gray. There is no affected pull towards artificialism as in the case of Burns's letters. He has Byron's frankness, if he lacks his sparkle. Colloquial turns are lavishly introduced.[2] With certain correspondents —most of all with Atticus—he sprinkles his sentences with Greek, as we might use a handy French word in a letter,[3] but sometimes solely because of Atticus's Greek tastes. In the more familiar and unstudied notes, the parallelism to the language of the comic stage is a natural phenomenon.[4] While the majority exhibit this free-and-easy style, others are restrained, others again stilted and awkward. Those especially which are written by Cicero as a politician to politicians are laboured and artificial, and, it may be, hampered by caution and dissimulation. For example, the letters to Lentulus, Appius, and Plancus are couched in most literary language, and letters of consolation are inevitably formal. Rhythm naturally plays in the correspondence a humble part. Yet in in the more carefully composed epistles its principles are illustrated in a way that recalls the finish of the orations.[5] The presence of letters by others affords proof of the superiority of Cicero's Latin, whether he writes in the formal or the informal manner.[6]

It remains to examine the treatises on political science, rhetoric, and

[1] Many letters in the *Ad Fam.* are as stately in construction as the speeches.

[2] P. Meyer, *De Ciceronis in epistulis ad Att. sermone*, 1887; A. Stinner, *De eo quo C. in epist. usus est sermone*, 1879; *cf.* A. Dräger, *Historische Syntax*, ed. 2, 1878–81, and C. F. Nägelsbach, *Stilistik*, ed. 9, 1905.

[3] In such cases, but not in every case, a translation might admit French, German, or Italian words, *e.g.*, σφάλμα, *faux pas*; ἐπίτευγμα, *coup*; ἀπότευγμα, *fiasco*. See R. Y. Tyrrell, *Class. Rev.*, xiv., 1900, pp. 471–2.

[4] J. Lebreton, *Études sur la langue et la grammaire de Cicéron*, 1901, considers this parallelism has been exaggerated. The extent of the similarity with the comic vocabulary is discussed, Tyrrell and Purser, *Corresp. of Cic.*, vol. ii., ed. 2, pp. lxv. *sqq.*

[5] There is too arbitrary a dissection of the letters in Bornecque, *La prose métrique dans la correspondance de Cicéron*, 1898. Tyrrell and Purser, *op. cit.*, ii, pp. lxvi–lxvii, consider the conformity of the more elaborate letters to Zielinski's law of clause-endings.

[6] For the language of Cicero's principal correspondents, see list of monographs by German scholars in Tyrrell and Purser, *op. cit.*, i., ed. 3, 1904, pp. 91, 92. Caelius's language is especially discussed, *op. cit.*, iii. (1890), pp. ci–cix. Caelius did not aim at being literary, but adopted the style of everyday life, with jerky sentences, vulgarisms, and a tone suited to the frivolous set.

philosophy. The *De Republica*, due, like the *De Oratore*, to Cicero's first political eclipse, was begun in 54, and had been published before his provincial governorship.[1] It was composed in six books. Through the Middle Ages and in modern times it was unkuown except for quotations in writers like Lactantius and St. Augustine, and except for the *Somnium Scipionis*, which had at an early date been separated from the sixth book and commented on by Macrobius. What then was the excitement of the learned world when a palimpsest discovered in 1822 by Cardinal Mai proved to contain about one-third of the vanished work! To its speculative sources in Plato, Aristotle, Theophrastus, and Polybius, Cicero added copious contributions from Roman history and his own experience. The aim is to discover the best form of government and to examine the bases of national prosperity. After a proem advocating active patriotism and the study of the art of government, Cicero defines the commonwealth as 'a union of the population linked by a common recognition of rights and by community of interests.'[2] In his examination of the three primary forms—monarchy, oligarchy, and democracy—the Roman distrust of democracy frequently emerges.[3] Cicero's own view is expressed in the dialogue by Scipio's preference for a mixed constitution, with all three principles in equilibrium.[4] If he had to choose one definitely, he would select kingship. Clearly he had Plato's 'philosopher-king' in view. After a second book largely devoted to the Roman kings, a third considers justice as the basis of the 'common recognition of rights.' Like Thrasymachus in Plato's *Republic*, Philus is put up as *advocatus diaboli* to argue that all government implies injustice. He canvasses the fairness of the Romans in their rule of and treaties with other peoples.[5] Laelius in reply maintains the eternal nature of justice. The last three books are more fragmentary. The fourth holds that civil institutions should secure an honourable and happy life for the citizen (*beate et honeste uiuendi*)—an object as Aristotelian as it is Benthamite. The relations of the community to education, property, poetry, and the drama are touched on. The typically Roman attitude of opposition to outspoken literature which is adopted contrasts with the licence permitted at Athens, and explains how the growth of Latin comedy was checked. Roman opinion preferred that a censor rather than a dramatist should stigmatise moral obliquities. The fifth book, opening with a note of sadness over political degeneracy, declares that the best means of achieving the happiness of the community is the discovery of a *moderator rei publicae*. On such a governor social welfare

---

[1] Caelius writes to Cicero in Cilicia, 'tui politici libri omnibus uigent,' *Ad Fam.*, VIII. i. 4.
[2] *De Rep.*, I. xxv, 'coetus multitudinis iuris consensu et utilitatis communione sociatus.'
[3] I. xlii, xliii.
[4] I. xxxv.
[5] III. xv., xvii.

depends as vitally 'as a safe voyage on the helmsman, health on a doctor, victory on a general.' It is here that Cicero has Pompey in view. The sixth book contains the famous *Dream of Scipio*, a distant imitation of the vision of Er in Plato's *Republic*. With its throbbing music of style, responsive, as it were, to its own description of the Harmony of the Spheres, with its warm tearfulness, its vivid question and answer, its inspired monitions, its depth of vision and recognition of barriers fixed immutably by God for the universe and for the human soul, the *Somnium* affects one after some such fashion as Dante does. Preserved by Macrobius, it is a bridge between the ancient and the medieval spirit.

The title *De Republica* suggests a comparison with Plato's *Republic*. The differences outnumber the resemblances. Though he had gleams of Plato's idealism, Cicero was too Roman to sympathise with the Greek thinker's indifference to the possibility of realising the ideal state in hard fact. To him the 'pattern laid up in heaven,' the community of goods, the community of wives and children, would be stumbling-blocks. Roman-like and riveted to the practical, Cicero contemplated no far-reaching scheme of social reform such as Plato sketched. Accepting the prevailing order, he exhibits far more *laissez faire*. Hence some of his limitations. A lack of penetration into the tangle of politics prevented him from seeing that his advocated combination of senate and *equites*, with Pompey as a Lord Protector of the Commonwealth, could only be a temporary remedy, incapable of touching the radical rottenness of the oligarchic cabal. Blindness to the needs of the democracy barred any broad attitude on corn distribution, agrarian legislation, and colonisation. Some faintness of interest in what we should call 'imperial questions' might perhaps be suspected from the absence of any discussion on provincial government—that is, on the duty of Rome to the world at large.[1] This is the more regrettable because Cicero could be 'imperialist' enough in his genuine enthusiasm over the conquests of Pompey and Caesar; and it is notorious that while Cicero felt his absence from the capital insufferably irksome, he proved a fair-minded governor, with an interest in the governed keener and sounder than that of any other man of his time, so far as is known. The value of the *De Republica* lies not in any constitutional scheme or political panacea, but in its application of ethical ideas to politics. The social duty of interesting oneself in questions of government—so different from the Epicurean attitude—is repeatedly insisted on. It receives a sacred sanction in the *Dream*, where for those who save, help, and strengthen their country there is assured a place in heaven, while spirits of indolent pleasure-lovers whirl in a ceaseless round, like the souls of Paolo and Francesca.

---

[1] Perhaps the most definite approach to this subject by Cicero is in his letter, already mentioned, drawing up for his brother instructions on the duties of a Roman governor, *Ad Q. Frat.*, I. i.

The doctrine of the need for moral worth in governors is parallel to Cicero's high conception of the qualifications of an orator, who, to be effective, must be no sophistic charlatan, but an upright statesman. This idea, shared with Plato, is a natural corollary to the recognition in ancient politics of the social danger of vice and luxury. The store set on freedom appears in Cicero's hatred of tyranny as ruinous to the state and in his allowance to democracy of its signal glory of *libertas*. It is among the outstanding merits of the treatise that its social conscience is strong and its love of country and of freedom sincere.

As Plato's *Laws* came after his *Republic,* so Cicero proceeded to add the treatise *De Legibus* about 52 B.C. It may have been left incomplete. Three books remain; but it is certain there were at least five.[1] It is a monologue by Cicero, interspersed with comments by Quintus and by Atticus. That its central ideas are based on the Stoic conception of law is a natural result of the currency of the Stoic views among Roman lawyers. Law is glorified as possessing a universal sanction in reason, which is ultimately divine. This harmonises with the Stoic doctrine that the wise man in the ideal state frames laws in accordance with the mind of God. Law is viewed, then, as a gift of Providence. Book II examines laws applied to religion; Book III laws as applied to magistrates; Book IV was designed to treat of law courts (*de iudiciis*).

While Cicero's political philosophy was the reflection of so much in his life and letters, his rhetoric treatises formed a theoretical counterpart to what was greatest in his genius. They all prove the astounding technical diligence which underlay his success. Four of them need not detain us long. One is his *De Inuentione*, or *Rhetorica* (*c.* 84 B.C.), whose two books of dull divisions and rather less dull examples of argumentation are dismissed by Cicero about thirty years later as imperfect efforts of youth.[2] The compilation often refers to Hermagoras and Aristotle. It is much indebted to the treatise *Ad Herennium.*[3] The others of the four belong to his last twelve years. The *Partitiones Oratoriae* (*c.* 54), a far from exhilarating dissection of rhetoric by means of question and answer between Cicero's son and himself, leaves little but dry bones. The *Topica* (44) was Cicero's response to a request for an exposition of Aristotle's *Topics*, a copy of which had puzzled Trebatius in Cicero's library at his Tusculan villa. Written partly at sea and largely from memory, it illustrates the Aristotelian types of argument with examples bearing on Roman law. The brief *De Optimo Genere Oratorum* (46), prefatory to Cicero's translations of the Greek speeches *De Corona*, is less technical. It touches the fringe of literary criticism. Attic oratory,

---

[1] See J. B. Mayor, *Ancient Philosophy*, 1881, p. 235. Macrobius quotes from Book V.
[2] *De Or.*, I. ii. 5, 'quae pueris aut adulescentulis nobis ex commentariolis nostris incohata ac rudia exciderunt.'
[3] Spengel, *Rhein. Mus.*, xviii. 495.

exemplified in Lysias's simplicity, is proclaimed the excellent and
Asianism the faulty type. Rounding on his critics, Cicero claims to
speak in Attic style. As the best of Greek orators were the Athenians,
and of these Demosthenes best beyond compare (*princeps facile*), it
follows that 'to speak well is to speak in the Attic way.'[1] Having alluded
to Thucydides's style as irrelevant in matters of oratory and to weak
points in Isocrates, Cicero defends his project of translating from
Demosthenes and Aeschines. Objectors who ask, 'Why should I read
them in Latin rather than in the original?' are the very people who read
adaptations by Terence and Caecilius as much as they do Menander,
and who study Ennius, Pacuvius, and Accius more than Euripides and
Sophocles.[2]

A much more important triad consists of the *De Oratore*, 55 B.C., and
the *Brutus* and the *Orator*, both written about ten years later. The *De
Oratore* is an imaginary discussion in 91 B.C. at the Tusculan villa of the
great orator, Licinius Crassus, in which he and his rival Antonius take
the chief part. In Book I Crassus speaks on the wide knowledge requisite for oratory; in Book II Antonius discusses matter and arrangement
and induces one of his hearers, Caesar, to propound and illustrate his
theory of humour; in Book III Crassus is again the main speaker, on
style and delivery. Cicero's aim in the work was to construct a system of
oratory, so as to correct for his brother Quintus the crudities of the
De Inuentione. While Antonius maintains that oratory can be studied
quite independently of law, philosophy, and other departments, the
exalted view of the orator's training and *métier* maintained by Crassus
represents Cicero's own feeling. By the use of dialogue—though
inferior in dramatic power to Plato—Cicero enlivens an abstract subject.
None of his works is in more richly polished Latin. *Brutus*, or *De Claris
Oratoribus*, is a record of actual achievement. Its contents include a
sketch of Greek eloquence and notices of nearly two hundred Roman
orators. The avowed intention to omit living orators is departed from
in the four cases of Caesar, Servius Sulpicius Rufus, M. Marcellus, and,
fortunately, Cicero himself. The sections on Cicero's training[3] and his
rivalry with Hortensius lend great interest to the work. Nowhere else
does Cicero attain such vivacity of dialogue, which flags frequently in
his philosophical books. One of the motives in the composition was the
patriotic desire to display a galaxy of Roman orators. It is to impress his
readers with the great traditions of the national eloquence that Cicero

---

[1] *De Opt. Gen. Or.*, iv. 13, '. . . ut, quoniam Attici nobis propositi sunt
ad imitandum, bene dicere id sit Attice dicere.' The Attic style might take a
suitable motto from Dionysus's advice in Aristophanes's *Frogs*, 906, 'neat
urbanity, without figures and without commonplace' (ἀστεῖα καὶ μήτ' εἰκόνας
μήθ'οἷ' ἂν ἄλλος εἴποι), *i.e.*, free from excessive ornament and yet characteristic
of the individual. It is the kind of prose to which the closest English analogues
might be found in Swift and Addison.
[2] *Ibid.*, v. 18.
[3] For autobiographic portion see *Brut.*, lxxxix, 304 *sqq.*

confines himself to a sketchy introduction on the Greeks.[1] He had the further motive of a constant desire to impart knowledge — strengthened in the case of rhetoric, by hopes of training a generation of younger speakers who might prove champions of freedom. The *Orator ad M. Brutum*, also called *De Optimo Genere Dicendi*[2] from its contents, puts the coping-stone on Cicero's rhetorical work. It seeks to delineate the perfect orator. The quest after perfection is taken up in a spirit of Platonic idealism consistent with Cicero's belief in the philosophic basis of oratory.[3] He owed more, he says, to the walks of the Academy than to the workshops of rhetoricians.[4] The scheme pursues the delineation of the consummate orator as to management of a speech; as to the three styles, the grand, the intermediate, and the plain (*grande, medium, tenue*); as to the threefold function of proof, pleasure, and per-suasion (*probare* or *docere, delectare, flectere* or *mouere*); as to depart-ments of knowledge; as to qualities, ornaments (*lumina uerborum* and *ornamenta sententiarum*) and rhythm of style (*numerus oratorius*). The professed aim is criticism rather than systematic teaching.[5] In a spirit of preferring example to precept, Cicero passes comments on Demos-thenes and other Greek orators and draws illustrations of oratori-cal qualities, like rhythmic endings, from his own speeches. The minute analysis in the *Orator* explains that scrupulous nicety of taste and ear which strikes one in the recital of Ciceronian Latin.

Latin literary criticism[6] may be said to have its real beginning in Cicero rather than in sundry passages of Ennius, Terence, and Lucilius, or in canons like Sedigitus's classification of poets on Alexandrian lines. The Romans had the advantage over the Greeks of having another literature for a touchstone. The very process of modelling on Greek originals implied some critical appreciation. Yet stimulating criticism came slowly. From such a collector, student, and maker of books as Cicero, more might have been expected in the way of criticism — if not in a special treatise, then as *obiter dicta*. But in the letters we have to

---

[1] For Greek oratory and rhetoric, F. Blass, *Die Griechische Beredsamkeit,* u.s.w., 1865; and *Die Attische Beredsamkeit,* 4 vols., 1868–80; E. M. Cope, *Aristotle's Rhet.,* 1877 (Introd.); R. C. Jebb, *The Attic Orators from Antiphon to Isaeos,* 2 vols., 1876; J. E. Sandys, ed. of Cic., *Orator,* 1885, Introd., pp. ii–xxxviii (followed by retrospect of Roman oratory); A. S. Wilkins, Introd. to vol. i of ed. of *De Or.,* § 4. A list of Latin rhetoricians accompanies the sketch of Greek oratory in A. E. Chaignet's *La Rhétorique et son histoire,* 1888, pp. 1–69; and there is a 'breuis eloquentiae Romanae ante Caesares historia' in F. Ellendt's *Brutus,* 1844, pp. 1–150. R. Volkmann, *Die Rhetorik d. Griechen u. Römer,* ed. 3, 1901, is an exhaustive treatise on formal rhetoric. A broader field is covered by E. Norden, *Die antike Kunstprosa,* u.s.w., 2 vols., 1898.

[2] *Ad Att.,* XIV. xx. 3; *Ad Fam.,* XII. xvii. 2.

[3] *Or.,* ii. 7, 'In summo oratore fingendo talem informabo, qualis fortasse nemo fuit.'

[4] *Or.,* iii. 12, 'Fateor me oratorem, si modo sim aut etiam quicunque sim, non ex rhetorum officinis, sed ex Academiae spatiis exstitisse.'

[5] *Or.,* xiv. 45.

[6] See H. Nettleship, *Lectures and Essays,* vol. ii., 1895, p. 44; G. Saints-bury, *A Hist. of Criticism,* etc., vol. i, 1900, pp. 211 *sqq.*

content ourselves with morsels like his words on Lucretius, unsatisfying
as criticism whatever the reading, or his facetious allusion to Aristarchus's way of rejecting for spurious what he disliked, or the characterisation of his own Greek prose style in describing his consulate

> My book has used up the whole perfume-shop of Isocrates, and
> the scent-boxes of his followers — and even a dash of Aristotelian
> colouring.[1]

The *Brutus* notably breaks away from formal rhetoric into the wider
field of literary criticism; and the history of literature owes much to
Cicero's patriotic love of the old Latin poets and his habit of quoting
them. All, however, is ancillary to his master-passion: it is as a critic of
oratorical prose that he is singularly authoritative. His services to the
critical vocabulary — though not comparable to his enormous services in
creating a philosophical vocabulary in Latin — were also noteworthy.
He was the introducer or translator of many technical terms from the
Greek rhetoricians; and he crystallised, within the zone of criticism, the
use of many Latin adjectives and nouns, particularly the metaphorical
extension of words like *exsanguis, lacerti, nerui*, and *sucus*. Yet nothing in
Cicero equals the rapid survey in Quintilian's Tenth Book for varied
suggestiveness.

Some of Cicero's speculations on ethics, theology, and epistemology
call for further notice. The essays *De Senectute* and *De Amicitia* have
sub-titles, *Cato Maior* and *Laelius*, after the principal speakers in each.
They have a perennial winsomeness. The significance of that *On Friendship* does not lie in imperfections of arrangement or in its borrowings
from Theophrastus, Chrysippus, and indirectly from Aristotle: for
pure beauty it is unsurpassed in Cicero. Its noble calm, its melodious
sentences, and its hold upon pellucid brevity give it a rank in literature
beside Montaigne's inimitable portrayal of the fervency in affection and
community of will which must ally friends. The *De Natura Deorum* and
De Diuinatione may be grouped together as theological. The latter, a
conversation on Stoic and Academic tenets regarding human means of
learning the divine will, is a supplement to the theoretical investigations of the former. The *De Natura Deorum* is one of five philosophical
works dedicated by Cicero to Brutus, afterwards Caesar's murderer.
Brutus's name appears in the title of the *De Claris Oratoribus*; he was
himself a man of philosophical attainments and an author. In Book I
(based possibly on a tract by Philodemus discovered imperfect among
the Herculanean MSS.) C. Velleius is the spokesman of Epicureanism;
in Book II (based on Posidonius) Q. Lucilius Balbus speaks for the
Stoics; in Book III (based on Clitomachus, the pupil of Carneades, and
partly lost) C. Aurelius Cotta speaks for the Academic view. The

---

[1] *Ad Att.*, II. i. 1, 'Meus autem liber totum Isocratis μυροθήκιον, atque
omnes eius discipulorum arculas ac nonnihil etiam Aristotelia pigmenta con-
sumpsit.'

theology thus corresponds, school for school, to the theories of the ethical end in the *De Finibus*. The work is often superficial and loose-jointed. The summary in Book I of the views of various philosophers contains inaccuracies.[1] Velleius—whose blustering style is an intentional suggestion of Epicurean arrogance—makes strong points against the theory of creation, which are never refuted. On the whole, the Academic criticism does not shine here; and it must be remembered that Cicero on moral and theological problems sympathised largely with the Stoics. The greatest thing in the work is the attempt in Book II to prove divine providence. The defects of the *De Natura Deorum* scarcely weaken its value as a historical document. It is a summary of the prevailing modes of thought in Rome, half a century before the birth of Christ, concerning questions of permanent interest to mankind. It appealed strongly to early Christian writers, and furnished Minucius Felix, Tertullian, Lactantius, and St. Augustine with arguments against polytheism.

Among Cicero's philosophical works the most careful is the *De Finibus*, written in the year before the *De Natura Deorum*. The rival theories of the *summum bonum* are reviewed. The Epicurean theory is stated in Book I by L. Torquatus near Cumae and refuted in II by Cicero; the Stoic is stated in Book III by M. Cato within the library of Lucullus at Tusculum and refuted by Cicero in IV; and the Peripatetic is expounded in Book V by M. Pupius Piso, with the scene appropriately changed to the Academy at Athens. Corresponding to this treatment of the foundations of conduct, the *Academics* treats the theory of knowledge. For both works Cicero drew largely from late Greek speculation. In the absence of many of his sources, he is a valuable authority, especially on the doctrines of the Academy. Cicero wrote the *Prior Academics*—the earlier edition—in two books entitled *Catulus* and *Lucullus*. The second edition—the *Posterior Academics*—was due to a hint that some of his works should be dedicated to Varro. Some days of continuous rain during a stay at Arpinum gave Cicero time to recast the work. He divided it now into four books, and made the interlocutors Varro, Atticus, and himself. This edition he declared would be 'more brilliant, more terse, and altogether better than the last.'[2] He mentions the care and polish bestowed on it.[3] Only the *Lucullus* has survived of the *Prior Academics*; of the *Posterior Academics* the greater part of Book I, with quotations from the other three. We possess, therefore,

---

[1] J. S. Reid wrote to the author: 'As to the inaccuracies in *N.D.* I, and elsewhere, some of those imagined by modern scholars are not there; many of them were the views of the earlier philosophers which were currently accepted in the schools of Cicero's time – very few anywhere can be proved to be Cicero's own errors. On the whole, Cicero's philosophical works are translations (as he himself often implies) and fairly faithful translations too.'

[2] *Ad Att.*, XIII. xiii. 1.

[3] *E.g.*, *Ad Att.*, XIII. xix. 3 and 5.

almost three-quarters of the whole. Cicero's object was to justify the
sceptical criticism of the New Academy. So the bases of knowledge and
the possibility of dogmatic certitude come under examination. The
Tusculan Disputations are on the essentials that make for happiness.
Unencumbered with learned terminology, this is the most readable of
the philosophic works for its plain human interest. The five books are,
in order, on the contempt of death; on the endurance of pain; on the
control of grief; on the conquest of other trials and passions; on the
sufficiency of virtue for happiness. Of the *De Officiis*, the last philosophic fruit of Cicero's leisure, Book I handles classes of duties in
relation to the four cardinal virtues of Plato; Book II, turning from the
honestum to the *utile*, handles expediency in actions; Book III handles
the conflict between expediency and virtue, and settles problems in
casuistry by deciding that only apparent expediency is opposed to
virtue. Honour is the true expediency. The first two books were based
on a lost treatise by Panaetius περὶ τοῦ καθήκοντος; the third book —
much the least systematic — was based on Posidonius and others.
On the Greek foundation was raised a fabric of practical rules fortified
by copious Roman examples. Though in a very different tone from Lord
Chesterfield, Cicero had a similar aim — to exhort a son. He produced a
handbook for a Roman gentleman in his daily occupation. Whatever its
defects, it is an honest endeavour after a science of conduct, founded on
the thought of the past and on the ripe experience of the author. The
resounding praises won by the work from the elder Pliny and St.
Ambrose, from Erasmus and Frederick the Great, may seem disproportionate on the score of scientific merit; but the elegance of its
Latinity and its continuance of the task of building up a philosophical
language capable of diffusing Roman culture have deservedly given to
'Tully's *Offices*' a prominent place among Latin works in the eyes of
the world.

Cicero's widely differing teachers in Rome, Athens, and Rhodes, his
multifarious reading, his insatiate craving for discussion, produced in
one of his impressionability and indecision neither absolute scepticism
nor original theorising, but an eclectic tolerance. Although mistakes
prove he was not a perfect master of Platonic philosophy, yet his profound veneration for Plato's idealism, dialectic and style endeared the
traditions of the Academy to him. Little as he cared to parade Greek
tastes too openly — he carefully minimises acquaintance with Greek art
in the *Verrines* — he did not shrink from the avowal of his Platonic and
Aristotelian sympathies in court.[1] This homage largely determined the
prevailing element in his eclecticism. In general an adherent of the
revived Academicism of Carneades, he could not go so far as to accept
the tenet of the impossibility of knowledge. Clearly Cicero would
defend the usefulness of a limited scepticism in a Carneades who would

[1] *E.g., Pro Mur.*, xxx. 63.

lead men to examine doctrines in the light of reason[1] —like some Hume
waking the ancient world from its 'dogmatic slumber.' So he does
battle against dogmatism as presumptuous. He is the champion of
qualified assent to the most probable opinion.[2] For him this is freedom
of thought. The wars among mighty intellects overawe him into caution,
and even humility, in assertion. He contemplates with complacency
change of view. It is the condition of mental advance. Traversing an
extensive range of thought, he refuses —and who shall blame him?—to
be trammelled by his own previous conclusions.[3] This Academic re-
servation of judgement suited admirably the Cicero of politics. Its effect,
too, is manifest in the arguments of his speeches.[4] But Cicero was more
than Academic. In him with more than usual clearness, many forces
met.[5] It is true that for Epicureanism he felt a dislike all the stronger
because he never fully appreciated the intellectual position of its founder
or the commanding genius of his own contemporary Lucretius. The
dislike of formal Epicureanism was almost universal at the time. We
have to come down to Seneca before we can find a non-Epicurean who
will allow anything good of the school. In any case its self-centred
egoism was certain to clash with the public and practical instincts of a
spirit so Roman. It is true also that Stoicism in its most inflexible form
would not naturally commend itself to a Roman mind. Its paradoxes
adumbrated unattainable ideals. Its notion of the unchangeable condition of virtue and its denial of degrees in good and evil made moral
progress look impossible. Its fantastic idealism and intellectual self-
sufficiency deserved the satire of the *Pro Murena*. But it was not
the pedantry of a Zeno or the unbending Stoicism accepted by Cato
which was to win so many adherents in Rome. It was Scipio's friend
Panaetius who, by an adroit departure from the stricter lines laid
down by predecessors had given to Stoicism the turn necessary to
appeal with some force to a mind like Cicero's. Stoicism for Cicero had
much that was attractive —for example its sublime belief in the
sovereignty of virtue. Scepticism in matters of the intellect might be a
stimulus; but scepticism in the region of morals would mean anarchy of
conduct. So it is on Panaetius that Cicero founds his treatise *On Duties*;
and his ethical system is deeply coloured with Stoicism and neo-
Stoicism.[6]

[1] *De Nat. Deor.*, I. iv. 10.
[2] See his brief answer to his critics, *De Off.*, II. ii. 7–8; cf. *Tusc. Disp.*, IV.
iv. 7, 'quid sit in quaque re maxime probabile semper requiremus.'
[3] *De Off.*, III. vii. 33, 'tum hoc tum illud probabilius uidetur.'
[4] *Tusc. Disp.*, II. iii. 9, 'Itaque mihi semper Peripateticorum Acade-
miaeque consuetudo de omnibus rebus in contrarias partes disserendi non ob
eam causam solum placuit, quod aliter non posset quid in una quaque re
uerisimile esset inueniri, sed etiam quod esset ea maxima dicendi exercitatio.'
[5] His eclecticism, expressed in words almost echoed by Horace, appears
Tusc. Disp., IV. iv. 7, 'Defendat quod quisque sentit: sunt enim iudicia libera:
nos institutum tenebimus, nulliusque unius disciplinae legibus adstricti,' etc.
[6] *De Off.*, I. ii. 6, he claims to follow the Stoics freely, 'Sequimur . . .

On such data no original system of philosophy is to be expected from Cicero. He did not claim to be an original thinker. Much modern criticism of his philosophical writings is based on the tacit assumption that he did. Such originality as he possesses consists in his power of combination and his claim to criticise—to accept or reject *iudicio arbitrioque suo.* He belonged to no school: he founded no school. He was a philosopher not by choice but by the compulsion of circumstances. His primary interest in philosophy hung on its usefulness for oratory. But in retirement and depression a secondary interest came to the front; and his motives for composing treatises were the desires worthily to occupy the mind[1] and to disseminate thought.[2] It costs his facile genius little trouble to make elegant transcripts[3] from Greek philosophy; and it would have been more than a miracle if works concocted with such speed from different authors had been flawless and systematic. If he was not an original philosopher, Cicero was the ablest of philosophic amateurs. He was an amateur in the best and original sense of the term: he loved learning and he made it influence the world. There are many reasons why that world should not let the philosophical works of Cicero die. Their proems are vital with personal interest. Their Latin moves in a stately pomp, so that it is often a pleasure merely to dwell on the cadence of the clauses and the vowel-music of the syllables. But beyond everything there is the historical reason. St. Augustine may be taken as an example of the power exerted by Cicero. The writers of the Church fell far short of the glories of his style; but it was the Church that kept his influence alive and the lamp of his fame burning.

Contemporary orators were outshone by Cicero. The most famous was Q. Hortensius Hortalus (114–50 B.C.). His slight seniority to Cicero gave him ascendancy in the law courts up to his defence of Verres in 70. Senatorial sympathies placed him on the losing side. Thenceforward he was recognised, and recognised himself, as the second speaker of his day. A growing Epicureanism lessened his ambitions and exertions. It was his custom, when acting for the same client, to yield the more important duty of closing to Cicero. That his eclipse by the new luminary did not prevent friendly relations was a credit to both.[4] Fleeting jealousies troubled the sensitive junior; but he was a sincere admirer of Hortensius, and after his death paid him a fine tribute at the beginning of the *Brutus*, in the latter part of which he gives an admirable

---

potissimum Stoicos, non ut interpretes; sed ut solemus, e fontibus eorum, iudicio arbitrioque nostro, quantum quoque modo uidebitur, hauriemus.'

[1] *Acad. Post.*, I. iii. 11, 'Doloris medicinam a philosophia peto et otii oblectationem hanc honestissimam iudico.'

[2] *De Nat. Deor.*, I. iv. 7, 'Ipsius reipublicae causa philosophiam nostris hominibus explicandam putaui.'

[3] *Ad Att.*, XII. lii. 3, 'ἀπόγραφα sunt: minore labore fiunt; uerba tantum affero, quibus abundo.'

[4] *Brut.*, xciv. 323.

estimate of his genius.[1] To gifts of voice, enthusiasm, and memory, Hortensius added a youthful diligence which won striking power in expression and in summarising arguments. He became the master of the flamboyant style. Though clear, he inclined to the use of inflated periods, luxuriant ornament, and monotonous rhythm—a rich Hellenism of the later or Asiatic type, from which Cicero in early times had not been free.[2] Hortensius was a man of wide interests. He passed through the public offices; and though it was said that he spoke better than he wrote,[3] his literary record included published speeches, a *Rhetoric*, *Annals*, and love poems.[4]

Most public men at Rome spoke effectively. The triumvirs, disreputable governors like Memmius, and a host of Caesarians, anti-Caesarians, and waverers, were orators. But they have left little mark upon literature.[5] A few main tendencies and names deserve special note. The struggle between 'Asianism' and 'Atticism' at Rome has part of its fortunes recorded in the *Brutus*.[6] It is, however, a recurrent phenomenon in literature. If 'Asianism' had its Roman heyday in Hortensius, it had a recrudescence in Bossuet and in Burke. Cicero, though claiming to be 'Attic,' represented the eclectic Rhodian school, eschewing the extremes of flamboyance and of severity. The stricter Attic form was exemplified in the pioneer of a reaction against Cicero's style—M. Calidius. The aim was a simplicity and restraint which should contrast with Cicero's rich Isocratean elaboration. The Greek models—not always widely used—were sometimes Lysias and Hyperides, sometimes the historians Thucydides and Xenophon. The besetting dangers of the reaction were baldness, coldness, and positive sleepiness. Calidius—whose characteristics Cicero had full opportunity of judging in court, both on the same and on the opposite side[7]—affected such unconcern and spoke so 'yawningly' (*oscitanter*) that Cicero twitted him with not believing in his own case.[8] To this reactionary group belonged Caesar, and many of the younger generation—Caelius Rufus, once a pupil of Cicero's,[9] Curio, M. Brutus, and Catullus's diminutive friend, Licinius Calvus. In reference to Calvus, as a leading representative of the school, Cicero remarks that the Atticists found that their

[1] *Brut.*, lxxxviii. 301 *sqq.*
[2] For Hortensius's Asianism, see *Brut.*, xcv. 325.
[3] *Or.*, xxxviii. 132, 'Dicebat melius quam scripsit Hortensius.'
[4] Quint., *Inst. Or.*, II. i. 11; Vell., II. xvi. 3; Ovid, *Tr.*, ii. 441; Plin., *Ep.*, V. iii. 5.
[5] It must be enough to refer to Teuffel, §§ 171, 202, 209, 210, for their names, and for his citation of Cicero's criticisms in the *Brutus*.
[6] The contrast over the range of Roman literature, as a whole, is dealt with by Norden, *Die Antike Kunstprosa*, u.s.w.
[7] Teuffel, § 202, 1.
[8] *Brut.*, lxxx. 277-278. The 8th Duke of Devonshire, when Marquis of Hartington, yawned during one of his own speeches – to the unbounded delight of Disraeli, who remarked 'He'll do!' Cicero judged Calidius otherwise.
[9] Quint., *Inst. Or.*, XII. xi. 6.

L

audiences speedily melted away,[1] and that Calvus's attention to *minutiae* led to a loss of force.[2] Yet he was no pale and strengthless copy of Lysias. It is of him as prosecutor of Vatinius that the elder Seneca records the indignant protest by the accused against being brought in guilty simply because Calvus was an eloquent speaker.[3] Slightly later come M. Valerius Messalla Corvinus and Asinius Pollio. Regarding this Attic school, which would fain have classed Cicero as 'Asian,' Blass approves of Mommsen's judgement: 'Undeniably there was more taste and more spirit in the younger oratorical literature than in the Hortensian and Ciceronian put together.'[4] But it is useless so to praise men who have left nothing by which we can judge. Time has judged them. The plain fact remains — they did not establish a school of eloquence to rival Cicero's influence; nor did they arrest the decay of eloquence which the loss of political freedom brought about. They rather hastened that decay by opposing the most vigorous oratory which their country had produced. Cicero justifiably derides their vaunted Atticism — *si anguste et exiliter dicere est Atticorum, sint sane Attici.*[5] In taste he was right. Latin, as a spoken language, needed more ornament than Greek; and Roman audiences took genuine pleasure in amplitude of rhythm and affluence of expression. Had Cicero not perceived this, he would never have been the typical orator of Rome.

[1] *Brut.*, lxxxiv. 289.
[2] *Brut.*, lxxxii. 283.
[3] Sen., *Contr.*, VII. iv. 6. The incident has been mentioned and the text cited *supra*, p. 227.
[4] Mommsen, *Hist. R.*, IV. 644; Blass, *Griech. Bereds.*, pp. 122 *sqq.*
[5] *Brut.*, lxxxiv. 289.

Chapter V

CAESAR AND HISTORY

C. Julius Caesar – His early career – The fifteen years before his consulship – The dawning sense of greatness – His Gallic command and what came of it – Caesar's murder, and his work as the bridge to the Augustan age – Lost literary works – Extant works; *De Bello Gallico*, its aim and style – Vigour and dignity – Are the enlivening touches too scarce – *De Bello Ciuili* – Caesar's continuators, *De Bello Gallico, VIII* and *Bellum Alexandrinum* – *Bellum Africum* – *Bellum Hispaniense*.
C. Sallustius Crispus – *Catiline, Jugurtha* and other works – Sallust made Roman history more scientific and more literary – Sources and models – Plagiarism and originality – Influence.
Cornelius Nepos – Works – Faults and merits – His Latin.
Caesar and the Mime – The plays of D. Laberius – Publilius Syrus.

FRAUGHT with illimitable issues, the life of C. Julius Caesar[1] (102–44 B.C.) affected men more than letters. Its details belong rather to political history. It is not as with Cicero's life, where every event coloured his writings. Yet no one can pretend to isolate Caesar the writer from Caesar the greatest Roman of them all. Few phenomena so absolutely defy explanation as a supreme 'maker of history' who exercises lasting influence on his country and the world.

[1] Text of 'Corpus Caesarianum': F. Kraner (Dittenberger), *Bell. Gall.*, ed. 15, 1890; F. Kraner (Hofman), *Bell. Ciuile*, ed. 10, 1890; H. Meusel, *Caesaris Bell. Gall.*, i–vii, *Hirti liber*, viii, 1894. [This last and B. Kübler's ed. (Teubner, 1894–97, including in vol. iii, pt. i, *Bell. Alex.* and *Bell. Afric.*, pt. ii, *Bell. Hisp.* and *Fragmenta*) mark a reaction from the ground-principle of Nipperdey's text, that the longer MSS. are the more interpolated.] R. du Pontet, i, *Bell. Gall. libri vii cum Hirti supplemento*, ii., *Libri iii de Bell. Ciuili cum libris incertorum auctorum De Bell. Alex., Afric., Hisp.*, 1900; E. Wölfflin and A. Miodoński, *C. Asini Polionis De Bell. Afric. Comment.*, 1889. Life and work: J. A. Froude, *Caesar: A Sketch*, 1876; W. Warde Fowler, *Julius Caesar and the Foundation of the Rom. Imp. System*, 1892; T. Rice Holmes, *Caesar's Conquest of Gaul*, ed. 2, 1911; Petsch, *Die historische Glaubwürdigkeit der Commentarien Cäsars vom gallischen Kriege nach gegenwärtige Stande der Kritik*, i, 1885; ii, 1886. Ancient authorities for his life are partly contemporary: his own writings, the account of his wars by his continuators, Cicero's speeches and correspondence, the Julian laws in the *Corpus Iuris Ciuilis*, Sallust's *Catiline*, a lampoon by Catullus, and the *periochae* to some of the lost books of Livy (ciii *sqq.*). Asinius Pollio, who was present at the Rubicon, as Suetonius and Plutarch record, passed on much information in his history of the Civil War. The main secondary authorities are Plutarch, Suetonius, and Appian, separated from Caesar's time by a century and a half, and Dion Cassius, about half a century later still.

Innumerable questions circle round such a Herculean child of his age
as Caesar. How is his life-work to be interpreted? What distinguished
him from his less prominent fellows? Are the grounds of success in his
unique personality, or in favouring circumstances, or in both; and, if
in both, in what proportions? Would such another man have proved
equally eminent in a totally different epoch? Did the conditions of his
time tend so inevitably in the very direction of his actions that others
might have filled his place with equal influence on the destiny of Rome?
Is it merely the success of such bold policy as Caesar's that justifies it?
Or would his deeds have been equally great had they failed? The complexity of human affairs baffles nice estimation. The historian can
seldom pretend to exhaust the innumerable factors of a given event,
much less of a life. On many causes he can at best speculate without
dogmatising. No historical or literary chemistry, therefore, can adequately analyse a great leader of men. Yet two elements seem constant —
discernment to read in the signs of the time its ripeness for new principles, and determination to act unhesitatingly on insight. Both characteristics united in Caesar. Complete insight came to him comparatively
late: but perhaps no man ever displayed such promptitude in action.
And if his soldiership was transcendent, his statesmanship was scarcely
inferior, while his power over language, spoken and written, reached the
acme of clearness and force. His career reads like a romance, albeit
there was little romance in himself. His advice that a ' far-fetched word
should be shunned like a rock'[1] is characteristic of the man and his
style. It typifies his preference for unadorned Latin and that absence of
the romantic which is so conspicuous in his writings. Eminently practical, whether he gave himself to mighty problems like tangled diplomacy and the plan of a campaign, or turned to niceties of grammar
and the details of the calendar, he was in many ways the most Roman
of Romans. Caesar bequeathed from his short undisturbed period of
absolutism a goodly number of laws and precedents which prove his
desire to serve social and imperial interests of far wider import than
those of the old, narrow city-state. He was the inaugurator of a better
system of government, and in a real sense the founder of the Roman
Empire.

Ancient writers place his murder in his 56th year.[2] This implies his
birth in 100 B.C. But Mommsen's contention in favour of 102 is now
generally accepted, because, if Caesar had been born in 100, he would
have held his offices two years under the legal age, and we should have
expected mention of the departure from usage. He came of a Roman
family of some distinction in public life, and of much greater distinction
in its traditions. As young Caesar declared in his laudation at his aunt
Julia's funeral, the family claimed to be of both royal and divine

[1] Quoted Gell., *N.A.*, I. x. 4, from Caesar's *De Analogia I.*
[2] Plut., *Caes.*, lxix; Suet., *Iul.*, lxxxviii; Appian, *Bell. C.*, II. xxi. 149.

descent.[1] This claim has a permanent value for literature. It was to be the inspiration of the *Aeneid*. Caesar virtually inherited democratic associations. His aunt had married Marius. That rugged old general selected his nephew by marriage, before he was sixteen, for a priesthood of Jupiter—much as boy bishops were made in medieval times. Julius was not twenty when he married Cornelia, the daughter of the Marian consul, Cinna. During Sulla's ascendancy, the young husband's characteristic refusal to put his wife away at the dictator's bidding led to a price being set on his head. Only bribery of Sulla's detectives and influential intercessions saved him. Sulla reluctantly forewent his designs against a youth in whom, according to a tale which deserves to be true, he saw 'many Mariuses.'[2] Similar contumacy marked Caesar's parade of the proscribed Marian images in his aunt's *cortège* at a later date. Meanwhile, the East was safer for him than Rome. His valour won the 'civic wreath' at the siege of Mytilene. His rumoured vices at the court of Bithynia were, save for the mouth of political enemies, unmentionable.[3] From campaigning in Cilicia, he returned to Rome, on Sulla's death. It was easier now to attack Sullan grandees, and to make a *début* in political self-advertisement. Caesar's impeachments of Dolabella, ex-governor of Macedonia in 77, and of Antonius Hybrida the year after, though, of course, unsuccessful in moving senatorial juries, afforded opportunities of attesting his popular leanings and of practising oratory. But he coveted higher place as a speaker. So he paid another visit to the East, to study rhetoric, as Cicero did, at Rhodes under Apollonius Molo. Of his journey the incident of his capture by pirates is related. The young Roman gentleman proved an entertaining captive for thirty-eight days till his ransom was forthcoming. He behaved, Plutarch says, more like a prince than a prisoner.[4] He wrote verses and speeches which, one may fancy, amused the buccaneers less than his joke that he would one day crucify them. They did not know their man. No sooner was he free than he raised a force, surprised the corsairs, recovered the ransom, and kept his promise to them of crucifixion— with the indulgence of cutting their throats first in consideration of their merry weeks together. Before his return to Rome the outbreak of the third Mithradatic war let him see more service, and his energetic levy of troops led to a repulse of Mithradates's general.

The fifteen years after his home-coming in 74 form a period during which Caesar made gradual, and sometimes stumbling, progress towards the greatness of his final fifteen years. It might have been guessed that he would make his mark; but in what sphere? In the world of fashion? Among speakers? Among writers? or through political

[1] Suet., *Iul.*, vi.
[2] Suet., *Iul.*, i; Plut., *Caes.*, i.
[3] Suet., *Iul.*, xlix.
[4] Plut., *Caes.*, ii., ὥσπερ οὐ φρουρούμενος ἀλλὰ δορυφορούμενος ὑπ' αὐτῶν. Cf. Suet., *Iul.*, lxxiv.

agitation? or in civic office? 'All rising to great place is by a winding stair.' The Baconian aphorism is eminently true of this tall, thin, pale-faced, courteous dandy, with keen dark eyes, the intellectual stamped on his refined features, the sensuous on his full lips, scrupulously par-ticular over his toilette and the fringes of his toga.[1] Many windings of the stair were yet before this gallant so dangerous to the peace of Roman households,[2] this abettor of turbulence on assembly days, this heavily encumbered debtor, this friend of anarchists. He was quaestor in Spain in 68; he supported the democratic bills of 67 and 66 conferring un-exampled powers on Pompey; he used his aedileship of 65 partly at his colleague's cost, partly at well-nigh ruinous cost for himself, to capture popularity by sensational displays of gladiatorial games and impressive public works; he was suspected of complicity in Catiline's schemes; and in the year of Cicero's consulate he secured the position of Pontifex Maximus to the chagrin of the optimates. Till now, no one, not even Caesar himself, had divined his strength. Cicero had inklings of what lay under an exterior so free and debonair, but he felt bound to dismiss suspicions of deep designs as incompatible with such manifest foppish-ness.[3]

Caesar has been portrayed by enthusiasts as if from early years he was conscious of an intuition summoning him to the rule and ameliora-tion of his country, as if his life-long aim had been the political, military, and moral regeneration of his deeply decayed fatherland. Mommsen's suggestion of regal stirrings within Caesar's youthful breast is an ima-gination founded on the close of his career. To picture Caesar with altruistic yearnings towards humanity is to credit him with a miraculous foresight of what actually resulted from his achievement. That he was eventually an uncrowned king and saviour of the state is no proof that at first he intended or hoped to be either. In fact, circumstances greatly shaped his aim. Doubtless he had always harboured ambitions. It was well that he did. The ambitions only needed direction to become serviceable. In Spain, when quaestor, he had sighed before an image of Alexander the Great to think that he had as yet done nothing memor-able, though he had reached the age at which Alexander had subdued the world.[4] It was not long before he grasped the part which force could

---

[1] Suet., *Iul.*, xlv: 'Fuisse traditur excelsa statura, colore candido, tere-tibus membris, ore paulo pleniore, nigris uegetisque oculis. . . . Circa corporis curam morosior. . . . Etiam cultu notabilem ferunt; usum enim lato clauo ad manus fimbriato.'

[2] In the elder Curio's estimation he was 'omnium mulierum uir et omnium uirorum mulier' (Suet., *Iul.*, lii). The man who insisted that Caesar's wife should be 'above suspicion' (Suet., *Iul.*, lxxiv), and who was, when dictator, to uphold morality by penal code, himself had *liaisons* with many married ladies in Rome and with princesses abroad (Suet., *Iul.*, l–lii). The free jests of the soldiers at his Gallic triumph, and Catullus's lampoon, which he treated with silent con-tempt, imply this and more.

[3] Plut., *Caes.*, iv.

[4] Suet., *Iul.*, vii.

play in a tottering commonwealth. So far he saw his best chances in a *coup d'état*. That would infallibly relieve his debts. In the revolutionary schemes of Catiline, which at one time he almost certainly favoured, he had been content with a place less than the highest. But about his fortieth year, during the Lusitanian campaign of his Spanish propraetorship, there must have first dawned on him the consciousness of ability as a general. No warrior of first rank, save Cromwell, realised his strength so late in life. Alexander the Great, Hannibal, Bonaparte, were soldiers from boyhood. Now it was that Caesar inferred what the command of an army might mean for him. Catiline's method had failed. Pompey had failed, too, because he habitually let 'I dare not wait upon I would,' and because he blundered irretrievably in disbanding his veterans. It remained to try what could be done with the mightier will-power of which Caesar was clearly conscious. This determined his line. The covenant of 60 was made. Pompey was to have his claims satisfied and Caesar a consulship, which must be followed by a military command so extended in time as to rival Pompey's long-term mandates. Pompey and Crassus could not read him. When they entered into their bargain, none but Caesar himself could have dreamt of eclipsing the greatest general and the wealthiest capitalist of the day.

The measures of 59 B.C., flagrant in their defiance of colleague, senate, and auspices, do not here concern us. This was the consulate of 'Julius and Caesar.' In one way it marked a democratic advance towards journalism; for Caesar arranged that whitewashed walls should be inscribed with a summary of the leading news, and that the proceedings in the senate should be more regularly recorded. When the senate added Transalpine Gaul for five years to Caesar's provincial jurisdiction over Cisalpine Gaul and Illyricum, it gave him the chance of a lifetime. Plutarch sagely regards the Gallic command as opening a new career for Caesar.[1] His main purposes were to establish his reputation and to train an army of devoted legionaries; his secondary purposes were to Romanise Gaul and afford fresh outlets for Roman commerce. For seven of the nine years of conquest and administration we have precise information in his own *Commentaries* on the wars against the Helvetii and Germans (58), the Belgae (57), the coast tribes (56), the peoples on both sides of the Rhine (55); against the Britons in two expeditions (55 and 54); and against the forces of disaffection in Gaul, which led to a widespread but vain effort for freedom (52). In 55, thanks to a new *concordat* made with Pompey and Crassus at Luca in 56, Caesar had secured an extension of his command. But the death of his daughter Julia, Pompey's wife, and the fall of Crassus in battle against the Parthians, accentuated Pompey's jealousy. The senatorial attitude on the question of Caesar's command drove him to carry arms into Italy to enforce his

---

[1] Plut., *Caes.*, xv., ὥσπερ ἄλλην ἀρχὴν λαβόντος αὐτοῦ καὶ καταστάντος εἰς ἑτέραν τινὰ βίου καὶ πραγμάτων καινῶν ὁδόν.

demands of 49. An incredible *débâcle* ensued. Pompey, who had boasted of the armament which a stamp of his foot could call forth, fell back on Brundisium. Caesar carried all before him in the peninsula, displaying towards opponents who surrendered a politic generosity in striking contrast to his remorseless vengeance, which had swept a million of Gauls from the face of the earth.[1] When Pompey crossed to Epirus, Caesar did not at once pursue him, but first quelled the Pompeians in Spain. The spade-work of his entrenchments next year at Durazzo — more astonishing even than that round Alesia, in Gaul — appeared to have gone for naught when Pompey inflicted a serious reverse on him; but this was retrieved in Thessaly, whither Pompey had followed. Pharsalia sealed Pompey's fate. In his wake Caesar made for Egypt, to find his enemy murdered. Caesar's temerity in taking inadequate troops, and his dalliance with Cleopatra, placed him in dangers from which luck more than anything else rescued him. Then campaigns in Syria and Asia Minor claimed his attention; and his victory at Zela was the occasion of that notorious message of brief fustian, 'Veni — Vidi — Vici.'[2] He spent only a few weeks of 47 in Rome before he had to sail for Africa to face Scipio, Cato, and Juba. There the victory of Thapsus in 46 freed him temporarily to use his dictatorship for the good of Rome. But another interruption came in the shape of his last war. This was against Pompey's sons in Spain, and closed with the battle of Munda in 45.

One evening less than a year later, at a supper-party, Caesar had documents to sign, while the other guests talked. The conversation turned on the death most to be desired. Instantly, before any opinion could be expressed, Caesar looked up from his papers with the answer: 'The unexpected.'[3] Next day in the senate he suddenly found himself confronted by a ring of sixty murderous poniards. For some time he had dispensed with guards, and defence was impossible. Wrapping his toga round his head, and gathering its lower folds that he might fall decently, he sank at the base of Pompey's statue. Most of his assassins were pardoned enemies whom he had befriended. Many had taken part in showering on him those honours and adulations, the bare recital of which makes Appian and Dion Cassius tedious reading. There were signs that Caesar had been wearying of his task. His health had weakened. He had been heard to say that he had lived long enough. Yet death found him full of schemes.[4] In five years during which he had

---

[1] That is the estimate of Plut., *Caes.*, xv. Like all devotees of ambition, Caesar was prepared to use men as unconsidered pawns in his game. He was not bloodthirsty, but he would not hesitate to shed blood if he deemed it policy. No doubt he valued Roman lives as intrinsically higher than Gallic. The good impression he produced is evident from Cic., *Ad Att.* VIII. ix. 3; VIII. xiii. Later in 46, Cicero says (*Ad Fam.*, VI. vi. 8): 'In Caesare haec sunt: mitis clemensque natura,' etc.

[2] Plut., *Caes.*, l. [3] Plut., *Caes.*, lxiii; Suet., *Iul.*, lxxxvii.

[4] Suet., *Iul.*, xliv.

been master of Rome, seven campaigns had allowed him to reside about
fifteen months in the capital. But his work went far to make a new Rome.
His remedy for a rotten state was despotism resting on a trained
soldiery. He was an autocrat at once democratic and imperialist. So
his constitutional reforms embodied the essential ideas of Roman
democracy—alleviation of debtors' burdens, trans-marine colonisation
to Carthage and Corinth, liberation of the executive from the senate.
Through his nomination to commands, imperial administration passed
under his control. In finance, land-tenure, morals, and the calendar, he
effected improvements of high social value. Law he served by ordaining
a digest; learning, by inaugurating public libraries and by honouring
with the freedom of the city[1] professors and physicians. It is admitted
that in his mode of procedure, his recommendations to magistracies, his
increase of the number of senators, he was arbitrary. Even democratic
projects were carried in an undemocratic way. It is a plausible criticism
that Caesarism involved the degradation of ancient civic ideals and the
throttling of aspirations after self-government. But Caesar's was the only
course for his time. Dante's placing of Brutus and Cassius beside Judas
is profounder historical criticism than Shakespeare's idealisation. The
folly of his murder is proved by events. An interval of bloodshed ended
in the inevitable establishment of empire. On Caesar's work, and largely
on his lines, his grandnephew built the social fabric which not only
made the Augustan literature possible, but furnished it with vital
inspiration.

Much of his contribution to literature is lost. His orations, praised
by Cicero and Quintilian in words which outweigh the sneer in the
Dialogus de Oratoribus,[2] are now best represented by Sallust's report of
his speech in the Catilinarian debate. His collected despatches and
letters—some of them written in a surprisingly simple cipher[3]—no
longer exist. Nor have we his treatise upholding *Analogy* in Grammar,
written on a journey across the Alps and dedicated to Cicero; his astronomical inquiry *De Astris*; or the *Apophthegmata*, otherwise *Dicta
Collectanea*, a store of witticisms which may have made him a kind of
Sheridan in his day. The two books of the *Anticatones*[4]—a counterblast
to Cicero's eulogy of Cato—would, if they survived, only lessen his

---

[1] Suet., *Iul.*, xliv.
[2] In Tac., *Dial.*, xxi, the champion of the new imperial oratory is made to
estimate Caesar's eloquence as comparatively ineffectual for such a genius
('ut . . . minus in eloquentia effecerit quam diuinum eius ingenium postulabat'),
and he implies that Caesar degenerated into dullness and languor ('eiusdem
lentitudinis ac teporis'). But Tac., *Ann.*, XIII. iii, calls him 'summis oratoribus
aemulus.' *Cf.* Cic., *Brut.*, lxxii. 252; Quint., *Inst. Or.*, X. i. 114.
[3] Suet., *Iul.*, lvi., gives the key. To read the cipher, for each letter one must
substitute the third letter following – 'id est, D pro A et perinde reliquas com-
mutet.'
[4] A. Dyroff, *Rh. Mus.*, vol. 50, pt. 3, 1895, argues that only one of the books
was by Caesar, the other by Hirtius; but this is not the usual view.

reputation for magnanimity. Of his poetry, the one thing left is the well-known criticism on Terence. His juvenile *Praises of Hercules*, his tragedy of *Oedipus*, his lines written in captivity for his piratic hosts, the *Iter* which he wrote when bound for Spain in 46, and the love-poems which the younger Pliny mentions, have all perished.

His extant works are the seven books of commentaries *De Bello Gallico* and the three books *De Bello Ciuili*. The books on his Gallic campaigns from 58 to 52 were published in 51. They were composed probably in the preceding winter, and based partly on notes and despatches, but also on memory—for there are slips.[1] The purpose was primarily to defend his administration. The *Commentaries* are at once a public record and a personal justification. The style is the exact reflection of Caesar's character and practical aim. The spirit is as the antipodes to Cicero's egoism. In tone impersonal—or shall we say third-personal?[2]— he delivers an unvarnished tale of labour momentous for the civilisa- tion of Western Europe. The studied repression comports well with the author's greatness. But the bare style harbours a skilful design. Appar- ently artless explanations and scarcely discoverable suppressions of fact make Caesar's plain story tell uniformly in his own favour. Passionless and restrained, his writing seems above self-interest and party. But in effect Caesar is answering beforehand possible attacks by political opponents. There is nothing to betray the fact that in the senate there were members, like Cato, who thought Caesar ought to be handed over to the barbarians as a perfidious violator of truce.[3] The work, then, without being apologetic in tone, is Caesar's *Apologia*. Midway between notebook and finished history, his memoirs have no superior as military narratives. They won Cicero's praise for a naked and straightforward grace comparable to that of undraped statuary. Commending Caesar's directness, Cicero flings out a passing quip at those 'silly writers who will needs be frizzling up his exploits with the curling-tongs!'[4] Wise men, he argues, would see that by marshalling the material with such clearness, Caesar had left them no chance of traversing the same his- torical ground.[5]

---

[1] Suet., *Iul.*, lvi., quotes Pollio as to his mistakes. 'Pollio Asinius parum diligenter parumque integra ueritate compositos putat, cum Caesar pleraque et quae per alios erant gesta temere crediderit et quae per se uel consulto uel etiam memoria lapsus perperam ediderit.' Hirtius, *B.G.*, viii, *praef.*, alludes to the rapidity of Caesar's composition.

[2] One might borrow Shakesapeare's words as a motto for his grammar: 'Always I am Caesar.' Only in two or three passages does he lapse into the first person.   [3] Suet., *Iul.*, xxiv; Plut., *Caes.*, xxii.

[4] Cic., *Brut.*, lxxv. 262, 'nudi enim sunt, recti et uenusti, omni ornatu orationis tamquam ueste detracta: sed dum uoluit alios habere parata unde sumerent qui uellent scribere historiam, ineptis gratum fortasse fecit qui uolent illa calamistris inurere. Sanos quidem homines a scribendo deterruit: nihil enim est in historia pura et illustri breuitate dulcius.' For notices in other Latin writers see E. G. Sihler, 'The Tradition of Caesar's Gallic Wars from Cicero to Orosius,' *Trans. Amer. Philol. Assoc.*, 1887.

[5] *Cf.* Hirt., *B.G.*, viii, *praef.*, 'adeoque probantur omnium iudicio ut praerepta, non praebita, facultas scriptoribus uideatur.'

A portion of the mighty commander's vigour animates his words. This is especially observable in the struggle with the Nervii; the marine operations against the Veneti; the landing in Britain; the squabble at the council of war over the treacherous Gallic advice that Sabinus should withdraw his troops to Labienus's camp or to Quintus Cicero's; the gallant behaviour of Cotta during the ill-judged and ill-fated march which followed; Caesar's rescue of Cicero and the incident of the urgent letter of exhortation in Greek script tied to a javelin which stuck to a camp-tower for two days without being noticed; the description of military works, entanglements, and manœuvres round Alesia. All is clearness itself. He can verge on the thrilling too, if he has to describe the imminent danger of Sabinus or the hairbreadth escape of Cicero when the fort at Aduatuca was imperilled by a swoop of German marauders.[1] This last most dangerous episode closes with the brief repression so characteristic of the whole — *quem timorem Caesaris aduentus sustulit*. It matches the tempered rebuke administered to Quintus Cicero in the next chapter. This restraint reflects the majestic calm of Caesar, as the clearness reflects his practical qualities. Caesar's own dignity and the dignity of Rome — the juxtaposition, like the order of the words, is his own[2] — are consulted throughout. The assumption of superiority to the natives appears as clearly as anywhere in the calm irony with which he registers their well-understood duplicities and subterfuges, their half-expected perfidies, their subsequent apologies valued at the true worth. He makes one feel that the peoples dealt with are in the clutches of a strong man. They are puppets. He knows how the drama must go. There is no need for excited scoldings. He can wait — and meanwhile the grim chronicle proceeds. The *Pax Romana* is established by strenuous and unrelenting measures. The impression is that of an irresistible force of nature. National aspirations in Gaul are trampled down. Vercingetorix for his patriotism gets no more chivalrous treatment from Caesar than Wallace did from the English. Tribes are nothing, weighed in the scale against Rome. Even their distinctive customs call only for a few broad strokes of description.[3] Caesar had little time for anthropology. His task was civilisation, and its common price is blood and tears.

Amid so much that is business-like and cold, one welcomes occasional human touches. It is something to have signal bravery honoured, like Cotta's or Baculus's;[4] or in the *Civil War*, that of the centurion Scaeva, whose shield had 120 holes.[5] Or, again, there may be a passing but

[1] *B.G.*, VI. xxxvi–xli.
[2] *E.g.*, *B.G.*, IV. xvii, to cross the Rhine in boats (*i.e.* without building a bridge) he considered not quite safe, and not quite consistent with his own or the national dignity — 'neque suae neque P.R. dignitatis esse statuebat.'
[3] The chief exception is the digression, *B.G.*, VI. xi–xxviii, on Gallic and German customs, including the interesting account of Druidism. Rather short measure is given on the Britons; but information was admittedly hard to obtain.
[4] *B.G.*, V. xxxiii and xxxvi; VI. xxxviii.
[5] *B.C.*, III. liii.

THE LITERATURE OF THE GOLDEN AGE

penetrating note on Gallic impulsiveness,[1] or an allusion to Caesar's belief in fortune.[2] Yet this manner of writing, where the clear extrudes the picturesque and where fact reigns supreme in chilly elegance, seldom rises into great literature. Honestly one must confess to weariness, if one reads the *Commentaries* in the mass. Admirable as is their Latinity, admirably as they serve their purpose, they provoke what is doubtless, in the circumstances, an illegitimate yearning after something more imaginative. And if that might imply the use of the 'curling-tongs' derided by Cicero, then one cannot help wishing that Caesar's purpose had permitted him to indulge in more generalisation and reflection. It is the penalty of his self-denying sobriety of style that he does not enchain us as Livy and Tacitus can.

The *Civil War* has gaps and was never completed.[3] Book I describes the opening phases of the contest; Book II continues the operations by sea and land against Massilia resulting in its surrender; and Book III traces the Caesarian and Pompeian strategy which culminated in Pharsalus. The author's impassive restraint becomes more than ever remarkable in relating his quarrel with the senate. The great struggle of his life begins with no record of a dramatic crossing of the Rubicon. He recalls no heart-searchings or omens. There is no '*Iacta alea est.*' Other authors supply all this.[4] And yet Plutarch's tale of Caesar's long pause for silent thought and for debate with his officers comes presumably from Asinius Pollio's recollections as an eyewitness. It is likely enough to be true; but its omission is typical of Caesar. He makes repeated reference to his grievances and the intrigues of his enemies. The method, however, is that of statement without comment. His grim humour is admirably effective in his matter-of-fact mention of the Pompeian general who styled himself *imperator* 'for sundry disasters experienced,'[5] or in his recital of the bickering of the nobles over their chances of succession to his own pontificate. Our sympathies are enlisted by the quiet register of Caesar's frequent overtures for peace, and of that cruelty, treachery, insolence, and greedy haggling among the Pom-

---

[1] *B.G.*, III. viii. 3; x. 3.
[2] The sceptical pontiff's belief was, I think, more superstitious than Warde Fowler concedes in *C.R.*, xvii, 153 *sqq.* It went beyond a vague conception of chance, and beyond reliance on his own good luck – the glorified self-confidence of the story recorded by Plutarch, Suetonius, Valerius Maximus and Appian about his encouraging the boatman in a storm, 'Fear nothing: you carry Caesar and his fortunes.' Passages in *B.G.*, VI. xxx and xxxv, *B.C.*, III. lxviii ('Fortuna quae plurimum potest cum in reliquis rebus tum praecipue in bello'), and especially III. lxxiii, prove that Caesar quotes 'Fortuna,' both in his historical comments and in his addresses to his soldiers, as a controlling principle in human affairs – a power to be reckoned with, who could upset plans and whose caprices must be remedied by industry.
[3] It is certainly Caesar's. Vossius made an unanswerable defence of the authorship on the ground of Suetonius's statement – backed by the argument from style.
[4] Luc., *Phars.*, I. 183–230; Suet., *Iul.*, xxxi–xxxiii; Plut., *Caes.*, xxxii.
[5] *B.C.*, III. xxxi.

peians which made their friend Cicero shudder to think of their possible
victory.[1] When, with undiminished gravity, he relates how his crowning
victory was accompanied by marvels elsewhere — by a statue turning in a
temple at Elis, by a sound of trumpets at Antioch, and of drums at
Pergamum[2] — we are much fascinated with the surviving strain of superstition. Very often thin partitions divide scepticism from mysticism.

The authorship of the continuations of Caesar's wars presents considerable difficulty. They were supplements published after his death
by, or under the auspices of, his friends. It is not absolutely impossible
that his officer Hirtius, who died at Mutina in 43, and who is the
author[3] of *De Bello Gallico VIII*, may also be author or editor of the
Bellum Alexandrinum.[4] The title *Alexandrinum* is inapplicable beyond
chapter xxxiii, for the book turns from Egypt to affairs in Spain, Syria,
and Asia. It is conceivable that the notes for the Spanish section
(xlviii–lxiv) were furnished to Hirtius by Pollio, who was governor of
Farther Spain in 45. Landgraf[5] suggests that after Hirtius's death Pollio
recovered and edited his own notes along with Hirtius's incomplete
work, and even touched up Hirtius's conclusion to the *Gallic War*.
But on this hypothesis of composite authorship, to allot minutely to
authors their several shares in the composition is to land eventually in
guesswork.[6] Broadly, the style strikes one as more artificial than
Caesar's; and as compared with *Bellum Gallicum VIII*, whether owing
to different authorship or to greater enthusiasm for the subject, it shows
an advance in vigour. It is a clear narrative, evidently by one experienced in war. The author is an admirer of his general, and will not
have Caesar's wisdom called in question by unthinking critics, who, for
example, dismiss his indulgent treatment of young Ptolemy as quixotic.[7]

[1] *B.C.*, III. lxxxii; Cic., *Ad Fam.*, VII. iii. 2, 'primum in ipso bello
rapaces, deinde in oratione ita crudeles ut ipsam uictoriam horrerem.'
[2] *B.C.*, III. cv.
[3] On the evidence of MSS. and of Suet., *Iul.*, lvi: '*Alexandrini Africique* et
Hispaniensis incertus auctor est; alii Oppium putant, alii Hirtium qui etiam
Gallici Belli nouissimum imperfectumque librum suppleuerit.' Nipperdey
ascribed *B. Alex.* to Hirtius on linguistic grounds (*e.g.*, absence of *licet, quamuis,
antequam, subito* from *B.G. VIII.* and *B. Alex.*). But Nipperdey felt bound to
prefer *a nostris* to *a nobis* in iii. 1 and xix. 6, so as to square the book with
Hirtius's express statement (*B.G. VIII., praef.* 8) that he took no part in
the Alexandrine and African wars. R. Schneider, ed. *B. Alex.*, 1888, *Einleit.*,
quotes evidence collected by E. Fischer (Progr. Passau, 1880) and F. Fröhlich
(Festschrt., Zürich, 1887), to prove linguistic differences. Common words like
subsidium, incolumis, praeterea, which occur 8, 5, and 7 times respectively in *B.
Alex.*, are never used in *B.G. VIII.*
[4] J. S. Reid, in a note on Introductory Epistle to Eighth Book of
Caesar's *Gallic War*, *Class. Phil.*, iii, No. 4, 1908, p. 442, says, 'I agree with
what seems now to be the general opinion, that *Bell. Gall. VIII.* is all that we
have from the hand of Hirtius.'
[5] G. Landgraf, *Untersuchungen zu Caesar u. seinen Fortsetzern*, 1888.
[6] Landgraf's grounds for distinguishing Caesarian, Hirtian, and Pollion-
ian parts are not convincing. J. Zingerle, *Zur Frage nach d. Autorschaft d. Bell.
Alex.*, u.s.w. (see *Wien. Stud.*, xiv.), seeks to trace Caesar's genuine work up to
chap. xxi.   [7] *B. Alex.*, xxiv, 7.

The *Bellum Africum* is the supplement on Caesar's conflict with Scipio, Cato, and King Juba. Its contrasts in expression and usage to *Bellum Gallicum VIII* and to the *Bellum Alexandrinum* are such that statistics prove the different authorship.[1] Every reader must agree that at least the original draft was by a participator in the African War. It smacks of a diary-style which rules Hirtius out of the question.[2] Wölfflin argues from effective turns, from the speeches introduced,[3] and from what he regards as acquaintance with sound Latin, that the author was well trained in the arts of style. Like Landgraf he declares for Pollio. But he overrates the style. Cleared of a crowd of interpolations, it deserves a higher place than Nipperdey allowed, and yet its faults of ignorant and hasty composition somewhat discount Justus Lipsius's claim for it—*ad comicum morem pura dictio*.[4] Irrespective of style, other considerations conflict with the ascription to Pollio. There is much likelihood that the composer was a member of the fifth legion, with which Pollio stood in no connexion; and there is little likelihood that Pollio was a spectator of all the actions of the African War, which the composer describes.[5]

For the *Bellum Hispaniense*, on the overthrow of Pompey's sons, there is no claimant. Its Latin is too bad to suggest any author but an inferior subaltern.[6] Even more than by solecisms and vulgarisms, the writer's lack of literary training is betrayed by ill-timed grandiloquence. Such are his grotesque comparison of a combat to that recorded between Memnon and Achilles, and his bombastic quotations from Ennius, *nostri cessere parumper* and *pes pede premitur, armis teruntur arma*.[7]

In the year that saw Athens taken and Sulla victorious in the East,

[1] This amount is proved by E. Wölfflin (*Sitzungsberichte d. k. b. Akad. d. Wissenschaften zu München*, 1889, pp. 323 *sqq.*, and in pref. to his ed. with Miodoński of *C. Asini Polionis De Bell. Afric. Comm.*, 1889, p. xxxii). *E.g.*, *B. Afr.* has *grandis, subito, conuulnero*, where *B. Gall. VIII.* and *B. Alex.* use *magnus, repente, uulnero*, etc. What is not convincing is Wölfflin's acceptance of Landgraf's identification of the author with Pollio (or 'Polio') on the alleged ground of the educated style of *B. Afr.*, and on the shaky foundation of coincidences in extant letters by Pollio.

[2] Hirtius, it has been pointed out, *B.G. VIII, praef.*, says he did not take part in the Alexandrine or in the African war. Wölfflin is entitled to insist that the writer of the *B. Afr.* took part in it: 'cum scriptorem rebus interfuisse quaeuis pagina doceat,' *Praef.* to ed. of *B. Afr.*, p. xxxii.

[3] *B. Afr.*, xxii, xxxv, xliv, xlv, liv.

[4] Cited in Wölfflin's ed., pref., p. xxxi. Its familiar style is seen in usages like 'quantum pote,' which is common to Afranius and Cicero (*Ad Att.*, IV. xiii. 1, 'rescribas ad me quantum pote'; *cf.* Catullus, xlv. 5).

[5] These are the conclusions of T. Widmann, *Über d. Verfasser d. B. Afr. u. die Polliohypothese Landgrafs*, in *Philol.*, l, 1891, p. 565.

[6] Prof. J. S. Reid, *Class. Philol.*, iii, No. 4, 1908, p. 442 (note) says, 'The *Bellum Hispaniense* seems to be a rough soldier's report, prepared as material for a literary man. For a similar purpose, L. Verus demanded *commentarios* from provincial commanders (Fronto, p. 131, Nab.).'

[7] *B. Hisp.*, xxv, xxiii, xxxi. In the latter quotation he alters the metrical order.

C. Sallustius Crispus[1] (86–35 B.C.) was born at Amiternum.[2] Unless political opponents maligned him unconscionably, Sallust speedily outgrew the primitive virtues of his native Sabine uplands. In Rome he joined the democrats. Belonging to a plebeian family, he became tribune in 52. He was instrumental in exciting odium against Milo after his fatal affray with Clodius, less because he thought Milo guilty than because he remembered a horse-whipping endured for an intrigue with Milo's wife.[3] Possibly all the evil told of him is not gospel-truth. Certainly, Lenaeus, Pompey's freedman, repaid in kind Sallust's description of his master as *oris probi, animo inuerecundo*, by maligning his character and his style.[4] So what political rancour may have exaggerated, but did not entirely invent, lived on through the forgery called Cicero's *Invective against Sallust*, to be the verdict of posterity.[5] Yet, if less black than he was painted, he was bad enough to be removed from the senatorial roll in 50; and his disquisitions on morality serve but to draw the thin veil of a censorious pose over a discreditable past. His adhesion to Caesar in the Civil War brought a quaestorship which reopened the senate to him, and a command in Illyricum. Service in Africa ended in his being left as proconsul of the province newly made out of the Numidian kingdom, which was to enter so prominently into his *Jugurtha*. His subsequent splendour of living and the noble pleasure-grounds at Rome which kept the memory of Sallust green for centuries, tend to confirm rather than merely explain allegations of extortionate misgovernment. His contemptuous words on covetousness[6] tally perhaps as little with his treatment of a province as his moral platitudes do with his early life. Age had reformed the rake, and ill-gotten gear satisfied his greed; but sermonising nauseates even if it does imply a farewell to debauchery and peculation. After 44 B.C. he had nine years of leisured private life. Frankly disliking the favourite Roman pursuits of agricul-

---

[1] Text: E. W. Fabri, ed. 2, 1845; R. Dietsch, 1843–46, (w. Germ. notes) 1864; H. Jordan, ed. 2, 1876, ed. 3, 1887; R. Jacobs (ed. 10, H. Wirz), *Cat. et Iug., ex Hist. . . . Orationes et Epistulae*, 1894; F. Kritz., *Cat. Iug. Fragm.*, 1828–53; W. W. Capes, *Cat.* and *Iug.*, 1884; A. M. Cook, *Cat.*, 1888; B. Maurenbrecher, *Hist. reliq.*, 1891–93. On Sallust as historian: C. John, *Die Entstehungsgesch. d. Cat. Verschworung*, u.s.w., 1876; Bellezza, *Dei fonti e dell' autorità storica di C. Sallustio Crispo*, 1891. Style: L. Constans, *De Sermone Sallustiano*, 1880; I. Uri, *Quatenus ap. Sall. sermonis lat. plebeii aut cotidiani uestigia appareant*, 1885.
[2] Dates and birthplace are known from Jerome.
[3] Gell., *N.A.*, XVII. xviii, 'M. Varro . . . C. Sallustium scriptorem seriae illius et seuerae orationis, in cuius historia notiones censorias fieri atque exerceri uidemus, in adulterio deprehensum ab Annio Milone loris bene caesum dicit.'
[4] Suet., *De Gramm.*, xv.
[5] Macrob., *Sat.*, II. ix., 'Sallustius grauissimus alienae luxuriae obiurgator et censor'; Serv. ad Verg., *Aen.*, vi. 612, 'Sallustius quem Milo deprehensum sub serui habitu uerberauit,' etc.; Lact., *Inst. D.*, II. xii, 'hominem nequam Sallustium'; cf. Asconius cited in schol. ad Hor., *Sat.*, I. ii. 41; Dion. Cass., XL. lxiii.
[6] E.g., *Cat.*, xi. 3, 'Auaritia pecuniae studium habet, quam nemo sapiens concupiuit.'

ture and the chase, he found his chief pleasure in writing history.[1] To this period all his works belong.

The *De Catilinae Coniuratione* or *Bellum Catilinae*—an eminently readable monograph—has some of the effect of a party pamphlet.[2] Minutely to assess the perversion of facts and dates indulged in by Sallust while sketching the years 66 to 63 is a historical problem. By a clever re-writing of events he screens Caesar's fame from too close association with Catiline. At the same time, to depict Catiline as a fire-breathing renegade from the outset, and to antedate his treasonable machinations, had for Sallust the attraction of admitting heightened literary colour. So both hero-worship of Caesar and a gift of rhetoric led to a sacrifice of historical accuracy. But the result is a terse and vigorous book, with unforgettable speeches and character-drawing. The *Bellum Iugurthinum*, on the struggle with Jugurtha from 112 to 106, has, along with considerable maturity, the freshness of a good book for boys. If one excepts its politics and reflections, it contains much that, read in youth, will be remembered for a lifetime—the realistic sense of North-African landscape, the wiliness of the Numidian, the deadly grapple and vicissitudes of battle and siege, and the thrilling description of more than one unscrupulous murder. Sallust assigns two reasons for his choice of this theme—it was a war appalling in its chequered fortunes, and as a constitutional landmark it involved the first check administered to senatorial arrogance.[3] Marius, the democratic general, is the hero; and the worst side of aristocratic corruption is emphasised by examples, repeated like a refrain, of the venality of Rome.[4] The *Historiae* dealt with events for slightly over a decade from Sulla's death, 78 to 67. The work was a continuation of Sisenna's. Its extant parts consist of fragments, four speeches, and two letters.[5] Of pseudo-Sallustian works, the pretended *Invective* of Sallust against Cicero and the pretended reply by Cicero are debating show-pieces (*controuersiae*)

---

[1] *Cat.*, iv. 1, 'Ubi . . . mihi reliquam aetatem a re publica procul habendam decreui, non fuit consilium socordia atqua desidia bonum otium conterere, neque uero agrum colundo aut uenando seruilibus officiis intentum aetatem agere; sed . . . statui res gestas Populi Romani carptim ut quaeque memoria digna uidebantur perscribere.'

[2] Mommsen, *H.R.*, 1877, iv. 184 footnote.

[3] *Iug.*, v. 1, 'primum quia magnum et atrox uariaque fortuna fuit, dehinc quia tunc primum superbiae nobilitatis obuiam itum est.'

[4] *Iug.*, viii, xx, xxviii, xxxv. In xxxv. 10, it rises to dramatic force as Jugurtha leaves Rome: 'postquam Roma egressus est, fertur saepe eo tacitus respiciens postremo dixisse urbem uenalem et mature perituram, si emptorem inuenerit.'

[5] There is a strong democratic speech by Lepidus against the Sullan constitution, an energetic tirade by Philippus rousing the senate against Lepidus, a protest against senatorial privileges by the tribune Licinius Macer, and an oration by the consul Cotta in time of famine. The letters are an angry one by Pompey to the senate, and an anti-Roman one by King Mithradates to King Arsaces. These owe their survival to inclusion in some rhetorical selection made about the second century.

composed by some professor of rhetoric. The two epistles *Ad Caesarem senem de re publica* are filled with imaginary advice patently concocted, in imperial times, out of a knowledge of what Caesar had actually done.

In two ways Sallust marked an advance among Roman historians. He abandoned the annalistic method which culminated in Caesar, and he raised the literary level of history.[1] The abandonment of the annalistic method involved for him an indifference to chronological detail—a vagueness content, for instance, to leave a whole year of the Jugurthine War unaccounted for and to annihilate the times essential for traversing vast distances. The aim at higher literary effect was responsible for occasional flights of rhetoric. But these were inconsiderable drawbacks compared with what was gained. Sallust produced work at once more scientific and more pleasure-giving than any Roman historian before him. History, he realised, must do more than narrate; it must observe tendencies; it must explain. He is a historian with some grasp. He appreciates movements and their mainsprings. He interprets political intrigues. He makes the outlines of democratic policy during two generations stand out plainly. True, he harboured purposes other than scientific. Caesar's underlying purpose in his *Commentaries* had been political self-justification, and his method the ostensibly artless one of simple statement. Sallust's purpose was political justification for others, and his method only apparently more artful in ascription of motives and in digressions for reflection. Even if the motives might not always be correctly divined, nor the reflections be free from pharisaism, still history had become more philosophic. Bias notwithstanding, he had enough of the student's detachment to justify his claim to noteworthy impartiality.[2] He can be fair to both sides. He sees faults in his own party. He sees merits in optimate generals like Calpurnius and Metellus. His reverence for Caesar does not blind him to the qualities of Cato. Though a democrat, he does not fail to approve of Cicero's steps against the Catilinarian plot. Partly a philosophic desire to pierce to the mind behind a deed, partly pure literary instinct, interested Sallust in character. He likes to analyse a personality. So in his pages the events assume meaning and the figures live. Their variety is impressive—Catiline with unfathomable abysses in his soul;[3] Cicero distracted with anxieties for his country; Caesar calmly utilitarian in his humane liberalism; Cato rigorous in his conservative austerity; Jugurtha as cunning and conscienceless as an African prowler on the trail of prey; Metellus with the sententious pride of ancient blood; Marius with the confidence of the self-made man; and Sulla with the insinuating address of a youthful aristocratic officer. His demagogues—Memmius,

[1] For Cicero's views on the inferiority of Roman historical works, see *De Legg.*, ii; *De Orat.*, II. xii. 51; *Brut.*, lxiv. 228.

[2] *Cat.*, iv. 2, 'mihi a spe, metu, partibus rei publicae animus liber erat.'

[3] *Cat.*, v. 5: 'Vastus animus inmoderata, incredibilia, nimis alta semper cupiebat.'

Marius, Lepidus, Macer, Catiline —get each a different aspect of policy to uphold. Foreign princes, too, display distinct individuality. The humility of Adherbal, so flattering to Roman influence in Numidia, has a counterfoil in the uncompromising Orientalism which animates Mithradates's letter.[1] A similar psychological gift is visible in the speeches. They are, as a rule, dramatically adapted to the speaker (by an assumption of thought-reading), rather than historically accurate.[2] The energy which they share with Sallust's style in general is nowhere more powerfully felt than in denunciations of the nobility. Thus Marius expresses undisguised contempt for those incompetent scions 'of ancient stock, with statues galore but never a campaign,'[3] who, when elected to office, rush to the study of their hitherto neglected Roman histories and Greek manuals on strategy. They begin at the wrong end (*praeposteri homines*): he claims to be more practical:

> With their arrogance, fellow-citizens, compare now me, the self-made man. What they generally hear or read about I have either witnessed or myself performed. What is book-knowledge for them, I have learned on active service. It is for you to consider whether deeds or words are better value. They despise my origin; I, their slackness. The reproach against me is my luck; against them, their infamy. Yet to my thinking all men have one common nature — only, the bravest is the noblest. If the question could now be put to the forefathers of an Albinus or a Bestia whether they would prefer me or them for offspring, what do you suppose the answer would be, but that they wished the best to be their children? Nay, if my opponents are entitled to disdain me, let them do the same to their own ancestors. Their nobility started like mine — in merit. They grudge me my high office: well then, let them grudge me toils, integrity, and my dangers too, since it is through these that I have gained it. . . . To win credit I have no statues, triumphs, or consulships of my ancestors to display: but, should occasion call, I have spears, a standard, decorations, and other military prizes — I have scars too, in front. These are my statues, these my patent of nobility — not left me as a legacy like theirs, but gained by very many toils and risks of my own. My words have no studied elegance. That I value slightly. Merit can display itself unaided. My detractors require artificiality to screen low deeds behind rhetoric. I never studied Greek literature. I had no wish to — it had been of no use to its teachers in the direction of virtue. My skill lies in what is far the most serviceable for my country — to smite a foe, to keep good watch, to fear nothing save discredit, to endure winter and summer alike, to sleep on the ground, to undergo hunger and fatigue together. With such training I shall stimulate my soldiers.[4]

[1] *Hist.*, fragm.
[2] Some are obviously unreal. *Cat.*, xx, does not harmonise with the audience. *Iug.*, lxxxv, though outspoken, is too polished for Marius.
[3] *Iug.*, lxxxv. 10, '. . . hominem ueteris prosapiae ac multarum imaginum et nullius stipendi.'
[4] *Iug.*, lxxxv., 13: 'Conparate nunc Quirites, cum illorum superbia me

Sallust made considerable, though not exhaustive, use of document-
ary sources. For the *Catiline* he depended on his own memory, on hearsay, on impressions formed from reading Cicero, on public archives,
and possibly on a *résumé* of facts supplied by Ateius Philologus.[1] For
earlier events he drew from Sisenna, of whose diligence he speaks
respectfully;[2] from the old annalists, and from memoirs by Scaurus,
Rutilius, and Sulla. Observation and inquiry in Africa must have
furnished geographical and ethnological data for the *Jugurtha*. Sallust
also consulted Carthaginian records said to have belonged to King
Hiempsal's library.[3] Cato was to some extent a source and a model.
Besides affecting his style, Cato may have stimulated Sallust's interest
in the picturesque and in tribal origins. The introductions owe something to Posidonius. But his model *par excellence* was Thucydides,
beside whom it was his ambition to take rank, and with whom Quintilian
in a fit of enthusiasm ventures to match him.[4] Reflections, character-
drawing, and speeches are indebted to Thucydides. But neither the
Jugurtha nor the *Catiline* has the intellectual depth, the marmoreal
impassivity and dramatic impressiveness of the *Peloponnesian War*.
Notably in his philosophy of history Sallust is eclipsed. Thucydides's
rapid view of the early age of Greece is far more incisive than Sallust's
sketch of the development of Rome. Throughout he has an amplitude
and penetration missing in Sallust, who is given to mask vagueness
under effective words. Sallust is not so profound, but he is often more
vivacious.

His inwardness of view and epigrammatic terseness entitle Sallust to

hominem nouom. Quae illi audire aut legere solent, eorum partem uidi, alia
egomet gessi; quae illi litteris ea ego militando didici. Nunc uos existumate
facta an dicta pluris sint. Contemnunt nouitatem meam, ego illorum ignauiam;
mihi fortuna, illis probra obiectantur. Quamquam ego naturam unam et communem omnium existumo, sed fortissumum quemque generosissumum. Ac si
iam ex patribus Albini aut Bestiae quaeri posset, mene an illos ex se gigni
maluerint, quid responsuros creditis, nisi sese liberos quam optumos uoluisse?
Quodsi iure me despiciunt, faciant idem maioribus suis, quibus, uti mihi, ex
uirtute nobilitas coepit. Inuident honori meo: ergo inuideant labori innocentiae
periculis etiam meis, quoniam per haec illum cepi. . . Non possum fidei causa
imagines neque triumphos aut consulatus maiorum meorum ostentare, at, si res
postulet, hastas uexillum phaleras alia militaria dona, praeterea cicatrices
aduorso corpore. Hae sunt meae imagines, haec nobilitas, non hereditate relicta,
ut illa illis, sed quae ego meis plurumis laboribus et periculis quaesiui. Non sunt
composita uerba mea. Parui id facio. Ipsa se uirtus satis ostendit. Illis artificio
opus est ut turpia facta oratione tegant. Neque litteras Graecas didici: parum
placebat eas discere, quippe quae ad uirtutem doctoribus nihil profuerant. At
illa multo optuma rei publicae doctus sum – hostem ferire, praesidium agitare,
nihil metuere nisi turpem famam, hiemem et aestatem iuxta pati, humi requies-
cere, eodem tempore inopiam et laborem tolerare. His ego praeceptis milites
hortabor.'

[1] Suet., *De Gramm.*, x.
[2] *Iug.*, xcv. 2.
[3] *Iug.*, xvii. 7, '. . . uti ex libris Punicis, qui regis Hiempsalis dicebantur,
interpretatum nobis est.'
[4] *Inst. Or.*, X. i. 101: 'Nec opponere Thucydidi Sallustium uerear.'

a high place, if not exactly to that which Martial assigned him—*primus Romana Crispus in historia*. Yet what ancient critics principally detected in him was an archaising affectation with which Pollio said his writings were 'besmeared.'[1] Lenaeus ill-naturedly called him 'a most unscholarly plagiarist of Cato and the ancients.'[2] There is admittedly an old-fashioned ring in words like *prosapia*, in forms like *nequitur*, in scarcely unpleasant mannerisms like *multi mortales*, in a certain monotony of connectives or of sentence-build. Still, some ages have admired him the more for it. What was a fault to Augustan purists was a merit to the circle of Fronto. A modern charge is that he wrote the Latin of a vulgar democrat.[3] And it is true that with his spice of the archaic he has what sometimes coincides therewith—a colloquial turn. He shares old forms with Plautus, Pacuvius, Terence, Cato, Sisenna, and Lucretius; he has bits of the common speech which reappear only in Apuleius and Vitruvius.[4] It is a mistake, however, to consider his compositions, as a whole, either obsolete or common. Sallust maintains an elevation as much removed from obsolescent oddity as from undistinguished vulgarity. Far more significant than his excursions into the colloquial or his piracies from the antique—even if they could be exactly numbered— are the qualities that are his own. Sallust was no more bound to 'play the sedulous ape' to Cato's quaintness than to Cicero's copiousness or Caesar's bareness. So much was he himself that the alleged plagiarist struck some critics more appropriately as an innovator.[5] And it is to be an innovator to attain in Latin prose an unprecedented union of rapidity, brevity, and variety. It is a rapidity which fastens the attention —subserved not merely by brevity and by usages like the historic infinitive, which he did much to popularise, but by the gift of visualising with intense vividness an action or scene.[6] Brief Sallust is not, in the sense of adhering to strict relevance. He has a weakness for introductions and digressions. But he economises in the length of sentences and the number of words. His structure can be short—to jerkiness. His variety is far more than linguistic. It was not merely that he broke

---

[1] Suet., *De Gramm.*, x.: '. . . nimia priscorum uerborum affectatione oblita.'
[2] Suet., *De Gramm.*, xv.: 'Catonis priscorumque uerborum ineruditissimum furem.' Quintilian, *Inst. Or.*, VIII. iii. 29, cites the epigram:

'Et uerba antiqui multum furate Catonis,
    Crispe, Iugurthinae conditor historiae.'

Augustus had expressly noted Sallust's debt to Cato for words 'quae . . . excerpsit ex Originibus,' Suet., *Aug.*, lxxxvi.
[3] E. Wölfflin, *Philol.*, 1874, p. 137.
[4] *E.g.*, the conversational 'pergnarus' and the use of 'priuus' to mean 'without' are common to Sallust and Apuleius: 'portatio' is common to Sallust and Vitruvius. For the other exx. see A. M. Cook, *Cat.*, whose Introd., pp. 29–43, gives a useful summary of Sallust's style.
[5] Gell., *N.A.*, IV. xv. 1, refers to his 'nouandi studium.'
[6] *E.g.*, the murder of Hiempsal, *Iug.*, xii. 5; or the graphic escalade of the fort near the Mulucha, *Iug.*, xcii. 5–xciv, a passage comparable to Livy's description of the Gallic attempt on the Capitol in Book V.

away from the Ciceronian balance of phrase and of grammatical form. He was a free artist, quick to see new values in a juxtaposition of elements drawn from history, rhetoric, psychology, geography, and ethics.

By such qualities Sallust turned historical prose into the path along which it was developed by Livy and Tacitus. While the former criticised Sallust adversely,[1] and was infinitely his superior in harmonious modulation, he owed something to his predecessor's endeavour after artistic refinement. Tacitus was a close student of Sallust's style.[2] Quintilian, though not an indiscriminate, was a sincere admirer, and by praise of his 'immortal swiftness' must have strengthened his vogue. Sallust's fame has had its fluctuations; but it seldom rose higher than in the days of Marcus Aurelius. His influence is traceable in Justin's abridgement of Trogus, and the imitation of him by many historians of the fourth and fifth centuries made a fitting prelude to the esteem which he enjoyed in the Middle Ages.[3]

The Insubrian Gaul, Cornelius Nepos[4] (*circ.* 100–*circ.* 25 B.C.), represents the fresh note of cosmopolitan biography. He was probably a native of Ticinum.[5] At Rome, he belonged to the circle of his fellow-northerner Catullus, of Cicero, and of Atticus. Catullus, in dedicating his poems to him, politely exaggerates the learning in Nepos's compendious history of the world.[6] Cicero writes in 44 of Nepos's distaste for works—doubtless philosophical—on which Cicero plumed himself, and with scarcely intelligible jocularity calls him 'an immortal' ($\overset{\smile}{\alpha}\mu\beta\rho\sigma\tau\sigma$).[7] With Atticus his intimacy dates from Atticus's return to Rome in 65 after his prolonged stay in Athens. It is only in his biography of Atticus that Nepos is an original authority. Written in part during its subject's lifetime, it was completed before Octavian's acceptance of the title of 'Augustus' in 27.[8] Of equestrian fortune and senatorial sym-

---

[1] Livy's hostility to Sallust is illustrated by Seneca, *Contr.*, IX. i. 14.

[2] *E.g.*, a portion of the battle in Tac., *Agric.*, xxxvii, is modelled on *Iug.*, ci. For Tacitus's borrowings see A. Dräger, *Ueber Syntax u. Stil des Tacitus*, ed. 3, 1882, p. 125.

[3] Teuffel, *op. cit.*, § 206, 10.

[4] Text: K. Nipperdey (ed. B. Lupus), Germ. notes, 1895; K. Halm (ed. A. Fleckeisen), 1898; O. Browning and W. R. Inge, Eng. notes, ed. 3, 1888; E. O. Winstedt, 1904.

[5] He was 'Padi accola' (Plin., *N.H.*, III. 127), and a townsman of T. Catius (Plin., *Ep.*, IV. xxviii. 1). Since Catius was Insubrian (Cic., *Ad Fam.* XV. xvi. 1), it is a fair inference that Nepos came from the one Insubrian town on the Po – Ticinum, now Pavia. Before Mommsen (*Herm.*, iii., 1, p. 62), his birthplace was considered Hostilia, now Ostiglia, near Verona. His praenomen is unknown.

[6] Catull., i. 5–7:
'. . . cum ausus es unus Italorum
Omne aeuom tribus explicare chartis,
Doctis, Iuppiter, et laboriosis.'

[7] Cic., *Ad Att.*, XVI. v. 5.

[8] Nep., *Att.*, xix. 1, 'Hactenus Attico uiuo edita a nobis sunt.' In xix. 2, Octavian is still 'imperator.'

pathies, Nepos was a man of letters, not of action. His distrust of philosophising, which piqued Cicero, emerges in his praise of Atticus's preference for the practical rather than the showy in speculation.[1] His observation in a letter to Cicero that none have more need of masters in conduct than some professed masters of philosophic theory, is caustic and Roman.[2] But the attitude brought its penalty. He has no depth, no synthesis, in his historical outlook. In fact, he is at pains to insist that his business is biography, not history.[3]

His lost works consist of a universal history (*Chronica*), a 'Golden Treasury' (*Exempla*) of great things in Roman history, a *Life of Cato*, and a *Life of Cicero*, besides a geographical treatise known to Pliny the elder, and erotic poems mentioned by Pliny the younger. The twenty-five *Lives* which we possess belong to his last work, *De Viris Illustribus*, originally in at least sixteen books.[4] It seems to have treated kings, generals, jurisconsults, orators, poets, historians, philosophers, and scholars, each in two books devoted to foreigners and Romans respectively. The extant *Lives* are those of nineteen Greeks and one Persian (*Datames*); the sketch *On Kings*; *Hamilcar*; *Hannibal*; and from *Latin Historians* the scrappy paragraphs of his shorter *Cato*, followed by the much more interesting *Atticus*. The *Lives* were first printed in 1471, entitled *Aemilii Probi... de Vita... Excellentium Liber*. A dedication[5] to Theodosius and the fact that no MS. ascribes anything but the *Cato* and the *Atticus* to Nepos favoured the supposition that the work *On Generals* was a composition, or at any rate an abridgement, of the fourth century. Nepos's performance, too, seemed unworthy of the high encomia of antiquity. Lambinus, however, in his edition of 1569, was the first to vindicate the authorship by Nepos. Both style and political allusions prove that he was right.

His sources include Thucydides, Theopompus, Xenophon, and the *Agesilaus* now considered to be Xenophon's; for Sicilian history, Timaeus, and for Persian, Dinon. But he does not use them to advantage, or with care. He even mistranslates. Some authorities, like Ephorus, he never acknowledges. Herodotus he unaccountably neglects. For his *Hannibal*, besides Polybius, Sulpicius Blitho, and Atticus, who are mentioned,[6] he drew from the obscure writers Sosilus and Silenus.[7] What use

[1] Nep., *Att.*, xvii. 3, 'ad uitam agendam non ad ostentationem.'
[2] We owe its preservation to Lactantius, *Inst. D.*, III. xv. 'Tantum abest ut ego magistram esse putem uitae philosophiam beataeque uitae perfectricem, ut nullis magis existimem opus esse magistros uiuendi quam plerisque qui in ea disputanda uersantur.'
[3] Nep., *Pelop.*, i. 1. 'Vereor, si res explicare incipiam, ne non uitam eius enarrare sed historiam uidear scribere.'
[4] Charisius (*G.L.*, ed. Keil, i. 141) quotes from the sixteenth book.
[5] Lines 9–10 run:
'Si rogat auctorem, paullatim detege nostrum
Tum domino nomen; me sciat esse Probum.'
[6] Nep., *Hann.*, xiii. 1.
[7] G. Hähnel, *Die Quellen des Corn. Nepos im Leben Hannibals*, Diss., Jena,

he made of Roman chroniclers in general there is little to show. As history, his work is marred by glaring inaccuracies, bad chronology, and a lack of proportion. One Miltiades is confused with another. A Brasidas is omitted, and a Datames gets more than his share. Nepos's enthusiasm, too, is unchastened. It is refreshing in his handsome tribute to Rome's great enemy, Hannibal; and it is intelligible in the case of Alcibiades, who is warmly defended as retaining affection for his country all through his quarrel with his personal opponents. But it is an enthusiasm too all-embracing and too uncritical. Great and small are alike heroes to Nepos. Yet two merits at least are his. They are the counterparts of his negligence and his enthusiasm. He is lively and he is cosmopolitan. His aim was popular biography. We must, then, look for incident, manners, character-drawing, and descriptions of personal appearance, rather than inductive reasoning or investigation of causes. His catholic sympathy with foreign types of manhood is in harmony with the imperial *rôle* which Rome was now playing among the nations. A citizen of the world is already speaking in his dedication to Atticus. Claiming that there is no triviality in noting Greek customs, Nepos enters a caveat against a national bigotry in matters of biography.[1] It is his misfortune that we have not more of the Roman *Lives* to judge him by. The *Atticus* is distinctly good. Not only is it a clear picture of the man, but it makes clear his intellectual interests and his services to literature.[2] It contains Nepos's wise judgement on the historical and social value of the sixteen books of Cicero's *Letters to Atticus*: 'He that reads them will not much require a regular history of those times.'[3] Of the Greek *Lives* the most interesting is the *Alcibiades*. Though the sketch does not fully respond to the inspiration of a subject so brilliant, it still catches glimpses of this dazzling and Machiavellian time-server (*temporibus callidissime seruiens*). Nepos has nothing better in the way of summarising character:

It looks as if in him Nature tried what she could turn out. For there is a consensus among his biographers that for good and for bad, there was nothing to surpass him. Born in a magnificent city, of exalted family, the handsomest man of his day, he was a paragon of versatility, abounding in resource—he acted both as High-admiral and as Generalissimo. Fluency gave him signal power in speech, because look and language were so winning that no one could resist him. Wealthy, hard-working and enduring whenever need demanded,

---

1888. For the imperfect use of Thucydides, Ephorus, and Theopompus, see Lippelt, *Quaest. Biograph.*, Diss., Bonn, 1889. For additional authorities, see Teuffel, § 198, 11.

[1] Nep., *Praef.*, 1–3. Hostile critics, he says, 'ii erunt fere, qui expertes litterarum Graecarum nihil rectum, nisi quod ipsorum moribus conueniat, putabunt.'

[2] Nep., *Att.*, xiv and xviii.

[3] *Ibid.*, xvi. 3, 'Quae qui legat, non multum desideret historiam contextam eorum temporum.'

generous, splendid no less in life than in living, approachable and courteous, he proved a consummate opportunist. But give him a leisure hour with no reason for mental exertion, and he was discovered to be luxurious, profligate, lustful, and intemperate, so that it was a world's wonder that within one human being there could be so much unlikeness — such a conflict of nature.[1]

Nepos's clear and simple sentences are well adapted to his purpose of sketching object-lessons from the past. But they have small literary grace. At times brevity is overdone, and the result is jerkiness and obscurity. His deviations from classic usage are not sufficient to relegate our present form of his works to a later age. Indeed, much in him is best explained as linguistic survival, and as borrowing from the popular language of the day.[2] Such homely Latin would commend itself to the average reader, whom Nepos desired to attract.

The account of the Caesarian age may fittingly close with a notice of the two prominent mime-writers with whom Caesar came into contact — Decimus Laberius (*circ.* 105–43 B.C.)[3] and Publilius 'Syrus.' The mime has been already briefly characterised. An import from Magna Graecia, it once consisted chiefly in extempore mimicry and mockery of personal peculiarities in well-known persons or bystanders. Mimicry it always retained, but as it absorbed much from the other kinds of light drama, its travesties of life and personages became in time more literary and more varied, if no less indecent. By gesticulations, grimaces, imitations of man, beast, or bird, and the roughest buffoonery, it guaranteed laughter. Actresses (*mimae*), scantily but gaudily attired in a mantilla, improved the dancing and singing, and often won an undesirable notoriety. Such was the performance which, according to Valerius Maximus, was too loose to be permitted in Massilia. But at Rome from

---

[1] Nep., *Alcib.*, i. 'In hoc quid natura efficere possit uidetur experta. Constat enim inter omnes qui de eo memoriae prodiderunt nihil illo fuisse excellentius uel in uitiis uel in uirtutibus. Natus in amplissima ciuitate summo genere, omnium aetatis suae multo formosissimus, ad omnes res aptus consiliique plenus (namque imperator fuit summus et mari et terra), disertus ut in primis dicendo ualeret, quod tanta erat commendatio oris atque orationis, ut nemo ei posset resistere, diues, cum tempus posceret laboriosus patiens, liberalis, splendidus non minus in uita quam uictu, affabilis, blandus, temporibus callidissime seruiens: idem, simul ac se remiserat neque causa suberat quare animi laborem perferret, luxuriosus, dissolutus, libidinosus, intemperans reperiebatur, ut omnes admirarentur in uno homine tantam esse dissimilitudinem tamque diuersam naturam.'

[2] Nepos uses the old gerundive in -*iundus*; *fungor* and *potior* with the accusative; colloquialisms common to Plautus and Terence, like the datives *totae* and *alterae*; bits of old Latin like *parserat* for *pepercerat*, *face* for *fac*, *se emergere* for *emergere*, *dispalor*, etc. Among his mannerisms are a loose employment of the present participle – contrary to the usage of Cicero and Caesar – to express cause or concession; the poetic habit of connecting the indicative with *quamuis*; abrupt changes of tense, and awkward ellipses and inversions.

[3] It was in 45 B.C. that Laberius acted in his own mime (see Suet., *Iul.*, xxxix); his own prologue says he was then sixty: he was therefore born in 105. The date of death comes from Hieron., *Euseb. Chr.*, ad ann. Abr. 1974=43 B.C.

the time of Caesar the mime became increasingly popular. Under the
emperors its noisy mimicry competed for favour with the silent gestures
of the *pantomimus*. Here it may be noted that both Laberius and
Publilius were critics of society.[1] Laberius was more. He was a political
critic; and it was the bluff outspokenness of this veteran knight that
brought down upon him Caesar's invitation in 45 B.C. to appear on the
stage in one of his own mimes.[2] The invitation, as Macrobius observed,
was a command, and the intention was to humble the poet in the competition to which the foreigner Publilius had challenged all rivals. From
a part of the prologue we have the protest of Laberius:

> After a life of sixty years unstained,
> I left my house a Roman knight, but must
> Go home a mummer. Certes, this same day
> My life has grown to be a day too long.[3]

But he had the spirit to introduce double-edged lines which turned the
eyes of the audience on Caesar:

> *Porro Quirites! libertatem perdimus,*

and

> *Necesse est multos timeat quem multi timeant.*

Caesar awarded the prize to the alien competitor, but handed to the
Roman the ring which outwardly restored his knighthood. Laberius
accepted the situation. The time had come, he recognised, when he
must make room for another.[4] Horace's contempt[5] for the mimes of
such an anti-Caesarian doubtless was a correct attitude at the court of
Augustus; besides, their hasty workmanship would annoy him.
Laberius's sharp tongue could make Cicero wince. When in the theatre
Cicero apologetically expressed his inability to make room for Laberius
among the knights' stalls, as they were so crowded, the retort came

A novelty for you; for you generally sit on two stools at once.

Little wonder that Cicero should mischievously assure a correspondent

[1] See Petronius, *Sat.* 55, where the lines either are by Publilius or are a
parody on his manner.
[2] The whole incident is recounted in Macrob., *Saturn.*, II. vii, 'Laberium
asperae libertatis equitem Romanum Caesar quingentis milibus inuitauit ut
prodiret in scaenam et ipse ageret mimos quos scriptitabat,' etc.

[3]   'Ego bis tricenis annis actis sine nota
          Eques Romanus e Lare egressus meo,
          Domum reuertar mimus. Nimirum hoc die
          Uno plus uixi mihi quam uiuendum fuit.'
                                        Macrob., *loc. cit.*

[4]   'Non possunt primi esse omnes omni in tempore . . .
          Cecidi ego: cadet qui sequitur'
were words introduced into his next mime (Macrob., *loc. cit.*).
[5] Hor., *Sat.*, I. x. 5:
                'Nam sic
          Et Laberi mimos ut pulchra poemata mirer.'

that he had grown case-hardened (*obdurui*) to *ennui* when he could sit through performances of Laberius and Publilius.[1]

Among forty-four known titles[2] of the plays of Laberius, some in themselves provoke curiosity, like *Lacus Auernus, Late Loquentes, Cancer* and *Carcer*. Others show how the mime had annexed the remaining divisions of light drama. Laberius shares with the Atellan farce titles such as *Gemelli, Nuptiae, Piscator*; with the *togata*, such as *Aquae Caldae, Compitalia*, and the ever recurrent *Fullo*; and with Greek comedy and the *palliata, Colax, Ephebus, Necyomantia*, and *Aulularia*. His prosody in the main follows comic usage. His diction is marked on the one hand by bold inventiveness, on the other by inroads upon plebeian Latin — sometimes of the lowest sort.[3] Occasionally the desired effect was produced by a homely simile:

I fell in love like a cockroach into a basin![4]

Publilius, the Syrian, was a slave — probably from Antioch.[5] High in his master's good graces, he earned his manumission by his wit.[6] Presumably he gave to the mime some novel turn or an added popularity, that justified the elder Pliny in calling him 'the founder of the mimic stage.' Publilius may have long survived his contest with Laberius. His mimes were still in vogue under Nero. The fact that we know only two of his titles suggests that his improvisations were precariously enshrined in actor's copies. We know him best through the collection of *Sententiae*[7] drawn from his mimes in the first century A.D. These saws were increased by paraphrasing some of his own lines and by incorporating similarly proverbial lines from others. Something like seven hundred lines may be genuine. They are mostly iambic senarii, but some are trochaic septenarii. As wisdom and morality in tabloid form they were found useful to administer in school.[8] A few specimens will show their quality:

[1] Cic., *Ad Fam.*, XII. xviii. 2.
[2] In O. Ribbeck. *Com. Rom. Fragm.*, ed. 3, 1898. Over 145 lines survive.
[3] Gell., *N.A.*, XVI. vii. 1, says, 'oppido quam uerba finxit praelicenter,' and gives among other instances his use of ' "depudicauit" pro "stuprauit," et "abluuium" pro "diluuio," "manuatus est" pro "furatus est," ' etc.; *N.A.*, XIX. xiii. 3, 'quae a Laberio ignobilia nimis et sordentia in usum linguae Latinae intromissa sunt.'
[4] 'Amore cecidi tamquam blatta in peluim.'
[5] Plin., *N.H.*, xxxv. 199, 'talem (*i.e.* pedibus cretatis, as an imported slave) Publilium † lochium (Antiochium, O. Jahn, *Phil.*, 26, 11), mimicae scaenae conditorem, et astrologiae consobrinum eius Manilium Antiochum, item grammaticae Staberium Erotem eadem naue aductos uidere proaui.' His name 'Publilius' was established by Wölfflin to replace the false form 'Publius' in the MSS. of Cicero, the Senecas, Gellius, Macrobius, and Jerome.
[6] Macrob., *Saturn.*, II. vii. 4–8.
[7] Text: in O. Ribbeck, *op. cit.*; E. Wölfflin, 1869. W. Meyer, 1880 (critical text of 723 'sententiae,' of which 84 are not accepted in Wölfflin's edn.); O. Friedrich, 1880 (761 'sententiae' followed by others from Caecilius Balbus, from Pseudo-Seneca, proverbs, and maxims falsely considered Publilian); R. A. H. Bickford-Smith, 1895 (contains orderly account of MSS. and editions.)
[8] Teuffel, *op. cit.*, § 212. 5. *Cf.* Gell., *N.A.*, XVII. xiv. 3, 'Huius Publilii

'A witty companion is a good lift on the way':

> *Comes facundus in uia pro uehiculo est.*

'The only right thing a miser does is to die':

> *Auarus nisi cum moritur nil recte facit.*

'To ape the accents of goodness is double-dyed wickedness':

> *Bonitatis uerba imitari maior malitia est.*

'Fortune is like glass—amid its glitter it breaks':

> *Fortuna uitrea est: tum cum splendet frangitur.*

'Nature, not rank, makes the gentleman':

> *Virum bonum natura non ordo facit.*

'Looking wise is not the same as being born so':

> *Vultu an natura sapiens sis, multum interest.*

Thanks to such industrious culling, it is only the better side that has survived from the mimes of the Caesarian age.

---

sententiae feruntur pleraeque lepidae et ad communem sermonum usum commendatissimae' (of fourteen lines quoted by Gellius, all but one are in the extant collection). Sen., *Contr.*, VII. iii. 8, '. . . quae apud eum melius essent dicta quam apud quemquam comicum tragicumque aut Romanum aut Graecum.' Jerome (*Ep. ad Laetam*, 107) records that as a schoolboy he read the line 'Aegre reprendas quod sinas consuescere,' which has been proved to be by Publilius.

Part III: *The Augustan Period*
43 B.C.—14 A.D.

Chapter I

VIRGIL

The Augustan period and poetry – Imperial patronage – The life of
Virgil – Virgil the man – Early pieces – The *Eclogues* – Theocritean
and other influences – Artificiality and beauty – Distant echoes of
contemporary events – 'Nature' in the *Eclogues* – Distinction
achieved in imitation – Borrowed and original elements in the
Georgics – Relation to Lucretius – Relation to Octavian Caesar and
Maecenas – Love of Italy – Sympathy with the animate and the
inanimate – Complex attitude to nature – Is it 'the best poem of
the best poet'? – The preparation of the *Aeneid* – Sources – Homer
and Virgil – Virgil more critical, urbane, and emotional – Relation
to the age – Legend and character of Aeneas – The broadened idea
of Italy and Rome in the *Aeneid* – Attitude to the emperor –
Tender melancholy – Dido – Virgilian romance – The 'symbolism'
of Virgil – Beauty of style – Influence on literature of early empire
– Influence through education – Ancient criticism on Virgil –
Centos – Fame as prophet and wizard – Summary of Virgil's
claims.

THE political changes which distinguished the Augustan from
the Ciceronian period were reflected in literature. In the
republic no human being could have been praised in the terms
of deification applied by Augustan poets to the new ruler. The altered
tone was facilitated by the complete passing within a very few years of
the previous generation of writers. Strictly, the term 'Augustan' might
be limited to the period from the defeat of Antony at Actium in 31 B.C.
to the death of Augustus in A.D. 14, or, more appropriately in a
history of literature, to the death of Ovid in A.D. 17 or 18. But, in a
broad sense, the Augustan period may be said to begin with the death
of Cicero in 43 B.C. The one age follows hard on the other. Yet remarkably few *littérateurs* of Ciceronian times survived to be contemporaries
of Virgil. Helvius Cinna is common to Catullus and to the *Eclogues*;[1]

[1] *Ecl.*, ix. 35.

and Catullus's Varus may be the Quintilius mourned by Horace.[1] A more famous link between the two eras is Asinius Pollio,[2] Virgil's earliest patron. Seldom, however, is there so little transition. Thus the new era presents an entirely new group of poets—Virgil, Horace, Tibullus, Propertius, Ovid. Of these all were born, and some were grown men, before Philippi sealed the doom of the republic in 42 B.C. But all of them—including Horace, who had served in the army of the republic—are imperial in sympathy, even though, in the case of the elegists, the imperial note finds little expression. Much is explained by the social relations between the new writers and the organiser of empire. While still one of the triumvirs for 'establishing the republic,' Octavian possessed the gift of winning the confidence of the wise. He was the coming man, or rather the man who had come to establish order. The revulsion of feeling against the murder of Caesar aided his great-nephew; and when the choice lay between Octavian's business-like capacity and Antony's dissolute Orientalism, patriotic writers hardly needed to hesitate. Octavian's shrewdness realised the advantage to be drawn from the support of literature. Both he[3] and his adviser Maecenas had their own *penchant* for writing and for literary society; but, at least to an equal extent, state reasons determined them to befriend authors. So a new kind of patronage arose. Patronage itself was no new thing. It had existed at Rome since the days of Scipio. But never till this epoch had the patron been the arbiter of Rome's destiny the head of the state, combining supreme military, civil, and religious powers, the giver of peace, the consolidator of empire, the lawgiver in the cause of justice and morals, the restorer of ancient temples and ceremonial, the beautifier of the capital, and the scion of a family which claimed divine descent.

In itself, the imperial system, even before it could be fully understood, contained for writers the most fertile possibilities. Much in it might stir the imagination of a Virgil or the historic sense of a Livy. But even the single factor of imperial patronage—outshining, as it did, the patronage of Maecenas, Pollio, and Messalla—had far-reaching effects. It left its *protégés* less free in choice of theme and words. It was thus accountable for a certain want of outspokenness—a limitation of outlook which matched the typically 'Augustan' restraint of style. It is true, then, that this imperial protectorate over letters did not foster daring. But there were compensations. It guaranteed for the poets social security and affluent circumstances. They could live for art. Their ideal could be perfect form. Fairness demands that, if we debit the

[1] Catull., x. 1; Hor., *Od.*, I. xxiv. 4.
[2] Catull., xii. 6–9.
[3] For Augustus as an orator see Suet., *Aug.*, lxxxiv.; Tac., *Ann.*, XIII. iii. For his tragedy *Ajax* which he destroyed as a failure, Macrob., *Sat.*, II. iv. 1. When the tragic poet Varius inquired after his *Ajax*, the emperor's jest on its fate was 'In spongiam incubuit.'

Augustan supremacy with the absence of adventurous literature and
with the decay of oratory, so also must we credit it with inspiring
masterpieces by Virgil and Horace. Admitted that both poets are, to
modern taste, extravagant in eulogies of the emperor, admitted, too,
that deference to Augustus might produce such unhappy results as the
excision of the praises of Gallus from the conclusion of the fourth
Georgic, still the same patronage yielded rich fruit. But for the kindness
of Octavian to Virgil, when dispossessed of his farm, the *Eclogues*
would have been in far different notes. To Maecenas he owed the suggestion of the *Georgics*. The emperor personally proposed the idea of an
epic which Virgil shaped into the *Aeneid*; and from his encouragement
and even solicitude, a diffident nature like Virgil's must have drawn
valued support. As for Horace, he never sounds a note more masculine
and sincere than in the opening six *Odes* of his third book, inspired by
an appreciation of the great work being done for his country by
Augustus.

For the life of P. Vergilius Maro (70–19 B.C.) our fullest source is the
biography once prefixed to the now lost commentary of Aelius Donatus.
Stripped of interpolations, it probably represents part of Suetonius
De Poetis.[2] Virgil was born on October 15, 70 B.C., at Andes, near

---

[1] Text: Wks. and Comm., J. Conington; new ed., w. corrected orthography, etc., H. Nettleship, 3 vols., 1881–84; ed. 5 of vol. i rev. F. Haverfield,
1898; O. Ribbeck, ed. 1, 1859–68 (signalised, in spite of some notoriously bad
emendations, an enormous improvement on text), ed. 2, 1894–95; recogn. H.
Nettleship, in Postgate's *C.P.L.*, i., 1894; T. E. Page (notes), 3. vols., 1894–
1900; F. A. Hirtzel (*Script. Class. Biblioth. Oxon.*), 1900; *Oeuvres, avec un
commentaire*, E. Benoist, i., ed. 3, 1884; ii., ed. 3, 1882; iii., ed. 4, 1890; *Aeneis*,
G. G. Gossrau, 1876.
　　English translations: *Poems* (Eng. prose), J. Conington, new ed., 1884; *Aen.*,
J. Conington (verse, mainly octosyllabic), ed. 3, 1870; *The Aeneids* (rhymed
fourteeners), W. Morris, ed. 2, 1876; *Aen.*, text w. tr. (blank verse), C. J.
Billson, 2 vols., 1906; *Aen.* (blank verse), J. Rhoades, new ed., 1907; *Aen.*
(prose), J. W. Mackail, 1885; *Bucolics* and *Georgics*, do., 1889; *Eclog.*, new ed.
(with *Theocritus*), C. S. Calverley, 1908; *Georgics* (blank verse), Lord Burgh-
clere, 1904.
　　Commentaries, etc.: *Servii Grammatici qui feruntur in V. carmina Commentarii*, G. Thilo and H. Hagen, 3 vols., 1881–87; H. Nettleship, *Anct. Lives
of Vergil, w. Essay on the Poems*, etc., 1879; do., *Suggestns. introd. to a Study of
Aeneid* in his *Lectures and Essays*, 1885; J. Henry, *Aeneidea* (crit., exeget., and
aesthetic remarks . . . w. personal collation of all first-class MSS., upwards of
100 second-class MSS.), 5 vols., 1873–92; C. A. Sainte-Beuve, *Étude sur
Virgile*, new ed., 1891; W. Y. Sellar, *Roman Poets of the Augustan Age: Virgil*,
1877; G. Boissier, *Nouvelles Promenades Archéologiques* (Eng. tr. as *Country of
Horace and Virgil*, 1876, pp. 119 sqq.); do., *La Religion romaine d'Auguste aux
Antonins*, ed. 6, 2 vols., 1906, pp. 221–314; M. Patin, *Études sur la poésie latine*,
ed. 4, 1900 i. chap. viii–xii; F. W. H. Myers in *Essays Classical*, 1888; T. R.
Glover, *Studies in Virgil*, 1904; J. A. Hild, *La Légende d'Enée avant Virgile*,
1883; R. Sabbadini, *Studi critici sulla Eneide*, 1889; R. Heinze, *Virgils epische
Technik*, 1903; D. Comparetti, *Virgilio nel medio evo*, 2 vols., 1872 (Eng.
tr., E. F. M. Benecke, 1895); C. G. Leland, *The Unpublished Legends of Virgil*,
1899.
　　[2] Nettleship, *Anct. Lives of Virgil*, pp. 28–31.

Mantua. His father—either a potter or a day-labourer—belonged
to the peasantry. He married his employer's daughter, Magia Pollia; the
guess has been hazarded, and denied too, that her name aided the
medieval belief in Virgil's gifts of sorcery. Virgil, then, was a boy of
eleven when Caesar came to govern Gallia Cisalpina. By a coincidence,
his young mind had thus early forced upon it the greatness of the
Julian family, which he was to celebrate in the *Aeneid*. Whether his
descent, name, and 'note' were Keltic or not, Virgil was in law born a
Gaul. It was only to Caesar, and at a later date, that the natives of his
province were to owe the Roman citizenship. His early education was
received at Cremona and at Mediolanum, in whose school the younger
Pliny showed his interest generations later. For higher training Virgil
went to Rome. Philosophy, rhetoric, medicine, and mathematics
engaged his attention. Of the two chief careers of the day, military and
forensic, Virgil aimed at the latter. But he spoke only once at the bar.
It is recorded of him at a later date—probably by some courtier—that
in society he was hesitating of speech: and certainly constitutional shyness would not set him at ease either in a law court, or in the imperial
presence among the uncertain company which inevitably gathers round
a new throne. From Epidius Virgil learned to appreciate Alexandrine
Greek, and from Siro that Epicureanism which heralded the influence
of Lucretius over him. His early manhood he spent, principally in study,
on his northern farm, till the evil days of confiscation came in 41.
Among many others, he lost his property when Antony's soldiers had
to be satisfied with land allotments.[1] The commissioners, Gallus, Varus,
and Pollio (then legate of Gallia Transpadana), urged him to appeal to
young Caesar in Rome, and the gratitude of the poet for amended
fortunes appears in the first *Eclogue*, which records the indulgent reply
to his petition:

Pascite ut ante boues, pueri, submittite tauros.

Whether a second eviction followed is doubtful.[2] In those turbulent
times Virgil's life seems to have been endangered. His father and he
found refuge in the villa of Siro, his teacher. But thenceforward he lived
chiefly in the South—sometimes in Rome, sometimes at a country-
house near Nola, and mostly at Naples, where he composed the
Georgics.[3] The four books took seven years to complete. So consummate
was their elaboration that progress seldom exceeded the rate of a few
verses a day.[4] The total of 2,188 lines gives an average of less than one
line a day over the period of writing. His slow method of composition is

[1] *Ecl.*, i. 71:
    ' Impius haec tam culta noualia miles habebit?
    Barbarus has segetes?'
[2] Nettleship thinks not, *op. cit.*, p. 42.
[3] *Georg.*, iv. 563-4.
[4] Quint., *Inst. Or.*, X. iii. 8.

illustrated by his own remark about licking his lines into shape as a bear does her cubs.[1] Octavian's bounty furnished him with a Neapolitan home. He had entered the ruler's circle on the introduction of Maecenas. It was for Virgil in turn to introduce Horace to Maecenas in 38 B.C.[2] To Horace he was *animae dimidium*[3]—no other 'Vergilius' could be that: Horace counted Virgil with their common friends Plotius Tucca and Varius as one of those

> Souls than whom earth yields none more fair.

This last is the glimpse we obtain of him on the famous journey to Brundisium of 37 B.C. in Horace's company.[4] It was then, too, that physical infirmity debarred the two poets from the games in which their fellow-travellers indulged—Horace had sore eyes and Virgil was suffering from indigestion. The remainder of his life, after the completion of the *Georgics* in 30, Virgil devoted to his epic on Aeneas. Through a marvellously interwoven texture of the legendary and the historical, the poet honours the established power of Augustus, and at the same time gives expression to the patriotic sentiment and the loftiest aspirations of his day. After a decade of toil, Virgil intended to devote three years more to revision. He projected a tour in the East to visit some of the scenes in his poem. Exposure to excessive heat at Megara induced an illness which grew more serious as he hastened homewards. He had barely reached Italy when death overtook him at Brundisium in 19 B.C. He was buried at Naples, where the *tomba di Virgilio* became in after ages an object of superstitious reverence. The epitaph, credulously alleged by Donatus to be his own composition, records his life and works in brief:

> *Mantua me genuit, Calabri rapuere, tenet nunc*
> *Parthenope: cecini pascua, rura, duces.*

Tall and dark, Virgil retained the looks of a countryman.[5] His pure character won him the epithet of 'Parthenias'[6] among the Neapolitans. Weak health and devotion to composition encouraged him in the habits of a recluse. His visits to Rome became few. Popular demonstrations in his honour gave him pain, just as they rather pleased his friend

---

[1] Recorded probably by Varius, and quoted by Gellius, *N.A.*, XVII. x. 2, 'parere se uersus more atque ritu ursino': cf. Donat., *Vit.*, 22, 'carmen se ursae more parere dicens et lambendo demum effingere.'
[2] Hor., *Sat.*, I. vi. 54:   ..
> 'Optimus olim
> Vergilius, post hunc Varius, dixere quid essem.'
[3] Hor., *Od.*, I. iii. 8.
[4] Hor., *Sat.*, I. v.
[5] Donat., *Vit. Verg.*, 8, 'Corpore et statura fuit grandi, aquilo colore, facie rusticana,' etc.
[6] *Ibid.*, 11.

Horace.[1] Virgil would take refuge in the first available house.[2] Once he had the overwhelming experience of a greeting from the audience in the theatre where some of his verses were being recited.[3] This was probably one of those occasions on which the stage used his *Eclogues*. His diffidence in society found a parallel in his distrustfulness of his artistic powers. Despite incessant pains, he fell short of his own ideal of finished workmanship. Pressed by the emperor for a rough draft and extracts to show how the *Aeneid* was progressing, he wrote of his task as so great that he felt he must have entered on it in a fit of mental aberration.[4] The unfinished lines and inconsistencies left in the *Aeneid* so troubled him that his dying desire was for the destruction of the unpublished work. The emperor's intervention rescued it. Augustus commissioned Varius and Tucca to edit the poem, excising the superfluous, but adding nothing. Thus about 17 B.C., the second year after Virgil's death, his great epic was given to the world.

Of the minor poems traditionally ascribed to Virgil's youth few can be definitely pronounced genuine. For example, though Virgil certainly wrote a poem entitled 'The Gnat' (*Culex*), it is hard to believe that the *Culex* which has survived is his. Again, 'The Salad' (*Moretum*) is just conceivably an early study in realism by Virgil: if so, it makes an entertaining contrast to the idyllic beauty of the *Eclogues*. Great difficulties arise regarding the authorship of the *Ciris*. But fuller reference to the longer *Pseudo-Vergiliana* may be deferred. Of the short pieces grouped as *Catalecta*, or preferably as *Catalepton*,[5] one is vouched for by Quintilian[6] and a few more are likely enough to be genuine. That as a tiro Virgil should imitate or parody Catullus is consistent with the known influence of Catullus elsewhere upon him. The three which markedly show this influence (*e.g.*, *Sabinus ille quem uidetis hospites*) are therefore credibly Virgil's. The farewell to rhetoric:

> *Ite hinc, inanes, ite rhetorum ampullae —*

proclaims a vigorous rebellion against the 'nation of grammarians dripping with fat,' in which the name of Varro is included. The writer in fancy leaves his poetic companions (*iam ualete formosi!*), and sets sail for havens of bliss where Siro's Epicureanism will free the mind from care:

[1] Horace thanks Melpomene, *Od.*, IV. iii. 22:
' Quod monstror digito praetereuntium
Romanae fidicen lyrae.'
Unlike Persius, Virgil thought it anything but fine 'digito monstrari et dicier *hic est*,' Pers., i. 28.
[2] Donat., *ibid.*, 11, 'ut . . . si quando Romae, quo rarissime commeabat, uiseretur in publico, sectantes demonstrantesque se suffugeret in proximum tectum.'
[3] Tac., *Dial.*, xiii.
[4] Macrob., *Sat.*, I. xxiv. 'Tanta incohata res est ut paene uitio mentis tantum opus ingressus mihi uidear,' etc.
[5] *Catalecta* means 'collected pieces.' *Catalepton* means 'minor pieces,' 'trifles,' τὰ κατὰ λεπτόν (a title given to a work by Aratus). Of the fourteen pieces included, eight are in elegiacs, the rest in iambics or choliambics.
[6] Quint., *Inst. Or.*, VIII. iii. 28.

M

> *Nos ad beatos uela mittimus portus,*
> *Magni petentes docta dicta Sironis,*
> *Vitamque ab omni uindicabimus cura.*

Once the Muses were sweet to him; and even now will they not some-times revisit him, *sed pudenter et raro?* A piece, in three elegiac couplets, apostrophises Siro's country-house, where Virgil and his household found refuge after eviction. Whether by Virgil or not, the solicitude therein expressed for a father recalls a winning trait in Horace's charac-ter.

Virgil's pastorals are better known, under the colourless title of the MSS., as *Eclogues* (ἐκλογαί, 'Selections'), than under the more descriptive title of *Bucolics* (βουκολικά, 'Songs of the Neatherds'). The ten poems were composed between 43 and 37. They are not in the order of composition.[1] Some can be definitely dated. For example, the fifth, on the apotheosis of Daphnis, is best understood as written for the first celebration of the dead Caesar's birthday in July, 42. The fourth, the so-called 'Messianic Eclogue,' belongs certainly to the year of Pollio's consulship, 40 B.C. Historical allusions fix the eighth to 39 and the tenth to 37. The earliest of all is probably the second. It is markedly Theocritean in the amorousness and banter which are so traditional in pastorals that it is absurd to interpret the passion for Alexis as besmirch-ing Virgil's own life. It is scarcely of vital moment whether the ninth was written before the first Eclogue —the shepherd's thanksgiving to Octavian in 41 —or whether it belongs to the next year. Both reflect the hardships of rustics dispossessed by soldiers.

In these poems Virgil imitated, not primitive shepherds' songs racy of the soil, but the Sicilian idylls of Theocritus. Virgil, in a sense, is more 'Alexandrine' than he; for the Doric of Theocritus, his stronger dramatic power, his greater simplicity, are much closer to real life than Virgil is. The second and third Eclogues show most directly the influence of Theocritean incident and language. But Virgil, though the very names of his shepherds are standing reminders of the Greek, is not slavishly bound to his model. He is not always careful even to translate correctly.[2] The seventh may serve to illustrate his freely imaginative treatment of a singing match. The suggestion comes from Theocritus. The competitors are 'Arcadian' (*Arcades ambo*). The scenery is Sicilian —at least the background is —but the details are from the poet's own Northern Italy, where the Mincio 'fringed its green banks with tender reeds.'[3] Theocritus is by no means the only influence

---

[1] See M. Sonntag, *Vergil als bukolischer Dichter*, 1891.

[2] *E.g.*, *Ecl.*, viii. 58, 'omnia uel medium fiant mare' is a blunder for πάντα δ' ἔναλλα γένοιτο and at viii. 41, in the famous 'ut uidi, ut perii,' the second 'ut' misrenders ὡς in χὠς ἴδον ὡς ἐμάνην, Theocr., ii. 82 – if, at least, that Greek word should bear an accent here.

[3] *Ecl.*, vii. 12: 'Hic uirides tenera praetexit arundine ripas
    Mincius.'

at work. Virgil was already deep-read in Greek literature and mythology. In the 'verse of Chalcis' he alludes to Euphorion, the fashionable
model of contemporary poetry. Already, before the days of the *Georgics*,
he reveres Hesiod as 'the sage of Ascra.' His Alexandrine studies force
allusions upon him. Arrows are 'Cydonian,' spikenard 'Assyrian,' wine
is 'Ariusian,' and yews, 'Cyrnean.' One cannot hope to exhaust his
sources. Blended with his conscientious exactitude, a shyness half-
reticent and mysterious characterises the learning of Virgil, and, as
Macrobius had the penetration to observe, makes its well-springs hard
to trace.[1] Roman poets also influence him. Some of his metrical movements are reminiscent of Catullus. The wonderful song of Silenus, in
the eclogue dedicated to Varus, opens with a Lucretian account of the
universe in Lucretian phraseology and rhythm. It shows Virgil accepting philosophic inquiry alongside of mythology as poetic material.

Obviously this is the most artificial of poetry. Pictures of actual
nature—drawn often with whole-hearted fidelity—and references to
straying flocks and the simple life, cannot give reality to the whole. In
truth, Virgil is not concerned with consistency[2] and realism, but with
beauty. That effect he achieves. He makes his rustics sing as rustics
never sang. In an Arcady modelled on Theocritus but elaborated by
Virgil, Sicilian and Italian landscapes interchange with a dream-like
inconsistency. Ideal shepherds pipe and sing of equally ideal shepherd-
esses, and of their hopes and despairs. They contend inimitably in
amoebean verses: an umpire may reasonably fail to decide between their
skill. The lamentations of one over confiscated land are answered by the
grateful homage of another to Octavian as a divine establisher of peace —
deus nobis haec otia fecit. It is an Arcady to appreciate, not to analyse —
a southern land of brilliant sunshine and cool shade and slow-moving
rustics among meadows and flocks, greensward and flowers, hills and
grottoes. The lizards dart to and fro, the cicalas chirp noisily, the trees
are 'shrill-voiced' in the air. As in *The Scholar Gipsy*, on one's ear is
borne

All the live murmur of a summer's day.

A poetry languorous in its suggestion of leisure and music and love
invites to drowsiness on grass 'more soft than sleep.'[3]

[1] Macrob., *Sat.*, V. xviii. *ad init.* 'Fuit enim hic poeta ut scrupulose et
anxie ita dissimulanter et quasi clanculo doctus, ut multa transtulerit, quae
unde translata sint difficile sit cognitu.' The Greek element in the *Eclogues* is
discussed in P. Jahn's programmes (*Köln. Gymn.*, 1897–99), and his article 'Aus
Vergils Frühzeit' (*re* Skutsch's work on the subject) in *Herm.*, xxxvii. (1902),
pp. 161–72.
[2] He mixes his geography regularly, mixes his seasons (ploughing does not
go naturally with midsummer heat), mixes together an Italian vinedresser and
the conventional shepherd of Sicily, and even mixes different ages in the same
shepherd; for Tityrus, presumably a youthful lover of Amaryllis in i. 5, is later
in the eclogue hailed as 'fortunate senex.'
[3] Virgil has transferred Theocritus's phrase about fleeces ὕπνω μαλακώτερα
to grass – 'somno mollior herba,' *Ecl.*, vii. 45.

Literature so artificially beautiful is best appreciated in an age of high civilisation. There is piquancy in watching a poet play at shepherd life, and, with a pretty grace, ignore all sordid detail. Certainly the refreshing unreality of the earlier and more Theocritean eclogues contrasts with the earnestness of the contemporary struggle among Roman citizens which ended at Philippi. Even when echoes of war—or of resultant confiscations—are heard, they are muffled in the Virgilian music. They sadden the shepherd, but he is still vocal. Nowhere in the *Eclogues* is Virgil so serious as in the fourth. 'Let us sing a loftier strain, O Muses of Sicily,' are the opening words, which are justified by the stateliness of the whole. Written two years after Philippi, it expresses yearning after peace and happier times. The relations between Octavian and Antony gave promise of security in the state. Virgil had a confident prevision of the return of a golden age, and under the symbol of the nativity of a divine child (*magnum Iouis incrementum*) he prefigured its dawn. The extraordinary similarity to the language of Isaiah produced in the Church, after the time of Constantine the Great, a general acceptance of this eclogue as a prophecy of the advent of Christ. Few now credit this; but much of the imagery may fairly be termed 'Messianic' in the sense that it is ultimately traceable to Jewish ideas, which spread considerably in Italy in the latter half of the first century B.C.[1] The feeling of the age, then, does affect even poetry which appears so remote from everyday concerns as the *Eclogues*.

When all has been said that can be said about the imitative, unreal, and inconsistent features of the *Eclogues*, two things must be added. Firstly, they are poetry; secondly, under all the artificiality they are absolutely sincere and serious in their love of Nature. The union of the artificial and the natural is nothing uncommon in pastoral verse. Pierre de Ronsard is as artificial as Virgil in turning Elizabeth of England and Mary of Scotland into two Venuses and the chief poets of his day into rustics. That is like the disguise of Virgil as 'Tityrus,' of Julius as 'Daphnis,' of Gallus as a love-sick shepherd. But, artificial as he is, Ronsard commends the beauty of Nature wild and unadorned as something beyond embellishment:

> *Car tousjours la nature est meilleure que l'art.*

This is more than a pious sentiment to Virgil. He loves the smiling

---

[1] It is poetic to regard the marvellous babe as purely symbolic – the figurative incarnation of the new era. Sir W. M. Ramsay refuses to admit that any definite child is denoted (*Expositor*, June and August, 1907). But I find it extremely difficult to believe that the homely realism of lines 60–61 does not refer to an actually expected birth. If that be so, then, beyond all question, language and circumstances apply best to the looked-for child of Octavian. That the child proved to be a girl instead of the 'puer' acclaimed by the poet need not have been so disconcerting as is sometimes alleged, in a poem which, on any theory, remains a mass of symbolism. For further discussion on the subject, see *Virgil's Messianic Eclogue*, by J. B. Mayor, W. W. Fowler, R. S. Conway, 1907: *cf.* W. R. Hardie, *Lectures on Class. Subjects*, chap. iv., on 'The Age of Gold.'

countryside with unmixed delight. Pastoral scenery may be an artificial taste for the town-dweller; but Virgil's own joy in external nature springs from his susceptibility to beauty.[1] His shepherds feel it worth while to leave flocks to stray and let the influences of a fair scene pass into the mind, while they enjoy cool shade and the murmur of water to the accompaniment of music. The result is a kind of pensive melancholy as often as rapturous pleasure. The 'Nature' of the *Eclogues* invites to idleness, as the 'Nature' of the *Georgics* invites to work. It is not unlike the contrast between Watteau's art and Millet's. In the *Eclogues* there is a sense of Nature's witchery; in the *Georgics* a Lucretian sense of Nature's stubbornness. Yet in the latter, Nature is less of a taskmistress than in Hesiod: the duel between husbandman and Nature ends in an alliance which guarantees bountiful increase. A Providence—which Lucretius rejects--secures the mastery for mankind, if man will work and watch and pray aright. The easier and less philosophic—or shall we say less theological?—attitude of the *Eclogues* finds in Nature refreshment and even something like Wordsworth's 'healing power.' This appears in praising the first part of the song on Daphnis:

> Thy song, O godlike poet, is for us
> As for the tired to sleep on grass, or quench
> Hot thirst in dancing rills of water sweet.[2]

And the second part is praised in terms likewise drawn from Nature:

> What guerdon shall I pay for such a song?
> Nor whisperings of the South Wind as it comes
> Can charm so much, nor billow-stricken shores,
> Nor hurrying streams adown the rocky glens.[3]

This is one of repeated touches indicative of a romantic sentiment for wild Nature, and a passion for escape from civilisation, so characteristic of much in Rousseau and Byron.[4] Less romantic, but still beautiful, is the picture drawn in the first eclogue:

> Mid streams of boyhood, old man fortunate,
> And haunted springs thou'lt woo the sombre cool.
> Here the old hedge, thy neighbour's boundary,

[1] This was the quality Horace, *Sat.*, I. x. 44, saw in his *Eclogues*:
'Molle atque facetum
Vergilio adnuerunt gaudentes rure Camenae.'

[2] *Ecl.*, v. 45:
'Tale tuum carmen nobis, diuine poëta,
Quale sopor fessis in gramine, quale per aestum
Dulcis aquae saliente sitim restinguere riuo.'

[3] *Ecl.*, v. 81:
'Quae tibi, quae tali reddam pro carmine dona?
Nam neque me tantum uenientis sibilus Austri,
Nec percussa iuuant fluctu tam litora, nec quae
Saxosas inter decurrunt flumina ualles.'

[4] Byron's attitude to nature become eventually more composite and philosophic: see discussion, J. Wight Duff, *Byron: Selected Poetry*, 1904, Introd., pp. xlix–lvi.

> Whose willow-blooms the bees of Hybla sip,
> Will lure thy slumber oft with gentle hum.
> There 'neath high crags the woodman's song will rise,
> Nor yet will those hoarse pigeons thou dost love,
> Nor turtles, fail to moan from windy elm.[1]

To appreciate Virgil's power one has but to compare the feebleness of his imitators—Calpurnius Siculus in Nero's time, and Nemesianus two centuries later. Virgil, even when most imitative, could write with distinction. There is no better example of what a master-hand can do when he borrows than the Latin into which Virgil turned Theocritus's description of boyish love at first sight. It is one of the most powerfully simple things in literature, and one writes an English version with hesitation:

> 'Twas in our garden-close I saw you pull
> The dewy apples by my mother's side.
> You were a little girl—I showed you both
> Where apples grew. My years were twelve: I just
> From off the ground could reach the brittle boughs.
> I looked and lost my heart: and all my thoughts
> Were sent awhirling by some cruel power.[2]

The *Georgics* (Γεωργικά, 'Points of Husbandry'), the fruit of seven years of elaboration between 37 and 30 B.C., are in four books. Book I treats crop-raising; II, tree-growing, especially the vine and the olive; III, cattle-rearing; IV, bee-keeping. Virgil's acknowledged model is Hesiod's Ἔργα καὶ Ἡμέραι:

Ascraeumque cano Romana per oppida carmen.

But his relation to Hesiod, closest in the first book, is not so close as his relation to Theocritus in the *Eclogues* and to Homer in the *Aeneid*. His sources are multitudinous. He had studied the natural history and agriculture of Greece, as represented by Democritus, Xenophon, Aristotle, and Theophrastus.[3] He made much use of the didactic side

[1] *Ecl.*, i. 51:
> 'Fortunate senex, hic inter flumina nota
> Et fontes sacros frigus captabis opacum.
> Hinc tibi quae semper uicino ab limite saepes
> Hyblaeis apibus florem depasta salicti
> Saepe leui somnum suadebit inire susurro:
> Hinc alta sub rupe canet frondator ad auras;
> Nec tamen interea raucae, tua cura, palumbes,
> Nec gemere aëria cessabit turtur ab ulmo.'

[2] *Ecl.*, viii. 37:
> 'Saepibus in nostris paruam te roscida mala
> (Dux ego uester eram) uidi cum matre legentem.
> Alter ab undecimo tum me iam ceperat annus;
> Iam fragiles poteram a terra contingere ramos.
> Ut uidi, ut perii, ut me malus abstulit error!'

[3] For the influence of Theophrastus see P. Jahn in *Herm.*, xxxviii. (1903), pp. 244 *sqq.*, on 'Eine Prosaquelle Vergils u. ihre Umsetzung in Poesie durch den Dichter.'

of Alexandrinism. For instance, he consulted Eratosthenes on the heavenly bodies,[1] and the Διοσημίαι of Aratus for the signs of disturbed weather.[2] He copied the description of a serpent[3] in the extant Θηριακά of Nicander. It may be assumed that the fourth book included imitations of the lost Μελισσουργικά of Nicander, who probably used Aristotle's researches on bees before Virgil did. Virgil's Roman sources include priestly books, rural proverbs, and the agricultural treatises of Cato and Varro. To Lucretius he owed a deep debt. Besides, Virgil's own position as a son of the soil and a practical farmer must not be overlooked. He was not a mere *dilettante*, but practically interested and a keen observer. Though he writes poetry, it is science as well, and he is quoted seriously by Columella and Pliny. Virgil's obvious borrowings must not be allowed to obscure the true nature of his performance. He planned and achieved something more than a didactic poem on Alexandrine lines. To a degree beyond the reach of an Aratus or a Nicander, he interspersed his teaching with national, religious, imaginative, and subjective elements. Many of the agricultural details cannot interest universally. Some frankly are dull. Virgil grasps this difficulty of elevating the humbler themes,[4] but he can make poetry out of what seemed to promise none.[5] Hesiod's didacticism had been desultory; his precepts were loosely connected. Then, Alexandrine didacticism consisted in a narrower, a more specialised treatment of a subject—of which the author frequently had only a book-knowledge. Now Virgil retains much of the methodical treatment of Alexandria, but he imports far more variety of thought and adornment. This is one reason why the greatness of the *Georgics* lies in the episodes. Both Hesiod and Virgil's Alexandrine models were artistically his inferiors. Like every consummate artist, Virgil conferred honour on his literary creditors. The result of his borrowing is an original masterpiece. The attitude to life— man, beast, and plant—the sympathy with the farmer, the love of natural beauty, and the magnificent finish of the hexameters, are Virgil's own.

Virgil's individuality, again, emerges distinctly in any estimate of his relation to Lucretius. Virgil was too independent to tie himself to one philosophy of nature. His thought is composite—inconsistent indeed.

---

[1] *G.*, i. 231 *sqq.*
[2] *G.*, i. 356–465.
[3] *G.*, iii. 425.
[4] *E.g.*, iii. 289, approaching the subject of sheep and goats:
'Nec sum animi dubius uerbis ea uincere magnum
Quam sit, et angustis hunc addere rebus honorem.'
Cf. his diffidence regarding the subject of bees; 'slight the field of work, but not slight the glory, if Apollo aid,' iv. 6:
'In tenui labor, at tenuis non gloria,' etc.

[5] This will be plain to anyone who cares to compare Virgil's lines on the growing of trees in *G.*, ii. 9–34, with their Greek original in Theophrastus, *Hist. Plant.*, ii. 1.

Permeated with Lucretian speculation,[1] the *Georgics* have not that abiding fidelity to the reign of natural law which is a tower of strength in the *De Rerum Natura*. From Epicureanism the poet passes freely to Stoic views of an overruling Providence. Echoes of the materialistic and evolutionary doctrines of Lucretius give place to teleological conceptions of the universe. Miracles, such as the finding of bees in a carcass, and portents such as those heralding the death of Caesar,[2] are accepted. There is a primitive piety, partly Hesiodic, partly Italian, which would be anathema to Lucretius. Virgil's gods are not the far-distant dwellers in the interspaces of the world. He could not banish the bright creations of Hellenic fancy. He gives them a Roman colour. His gods care for the land and the toiler; they must be propitiated by prayer and sacrifice. Ritual, disdained by Lucretius, is dear to Virgil. Already in the *Georgics*, he fosters the national religious sentiment which pervades the *Aeneid*. His purpose is different from that of Lucretius. The older poet conceived the goal of his system to be a philosophic quietism or resigned aloofness. No such retirement from the work of the world is in Virgil's view. The opposition of nature calls not for despair but for conquest. Man must exert himself to gain the dominion.[3] It is an evangel of work. Herein Virgil is truly national. The *Georgics* proclaim the Italian's *imperium* over the soil,[4] as the *Aeneid* was to proclaim the Italian's *imperium* over the world.

The outward sign of the national tone in the *Georgics* was the relation in which the poet stood to Octavian and Maecenas. Maecenas was the patron, and, in virtue of what Virgil calls his 'orders' (*iussa*), the 'begetter' of the work. Maecenas must have felt far deeper interest in it than Memmius did in Lucretius's poem. Here was not simply a versified handbook, but a poem in perfect style, fitted to throw a halo round the agrarian policy of the new government. If it could not actually tempt cultivators 'back to the land,' it accorded admirably with statesmanlike efforts to alleviate agricultural depression, to arrest the depopulation of rural districts, and to restore the manly life of the ancient yeomen of Italy. So Virgil concludes the first *Georgic* with a prayer that Octavian be spared as the one who can raise Italy out of the ruin of civil bloodshed. Unfeignedly he mourns the staggering blows dealt to agriculture by demoralising warfare:

> *Tot bella per orbem;*
> *Tam multae scelerum facies; non ullus aratro*
> *Dignus honos.*

[1] *E.g.*, *G.* i. 89–90 uses the Lucretian theory of the constitution of the earth; i. 121 *sqq.*, follows the sketch of primitive man in Lucret., v; i. 415 *sqq.*, the denial of divine origin for the instincts of birds is on the lines of materialistic speculation (and contrasts, therefore, with iv. 219, the acceptance of the notion of bees sharing in the Soul of the Universe); the pessimistic ideas at i. 199, and elsewhere, resemble those of Lucretius; the passages, iii. 242 *sqq.*, on the instincts of sex, and iii. 478 *sqq.*, on the plague, are clear cases of borrowing.
[2] *G.*, i. 461–97.   [3] *G.*, i. 118–46, 159, 200–3.
[4] *G.*, i. 99: 'Exercetque frequens tellurem atque imperat aruis.'

The prayer rings more genuine than the invocation to Caesar which opens the poem. With mythology incredibly frigid to modern tastes, it enrols Octavian among the gods. It speculates on the chance of Tethys purchasing him, 'for son-in-law with dower of all her waves'—in other words, it suggests that he may marry a Nereid; alternatively, it fancies the Scorpion and other celestial bodies contracting themselves to make room for his majesty in the heavens! All this shows what might have happened to Virgil in the way of literary conceit had he pursued too diligently the mythological track. It is the more refreshing to read, in the introduction to the third *Georgic*, his recoil from the hackneyed themes of his own period.[1] We know that the *Georgics*, when completed, were read aloud in four days by Virgil—relieved occasionally by Maecenas—to the emperor at Atella, when he was undergoing a rest-cure for a throat complaint. Perhaps it was then[2] that he composed this brilliant prologue of defiance to Alexandrinism run wild. Anyhow, he announces his intention of writing a national Roman epic, and appropriately introduces an Ennian echo:

Victorque uirum uolitare per ora.

He promises to gird himself 'to relate the fiery battles of Caesar.' Fortunately, Virgil modified his plan. He did not compose a strictly historical epic, as Lucan was to do. The wars against Brutus and Antony would not have yielded the rich material of the *Aeneid*. Virgil found subtler means of glorifying Caesar.

But in nothing is Virgil more national than in his love of Italy. This is the feeling which inspires his enthusiasm for his task. It accords with this national feeling that he should interest himself in the simple joys of country life and in the apparently prosaic details of farm-management. It is a point of honour with him that a reader should learn the make of the old Italian plough, the weather-lore, and the rustic festivals of Italy. To the warm praise of Italy expressed by Varro, Virgil adds poetry. He dwells[3] lovingly on her climate and fertility:

> perpetual spring,
> Summer in months that are not summer's own;[4]

her lakes, which he so beautifully invokes,

> And rivers gliding under ancient walls;[5]

her valorous tribes and her renowned families. The end is a transport of admiration:

[1] *G.*, iii. 3–5:
'Cetera, quae uacuas tenuissent carmine mentes,
Omnia iam uulgata. Quis aut Eurysthea durum,
Aut illaudati nescit Busiridis aras?'
[2] G. Boissier, *Country of Horace and Virgil*, p. 165.
[3] *G.*, ii. 136–76.
[4] *G.*, ii. 149:
'Hic uer assiduum, atque alienis mensibus aestas.'
[5] *G.*, ii. 157:
'Fluminaque antiquos subterlabentia muros.'

> Salue, magna parens frugum, Saturnia tellus,
> Magna uirum!

Interlaced herewith is a corresponding affection for Rome. His portrayal
of the hardy country life closes in his declaring it to be the secret of
Etruria's strength, and the cause why

> Rome hath become the fairest thing on earth.[1]

It is curiously parallel to Wordsworth's attitude towards London in his
Sonnet Composed upon Westminster Bridge:

> Earth hath not anything to show more fair.

The combined love of nature and humanity in both poets makes the
parallel more striking.

Under Virgil's elaboration lies a simplicity of feeling apt to be overlooked. Very unlike Wordsworth in his theory of style, Virgil is like
him in finding beauty in some 'unassuming commonplace of nature.'
In the *Georgics* he is not afraid of the humble. With genuine sympathy
he ascribes life and feeling to things: the sun 'feels compassion,' the
south wind 'lays plans,' the moon 'mantles her face in a maiden-blush,'
fruit trees 'feel' their strength; and with the true Virgilian suggestiveness contained in a single word, the ploughlands have the 'wild look of
mourners' (*squalent*) for the tillers they have lost.[2] His epithets are those
of personality. Earth is 'most righteous' (*iustissima tellus*); the slopes
can be 'niggardly' (*maligni*); the ground 'genial' (*facilem*).[3] So it is
with a humour not so much mock-heroic as kindly that in the fourth
Georgic he enters on a miniature epic which has 'the kindred' of the
bees for theme, and their 'high-souled captains' (*magnanimosque duces*)
for heroes. Into their statecraft, their polity, their thrift, and battles he
penetrates with the understanding of genius. Sympathy animates his
sorrow over the destruction of birds' nests,[4] and over the bullock that
loses a mate.[5] Similar sympathy animates pictures of family life, such
as the cottar's winter-night spent in pointing torches with a sharp knife
while his wife beguiles her spinning with song or boils the must.[6] The

---

[1] *G.*, ii. 533:
> 'Sic fortis Etruria creuit;
> Scilicet et rerum facta est pulcherrima Roma.'
Plutarch judged Rome similarly, τῶν ἀνθρωπίνων ἔργων τὸ κάλλιστον, *De Fortuna Romanorum*, 316 E.
[2] *G.*, i. 466; i. 462; i. 431; ii. 426; i. 507.
[3] *G.*, ii. 460; ii. 179; ii. 223.
[4] *G.*, ii. 209:
> 'Antiquasque domos auium cum stirpibus imis
> Eruit: illae altum nidis petiere relictis.'
[5] *G.*, iii. 517:
> 'It tristis arator
> Maerentem abiungens fraterna morte iuuencum,
> Atque opere in medio defixa relinquit aratra.'
[6] *G.*, i. 291 *sqq.*

farmer's home is lit up by the clinging affection of his children, introduced in a less touching situation than in Lucretius, but with beautiful
tenderness:

> *Interea dulces pendent circum oscula nati.*[1]

His own observation furnishes him with a store of incidental descriptions—the wind-storm uprooting the crops; the Po in flood in his own
north country; the charming glimpse back on the old Cilician pirate
turned gardener among his early roses; the vigorous emulation of the
chariot-race.[2] It is the poet's eye that gives so much life and beauty to
his treatment of agricultural instructions—as when, after the practical
specification for a threshing-floor, one comes on a passage like this:

> Mark too when most the walnut in the woods
> Is blossom-clad and bends its fragrant boughs;
> Abundant fruit will bring like crops of corn,
> And with great heat great threshing sure will come.[3]

Virgil's attitude to nature, however, is complex. Two principles strive
to assert themselves. The one is philosophic, the other is romantic.
Virgil is conscious of these contending tastes. Reverently impressed by
Lucretius, he cherishes an aspiration to solve the riddle of the universe
on scientific principles. Philosophy remained an aspiration to Virgil.
Even at the close of life he was still on the quest: he knew he had not
'attained.' So in the *Georgics*, he feels that if this passion for a profounder investigation of nature is not fulfilled, he must fall back on a
simple love of nature's beautiful things (*flumina amem siluasque inglorius*). He has himself placed both attitudes side by side in the second
Georgic:

> First may the Muses, sweet beyond compare,
> Whose acolyte I am, deep smit with love,
> Receive and teach me of heaven's star-lit paths;
> The sun's eclipses; travail of the moon;
> Earthquakes; the force by which deep oceans swell,
> Burst bars and ebb upon themselves again;
> Why winter suns make so much haste to dip
> At sea: what sloth besets the laggard nights.
> But if tame blood at heart shall bar my hopes
> To track such portions of the universe,
> Then fields and brooks in glens shall gladden me,
> Lover of stream and wood, unknown to fame.

[1] *G.*, ii. 523.
[2] *G.*, i. 316–321 ('Saepe ego ... uidi'); i. 481 *sqq.*; iv. 125 *sqq.* ('Namque...
memini'); iii. 103 *sqq.* ('Nonne uides cum praecipiti certamine campum,' etc.).
[3] *G.*, i. 187:
> 'Contemplator item cum se nux plurima siluis
> Induet in florem et ramos curuabit olentis;
> Si superant fetus, pariter frumenta sequentur,
> Magnaque cum magno ueniet tritura calore.'

Oh, where Spercheos? Where the plains? or scene
Of revelling Spartan maids, Taÿgetus?
Oh, who will set me in cool Haemus' dales
Beneath the shield of giant shady boughs?
   Blest he who could unveil the cause of things,
And trample upon Fate inexorable,
On Fears, and roar of Hell insatiate!
   Happy he too who knows our rural gods,
Pan and Silvanus old, and sister-Nymphs.
Him not a nation's rods nor purple robes
Of king could sway, nor brothers' trait'rous feud.[1]

So in his desire to wed the scientific conception of nature to his own passionate love for beautiful scenery, he distinguishes in unsurpassable words between the two attitudes—the Lucretian and the Virgilian.

On comparison with his predecessors, it will be found that no one had given to didactic poetry the beauty of thought, of phrase, and of metrical technique which distinguishes the *Georgics*. And there has been no didactic so beautiful since. Dryden's enthusiasm led him to pronounce the *Georgics* 'the best Poem of the best Poet.' Critics are less dogmatic now. Within the range of Virgil's own works, and with other poets left out of count, there will always be those who prefer the *Aeneid* for its wider human interest and greater stir, and so overlook its less finished art.

The last eleven years of Virgil's life were spent on the twelve books of the *Aeneid*. He began it when he was forty, and worked at it chiefly in the seclusion of Campania. He had long meditated an epic. Like Milton, he cast about among many themes. According to Servius, he

---

[1] *G.*, ii. 475 *sqq.*:

  'Me uero primum dulces ante omnia Musae,
  Quarum sacra fero ingenti percussus amore,
  Accipiant caelique uias et sidera monstrent,
  Defectus solis uarios lunaeque labores,
  Unde tremor terris, qua ui maria alta tumescant
  Obicibus ruptis, rursusque in se ipsa residant,
  Quid tantum Oceano properent se tinguere soles
  Hiberni, uel quae tardis mora noctibus obstet.
  Sin, has ne possim naturae accedere partis,
  Frigidus obstiterit circum praecordia sanguis,
  Rura mihi et rigui placeant in uallibus amnes;
  Flumina amem siluasque inglorius. O ubi campi
  Spercheusque, et uirginibus bacchata Lacaenis
  Taÿgeta? O, qui me gelidis conuallibus Haemi
  Sistat, et ingenti ramorum protegat umbra?
    Felix qui potuit rerum cognoscere causas,
  Atque metus omnis et inexorabile fatum
  Subiecit pedibus strepitumque Acherontis auari!
    Fortunatus et ille, deos qui nouit agrestis,
  Panaque Siluanumque senem Nymphasque sorores.
  Illum non populi fasces, non purpura regum
  Flexit et infidos agitans discordia fratres.'

once felt attracted to the Alban kings.[1] Virgil himself in the *Georgics* promised to celebrate the emperor's wars.[2] But time matured his preference for an epic which should be national without being purely historical.[3] The heroic age, he saw, would admit the glamour of the legendary and the supernatural; the Roman race and the ancestors of its ruling house could be cradled under divine protection; and prophecy could rehearse the historic glories of Rome and Romans. In the story of Aeneas Virgil found his groundwork. His method of composition was to make a prose sketch of the whole, and to elaborate parts in verse at his pleasure. The books, then, were not written in the order of their numbers. Episodes were freely inserted or altered in place. The work was never finished. When dying, Virgil thought three years necessary to perfect it. What Newman called the 'pathetic half lines' are proofs of its unfinished state: there are no such broken lines in the *Georgics*. True, some have wonderful force in the pause they secure —*numina magna deum*; *disce omnes*; *quem tibi iam Troia*. But others are manifestly awkward;[4] and there is no good reason to think them other than first forms of lines which Virgil intended to complete.[5] Much interest was taken in the progress of the work. Propertius sums up the high expectations of literary talk about a Roman poem to eclipse Homer:

Nescio quid maius nascitur Iliade.

In the imperial presence there were readings of verses made doubly melodious by a voice of whose sweetness record has been left. On one such occasion Augustus's sister, Octavia, fainted at the vision in the lower world of the son she had lost in 23 B.C.:

[1] *Cf. Ecl.*, vi. 3:
'Cum canerem reges et proelia, Cynthius aurem
Vellit et admonuit: "pastorem, Tityre, pingues
Pascere oportet oues, deductum dicere carmen".'
[2] *G.*, iii. 46.
[3] Acc. to Donat., *Vit.*, 19, he had felt disappointed with early attempts on historical subjects: 'cum res Romanas incohasset, offensus materia, ad *Bucolica* transiit.'
[4] *E.g.* Aen. i. 534, 'Hic cursus fuit'; i. 560, 'Dardanidae.'
[5] The point is well put by Joseph Trapp, *Praelectiones Poeticae*, ed. 3, 1736, p. 122: 'Versus istos mutilatos quod attinet, qui in *Aeneide* passim occurrunt, sentiunt non pauci, illos a poeta consulto factos fuisse, et stylo poetico venustatem quandam adicere. Adducor tamen potius ut credam, hiatus istos indicia esse operis imperfecti, qui a Virgilio adimpleti fuissent, si divino poemati ultimam manum adhibuisset.' The question can be fairly judged only on consideration of all the cases, not chiefly those where the pause is effective, as in the painful emotion of Andromache at iii. 340. Here Leo, *Plaut. F.*, ed. 2, 1912, p. 41, sees only a sign of the publication of the text exactly as left by Virgil: 'die halben Verse blieben wie sie waren . . . auch der unfertige Satz . . ., iii. 340, blieb.' All the same, attempts were made in quite early editions to supply gaps: *e.g.*, Seneca read in his text at x. 284, 'Audentis Fortuna iuuat, piger ipse sibi obstat.' The attempt shows the great superiority of Virgil's 'imperfection': see Bücheler, *Rh. Mus.*, xxxiv., 623.

Ah, piteous boy! Couldst thou but cleave grim doom!
Marcellus thou shalt be! Come, lilies bring
In handfuls! Let me strew bright blooms and heap
Such gifts for my young kinsman's soul, and pay
A duty unavailing.[1]

Of the twelve books, the first six—recounting the wanderings of Aeneas—were broadly modelled on the *Odyssey*; the last six—recounting his wars and settlement in Italy—on the *Iliad*. Besides Homer, the Cyclic poets and the Homeric hymns were drawn on, especially for Virgil's treatment of Troy and the gods. The Medea in the *Argonautica* of Apollonius Rhodius was a model for much of the passion of Queen Dido in Book IV. Lost, as well as extant, Greek tragedies also affected Virgil's incidents and view of human destiny. An excellent example of his composite method is afforded by the Descent into Hell in Book VI. Modelled on the eleventh *Odyssey*, and destined in turn to mould Dante's *Inferno*, Virgil's underworld gives him scope for coupling Hellenic mythology with Hellenic philosophy. In a Homeric framework he sets Stoic pantheism, Pythagorean doctrines on transmigration of souls, and Platonic myths on the other life. And the whole is inwrought with a mysterious pageant of the great figures of Roman history, in whom the souls shown to Aeneas shall be incarnate. With all this borrowing from Greek, Virgil is one of a national line of poets, even if he is judged solely by his literary debt to Roman writers. Naevius, Ennius, Pacuvius, Accius, Lucilius, Lucretius, are among those who can be cited in poetry; Cato and Varro in prose. And the national ring, which characterises the religious as much as it does the political aspect of the *Aeneid*, is due to Virgil's love for the legends of his native land and to his sympathetic study of books on ritual and augury belonging to the sacred colleges.

To Homer Virgil owed both merits and defects. The general scheme, the duodecimal system of books, the divine 'machinery,' the adventure into the lower world, the description of the shield of Aeneas, the exploit of Nisus and Euryalus, are obvious examples of borrowing. The Homeric influence is not invariably for good. Book V, the feeblest of all, and perhaps an unlucky afterthought, relates the games in honour of Aeneas's dead father because Homer had related the games in honour of the slain Patroclos. Some inapposite incidents and similes would not have been introduced but for the desire to emulate Homer. We could spare much of Book X, with its endless battles and wounds. It has not, as a redeeming feature, the battle-glee which the *Iliad* shares with the

---

[1] *Aen.*, vi. 882 *sqq.*:

'Heu miserande puer! Si qua fata aspera rumpas!
Tu Marcellus eris. Manibus date lilia plenis:
Purpureos spargam flores, animamque nepotis
His saltem accumulem donis, et fungar inani
Munere.'

Icelandic sagas and such Anglo-Saxon poems as *Beowulf*.[1] Virgil does
not enjoy the slayings any more than his reader; he is merely overborne by convention. Similarly, we could spare such a piece of incon-
gruous aping as the beautifying of the hero by his goddess mother to
ensure his captivating Dido. The Greek parallel is at once simpler and
more credible. Yet Virgil was by no means always in mental servitude to
the Homeric tradition. His deepest ideas are not from Homer. He
represents a different class of epic, for he belongs to a more advanced
period of civilisation. He could not possibly have reproduced Homer's
simplicity. Too conscious a purpose pervades the *Aeneid* to admit
naïveté. Homer was much nearer to the primitive epic. But in its calculated art subserving a definite national aim, in its elaborate style, its
learning reared on so much poetry and philosophy of the past, the
Virgilian type has travelled far from the semi-balladic—from a *Kale-
wâla* or a *Nibelungenlied*. There must always be a gulf unbridgeable
between the poetry of perfected form and the poetry of spontaneous
inspiration. On the one side is artistic convention and devoted regard
for technique and music; on the other, a divine possession, a half-
unconscious outwelling of the spirit.[2] It is pointless to range such poets
in classes with the idea of setting the more 'conscious' artist on a lower
plane than the less 'conscious.' There is something as miraculous and
inexplicable in the finish of Virgil, Dante, Milton, as in the apparently
easier effects of Homer, Shakespeare, Burns. It is an antinomy of the
'critical' reason. The difference may be as vast as that between freewill and predestination; but criticism, if it may not reconcile the two
types in the higher unity of genius, must find a welcome for both. In the
temple of literary fame there are many mansions: Virgil has his own
place between the simple vigour of Homer and the exaggerated artificiality of Ovid or Lucan. Elaborate, he remains clear. To compensate
for the absence of fire, he has exactitude of workmanship and equilibrium of style. It is a point Quintilian makes—*quantum eminentioribus
uincimur fortasse aequalitate pensamus.*

As befits his times, Virgil is more critical, urbane, emotional, than
Homer. Conformably to a simpler age, Homer was content to draw his
gods endowed with fluctuating human passions—in Sainte-Beuve's
words, 'tour à tour débonnaires, brusques, colères, personnels, doués de
passions humaines, mais avec des facultés et des forces surnaturelles.'
On Virgil's theology the speculations of philosophy are not wholly lost.
If for poetic purposes he accepts the gods from mythology, he does not
believe in the mythological representation. He turns critically upon his

---

[1] J. Wight Duff, *Homer and Beowulf*, in the Saga-Book of the Viking Club,
vol. iv, pt. ii, 1906, pp. 382–406.
[2] It is the old distinction between the εὐφυής and the μανικός in Aristotle,
Poetics, xvii. 2, διὸ εὐφυοῦς ἡ ποιητική ἐστιν ἢ μανικοῦ· τούτων γὰρ οἱ μὲν εὔπλαστοι
οἱ δὲ ἐκστατικοί (ἐξεταστικοί *codd.*) εἰσιν.

own account, with a saving clause, *si credere dignum est*,[1] or with a question, *tantaene animis caelestibus irae?*[2]

A simplicity, too, that is charmingly natural in older epics would be grotesque in the *Aeneid*. The hero of the *Odyssey* shoots a stag: the poet tells how he ties its legs together, slings it round his neck, and carries it off. 'Tout cela est naïf et d'une bonhomie à la Robinson Crusoe, que Virgile n'a garde de prêter au fondateur du futur empire romain,' to quote Sainte-Beuve again.[3] One cannot imagine Aeneas so acting. Virgil, with a not infrequent tendency to exaggeration, as if he must outbid his epic masters,[4] makes his hero shoot seven stags. But it would not be dignified to make him carry them, even with the help of his *fidus Achates*.[5] The heroic age had long passed. *L'urbanité était née.* But with greater care for the proprieties there is less nature. Homer keeps the attention more closely, and is more fully believed. What reader can accept the legendary if it is artificially Romanised? Virgil allows ideas from developed civilisation to deprive his mythology of the requisite simplicity and remoteness.[6] Again, he has elements of personal emotion tending towards a certain restlessness under the workings of fate. He has not the imperturbable calm of Homer.[7] The depth of feeling which we shall find in him is a part of the romantic in Virgil. One could not define 'romance' in such a way as to exclude the *Odyssey*; and yet one sort of romantic interest is present in Virgil and absent from the more direct, concrete, unreflective Homer. There is in Virgil already more than a presage of the *Weltschmerz*. *Sunt lacrimae rerum* were words born of personal brooding over sorrow. Tears come lightly in the Homeric poems: they are not curiously inquired into or mournfully pondered. Grief and its causes, fate and its ways, are accepted as part of the natural order of things. But this saga-like spirit of acquiescence is not Virgil's. Another element of emotion, and of romance as well, which

---

[1] *Aen.*, vi. 173 (repeated from *G.*, iii. 391), of Triton's jealousy which led to the drowning of Misenus.

[2] *Aen.*, i. 11, of Juno's unrelenting hostility to Aeneas.

[3] *Étude sur Virgile*, 1891, p. 243.

[4] *E.g.*, the boulder thrown by heroes in combat, greater than could be lifted by *two* of later days in Homer, by *four* in Apollonius, by *twelve* in Virgil!

[5] *Aen.*, i. 184–94. Virgil takes care not to say how the carcasses reached the shore.

[6] *E.g.*, the nymph promised by Juno to Aeolus as a reward for raising the storm in *Aen.*, i. is pictured as a Roman matron to be united to him in 'steadfast wedlock' ('conubio stabili'), to spend 'all her years' with him, and make him 'a father with fair progeny.' It is the Roman ideal of the *familia*. It is not poetry.

[7] Prof. W. R. Hardie, *Lects. on Class. Subjects*, 1903, p. 159, illustrates the romantic attitude of Virgil by contrasting one of his imitations with the Homeric original. 'Achilles in Book XX (l. 391) says to Iphition, whom he has mortally wounded: "Here is thy death – thy birth was by the Gygean lake." Virgil in similar words himself addresses a fallen hero: "Here thy race was run, thy goal reached; under Ida stands thy high home, thy high home at Lyrnessus, in Laurentian earth thy grave." The poet himself addresses the dying warrior in sympathetic tones: he rebels against the hardness of fate.'

distinguishes Virgil from Homer is the treatment of love. Made possible by Alexandrine precedent, Virgil's Dido is a finer, stronger, more romantic creation than the Medea of Apollonius. Dido would have been an impossibility to Homer. Equally out of Virgil's range would have been anything so domestic as the parting of Hector and Andromache, or many scenes in the home of Odysseus. With all his tenderness Virgil is not so much concerned with the plainer facts of man's feelings or plainer details of his life. Virgil is more humane; he is less simply human.

The originality of Virgil is most manifest where he is most national. Where he is most national, he is most in touch with his own times. Responsive to the imperial spirit, conscious of the destiny of Rome, possessed with a noble pride in her civilising mission among the nations, and auguring a great future from great prestige, Virgil is pre-eminently the poet of his age. Round imperial aims, religious observances, rural customs, round Italy and Rome, Virgil sets a halo of high sanctions. The sanctions are more than historic. They are divine. So he welds together the historical and mythological epic. The gods have cared for Rome from heroic times. The ages have been ordained to shape her destiny. Aeneas is the pattern of an emperor who shall be father to his people — the *Aeneadae*. His mission is to found a state which shall evolve into empire; to found usages which shall be observed in government, ritual, even in games; to found a family which shall produce Julius and Augustus. To achieve his purpose of glorifying Rome and her ruler, Virgil served himself heir to traditions which formed a precious appanage among the national possessions. His Roman reader could enter into this heritage with him. He could realise how the national life was enriched through the stimulus given to Roman patriotism when genius created pictures of a noble past half mythic, half real, which, like an eternal and silent monitor of the present, offered the surest guarantee of an exalted future. The *Aeneid* is in the mid-current of the national life, not in virtue of any exact reflection of contemporary movements, but in virtue of its fidelity to the essential spirit of Rome, its homage paid to fortitude, endurance, and piety, its lines and scenes reminiscent of glorious deeds. It is a partial view which over-emphasises in Virgil and in Horace their recoil from a current fashion in literature.[1] They are appropriately viewed as types rather of a new age than merely of a new literary fashion. Virgil is the idealist of his day. He reflects its highest aspirations and deepest meaning as Horace reflects its social customs and polite pursuits. Horace stands for the externals of the Augustan age, Virgil for its inwardness. Virgil is spiritual, touched with doctrine, reverie, regrets, misgivings, consecration; he is national, heartened by Rome's achievement and hopeful for her continued great-

[1] H. J. G. Patin, *Études sur la poésie latine*, ed. 4, 1900, tom. i, chap. viii, on 'Des écoles littéraires et des poètes du siècle d'Auguste.'

ness. His brooding melancholy he wedded mystically to this strong confidence in the service which his country must render to the world. Great art is contemporary with all the ages. Doubtless, Virgil can touch universal humanity. So while he has his definite historic position in the new empire, he is also the link between that new empire and the modern world. He had that prophetic instinct which placed him in advance of his time. His Stoic acceptance of destiny relates him in thought more closely to Marcus Aurelius than to Augustus. His regard for the things of the spirit struck harmonious chords in early Christian hearts and led to such legends as that enshrined in the old Mass at Mantua of St. Paul's lament that the poet died in paganism:

> *Ad Maronis mausoleum*
> *Ductus fudit super eum*
> *Piae rorem lacrimae;*
> *'Quem te,' inquit, 'reddidissem*
> *Si te uiuum inuenissem,*
> *Poetarum maxime!'*

The legend of Aeneas had signal advantages as a groundwork. While it could be linked with associations as truly Roman as the story of Romulus could be, it had attractive associations with Greek. Aeneas is not a mighty man of valour in the *Iliad*; still, he is one in whom the gods take interest enough to save him when in peril. The very vagueness of his personality left room for imaginative amplification. The prophecy known to Homer, that he would one day reign over the Trojans, marked him for an exalted destiny. Post-Homeric legend did more for him. He became a prince, not in the Troad, but in Thrace. Thence his travels were fabulously extended to places connected with the cult of his goddess-mother, Aphrodite. In time, through Greek colonies, his fame reached Italy; and we have already noted the employment by Naevius of the myth. For two hundred years the connexion of Aeneas with the Romans as their distant Trojan ancestor had been officially recognised. It remained for Virgil to give the legend final form. What does Virgil make of Aeneas? He does not make him uniformly interesting. Aeneas is dutiful (*pius*) to his old father and to the gods. Though he sometimes needs reminding, he is usually conscious of his divinely appointed destiny to found a new Troy. But the high purpose of heaven becomes oppressive for the reader. This fate-driven exile (*fato profugus*) is too little of a free agent. His desertion of Dido is inevitable on Virgil's hypothesis—for how could Carthage and Rome unite? Yet it leaves Aeneas either more or less than human—either demigod or brute. Hereby the poet proclaims the irresistible power of the celestial will, overruling human hopes and callous to the tragedy of Dido's misplaced love. A woman is nothing, weighed in the balance against the origin of the Roman race. Virgil has won the sympathies of all readers for Dido against his chosen favourite of the gods—so well has he portrayed a woman's passion and despair. Thus the *Aeneid* succeeds in spite of its hero—especially because of the energy thrown into the tale of the last agonies of Troy in Book II, the romantic passion in Book IV, the awe-inspiring visit to the nether regions in Book VI. The character of Aeneas develops as the epic proceeds. In Book VI he gains reflected glory from his mystic guidance by the Sibyl, from his wielding the talisman of the Golden Bough, from the exceptional revelation of the other world to a living man, from the pageant of his descendants passing before his eyes, from the profound instruction of his sire Anchises. In the six books which follow, his wars show Aeneas to be the preordained bringer of civilisation into Latium and the conqueror of barbarous Italian tribes.[1] His enemies may be brave, but they are mainly violent boasters like Turnus, or impious monsters of tyranny like Mezentius. Juno raises Allecto the Fury to stir up Italian resistance but the very powers of hell cannot prevail against Aeneas. Yet in Book XII—the book which next to IX is best in the later half—it is impossible to avoid sympathising with Turnus. He is so utterly foredoomed. The gods trick him. In his struggle with destiny, he remains a man. Aeneas is too often a puppet.

Virgil's love of Italy and of Rome have in the *Aeneid* grown more imperial. It is the enthusiasm of the *Georgics* broadened. There is the old feeling for picturesque Italy of the melodious place-names. Italy is a passion—the land as a whole and the land in detail. The land as a whole is always before Aeneas as the object of his quest.[2] In detail, the love of the land, so evident in *Eclogues* and *Georgics*, is not lost amid the national and human interests of the *Aeneid*. Virgil remained 'lover of stream and wood,' though not 'unknown to fame.' He makes his reader see 'the Mincio from the parent lake Benacus, crowned with grey reed,' 'blue Tiber, river dearest to the sky,' 'the Hernican crags bedewed with becks,' 'the Massic lands glad with the Vine-god,' and the apple-orchards of lofty Abella.[3] In a spirit anticipative of *Balder Dead*, he makes nature weep for a slain warrior skilled in spells:

[1] This view is implicitly accepted in the epithet of Tibullus, II. v. 48, 'barbare Turne.'
[2] *E.g.*, in Aeneas's Cretan vision sent to instruct him, *Aen.*, iii. 163:
'Est locus, Hesperiam Grai cognomine dicunt,
Terra antiqua, potens armis atque ubere glebae.'
Cf. the enthusiastic greeting of the low-lying coast of Italy, surely a reminiscence from some of Virgil's own voyages, iii. 522:
'Cum procul obscuros colles humilemque uidemus
Italiam. Italiam primus conclamat Achates;
Italiam laeto socii clamore salutant.'
[3] *Aen.*, x. 205:
'patre Benaco uelatus arundine glauca
Mincius';
viii. 64:
'Caeruleus Thybris caelo gratissimus amnis';

Anguitia's grove and glassy Fucinus
Mourned thee: for thee the crystal tarns shed tears.[1]

Many epithets flash upon the eye pictures of towns perched on hill-tops
or situated hard by forest, river, or marsh. But there is much more than
the eye for externals. Virgil unites Italy with her own past. There is an
abiding keenness for the historic and the antiquarian interest. This
spirit pervades the gathering of the Italian clans in Book VII or of the
men from Etruria and the North in Book X, the speech by Remulus in
Book IX describing the hardy customs of ancient Italian tribes, or,
again, the woodland rearing of the warrior-maid Camilla in Book XI.
The imperial city is honoured in glimpses of her primeval condition —
as at the festal reception of Aeneas[2] when the Salii perform their ritual
and Evander tells the early history of the land and points out to his
guests spots famous in the Rome of after-days — the Asylum, the cave of
Lupercus, the Argiletum, the Tarpeian rock, and the Capitol:

Now golden, once o'ergrown with salvage brakes.[3]

So with the religious element in Roman life. The native gods find a
place in Virgil, even if they have to be identified by a sort of Ennian
Euhemerism with a dynasty of native kings. Festivals and ritual receive
the sanction of hoary antiquity.[4] Popular beliefs Virgil, as became a
national poet, knew how to employ all through his works. His knack of
turning anthropology into literature is seen in his use of Italian superstitions, saws, and folk-tales. The incantations of the eighth eclogue
are admirably wrought on the principle of 'homoeopathic magic'[5].

---

vii. 683:

                             'roscida riuis
        Hernica saxa';

vii. 725:

                             'felicia Baccho
        Massica';

vii. 740:

        'Et quos maliferae despectant moenia Abellae.'

[1] *Aen.*, vii. 759:

        'Te nemus Anguitiae, uitrea te Fucinus unda,
        Te liquidi fleuere lacus.'

[2] *Aen.*, viii. 280–368.

[3] *Aen.*, viii. 348:

        'Aurea nunc, olim siluestribus horrida dumis.'

[4] *E.g.*, the passage on the true ritual of prayer with fitting vestments and
veiled head, ending in the command, iii. 408:

        'Hunc socii morem sacrorum, hunc ipse teneto;
        Hac casti maneant in religione nepotes.'

[5] The phrase aptly describes Amaryllis's mode of charming Daphnis home,
esp. at *Ecl.*, viii. 80:

        'Limus ut hic durescit, et haec ut cera liquescit
        Uno eodemque igni: sic nostro Daphnis amore.'

J. G. Frazer, *Lects. on the Early Hist. of the Kingship*, 1905, p. 38, prefers this
phrase quoted from Y. Hirn's *Origins of Art*, 1900, to the older phrases
'imitative' or 'mimetic magic'; see S. Hartland, *Folklore*, viii, 1897, p. 65.

There is more poetry, if less realism, than in Horace's witch Canidia. Virgil returns to the subject of sorcery in the *Aeneid* when he introduces the Sibyl or the wizard for whom the groves and lakes shed tears. To the *Georgics* humble life had contributed proverbial expressions like *hiberno laetissima puluere farra*; *nudus ara, sere nudus*; *quid uesper serus uehat*.[1] The heroic epic has its elements of popular origin. The sign that Aeneas has won his appointed destination is of the homeliest order — of the type which in folk-story has so often associated the foundation of a city with an animal. It is a sow and her litter. The apparently dread prophecy that Aeneas and his followers will be reduced to 'eating their tables' is realised, after the true manner of the folk-tale, by circumventing destiny. Just as an evil omen may be among primitive tribes annulled by a mimic fulfilment, so Virgil is probably parodying some Italian folk-story when he replaces a real calamity by a mock one. All this proves the breadth of Virgil's interest in his native land. But what crowns her most with honour is her imperial destiny. Her mission to rule Virgil conceives to be as firmly ordained by fate as Aeneas's mission to found a settlement in Italy. The promise of empire is among the earliest notes of the poem:

> *Populum late regem belloque superbum.*[2]

Jupiter's assurance is one of boundless possessions and sway:

> *His ego nec metas rerum nec tempora pono:*
> *Imperium sine fine dedi.*[3]

The vision at Crete foretells exaltation for the Trojan descendants and power for the city:

> *Idem uenturos tollemus in astra nepotes*
> *Imperiumque urbi dabimus;*[4]

and so on, through the epic, when Jupiter decides that Aeneas must part from Dido,[5] when in Elysium the Roman's task is contrasted with the artistic eminence of the Greek,[6] when the native oracle of Faunus warns King Latinus of the future greatness of the strangers,[7] and when the figures hammered on the shield of Aeneas mark out the extent of the Roman dominions.[8] It is no matter for wonder that this patriotic

---

[1] *G.*, i. 101, 299, 461. At the second of these Virgil's detractors mocked in the line:
> ' "Nudus ara, sere nudus": habebis frigore febrim!'
[2] *Aen.*, i. 21.
[3] *Aen.*, i. 278.
[4] *Aen.*, iii. 158.
[5] *Aen.*, iv. 229–34.
[6] *Aen.*, vi. 851:
> 'Tu regere imperio populos, Romane, memento.'
[7] *Aen.*, vii. 98–101:
> 'Omnia sub pedibus,' etc.
[8] *Aen.*, viii. 724–31.

sentiment should involve a disdain in Virgil for other nations—a sense
of Italy against the world. Thus, foreign gods of monstrous birth like
the dog-headed Anubis are introduced on the shield of Aeneas in vain
opposition to the Roman gods.[1] The poet, too, takes evident satisfaction
in regarding the subjection of Greece to the overlordship of Rome as
fair revenge for the Greek capture of Troy.[2] Still, this imperialism is no
vulgar lust of conquest, but a confidence in civilising and pacifying
power. The rule of mercy (*parcere subiectis*) laid down by the poet is
the same as Augustus's own claim on the *Monumentum Ancyranum*.[3]

The imperial note centres in Virgil's attitude to Augustus. Emperor-
worship, so strange to modern views, was favoured by many circumstances at Rome. The veneration of departed ancestors and the belief
in the individual's *genius* facilitated the recognition of a divine principle
in a dead or a living emperor. In any case, to an ancient Italian the terms
deus and *diuinus* conveyed less than to a modern mind. It was a 'divine'
thing to be a great benefactor of humanity. A Caesar who could restore
the Golden Age of security was like a Hercules or a Bacchus. There was,
too, a strong sanction, half-political, half-religious, attaching to the
supreme ruler. The religious idea of *Roma* centred in the *Fortuna Urbis*.
It was outwardly embodied in the emperor. He represented and
guarded the success of the state. So temples might appropriately be
dedicated to Augustus and Rome jointly—such as that at Ancyra on
whose walls the famous *Monumentum* was found. Naturally, it was in
the East that the doctrine of a god-emperor would be most literally
accepted, for it fitted into the traditional belief of Orientals. Virgil's
eulogies came, not from servility, nor from merely friendly admiration,
but from a recognition of the god-like gifts which had brought to mankind the blessings of ordered government. Implicit compliments to the
ruler are traceable now in a trait of Aeneas, now in a prophecy, now in
the establishment of games, such as those at Actium suggestive of the
victory over Antony. But there are three outstanding passages where
notable honours are conferred on the emperor or his house, as culminating figures to whom all Roman history has led up. The deification prophesied in Book I[4] may apply to Julius Caesar or to his adopted
son—it is doubtful which. In the other two Augustus is named. The
Elysian vision of souls beholds in him a god's son who will re-establish

[1] *Aen.*, viii. 698:
'Omnigenumque deum monstra et latrator Anubis.'
[2] *Aen.*, i. 283:
'Veniet lustris labentibus aetas
Cum domus Assaraci Phthiam clarasque Mycenas
Seruitio premet ac uictis dominabitur Argis.'
[3] *Mon. Ancyr.*, 3, 'Victorque omnibus [superstitib]us ciuibus peperci.
Exte[rnas] gentes quibus tuto [ignosci pot[ui]t co]nseruare quam excidere
m[alui].'
[4] *Aen.*, i. 290: 'uocabitur hic quoque uotis.'

for Latium the Golden Age as it was in the reign of Saturn:[1] the shield
pictures him triumphant and miraculously attended by the star[2]
emblematic of the legendary descent from Venus alluded to in the ninth
eclogue

> *Ecce Dionaei processit Caesaris astrum.*

In sum and substance, this attitude constitutes Virgil the poetic apostle
of imperial autocracy. His central idea is to uphold the new monarchy as
one foreshadowed in the fatherly leadership of Aeneas, and predestined
to follow the long and glorious evolution of the republic. It is a historic
idea majestic in its historic associations. It flattered the national pride.
But it does not stir the heart. The appeal from Roman patriotism to
human emotion at large comes elsewhere — in the fortunes of those who
struggle against the fate which looms so big in the epic, in Virgil's own
pity for the victims of his central idea, in his moments of brooding
over the mysteries of life and death.

Virgil's tender melancholy is merged in his profound reflections. He
both thought and felt deeply on life. The world viewed strictly from a
physical standpoint had always been for him an attraction and a riddle.
This tendency marks Silenus's song in the *Eclogues*, the aspirations
after the 'causes of things' in the *Georgics*, and the song of creation
given to Iopas at the court of Dido. But there were enigmas more per-
plexing still. Man's place in the world, the meaning of life, the origin
and destiny of souls, the issues of death, are problems on which
Anchises expounds the Virgilian philosophy. The same mind which
struggled under the burden of all this unintelligible world was most
sensitively responsive to the suffering of human beings:

> Tears haunt the world; man's fortunes touch man's heart.[3]

This tenderness is one secret of Virgil's perennial power. A spirit of
humanity saves his patriotism from being too exclusive — too entirely
Roman. His breadth of sympathy gives to him an aspect of modernity.
Yet it simply means that he is universal. His feeling is at times as
natural as Homer's, but it is expressed with a subtlety inseparable from
a more advanced civilisation. As an embodiment of the classic spirit
Virgil does not seek to evoke rare and remote emotions. He does not
pursue the romantic quest after dazzling surprises in passion or invention. Rather he expresses depths of feeling common to mankind, and
while touching chords to which all hearts can respond, he gains his

---

[1] *Aen.*, vi. 791:
> 'Hic uir, hic est, tibi quem promitti saepius audis,
> Augustus Caesar, Diui genus, aurea condet
> Saecula qui rursus Latio.'

[2] *Aen.*, viii. 678–81.

[3] *Aen.*, i. 462:
> 'Sunt lacrimae rerum, et mentem mortalia tangunt.'

triumph in art by perfection of utterance. Words are combined with theme so that the Virgilian musings, descriptions, speeches, rich in a compassionate tenderness, attain the finished beauty of a solemn music. All is stately and impressive. There is no *abandon*—unless perhaps momentary suggestions in the frenzy of the Trojan at bay (*arma amens capio*) or of Dido in despair. This calm pathos, then, centres in element- ary human affections. Aeneas is touched to see his countrymen's woes depicted in art;[1] Daedalus is unnerved when he comes to represent the death of his boy;[2] the young warrior, Euryalus, on the eve of a perilous enterprise, is unable to say 'good-bye' to his mother; he commends to the care of Iulus that mother who is so soon to be frenzied with grief;[3] but his own death comes like a thing of beauty:

> As when, by ploughshare lopped, a crimson flower
> Droopeth in death: or poppies weary-necked
> Have bowed the head, laden mayhap with rain.[4]

With this gift for seeing beauty in sorrow, Virgil describes the dead prince Pallas on his bier about to be carried home to his old father:

> Like flower cropt by maiden's hand, perchance
> Soft violet or drooping hyacinth,
> Its brilliance dimmed, though beauty be not gone:
> No longer mother-earth gives food and strength.[5]

It is Virgil's own heart that gives to Aeneas his allied piety and pity.[6] Aeneas is deeply moved when he slays Lausus in the act of succouring his father. The sword pierced the tunic which the lad's 'mother had spun with thread of gold; and blood drenched his bosom':

> But when he saw that dying look and face—
> Face pale in wondrous wise—Anchises' son
> In ruth groaned deeply and outstretched his hand:
> His mind drew pictures how he loved his sire.[7]

---

[1] *Aen.*, i. 462.   [2] *Aen.*, vi. 30–33.
[3] *Aen.*, ix. 288, 290, 475 *sqq.*
[4] *Aen.*, ix. 435:
> 'Purpureus ueluti cum flos, succisus aratro,
> Languescit moriens, lassoue papauera collo
> Demisere caput, pluuia cum forte grauantur.'
[5] *Aen.*, xi. 68:
> 'Qualem uirgineo demessum pollice florem
> Seu mollis uiolae seu languentis hyacinthi,
> Cui neque fulgor adhuc nec dum sua forma recessit;
> Non iam mater alit tellus uiresque ministrat.'
[6] Sainte-Beuve, *op. cit.*, p. 100, 'Virgile, comme son héros, a la piété et la pitié, parfois une teinte de tristesse, de mélancholie presque.'
[7] *Aen.*, x. 821:
> 'At uero ut uultum uidit morientis et ora,
> Ora modis Anchisiades pallentia miris,
> Ingemuit miserans grauiter dextramque tetendit:
> Et mentem patriae subiit pietatis imago.'

This tenderness dictates lines over which the voice may falter, as Virgil's own voice did; lines that wrung imperial tears or made a bereaved mother swoon; lines to haunt a mystic, and to beckon a Savonarola towards a heavenly life;[1] lines of expected comfort or warning for believers in the *Sortes Vergilianae*.

Chiefly to this power of reading the heart is due Virgil's success in Dido. Her place in the story of Aeneas has been already glanced at. Dido blocks the advance of fate. She must perish. It is the conflict familiar in Greek drama—the individual against the divine will. To resist the destined establishment of Aeneas in Italy is to tread the way of madness and doom. Aeneas's alliance with Dido was wrong. His interests were the interests of Rome. Virgil meant readers to feel that. Desertion of Dido became a duty: it cannot be judged—or at least understood—by standards of chivalry. Dido represented Rome's enemy, Carthage. But at this point Virgil's tenderness intervenes. She is no temptress: she is *infelix Dido*. From the outset the poet sets himself to compel admiration for the queen. And he succeeds in making her the most engrossing of all his figures. Interest is awakened by her royal demeanour, her sorrowful past, her generosity towards strangers, her passion for their prince, her desertion by him, and her tortures of despair. How well Virgil succeeded in drawing a woman[2] is proved by that sympathy which he wins for her against his hero. A melancholy haunts her life. Her ready kindness to the Trojans is the outcome of a fellow feeling:

> Well schooled in ill, I learn to aid distress.[3]

The pleadings with her betrayer, the half-confidences to her sister, the well-concealed resolution to die, are full of tragic power. Her death is expressed in a line of wonderful sadness

> Sought light in heaven—groaned when light she found.[4]

Then the flames of her funeral pyre light up the sea over which the Trojan has set sail: and the reader feels how little Aeneas deserves his kingdom in Italy. Certainly, one of the finest things in Virgil is the silent disdain with which Dido's shade turns from Aeneas's tearful entreaty in Hades.[5] St. Augustine shed over Dido tears that were surely

---

[1] *Aen.*, iii. 44:
> 'Heu! fuge crudeles terras, fuge litus auarum.'

[2] Sainte-Beuve, *op. cit.*, p. 100, 'Il a dans la peinture de sa touchante victime, de sa Didon immortelle, toutes les tendresses et les secrets féminins de la passion.'

[3] *Aen.*, i. 630:
> 'Non ignara mali miseris succurrere disco.'

[4] *Aen.*, iv. 692:
> 'Quaesiuit caelo lucem ingemuitque reperta.'

[5] *Aen.*, vi. 466:
> 'Quem fugis? extremum fato, quod te alloquor, hoc est.'

pardonable. Her own words, *agnosco ueteris uestigia flammae*, were used worthily to express Dante's love for Beatrice in Paradise.

To the romantic aspect of Virgil's emotional power we have already adverted. Romanticism pervades the story of Dido. But Virgil's romance is not confined to this element. He is romantic in his command over dread, over the adventurous, even over the grotesque—as in the episode of the foul Harpies. He transports his reader into the most marvellous of surroundings—the Cave of the blustering Winds,[1] or the Forge of the Cyclopes.[2] It is in the sixth book that this manner is best exemplified. The book is one mass of romance. The note of unearthly awe is struck in the eerie abode of the Sibyl and her inspired frenzy. Then follows a pageant of marvels—the quest of the Golden Bough; the guidance by the doves of Venus; the Sibyl's invocation to Hecate; Aeneas's sacrifice to Night, Earth, Proserpina, and Pluto; the frightful Shapes at the entrance to Hell; the Tree of Empty Dreams; monsters of the Shadow-land; the way to Acheron; Charon's boat; the mystery why some embark and some are left; the ghosts of those lost at sea; the ferrying of the infernal stream; the hell-hound Cerberus; spirits of human beings in contrast with goblin forms which may not cross the Styx; the Bourne of the infants; the Bourne of the unjustly condemned; the Bourne of guiltless suicides; the Mourning Plains; the eternal farewell to Dido; haunts of warriors; the prison-house of Tartarus confining rebellious demigods and the worst human offenders; the groves of Elysian bliss where the wraith of Anchises expounds the purgatory and reincarnation of spirits in conjunction with the doctrine of the World-soul; the mystic vision of the great men of Rome; and the paradoxical dismissal of Aeneas and the Sibyl back to workaday life through the Ivory Gate whence issue false dreams.[3] The description of the Gates of Hell may be quoted as a typical illustration:

> A cavern deep there was,
> Immeasurable in its desolate gape,
> Of ragged rock, and sheltered with black mere
> And darkling groves around. O'er it no thing
> That flies could flit unscathed nor stretch its flight
> On wing; so rank a breath, from inky jaws
> Outpoured, was wafted to the vaulted sky.[4]

---

[1] *Aen.*, i. 50 *sqq.*

[2] *Aen.*, viii. 416 *sqq.*

[3] Servius comments gravely 'et poetice apertus est sensus, uult enim intellegi falsa esse omnia quae dixit.' To this he adds a physiological interpretation that the 'porta cornea' symbolises the eyes, which see 'uera'; and the 'porta eburnea' the mouth ('a dentibus'), which may utter falsehood!

[4] *Aen.*, vi. 237 *sqq.*:

> 'Spelunca alta fuit, uastoque immanis hiatu,
> Scrupea, tuta lacu nigro nemorumque tenebris;
> Quam super haud ullae poterant impune uolantes
> Tendere iter pennis: talis sese halitus atris
> Faucibus effundens supera ad convexa ferebat.'

Here, under the Sibyl's direction, Aeneas offers victims to the powers of darkness; then with sword drawn and steadfast heart (*pectore firmo*) plunges, like the Sibyl, wildly (*furens*) into the yawning cave. It is a moment of breathless suspense, and the poet pauses to utter a fresh invocation:

> Ye Gods whose realm is Soul, ye silent Shades,
> Chaos and Phlegethon, hush'd tracts of Night,
> Grant me to utter that which I have heard
> And by your grace to show realities
> O'erwhelmed in gloom beneath the depths of earth![1]

Then the venture into Hell continues:

> Through mirk they fared unwrapt in lonely night,
> Through Pluto's halls unfilled and ghostly realms,
> E'en as 'neath niggard light of fitful moon
> There runs a road through trees, when Jupiter
> Shrouds heaven, and inky night steals every hue.
> Before the Door—the opening jaws of Hell—
> Grief and the Venging Cares have set their couch;
> There wan Diseases dwell and dolorous Eld,
> Fear, ill-advising Famine, loathly Want,
> Dread shapes to look upon—and Death and Toil,
> Then Death's own brother Sleep, and Evil Joys
> Of mind, and on the threshold full in view
> Death-dealing Warfare and the iron cells
> Of the Eumenides and maddening Strife,
> Her viper tresses twined in bloody wreaths.[2]

Much of Virgil's utterance to his times took the form of a symbolism borrowing, as it were, ethereal colours from distant spheres of imagination and bearing on things present with an intangible suggestiveness. Words were by Virgil so experimented on as to raise in the mind

[1] *Aen.*, vi. 264 *sqq*:
'Di quibus imperium est animarum, Vmbraeque silentes,
Et Chaos et Phlegethon, loca nocte tacentia late,
Sit mihi fas audita loqui; sit numine uestro
Pandere res alta terra et caligine mersas.'
[2] *Aen.*, vi. 268 *sqq.*:
'Ibant obscuri sola sub nocte per umbram
Perque domos Ditis uacuas et inania regna:
Quale per incertam lunam sub luce maligna
Est iter in siluis, ubi caelum condidit umbra
Iupiter, et rebus nox abstulit atra colorem.
Vestibulum ante ipsum primisque in faucibus Orci
Luctus et ultrices posuere cubilia Curae;
Pallentesque habitant Morbi, tristisque Senectus,
Et Metus et malesuada Fames, ac turpis Egestas –
Terribiles uisu formae – Letumque Labosque;
Tum consanguineus Leti Sopor, et mala mentis
Gaudia, mortiferumque aduerso in limine Bellum,
Ferreique Eumenidum thalami, et Discordia demens
Vipereum crinem uittis innexa cruentis.'

indefinable associations transcending the ordinary meaning and transcending ordinary experience. A sense is constantly produced as of some
dim realm of moods almost beyond expression—a background consisting of another world. The implication within a single word, or the
juxtaposition of several, or perhaps their very music, may possess an
incommunicable hint of awe or sadness. It is a symbolism inherent in
the Virgilian temperament. In some of its effects it anticipates the
modern symbolism of Poe, Baudelaire, Verlaine, and Maeterlinck. One
confirmation is to be found in the new light and new emotions discoverable at each new reading of the *Aeneid*. This wealth of varied
suggestion seems to begin almost in Virgil's vague use of cases. He has
surprising genitives, and fascinating ambiguities between an ablative
and a dative, so that phrases like *facilis descensus Auerno* and *it clamor
caelo* can be taken in more ways than one. But, of course, it is something
far more than grammatical fluidity. It is to be expected of an artist so
consummate that by fresh applications or cunning union of words—
Horace's *callida iunctura*—he shall obtain absolutely novel effects in
language. The true meaning does not always lie on the surface. Virgil
loves to wield this infinite power of raising other trains of thought and
to leave ambiguous his real meaning. So there are esoteric suggestions
in such phrases as

> *Hi motus animorum atque haec certamina tanta*
> *Pulueris exigui iactu compressa quiescunt,*

or

> *Facilis iactura sepulcri,*

or

> *Sunt lacrimae rerum,*

or

> *Distulit in seram commissa piacula mortem,*

or

> *Quisque suos patimur manes.*[1]

Apart from the symbolism in language, there is a symbolism of incident
and character in the *Aeneid*—a meaning for Golden Bough and Ivory
Gate, a hazy foreshadowing of Augustus in Aeneas, and a clearer foreshadowing of many observances adopted in Virgil's own day. But it is
dangerously easy to overstate Virgil's allusions to his own times, and
to see allegory where none was intended.[2]

The beauty of Virgil's style was produced by a minute and sedulous
shaping of words in the endeavour to satisfy the imperious demands of a
refined self-criticism and an ear divinely attuned. His horror of hurried
workmanship implied the passion for the finishing hand. In this critical
attitude he was at one with Horace. Virgil's ideal was the choice of

---

[1] *G.*, iv. 86–87; *Aen.*, ii. 646; i. 462; vi. 569; vi. 743.
[2] *E.g.*, it hinders the appreciation of Dido's character to regard her as suggesting Cleopatra.

words which in themselves and in association are winsome, impressive, and worthy of a noble theme. By touching and retouching—which, however, frequently fell short of his own exalted standard—he achieved unrivalled mastery over the music of Latin verse. No Roman poet ever used the hexameter with such power and variety. It ranged in his hands from the rapidity of the galloping horse,

Quadrupedante putrem sonitu quatit ungula campum,[1]

to the slow toil of the Cyclopes at their forge,

Illi inter sese magna ui bracchia tollunt.[2]

He could copy or refine upon the Ennian alliteration, and imitate the hissing surge of the salt sea-spray among the rocks in

Obiectae salsa spumant aspergine cautes;[3]

he could introduce a verse stately as with the tone of ancient ritual

Cum patribus populoque penatibus et magnis dis,[4]

or resounding like

Romanos rerum dominos gentemque togatam,[5]

or filled with compassion in

Venit summa dies et ineluctabile tempus,[6]

or in

Vrbs antiqua ruit multos dominata per annos,[7]

or lines touched with the fairness of another world

Deuenere locos laetos et amoena uireta
Fortunatorum nemorum sedesque beatas.[8]

His faculty of compact utterance, too, is seen in phrases grown almost proverbial from frequent quotation—*dis aliter uisum*; *dux femina facti*; *auri sacra fames*; *mens agitat molem*; *audentes fortuna iuuat*. But it is to beauty that, like Dante, one returns as the final fact and feature of his style. Under Virgil's verbal sorcery, Latin becomes a golden language of exquisite richness, veined with a delicate melancholy and wistful reverie upon the abundant travail of life. If his wealth of tremulous pities and mystic dreams do not make true poetry, then poetry was never written.

Virgil had an assured fame during his lifetime. Eagerly expected, the *Aeneid* acted on literature instantaneously. Tibullus and Propertius

---

[1] *Aen.*, viii. 596.
[2] *G.*, iv. 174, repeated *Aen.*, viii. 452.
[3] *Aen.*, iii. 534.
[4] *Aen.*, viii. 679.
[5] *Aen.*, i. 282.
[6] *Aen.*, ii. 324.
[7] *Aen.*, ii. 363.
[8] *Aen.*, vi. 638.

show this. Horace in an ode of his fourth book alludes to the theme of
the recently published epic. The influence operated more definitely
upon Ovid and Manilius, and during the first century it operated
through the Virgilian tradition in epic—the tradition which had supplanted the Ennian—upon Lucan, Statius, Silius, and Valerius Flaccus.
The didactic poem *Aetna* was so charged with Virgilianisms that
it was long ascribed to Virgil. But outside epic, didactic, and descriptive poetry, Virgil's influence appeared in Juvenal's *Satires* and
Martial's *Epigrams*. Among historians it affected Livy, and, in a very
decided manner, Tacitus.

As a manual in schools of grammar and rhetoric, the text of Virgil
exerted an influence not only on literature, but on the Latin language as
a whole. It marked a vast change in style from the work of Livius
Andronicus, which had enjoyed an educational vogue for two centuries.
Q. Caecilius Epirota, a freedman of Atticus, was the first to use Virgil
and other Augustans (*alios poetas nouos*) as reading-books.[1] Virgil
became the standard authority in language. His influence on society,
through education both elementary and advanced, was enormous.
Juvenal is our witness for the use of Virgil and Horace as school-books
in the first century.[2] He is also our witness for the part played by the
Aeneid in literary talk; he instances a lady who discussed Dido's character and compared Virgil and Homer.[3] An upstart like Trimalchio in
Petronius felt he must pretend to know Virgil, and quotations scratched
on the walls at Pompeii are eloquent of the wide dissemination of his
lines.

The predominance of Virgil is manifest in the amount of grammatical, exegetical, and literary commentary upon him.[4] Between the
first edition of the *Aeneid* by Varius and Tucca about 17 B.C., and the
first critical edition by the deservedly famous Probus in the time of
Nero, there had been much criticism. It was not invariably flattering.
Indeed, Virgil had never been without detractors.[5] In his own days
there was the enmity of a Bavius and a Mevius to contend with.
There were also charges of affectation, plausibly founded on Virgil's
use of old words after a fashion difficult in its novelty. Horace defended
him implicitly in the *Ars Poetica* when he prescribed a 'cunning juxtaposition' as a bit of good style (*dixeris egregie*). He defended Virgil
explicitly against charges of being new-fangled when he asked why
Virgil and Varius should not use new words as Ennius and Cato had
done. From the time of the *Vergiliomastix* there were several foolish

[1] Suet., *De Gramm.*, 16.
[2] Juv., vii. 227.
[3] Juv., vi. 434 *sqq.*
[4] Comparetti, *op. cit.*, chaps. iii and iv; J. E. Sandys, *Hist. Class. Scholarship*, ed. 3, 1921, vol. i, p. 196.
[5] Donat., *Vit.*, 43, 'Obtrectatores Vergilio numquam defuerunt; nec mirum,
nam ne Homero quidem.'

books on Virgil's 'blemishes' (*uitia*) and 'plagiarisms' (*furta*), by
authors whose names do not call for record. Some were answered by
Asconius, the renowned commentator on Cicero. Of such carping
criticism no more need be said. The Verona scholia include inter-
pretations as far back as those of Cornutus—the friend and teacher of
Persius—Velius Longus in Trajan's time, and Asper at the end of the
second century. Part of the fanciful allegorising by Aelius Donatus
survives in the more sober commentary of the learned Servius, composed about the end of the fourth century and transmitted with the
encumbrance of later interpolations. The Virgilian influence was strong
enough to hold its own despite the preference of the Frontonianists in
the second century for earlier work by Ennius, Lucilius, and Lucretius.
It was Virgil's good fortune to keep the favour of two opposing literary
schools in the early empire—of the leaders of the modern group like
Seneca, and (though it is true that Fronto hardly quotes him) of the
antiquarian enthusiasts like Gellius. What Virgil meant to scholars of
the fourth and fifth centuries may be illustrated by the facts that Nonius
quotes nearly 1,500 passages from him, and that Macrobius discusses
his poetry with such fulness in the *Saturnalia*.

The patching together of Virgilian phrases into centos[1]—once
esteemed for their ingenuity—has at least the value of proving the
intimate acquaintance with Virgil's words on the part of people barren
of ideas. In Tertullian's time Hosidius Geta put together a tragedy,
Medea, out of Virgil. Christian centos devoted to themes like Old
Testament history, the Passion, the Incarnation,[2] multiplied so plenti-
fully that they had eventually to be declared apocryphal by papal
authority. During the late decadence of Latin poetry the Virgilian
tradition assumes such strange guises as one finds in the opening of an
idyll by Pope Damasus I:

Tityre tu fido recubans sub tegmine Christi.

A different spirit had animated Ausonius's prostitution of Virgil's lines
to convey obscene ideas in his *Cento Nuptialis*. The Emperor Valen-
tinian had the demerit of trying his hand at such work, and of ordering
Ausonius to compete. Yet it is doubtful if this kind of cento—certainly
clever in the case of Ausonius—implied any more disrespect than the
comparatively modern travesties by Scarron in French, by Milton's
nephew Phillips in English, and by Blumauer in German.

Virgil's renown became something far deeper than a literary or
grammatical fashion. It was almost a worship. Silius Italicus kept

---

[1] Comparetti, *op. cit.*, chap. v.; O. Delepierre, *Tableau de la litt. du centon
chez les anciens et les modernes*, 1875. The earliest collection of Virgilian centos
is in the Codex Salmasianus (eighth century), which forms the bulk of the first
vol. of Bücheler and Riese's *Anthologia Latina*.
[2] Among later examples may be cited Gryphius's *Virgiliocentones con-
tinentes uitam Saluatoris nostri Domini Iesu Christi*, and Ross's *Christiad*.

Virgil's birthday, revering his tomb as Statius did. Martial regarded the Ides of October as a kind of Saint's Day.[1] By the second century Virgil had come to be esteemed as more than a guide in language—his words might throw light on the future. Hadrian consulted the *Sortes Vergilianae*. Gradually the superstition grew. Virgil's tenderness and spirituality appeared half-Christian: his reputed omniscience appeared magical. One set of legends made him a prophet of Christ: another made him a necromancer. By the twelfth century at Naples the common people attributed to Virgil the most astounding powers of working wonders. He was 'il gran matematico'—a marvellous builder, engineer, changer of shapes, and controller of fiends. Elements in the popular notion are by Dante wedded to the learned tradition. But with all the mysterious powers and profound lore ascribed to Virgil as *magus* and *sapiens*, Dante does not underestimate his lofty art. The purely literary side of Virgil is acknowledged in declaring him to be the 'master' from whom he borrowed 'the fair style' of the *Divina Commedia*.'[2]

Virgil has many claims to greatness. His amazing verbal art is one. His power to touch the feelings is another. His influence on literature, and even his fame in the Middle Ages, are others still. But his historic position alone, as the poet of the empire, would assure him one of the highest places. To minimise his creative gifts—either on the ground of his borrowings and conventions, as if he were a second-hand plagiarist, or on the ground of his conscious aim, as if he overdid the didactic—is to miss the significance of Virgil's relation to his age. In this respect French criticism has more consistently appreciated Virgil than German criticism. English criticism has had its fluctuations. But to write the supreme epic of an empire like the Roman is not given to any but a deep thinker and a great artist. Virgil's wide scholarship yielded materials of which an inferior craftsman would have made patchwork. He created a unity. The obligations to Greece leave the poem entirely national. His poetic insight recognised the continuity of Italy past and present, recognised the incarnation of her greatness in the ruler of the day, and recognised her queenship among the nations. To Virgil more than to any other, the imperial grandeur of Rome was revealed.

[1] Mart., XII. lxvii. 3:
        'Octobres Maro consecrauit Idus.'
[2] *Inferno*, i. 85–87:
                'Tu se' lo mio maestro e il mio autore:
                Tu se' solo colui da cui io tolsi
                Lo bello stile che m' ha fatto onore.'

Chapter II

THE MINOR POEMS ATTRIBUTED TO VIRGIL

The contents of the *Appendix Vergiliana* – *Catalepton* – A suggested time-grouping of the seven chief poems – The *Ciris* in relation to a Virgilian circle – Likelihood that it preceded the *Eclogues* – *Dirae* and *Lydia* – *Copa* – *Moretum* – *Culex* – Qualities of *Aetna* – Theories on its date.

AMONG the most vexed problems in Latin literature are those that turn on the authorship of the minor poems ascribed to Virgil.[1] Donatus (that is, virtually Suetonius) quotes as Virgil's first essay in poetry a distich on the bandit Ballista. Then follows this list: *Catalepton*, *Priapea*, *Epigrammata*, *Dirae*, *Ciris*, and the *Culex*, written, he states, when Virgil was sixteen. After a summary of the *Culex*, not absolutely consistent with the poem as we have it, he adds that Virgil wrote also *Aetna*, 'which is a subject of dispute,' and that after starting on a historical theme, he found the subject-matter irksome, and took up pastoral poetry.[2] Donatus's evidence, then, makes them juvenile poems, earlier than the *Eclogues*. The life prefixed to the Commentary of Servius gives the same titles in a different order, inserting the *Copa*.[3] The usual contents of the *Appendix Vergiliana* consist of these pieces, with the exception of *Aetna*, which few believe to be Virgil's, but with the addition of the *Moretum*, for which there is no external evidence, and of four pieces which nobody can refer to Virgil, *Est et non*, *Vir Bonus*, and the two *Elegiae in Maecenatem*. About most of these, critics differ widely on the assessment of their claims to be poetry and to be Virgil's. Thus when Professor Mackail discussed the ascrip-

[1] Text: *Appendix Vergiliana* (*Culex, Dirae, Copa, Aetna, Ciris, Priapea, Epigrammata* [*Catalecta*], *Moretum*) in Bährens's *Poet. Lat. Min.*, vol. ii., 1880; *Culex*, F. Leo (acc. *Copa*), 1891; *App. Verg.* (*Culex, Ciris, Copa, Moretum, Catalepton, Dirae, Lydia*), O. Ribbeck, ed. 2, 1895; *App. Verg. siue carmina minora Vergilio adtributa* (as in Ribbeck's ed., without *Aetna*), R. Ellis, 1907; *Aetna*, H. A. J. Munro, 1867; S. Sudhaus, 1898; proleg., trans., comment., and bibliography, R. Ellis, 1901; (w. Fr. trans. and comm.) J. Vessereau, 1905. Translations: *Virgil's Gnat*, Ed. Spenser, 1591 (in the eight-lined stanza fitted by Pulci and Berni to burlesque narrative or satire, and familiar in Byron's *Beppo* and *Don Juan*); *The Ceiris* (verse), E. B. Greene, 1780.
[2] Donat., *Vit. Verg.*, 19. 'Scripsit etiam de qua ambigitur *Aetnam*. Mox cum res Romanas incohasset, offensus materia ad *Bucolica* transiit.'
[3] Serv., *Vit. Verg.*, 'Scripsit etiam septem siue octo libros hos: *Cirin, Aetnam, Culicem, Priapea, Catalepton, Epigrammata, Copam, Diras.*'

tion to Virgil of the *Culex*, *Ciris*, and *Moretum*, he found 'a greater or less amount of *prima facie* plausibility in the case of all three.'[1] Professor Robinson Ellis, though he believed the rhetorical style of *Aetna* and other arguments were against its being Virgil's (or even Augustan), added the qualification, 'yet the ascription to him should not be entirely overlooked';[2] and Kruczkiewicz defended the old belief in the Virgilian authorship.[3] On the other hand, Professor Housman declared that the authors of *Culex* and *Ciris* and *Aetna* were mediocre poets and worse, and that the gods and men and booksellers whom they affronted allotted them to worse than mediocre scribes. Between the extreme views on nearly every poem there is room for the most varied refinement of theory.

The *Catalepton*—already mentioned in connexion with Virgil's life— does not call for much further comment. It is probably identical with the *Epigrammata* of the lists in Donatus and Servius.[4] For literary history, the fact of value in the collection is that certain poems betoken the continuance of the influence of Catullus either on Virgil, or, if they are not his, upon the poetic school contemporary with his youth. It is the same influence which is so strongly marked in the *Ciris*. The three short *Priapea* may also be among the light verses which Pliny says Virgil composed.[5] The Maecenas elegies are manifestly not by a poet whom Maecenas outlived by eleven years: they may even be rhetorical exercises of post-Augustan date. The *Est et Non* and the *Vir Bonus* bear the impress of the Ausonian literary revival in the fourth century.

It remains to consider seven poems more fully. Professor Mackail, in the article alluded to, groups with the time of the *Eclogues* the *Ciris*, the *Dirae*, and (what until modern times was not seen to be separate from the latter), the *Lydia*. He refers the *Copa* to the same period. The *Culex* and *Moretum* he links with the immediately subsequent period of the *Georgics*. This grouping is attractive. It is true to the literary qualities and affinities of the poems: and if, where varied hypotheses are so rife, the order will not commend itself to all, it has the merit of placing in the forefront the *Ciris* as the poem round which the most crucial problems revolve, and which is most representative of the literary tendencies in the quarter century following the death of Catullus (54 B.C.). It will be observed that the order implies placing the *Aetna* in a later category.

The *Ciris* turns on the infatuation of the Megarian princess Scylla for Minos, the enemy of her country, and on her treacherous cutting of the

---

[1] *Cl. Rev.*, xxii. 3, May, 1908, art. on 'Virgil and Virgilianism.'

[2] R. Ellis, *Aetna*, 1901, *Proleg.*, xxi.

[3] See *infra*, p. 361 n. 3.

[4] Ribbeck argued that the title *Catalecta* once embraced not only *Epigrammata*, but the *Priapea* and *Dirae*, and was later cut down to the fourteen pieces now included.

[5] *Ep.*, V. iii. 2, 'uersiculos seueros parum'.

fateful lock from the head of her father, Nisus, the king. It ends in her transformation into a bird —ever to be pursued by Nisus. The theme is a mythological triviality. Alexandrinism is stamped on the face of it. The grotesque is most obvious in the qualms about turning Scylla into a fish —she might be eaten![1] —or in the minute realism which furnishes details of the growth of beak, feathers, and claws. The style of this playful epyllion marks its place in Roman literature within definite limits. It opens with phrases and metrical movements which are unmistakably those of Catullus. It shows quite distinctly Lucretian elements, though, as might be expected from the subject, to a less extent. Before fifty lines are passed it becomes Virgilian. Sharing passages and separate lines with both *Eclogues* and *Georgics*, and introducing phrases infallibly suggestive of the *Aeneid*, it reads like a Virgilian cento interwoven with patches of Catullus. The critical problem hinges on the Virgilian lines. An easy inference is that the *Ciris* is the work of a gifted versifier to whom Virgil's poems were known.[2] It is scarcely less easy to imagine it an early work by Virgil himself, containing lines which he afterwards incorporated in more finished work. But another explanation, if not so easy, is more plausible. The lines common to Virgil and the *Ciris* may not have been borrowed from Virgil. He may have been the borrower. A fair estimate has been made out for Virgil's indebtedness to Cornelius Gallus in the sixth and tenth *Eclogues*.[3] Professor Skutsch of Breslau has made it appear at least possible that Gallus was the author of the *Ciris*, and that such parts of it as reappear in Virgil were drawn from the work of his brilliant young friend.[4] But if the author cannot be absolutely identified with Gallus, still the likeliest explanation lies in

---

[1] *Ciris*, 486:

'Nimium est auidum pecus Amphitrites.'

[2] This is Prof. Leo's theory. Reviewing the first volume of Prof. Skutsch's *Aus Vergils Frühzeit* (in *Herm.*, xxxvii., pp. 14 *sqq.*, 1902), Prof. Leo rejects Skutsch's contention that the *Ciris* could not have been written after the appearance of Virgil as a literary force. If the *Ciris* was published before the *Aeneid* at all, then, according to Prof. Leo, the author must have seen or heard portions of the *Aeneid* before publication, to account for the resemblances to the earlier books. Its author on this theory is not Gallus (Skutsch's candidate), but a learned *dilettante* who has retained till the very end of Virgil's career the literary characteristics of a preceding period. 'Das Gedicht ist ein Product des aus dem hellenistischen hervorgegangen gebildeten römischen Dilettantismus der der Technik, wie wir das auch sonst aus Beispielen und vielfacher Ueberlieferung wissen, mächtig ist.' It is then a neoteric survival.

[3] R. Bürger, *Herm.*, xxxviii. 1, 1903, pp. 19 *sqq.*, attempts to show the contents and nature of the elegy of Gallus which was the foundation of Virgil's tenth eclogue.

[4] F. Skutsch, *Aus Vergils Frühzeit*, 1901, and vol. ii., *Gallus u. Vergil*, 1906. His position is thus summed up: 'In der zehnten Ekloge sind besonders die Verse 31–69 im wesentlichen eine Blüthenlese aus Gallus, der Gesang des Silen in der sechsten Ekloge katalogisirt gleichsam die Dichtungen des Gallus, und Gallus ist der Verfasser der *Ciris*, die von Vergil in seinen sämmtlichen Dichtungen mehr oder weniger stark benutzt ist.' P. Jahn, *Herm.*, xxxvii., 1902, pp. 161 *sqq.*, criticises Skutsch and concludes: '(1) dass Ecl. x (nicht 31 sondern erst 43–64 u. 69) eine Anzahl von Anklängen an Gallus enthalten kann: (2) dass

believing that the poem emanated from the circle of youthful poets to which Gallus, like Virgil, belonged. It may be pictured as a circle permeated by a common 'neoteric' note as completely as were Spenser's youthful companions by a common 'Elizabethan' note. Such community of note is traceable partly to the action of a common environment, partly to the reaction of individuals on that environment, and partly to the interaction of individuals one on another. In this sense a work for which Gallus, say, was nominally responsible would be due in part also to his circle. What baffles exhaustive disentanglement is the manifold interplay of genius. Professor Mackail cites the parallel of the *Lyrical Ballads* of 1798. The *Ancient Mariner* is Coleridge's, but it owes to Wordsworth elements which we definitely know, and others which we might guess but can never know. Similarly the Wordsworth of these *Ballads* is not entirely himself: he is in part Coleridge. Analogously in Rome, the poetic fraternity which included Gallus, Macer, Varius, and Cinna produced work which could not be strictly individual. Whatever member of it composed the *Ciris* must have owed something to the mere stimulus of contact with Virgil. Quite conceivably, Virgil contributed verses to it which he afterwards resumed in works of his own. But at all events he would not hesitate to borrow from one of the brotherhood, any more than he hesitated to borrow from Varius in the *Aeneid*.[1]

The queries then amount to these—Did Virgil borrow from the author of the *Ciris*? or did the author of the *Ciris* borrow from Virgil? or did Virgil himself write the *Ciris*, incorporating some of its verses in his later works? As to date, the option clearly lies between putting it before the *Eclogues* were published (that is, before 37 B.C.) and putting it after the *Aeneid* was at least in great part composed. The earlier date presents least difficulty. It is consistent with the internal evidence of a poem so full of phrases and rhythms from Lucretius and Catullus. It agrees with the Alexandrinism of *motif*. It accounts more readily for the tradition that the poem was one of Virgil's early works. So far from the *Ciris* being the work of a man of advanced years,[2] it seems to me

---

der Dichter der *Ciris* nicht Gallus war, sondern ein Späterer, dem zum mindesten Vergils *Eclogen* und *Georgica* vollständig vorlagen.' This supports Leo's case. The divergence of opinion will be further illustrated by comparison of the following: S. Lederer, *Ist Vergil der Verfasser von Culex u. Ciris? Zugleich ein Beitrag zur Geschichte des Hexameters*, 1890 (contention is that *Culex* is by Virgil and *Ciris* not); F. Vollmer, *Rh. Mus.*, lxi. 4, 1906 (discusses the connexion between proem and body of *Ecl.* vi, and believes Virgil's authorship of *Ciris* possible). G. Némethy, *Rh. Mus.*, lxii. 3, 1907 (finds parallelisms to the pseudo-Tibulliana in both *Ciris* and *Culex*, and pronounces the *Ciris* a forgery like the *Culex*); W. R. Hardie, *Journal of Philol.*, xxx, 60, 1907 (considers some non-metrical arguments bearing on the date of the *Ciris*).

[1] *Aen.*, vi. 621–22.
[2] Teuffel, *Rom. Lit.*, § 230, 2, thinks of the author as seeking retirement after an 'eventful political life.' This is presumably based on l. 2 ('Irritaque expertum fallacis praemia uulgi'). In the *Ciris* this is no more proof of a long public career than the line, 'My days are in the yellow leaf,' from Byron's poem

impossible to think of it as other than a poem written by a youngish man who pretends at the opening to feel a fit of *Weltschmerz*. This would accord with, though of course it does not prove, the ascription to Gallus. It should also be borne in mind that the fall of Gallus might provide reasons for a diplomatic concealment of the real authorship under the name of Virgil.

From the same circle, but from a different poet, sprang the *Dirae*. With its 103 lines used to be coupled the 80 lines which survive of the *Lydia*.[1] Allusions in the *Dirae* to partition of lands and to the interloping agriculturist[2] must have appeared sufficiently suggestive of the *Eclogues* to foster the old belief in a Virgilian origin. The common mention of Lydia led to a hasty amalgamation of the poems; but the *Lydia* almost certainly preceded the *Dirae*.[3] Scaliger, who took the two for one poem, conjectured Valerius Cato to be the author, and, notwithstanding disproof by Merkel, Keil, and Hermann, this ascription still has its supporters. Rothstein's contention,[4] that style and subject of the two preclude the possibility of their having been written by the same poet, is no more proved than the contention that the *Dialogus de Oratoribus* is not by the author of the *Agricola*. The dealings of time with the text of the *Dirae* place some arguments on the shakiest foundations. But without losing ourselves in critical subtleties, it is enough here to recognise what is broadly the identical literary note in both. There is a flavour in which Professor Mackail detects the 'Latin of the South' and which at any rate agrees with the Sicilian landscape. There is a simplicity alien to the *Ciris*. There is a precision of eye for the processes and colours of nature. It looks like the same mind which notes in the *Dirae* the 'steaming rains upon the high hills' (*altis fumantes montibus imbres*) and invokes

> Ye waves that beat the seashores with your surge,
> Shores that disperse sweet breezes o'er the land;[5]

written on his thirty-sixth birthday, would prove him to have been a man of fifty-five or sixty. Yet that would be a possible inference from internal evidence alone, if the piece were anonymous. The tone of the address to Messalla (ll. 36 *sqq.*) is that of a compeer in age, who has spent pains, but probably not years, over the elaboration of his poem (l. 46, 'meo multum uigilata labore.').

[1] Friedrich Jacobs in the eighteenth century saw that the two were different pieces, and Näke has shown that we possess only part of the *Lydia*.

[2] *Dir.*, 80:
'Piscetur nostris in finibus aduena arator.'

[3] R. Ellis, *Amer. Jrnl. of Philol.*, No. 41, April, 1890, supports Näke's view that if the scene of the *Dirae* is the same as that of *Lydia*, then on grounds both of matter and language the latter was written first. This view holds good even if the *locale* in each is different. The Lydia of the *Dirae* is a woman; the other Lydia a girl.

[4] M. Rothstein, *De Diris et Lydia carminibus*, in *Herm.*, xxiii., 1888.

[5] *Dir.*, 48:
'Vndae quae uestris pulsatis litora lymphis,
Litora quae dulcis auras diffunditis agris.'

as that which in the *Lydia* seizes on a characteristic aspect of an evening sky

> When mid the sunset green wan stars return,
> And the Moon's course begins and all is gold,
> Thy love is with thee, Moon; why is not mine
> With me? Thou knowest what pain is, O Moon;
> Have ruth on mine.[1]

The *Copa* is a short sketch of a 'Hostess' or 'Barmaid' who exhibits her skill in the castanet dance to the frequenters of her tavern. Its elegiacs are in a style worthy of Virgil, and Charisius thought it was Virgil's. But its *insouciance* is unlike him. It is sprightly to the verge of *abandon*, as may be seen in its closing couplet

> Ho! wine and dice! To-morrow's thoughts be damned!
> Death at the ear saith, 'Live your life; I come.'[2]

The *Moretum*, or 'The Salad,' is said to be modelled on a Greek idyll by Parthenius of Nicaea. Gallus was his patron. Parthenius consequently was in touch with the Virgilian circle. There is no external evidence in favour of Virgil's authorship of these 123 hexameters. The most that can be said is that the poem is good enough to be his. As a close study of humble life, it might serve as a poetical excursus on the *Georgics*. It is full of pictures impressive in their unaffected realism — the peasant rising betimes on a dark winter morning, the making of a fire, the grinding of corn in the old Italian hand-mill, the ugly old negress who is housekeeper, the vegetable garden, the estimation of the lettuce in contrast with the fastidious daintiness of Martial's day,[3] the mortar for the salad, the pungent odour that rises as the pestle pounds the herbs, the two fingers passed round the mortar to bring all clean off the sides, and the start of the peasant for his ploughing secured against hunger for the day.

The *Culex* is rather shorter than the *Ciris* or than a book of the *Georgics*. It recounts the fate of a gnat which stings a sleeping shepherd at the critical moment when he is endangered by a serpent. Awakened by the smart, the man kills the gnat and batters the serpent to death. At night the ghost of the gnat appears to him and relates the tortures and the bliss of the other world. The vision inspires the man to clear a grassy spot near a stream for a tomb, on which he inscribes the epitaph:

[1] *Lyd.*, 39:
> 'Sidera per uiridem redeunt cum pallida mundum,
> Inque uicem Phoebe currens atque aureus orbis,
> Luna, tuus tecum est: cur non est et mea mecum?
> Luna, dolor nosti quid sit: miserere dolentis.'

In l. 40 I do not feel convinced either by Ribbeck's 'Phoebi currus fugat' or by Ellis's 'Phoebae coiens atque.'

[2] *Copa*, 37:
> 'Pone merum et talos. Pereat qui crastina curat!
> Mors aurem uellens, "Viuite," ait, "uenio".'

[3] Cf. *Mor.*, 76, and Martial, XIII. xiv. 1.

> Small gnat, the shepherd whom thy sting did save,
> In lieu of guerdon giveth thee a grave.[1]

That Virgil wrote a *Culex* is well attested —by Suetonius, Statius, and Martial.[2] Considerable weight must be given to the opinion of Statius, who was a Virgilian scholar and enthusiast. A review of the evidence suggests a mistake of ten years in the age at which, according to the *Life* ascribed to Donatus, Virgil wrote his *Culex*.[3] Virgil's poem, in that case, was written about 44 B.C., and dedicated to the young Octavius.[4] But is our *Culex* his? Here the question turns on the view adopted about its three outstanding parallels to Virgil —the praise of the pastoral life resembling *Georgics*, ii. 458–540; the episode of Orpheus and Eurydice resembling *Georgics*, iv. 453–527; and the gnat's description of the infernal regions resembling parts of *Aeneid*, vi. Are these imitations of Virgil or early studies by himself? The depravity of the text[5] increases our difficulty in judging the quality of the poetry. It is safe to admit that there is technical skill. But the specific Virgilian note is absent, and what most readers of any text now available must be conscious of is an uneasy feeling of its unworthiness to be Virgil's. On the evidence it is impossible to dogmatise. One is left in the realm of conjecture. It strikes one as a paradox to believe that there was a second *Culex* treating Virgil's idea in a manner to be called 'Virgilian' only in the sense of emanating from Virgil's circle and catching echoes from his poems, and that this *Culex* in time displaced the genuine poem. On the whole, it seems a less remote possibility that we have after all in the *Culex* a juvenile production by Virgil which his fastidious taste never

---

[1] *Cul.*, 412:

> 'Parue culex, pecudum custos tibi tale merenti
> Funeris officium uitae pro munere reddit.'

[2] Suet., *Vit. Lucani*, 'ut praefatione quadam aetatem et initia sua cum Vergilio comparans ausus sit dicere "et quantum mihi restat ad *Culicem!*"' Stat., *Sil.*, II. vii. 73, 'ante annos *Culicis* Maroniani'; *Sil.*, i, *praef.* (referring to the *Culex* and *Batrachomyomachia*), 'nec quisquam est illustrium poetarum qui non aliquid operibus suis stilo remissiore praeluserit.' Mart., XIV. clxxxv:

> 'Accipe facundi *Culicem*, studiose, Maronis,
> Ne nucibus positis "Arma Virumque" legas.'

Cf. Mart., VIII. lvi. 20. Nonius, 211, also assumes the authenticity by citing the use of *labrusca* in neuter gender: 'neutro Vergilius in *Culice*.'

[3] *I.e.* that xvi is an error for xxvi in '*Culicem cum esset annorum xvi*' (Donat., *Vit. Verg.*, § 17).

[4] 'Octaui uenerande,' l. 25, and 'sancte puer,' ll. 26 and 37, can only be meant for the future emperor. R. Ellis in 'A Theory of the *Culex*,' contributed to *Cl. Rev.*, x. pp. 177–83, 1896, indicates other periods in the life of Octavianus from which we might date the conception of the poem by 'some learned visitor to the region of Epirus' who may have planned an epyllion in imitation of the ideas of Virgil and worked into it two famous episodes of the *Georgics*. A look of genuineness would be added by dedicating it to the man who, as Octavius, had been Virgil's early patron.

[5] What the scribes are responsible for may be illustrated by the distortion of 'Zanclaea' into 'metuenda' at l. 332, and 'Cui cessit Lydi timefacta' into 'legitime cessit cui facta' at l. 366.

passed for publication, and which may have survived in private hands unauthorised by his executors. It would so escape destruction, but so would it miss final revision.

Aetna is a hexameter poem of 644 lines assigned by its MSS. to Virgil. We have seen that as early as Donatus's days the ascription was doubted. The opening invocation is to Apollo. The poem then turns to its didactic purpose of explaining the causes of Aetna's eruptions after an express dismissal of mythological subjects. This is a recoil from the hackneyed and trivial, and is rather more in the solemn mood animating Lucretius than in the spirit of the openings of Virgil's third *Georgic* or Juvenal's first satire. The author insists that his aim is science, not legend.[1] He is enamoured of truth. His affinity with Lucretius lies deeper than verbal imitation, though that is frequent. He unites a Lucretian contempt for fable with a Lucretian pursuit of a *uera causa*. He has, too, a Lucretian aptitude for analogy, as where currents of air within the earth are likened to the circulation of the blood, and the less compact portions of earth are likened to the interstices in random heaps of stones. But some of the main Lucretian characteristics are absent. The author has no defiance of religion.[2] Nor has he anything like the vigour and passion of Lucretius. It is unusual to find passages with the energy of that on the battle of the flames.[3] Most are like his theories of wind-pressure as the cause of volcanic disturbance — dull. They are not poetry.[4] If there is little attempt to link thought with human life, as the manner of Lucretius is, it is mainly because the author of *Aetna* has a high disdain for the human document. Nature is his entrancing volume: 'You shall see no such marvellous sights mid the rabble of mankind.'[5] Quite rarely, then, have we such ethical illustrations as that on the cumbersome vanity of possessions in the evil days of eruption,[6] or the

---

[1] *E.g., Aetn.*, 74:
> 'Haec est mendosae uulgata licentia famae.'
Ibid., 91:
> 'Debita carminibus libertas ista, sed omnis
> In uero mihi cura.'
[2] See, *e.g., Aetn.*, 631–32.   [3] *Aetn.*, 463 *sqq.*
[4] Occasionally the eye for the picturesque enlivens matters, as where the poet pauses to indicate the colour-effects which the ancients associated with sun and moon, l. 236:
> 'Quo rubeat Phoebe, quo frater palleat igni.'
But his best touch is to describe the cooling lava losing its appearance of a waving field of flame, l. 497:
> 'Ac flammea messis
> Excutitur facies.'
[5] *Aetn.*, 599:
> 'Nulla
> Tu tanta humanae plebis spectacula cernes.'
[6] See the passage beginning l. 613. It leads up to the satiric hit – for which one respects the author – at the poet trammelled by the endeavour to save his poems:
> 'Defectum raptis illum sua carmina tardant.'

incident of the devoted sons rescuing the parents who were their true
wealth.[1] The general attitude cannot be better summed up than in the
fine assertion that the stupendous work of the artificer Nature before
one's eyes contains marvels that equal anything in antiquity, literature,
or art.[2]

The various dates proposed for the *Aetna* have a range of a century
and a quarter. The extreme *terminus a quo* is the death of Lucretius
about 55 B.C. —the poem must be later than that. The extreme *terminus
ad quem* is the eruption of Vesuvius in A.D. 79—the poem must be
earlier than that; for Vesuvius is not in its list of volcanoes. Alzinger's
theory places it earliest, about 49 B.C. The modern reassertion of its
Virgilian authorship has been mentioned.[3] The prevailing theory since
Wernsdorf[4] has been that the author was Lucilius Junior, the correspondent of the younger Seneca and procurator in Sicily. The problem
really narrows itself down to the question whether the poem is Augustan
or Neronian. Neither answer is free from difficulty. On the one hand,
the later the *Aetna* is placed the harder it is to account for its ancient
ascription to Virgil; while the absence of genitives in *-ii* and certain
points of metric are slightly against a Neronian date.[5] On the other hand,
it is difficult to see how, if *Aetna* were Augustan, it was not mentioned
by Seneca[6] in his enumeration of poetic descriptions of the mountain —
unless, indeed, we are to agree with Kruczkiewicz that it is Virgil's, or
with some MSS. of the fifteenth century, backed by Scaliger, that it is
by Cornelius Severus,[7] whom Seneca mentions in the said enumeration.
But I cannot say that the identification of the author with Lucilius has
ever impressed me as convincing. Seneca writes asking him as a favour
to climb Aetna and then send information:

> Not that I need ask you: your own keenness would be enough to
> urge you. I bet you anything you'll be describing Aetna (*Quid tibi do
> ne Aetnam describas?*) in your poem, and setting your hands on this
> common-place of all the poets. Virgil's complete treatment (*quod
> iam Vergilius impleuerat*) did not bar Ovid from handling it:[8] Cornelius
> Severus tried it in spite of both. . . . Either I am mistaken in you, or
> Aetna is making your mouth water (*Aetna tibi saliuam mouet*): you
> are already set on writing something fine to match former attempts.

---

[1] *Aetn.*, 623 *sqq.*, esp. 629:
        'Illis diuitiae solae materque paterque.'
[2] *Aetn.*, 567–601.
[3] B. Kruczkiewicz, *Poema de Aetna monte Vergilio auctori praecipue tri-
buendum*, dissert., 1882.
[4] J. C. Wernsdorf, *Poet. Lat. Min.*, vol. iv, 1785.
[5] For the question, 'Is *Aetna* Augustan?' see R. Ellis's ed., *proleg.*, xxxiii
sqq.
[6] Sen., *Epist.*, lxxix.
[7] Severus was the author of a lost hexameter poem on the war against
Sextus Pompey in Sicily.
[8] Virg. *Aen.* iii. 571 *sqq.*; Ov. *Met.* xv. 340 *sqq.*

This does not prove more than that Seneca suggested the introduction of a description of Aetna into a poem on which Lucilius was at work; and the arguments that the author must have known Sicily, must have known the vicinity of Naples, and combined Epicurean with Stoic leanings, would, it is only fair to state, equally fit Virgil. More stress can fairly be laid on the argument from style. Munro could not believe the poem to be older than the Silver Age. Certainly *Aetna* has not the simplicity of the other *Vergiliana*, though for this its theme may be in some degree accountable. Its rhetorical turns point rather in the direction of post-Augustan Latin: and its compactness savours of the age rather of Persius than of Virgil.

Chapter III

HORACE

Descent and education of Horace – Anti-Caesarian and Bohemian – The patronage of Maecenas – The mellowing of later life – Horace's literary periods – *Epodes* – The date of the *Satires* – Their alternative title – Horace's debt to Lucilius – Opening for a new satirist – The language of the *Satires* – The Horatian hexameter – Horatian geniality – The range of the grave and the gay – Horace and the bore – Deeper moral tone of the second book – The date of the *Odes* – Horace and Greek lyric – His chief metres and their effects – Alcaics – Sapphics – Asclepiads – Attitude to the new *régime* – Support of moral reforms – Religious ideas and Caesar-worship – Horace's sincerity as a 'laureate' – Virgil and Horace as political assets – Horace as moralist in *Epistles*, Book I. – Date of the literary *Epistles* – Horace as critic in the *Epistle* to Augustus – The *Epistle* to Florus – The *Ars Poetica* as a manifesto of dramatic principles – Its sources and central themes – Influence on criticism – Interest of Horace's self-revelation – His reflection of his own times – His appeal to the world – His poetic charm – Love of rural nature – Limitations and strength – *Non omnis moriar.*

N O ROMAN author except Cicero has left anything like so complete a self-revelation as Horace.[1] His own works tell all that is essential. The most important additions in Suetonius's *Life* are the date of death and details about the emperor's relations to

---

[1] Text: *Q.H.F. ex rec. et cum not. et emend.* R. Bentleii, 4to, Camb., 1711, Amsterd., 1713; 2 vols. (Zangemeister's index), Berlin, 1869 [Bentley's boldness is always stimulating, and often provocative]; Io. G. Orellius, cur. Io. G. Baiter, ed. 3, 2 vols., 1850–52; revised W. Hirschfelder and W. Mewes, 1886–92; A. Kiessling, 1889–95; O. Keller and A. Holder, 2 vols., crit. app., 1864–76; new ed., 1899 *sqq.* (O. Keller, *Epilegomena zu Horaz*, 3 vols., 1879–80); J. Gow in Postgate's *C.P.L.*, i, 1894. *Odes*, T. E. Page, ed. 1, 1883, new edd., 1890 *sqq.*; E. C. Wickham, ed. 2, 1874; ed. 3, 1896; *Oden u. Epoden*, erkl. L. Müller (ed. Goetz), 2 vols., 1900; *Sat.*, A. Palmer, ed. 1, 1883, new edd., 1885 *sqq.*; *Epist.* (w. *Ars Poet.*), A. S. Wilkins, 1885 *sqq.*; *Sat. u. Epist.*, anmerkn., L. Müller, 1893. Translations in Eng. verse: J. Conington, *The Works* [with the main exception of the *Epodes*], 1870, new ed., 1905; Th. Martin, *Odes*, 1860; *Odes and Sat.*, 1869. [For enumeration of translations into English, as well as French, German, and Italian, see E. Stemplinger, *Das Fortleben der Horazischen Lyrik seit d. Renaissance*, 1906]. Commentaries, Literary Studies, etc.: *Scholia Horatiana quae feruntur Acronis et Porphyrionis*, etc., F. Pauly, 2 vols., ed. 2, 1861; A. Holder, *Porphyrion*, 1894; *Pseudacronis Scholia in Hor. uetustiora*, O. Keller, 2 vols., 1902–4; C. Franke, *Fasti Horatiani*, 1839; C. A. de Walckenaer, *Hist. de la vie et des poésies d'Horace*, ed. 2, 1858; Th. Plüss, *Horazstudien*, 1882 [valuable for original elucidation of *Odes*]; A. W. Verrall, *Studies in the Odes*, 1884;

him. Q. Horatius Flaccus[1] was born at Venusia, on the confines of
Lucania and Apulia, December 5, 65 B.C.[2] He was thus five years
junior to Virgil. North and South Italy were again represented in the
two great poets of a period, as they had been in Plautus and Ennius.
Like Virgil, Horace was of humble origin. His father had been freed,
and was a collector of taxes or auction debts — or, some said, a vendor
of salted fish.[3] Horace's servile descent may have been an outcome of the
Samnite wars. It is a probable speculation that he was of Sabellian, and
not Greek, ancestry.[4] His qualities and sympathies are in any case those
of an old Italian stock. We can only guess how his father 'Flap-ear'
(*Flaccus*) got the Roman gentile name *Horatius*. A clue may be found in
the fact that Venusia was a colony enrolled in the Horatian tribe. If,
then, Horace's father was a public slave in the service of that community, the Horatian name would be the most natural one to adopt.
Libertinus though he was, the father decided that his son should have an
education equal to that of any Roman senator or knight. He took him
to Rome.[5] There the boy was placed under the severe tuition of the
grammarian Orbilius from Beneventum. Lively recollections of thrash-
ings associated with the text-book used — Livius Andronicus's rendering
of Homer into saturnians — must have intensified his distaste for early
Latin verse, as Horace himself was destined to be hated in later ages by
Byron and others for similar reasons.[6] With his intellectual education

---

H. Nettleship, *Lects. and Essays*, 1885; G. Boissier, *Nouvelles promenades
archéologiques*, 1886 [a careless Eng. trans., *The Country of Hor. and Virg.*,
1896]; M. Patin, *Études sur la poésie latine*, ed. 4, 1900; W. Y. Sellar, *Roman
Poets of Augustan Age: Horace and the Elegiac Poets*, ed. 2, 1899; J. J. Hartman, *De Horatio Poeta*, 1891 [shows admiration for Peerlkamp, whose edition
is based on adventurous treatment of the text]; A. Cartault, *Études sur les satires
d'Horace*, 1899.

[1] Each part of his name is proved in turn by *Sat.*, II. vi. 37; *Od.*, IV. vi.
44; *Sat.*, II. i. 18.
[2] *Sat.*, II. i. 34:
'Lucanus an Apulus anceps,
Nam Venusinus arat finem sub utrumque colonus.'
Epist., I. xx. 26:
'Forte meum siquis te percontabitur aeuum,
Me quater undenos sciat impleuisse Decembris,
Collegam Lepidum quo duxit Lollius anno.'
Suet., *Vit. Hor.*, 'Natus est VI Id. Decembr., L. Cotta et L. Torquato Coss.'
[3] *Sat.*, I. vi. 6, 'me libertino patre natum'; cf. *Sat.*, I. vi. 83; Suet., *Vit.
Hor.*, 'Patre, ut ipse tradit, libertino et auctionum coactore, ut uere creditum est,
salsamentario.'
[4] See Sellar, *Horace*, 1899, p. 9; E. A. Sonnenschein, *C.R.*, xi, 339,
October, 1897; and xii. 305, 1898.
[5] *Sat.*, I. vi. 76:
'Sed puerum est ausus Romam portare docendum
Artes quas doceat quiuis eques atque senator
Semet prognatos.'
[6] Yet he says with a kind of rueful generosity, *Epist.*, II. i. 69:
'Non equidem insector delendaue carmina Liui
Esse reor, memini quae plagosum mihi paruo
Orbilium dictare.'

his father coupled sound moral instruction. He acted as a watchful
paedagogus to his son, laying the foundations of that ethical interest
which grew steadily into the mellow wisdom of the *Epistles*. Horace
expressed gratitude for many things in life—for the inspiration of the
Muse, and for the grant of his Sabine farm; but he valued nothing more
highly than the precept and example of his father. To Horace education
was more than a leveller of the high-born and the slave's son: it was a
pilot in the dangers of life.[1]

At Athens a wider survey of literature and philosophy opened before
him.[2] Horace was there, a student of twenty, when Caesar's assassination startled the world. Nowhere was the news more welcome than
among young Romans abroad. Filled with Greek notions of liberty, they
applauded the tyrannicides as the new Harmodius and Aristogiton. It
was natural that when Brutus visited Athens six months after the fateful
ides of March, Horace should accept his offer of a commission in the
army. So he became a *tribunus militum* in the forces of the republic: he
would strike a blow against despotism. In the retinue of Brutus, Horace
saw a little of the nearer East. One of his early satires, the seventh of
Book I, is a sketch of a suit conducted uproariously by two rowdies
before Brutus; and long years after, in his Epistle to Bullatius, he writes
with familiarity about Asiatic towns and Aegean islands. The field of
Philippi in 42 decisively ended both the old republic and Horace's
military career. He found war magnificent only in theory. When success
declared for the Caesarians, Horace had the discretion to join the run-
aways. Later he had at least the moral courage to sing, Alcaeus-like,
about his flight.[3] Whatever he might do, the cause was a lost one. Half
distrustful, it may be, at first of any amnesty, he subsequently returned
to Rome 'with wings clipped.'[4] It was not merely that he was a discredited soldier. Confiscation had beggared him. His father was dead.

[1] *Sat.*, I. vi. 65:
> 'Atqui si uitiis mediocribus ac mea paucis
> Mendosa est natura, alioqui recta, . . .
> Causa fuit pater his,' etc.

Ibid., I. vi. 81:
> 'Ipse mihi custos incorruptissimus omnes
> Circum doctores aderat.'

Ibid., I. iv. 105:
> 'Insueuit pater optimus hoc me
> Ut fugerem, exemplis uitiorum quaeque notando.'

[2] *Epist.*, II. ii. 41:
> 'Romae nutriri mihi contigit atque doceri
> Iratus Graiis quantum nocuisset Achilles:
> Adiecere bonae paulo plus artis Athenae,
> Scilicet ut uellem curuo dignoscere rectum,
> Atque inter siluas Academi quaerere uerum.'

[3] *Od.*, II. vii. 9:
> 'Tecum Philippos et celerem fugam
> Sensi relicta non bene parmula.'

[4] *Epist.*, II. ii. 49:

He was glad to secure a clerkship in the Treasury.[1] Poverty drove him to write verses — not because poems would bring in money direct, but because they might win him notice and patronage. This was his period of struggle, when he mixed with the Bohemian section of the capital, its *ambubaiarum collegia, pharmacopolae, mendici, mimae*.[2] The echoes of strange acquaintanceships, coarse amours, and virulent hatreds ring out in the earlier satires and epodes. Talent, however, won him better friends. Among the poets of the day Horace became intimate with Virgil and Varius at the very time when the *Eclogues* were being written. Through them came the introduction which moulded his whole career. Maecenas, the able adviser of the future emperor, was himself interested in literature and constant in his endeavour to attach intellect to the new order of things. He had talked to his poet friends about this young writer of twenty-six, whose privately circulated verses had made a stir and damaged some reputations. Virgil and Varius evidently assured their patron that Horace had more in him than scurrilous lampoons.[3] Yet when the interview took place it proved to all appearances a *fiasco*. The newly introduced poet felt awkward; he stammered nervously; he had the fatal suspicion that he was not impressing the great minister. Maecenas, besides, was reticent as usual. Once Horace left his presence, nine months elapsed before further notice was taken of him. But he had not been forgotten. At last an invitation came which marked his entry into the coveted circle.[4]

Close touch with the governors of the Roman world and with the highest society in the capital had at once an elevating and a sobering effect on Horace. His bitterest and coarsest work preceded his introduction to Maecenas. Thereafter he was no longer a free-lance. On the other hand, as time passed, he divined what it meant to organise an empire. Hence sprang his admiration for the controlling hands and his insistence upon civic responsibilities. For thirty years the friendship with Maecenas continued. The poet fancied there was a similarity in their horoscope.[5] His prophecy[6] that he could not long survive his

---

'Unde simul primum me dimisere Philippi,
Decisis humilem pennis inopemque paterni
Et Laris et fundi, paupertas impulit audax
Ut uersus facerem.'

[1] Suet., *Vit. Hor.*, 'uictisque partibus, uenia impetrata scriptum quaestorium comparauit.'

[2] *Sat.*, I. ii. 1.

[3] *Sat.*, I. vi. 54:
'Optimus olim
Vergilius, post hunc Varius dixere quid essem.'
Horace's recollections of the interview follow.

[4] *Sat.*, I. vi. 61:
'Abeo et reuocas nono post mense iubesque
Esse in amicorum numero.'

[5] *Od.*, II. xvii. 21:
'Vtrumque nostrum incredibili modo
Consentit astrum.'

[6] *Od.*, II. xvii. 5–12.

patron was fulfilled; for when Maecenas in 8 B.C., on his death-bed, committed Horace to the special regard of the emperor (*Horati Flacci, ut mei, memor esto*), his *protégé* had but a few months to live. It was an intimacy based on affection[1] and allied tastes. As the bore of the Sacra Via found, Horace resented nothing more than the insinuation that tortuous intrigue could win the favour of Maecenas. He insisted that with Maecenas it was worth, not birth, that counted. He insisted, too, that he himself was not the confidant of state secrets. Pestered by the curious, he had no statements to make 'on the highest authority.' If he went driving with Maecenas it was to talk something lighter than politics—to pass the time of day, to criticise a pair of gladiators, to discuss the weather.[2] At other times the conversation was of that reasoned kind for the sake of which Horace most esteemed convivial gatherings. His advice on living with the great, contained in two epistles,[3] proves that he could steer the middle course between obsequiousness and *brusquerie*. Throughout he maintained his own freedom of action. In another epistle[4] he firmly claims that not all his indebtedness to Maecenas must constrain him into doing things against the grain—for example, going to Rome in the unhealthy season. The suggestion that coolness arose between the two, and that Augustus to some extent supplanted Maecenas in Horace's heart, will not bear investigation.

In 37 Horace was one of Maecenas's train, including Virgil and Varius, on the diplomatic mission to Brundisium immortalised in the fifth satire of Book I. To Maecenas a few years later Horace owed the Sabine farm in which he took unalloyed delight. It lay some miles east of Tibur, in a valley watered by the Digentia (the modern Licenza).[5] Horace writes in the first book of the *Satires*, that is, up to 35 B.C., for the most part as a man of the town; but in the period of the second book, between 35 and 30 B.C., he has become an enthusiastic landholder. We learn from Suetonius that Horace, without losing the imperial favour, declined the emperor's offer of a private secretaryship. His tact would furnish a plausible excuse. For him regular duties would have been as distasteful and punctuality as difficult as for Charles Lamb at the India Office. Horace preferred a life of comfort, free to follow each transient caprice, within hail of congenial friends who could talk and enjoy good cheer, and yet know at other times how to leave him alone. Routine was not suited to one who liked lying abed till ten.[6] Clearly, he would feel

---

[1] Suet., *Vit. Hor.*, 'Maecenas quantopere eum dilexerit, satis testatur illo epigrammate:

> 'Ni te uisceribus meis, Horati,
> Plus iam diligo, tu tuum sodalem
> Ninnio uideas strigosiorem.'

[2] *Sat.*, II. vi. 42–58.   [3] *Epist.*, I. xvii and xviii.
[4] *Epist.*, I. vii.
[5] The site was fixed in the eighteenth century by the investigations of the Abbé Capmartin de Chaupy; see G. Boissier, *Nouv. promen. arch.*, chap. i.
[6] *Sat.*, I. vi. 122, 'Ad quartam iaceo.'

less fettered, and do himself more justice, as a guest than as an official of the emperor. Love of ease, backed by a sunny Epicureanism, bore its fruit in indolent procrastination. He did not always meet his friends or write to them as promised. He might pack up his Plato and Menander to help his composition in the country; but it did not follow that he would produce the work designed. The well-dressed, dark-haired, once attractive youth[1] grew into a short, fat, prematurely grizzled bachelor,[2] who felt only a mild thrill in recalling his flirtations. He jested at himself as a 'porker from Epicurus's sty':[3] so he can hardly have objected to the emperor's chaff on receipt of one of his volumes, that the author seemed afraid of his books proving bigger than himself —he might not have *statura*, but he certainly had *corpusculum*! His temper improved with years and philosophy. He knew he was *irasci celer*: he introduces a slave twitting him upon it —a sure sign of amelioration —but he could remember the day when he would not have tolerated what amused him in later life (*lenit albescens animos capillus*). As early as his encounter with the bore, he had reason to envy a more fiery disposition.[4] Indeed, the Horatian placidity inevitably outgrew anger like other passions. It also outgrew keenness for exertion. But in great men much seeming sloth is activity of brain. His own answer to charges of idleness was that he must have leisure to think. Under apparent lethargy, Horace matured those reflections on life which found fullest expression in the *Epistles*. If he was constitutionally averse to an energetic life, he had what is not uncommon in the thinker —an admiration for men of action and of affairs.

His literary career falls broadly into three periods —that of the *Epodes* and *Satires*, down to 30 B.C.; that of the first three books of the *Odes*, to 23 B.C.; and that of the *Epistles*, and the largely official *Odes* of Book IV published about five years before his death in 8 B.C. It is a varied performance by a satirist, lyrist, moralist, and literary critic. But, what is of striking significance, it is a performance of constantly widening interest. Beginning in the rancour of merely personal animosities, it turns to a genial mockery of types instead of individuals; from initial despondency over the future of Rome it rises to an enthusiasm for the national prowess and to an elevated consciousness of the obligation to

---

[1] *Epist.*, I. xiv. 32:

    ' Quem tenues decuere togae nitidique capilli,
    Quem scis immunem Cinarae placuisse rapaci,' etc.

[2] Suet., *Vit. Hor.*, 'Habitu corporis fuit breuis atque obesus.' Hor., *Epist.*, I. xx. 24:

    ' Corporis exigui, praecanum, solibus aptum.'

[3] *Epist.*, I. iv. 15:

    ' Me pinguem et nitidum bene curata cute uises,
    Cum ridere uoles, Epicuri de grege porcum.'

[4] *Sat.*, I. ix. 11:

                          ' O te, Bolane, cerebri
    Felicem!'

secure an inward dignity of character worthy of the external grandeur of the state. The cause of art Horace served by resolute advocacy of finish in style; and in the *Ars Poetica* he transmitted rules which, as he stated them, have left a deep impress on the literatures of Europe.

The *Epodes* were not collected till about the same time as the second book of the *Satires*, 30 B.C. But they may be conveniently considered first, for they contain some of Horace's earliest things, and they are his least attractive work. Their essential form is a couplet of lines of different length, and the prevailing foot is the *iambus*. He refers to his *Epodes* as *iambi*.[1] Both metre and abusiveness testify to the influence of Archilochus of Paros.[2] Horace's rapid Archilochian iambics differ from the iambics of tragedy or comedy in comparative freedom from spondees or equivalent feet. The arrangement of the seventeen poems is metrical, not chronological. The first ten are in the *versus ἐπῳδός* — an iambic trimeter and an iambic dimeter alternately. The next six are more complex. Most combine iambic lines with hexameters constructed on principles as developed as those of Varro Atacinus and of Virgil in the *Eclogues*. The last of all is not in couplets, but in iambic trimeters. Most frequently, the iambic metres have a satiric ring: the dactylo-iambic metres are rather convivial and anacreontic. This brings us to subject-matter. The chief part is played by invective, love, and wine. Among the victims of his mockery are an upstart officer, a cowardly libeller of himself, the hateful 'witch' Canidia, the poetaster Mevius who caused annoyance to Virgil also, and Neaera—that sweetheart 'clinging fast as ivy,' whose falsity Horace's supplanter will yet discover. He humorously curses garlic as a deadly herb, and warns his 'merry Maecenas' that it spoils his chance of getting kisses! The second epode reads like an idyllic eulogy on country life with a profusion of detail in strong contrast to Horace's later terseness of manner. But its last four lines pull one up with a jerk. Only at the end one learns that the eulogy comes from the mouth of an absolute townsman:

> These words the money-lender Alfius said
>   As if for rural life athirst;
> On the fifteenth he had his loans repaid,
>   And wants to place them on the first!

The reader feels like those who in Rome used to suspect Horace of befooling them—*ut tu semper eris derisor*! It is suggested that the satiric tag is added 'to prevent his being taken too seriously.'[3] But Horace hardly needed to make a shamefast apology for his rural tastes. Probably he rather wished to ridicule unreal praises of the country by townsfolk who may have caught the infection from the *Eclogues* and

---

[1] *Epod.*, xiv. 7; *cf. Od.*, I. xvi. 3.
[2] Horace likens himself to both Archilochus and Hipponax, *Epod.*, vi. 13, and names Archilochus definitely as his model, *Epist.*, I. xix. 23–5.
[3] Sellar, *op. cit.*, p. 130.

aped their vogue in season and out. To balance the untranslatable foulness of two of the pieces, there are others in a nobler strain. The first epode expresses loyal anxiety to follow Maecenas through all perils of war, and acknowledges his handsome liberality

> *Satis superque me benignitas tua*
> *Ditauit.*

Concern for national welfare is patent in his protests against internecine strife, *Quo, quo scelesti ruitis?* and *Altera iam teritur . bellis ciuilibus aetas.* Their fullest meaning, perhaps, is not, as Porphyrion thought, in relation to the Perusine War of 41 (in which case they must have found their chief welcome in the older republican coteries), nor yet in relation to the struggle against Sextus Pompey in 36. The former may bear on frontier troubles in East and West about 32, and on the prospects of a new civil war; and the latter may derive its pessimistic view of Rome's fortunes from the actual outbreak of hostilities. One thing, however, is certain. Jeremiads are not usual in Horace after he realised the strength of empire. For him, as for his country, Octavian's victory at Actium in 31 settled many doubts. It is with special curiosity that one realises in the ninth epode a poem written in two parts—the one immediately before, the other immediately after Actium. The reference to sea-sickness (*fluentem nauseam*) produces the impression that Horace was a spectator of the engagement.

The first book of the *Satires* appeared about 35 B.C. It must precede Horace's acquisition of his Sabine estate; and he was established there at any rate before December, 33.[1] Possibly the presence at Rome in 35 B.C. of Antony's political agent, Bibulus, is referred to in the last satire of the book.[2] The satires are not in the order of composition. The fifth sixth, ninth, and the introductory one—probably written last—imply acquaintanceship with Maecenas, and are therefore later than 38 B.C. Others are in Horace's very earliest manner. The seventh, on the rapscallions before Brutus in 43 or 42, was presumably a sketch written at the time of the occurrence. The second seems to be next oldest. Its virulence, coarseness, and traces of archaism point to its being one of Horace's first essays in the manner of Lucilius. The third and fourth also precede the introduction to Maecenas. About five years intervened before the publication of the second book. It is contemporaneous with the *Georgics*. Actium, 31 B.C., had been fought before Octavian could be called *iuuenis Parthis horrendus.*[3] The latest clear allusion in the book is to his return resolved to satisfy with allotments his troops disbanded after Actium.[4] The first piece was probably, as in so many books, the last written; and its attitude to Octavian as war-lord[5] rather than peace-

---

[1] *Sat.*, II. iii. 5 and 185. [2] *Sat.*, I. x. 86.
[3] *Sat.*, II. v. 62. [4] *Sat.*, II. vi. 55.
[5] *Sat.*, II. i. 11–15.

giver suggests that it preceeded the closing of the Temple of Janus in 29 B.C.

Horace regarded both *Satires* and *Epistles* as *sermones*[1] —chatty essays or *causeries* in verse. The MSS. have restricted the title *sermones* to the *Satires*; but since Horace used *sermones* in the wider sense indicated, and since he employed the word *satura*[2] as well, it is clearer to distinguish them from the *Epistles* by the term which suggests their purpose.

Horace's attitude and debt to Lucilius have been noted in an earlier chapter. Lucilius was his master, but a master not beyond criticism. Horace devotes considerable space[3] to strictures on his faults of harsh and careless composition, and to admiration of his shrewdness, moral force, and autobiographical frankness. Much of him Horace would fain imitate. He likes the charming openness of his self-revelation and his boldness in unmasking shams. He likes to think of him as at once the friend of virtue and the friend of distinguished men. Here Horace could picture himself as a parallel; for he prided himself somewhat complacently on knowing how to live with the great, and wrote two epistles for the guidance of others.[4] It had been the task of Lucilius to divert the old discursive and semi-dramatic *satura* into the path of censorious criticism. 'He rubbed the city down with plenty of salt.'[5] Horace sees Lucilius's likeness to the old Attic comedy in his attacks upon the infamous and in the political bearing of his censures. But along this line he does not follow him. There was much to retain and much to reject in his model. Horace kept the desultory and dramatic nature of the ancient *satura* transmitted through Lucilius. He adhered strictly to Lucilius's prevailing form, the hexameter. But he dropped the bitterness and carelessness largely, and the political tone entirely. Where he most resembles Lucilius is in the less restrained satires of the first book —in the 'low company' of the second satire and the seventh, and in the nature of the fright administered in the eighth to the witches haunting the disreputable Esquiline. The journey to Brundisium, in the fifth,

---

[1] *Sat.*, I. iv. 41:
> 'Neque siqui scribat uti nos
> Sermoni propiora, putes hunc esse poetam';

Epist., II. i. 3:
> 'In publica commoda peccem,
> Si longo sermone morer tua tempora, Caesar';

Ibid., 250:
> 'Nec sermones ego mallem
> Repentis per humum quam res componere gestas.'

[2] *Sat.*, II. i. 1:
> 'Sunt quibus in satura uidear nimis acer';

Sat., II. vi. 17:
> 'Quid prius inlustrem saturis musaque pedestri?'

[3] *Sat.*, I. iv. 6–12, 57; x. i–5, 20–24, 48–71; II. i. 17, 29–34, 62–75.

[4] *Epist.*, I. xvii. and xviii.

[5] *Sat.*, I. x. 3, 'sale multo urbem defricuit.'

borrowed hints from the old poet's journey to the Sicilian Straits. In the second book, Horace is most Lucilian where, as in the second, third, fourth, and eighth satires, a dialogue discusses questions of philosophy or gastronomy.

The example of Lucilius pointed Horace to fame. If it is asked why he took to satire, the answer is not simply that he had the genius for it. Lucilius's works were well known in Roman literary circles, and they suggested to Horace one mode of writing·which in his day had not been overdone. Other fields were already occupied—comedy by Fundanius, tragedy by Pollio, epic by Varius, pastoral by Virgil.[1] But after the failure of Varro Atacinus there was an opening for a satirist—if only in adapting Lucilius to Augustan taste and freely rewriting his now antiquated sketches. So Horace served his apprenticeship to satire by modernising pieces from Lucilius, much as Pope served Chaucer up for readers of the Queen Anne period, who had come to think fourteenth-century English barbarous. Horace modestly owns his inferiority to his predecessor (*inuentore minor*), and disclaims any thought of daring to pull away

> The clinging wreath of glory on his head.[2]

All the same, a few experiments sufficed to prove that the apprentice would be the next master. Horace was like all artists: he imitated till he discovered his own strength. He could then find new motives, new subjects, and new uses for satire.

Horace had a high conception of the divinity that hedges the poet. With the poet he associated genius, a heavenly afflatus, and the grand style.[3] But in his satires (*sermoni propiora*) he explicitly renounces any attempt at poetry. His title to be a 'bard' (*uates*) or a 'priest of the Muses' (*Musarum sacerdos*) he would base upon the lyric mastery towards which he was at this period gradually feeling his way. He contrasts himself and Lucilius with Ennius, whose poetic diction would be still evident (*disiecti membra poetae*[4]) even after it had been taken out of metrical order. The disavowal of a poetic standard left Horace free to adopt an offhand style, colloquial phrases, and words from the common speech, jumbled occasionally with foreign importations. This gave vigour and variety to compositions which aimed at the portrayal of real life. So the *Satires* often smack of the qualities and phraseology observable in a comic scene on the Roman stage or in a note hastily tossed off by Cicero. There are conversational phrases like *pulchre est, ohe iam*

---

[1] *Sat.*, I. x. 40–49.
[2] *Ibid.*, 48:
> 'Neque ego illi detrahere ausim
> Haerentem capiti multa cum laude coronam.'
[3] *Sat.*, I. iv. 43:
> 'Ingenium cui sit, cui mens diuinior atque os
> Magna sonaturum, des nominis huius [*sc.* poetae] honorem.'
[4] *Sat.*, I. iv. 62.

satis est, numquid uis?, uin tu?, disperam ni, and downright slang like *nodosus* (cunning), *dolare* (belabour), *serua* (look out!). There are anticipations of the transition into the Romance languages in syncopated forms like *soldum, caldior, euasti,* in substitutes for the classic superlatives like *multum celer, bene sanus,* in words like *caballus* and crowds of diminutives. The actual sound of the *sermo cotidianus* is faithfully represented by altering *au* to *o* in *plostrum, plostellum* and *cole.* Some of his rare words and ἅπαξ εἰρημένα are, no doubt, of his own invention—he defended the use of new terms, everyone remembers, in the *Ars Poetica.* Some may come from old plays which have been lost. Some, one may be sure, are relics of his Bohemian days. One might expect that, treating ordinary life in ordinary words, the *Satires* would be easy reading. The reverse is true. Problems textual and exegetical place the *Satires* among quite the hardest books in Latin. There are passages where no editor could support the universal reading of the MSS. There are some where no conjecture has won absolute conviction. There are interpolations. But the difficulties are not all of this sort. Some are due to his desultory mode of composition: others are due to the fact that Horace had not yet reached the lucidity of the *Epistles.* The expression is not always adequate to the thought. His habit of blending prosaic and vulgar Latinity with the rhetorical and poetical artifices of the schools is more compatible with the traditions of the old medley than with an artistic standard of clearness.[1]

Despite, then, his avowal of writing something allied to prose, Horace keenly appreciated the main virtues of satiric style. He saw the need for brevity, variety of tone, and distinction of language.[2] He inveighs against hasty workmanship. His hexameter was polished as compared with that of Lucilius, though he did not equal the finish which he afterwards attained in the *Epistles.* Carelessness regarding the caesura, the use of pentasyllabic, quadrisyllabic, and monosyllabic endings, the prevalence of elision (rising once to a fourfold elision in a line), the elision of long syllables before short, and the retention of the quantity of short final syllables before *sp, st, sc,* are among the rugged features of his hexameter. It would be unfair to pit him against Virgil. Horace's themes did not call for the same music: and he had not the skill to ring the changes with such miraculous variety on spondees and

[1] For Horace's employment of vulgar Latin, desultory mode of composition, recourse to devices of orator and poet, see A. Cartault, *Études sur les satires d'Horace,* 1899, supplemented by his article *L'Inexprimé dans les satires,* etc., in *Revue de Philol.,* vol. xxvi, i, January 1902.
[2] *Sat.,* I. x. 9:
'Est breuitate opus, ut currat sententia neu se
Impediat uerbis lassas onerantibus auris;
Et sermone opus est modo tristi saepe iocoso,
Defendente uicem modo rhetoris atque poetae,
Interdum urbani, parcentis uiribus atque
Extenuantis eas consulto.'

dactyls. It is more to the point to say that, within Horace's own sphere of satire, Juvenal's verse far outshines his for dignity. But then Juvenal had studied Virgil from youth.

Through a variety of purposes and still greater variety of themes the general spirit of the Horatian satire remains fairly uniform. True, Horace began with vindictive acrimony and personal detraction. On the extent to which he introduced the names of living persons authorities are not agreed.[1] Certainly he borrowed some names from Lucilius to serve as types, like *Nomentanus* for a spendthrift. Others are suspiciously like thin disguises parodying a real name, like *Ceruius* for Seruius. Just possibly the *Catius*, who summarises for Horace a lecture on the science of dining, is Cicero's correspondent Matius. Others carry their fictitious origin imprinted on them. If a modern writer used 'Grab-all' for a borrower, 'Rich-hard' for a wealthy skin-flint, 'Newly' for an upstart, and 'Mr. Piggins' for a man who made whole cakes disappear at a banquet, he would only be repeating Horace's *Pantolabus*, *Opimius*, *Nouius*, and *Porcius*. Horace, however, came increasingly to satirise a class rather than an individual, and a sin rather than a sinner. We rightly associate him with something more sunny than the 'juice of the black cuttlefish' and 'absolute verdigris' to which he compared back-biting.[2] He preferred the method of the open jest. A joke may settle weighty matters better than a sharp word.[3] Yet even to laugh at people may hurt. Without the abusiveness of his early work, and without con-tinuing to use actual names, he could draw speaking likenesses. Victims are in general only too ready to fit the cap on their own heads. He realised it. In one satire he pictures people shunning the satirist as a dangerous person among them who used his circle of intimates as merely so much 'copy': 'He has a hay-wisp on his horn; give him a wide berth: provided he can raise a laugh for himself, he'll not spare any friend; and what he once scrawls on paper, he'll yearn for all to know, slave-boys and old women, as they come back from the bakery or the water-tank.'[4] Horace felt he had to reason with those who told him

---

[1] *E.g.*, Palmer (pref. to his ed. of *Satires*) thinks the names largely fictitious: Nettleship (*Lectures and Essays*, p. 151) objects.

[2] *Cf. Sat.*, I. iv. 81 *sqq.*, and *ibid.*, 100:

> 'Hic nigrae sucus lolliginis, haec est
> Aerugo mera.'

[3] *Sat.*, I. x. 14:

> 'Ridiculum acri
> Fortius et melius magnas plerumque secat res.'

[4] *Sat.*, I. iv. 34:

> 'Faenum habet in cornu; longe fuge: dummodo risum
> Excutiat sibi, non hic cuiquam parcet amico;
> Et quodcumque semel chartis illeuerit, omnis
> Gestiet a furno redeuntis scire lacuque
> Et pueros et anus.':

like Burns's warning:

'you like to sting' (*laedere gaudes*).[1] He opens the second book by owning that to some he appeared too sharp in his satire, and he introduces the lawyer Trebatius admonishing him about the risks of an action for libel. Yet the dominant note is good humour. Foibles are treated in the spirit rather of Chaucer than of Pope. The typical Horace speaks when he entreats an indulgent view of his outspoken mirth;[2] when he recalls the harsh judgments of the world;[3] when he pleads for leniency in criticism upon the most human of all grounds — *uitiis nemo sine nascitur*; and when he banters the Stoic doctrinaire on the absurdity of reckoning all sins alike. Some pieces are not what we should now call 'satire' at all. Some are written frankly to amuse himself as much as others. It was one of his peccadilloes so to trifle.[4] The most entertaining of all — Horace in the clutches of the bore — is really a dramatic sketch in which he laughs at himself as much as at his tormentor. Others are full of reflection, and are indicative of the growing seriousness of his aim. If his object at one time was to retort, at another it was to reform, and at another to 'indulge his genius.' The total impression is one of prevailing geniality in the midst of variety.

The primitive medley bore in Horace its pleasantest fruit. Juvenal, who called his own work a hotch-potch (*farrago libelli*) and claimed mankind for his study (*quicquid agunt homines*), has really a narrower outlook. His fierce indignation restricts his horizon. Now, here it is that Horace's kindlier nature conferred its greatest benefit on literature. Horace learned the secret of that broad sympathy which finds material in unsuspected quarters — in quite unpromising things and people. Any subject, except perhaps politics, served for his chameleon-like satire. Such was his knowledge of human nature that to be effective he only needed to sketch it with a smile — his own life and failings, his own and other philosophies, a long journey, a few moments in the green-market to price vegetables, an evening stroll through the forum to watch the fortune-tellers, a morning walk down the Sacra Via, a dinner-party, an authority on festal delicacies, the pearl dissolved to make a costly drink, the nightingale luncheon, the peacock course, and all the little things that matter or seem to matter at table. Then, becoming graver,

---

> 'If there's a hole in a' your coats
>   I rede you tent it:
> A chiel's amang you takin' notes
>   And, faith, he'll prent it.'

[1] *Sat.*, I. iv. 78.
[2] *Sat.*, I. iv. 103:

> 'liberius si
> Dixero quid, si forte iocosius, hoc mihi iuris
> Cum uenia dabis.'

[3] *Sat.*, I. iii. 55 *sqq.*
[4] *Sat.*, I. iv. 138:

> 'ubi quid datur oti
> Inludo chartis.'

he would analyse the literary qualities of satire, or discuss the 'false-hood of extremes,' the ineradicable inconsistency of mankind, the unhappiness of the avaricious, the incredibly mean tricks of the legacy-hunter, and the simple life practised by a rustic sage who is 'wise with-out the rules' (*abnormis sapiens*). And so on, till the manners and customs of the Augustan age stand out as clear as his own personality. He himself insisted that the grave and the gay should meet in satire. In his gay moods, he views human failings merrily; in his grave moods, more in sorrow than in anger. The jocular side yields such things as the fable of the ambitious frog that burst; the town and the country mouse; the conundrum whether it was madder to turn a pet lamb into a daughter or a daughter into a sacrificial lamb; the host who spoiled his dainties by lecturing the guests on the *menu*; and the sarcastic old lady of Thebes who ordained that her heir must carry out for burial her corpse smeared with oil—she had never slipped through his fingers when alive! The lively incidents on the way to Brindisi are among the good things too. It is all so realistic. The short stages suitable to an easy-going traveller like Horace along the tedious Appian Way, knavish inn-keepers, villainous drinking-water, squabbles about overcrowding on the canal-barge, sleeping made difficult by nasty mosquitoes and croaking frogs (*mali culices ranaeque palustres*), the drunken bargee's maudlin song about 'the girl he left behind him' (*absentem ut cantat amicam*), his rascality in turning the mule off the tow-path to graze once his passengers are asleep, and the trouncing which he earns, are among the opening strokes in a satire which has scarcely a dull line.

The liveliest satire of all is the ninth of the first book. As Horace writes *sermoni propiora*, it is tempting to translate it in prose as a dramatic sketch:

SCENE. — ROME ON THE SACRED WAY.

The poet Horace is walking down the street, as his habit is, composing some trifle—in a brown study (totus in illis)—when a person known to him only by name rushes up and seizes his hand.

THE BORE (*effusively*): How d'ye do, my dear fellow?

HORACE (*politely*): Nicely, at present. I'm at your service, sir.

      (*Horace walks on, and as the bore keeps following, tries to choke him off.*)

You don't want anything, do you?

BORE: You must make my acquaintance; I'm a *savant*.

HOR.: Then I'll think the more of you.

      (*Horace, wretchedly anxious to get away, walks fast one minute, halts the next, whispers something to his attendant slave, and is bathed in perspiration all over. Then, quietly to himself:*)

Lucky Bolanus, with your hot temper!

BORE (*whose chatter on things in general, and pretty remarks about the*

streets and about Rome, have been received with dead silence:) You're
frightfully keen to be off. I've noticed it all along. But it's no good. I'm
going to stick to you right through. I'll escort you from here to your
destination.

Hor. (*deprecatingly*): No need for you to make such a *détour*. (*Inventing a fib as he goes along*) There's someone I want to look up —a person
you don't know —on the other side of the river —yes, far away —he's
confined to bed —near Caesar's park.

Bore: Oh, I've nothing to do, and I don't dislike exercise. I'll follow
you right there. (*Horace is as crestfallen as a sulky donkey when an extra
heavy load is dumped upon its back. The bore continues*) If I know myself,
you'll not value Viscus more highly as a friend, or Varius either; for
who can write verses faster, and more of them, than I can? Who's a
greater master of deportment? As for my singing, it's enough to make
even Hermogenes jealous.

Hor. (*seizing the chance of interrupting*): Have you a mother —any
relatives to whom your health is of moment?

Bore: Not one left. I've laid them all to rest.

Hor.: Lucky people! Now I'm the sole survivor. Do for *me*. The
melancholy fate draws near which a fortune-telling Sabellian crone once
prophesied in my boyhood; 'This lad neither dread poison nor hostile
sword shall take off, nor pleurisy, nor cough, nor crippling gout. A
chatterbox will one day be his death! Let him, if wise, avoid the
garrulous, as soon as he has grown to man's estate!'

Bore (*noticing that they are close to Vesta's temple, and that, as it is the
hour for opening the law courts, he must answer to his recognisances or lose
a suit to which he is a party*): Oblige me by giving me your assistance in
court for a little.

Hor.: Deuce take me if I've the strength to hang about so long, or
know any law. Besides, I'm hurrying you know where.

Bore: I'm in a fix what to do —whether to give you up or my
case.

Hor.: Me, please.

Bore: Shan't!

(*Starts ahead of Horace, who, beaten at every point, has to
follow. The bore opens conversation again.*)
On what footing do you and Maecenas stand?

Hor. (*haughtily*): He has a select circle of friends, and thoroughly
sound judgement.

Bore (*unimpressed*): Ah! no one ever made a smarter use of his
chances. You'd have a powerful supporter, a capable understudy, if
you'd agree to introduce your humble servant. Deuce take me, if you
wouldn't clear everybody out of your way.

Hor. (*disgusted*): We don't live on the terms *you* fancy. No establishment is more honest than his, or more foreign to such intrigues. It does
me no harm, I tell you, because this one has more money or learning
than I. Everybody has his own place.

Bore: A tall story —hardly believable!

Hor.: A fact, nevertheless.

BORE: You fire my anxiety all the more to be one of his intimate friends.

HOR. (*sarcastically*): You've only got to wish it. Such are *your* qualities, you'll carry him by storm — and he is the sort than can be won; that's why he always keeps the first approaches hard.

BORE (*on whom the irony is lost*): I'll not fail myself. I'll bribe his slaves. If I find the door shut in my face, I'll not give up. I'll watch for lucky moments. I'll meet him at the street corners. I'll see him home. Life grants man nothing without hard work.

> (*Enter on the scene Aristius Fuscus, a friend of Horace. Well acquainted with the bore's ways, he reads the situation at once. A few questions pass about their respective engagements. Horace furtively tugs at Fuscus's gown, pinches his arms without producing any effect, nods and winks to Fuscus to rescue him. Fuscus smiles, and with a mischievous fondness for a joke he pretends he does not understand.*)

HOR. (*angry with Fuscus*): Of course, you *did* say you wanted to talk over something with me in private.

FUSC.: Ah yes, I remember quite well, but I'll tell you at a more convenient season. (*Inventing an excuse with mock solemnity*) Today is the thirtieth sabbath. You wouldn't affront the circumcised Jews, would you?

HOR.: I have no scruples.

FUSC.: But I have. I'm a slightly weaker brother — one of the many. Pardon, I'll talk about it another time. (*Exit, leaving Horace like a victim under the knife*).

HOR. (*to himself*): To think that this day should have dawned so black for me!

> (*Suddenly enter the plaintiff in the suit against the bore.*)

PLAINTIFF (*loudly, to the bore*): Where are you off to, you scoundrel? (*To Horace*): May I call you as witness to his contempt of court?

> (*Horace allows his ear to be touched according to legal form. The bore is haled away to court, he and the plaintiff bawling at each other. The arrest attracts a large crowd.*)

HOR. (*quietly disappearing*): What an escape! Thank Apollo!

The solid morality with which Horace interwove his jocund merriment is part of his versatility. Again and again, even in the first book, a serious ethical note is sounded. You laugh at the fable of Tantalus, Horace says; but it has its application: 'Thou art the man' (*mutato nomine de te fabula narratur*). His treatment of avarice may not abide in the memory like Plautus's or Balzac's: yet he limns an impressive picture of the miser who has failed to gain love (*non uxor saluum te uolt*). The lesson to be drawn from a paragon of inconsistency (*nil fuit umquam sic impar sibi*) is ultimately one of charity.[1] Horace rises indeed to moral fervour and dignity where he appeals to the spendthrift:

[1] *Sat.*, I. iii. 19:
> 'Quid tu?
> Nullane habes uitia?'

Is there no better object than luxury to spend money on? No beggar at your gates? (*cur eget indignus quisquam te diuite?*). No temples to rebuild? Have you, worthless one, no measure of your great heap of money for your beloved country? . . . One day you will be the laughing-stock of your enemies. Which of the two shall trust himself best to meet the hazards of fortune—he who has accustomed to excess his mind and pampered body, or he who, content with little, and apprehensive of the morrow, has like a wise man made in peace the fit provision for war?[1]

This comes from the second book and is representative of the more reflective tone pervading it. There are two principal ways in which the second book contrasts with its predecessor. One indicates a development in form: it is more dramatic: dialogue is relied on to produce its effect. The other indicates a development in spirit. Horace has grown more definitely didactic. His Epicureanism is so far modified that he scoffs less at Stoic doctrine, and feels considerable sympathy with Damasippus's exhaustive analysis of the madness of mankind. With a fuller understanding of philosophy, he braces his slave Davus to portray the ideal escape from slavery of the mind:

> Who then is free? The sage with self-control,
> Whom poverty nor death nor chains affright,
> Steeled to refuse desire and trample fame—
> Complete, full-formed, and rounded in himself.[2]

The first three books of the *Odes* were issued together in 23 B.C. The *Maecenas atauis edite regibus* was the opening dedication, and the thirtieth ode of Book III was an *envoi*, intended to bid lyric poetry farewell. No historical allusion in the three books has been convincingly referred to a later date than 23.[3] The ode to the ship carrying Virgil to Greece need not apply to Virgil's last voyage in 19 B.C. There is nothing against, and there are certain presumptions in favour of, Virgil having visited Greece in other years; while in this particular ode, Horace's conventional notion that human daring is a temptation of Providence is, whether serious or ironical, suggestive of his less mature work. And two arguments still hold good. The reference to the Marcelli family[4] is surely earlier than the death of Marcellus in autumn

[1] *Sat.*, II. ii. 102 *sqq.*
[2] *Sat.*, II. vii. 83:
'Quisnam igitur liber? Sapiens sibi qui imperiosus,
Quem neque pauperies neque mors neque uincula terrent,
Responsare cupidinibus, contemnere honores
Fortis, et in se ipso totus teres atque rotundus.'
[3] The outstanding historical allusions are grouped under their years as bearing on the chronology, in Nettleship's *Lects. and Essays*, 1885, pp. 159 *sqq.* *Od.* II. ix is one of the crucial odes; its 'new trophies of Augustus' can refer quite as appropriately to 27 B.C. as to the recovery of the standards from the Parthians in 20. With Franke's *Fasti Hor.*, 1837, should be compared W. Christ, *Fastorum Horat. Epicrisis*, 1877, besides Wickham's Introd. to *Odes* and Verrall's *Studies in the Odes*.   [4] *Od.*, I. xii. 45.

23 B.C.; had publication followed Marcellus's death, Horace would have realised that the retention of the reference would cause needless pain. Secondly, the attitude adopted in two odes[1] towards Licinius Murena, brother of Maecenas's wife Terentia, though not necessarily implying deep affection, is still one which it would have been impolitic to parade after his execution for treason in 22. There is evidence, too, in proof of a long interval between the publication of *Odes* I–III and Horace's resumption of lyric activity. His lyric period would have ended absolutely fifteen years before his death but for the wishes of the emperor. It was to honour Augustus's revival of the secular games that the frigid *Carmen Saeculare* was composed in 17. Horace's work—no worse than what laureates usually achieve when on official duty—is recorded in an inscription commemorative of the *Ludi*, discovered in 1890. And it was in compliance with Augustus's desire that Horace returned to the composition of the most significant odes among those collected in Book IV.[2] That book is mainly political and national. Its fourth and fourteenth odes honour the campaigns of Drusus and Tiberius in the Tyrol and Grisons, 15 B.C. The second and fifth precede the emperor's return to Rome from Gaul in 13. The lighter odes of the book are virtually makeweights to fill it out.

The rich variety of metres and of musical power in Horace was signified by the epithet *numerosus* which Ovid applied to him. Horace was learned in the older lyric poetry of Greece. Verbal imitations are therefore not uncommon. Four odes in the first book open with phraseology modelled on Alcaeus; elsewhere there are borrowings from Pindar and Bacchylides;[3] and the apology to a lady (*O matre pulchra filia pulchrior*) was suggested by the palinode of Stesichorus. Some of the lighter odes may be free adaptations, but no complete poem can be shown to be a translation. Many deal with Roman things in so Roman a way that the effect dwarfs the contribution of Greece to metre or idiom. It was Horace's boast to have first wedded the Aeolian lyric to Italian measures.[4] Technically this claim is indefensible, for it ignores Catullus. But broadly Horace is justified in maintaining that he introduced a fresh kind of Roman poetry—the national lyric. The gift of

----

[1] One (II. x) is addressed to him; the other (III. xix) proposes a carousal in honour of his election as augur.

[2] Suet., *Vit. Hor.*: 'Scripta quidem eius [*sc.* Horati] usque adeo probauit [*sc.* Augustus] mansuraque perpetuo opinatus est ut non modo *Saeculare Carmen* componendum iniunxerit sed et Vindelicam uictoriam Tiberii Drusique priuignorum suorum, eumque coegerit propter hoc tribus *Carminum* libris ex longo interuallo quartum addere.' The opening words of IV. i are significant of the interval that had elapsed ('Intermissa, Venus, diu Rursus bella moues.').

[3] Points of resemblance to Bacchylides are traced in R. C. Jebb's Introd. to edn. of Bacchylides, 1905.

[4] *Od.*, III. xxx. 13:

> 'Princeps Aeolium carmen ad Italos
> Deduxisse modos.'

Catullus lay in producing effects other than moral dignity and patriotic fervour.

The opening nine odes of Book I are all in different metres, presumably to furnish specimens of the chief varieties in Horace. His commonest metre, the Alcaic, is named after Alcaeus of Lesbos, who is believed to have invented its Greek form. It is capable of great impetus and variety. It can carry sustained lyric themes with a fulness of rhetoric. It even admits delicate imagery. Horace sometimes followed his Greek master by employing the stanza for convivial and amorous poems—as in his winter song of hospitality (*Vides ut alta stet niue candidum*), in the invitation to his Sabine home, with its pretty fancy connecting Faunus and Pan (*Velox amoenum saepe Lucretilem*), in the apostrophe to a wine-jar (*O nata mecum consule Manlio*), in the verses on Lalage too young to wed (*Nondum subacta ferre iugum ualet*), in the withdrawal from the lists of love (*Vixi puellis nuper idoneus*), in the vigorous outburst on the news of Cleopatra's death (*Nunc est bibendum, nunc pede libero*), and in the congratulations on the restoration of civic rights to an old comrade (*O saepe mecum tempus in ultimum*)—a poem which ends merrily with anticipations of revel:

> recepto
> *Dulce mihi furere est amico.*

But experiment taught him effects unattempted by Alcaeus. At one time the Horatian Alcaics convey a sense of the power of God revealed in the bolt from the clear sky (*Parcus deorum cultor et infrequens*); at another, the pensive resignation of *Aequam memento rebus in arduis*, closing, in its final stanza, like a knell;[1] at another still, the solemn pathos of the fleeting years in *Eheu fugaces, Postume, Postume*. The Alcaics of the second book grow graver, as if in preparation for the series of six on imperial, moral, and religious themes which Horace arranged together for a majestic proem to his third book. To this metre he returns in the military paeans of the fourth book.

His next commonest metre bears the name of the Lesbian poetess Sappho. With predominating trochees and dactyls it subserves light and rapid movements. Structurally and musically it is more monotonous than the Alcaic; so Horace has certain rhythmical devices in his Sapphics whereby he seeks greater variety.[2] Animation is its pervading quality. Deftly managed, then, it can compass raillery, narrative, love, moral meditation, religious fervour. Its first appearance is to invoke

---

[1] *Od.*, II. iii. 25:
> 'Omnes eodem cogimur, omnium
> Versatur urna serius ocius
> Sors exitura et nos in aeternum
> Exilium impositura cumbae.'

[2] His frequent departures in Book IV and *Carm. Saec.* from the normal break after the fifth syllable in the first three lines seem to have this aim.

Octavian as the divine protector of Rome (*Iam satis terris niuis atque dirae*). It is used in praise of Jupiter, the other gods, and of heroic men who under them have served the world (*Quem uirum aut heroa*). In two stanzas it hymns Diana (*Montium custos nemorumque, Virgo*); in the same number, Venus (*O Venus, regina Cnidi Paphique*); in five stanzas, Mercury (*Mercuri, facunde nepos Atlantis*); and in eleven, Apollo (*Diue quem proles Niobea magnae*). Its capacity for combining the grave and the gay is well seen in the *Integer uitae scelerisque purus*. It is used to tell at length the story of the Danaids and of Europa, and again neatly to order a simple autumn repast (*Persicos odi, puer, apparatus*). It inculcates a judicious employment of money in *Nullus argento color est auaris*: in another ode (*Rectius uiues, Licini, neque altum*), it preaches the doctrine of the golden mean; and in moments of despondency it invokes a faithful friend (*Septimi, Gades aditure mecum*). But its rapidity, and the possibility of a sting in the brief last line, fitted it also for teasing Xanthias on his attachment to a slave girl (*Ne sit ancillae tibi amor pudori*), or for playfully reproaching the fair forsworn Barine (*Ulla si iuris tibi peierati*), or for ungallantly taunting Lyce on growing old (*Parcius iunctas quatiunt fenestras*). Its comic potentialities were duly noted by the author of 'The Needy Knife-Grinder' in the *Anti-Jacobin*.

The different Asclepiad measures owe to their characteristic choriambus a lightness of movement without precluding gravity. Horace has nothing to surpass the piquant grace of the ode to Pyrrha—the despair of so many translators, Milton himself not excepted. It is written in the 'fourth' Asclepiad stanza, consisting of two lesser Asclepiads followed by a Pherecratean and a Glyconic. Of this stanza's other six occurrences the best are the anxious lyric on the tempest-tossed ship of state (*O nauis, referent in mare te noui*); the lines of comfort to Asterie weeping for her absent lover (*Quid fles, Asterie, quem tibi candidi*), and the rapturous praise of the crystal well among the Sabine hills (*O fons Bandusiae splendidior uitro*). The 'second' Asclepiad, in couplets which place a Glyconic first and a lesser Asclepiad line second, attains marvellous speed. It is at its fastest in what is the closest approach to the dithyramb in Horace—*Quo me, Bacche, rapis?* It admirably fits the amoebean piece recording the lovers' quarrel and reconciliation (*Donec gratus eram tibi*). The examples cited are more than enough to substantiate Horace's wide control over metre. We may, then, forgo consideration of the other Asclepiads, and of some five exceptional metres, including the clever but unconvincing Ionics *a minore* which sketched a love-sick maid chafing against restraint.

This outline of metres in relation to theme conveys an idea of the width of Horace's lyric interest. Like some of the satires, certain odes were written mainly to amuse; others were written to inspire. There are songs of love and wine; there are praises and abuses of heroines wherein Horace is less than half-serious; there are purely occasional pieces; but there are others where he pitches his strain higher. He sings the lyrics of the new Rome. As in the *Satires*, a growing seriousness is traceable in the *Odes*. It is coupled with a firmer confidence in his country and her prospects. While he expresses admiration for the ruler and his successes, he is impelled to act the mentor to his age, and, as in the *Epistles*, to counsel caution and morality. More than any other portion of his works, the *Odes* raise the question of his attitude to the emperor and the system for which he stood. Horace in one sense was non-political. He was not concerned with details of government. He had no public career. The intrigues of ambition were in his eyes foolishness. But in another sense he was political. He was concerned with matters above 'politics' — not with the transient politics of the day, but with the super-politics of a nation's life and welfare. A boy during the civil war between Pompey and Caesar, afterwards a young enthusiast for the liberators against the triumvirs, he had realised later that the republican cause was shattered and leaderless. The liberators had destroyed security in destroying Caesar. It remained for Octavian and Antony to oust Lepidus, and then try conclusions one with the other. Horace's early poetry, we have seen, reflects the inquietude of critical times — the anxieties of the citizen during continuous turmoil and carnage. His pessimism in the sixteenth epode is in absolute contrast to the vision of a golden age which Virgil composed in the fourth eclogue — conceivably in reply to Horace. Horace's trust in Octavian sprang from sources deeper than weariness of strife and a longing for peace. Octavian's administration of the city impressed him favourably in comparison with Antony's enslavement to the queen of Egypt and his masquerading as the god Osiris. One-man rule was acceptable as a guarantee not only of personal security, but of Rome's existence. Before 31 B.C. Horace was in full sympathy with Octavian. A fair inference puts him on one of Octavian's galleys at Actium. Thenceforward the poet is his convinced eulogist. He shares the popular joy over Cleopatra's death. Republican dreams have long since been disillusioned. Horace symbolised the futility of any return upon the old constitution by Juno's declaration that Troy may not be rebuilt.[1] Every year brings fuller persuasion of the expediency of the new *régime*. Horace honestly believed in its promise of a noble future for the state; and, like Virgil, he supported its ingenious compromise between republic and monarchy.

About the business of the principate, about the workmanlike co-operation of Maecenas and Agrippa loyally placed at the ruler's disposal, about the reorganisation of departments relating to provinces, finance, roads, or public safety, we hear little in Horace. Such details are not for poetry. But the effects were not lost on him. Nor did he fail to note signs of national deterioration in the increase of Oriental sensuality, the eschewing of marriage responsibilities, the decline of the

---

[1] This is the view of *Od.* III. iii taken by Plüss, Sellar and Kiessling.

birth-rate. His praise of sound morals meant his practical support of the imperial legislation which aimed at social reform by penalising the unmarried, favouring fathers of children, and punishing adultery.

For ancillary schemes to resuscitate ancient religious practice,[1] the emperor had allies in the poets. Unlike the sceptical freethinkers, they saw beautiful and venerable ideals in the old ritual and beliefs. They even saw poetry in the novel homage to the head of the state. Many factors contributed to the development of Caesar-worship.[2] Its initiation owed something to the cult of the Ptolemies in Egypt, of the Seleucids in Syria, and of local dynasties in Asia Minor. Though Augustus declined divine honours at first, the very title *Augustus*, the organisation of *Augustales*, and the institution of the cult of his *Genius*, were all steps towards the consummated worship. At first the *Genius* of Augustus was associated with the plebeian cult of the *Lares*; he was the custodian of the empire safe-guarding the home physically, as the *Lares* safeguarded it spiritually. The fable of the divine descent of the Caesar family and the association with the Fortune of Rome won additional reverence for the new god. Altars spread his worship in Gaul, Africa, Spain, and other provinces. So time places Augustus among the greater public divinities, and Caesar-worship attained a universality which prepared a way for the ultimate predominance of Christianity. The prevision of a world-wide obeisance to the majesty of Rome and its emperor was calculated to inspire poetry; and it is noteworthy that some of Horace's best lyrics date from the time of the emperor's assumption of his majestic title. Yet the whole idea must have remained, for a mind like Horace's, political rather than religious. His religious sentiment was never so deep as Virgil's. Horace probably never entirely threw off the Lucretian scepticism with which he received the report of a miracle on his journey to Brundisium—*Credat Iudaeus Apella, non ego!* When he abjures his *insaniens sapientia*,[3] it must not be imagined that his 'conversion' by a thunderbolt was very thoroughgoing. The gods of the Greek mythology were chiefly to him fair creations of fancy and beautiful ornaments for poetry. Yet there is no need to call him atheistic. In some divine power ordering things he seems vaguely to believe, whether he conceives it to be above the gods of popular legend, or identifies it with Jove as impartial lord of all,[4] or with the mysterious Fortune to whom Romans attributed much of their greatness and whose harbinger Horace pictures as Destiny (*Necessitas*).[5] What remains clear

[1] *Od.*, IV. xv. 12, 'Et ueteres reuocauit artes.'
[2] J. Toutain, *Les cultes païens dans l'empire romain*, 1907.
[3] *Od.*, I. xxxiv.
[4] *Od.*, III. iv. 45:
    'Qui terram inertem, qui mare temperat
   Ventosum et urbes regnaque tristia,
    Diuosque mortalesque turbas
     Imperio regit unus aequo.'
[5] *Od.*, I. xxxv.

is his conviction that piety is a factor in social and national strength. He admires his rustic Phidyle whose humble offerings and prayers from a right spirit he believes to be acceptable to the gods.[1] This shows him at a loftier level than in the formal state-religion of the *Carmen Saeculare*. Whatever his personal religion, one may be sure that Horace theoretically, and sincerely enough, believed in the righteousness which exalteth a nation. It was at least good for the *profanum uulgus* to be taught reverence. Some opportunism doubtless alloys his acceptance of emperor-worship. He could bring himself, in moments of enthusiasm over the military successes of the empire, to rise from epithets like *inuictus*, *clarus*, *altus* into the extravagance of enrolling the *princeps* among the gods

> *Quos inter Augustus recumbens*
> *Purpureo bibet ore nectar.*[2]

But undeniably the praise of the emperor's reforms is marked by greater spontaneity than the adulation of the emperor himself. The tone of the six stately odes opening Book III dispels all suspicions as to the the poet's sincerity. They are lyrics absolutely unique in Roman literature. They owe their elevation to public spirit and patriotic instincts. With an abhorrence of the deadly sins of the day, Horace sings the praises of six types of civic virtue—the first four of which practically correspond to the Platonic cardinal virtues—moderation, courage, justice, wisdom, patriotism, and piety. When Horace consents to write the imperial lyrics of Book IV as a semi-official laureate, his panegyrics on Augustus are no less sincere. They are the work of a court-poet; but on the whole they are natural and justifiable. The emperor had really deserved well of his country for Roman victories over the barbarian; and the praise of his stepsons' military successes reflected credit on their guardian.[3] It was reasonable to honour him as head of an empire on whose greatness, Horace feels, 'the sun never sets.'[4] He was the restorer of morals and peace.[5] His policy was intensely national in its endeavour to link Italy with her own antique usages; and, appropriately, Horace echoed the *Aeneid* by referring to the connexion of the imperial house with the legendary past.[6]

[1] *Od.*, III. xxiii.
[2] *Od.*, III. iii. 11; *cf.* IV. v. 34:
> 'et Laribus tuum
> Miscet numen.'
[3] *Od.*, IV. iv and xiv.
[4] *Od.*, IV. xiv. 5–6:
> 'O qua sol habitabiles
> Illustrat oras,' etc.
IV. xv. 14:
> 'famaque et imperi
> Porrecta maiestas ad ortum
> Solis ab Hesperio cubili.'
[5] *Od.*, IV. v. 21, 'Nullis polluitur casta domus stupris.' For the closing of the Temple of Janus, *cf. Od.*, IV. xv. 8–9.
[6] *Od.*, IV. xv, *sub fin.*

O

Horace, though to a less extent than Virgil, stood aloof from the common people. Both wrote for court circles and the upper middle class, whose goodwill was essential to the permanence of the constitution. In this way Horace and Virgil were valuable political assets. But this was only at the dawn of the empire. Their real service has been rendered to universal literature and has outlasted the Roman empire. If neither repressive laws nor time-honoured religion could save Roman society, then Virgil's epic and Horace's songs were sure to fail on that side of their design. The futility of the emperor's efforts and the symptoms of ultimate ruin may be read in facts. Horace, the eulogist of Augustan regulations, braved their spirit by remaining a bachelor. Julia, the emperor's daughter, was banished for immorality; and Ovid, the favourite poet of high society, was kept in perpetual exile as the author of a scandalous manual of seduction.

The first book of the *Epistles* was published in either 20 or 19 B.C. This may be concluded with reasonable certainty from the closing words of its epilogue.[1] Here Horace is a moralist, as in the second book he is a literary critic. Letter-writing, whether in prose or verse, was essentially a Roman art. The prolonged separation from friends, due to official life, fostered it to an extent unthought of by the Greeks. In his *Epistles* Horace developed a form already used by Lucilius. Of these twenty poetical letters, the shorter ones—some of them little over ten lines long—are more personal and familiar. The longer ones—some of them over a hundred lines long—are more formal and didactic. The shorter show Horace, now a man of forty-five, pleasantly interested in the literary plans of the younger set on Tiberius's staff; they show him sending letters of recommendation—one a model of its kind to the future emperor—or inviting a friend to dinner on Augustus's birthday, or despatching certain *signata uolumina* (which need not be his *Odes*) to the emperor, or consulting a friend about health resorts, or emptying the vials of his scorn upon criticasters, or communing with his book on what comes of being published. The first epistle strikes the ethical note prevailing in the longer letters. Farewell is said to poetry, and attention is centred on philosophic inquiry.[2] But he must retain his independence of the schools.[3] True to this, Horace is eclectic. Though he closes this epistle with a quip at the self-sufficiency of the Stoic pedant ('rich, free, exalted, handsome, king of kings in short, sound beyond all—except when troubled by a cold!'), he proves by his insistence on virtue that his teaching is more Stoic than Cyrenaic. His heart is set on what is truly profitable. Wisdom is the supreme business of life; and it vexes

---

[1] These epistles belong in composition to different years from 24 to 20. Scholars who believe the *Odes* were published in 19 place *Epist. I* about 18 B.C.
[2] *Epist.*, I. i. 10:
      'Nunc itaque et uersus et cetera ludicra pono;
      Quid uerum atque decens, curo et rogo, et omnis in hoc sum.'
[3] *Epist.*, I. i. 14, 'Nullius addictus iurare in uerba magistri.'

him to watch the waste of human energy: so much eagerness is shown
for gold, so little for goodness. To this feverish restlessness[1] he returns
in that later one where he advocates as the secret of happiness the principle of caring for nothing overmuch—the principle of *Nil admirari*—a
philosophic calm in which Epicureanism and Stoicism might be recon-
ciled. The power of 'culture' to subdue the lower nature (I. i. 38 *sqq.*),
the need for the training of character (I. ii. 32 *sqq.*), the tendency of the
passions to ruin enjoyment (I. ii. 51), the adaptation of the self to company (I. xviii. 89), are among the many points of practical philosophy
which Horace represents himself as studying by the 'cool Digentia
stream' (I. xviii. 104). It is his desire to test his life by the tenets of
sound philosophy. Thus, to make a friend of oneself (*quid te tibi reddat
amicum*) is fittingly appended to his study of making friends among the
great. What Horace wishes for himself is typical of his philosophy—a
supply of books and a store of food sufficient to banish anxiety[2]

> Enough to pray to Jove who gives and takes,
> For life and means. Content be mine to find.[3]

The whole question touching the date of *Epistles*, Book II, and of the
Epistula ad Pisones, best known as the *Ars Poetica*, is intricate and
undecided. The second epistle of Book II is referred by various
authorities to different years between 19 and 10 B.C. Much the same
choice of dates is offered for the *Ars Poetica*. Considerable weight
attaches to the opinion that the '*sermones*' which Augustus complained
did not mention him[4] were the second epistle of this book and the *Ars
Poetica*. If that is so, they belong to years preceding the date of the
first epistle of the book, which is about 13 B.C.[5] But, then, the young

[1] *Epist.*, I. i. 82 *sqq. Cf.* I. xi. 27:
'Caelum non animum mutant qui trans mare currunt;
Strenua nos exercet inertia.'
[2] *Epist.*, I. xviii. 110, 'neu fluitem dubiae spe pendulus horae.'
[3] *Epist.*, I. xviii. 111:
'Sed satis est orare Iouem qui ponit et aufert,
Det uitam, det opes; aequum mi animum ipse parabo.'
[4] Suet., *Vit. Hor.*, '. . . post sermones uero quosdam lectos nullam sui
mentionem habitam ita sit questus "Irasci me tibi scito," etc. . . . expressitque
eclogam ad se cuius initium est "Cum tot sustineas, etc." (*i.e.*, *Epist.* II. i).'
Mommsen, *Herm.*, xv. 105, 1880, held that the *sermones* which piqued Augustus
were those of *Epist.*, Book I. This article (*Die Litteraturbriefe des Horaz*) discusses Vahlen's treatment of composition and date of the three epistles in
Monatsberichte d. Berl. Akad., 1878, 688 *sqq.* For *Ars Poet.*, *cf.* E. Norden on
Die Composition u. Litteraturgattung der Horazischen Epist. ad Pis., in *Herm.*,
xl, 481 *sqq.* (1905).
[5] *Epist.*, II. i. 15 bears on the institution of the cult of the *numen Augusti* in
14 B.C.; and ll. 252–254 bear on the victories of Drusus and Tiberius, as celebrated in *Odes*, IV. iv. and xiv. Two passages support the opinion that the
second epistle is earlier than the first: II. ii. 25 and 84–86 indicate that at the
time of writing Horace had not returned to lyric composition (*i.e.* since he
published *Od.*, I–III). The inference is that this second epistle precedes the
Carmen Saec. of 17 B.C. If the lines are taken to imply Horace's final abandonment of lyric poetry, then the epistle must be put after *Odes*, Book IV, *i.e.* after
13 B.C. Both views exclude the years 17–13 B.C.

men to whom the *Letter on Poetry* was addressed must, on an examination of dates, belong to another family than that which Porphyrion sur-
mised. In this case, too, we must abandon the idea that the *Ars Poetica*
was Horace's last work, left unfinished and unpublished by him. On
any view, however, Horace's writings on literary criticism belong to the
last ten or eleven years of his life.

In the first epistle of Book II—addressed to Augustus—Horace is a
champion for the new movement in literature in the battle of the
ancients and the moderns. Conscious of representing novel tendencies,
he did not feel for the old Latin poetry the enthusiasm of Lucretius and
Cicero. His Greek training, too, made the faults of old Latin writers
more glaring. Horace preferred chastened taste and refinement to
their virile ruggedness. So his remarks on Ennius, Naevius, Pacuvius,
Accius, Afranius, Plautus, Caecilius, Terence, and Livius are, even
where they praise, absolutely cold.[1] With the practical and didactic
genius of Rome he contrasts the artistic and speculative genius of
Greece.[2] He next sketches the native Italian drama and the spread of
Hellenism. His remarks suggest that three main factors militated against
Roman literature—a coarseness ingrained in the native Italian temperament; a tendency to careless composition; and, in Horace's own day,
the degenerate taste of audiences. With the sorry plight of contemporary
drama owing to the bad taste of Augustus's subjects Horace contrasts
the emperor's own discerning patronage of poetry. By recalling
Augustus's appreciation of Virgil and Varius, he realises he can compliment the *princeps*, even if, as he adds apologetically, he has not the
gift of the grand style needed for an epic upon him.

The second epistle was sent to the Julius Florus who was addressed
in a letter of the first book and who was a type of the younger literary
set. It is less critical. It includes valuable autobiographical reminiscences of Horace's education and early hardships, and complaints
against Rome as no place for peaceful composition. The pleasure, which
he notes in many poets, of nursing a fond delusion about their own
ability, diverts Horace from the literary to the ethical—the need for true
wisdom. Thus the queries towards the close are prompted by mellow
reflection on the value of character. Free from avarice you may be; but,
asks Horace, are you free from other human failings?

> Art thou thankful when thou numberest thy birthdays? Art
> forgiving to a friend? Dost grow a gentler and a better man as age
> draweth nigh? What doth it relieve thee to have but one thorn of
> many pulled out? If thou knowest not how to live aright, give place
> to those who have the skill.[3]

The two interesting things for literary criticism are the reference to

[1] *Epist.*, II. i. 50–72; *cf.* on Plautus, 170 *sqq.*   [2] *Epist.*, II. i. 93–107.
[3] *Epist.*, II. ii. 210:

Propertius's claim to be the Callimachus of his day,[1] and the unimpeach-
able doctrine of style laid down in terms[2] which go far to explain
Horace's own limpid ease. The points on which he insists are scrupulous
self-criticism; strength of will to delete; the choice of words now old,
now new; force, lucidity, and richness in diction (*fundet opes Latiumque
beabit diuite lingua*); and a process of pruning, of polish, and of rejection
unremitted until that ideal ease of movement be secured which comes of
taking adequate pains.

The *Epistula ad Pisones* is not to be judged as if Horace had himself
entitled it the *Ars Poetica*. If one looks in it for the whole art of poetry,
one inevitably discovers great omissions. There is a want of system,
fitting enough in what is half epistolary and half didactic. Most divisions
of poetry receive little more than mention. There is almost nothing
about Horace's own domain of lyric. Even in what he makes his main
theme, the drama, there is no inkling of the moral grandeur and eternal
problems of Greek tragedy. It strikes one as an extraordinary limitation
that, with his keenness to relate literature to life,[3] Horace should have
failed to grasp the universal import of the plays of Aeschylus and
Sophocles. But the book is best understood as conceived for the
guidance of intending dramatists. This was the age when tragedy was
attempted by Pollio, Varius,[4] and Augustus himself. Horace hoped for
a renascence of the Roman drama—probably of the satyr-play as well
as tragedy. His admiration for the magical power of the dramatist is
very forcibly expressed in the *Epistles*:[5] and it was natural that he should
desire to see a living Augustan drama—as living as he himself had made
lyric or Virgil epic. His real aim was to forward a national movement in
literature. He addressed his hints, then, through the Pisos, to the
younger generation of literary men. What he principally inculcated
was obedience to certain canons, for the avoidance of blunders, and
unwearying care in composition, for the attainment of success. There
could be no greater misconception than to imagine that the *Ars Poetica*
proposes the creation of poesy by rules and pains. Horace clearly
recognised that genius must combine with art[6]—by which latter he
meant what Carlyle meant by the former, an infinite capacity for taking

'Natales grate numeras? Ignoscis amicis?
Lenior et melior fis accedente senecta?
Quid te exempta leuat spinis de pluribus una?
Viuere si recte nescis, decede peritis.'

[1] *Epist.*, II. ii. 99 *sqq.*
[2] *Epist.*, II. ii. 109-125.
[3] *A.P.*, 309-318.
[4] Did Varius in his *Thyestes* follow the advice of Horace? or, if the *Thyestes*
preceded the *A.P.*, did Horace model his precepts on the practice of Varius?
This was discussed by G. Boissier, 'L'art poétique d'Horace et la tragédie
romaine,' in *Rev. de Philol.*, vol. xxi., October 1897.
[5] *Epist.*, II. i. 210-213.
[6] *A.P.*, 409 *sqq.*, 'nec studium sine diuite uena,' etc.

pains. He shows his contempt for that perennial phenomenon, the man who has a fatal facility for versifying[1] and who will inflict his recitations on any victim.[2] Therefore, for the good of Piso and others, he summarises three principles: only write if you have the afflatus (*nihil inuita Minerua*); submit your work to competent opinion (*in Maeci descendat iudicis auris*); keep it by you for nine years before publication (*nonumque prematur in annum*).

From Porphyrion we learn that the book was made up of selections from an Alexandrine scholar, Neoptolemus of Parium. Ultimately, a good deal of its teaching is Aristotelian. It is, however, impossible to say where exposition, and it may be translation, from the Greek ends, and where Horace's own contribution begins. The technical precepts on the five acts, the *deus ex machina*, the number of actors, the function of the chorus and the choral ode, bear on them the stamp of Hellenic origin; one may guess that the abstract principles laid down regarding poetry are from the same source. But Horace has a clear critical message for his times which is his own, and which is backed with definite pronouncements on the ever-reviving controversy touching the merits of ancients and moderns. Broadly, the *Ars Poetica* falls into three divisions.[3] After an introduction of over seventy lines on precepts of style, it devotes about two hundred lines to a special treatment of the drama among the different kinds of poetry, and concludes with about two hundred more on the essentials of literary success. If anything can confer unity on a rather discursive but none the less brilliant essay, it is the recurrent insistence on style in all its aspects. It is on more than language that Horace lays stress. With his eye upon the drama, he is emphatic that to beauty must be added feeling, and that the power to touch the heart involves true character-drawing.[4]

The *Ars Poetica* has exercised a powerful influence on both criticism and creation. It has swayed posterity more than it did its own age, for its wisdom did not arrest the Roman literary decadence. More accessible in the Middle Ages than Aristotle, this letter tended to be exalted into a court of appeal. Its weight with the writers of Elizabethan tractates on criticism was considerable, and Boileau's remodelling in *L'Art poétique* riveted some chains more tightly on the French 'classic' drama. The part it played in the Restoration period and in the eighteenth century, through the numerous versified essays on critical subjects, is familiar to all students of English literature. From it have descended many of the commonplaces and stock phrases of criticism, such as those relating to the purple patch (*purpureus pannus*), the gift of phrase-making (*callida iunctura*), the arbitrament of usage (*ius et norma loquendi*), the bathos born of bombast (*nascetur ridiculus mus*), the abrupt epic start (*in medias res*), the toil of filing (*limae labor*), the acme of polish (*ad unguem*), the

---

[1] *A.P.*, 372–384.
[3] (a) 1–72; (b) 73–288; (c) 289–476.
[2] *A.P.*, 453–476.
[4] *A.P.*, 99 *sqq.*

whetstone of criticism (*fungar uice cotis*), and the double function of all great literature (*omne tulit punctum qui miscuit utile dulci*). These and many others make the *Ars Poetica* a storehouse of phrases unsurpassable for sound sense and neat expression. But above all ranks the lofty ideal to which it beckons the artist in words. Horace is the foe of the slip-shod 'genius.' With anything less than the highest standard in literary revision he is malcontent.

There are many grounds for the attraction felt towards Horace by men differing in nationality, century, and time of life. Some have been drawn to his matter, others to his form, others to both combined. Certainly, one unfailing source of charm is his self-revelation. He makes his confessions, fears, musings, and judgements entertaining. No Latin author writes so openly and so winningly for the friendly reader. Horace has what Sir Thomas Browne discovers elsewhere, a 'magnetic alliciency.' He lures by his frankness and then plays round the very heart-strings: *circum praecordia ludit*—perhaps the best thing that his imitator Persius ever said. Horace possesses the gift, which he admired in Lucilius, of taking himself for theme and laying his life bare.[1] In an easy rambling habit of discourse, he listens to his own humours, and with sincerity registers reflections, memories and fancies, as they cross his mind. Here then is the autobiographic charm of Montaigne, who also had that mellowness of wisdom which led Sainte-Beuve to style him 'the French Horace.' So we are captured by everything Horace chooses to unfold about himself. His friendliness passes over into his writing. He wins readers now as he won comrades a score of centuries ago; for he unbosoms himself naturally. In conduct, as in literature, he has the self-criticism which marks and owns a fault. Thus, his egotism endears where Cicero's wearies. Through that sound commonsense which is his central attribute, Horace knew Horace better than Cicero knew Cicero. So far from offending, Horace can never tell us too much. We cannot but remember his moods, his likes and dislikes, his feelings on life. We note his constant desire to avoid extravagance in thought or behaviour, that preference for his own *aurea mediocritas* which saved him from excess. Amid banquets, wines, flowers, congenial company, peaceful seclusion, pleasures of nature, he enjoys life temperately. He advises others to do the same. Similar restraint underlies his detachment as a spectator of mankind. He touches human foibles for the most part gently and with a laugh. He can set himself in the place of others. His satire has the good-humoured tolerance of a Le Sage. If he works himself into no fury, neither does he work himself into passionate enthusiasm. He accepts life's goods without being enthralled—possesses without being

[1] *Sat.*, II. i. 32:

> ' quo fit ut omnis
> Votiua pateat ueluti descripta tabella
> Vita senis.'

possessed. It is his doctrine of *Nil admirari*. So he is overpowered by
no personage, no amour, no philosophy. He retains an independence,
cool, self-centred, manly. Even before the gods he will not cringe:

> *Sed satis est orare Iouem qui ponit et aufert,*
> *Det uitam, det opes; aequum mi animum ipse parabo.*

But this tranquil enjoyment can be momentarily ruffled. The inevitable
summons of death strikes Horace at times as suddenly as it came to
happy, thoughtless Everyman in the Morality play. Indeed, there is
something medieval in this aspect of Horace. The thought of life's
brevity, if not so ubiquitously arrestive as in Holbein's *Dance of Death*,
yet creates a dark presence which haunts the *Odes*. Horace sees the
spectre behind the wealthy rider (*post equitem sedet atra cura*). He
remembers that man goeth down surely whither kings have gone (*quo
pius Aeneas, quo Tullus diues, et Ancus*). He knows that every name is in
the capacious urn whose shaken lots will sooner or later tell us off for
the last voyage of all (*nos in aeternum Exsilium impositura cumbae*). Yet
it is not an unpleasant melancholy. There is no fretting or fuming.
There is no morbidity. On the other hand, there is no rebound towards
wild abandon. *Carpe diem* on Horace's lips implied reasoned pleasure
and respect for the moderation which, to the practical Epicurean, alone
secured happiness.

Another source of Horace's attraction lies in his reflection of his era.
He is the *index* to its men, manners, and ideas. He is in a kindly way its
iudex too. No other writer reveals Augustan society as he does. In his
pages we meet an extraordinary variety of figures—the commonest
folk in town or country, the middle-class, literary men: we touch the
imperial circle itself. There are nobles and parvenus, misers and spendthrifts, philosophers and singing-girls, and other types innumerable.
There is equal variety of scene and situation—the narrow, crowded
streets of Rome; Horace's 'little place in the country' (*modus agri non
ita magnus*); glimpses of the provincial towns of Italy; a rural festival;
a townsman's banquet; a theatrical audience stopping a play with
clamour for bears and boxers; the deathbed of a miser who grudges the
pence spent on gruel, while his heir chuckles; the insolvent debtor
coerced into hearing recitations from his creditor's histories; and Horace
himself in widely diverse surroundings. This representation of the times
takes its most concrete form, of course, in the *Satires*. There Horace is
most a realist. Yet, though the antithesis that Horace is the realist and
Virgil the idealist of the day is truer than most antitheses, it needs some
qualification. It does not mean that Horace had no idealism—his *Odes*
would correct that notion; and it does not mean that Virgil's *Georgics*
and *Aeneid* are unrelated to real life—on the contrary, they sprang out
of contemporary circumstances. But it does mean that we meet the
actual flesh and blood of the new Rome in Horace and not in Virgil;

and that Horace has not Virgil's sustained dignity and contemplative aloofness. Still, to think of Horace as a mere painter of externals would be a gross misconception. Even when he pictures social follies, he sets up ideal standards. And there is much else in him that is abstract. He represents the practical wisdom of his age in the earlier *Epistles*, its literary criticism in the later *Epistles*, and the national record and hopes in many of his *Odes*.

With all Horace's realism there is, then, a smack of the ideal, a truth of touch, a knowledge of universal humanity. If he had been solely for self, he would not have interested mankind. Complacent Epicureanism was not the greatest thing in Horace. He knew how to enjoy both society and solitude: he valued pleasures without enslavement of the reason. These pleasures were not merely material. He had what the Epicurean so often lacked—a sense of public duty. If he had been solely a narrow Roman, he would have failed to attract ages other than his own. But his patriotism was not confined to chanting paeans over national success. It rose into zeal for the moral welfare of the empire. This sprang from insight into human nature. Here, then, the Roman merges in the cosmopolitan. Mankind, in fact, interested and amused Horace. That is why he could draw types to interest mankind in turn. His strokes are vivid because of their fidelity to perennial human nature. It is, moreover, because humanity interested Horace that he endeavoured to cope with the maladies of his generation, and this broad outlook gave him words not simply for Rome, but for the world.

Still, self-revelation, the mirroring of a period, and truth to human nature are qualities of subject-matter. They may be found in prose. Horace has in addition the charm of excellent form in metre and phrase, while his best work attains high poetic dignity. This raises the question of Horace's claim to rank as a really considerable poet. He has met with severe critics like Goethe, who would make of him little more than a versifier possessed of technical skill and a 'frightful realism,' but without any true poetry, especially in the *Odes*.[1] It may be admitted at once that if Horace is no poet in the *Odes*, he is no poet anywhere. He rightly rested his poetic fame on them. No one will deny his inequalities. Apostle of care though he was, he has failures. Yet he falls into conceits with surprising rarity for so professed an elaborator. Only seldom have we lapses like the 'gadding harem of a noisome lord' (*deuiae olentis uxores mariti*),[2] or the gazing at treasure 'with eye untwisted back' (*oculo inretorto*), or the absurd conception of his transformation into a bird of song with a consciousness of the feathers sprouting! These and other such details do illustrate some degree of 'frightful realism.' But

---

[1] 'Nebst einer furchtbaren Realität ohne alle eigentliche Poesie besonders in den Oden,' F. W. Riemer, *Mittheilungen über Goethe*, xi. 644.

[2] Yet it is only the extension of Virgil's 'Vir gregis ipse caper,' *Ecl.*, vii. 7 ('sultan-goat of the herd').

he is not to be judged by his worst. To borrow one of his famous sayings, 'even Homer nods.' If not a genius of mighty originality with
transcendent flights of imagination, Horace yet possessed rare ability
to convey thought in exquisite form. Expressed in lowest terms, his
title to be a poet is that he had a marvellous mastery over phrase and
over unforgettable words—that he wrote many of what have become
the best-known quotations in literature. It is not to his discredit that
they are hackneyed after centuries of service. *Simplex munditiis*; *splen-
dide mendax*; *nil desperandum*; *carpe diem*; *auream mediocritatem*;
labuntur anni; *dulce et decorum est pro patria mori*; *uis consili expers mole
ruit sua*, and countless others, represent ordinary thoughts; but we
do not improve on Horace's expression. The two chief ancient criticisms on Horace united in emphasising this quality. Quintilian pronounced him 'most happily daring' (*felicissime audax*); Petronius
alludes to his 'painstaking happiness' (*curiosa felicitas*). Quintilian[1]
indeed thought him 'practically the one Roman lyric poet worth reading'; he recognises, besides his abundant grace and variety, the fact
that he can soar (*insurgit aliquando*). Though there is in him much of
'what oft was thought, but ne'er so well expressed'—the very ideal of
the English poets who have been called 'Augustan'—yet there is also
much that is not convention. There is genuine emotion over the sorrows
and shortness of life; true feeling for nature, and an elevated conception
of Rome's duty to herself and to the world.

Of these, some have been underrated. Horace's interest in the
country has been described as that of a townsman.[2] This view fails to
account for the glowing praises of Tibur and other places in Italy. Tibur
was a passion with him: the fairest scenes on earth and the great cities
of the East were not to be compared with it.[3] Later came that fondness
for his highland home in the Sabini which has immortalised the natural
features and the names so charming to him within his *ualle reducta*. His
love of nature was not merely derived from a sense of change from city
worries, although that counted, no doubt, and although even that sense
would distinguish his attitude from the typical attitude towards nature
in our own eighteenth-century literature:

'What trifles waste a day in town!' I sigh;
'When shall I see thee, country-home, that I
From classic book or idle hour or sleep
May for life's worry drink oblivion deep?'[4]

[1] *Inst. Or.*, X. i. 96, 'At lyricorum idem Horatius fere solus legi dignus:
nam et insurgit aliquando et plenus est iucunditatis et gratiae et uarius figuris et
uerbis felicissime audax.'
[2] J. P. Postgate, lecturing on *Horace as a Rustic* to the Eng. Classical Assoc.,
October 1906, held the poems gave no evidence that Horace, like Virgil and
Tibullus, was inspired by the country. 'Horace was by nature and bringing up a
townsman, and his interests were in Rome' (report in *Cl. Rev.*, December 1906).
[3] *Od.*, I. vii., 'Laudabunt alii claram Rhodon,' etc. *Cf.* II. vi. 13, 'Ille
terrarum mihi praeter omnis Angulus ridet.'
[4] *Sat.*, II. vi. 59:

There is strong love for country life even in his admiration for its simple
fare and simple talk (*O noctes cenaeque deum!*). His sympathies, it is
notorious, were with the country mouse of his own fable, and not with
its city cousin. More than this, he loved the external aspects of nature
for their own sake. True, it was without the philosophic, almost
religious, content of Virgil's attitude. But Horace's admirably vivid
descriptive touches can come only from loving observation. It was a
deep-rooted affection. With a thrill he noted on his way to Brundisium
the well-known Apulian mountains of his native district, where he had
wandered when a boy, and where the ring-doves had once covered him,
a child asleep, with forest-leaves.[1] The truth is, Horace was broad
enough in taste and feeling to love both town and country, both society
and retirement. Rural scenes were indispensable to him for much of his
poetry, and were a condition of its existence. This is why many have
discovered that, during travel in Italy, the words of Horace occur
oftener to the mind than those of any other Latin poet. Horace felt a
real sensuous pleasure in the sights and sounds of the country. This is
seen in epithets like those in *uda mobilibus pomaria riuis*; *domus Albuneae
resonantis*; *praeceps Anio*. Such vivid strokes of word-painting could
come only from a true admirer. Take, for example, his picture of the
timorous fawn 'in groundless dread of breeze or rustling wood':

> Or if thro' dancing leaves there chance to wake
> The quiverings that tell of new-come spring,
> Or if green lizards brush aside the brake,
> Tremors to heart and knee they bring.[2]

Take, again, his fancy of Nature's invitation to enjoy the cool under
the trees by a rivulet:

> Why are the giant pine and poplar white
> Impassioned to ally with boughs enlaced
> Their friendly shade? Why doth the brook take flight
> And bicker down its twining course in haste?[3]

With the same keenness he watches the changing seasons, and welcomes

---

'Perditur haec inter misero lux non sine uotis:
O rus quando te aspiciam? quandoque licebit
Nunc ueterum libris nunc somno et inertibus horis
Ducere sollicitae iucunda obliuia uitae?'

[1] *Sat.*, I. v. 77; *Od.*, III. iv. 9–20.
[2] *Od.*, I. xxiii. 5—8:
'Nam seu mobilibus ueris inhorruit
Adventus foliis, seu uirides rubum
Dimouere lacertae,
Et corde et genibus tremit.'
The unpoetic ingenuity of the suggested *uepris* is no inducement to alter l. 5.
[3] *Od.*, II. iii. 9–12:
'Quo pinus ingens albaque populus
Umbram hospitalem consociare amant
Ramis? Quid obliquo laborat
Lympha fugax trepidare riuo?'

spring in *Soluitur acris hiemps* and *Diffugere niues*. In a moment of delight he hails the fountain on his estate in verses which one might turn into a sonnet:

> Bandusia's Well, that crystal dost outshine,
>   Worthy art thou of festal wine and wreath!
> An offered kid to-morrow shall be thine,
>   Whose swelling brows his earliest horns unsheath,
> And mark him for the feats of love and strife;
>   In vain: for this same youngling from the fold
> Of playful goats shall with his crimson life
> Incarnadine thy waters fresh and cold.
> The blazing Dogstar's unrelenting hour
>   Can touch thee not; to roaming herd or bulls
> O'er-plied by plough, thou giv'st a shady bower.
>   Thou shalt be one of Earth's renowned pools;
> For I shall sing thy grotto ilex-crowned,
> Whence. fall thy waters of the babbling sound.[1]

It was the fancy of affection that brought the deities into touch with his rustic surroundings. Now it is Diana, 'maiden keeper of the woods and hills,'[2] to whom the pine-tree must be hallowed and a boar slain; now Faunus, as it were Pan fresh from Arcady, may be met on the neighbouring heights of Lucretilis;[3] now that same Faunus, grown more Italian again, has to be invoked at the villagers' *fête* to bless the younglings of the year:

> O Faun-god, wooer of each nymph that flees,
> Across my land, across those sunny leas,
> Tread thou benign, and all my flock's increase
>   Bless ere thou go —
>
> If each full year a tender kid be slain,
> If Venus' mate, the bowl, be charged amain
> With wine, and incense thick the altar stain
>   Of long ago.
>
> The herds disport upon the grassy ground,
> When in thy name December's Nones come round:
> Idling on meads the thorp, with steers unbound,
>   Its joy doth show.
>
> Amid emboldened lambs the wolf roams free,
> The forest sheds its leafage wild for thee,
> And thrice the delver stamps his foot in glee
>   On earth, his foe.[4]

---

[1] *Od.*, III. xiii, 'O Fons Bandusiae, splendidior uitro,' etc. The translation is reprinted from my article on 'Sonnets from the Antique' contributed to the Quatercentenary number of *Alma Mater* (Aberdeen Univ. Mag.), September 1906.
[2] *Od.*, III. xxii, 'Montium custos nemorumque, Virgo,' etc.
[3] *Od.*, I. xvii, 'Velox amoenum saepe Lucretilem,' etc.
[4] *Od.*, III. xviii, 'Faune, Nympharum fugientum amator,' etc.

In Horace one does not look for the sustained imagination or the mystic glamour of Virgil. His longest work, the *Ars Poetica*, is shorter than a book of the *Georgics*. He has not the patience to describe so protracted an adventure in the lower world as that of the sixth *Aeneid*. Glimpses sometimes genial, sometimes forbidding, satisfy him. Bacchus, it may be, is fawned on by Cerberus; or the black river Cocytus must one day be visited; or he has his own narrow escape from sudden descent into the realms of dusky Proserpina when the falling tree just missed him—a passing thought elaborated into a telling picture. Nor has Horace the spontaneity and passion of Catullus. He never writhes with an *Odi et amo*. He never utters a melodious moan like *Si qua recordanti benefacta priora uoluptas*. His love-trifles are weak beside Catullus's fervour. Contrariwise, Catullus was incapable of Horace's exalted patriotism and moral dignity. In Horace's best Alcaics are commanding tones worthy of an imperial poet. He discovered a new music in the Latin lyric. How inimitable he is may be seen if one compares the attempts by Statius in Horatian metres. The *Odes* contain more than polished and luminous versions of ordinary feeling and thought. They contain more than pretty occasional verses. The most powerful *Odes* possess majesty at once patriotic and moral. Horace had great things to sing. He is at his strongest in singing these. We have passed into a new world and hear a different music in his lyrics. It is a music serenely national in

> *Audire magnos iam uideor duces*
> *Non indecoro puluere sordidos!*

or in

> *Quis non Latino sanguine pinguior*
> *Campus?*

or in

> *Quibus*
> *Antris egregii Caesaris audiar*
> *Aeternum meditans decus*
> *Stellis inserere et consilio Iouis?*

It is serenely moral in

> *Non si trecenis quotquot eunt dies,*
> *Amice, places inlacrimabilem*
> *Plutona tauris*

or in

> *Latius regnes auidum domando*
> *Spiritum quam si Libyam remotis*
> *Gadibus iungas.*

Sometimes Horace pleasantly links a moral idea with lighter fancies. Thus, the all-sufficiency of a good conscience passes airily into the lover's light-heartedness in the *Integer Vitae* ode:[1]

[1] *Od.*, I. xxii.

The man of life unstained and free from craft
    Ne'er needs, my Fuscus, Moorish darts to throw;
He needs no quiver filled with venomed shaft
    Nor e'er a bow;

Whether he fare thro' Afric's boiling shoals,
    Or o'er the Caucasus inhospitable,
Or where the great Hydaspes river rolls
    Renowned in fable.

Once in a Sabine forest as I strayed
    Beyond my boundary, by fancy charmed,
Singing my Lalage, a wolf afraid
    Shunned me unarmed.

The broad oak-woods of hardy Daunia
    Rear no such monster mid their fiercest scions,
Nor Juba's arid Mauretania,
    The nurse of lions.

Set me where in the heart of frozen plains
    No tree is freshened by a summer wind,
A quarter of the globe enthralled by rains
    And Jove unkind;

Or set me neath the chariot of the Sun
    Where, overnear his fires, no homes may be;
I'll love, for her sweet smile and voice, but one —
    My Lalage.

It is probably not on those things which are artistically the most impressive and finished in Horace that his popularity chiefly rests. For one who appreciates the technique of the *Odes* and the organ-voice of his patriotic Alcaics, there are scores who prefer his lighter and less god-gifted utterances, whether in lyric, satire, or epistle. Horace suits moments less tense with idealism than those which befit the appreciation of Virgil. So while Virgil wins admirers, Horace wins friends. Without sustained inspiration, without profundity of thought, without impassioned song, he yet pierces to the universal heart. But his tempered and polished expression of common experience, free from transports and free from despairs, speaks more forcibly to ripe middle age than to youth. His secret lies in sanity rather than impetus. Kindly and shrewd observer of the manifold activities in life, he draws vignettes therefrom and passes judgements thereon which awaken undying interest. *Non omnis moriar* —he remains fresh because he is human.

Chapter IV

THE ELEGIAC POETS

THE elegiac couplet had served in classical Greek literature a diversity of purposes. It had been the form appropriate to epitaphs, and to inscriptions on votive offerings. It had been used to express warlike patriotism by Callinus and Tyrtaeus, political wisdom by Solon, proverbial wisdom by Theognis, and conviviality by Phocylides. Of the older poets Mimnermus had associated it notably though not exclusively, with love, in the spirit of his divine question:

$$\text{τίς δὲ βίος, τί δὲ τερπνὸν ἄτερ χρυσέης Ἀφροδίτης;}$$

But it was the Alexandrine age that abandoned its other themes and confined the elegiac to amorous pleasures and sorrows. Antimachus of Colophon had led the way, and in the poetic galaxy after him there shine out the names of Philetas, Hermesianax, Euphorion, and Callimachus. The loss of their elegiac works makes it impossible to assess the debt of Roman poets to them. It is certain that Callimachus influenced Propertius and Ovid, as he had done Catullus. Philetas, another of Propertius's models, possibly affected Tibullus, though he is least Alexandrine of Roman elegiac writers.

The elegiac was not a new metre to Latin.[1] Ennius used it for epigrams. Lucilius used it, perhaps for reflection—the traces are two few to judge by. Q. Catulus and Valerius Aedituus anticipated Catullus in its erotic employment; but Catullus widened its scope, and in turn anticipated Martial by developing the satiric capacities of the metre. It cannot be determined whether the couplet was used by Calvus for his dirge on Quintilia, by Varro of Atax for his love poems on Leucadia, or by Ticidas for his on Metella (the *Perilla* of his verses). But that in the hands of Augustan writers it had attained to freedom and vigour can be seen from the *Copa* and the surviving epigrams of the Virgilian circle.

Nor, of course, was love anything new in Roman literature either. Dramatised by Plautus and Terence, satirised—or was it only pondered over?—by Lucilius, analysed by Lucretius, the passion had found more romantic treatment from the poets whose names Ovid cites[2] to persuade Augustus that others had been sinners without being banished. This defence of himself by Ovid mentions Catullus, Calvus, Memmius, Cinna, Anser, Cornificius, Cato (the grammarian), the author of *Perilla* (Ticidas), the adapter of the *Argonautica* (Varro of Atax), Hortensius, Servius,[3] and adds in their proper succession Gallus, Tibullus, and Propertius. Later in the poem Ovid returns upon the presence of love in Virgil.

The Augustan elegists, then, had neither a new metre nor a new subject. Yet they were original and important in two ways. They gave to the Roman elegiac its consummate refinement of form, and they made it pre-eminently the metre of love. It is scarcely too much to say that love is with them their whole existence. Though Tibullus has praises for the exploits of Messalla, though Propertius awards patriotic recognition to Rome's past and present, though Ovid shows some historical sense in the *Fasti*, and is, indeed, at his best as a narrator, they are all in their different ways essentially poets of tender sentiment. Brooding over their passions, they utter their sweetest notes in pain. Thus, albeit votaries of pleasure, they remain true to the querulous traditions of the elegy. To turn from Virgil and Horace to Tibullus is to breathe a different atmosphere. The imperial note has gone. Tibullus never names either Caesar or Augustus. Here is a new empire—of the heart. Tibullus loathes war:[4] he has but languid enthusiasm for victories: it is in love's

---

[1] See chapter on 'Lucilius and Minor Poetry,' p. 172 and p. 181.
[2] *Trist.*, ii. 421 *sqq. Cf.* the names in the shorter list given by Propertius, II. xxxiv.
[3] *i.e.* Ser. Sulpicius; *cf. infra*, p. 448.
[4] Tib., I. x:

'Quis fuit horrendos primus qui protulit enses?' etc.

service that he is 'a goodly captain and campaigner.'[1] The quest after treasure is not worth the pang of separation from a loved one:[2] glory is nothing in comparison with Delia's presence;[3] and the country scenes, for which he had a warm affection, would lose their charms without her.[4] Tibullus protests he has no gift of writing verse save in honour of her who was his next love, Nemesis.[5] Poetry must serve the lover's interests. He will have none of the epics on war or didactics on the paths of sun or moon: his minstrelsy must open the path to his mistress's heart or be renounced[6]:

> 'My lady's grace to win through song I seek;
> Muses, I banish you, if song prove weak.'

This elegiac world is a narrower one than the world of the greater Augustans. There is a loss of variety, force, and manliness. This poetry of sentiment is a poetry of youth, and of youth in one phase only.

Distinct in tone, the Augustan elegy was also distinguished by its historical place in literature. The four elegiac poets of Rome whom Quintilian mentions are, in order, Gallus, Tibullus, Propertius, and Ovid. Of these he gives the palm to Tibullus for finish and elegance:[7] and in general terms this may be conceded without undervaluing the far wider and stronger poetic gift of Propertius. Certainly, Tibullus achieves a sweetness and smoothness undiscovered before in Latin elegiacs. The great technical distinction of the group as a whole is to have brought to perfection the single poetic form which still needed development. Drama, epic, lyric, had reached their zenith. Within these departments nothing so good was ever again done in Latin. It is clear that Horace had no high opinion of the elegiac metre, when he charac-

[1] Tib., I. i. 75:
'Hic ego dux milesque bonus.'
[2] Tib., I. i. 51:
'O quantum est auri pereat potiusque smaragdi
Quam fleat ob nostras ulla puella uias.'
[3] Tib., I. i. 57:
'Non ego laudari curo, mea Delia; tecum
Dum modo sim, quaeso segnis inersque uocer.'
[4] E.g., Tib. I. v. 21 sqq.:
'Rura colam frugumque aderit mea Delia custos,' etc.
[5] Tib., II. v. 111:
'Vsque cano Nemesim, sine qua uersus mihi nullus
Verba potest iustos aut reperire pedes.'
[6] Tib., II. iv. 15:
'Ite procul, Musae, si non prodestis amanti:
Non ego uos, ut sint bella canenda, colo,
Nec refero solisque uias et qualis, ubi orbem
Compleuit, uersis luna recurrit equis.
Ad dominam faciles aditus per carmina quaero:
Ite procul, Musae, si nihil ista ualent.'
[7] Inst. Or., X. i. 93, 'Elegia quoque Graecos prouocamus, cuius mihi tersus atque elegans maxime uidetur auctor Tibullus. Sunt qui Propertium malint. Ouidius utroque lasciuior, sicut durior Gallus.'

terised it as *exiguus*, and defined its province to be the lament (*querimonia*) or the votive inscription (*uoti sententia compos*).[1] But now it was the fortune of the elegiac poets in the Augustan Age to set up the final Roman trophies won from Greek literature.

The Roman elegy was a social as well as a literary phenomenon. It signalised the devotion of abundant leisure to personal enjoyment on the part of young men of talent. It also signalised the prominent part now being played in fashionable society by women. These women, who combined beauty with ability, were by no means invariably freed-women. Sulpicia, the authoress of half a dozen of the prettiest love-letters, was a kinswoman of Messalla. Cynthia, the granddaughter of the poet Hostius, was indisputably freeborn. So was Ovid's Corinna. Ovid pretends, in writing his excuses to the emperor, that his *Art of Love* was not meant for Roman ladies; but no one could be deceived into imagining that his feminine readers were merely courtesans. There were ladies in high places who were no better than the Princess Julia, and who enjoyed, if they did not always inspire, erotic poetry. With Ovid the elegy reaches its culmination in facility, lightness, and polish. But he is more than a literary landmark. He is a visible sign of forces sapping the moral life of the empire.

Cornelius Gallus (70–26 B.C:), who had the originality to make of the Latin elegy an independent province of art, was a native of Forum Iulii (now Fréjus) in Gallia Narbonensis. On the feelings and imaginations of contemporaries he produced a notable impression. His connexion with the sixth and tenth eclogues of Virgil, and Virgil's admiration for him, have been already glanced at. The conjecture that he wrote the *Ciris* has also been mentioned. His life-story is a tragedy. A contrast to the other elegists in being both soldier and man of affairs, Gallus was led by his public career to ruin. His gallantry and capacity at the capture of Alexandria were rewarded by his appointment as first Prefect of Egypt in 30. Ambition does not appear to have saved him from intemperance and indiscretion. His conduct and language incurred the suspicions of Octavian, and his forfeiture of the ruler's favour drove him to suicide at the age of forty-three.[2] His fame rested on an adaptation of one of Euphorion's works,[3] and on four books of elegies concerning Lycoris. These latter are his complaints over the fickleness of a mistress, generally identified with the actress Cytheris, whose relations to Mark Antony became notorious.[4] Quintilian observed that Gallus was in style

---

[1] Even to argue that these two functions might possibly include the sorrows and the successes of the lover is a proof that Horace gave no prominence to the aspect of love in elegy.

[2] Hieron., *Chron. Euseb.*, ann. Abr. 1990; Suet., *Aug.*, lxvi.; Ovid, *Trist.*, II. 445:

'Non fuit obprobrio celebrasse Lycorida Gallo,
    Sed linguam nimio non tenuisse mero.'

[3] Virg., *Ecl.*, x. 50.

[4] Serv. ad *Ecl.*, x. 1, 'amorum suorum de Cytheride scripsit libros iv.'

'harsher' (*durior*) than his immediate successors. But none can tell whether the disappearance of his works was due to neglect consequent on a comparative lack of charm, or was simply a stroke of bad luck.

The materials for a life of Tibullus[1] (*circ.* 55–19 B.C.), besides his own elegies, are an epigram by Domitius Marsus proving his early death about the same time as Virgil died,[2] and a lament upon him by Ovid.[3] If Ovid did not know Tibullus intimately,[4] he at least knew his works, and entered into what had been Tibullus's literary circle—that of Messalla. There is also an anonymous *Life* at the end of the Ambrosian and other MSS.[5] This *Life* may be ultimately based on Suetonius, but the corruption of the text at certain points weakens its authority. If we can accept the testimony of the *Life*—of the grammarian Diomedes[6]— of the Horatian commentator Porphyrion—and of the inscriptions in MSS. of Horace to *Odes* I. xxxiii and to *Epistles* I. iv—then we must agree with the usual view that the poet's name was Albius Tibullus. In that case the additional information to be gleaned from Horace is not much more than that the poet he addressed composed or strolled in the woods near Pedum in Latium, and took some interest, presumably transient, in philosophy. But difficulties have been found in the way of identifying Albius with Tibullus.[7] 'Glycera,' who according to Horace

---

[1] Text: E. Bährens, 1878; E. Hiller, *Tibulli Elegiae c. carmm. pseudo-Tibull.*, 1885; Postgate's *C.P.L.* also has Hiller's text; G. Némethy, vol. i, *Albii Tibulli carmina, acced. Sulpiciae Elegidia*, 1905; vol. ii, *Lygdami Carmina, acced. Panegyr. in Messallam*, 1906; J. P. Postgate, *Selections fr. Tibullus and others*, 1903 [valuable introd. and appendices]. Life, literary questions, etc.: C. Lachmann, *Klein. Schrift.*, ii. [for Messalla's circle and its literary productions]; E. Bährens, *Tibullische Blätter*, 1876 [for details of life, and for a denial of the identification with Horace's 'Albius']; W. Y. Sellar, *Horace and the Elegiac Poets*, ed. 2, 1899; H. Belling, *Kritische Proleg. z. Tibull*, 1893, *Quaestiones Tibullianae*, 1894, *Albius Tibullus, Untersuchung u. Text*, 1897; K. P. Schulze, *Röm. Elegiker*, ed. 5, 1910 [for bibliography].

[2]   'Te quoque Vergilio comitem non aequa, Tibulle,
            Mors iuuenem campos misit ad Elysios,
         Ne foret, aut elegis molles qui fleret amores
            Aut caneret forti regia bella pede.'

[3] *Amor.*, III. ix.

[4] *Trist.*, IV. x. 51:
         'Vergilium uidi tantum, nec auara Tibullo
            Tempus amicitiae fata dedere meae.'

[5] 'Albius Tibullus, eques † *regalis* (*R[omanus] e Gabiis*, Bährens; *R[omanus] ante alios aequalis*, Postgate), insignis forma cultuque corporis obseruabilis, ante alios Coruinum Messallam † *originem* (*or[atorem] ingenue*, Postgate) dilexit, cuius et contubernalis Aquitanico bello militaribus donis donatus est. Hic multorum iudicio principem inter elegiographos obtinet locum. Epistolae quoque eius amatoriae (*i.e.*, Sulpicia's love-letters) quamquam breues omnino utiles (*subtiles*, Bährens) sunt. Obiit adolescens ut indicat epigramma superscriptum.'

[6] P. 484, 17, Keil, '. . . Horatius cum ad Albium Tibullum elegiarum auctorem scribens,' etc.

[7] They are stated in Bährens, *Tibull. Blätter*, and in Postgate's *Selections*, Appendix A. A defence of the identity of the two poets was undertaken by Sellar, *Hor. and Eleg. Poets*.

is the heroine of Albius's elegies, is not the name of either of Tibullus's known mistresses. Horace rallies Albius on chanting 'miserabiles elegos' over Glycera's preference for a 'younger' (*iunior*) rival: in Tibullus a 'richer' one is the ground of annoyance. The Albius of the epistle is pictured as composing something superior to the *opuscula* of Cassius of Parma, and since Cassius's title to fame rests on his having been one of Caesar's assassins rather than on his lost literary works, it is submitted that Horace here pays Albius such a flimsy compliment as could not be meant for a master of elegiac verse. Further, Horace regards Albius as a rich man, and Tibullus protests to his mistress that he is poor. Some of the difficulties are serious only if we expect from Horace more accuracy in rallying a friend on that friend's love-affairs than he displays in singing about his own. But 'Glycera' need not in any case refer to Nemesis. It is not merely that the two words are not absolute metrical equivalents (Propertius's 'Cynthia' is not universally interchangeable with the name it represented, Hostia) — it is rather because it is perfectly credible that Tibullus wrote elegies on others than Delia and Nemesis. Next, why should we expect glowing compliments on the composition of elegies from one who called them *exiguos*? Further, what is there to prevent an improvement in the fortunes of Tibullus from having taken place — perhaps owing to Messalla's bounty — between the time of his complaints in the first book of the elegies and the date when Horace wrote the epistle to Albius? Or was his poverty, after all, only relative to the wealth of his ancestors,[1] and a pretty protestation for a love poem? One of equestrian rank, whose possessions had suffered, might feel himself comparatively impoverished without being really poor. There is, when all is said, a ring of comfort in Tibullus's words:

> *Ego composito securus aceruo*
> *Despiciam dites despiciamque famem.*[2]

It seems more likely that the traditional identification is well grounded than that an early commentator unwarrantably identified an obscure Albius with the recognised master of elegy.

Tibullus comes in order where Ovid placed him among the elegiac writers — between Gallus and Propertius.[3] Gallus had been writing love poetry about 39, when Virgil was engaged on the *Eclogues*: he had little leisure after 31. About that time the literary career of Tibullus begins. His opening poem is a farewell to war. The *Life* declares that he won military decorations, and that he shared the tent of his friend, the eminent orator and statesman, M. Valerius Messalla, during his campaign in Gaul. This was about 30 B.C. He wrote a poem[4] in honour of

---

[1] I. i. 41, 'diuitias patrum'; I. i. 19, 'felicis quondam nunc pauperis agri'; I. i. 5, 'mea paupertas'; I. i. 37, 'e paupere mensa.'
[2] I. i. 77.
[3] *Trist.*, IV. x. 53.
[4] I. vii.

Messalla's triumph in 27 B.C. The words there, 'Not without me was thy glory won' (*non sine me est tibi partus honos*), have been rejected by several critics as an outburst of egotism or pride incredible in one so modest as Tibullus. Yet in themselves the words may simply mean that he accompanied his patron and was a witness of his exploits.[1] It is what a friend could say without offence, but what a second-in-command dare not say. On another occasion he started with Messalla for the East. This time his friend's duties were performed 'without Tibullus,' for the poet was detained by illness at Corcyra, and uttered his depression and forebodings of death in the third elegy of Book I. His connexion with Messalla inspired another poem.[2] This celebrates the election of his patron's son, Messallinus, to the quindecimviral college in charge of the Sibylline books. It is here that Tibullus most clearly shows the influence of Virgil throughout the prophecy which he makes the Sibyl chant to Aeneas. Here, too, he sounds his one imperial note in turning from a glance at the primitive grass-grown pastures of the seven hills to the apostrophe:

O Rome, thy name is doomed to rule the earth![3]

Among his friends were Macer, a poet whom he mentions as departing for active service,[4] and Cornutus, addressed in two poems,[5] and plausibly identified with the Cerinthus to whom Sulpicia sent her love-letters. Of intimacy between Tibullus and Propertius, whose names are so inevitably coupled in literary history, there is no actual proof. But, though they never mention one another, the coincidences[6] in their thought and diction suggest that they may have heard each other give readings.

Three of Tibullus's poems are prompted by admiration for a fair youth, Marathus; but the chief inspiration of the elegies springs from his passion for two women whom he called by the names of goddesses — Delia and Nemesis. Apuleius tell us that Delia's real name was Plania.[7] She was probably of plebeian rank. During one period of Tibullus's infatuation for her she was living with her mother, for whom Tibullus entertained a sincere regard (*aurea anus* and *dulcis anus*), and who can hardly be the *lena* whom he curses for finding a new admirer for Delia. At another time Delia had a *coniunx*, who seems to have been more of a

[1] Bährens's conjecture, 'Non sine Marte ibi partus honos,' is more attractive than Housman's 'non sine re est tibi,' but equally unnecessary. Postgate sees in the traditional text 'ill-placed egotistical assertion.' Is there really more of it in this 'sine me' than in the same phrase at the opening of I. iii.: 'Ibitis Aegeas sine me Messalla per undas'?
[2] II. v.
[3] II. v. 57: 'Roma, tuum nomen terris fatale regendis.'
[4] II. vi.
[5] II. ii (a birthday poem) and iii.
[6] They are collected in H. Belling's *Albius Tibullus: Untersuchung*, 1897.
[7] Apul., *Apol.*, x, '. . . accusent . . . Tibullum quod ei sit Plania in animo, Delia in uersu' (δῆλος is Greek for *planus*).

'protector' than a regular husband. Her fickleness in the end killed love. There is an open field for guessing why his other lady-love was a 'Vengeance.' Here there is completer servitude on Tibullus's part to his passion, and even greater unhappiness. For Nemesis added rapacity to faithlessness.

Delia is the central theme in half the ten elegies of Book I, Marathus of three; one is devoted to the praises of Messalla, and the tenth to a contrast between war and peace. In Book II, Nemesis is the theme of half the elegies, as Delia was in the preceding book. The first elegy is a charmingly idyllic picture of the country spring festival of the Ambarvalia, where, after the holy ritual has been described, Tibullus couples the jollity with the toast of his patron's health, and then couples the lore of the rural gods with his recurrent theme of love by invoking Cupid to the banquet. Of the two remaining elegies one honours Cornutus, the other Messallinus. The book is not much over half the size of its predecessor: there are manifest gaps in the third elegy, and likely gaps elsewhere, which have produced the impression of inadequate finish. The received opinion in consequence has been that this book was not published during the author's life. But time rather than the poet is accountable for the imperfections. Verses which Ovid[1] wrote soon after Tibullus's death prove that the 'Nemesis' elegies were then generally known, and must therefore have been issued by Tibullus himself.

It is doubtful whether, beyond these two books, we have anything more by Tibullus. The remaining poems in the MSS. are of diverse origin. They constitute traditionally a third book. The comparatively modern division of these poems into a third and a fourth book tends to obscure their single element of unity. They are all, directly or indirectly, connected with the circle of Messalla. Someone belonging to that circle edited this poetic miscellany by various hands. There are six elegies whose author gives his name as 'Lygdamus.' They celebrate Neaera. Then follows, effectually dividing two love-stories, a *Panegyric* in 211 hexameters upon the consulship of Messalla in 31 B.C.[2] It is absolutely impossible to mistake it for a juvenile work by Tibullus. The *Panegyric* is distinguished for little but garrulous twaddle, extravagant rhetoric, misplaced learning, and clumsy digressions like that summarising the *Odyssey* in order to compare Messalla with Ulysses, or like that on the five zones of the earth. Valgius is next to Homer according to this pseudo-Tibullus. Protesting that he would not choose Homer's powers in preference to the sunshine of his patron's favour, the author works himself up to a closing absurdity—after death, after transformation into horse, bull, or bird, he shall no sooner regain human form than he will compose new elegies upon Messalla! These promised poems by an ex-

---

[1] *Amor.*, III. ix. 29–32. For a refutation of the opinion that only the first book was brought out by Tibullus himself, see R. Ullrich, *Studia Tibulliana*, 1892.

[2] III. vii. or IV. i.

horse or ex-bull or ex-bird could hardly be sillier than that which the unknown author actually wrote.[1] A sense of ease is at once felt in passing to the five succeeding elegies.[2] They treat the love entertained for 'Cerinthus' by Sulpicia, generally considered the niece of Messalla. They would not be unworthy of Tibullus. They have his style. Probably, however, they are the work of another author of the circle who knew how to make poetry out of the romance of Sulpicia's life. But she could write herself, and write well. The next six[3] are hers — *The Little Love-Letters of a Roman Lady*. The following elegy — to a lady unnamed — purports to be by Tibullus; but on the whole it is probable that this is a blind. For the authorship of the epigrammatic quatrain which closes this *Garner of Elegy* there is no clue.

The hardest problem of the third book is the identity of Lygdamus. Peculiarities in diction and weaknesses in Latinity support the view that 'Lygdamus' is not a pseudonym, but the real name of a cultured freedman. On this view, foreign extraction explains some of his lapses, and inferiority of rank can be occasionally detected in his tone.[4] It is tempting to identify him with Propertius's freedman Lygdamus, formerly his slave, and lent by him to Cynthia.[5] He was well-read in the Roman poets. The influence of Catullus, Virgil, and Horace is visible. He could rise to elegance, as in writing of the 'traitress, but though traitress still beloved':

Perfida, sed quamuis perfida cara tamen;

yet, as has been often pointed out, in the immediately preceding line he had shown to what his Latinity and verse could fall:

Perfida nec merito nobis inimica merenti.

One interesting literary problem arises in addition to that of his identity. How comes it that, in one passage of six lines in Lygdamus, there are coincidences with three different passages in Ovid which make the borrowing by one poet from the other indisputable?[6] One line is com-

---

[1] Both Lygdamus and Propertius borrowed from this *Panegyric*. Némethy (*Lygd. Carm.*, pp. 89 sqq.) definitely attributes it to Propertius when a youth, on the ground of agreements in language and sentiment which he enumerates. Many of the coincidences must be allowed to be remarkable; but the absence of the genuine Propertian note forbids one to think of it as even the earliest of his productions.

[2] III. viii–xii, or IV. ii–vi.

[3] III. xiii–xviii or IV. vii–xii.

[4] On the other hand, in Pauly-Wissowa, *R.E.*, (art. 'Albius'), the view is that he was not socially the inferior of Tibullus. Némethy thinks Lygdamus a Roman, 'certe uir Romanus, non peregrinus' (*Lygd. Carm.*, 1906, p. 29). It should be noted that his claim to Roman ancestry ('nostris . . . auis,' III. i. 2) is compatible with servile birth and quite appropriate in a newly made Roman citizen. (See Postgate's *Selections*, Introd., p. xlvi.)

[5] Propert., IV (V). vii. 35–36; viii. 37, 79–80.

[6] Cf. Lygd., III. v. 15–20, with Ovid, *A.A.*, ii. 669–670; *Tr.*, IV. x. 5–6; *Amor.*, II. xiv. 23–24.

mon to both—a line which proves that Lygdamus, like Ovid, was born in 43 B.C.:

Cum cecidit fato consul uterque pari.

It has been suggested that after Ovid's *Amores*, *Ars Amatoria*, and *Tristia* had appeared, Lygdamus incorporated lines from them in his 'Neaera cycle,' written long before, but till then unpublished.[1] The likelihood, however, is greater that here, as so often elsewhere, the greater genius was the borrower. Other parallels between Lygdamus and Ovid have been observed. Further, an undeniable allusion in the *Ars Amatoria* to the nineteenth piece in Book III proves that when Ovid was composing the *Ars* he was acquainted with the *Garner* which emanated from the Messalla circle. After getting as near as possible to the date of Ovid's works, 'we shall not be far wrong in affirming that Ovid became acquainted with the collection edited by Lygdamus some time between 15 B.C. and 2 B.C., that is to say, when the two writers were still *iuuenes* (*aet.* 28–41), and accordingly that it was published some time within this period.'[2] The likeliest explanation, then, of the appearance together of pieces so heterogeneous is that Lygdamus had some connexion with the Messalla household or with a member of the circle, and was author-ised to edit a group of poems concerned with the statesman, his kindred, and his literary set. It was not unnatural that the editor should open the volume with his own Neaera elegies.

The literary superiority of the first two books is unchallenged. The charm of Tibullus lies in the winning simplicity, lucidity, and smooth-ness of verse which he weds to the warm outpourings of his passion and to his joy in the country. The final impression left is one of idyllic love and peace, not in a Virgilian Arcady but amid actual landscapes in Italy. For no poet is more Italian. He is enamoured of Delia and of Nemesis, but he is as truly enamoured of the country:

Rura cano rurisque deos.

He values the white-robed procession 'to the shining altar.' The ancient and pious customs of the peasants' festivals are dear to him. He excels in vignettes which link the labour of the fields to domestic happiness.[3] He judges it to be an added horror in the nether world that it is unlike his own land:

There be no crops below, no vineyard trim.[4]

It is devotion to the country that prompts his idealising thoughts on a vanished golden age of Saturn[5] and colours his creation of a lovers'

---

[1] See E. Hiller, *Die Tibullische Elegiensammlung* in *Herm.*, xviii, pp. 360–361 (1883).
[2] J. P. Postgate, *Selections*, p. xlix.
[3] I. x. 39–42.
[4] I. x. 35.
[5] I. iii. 35 *sqq.*

paradise with perpetual dance and song, with warbling birds and fragrant cassia and roses.[1] So it comes that, though his Delia and Nemesis belong to the city, and though he does once threaten to imitate the rowdyism of urban gallants by breaking doors and indulging in brawls,[2] still it is mainly in rural surroundings that we picture Tibullus mourning over the crossed course of his affections. As a true lover he is a poet of fluctuating moods and of tender melancholy. He has a constant dread of the end: he exclaims against the 'folly of courting gloomy death in war':

> Death looms; his stealthy footsteps no man hears.[3]

How he combines simplicity with tenderness may be seen in his vision of his own deathbed:

> Dying I'd hold thee with my failing hand:[4]

or in his pathetic recollection of Nemesis's dead sister, 'sacred to me':

> So 'neath soft earth, my little maid, sleep well:[5]

or in his self-depreciation:

> I am not worth a single tear of hers.[6]

He combines equal simplicity and ardour in that fancy of Delia surrounded by her spinning-maids which leads up to the entreaty:

> Then, as thou art, thy wealth of hair undone,
> Barefoot to welcome me, my Delia, run.
> Dawn-goddess white on rosy steeds, I pray,
> Bring for our loves that radiant Star of Day.[7]

The simple delicacy of Tibullus has a winsomeness of its own, which is totally distinct from the bold inventions of Propertius and the sparkling vivacity of Ovid.

His management of the elegiac couplet made for clearness and beauty. The elaborate sentences of Catullus are dropped in favour of the distich containing complete sense in itself. By skilful variation of pauses, and by

---

[1] I. iii. 59 *sqq.* [2] I. i. 73.

[3] I. x. 34:
> 'Imminet et tacito clam uenit illa pede.'

[4] I. i. 60:
> 'Te teneam moriens deficiente manu.'

[5] II. vi. 30:
> 'Sic bene sub tenera parua quiescat humo.'

[6] II. vi. 42:
> 'Non ego sum tanti ploret ut illa semel.'

The translation of this line is that in R. Y. Tyrrell's *Lects. on Lat. Poetry*, p. 120.

[7] I. iii. 91–94:
> 'Tunc mihi, qualis eris, longos turbata capillos,
>   Obuia nudato, Delia, curre pede.
> Hoc precor, hunc illum nobis Aurora nitentem
>   Luciferum roseis candida portet equis.'

avoidance of a uniform break in the sense at the close of the hexameter, Tibullus eluded the danger of monotony. Technically, his elegiac measure is more akin to Propertius than to Ovid. Tibullus has a smaller proportion of non-disyllabic endings to the pentameter than Catullus. Propertius largely reduced his own proportion of such endings in his later work, though he never confined himself to disyllabic endings, as was Ovid's practice in his most finished poems. If Tibullus has not the antithetic sharpness of Ovid, he has more variety in metrical structure, while his ease of movement is free from the signs of labour traceable in Propertius.

Sextus Propertius[1] (*circ.* 50–16 B.C. or after) has his *praenomen* vouched for by Donatus.[2] His birth-year is matter for conjecture, but he can safely be regarded as junior to Tibullus and senior to Ovid. He was a native of Umbria[3]—of what town is not so clear, nor (in spite of vexed discussion, especially in Italy) is it so important. Among many claimants for the honour of being his birth-place, Asisium (Assisi) has received most support.[4] His boyhood was sad.[5] He was young when he mourned his father's death. Then, during the confiscations in 41, 'the dismal measuring-rod' (*pertica tristis*) of the surveyor deprived him of the family estate; and the siege of Perusia in 40 cost him the life of a kinsman.[6] His mother superintended his education in Rome. There he laid the foundations of his extensive acquaintance with Greek and Roman literature. The study of law, which he pursued for a time, was overborne by the fascinations of love and poetry.[7] He had not long

[1] Text: W. A. Hertzberg, 1843–45 (w. exhaustive *Quaestiones*); F. A. Paley, 1853, ed. 2, 1872 (antiquated); E. Bährens, 1880; A. Palmer, 1880; in *Corp. Poet. Lat.*, 1893, J. P. Postgate; H. E. Butler, 1905; *Selections fr. Tib. and Prop.*, G. G. Ramsay, ed. 3, 1900; *Select Elegies of Prop.*, J. P. Postgate, ed. 2, 1897 (valuable introd.). Translation (Eng. Prose), J. S. Phillimore, 1906. Life, literary questions, etc.: F. Plessis, *Études critiques sur Properce*, 1884 (account of MSS., editions, chronology, literary criticism, etc.); W. Y. Sellar, *Horace and Elegiac Poets*, ed. 2, 1899.
[2] For the additions 'Aurelius' and 'Nauta' in some MSS. there is no sound authority.
[3] I. xxii. 9; IV. i. 121; IV. i. 64: 'Umbria Romani patria Callimachi.' (It should be said that, in this chapter, the numeration of the references in Propertius presupposes the division into four, not five, books.)
[4] In IV. i. 125, for 'scandentisque Asis,' Lachmann's 'Asisi' has been accepted by many. Assisi is generally regarded as best suiting the touches of local description in Propertius, I. xxii. 9–10; IV. i. 65–66; *ibid.*, 121–126. The question has been re-opened in favour of Hispellum (Spello) by Giulio Urbini, *La patria di Properzio*, 1889. For the claims of Assisi, cf. Sellar's art. on 'The Birthplace of Propertius,' *Cl. Rev.*, November 1890, and his *Hor. and Eleg. Poets*, 1899, pp. 270–8.
[5] For his early life, see IV. i. 127–36.
[6] I. xxii. 5–8.
[7] IV. i. 133:
  'Tum tibi pauca suo de carmine dictat Apollo
    Et uetat insano uerba tonare foro:
  "At tu finge elegos, pellax opus, haec tua castra".' etc.

assumed the dress of manhood before he fell under the spell of his first love. This was the unknown Lycinna.[1] She did not enslave Propertius as his next passion did, but she was dangerous enough to awaken the jealous hostility of her who now entered his life to become the engrossing centre of his emotions and his poetry. This woman, whom he called 'Cynthia,' was really Hostia. She was the granddaughter of a learned man,[2] identified with the Hostius who in the preceding century wrote a historical poem on the Illyrian War. Cynthia is representative of a class of Roman women who, while higher than common courtesans, traded in their own charms and used their attractions to allure admirers. It is likely that her establishment was considerable: she had at least eight slaves. Her literary tastes and skill in playing and dancing enhanced the attraction of good looks and stately carriage. Her lover has immortalised the red and white complexion, the fine dark eyes, 'twin flambeaux, that are stars to me' (*geminae, sidera nostra, faces*),[3] and

> Hair auburn! tapering hands! full-formed and tall —
> A gait Jove's very sister to recall.[4]

Such was the imperious and fickle goddess whom he served for 'five years of thraldom.'[5] The course of the amour did not run smooth. Her perfidies drove him to retaliate in kind, and his lapse involved a breach for a year.[6] The opening elegy of all was written in a spirit seared by the memory of this unhappiness. Its very sadness argues the depth of the poet's desire for reunion. The publication of Book I, entitled *Cynthia*, and enshrining sunny memories among its shadows, sealed the reconciliation of 25 B.C. The book brought fame to both author and heroine. For Propertius it meant admission into the circle of Maecenas. For Cynthia it meant a singular gratification of pride, since she was capable of admiring such elegies, even if she had not been their theme. During nearly three years the *liaison* continued. Henceforward the lovers were more tolerant each of the other's frailties, but, even so, there were recriminations. Propertius, too, had gropings after some more sober occupation for his genius. He projected a voyage to Athens as a cure for love. Slowly his volcanic passions cooled, till in 23 there came the

---

[1] III. xv, esp. 3–10, 43–44.
[2] III. xx. 8:
      'Splendidaque a docto fama refulget auo.'
Cynthia also was called 'docta,' and so was especially gratified by Propertius's verses on her; II. xiii. 11; II. xxxiii.
[3] II. iii. 14.
[4] II. ii. 5:
      'Fulua coma est longaeque manus et maxima toto
        Corpore, ut incedit uel Ioue digna soror.'
[5] III. xxv. 3:
      'Quinque tibi potui seruire fideliter annos.'
[6] III. xvi. 9:
      'Peccaram semel et totum sum pulsus in annum.'

renunciation intended to be final.[1] That some sort of reconciliation, however, followed before Cynthia's death is an inevitable inference from the language assigned by Propertius to her ghost in his later vision.[2] Her death occurred about 18 B.C.

Of his subsequent history we can make but the meagrest surmise. The extinction of passion diverted him to other themes. This late-found interest in public and antiquarian matters is seen in the last book — possibly issued after his death. Arguments have been advanced that it contains some of his early work, but metrical and other reasons point rather to the pieces being his latest attempts in a serious vein. On the whole, they prove that with his love his gift of poetry had also gone. His commemoration of the *ludi quinquennales* for the festival of Apollo Palatine in 16 B.C.,[3] and an allusion to the consulship of Cornelius Scipio[4] in the same year, testify that he was alive then. But there is no exact clue to the end of his life. The most natural, but not the only defensible, conclusion from two passages in the younger Pliny[5] is that Propertius married and left issue. Legislation to encourage matrimony, mooted in 27, had threatened to interfere with the relationship between himself and Cynthia, and the affirmation of the policy in the *Leges Iuliae* of 18 B.C. may well have led Propertius to conform to the known pleasure of Augustus.

Propertius had friends, literary and non-literary, whom we meet in the elegies. But he had others whom he never mentions; for example, Ovid, who knew him well and often heard him recite. In gratitude for the intimacy of Maecenas after the issue of his first volume, Propertius addresses the introductory elegy of the second to his patron. There he deprecates any expectation of epic efforts from his pen — Callimachus, he urges, had no such mighty utterance. Diplomatically, he assures Maecenas that if he were endowed with epic gifts, his subject would not be mythological, but 'thy Caesar's wars and measures; beneath great Caesar thou shouldst be my second theme.'[6] In the other elegy addressed to Maecenas his attitude has both a personal and a literary significance. He discerns the minister's self-effacing loyalty to the emperor;[7] he also feels it due to Maecenas's encouragement to promise poetry on national legends[8] — the promise which some of his latest compositions endeavour to redeem. For Virgil, his most eminent fellow-member of the Maecenas circle, Propertius entertained the deep reverence which inspires his

---

[1] III. xxxiv and xxxv.

[2] IV. vii. See J.P. Postgate's arguments, *Selections*, pp. xxv–xxvii.

[3] IV. vi.

[4] IV. xi. 65.

[5] *Epist.*, VI. xv., 'Passennus Paullus . . . municeps Properti atque etiam inter maiores suos Propertium numerat'; IX. xxii., 'Propertium in primis a quo genus ducit,' etc.

[6] II. i. 25–6.

[7] III. ix. 34: 'Maecenatis erunt uera tropaea fides.'

[8] III. ix. 49–52.

praises in the epilogue to the second book — praises rendered the more
effective by subtle reminiscences of Virgilian diction.[1] While Propertius
regards Virgil as one of his predecessors in the province of love-poetry,
he here sounds a fanfare of welcome to the coming national epic, whose
appearance would eclipse all Greek and Roman fame.[2] Other literary
friends were Bassus, the iambic poet; Lynceus, a tragic author; and
Ponticus, the epic writer, whose verse he compares with Homer, after
that craze for exaggerated compliment which, to Horace's great disgust,
prevailed among certain poetic 'mutual admiration societies.' Tibullus
and Horace he does not name; nor they him. But Horace refers to him in
unfriendly tones. The Alexandrinism of Propertius's style and much in
his bearing would fail to commend him to the older poet, whose type of
art and temperament was totally different. So it is that in a passage
which cleverly parodies some of Propertius's mannerisms, Horace
sneers at him for posing as the Callimachus and Mimnermus of Rome.[3]
The supposition that he might have been Horace's bore in the first book
of the *Satires* is absolutely negatived by dates.

Propertius's life is mainly associated with the society and pleasures of
town. A visit to Tibur, a sojourn in the country watered by the Clitum-
nus, a sea-voyage, only serve to heighten the contrast. He was a servant
of Bacchus as well as of Venus:

> Joy! Joy! to fetter thought by drinking deep —
> Spring-roses ever round my brows to keep![4]

In one poem, after a late revel, he is fuddled with liquor when he visits
Cynthia.[5] Another — his very best attempt at rollicking realism —
describes a wine-party in questionable company which the sudden
arrival of Cynthia surprises and routs. His life was a round of indulgences varied with intellectual friendships. On personal appearance as
conducive to conquest he bestowed a lover's attention. The scented hair
and studied walk tended towards foppishness.[6] His pallor and thinness
were emblematic of his emotional temperament.[7] He had no prescribed
duties to steady his infirmity of will. Love only fostered moods and
moodiness. He made his nearest approach to consistent elevation of

---

[1] For a discussion of II. xxxiv. 59 to end, see M. Rothstein's art. on
'Properz und Vergil,' in *Herm.*, xxiv. 1 *sqq.* (1889).
[2] II. xxxiv. 65:
> 'Cedite Romani scriptores, cedite Grai:
> Nescioquid maius nascitur *Iliade*.'
[3] Hor., *Epist.*, II. ii. 87 *sqq.* See J. P. Postgate, *Selections*, pp. xxxii–xxxiv.
[4] III. v. 21:
> 'Me iuuat et multo mentem uincire Lyaeo
> Et caput in uerna semper habere rosa.'
[5] I. iii.
[6] II. iv. 5–6.
[7] I. v. 21:
> 'Nec iam pallorem totiens mirabere nostrum
> Aut cur sim toto corpore nullus ego.'

purpose in his quest after beauty. For he possessed the true artistic temperament —an ear for musical words, and an eye for noble statues and pictures which served his fancy with apt illustrations.

One of the many Propertian problems is that concerning the subdivision of the second book insisted on by Lachmann. His scheme splits the second book of the MSS. into two, ending Book II with the ninth elegy. Instead of the four books in the MSS., therefore, he and the editors who have followed him give five. The main reasons advanced for the division are the disproportionate length of the second book; the inference, based on *lacunae*,[1] that it represents a still larger mass of work; the turn to a new subject in the tenth elegy (*Sed tempus lustrare aliis Helicona choreis*); and the poet's anticipation of dying content, if he could but leave 'three books' to preserve his name.[2] On the last count, it is contended that the poet must refer to three virtually finished books, and therefore, that the lines in question must themselves belong to a third book. The reasoning is not of absolute cogency. Books still unfinished would suit the poet's despondency as well. Besides, there is a positive bit of evidence for the *status quo ante Lachmannum* in the citation by Nonius of *secundat*, in III. xxi. 14, as occurring in the 'third book.'[3] Most recent editors, therefore, have returned to the authority of the MSS. But Book II, by reason of its irregularity and disorder,[4] still remains a puzzling contrast to the artistic grouping of the elegies in Book I, whereby Propertius exhibited an Alexandrine skill in producing a unified effect out of diversity.

The dates of the various books, too, can only be given approximately. Where love-poems predominate, chronological traces are naturally rare. In Book I, the eighth elegy seems to have in it a shadow cast by the prospect in 27 of laws against celibacy, and there is good reason for the belief that the sixth was not written before that year.[5] The presumption is in favour of its publication in 26 or 25. In Book II the latest date likely for any poem is that presented by the tenth, 24 B.C. If the book was published in Propertius's lifetime at all, that is its conjectural date. Book III, which shows signs of better arrangement, is not earlier than 23 B.C.; for its eighteenth elegy laments the death of Marcellus in that year. Book IV, as we have seen, contains references to events of 16 B.C. It is incredible that it was prepared finally for publication by Propertius

---

[1] The evidence, however, does not amount to proving the loss of any one complete poem.

[2] II. xiii. 25–26:

'Sat mea sic magnast, si tres sint pompa libelli
   Quos ego Persephonae maxima dona feram.'

[3] See Postgate, *Selections*, p. li.

[4] Towards the close of the book, in II. xxxi, we have a piece referring to 28 B.C., *i.e.* of date prior to the issue of Book I. Again, xxviii, on Cynthia's illness, should chronologically precede the vows for her recovery in ix. See Sellar, *op. cit.*, pp. 298–9.

[5] See I. viii. 21, and Hertzberg's edn. I. 23 *sqq.*

himself. He could not have been so cynical as to follow the solemn elegy on the dead Cynthia's spirit (*Sunt aliquid Manes*) immediately with his Hogarthian sketch of a supper-party which incensed her in life.

When we come to his themes, we reach surer ground. The elegies bear their own witness. It is almost literal truth that Cynthia is the alpha and the omega of his writings (*Cynthia prima fuit, Cynthia finis erit*). Passion for her, as Martial said,[1] made a bard of him; and few of his poems on other subjects are successful. Of 22 elegies in Book I, 20 are given to her; of 34 in Book II, 31 spell Cynthia in one form or another—even the epilogue, in praise of Virgil, maintains that love is the genuine topic for the poet. Of the 25 elegies in Book III, far fewer celebrate Cynthia: three of them are tributes to other friendships, and three treat matters of national moment. Of the 11 pieces in the miscellaneous Book IV, Cynthia reappears in two; and nothing is quite so good in the book as these two, with the exception of the noble picture of a Roman matron's affection in the last elegy of all. It is, then, by his chronicle of love that Propertius is best remembered.

Plunged at an inexperienced age into a sea of passion, Propertius was the sport of its currents—dirigible only by the feeling of the moment. Such feeling was of an intensity that wrung expression from him. It fostered the poetic; but it quenched all else. To passion so full-blooded, ambition was nothing.[2] Propertius was more absolutely bewitched than Catullus himself was. Every phase of the devotee's love is in him. Taken solely as the history of a passion, the elegies are of engrossing variety. On the one side are the ebb and flow of Cynthia's affections, the favours, cajolery, accomplishments, waywardness, venality, and treasons of this 'light-of-love';[3] on the other, the succession of his moods, heavenly transports,[4] tortures of jealousy, forebodings of death, protestations of tireless fidelity, devil-may-care resolves of indiscriminate vice, earnest well-wishing, and splenetic curses. Now it is the lover's abasement before his enchantress, now it is the poet's assurance of immortal fame to be conferred upon her by his pages:

> Blest whoso art recorded in my quair;
> My songs shall live as proofs that thou art fair.[5]

In Propertius one is conscious of that type of unreserved absorption in love and intense sincerity in its expression which has been powerful in Italian literature right down to the novels and poems of D'Annunzio. So Propertius is master of the true lover's lore, declaring that 'Love has no why';[6] that love is a leveller—a democrat:

---

[1] Mart., VIII. lxxiii. 5: 'Cynthia te uatem fecit, lasciue Properti.'
[2] I. vi. 13 *sqq.*
[3] II. xvi. 12:   'Semper amatorum ponderat illa sinus.'
[4] *E.g.*, II. xiv. 10, 'immortalis ero,' etc.
[5] III. ii. 15–16: 'Fortunata meo si qua es memorata libello:
                        Carmina erunt formae tot monimenta tuae.'
[6] II. xxii. 14:   'Quod quaeris "quare?" non habet ullus amor.'

> Love knows no yielding to ancestral busts,[1]

and:

> Love knows no yielding to the might of wealth:[2]

again, that it transcends the general's fame:

> Conquest of tribes is nothing worth in love;[3]

and, in one of his greatest lines, that it partakes of the eternal:

> Great love o'ershoots the very shores of Doom.[4]

Intensity like this warranted his confidence that in his poetic gift lay his surest power of enchanting Cynthia:

> Her nor my gold could bend, nor Indian shells,
> But winning homage in love's villanelles.
> Muses then are; Apollo aids benign;
> Their grace defends love; Cynthia rare is mine.[5]

It warranted, too, his confidence in his own immortality as a poet: he can assert that his volume will be thumbed on the settle as an authoritative handbook treating affairs of the heart;[6] he can pit himself against Calvus and Catullus as eulogists of a beloved one;[7] and he can prophesy Rome's esteem for him among distant posterity.[8]

But there were reactions. Propertius is often melancholy, even sombre. In one of his most triumphant paeans over sensual delight, the thought of love's brevity strikes him:

> Feast we our eyes on love, while fate saith yea;
> The long night comes, with daybreak gone for aye.
> Thou must not, while 'tis light, life's fruit eschew;
> Give all thy kisses—they will still be few.
> See rose-leaves, fallen from a withered wreath,
> Float all bestrewn on wine-bowls underneath;
> So for us lovers, mightily elate,
> Mayhap to-morrow shall round off our fate.[9]

[1] I. v. 24:   'Nescit Amor priscis cedere imaginibus.'
[2] I. xiv. 8:   'Nescit Amor magnis cedere diuitiis.'
[3] II. vii. 6:   'Deuictae gentes nil in amore ualent.'
[4] I. xix. 12:   'Traicit et fati litora magnus amor.'
[5] I. viii. 39:
　　'Hanc ego non auro, non Indis flectere conchis,
　　　Sed potui blandi carminis obsequio.
　　Sunt igitur Musae, neque amanti tardus Apollo,
　　　Quis ego fretus amo; Cynthia rara mea est.'
[6] III. iii. 19:
　　'Vt tuus in scamno iactetur saepe libellus
　　　Quem legat exspectans sola puella uirum.'
[7] II. xxv. 3-4.
[8] III. i. 35:
　　'Meque inter seros laudabit Roma nepotes,'
cf. III. ii. 24:
　　'Ingenio stat sine morte decus.'
[9] II. xv. 23-24, and 49-54 (the order of the lines is doubtful, and, as in many of Propertius's poems, various transpositions have been proposed):

Death is constantly haunting him as a fact to shudder at rather than, as
Horace regarded it, a fact to face. He morbidly dwells on the hour that
will close his eyes for ever, on the reduction to ashes on the funeral pyre,
on the lamentation of friends, on the nether world. Yet this very gloom
has its compensations; for it forms part of his romanticism. From this
vein sprang his vision of Cynthia dead, from which portions are here
translated:

> Wraiths of the dead exist; death ends not all;
> The wan shade cheats the fires of funeral.
> Late buried by the marge of echoing road,
> My Cynthia hovering o'er my pillow showed,
> When slumber lagged for love's sad obsequies,
> And I bemoaned bed's queenless sovranties.
> I saw her hair, as on her bier, the same,
> The selfsame eyes —her robe was scorched with flame. . .
> It seemed the mind and voice of life: but, lo!
> Frail, bony fingers rattled to and fro.
>   (*Cynthia upbraids him for his lukewarm mourning.*)
> 'Traitor, whom woman ne'er could hope to mould,
> Can sleep so soon o'er thee dominion hold? . . .
> Guilty Propertius, I refrain from rage;
> Long did I hold the queendom in thy page.
> I swear by Destiny's chant ne'er yet untwined —
> So may the Triple Hound for me bay kind —
> I kept my troth. Let vipers in my tomb
> Hiss, if I lie, and 'mid my bones find room! . . .
>   (*She enjoins him to have regard to her neglected grave.*)
> Thrust struggling ivy-clusters from my mound;
> They choke my bones with tresses twisting round. . . .
> Write on the pillar's heart a verse for me —
> Brief, for quick drivers from the town to see;
> '*Here golden Cynthia lies in Tibur's ground,*
> *Whence, Anio, thy bank is more renowned.*'
> Disdain not dreams that leave the Holy Gate:
> When holy dreams come, they are dreams of weight.
> By night we roam abroad; night frees the ghost:
> E'en Cerberus may stray and quit his post.
> Dawn dooms us Lethe's pools again to view;
> We sail; the Boatman counts his freight anew.
> Others may clasp thee now —soon I alone;
> Thou shalt be mine, and mingle bone with bone!'[1]

'Dum nos fata sinunt, oculos satiemus amore:
  Nox tibi longa uenit nec reditura dies.
Tu modo, dum lucet, fructum ne desere uitae:
  Omnia si dederis oscula, pauca dabis.
Ac ueluti folia arentis liquere corollas,
  Quae passim calathis strata natare uides,
Sic nobis, qui nunc magnum spiramus amantes,
  Forsitan includet crastina fata dies.'
[1] IV. vii. 1-8, 11-14, 49-54, 79-80, 83-94:

P

Propertius won his fullest acquaintance with life through his passion. Love was his world. It may be asked whether, like Byron towards the close of a brief life, he was rising from a narrow groove to wider prospects. In the very sphere of love, he came to see beyond self. When his own amour ended its tangled chronicle in disillusion, he still cherished an ideal of true love in the imaginary epistle of Arethusa, and of a noble Roman matron's affection in Cornelia's charge to her husband.[1] But it is extremely doubtful whether the broadening interests indicated by his later work would have produced any striking success in a different field of poetry. His antiquarianism yielded little fruit. His retelling of Tarpeia's[2] love contains fine things, and the story of how Hercules came to found the *Ara Maxima* exhibits both beauty and humour;[3] but the semi-philological pieces on Vertumnus and Jupiter Feretrius are failures.[4] Propertius, indeed, judged rightly in declaring his *forte* to be love, not epic. Sundry gropings after other themes are noticeable in the third book, and they serve to emphasise his true bent. In the third elegy, Apollo in a vision discourages his attempt to set his 'puny mouth to the mighty well-springs from which Father Ennius drank'; in the fifth, Propertius thinks youth is his season for love-poems—science

'Sunt aliquid Manes: letum non omnia finit;
  Luridaque exstinctos effugit umbra rogos.
Cynthia namque meo uisa est incumbere fulcro,
  Murmur ad extremae nuper humata uiae,
Cum mihi somnus ab exsequiis penderet amoris,
  Et quererer lecti frigida regna mei.
Eosdem habuit secum, quibus est elata, capillos,
  Eosdem oculos: lateri uestis adusta fuit. . . .
Spirantisque animos et uocem misit, et illi
  Pollicibus fragiles increpuere manus:
"Perfide, nec cuiquam melior sperande puellae,
  In te iam uires somnus habere potest? . . .
Non tamen insector, quamuis mereare, Properti:
  Longa mea in libris regna fuere tuis.
Iuro ego Fatorum nulli reuolubile carmen,
  Tergeminusque Canis sic mihi molle sonet,
Me seruasse fidem. Si fallo, uipera nostris
  Sibilet in tumulis et super ossa cubet. . . .
Pelle hederam tumulo, mihi quae pugnante corymbo
  Mollia contortis alligat ossa comis. . . .
Hic carmen media dignum me scribe columna,
  Sed breue, quod currens uector ab urbe legat:
HIC TIBVRTINA IACET AVREA CYNTHIA TERRA
ACCESSIT RIPAE LAVS ANIENE TVAE.
Nec tu sperne piis uenientia somnia portis:
  Cum pia uenerunt somnia pondus habent.
Nocte uagae ferimur, nox clausas liberat umbras,
  Errat et abiecta Cerberus ipse sera.
Luce iubent leges Lethaea ad stagna reuerti.
  Nos uehimur, uectum nauta recenset onus.
Nunc te possideant aliae: mox sola tenebo:
  Mecum eris, et mixtis ossibus ossa teram".'

[1] IV. iii and xi.   [2] IV. iv.
[3] IV. ix.   [4] IV. ii and x.

(*naturae mores*) may be studied in old age;[1] in the ninth, he declares himself content with the task of handling love after the fashion of Callimachus and Philetas;[2] and in the prologue to the book he confirms this resolution and renounces heroics. The fact is that though he possessed patriotism he was not sufficiently possessed by it to compose anything like an *Aeneid*. Nor was he, like Horace, interested in social phenomena, or much troubled over corrupt civilisation. There is a transient glimpse of the damage done to the community by luxury:

Proud Rome doth break beneath her own success.[3]

There is a dislike, prompted by his own jealousy, of the surreptitious use made of theatres and temples for assignations.[4] There are pictures from that grade of society which as a voluptuary he knew best. But it remains the likeliest view that, with the death of love, his poetic gift withered. We owe the best of him to Cynthia.

Propertius several times owns his obligations to Callimachus and Philetas.[5] Pronouncing himself the Roman Callimachus, he also boasted that he 'first, from well-spring undefiled, made entrance as priest to bear Italian mysteries after the fashion of Greek measures.'[6] In plain words, this is a claim to be most strictly Alexandrine of Latin elegists. In that respect it is justifiable. From Meleager, the compiler of the first Greek anthology, and from other contributors to that collection Propertius drew suggestions. Doubtless, he had studied Theocritus and Apollonius Rhodius. But his Greek sources were not solely Alexandrine. He was obviously influenced by Homer and Mimnermus: there is reason to think that he was acquainted with the works of the Greek dramatists. Among his own countrymen he shows respect for Ennius as the time-honoured national examplar of epic, though, as we have seen, he considered epic alien to his own genius. It is uncertain whether the Roman scenic poets need be the source of his occasional lapses into conversational style.[7] With Catullus he naturally exhibits affinities, and he regards himself as one in a succession of amorous writers, among whom are Varro of Atax, Calvus, and Gallus. A good many Virgilian phrases occur, as might be expected from Propertius's admiration for Virgil. There are also coincidences with Horace and Tibullus, which

---

[1] III. v. 25.
[2] III. ix. 43.
[3] III. xiii. 60:
    'Frangitur ipsa suis Roma superba bonis.'
[4] II. xix. 9.
[5] III. i. 1; III. ix. 43; IV. i. 64.
[6] III. i. 3:
    'Primus ego ingredior puro de fonte sacerdos
    Itala per Graios orgia ferre choros.'
Cf. E. Maass, 'Untersuchungen zu Prop. u. seinen griech. Vorbildern,' *Herm.*, xxxi. pp. 375 *sqq.* (1896).
[7] J. P. Postgate believes Propertius had read Plautus and perhaps Terence (*Selections*, p. cxlii).

may be unconscious reproductions in a mind readily affected by the works of contemporaries.

The versification of Propertius shows greater vigour and variety than that of either Tibullus or Ovid. Both his hexameters and pentameters are of freer structure. It is typical of this greater freedom that the sense in Propertius frequently runs on beyond the couplet. Thus, if his poems have not Tibullus's smoothness, they avoid the regular appearance of being cut up into equal lengths. Polysyllabic endings for a pentameter are common in his earlier books, but markedly decrease in the later. Technically, this is a movement in the direction of Ovid's nearly invariable and too monotonous disyllable.[1] The great metrical triumph of Propertius was to dignify the pentameter with an elevation at once unprecedented and unrivalled. He did for the pentameter what Virgil did for the hexameter. The elegiac couplets of Tibullus and Ovid show normally a *crescendo* of feeling in the first line, and in the second a *diminuendo* — 'falling in melody back.' It is too much like incessant flow and ebb. The Propertian pentameter does not produce this uniform impression of subsidence or echo. It is often more powerful in sound and thought than the hexameter; and the spondees of the first half-line, whose musical value Propertius appreciated better than Ovid did, sometimes enable him to support this culminating effect. Many of Propertius's finest thoughts are therefore in his pentameters.

The language of Propertius presents considerable difficulty. Sometimes it is the vague in him, sometimes it is a spasmodic incoherence, sometimes his positively abnormal Latin[2] that makes him hard reading. Learning at one time, powerful emotion at another, torture his language into forced and troublesome turns. Seldom do six lines on end possess the limpidity of Tibullus. The *penchant* towards diffident, tortuous, remote ways of saying things unites with copious literary allusions to produce a rich and also obscure subtlety of style. Hence, of the *facundia* which Martial admired in Propertius, Alexandrine colour is but a fraction: there is his own individuality stamped on the Pindaric boldness which characterises his conceptions and use of words. A fresh *nuance* is given to a familiar term like *grauitas*: since its opposite, *leuitas*, is applied to fickleness, Propertius denotes by *grauitas* a lover's constancy. Metaphors and abstractions are employed with similar daring: *e.g.* 'sowed the arm-bearing ground with battle-seed' (*armigera proelia seuit humo*). There is thus in his language an unrestraint which matches the unrestraint of his feelings.

Learning affects him for good and for bad. It conduces to his elaborately variegated style. Beautiful names enamel his lines; beautiful

[1] A table of statistics of pentameter endings in Roman elegy is given in J. P. Postgate's *Selections from Tib.*, 1903, p. li.
[2] J. P. Postgate, *Selections*, Introd., p. lix. For full examination of his style and language, *ibid.*, lvii–lxxxviii.

legends enamel his complaints. But it also conduces to stiffness and
artificiality. It even acts as a hindrance. Tibullus's verses are like those
which Cynthia desired for her epitaph—such that he who runs may
read; with Propertius it is otherwise. At times the erudition overlays
feeling. His illustrations are so deliberate. The simplicity, for instance,
of a piece on Cynthia's sickness is spoiled by the speculation on the goddesses she may have offended.[1] The idea of nature's superiority to
artificial ornament is first illustrated by a group of charmingly simple
examples—lovely earth putting forth her colours, the ivies coming by
their own sweet will, the wild strawberry flourishing beside lonely
clefts, the water knowing to run its course untaught, the beach adorned
with native pebbles, and the birds that sing the sweeter for no training.[2]
Then the idea is laboured with parallels of mythological ladies who were
fair without adornment.[3] Perhaps it is on first acquaintance with
Propertius that this conventional side strikes one most: the recondite
Alexandrinism seems oppressive. But as one reads, the romantic in him
cannot be missed. It is present even in his treatment of an old legend
like that of Hylas.[4] His work has a mysterious loveliness to which his
melancholy, his passion, his dreams of another world contribute. Ideas
of gloom and wild nature are touched with an eerie glamour which
abides both in the thought and in the music. He makes us hear 'the
chafings of the maddened sea' (*uesani murmura ponti*). He conveys un-
erringly to the mind a full sense of the desolation attendant on departed
greatness:

> Thou once heldst empery, O Veii old,
> And sett'st in thy Great Square the chair of gold:
> Within thee now slow shepherds' bugle tones
> Are heard; men reap the fields amid thy bones.[5]

It is a graphic beauty in the portrayal of vanished grandeur, marvellously resembling that in *L'Oubli* and other sonnets by Heredia. A
kindred romanticism pervades the forebodings of a life beyond:

> There be in hell by thousands ladies fair,[6]

or

> Our loves must fare in Doom's one caravel,
> Dark-blue, with sails set for the meres of hell.[7]

[1] II. xxviii.   [2] I. ii. 9 *sqq.*
[3] II. ii. 15 *sqq.*   [4] I. xx.
[5] IV. x. 27:
> 'Heu, Veii ueteres, et uos tum regna fuistis,
>   Et uestro posita est aurea sella foro:
> Nunc intra muros pastoris bucina lenti
>   Cantat, et in uestris ossibus arua metunt.'
[6] II. xxviii. 49:
> 'Sunt apud infernos tot milia formosarum.'
[7] II. xxviii. 39:
> 'Una ratis fati nostros portabit amores
>   Caerula ad infernos uelificata lacus.'

In Latin there is only Virgil to equal Propertius for the faculty of evoking a dim consciousness of awe in lines which present an indefinable stimulus to the imagination. For poetic gifts of the highest order none of the elegists can rival him. His pre-eminently Italian intensity of warm luxurious passion finds vent in what Professor Sellar styled a 'desperate sincerity.' Because he is fearlessly true to his own feelings, he attains a strength which is beyond Ovid's reach. Because in his best work he freed himself from pedantry and monotony, he produces a greater impression of variety than his voluminous successor.

His influence on literature was practically instantaneous. Ovid's language owed him many turns of expression. The very notion of the *Heroides* and the *Fasti* is developed from Propertius; the former from the letter of Arethusa, the latter from the aetiological poems in the last book. All the leading poets of the early imperial age show acquaintance with him. Juvenal, Martial, and Statius are typical imitators. The influence is traceable in prose, too —in Seneca and Apuleius. Then, from the time of Justinian I, when the Greek epigrammatist, Paullus Silentiarius, imitated him, till the days of Petrarch, Propertius is as good as unknown. But, since the Renaissance, he has been sure of recognition, though not always of recognition as high as he deserves.

In Ovid, the last of the Augustan elegiac quartette, we have one whose fame, immeasurably greater than that of his fellows, rests not simply on his love-sentiments or his dexterity in elegy, but at least as much on narrative skill displayed in fifteen books of hexameters. P. Ouidius Naso[1] (43 B.C.–A.D. 18) was a native of Sulmo, some ninety miles from Rome, in the country of the Paeligni. It was a region which he liked to celebrate:

> Paelignian lands are crossed by crystal streams;
> Green o'er soft loam luxuriant herbage gleams.[2]

His birthday was the 20th of March in the year when both consuls,

[1] Text: P. Burmann (*cum integris Micylli, Ciofani, D. et N. Heinsiorum notis*, etc., of which Niklaas Heinsius's comments remain especially profitable), 4 vols., 1727; (*c. notis uariorum*) 12 vols., 1822–6; (w. notes of Lemaire, Bentley, etc.) 5 vols., 1827; R. Merkel, 3 vols., 1850–2 (new ed. R. Ehwald, etc., 1884–9); in Postgate's *C.P.L.*, 1894, by various editors. Separate works: *Heroides*, A. Palmer, 1898 (w. Gk. prose trans. of Planudes); *De Arte Amatoria*, P. Brandt, 1902; *Metamorph.* G. E. Gierig and J. C. Jahn (index), 2 vols., 1821–3; M. Haupt, 1867 (new ed. Korn and Müller, 1878–85); *Fasti*, R. Merkel, 1841; H. Peter, 1889; *Tristia*, V. Loers, 1839 (commentary, for its illustrative materials, more valuable than text); S. G. Owen, 1889; *Ibis*, R. Ellis, 1881. Literary criticism, etc.: A. Zingerle, *Ouidius u. sein Verhältniss zu den Vorgängern*, etc. (I, on Catull., Tib., Prop.; II, on Ennius, Lucr., Virg.; III, on Hor.) 1869–71; W. Y. Sellar in *Hor. and the Elegiac Poets*, ed. 2, 1899; H. de Mirmont, *La jeunesse d' Ovide*, 1905 (very detailed, but readable).

[2] *Am.*, II. xvi. 5–6:
> 'Arua pererrantur Paeligna liquentibus undis,
>   Et uiret in tenero fertilis herba solo.'
Cf. Tr., IV. x. 3:
> 'Sulmo mihi patria est gelidis uberrimus undis.'

Hirtius and Pansa, fell at Mutina, 43 B.C.[1] He uses the cognomen Naso in referring to himself: both the Senecas and Tacitus call him *Ouidius*: on the full name the MSS. agree. It was a point of pride with him that his equestrian rank was inherited, not merely a result of wealth.[2] A personality with narrower and more consistently selfish interests than Horace, Ovid gives a revelation of himself which is at once less full and more monotonous. If we except a fact or two from the elder Seneca about his rhetorical training, virtually all the essential details of his life may be drawn from one poem of his interminable *Sorrows*.[3] Along with a brother who was by exactly one year his senior and whom he lost in early manhood, he studied rhetoric at Rome under Arellius Fuscus and Porcius Latro.[4] Their influence is seen not merely in an occasional line borrowed,[5] but in the rhetorical cast of Ovid's work at large. He preferred the *suasoria* (the exercise in imaginary advice) to the *controuersia* (the prescribed debate). Much in the *Heroides* and —to take a notable instance from the *Metamorphoses*—the contest between Ajax and Ulixes are but poetic elaborations of his school practice. Ovid also studied at Athens.[6] He made an Eastern tour in the company of his poet friend Macer 'Iliacus.' He was well acquainted with Sicily from a residence of almost a year. His father's wish was that Ovid should shine in law; and he reproved the youth's taste for verse-writing as unprofitable[7] —Homer himself, he said, had not made money! But Ovid was constitutionally unfit to study jurisprudence or to write prose: his words ran into poetry. To him, as to Pope, 'the numbers came.'[8] Little wonder that his public career was brief. Apart from membership of the centumviral court and work as a *iudex*, it consisted of service on one of two boards of *tresuiri* within the 'vigintivirate.'[9] Though this suggests that he once aspired (or his father made him aspire!) to the senatorial *cursus honorum*, the duties were irksome, and civic honours were unalluring.[10] He was confessedly enamoured of ease, and any stirrings of ambition within set towards poetic glory. He yielded himself to a life of pleasure, while cultivating acquaintance with poets of whom his hero-worship made gods.[11] His early circle included Horace, Propertius,

[1] *Tr.*, IV. x. 5–6 and 13–14.   [2] *Tr.*, IV. x. 7–8.
[3] *Tr.*, IV. x.   [4] Sen., *Contr.*, II. x. 8.
[5] *Am.*, I. ii. 11, and *Met.*, xiii. 121 are mentioned as coming from Latro.
[6] *Tr.*, I. ii. 77.
[7] *Tr.*, IV. x. 21–22:
      'Saepe pater dixit "Studium quid inutile temptas?
         Maeonides nullas ipse reliquit opes".'
[8] *Tr.*, IV. x. 25–26:
      'Sponte sua carmen numeros ueniebat ad aptos
         Et quod temptabam dicere uersus erat.'
[9] *Tr.* II. 93–6; IV. x. 34; *Fasti*, iv. 383–4 (reading *bis denos*).
[10] *Tr.*, IV. x. 37–38:
      'Nec patiens corpus, nec mens fuit apta labori,
         Sollicitaeque fugax ambitionis eram.'
[11] *Tr.*, IV. x. 41–42:

Macer of Verona, Ponticus, and Bassus. Virgil he just saw (*Vergilium uidi tantum*). Tibullus's death prevented the growth of a close friendship. In time Ovid's work brought renown, when his turn came to be admired by a group of younger poets as he had once admired his elders.[1] The names of those to whom he addressed his *Letters from Pontus* in advanced life constitute a good index to his literary set.

He was a mere stripling when he recited poems that made a stir. They were pieces some of which survive in the *Amores*, while others have perished—for he freely consigned faulty work to 'flames that will emend.'[2] Gay society felt the appeal in his erotic poetry. The town was agog with speculation as to who his 'Corinna' was. Never had Roman poetry better earned the description of *lusus*. Ovid played with affections as with his pen. Yet, half in earnest, he declares the lover's existence no leisurely trifling: it is a hard campaign (*militat omnis amans*): he that would not grow a sluggard must turn lover.[3] Under much seeming laziness Ovid was conscious of high gifts. He writes one of the *Amores* to answer or forestall criticism. This *Defence of Poesy* declares that poets are not idlers, for their achievement is eternal honour (*carmina morte carent*):

> Why, gnawing Envy, tax with sloth my days,
> And call my song a work of idle ways?[4]

Is the charge, he asks, that he had no bent for dusty soldiering or prosy law?

> Thy quest is work that dies: mine, deathless fame,
> That all the world may ever know my name.[5]

Then to prophecies of the world-long survival of 'sublime Lucretius' and of Virgil's popularity with readers:

> While Rome is mistress o'er a captured world—[6]

he links his own confidence:

> 'Temporis illius colui fouique poetas
> Quotque aderant uates rebar adesse deos.'

[1] *Tr.*, IV. x. 55:
> 'Vtque ego maiores, sic me coluere minores.'
The group of Ovid's contemporaries is sketched in a succeeding chapter. His circle is well discussed in Hennig's monograph, *De P. Ouidii Nasonis poetae sodalibus*, 1883.

[2] *Tr.*, IV. x. 61–62:
> 'Multa quidem scripsi, sed quae uitiosa putaui
> Emendaturis ignibus ipse dedi.'

[3] *Am.*, I. ix. 46:
> 'Qui nolet fieri desidiosus, amet.'

[4] *Am.*, I. xv. 1–2:
> 'Quid mihi, Liuor edax, ignauos obicis annos,
> Ingeniique uocas carmen inertis opus?'

[5] *Am.*, I. xv. 7–8:
> 'Mortale est quod quaeris opus; mihi fama perennis
> Quaeritur, in toto semper ut orbe canar.'

[6] *Am.*, I. xv. 26:
> 'Roma triumphati dum caput orbis erit.'

So when the final fires my bones consume,
I'll live, and much of me survive the tomb.[1]

For about thirty years Ovid was the cherished poet of that smart set which had inherited the traditions of Clodia's circle. An inexhaustible facility poured out *Amours* real and imaginary, *Love-Letters of Heroines*, *A Lady's Toilet Directions*, *The Art of Love*, and *The Cures for Love*. They were productions after the heart of the thoughtless and fashionable. A task of wider compass, *The Metamorphoses*, occupied his attention for years, and friends possessed private copies of its fifteen books before publication. At the same time Ovid was engaged on his *Roman Calendar* or *Fasti*.

In domestic relationships the Ovidian temperament was little calculated to guarantee tranquillity. Of his three marriages only the last was of considerable duration. It was a union with a kinswoman of his influential patron, Paullus Fabius Maximus. During his banishment Ovid constantly commends her loyalty and trusts her tact to soften the Empress Livia. His daughter—probably by his second wife—was not, as if often stated, the poetess Perilla; the tone of Ovid's letter to Perilla[2] is not that of a father, and there are other objections to the supposition. His own father had reached the age of ninety and died, as his mother did, only a few years before the great calamity of his life overtook him.

It was in A.D. 8—some think a year later[3]—when Ovid was in Elba among the suite of M. Aurelius Cotta, that an imperial mandate ordered him to Tomis on the Black Sea. The sentence being *relegatio*, not *exsilium*, left him property and rights, but it inflicted on one who was still at fifty a butterfly of fashion the most crushing blow conceivable. He had to repair to Rome and say hasty farewell to its pleasures and society, to his wife and home. His place of retirement was a far-off town with uncouth inhabitants and barbarous neighbours. Dr. Johnson despatched to *Ultima Thule*, or Victor Hugo to Spitzbergen, could not have suffered more. The full reasons for his punishment, veiled by Ovid himself under mysterious hints, have been the subject of much speculation. He assigns two reasons—'a poem and a blunder.'[4] What 'the poem' was is unquestioned. It was the *Ars Amatoria*. It was now excluded from the public libraries of the capital. Written ten years before, its diabolical ingenuity as a pernicious counterblast to his social

---

[1] *Am.*, I. xv. 41–42:
> 'Ergo etiam cum me supremus adederit ignis,
> Viuam, parsque mei multa superstes erit.'

[2] *Tr.*, III. vii.

[3] The difficulties in accepting A.D. 9 are given by M. Schanz, *Gesch. d. Röm. Lit.*, § 291.

[4] *Tr.*, ii. 207:
> 'Perdiderint cum me duo crimina, carmen et error,
> Alterius facti culpa silenda mihi;
> Nam non sum tanti renouem ut tua uulnera, Caesar,
> Quem nimio plus est indoluisse semel.'

legislation had not been forgotten by Augustus. But it was not easy even for the emperor to attack the cleverest poet of the day for his urbane immorality. The chance came when the poet somehow directly hurt the imperial dignity. What was,'the blunder'? It has received all sorts of explanations, from an imagined violation of the mysteries of Isis to the grotesque supposition that he had seen the empress bathing![1] Nothing more probable has been advanced than the suggestion that Ovid connived at the adultery of the younger Julia with D. Silanus.[2] Ovid says his fault was 'to have possessed eyes'[3]—he had seen too much; and if he condescends on no particulars, it is expressly to avoid opening the emperor's wound. Augustus may well have discerned in his granddaughter's vice the fruits of Ovid's lax verses; if Ovid had-screened her misconduct, then his responsibility must have appeared more serious still.

The melancholy journey to Tomis, partly by sea, partly by land, took almost a twelvemonth. A decade of misery followed. The wretchedness of banishment was enhanced by *ennui*, illness, and climate. His lamentations are innumerable—over the want of books or literary friends, and over onslaughts by wild tribes shooting poisoned arrows. To kill time he took to learning the rugged Getic and Sarmatic; he had nearly forgotten his Latin, he said.[4] He even composed a panegyric on Augustus in Getic verse,[5] which, unfortunately for philology, has vanished. No results came of his entreaties for a remission of sentence, or at least a change to a less repellent place of abode. Ovid had a glimmering of expectation that Augustus, towards the end of his reign, would incline to mercy. But the accession of Tiberius in A.D. 14 made his case desperate. Appeals to a heart essentially inexorable were futile: there is no need to seek fanciful reasons in supposed umbrage given to the new ruler or his mother by lines of the *Metamorphoses* written long before to illustrate the deterioration from the golden age of the world:

> *Lurida terribiles miscent aconita nouercae;*
> *Filius ante diem patrios inquirit in annos.*

---

[1] This comes of an unluckily literal interpretation of Ovid's mythological illustration of his ruin, *Tr.*, ii. 103:
  'Cur aliquid uidi? Cur noxia lumina feci?
      Cur imprudenti cognita culpa mihi?
    Inscius Actaeon uidit sine ueste Dianam.'
[2] This view was ably advocated by T. Dyer in *Class. Mus.*, vol. iv, 1847, pp. 229–47, and is substantially the same as G. Boissier's in *L'Opposition sous les Césars*, 1875, chap. 3. A. Deville, *Essai sur l'exil d'Ovide*, 1859, clears the ground of untenable theories; *cf.* Appel, *Quibus de causis O. ab Augusto relegatus sit*, 1872. Schömann in *Philol.*, xli. 171, is not convincing. For more recent works on this subject see N. I. Herescu, *Bibl. de la litt. lat.*, 1943, § 365.
[3] *Tr.*, III. v. 49:
  'Inscia quod crimen uiderunt lumina, plector,
      Peccatumque oculos est habuisse meum.'
[4] *Tr.*, V. xii. 57:
  'Ipse mihi uideor iam dedidicisse Latine,
      Nam didici Getice Sarmaticeque loqui.'
[5] *Ex Pont.*, IV. xiii. 19–23.

So Ovid died heart-sick of hope deferred. Jerome's date for his death corresponds to A.D. 17, but the allusion in a revised passage of the *Fasti*[1] to the dedication of the Janus temple at Rome in October of that year makes 18 more probable. The news of the dedication would not reach Tomis for months.

The general chronology of Ovid's works is clear. He certainly made his *début* with love-elegies on Corinna.[2] Some of the *Amores*, then, are among his earliest things. But a well-known piece in the *Amores*[3] alludes to nine of the *Heroides*, with imaginary replies composed by Ovid's friend Sabinus to several of the heroines' letters. Clearly, then, some of the *Heroides* preceded the *Amores* as we have them. The solution of the difficulty lies in the issue of two editions of *Amores*, the earlier in five, the later in three books, as recorded by the prefatory epigram. The *Heroides* belongs to the interval between these first and second editions. More exact dates are unattainable, though we may note that in the *Amores* no event is prior to 19 B.C., the death of Tibullus, or later than Drusus's victory over the Sugambri in 12. One may place the first edition near 12 B.C., and the second before the publication of the *Ars Amatoria*. The *Amores, Heroides, Medicamina Faciei Femineae*, are all mentioned in the *Ars*,[4] which was being written shortly before the opening of the Christian era, for it alludes to the *naumachia* exhibited in 2 B.C.[5] A difficulty appears in what looks like a cross-reference between the *Ars* and the *Amores*. On the one hand, the third book of the *Ars* explicitly[6] mentions the issue of the *Amores* in three books. On the other hand, the piece in the *Amores* which mentions the *Heroides* also alludes[7] to Ovid's *Art of Love*. A reference to his *praecepta* gives the impression that the *Ars* was not simply in view, but partly written, before this poem was inserted in the *Amores*. His lost tragedy, *Medea*, praised by Quintilian[8] as indicative of high potentialities in Ovid, can only be vaguely fixed before the later *Amores*.[9] The *Remedia* manifestly followed the *Ars*.[10] His extensive *Metamorphoses* must have been at least in contemplation when Ovid gave a list of mythological themes in *Amores*, III. xii. 21–40. The fifteen books were composed before Ovid's banishment, for on the eve of his departure from Rome he rather theatrically consigned his own copy to the flames. He may have wished to emulate the dissatisfaction of Virgil with the *Aeneid*, as he explains its lack of the finishing file:

Defuit et scriptis ultima lima meis.[11]

---

[1] i. 223–6. [2] *Tr.*, IV. x. 57. [3] II. xviii.
[4] iii. 343–6, iii. 205. [5] *Ars Am.*, i. 171. [6] iii. 343.
[7] *Am.*, II. xviii, 19–20.
[8] *Inst. Or.*, X. i. 98, 'Ouidii *Medea* uidetur mihi ostendere quantum ille uir praestare potuerit, si ingenio suo imperare quam indulgere maluisset.'
[9] The *Medea* was written before *Am.* II. xviii. 13, but after *Am.* III. i, where Elegy and Tragedy are still contending for the poet.
[10] *Rem.*, 71, 361, 487. [11] *Tr.*, I. vii. 30.

But he admits that other copies were already in the possession of friends! His elegiac invective *Ibis*, directed, in imitation of Callimachus's attack on Apollonius, against a false friend unknown,[1] belongs to the first part of his banishment.[2] The *Fasti* had been interrupted by his *relegatio*, apparently half way through, at the sixth book. He had been engaged on this poetic calendar at the same time as the *Metamorphoses*. The second six books were probably never completed.[3] Ovid, who primarily addressed the work to Augustus, proceeded after that sovereign's death to dedicate it afresh to Germanicus Caesar. He hoped to remodel the whole, but only the first book was actually overhauled, and a few portions added elsewhere. Entirely belonging to his exile, are the five books of *Tristia*, begun on his journey to Tomis, and ending about A.D. 12; the *Epistulae ex Ponto*, in four books, written A.D. 12–16; and the *Halieutica*, on fish and other creatures of the Black Sea regions. It is only in this fragment, outside his *Metamorphoses*, that we have continuous hexameters from his hand. Pliny states that it was written about the close of Ovid's life.[4] His lost works include, besides the *Medea* and his Getic eulogy, a dirge on Valerius Messalla, an epithalamium in honour of Fabius Maximus, praises for Augustus and for Tiberius, and epigrams satirising poetasters. Among poems incorrectly ascribed to him, the most notable are the *Nux* and the *Consolatio ad Liuiam*. The former — a plaint by a nut-tre on its hard usage and on evil days — dates from a time after, but not long after, Ovid. The *Consolatio*, on the death of Drusus, must on grounds of diction and technique be referred to the first century A.D., and not, as Haupt held, to some humanist of the fifteenth century.

Our subsequent consideration of Ovid's chief works may fitly pursue an almost obvious grouping into amorous poetry, narrative poetry, and poems of banishment. From the outset he professes his theme to be love. Cupid has provided subject and metre to match. Ovid is conscious that, relatively to the heroic hexameter, the elegiac is *inferior uersus* — has not the love-god stolen a foot from it?[5] So in his proem to *Amores III*, when the Muses of Elegy and of Tragedy contend for his homage, it is by a grotesque conceit that he pictures comely *Elegeïa* 'of the scented hair' as having one foot longer than the other![6] In elegiacs, then, there are three books of *Amores* — for the most part lively sketches drawn from

---

[1] Corvinus (who cannot anyhow be Ovid's *friend* Messalla Corvinus), M. Manilius (author of the *Astronomica*), and the learned Palatine librarian, C. Iulius Hyginus, are candidates for this bad eminence. R. Ellis dismisses these in favour of some professional *delator* (*Proleg.* to ed. of *Ibis*, pp. xix *sqq.*). G. Gräber, *Untersuchungen über Ovids Briefe aus der Verbannung*, 1884, has shaken the foundations of the favourite Hyginus hypothesis.

[2] *Ibis*, 1, shows he had passed his fiftieth birthday, *i.e.* March 20, A.D. 9.

[3] There has been a good deal of discussion on *Tr.*, ii. 549:
'Sex ego *Fastorum* scripsi totidemque libellos.'

[4] Plin., *N.H.*, xxxii. 152, 'Id uolumen supremis suis temporibus incohauit.'

[5] *Am.*, I. i. 4.   [6] *Am.*, III. i. 7:

actual or imagined love-experiences. The central figure is 'Corinna.'
But she is a lay figure. She has not the reality of Lesbia, Delia, or
Cynthia: and Ovid has not the earnestness of Catullus, Tibullus, or
Propertius. The intolerable notion of Sidonius Apollinaris in the fifth
century that Corinna was the emperor's daughter ought not to have
lived to deceive many generations. Perhaps the bishop of Clermont must
not be blamed too severely for failing to recognise a *meretrix*. Ovid could
never have boasted openly of Corinna's favours if she had been the
Princess Julia. Little penetration is needed to divine that Corinna is an
epitome of many women. She is now married, now single; now adorable,
now shameless. There is no consistent story in the *Amores*. But they are
scarcely less interesting for that. They are the author's studies in varying moods of love. He is at one time the constant lover, yearning for the
requital of a true affection.[1] At another time he avows himself distracted
by equal passion for two sweethearts.[2] Again, he poses as the universal
gallant, susceptible to the charms of all fair women.[3] At one time he
claims to be animated by:

> Bare innocence and purple modesty:[4]

at another, and a good deal more truly, he proclaims himself 'Naso,
bard of my own naughtiness,'[5] uttering this warning:

> Away! strict ladies; Love this work ordains;
> No fitting audience ye for tender strains.[6]

It is hardly too extreme a thing to say that in the *Amores* Ovid is most
sincere when he is positively lascivious. No one can be for a moment
beguiled when he declares that the announcement of his lady's falseness
'left his face bloodless and brought deep night before his eyes.'[7] Nor
is one touched by the appeal to the keeper of his mistress's closed door,
though one likes its sweet refrain:

> *Tempora noctis eunt: excute poste seram.*[8]

'Venit odoratos Elegeïa nexa capillos,
Et, puto, pes illi longior alter erat.
Forma decens, uestis tenuissima, uultus amantis,
Et pedibus uitium causa decoris erat.'
[1] *Am.*, I. iii. 15:
'Non mihi mille placent, non sum desultor amoris.'
[2] *Am.*, II. x. 7:
'Pulchrior hac illa est, haec est quoque pulchrior illa.'
[3] *Am.*, II. iv. 10:
'Centum sunt causae cur ego semper amem.'
[4] *Am.*, I. iii. 14:
'Nudaque simplicitas purpureusque pudor.'
[5] *Am.*, II. i. 2:
'Ille ego nequitiae Naso poeta meae.'
[6] *Am.*, II. i. 3:
'Hoc quoque iussit Amor: procul hinc, procul este, seuerae!
Non estis teneris apta theatra modis.'
[7] *Am.*, III. vi. 45–46.   [8] *Am.*, I. vi.

The prayer to Dawn[1] that she hasten not makes one think more about
the Provençal *aubade* than about Ovid's love. The tablets with the
answer 'No' did not really wound his heart; nor was he really alarmed
over risks to Corinna on a voyage to Baiae—more than likely he wrote
the piece because Propertius had one upon Cynthia at Baiae. Ovid's
strength lies in grace, not depth. If he records a conflict of emotions
he has nothing like the agonised simplicity of Catullus's *Odi et amo*.
Ovid pauses to quote parallels to his own burdened heart:

> I'll hate you, if I can—else, love perforce;
> The bull hates yokes, yet wears what he abhors.[2]

So with his clever antitheses he proceeds to overlay natural feeling:

> I'd have you look less fair, or be less vile:
> Beauty so sweet keeps not with evil style.
> Thy deeds earn hatred, but thy face craves love;
> So, wretch! thy lady soars her faults above.[3]

It is much the same with his lament on his lady's pet parrot.[4] The treatment is full of fancy, but without the pathos of Catullus's grief for
Lesbia's sparrow.

While several of the 'amours' strictly so-called have no relation to
Corinna, there are also pieces with literary rather than erotic content.
Such are Ovid's apology for poets,[5] and his protestation to Macer that
he is incessantly driven from grander themes back upon love.[6] Another
piece turns on Juno's festival at his wife's birthplace.[7] But where the
least connexion with love appears is in his beautiful dirge for Tibullus.
For the nonce he has caught a portion of Tibullus's own sadness. It is
true he seeks to dovetail it into the collection by marking the different
task to which he is setting the elegiac metre:

> Thy guiltless hair loose, plaintive Elegy;
> Ah, now too sadly true thy name shall be![8]

---

[1] *Am.*, I. xiii.
[2] *Am.*, III. xi. 35:
> 'Odero, si potero: si non, inuitus amabo:
>   Nec iuga taurus amat: quae tamen odit, habet.'
[3] *Am.*, III. xi. 41:
> 'Aut formosa fores minus, aut minus inproba, uellem:
>   Non facit ad mores tam bona forma malos.
> Facta merent odium; facies exorat amorem:
>   Me miserum, uitiis plus ualet illa suis.'
[4] *Am.*, II. vi.
[5] *Am.*, I. xv.
[6] *Am.*, II. xviii.
[7] *Am.*, III. xiii.
[8] *Am.*, III. ix. 3:
> 'Flebilis indignos, Elegeïa, solue capillos:
>   A, nimis ex uero nunc tibi nomen erit.'

And he seeks to connect it with the Powers of Love by introducing Cupid as mourning for the dead poet and Venus as averting her face — 'some say she could not hold her tears.' Yet the significance of the poem lies in the assurance of Tibullus's immortality:

> If aught remains of us save name and shade,
> Then shall Tibullus haunt the Elysian glade:[1]

and in the very considerable feeling shown several times before the close:

> Rest, silent bones, in sheltering urn, I pray;
> Light may the earth upon thine ashes weigh.[2]

Still another point: it is noticeable that already in the *Amores* Ovid displays that taste for allegory wherein he heralds much of the medieval poetry. The poem which describes him as Love's captive introduces a triumphal pageant of Cupid with Good Sense and Shame and other foes to his camp as prisoners, but Blandishments, Error, and Frenzy as his attendants and warriors.[3] Similarly, the contest between the symbolic figures of Elegy and Tragedy 'amidst an ancient forest unhewn for many a year'[4] reads in spirit and setting like an antecedent of the *Romaunts* of the Middle Ages.

The full title of the *Heroides* was probably *Heroidum Epistulae*. Of the twenty-one in modern texts, the prevailing tendency is to reject the last six (xvi–xxi) — that is, the letters from Paris to Helen, Leander to Hero, Acontius to Cydippe, and the replies in each case. Yet these three pairs, though not strictly *Heroidum Epistulae*, have found modern defenders such as Palmer. Those who deny their Ovidian authorship at least admit their Ovidian inspiration. If Ovid did not write them, they were written by a poet, and by a poet who had caught his style. While they are marred by a double portion of Ovid's own diffuseness, they at the same time contain in Leander's epistle one of the most exquisite passages in Latin, where he recalls his swim for love in the moonlight with scarce a sound audible on the Hellespont save the notes of the kingfisher.[5] The three answers included in old editions, Ulixes to Penelope, Demophoon to Phyllis, and Paris to Oenone, are the work of the fifteenth-century poet Angelus Sabinus. Of the first fifteen *Heroides*, the one most doubted is the fifteenth — from Sappho, which has not the same MS. authority as its predecessors. It has had strong champions in Comparetti and

[1] *Am.*, III. ix. 59:
'Si tamen e nobis aliquid nisi nomen et umbra
Restat, in Elysia ualle Tibullus erit.'
[2] *Am.*, III. ix. 67:
'Ossa quieta, precor, tuta requiescite in urna,
Et sit humus cineri non onerosa tuo!'
[3] *Am.*, I. ii. 19–38.
[4] *Am.*, III. i. 1.
[5] *Her.*, xviii. 55–88.

others.[1] But on most of the *Heroides* sweeping attacks have been made, following the lead of Lachmann.[2] Starting with the unwarrantable assumption that absence of an epistle from among the nine *Heroides* mentioned by Ovid himself[3] threw doubt on its authorship, he brought to his support metrical and other reasons which have not compelled anything like general assent. Other scholars have proposed considerable excisions from those spared by Lachmann, and have secured still smaller following.[4]

Ovid claimed to have introduced a literary novelty in his *Epistulae.*[5] The departure did not consist in concentrating attention upon 'heroines'—that had been done in the *Eoiae*[6] and probably during the Alexandrine period in Theocritus's Ἡρωῖναι. As to the poetic *epistula*, Horace had just been employing that form, but for purposes entirely different from Ovid's. There had been a nearer foretaste of the Ovidian letter in that which Propertius assigns to Arethusa; only, she is not a 'heroine,' but a real Roman matron under a Greek name. Ovid's originality lay in the skill whereby he produced in letter-form the effect of a dramatic monologue and of a character-sketch. For he expends upon his enamoured women a psychological care lacking in his treatment of love from the man's standpoint. While the mental processes of the *Heroides* were mainly due to Ovid's own experience and observation in affairs of the heart, his subjects were borrowed.[7] He was pre-eminently indebted to the Greek drama—to Aeschylus for his Danaid *Hypermnestra*, to Sophocles for his *Hermione* and *Deianira*, to Euripides for his *Phaedra*, *Canace*, *Laodamia*, and *Medea*, which lady also came partly from Apollonius. Homer was the authority for the *Penelope* and *Briseis*. The *Cypria*, Sappho, the New Comedy, and Alexandrine authors were also laid under contribution. In Latin literature, he used Virgil notably for the *Dido* and Catullus for the *Ariadne.*

The letters are all alike in this, that each writer happens to be saddened by the absence of a beloved one. But there is considerable diver-

[1] D. Comparetti, *Sulla epistola Ovidiana*, etc. (Pubblic. dell Inst. di studi superiori, II. i, 1876); J. Lunak, *Quaestiones Sapphicae*, 1888; A. Palmer, *Heroides*, 1898, pp. 420–24.
[2] K. Lachmann, *Kleinere Schriften*, lvi–lxi. A succinct history of the discussions on the genuineness of the *Heroides* is given in Schanz, *Röm. Litteraturgesch.*, ed. 4, 1935, §294 (§ 295 in earlier edd.).
[3] *Am.*, II. xviii. 21–6.
[4] *E.g.*, K. Lehrs, *Adversarien über die sogenannten Ovidischen Heroiden*, *Jahrb.*, 1863, pp. 49–69 (cited by Palmer, *op. cit.*, Introd., p. xxix), leaves practically only the Canace letter intact.
[5] *A.A.*, iii. 345:

> 'Vel tibi composita cantetur epistula uoce:
> Ignotum hoc aliis ille nouauit opus.'

[6] Greek catalogues of heroines, each of whom was introduced by the words ἢ οἵη. The only complete extant specimen is Hesiod, *Shield* 1–56.
[7] His material is traced in J. N. Anderson's pamphlet, *On the Sources of Ovid's Heroides*, 1896; *cf.* Schanz, *op. cit.*, ed. 4, 1935, §§ 295–6 (§ 296 and § 296a in earlier edd.).

sity of situation and of character. Penelope and Laodamia are affectionate wives, anxious for a husband's welfare. Hermione implores her dear
cousin Orestes to rescue her from hated wedlock with Pyrrhus. Hypermnestra adjures her bridegroom to free her from the chains which she
owes to her compassion for him. Canace writes in despair over her
father's discovery and punishment of her passion. Phaedra reveals with
protestations and entreaties her forbidden longing for Hippolytus.
Briseis is amazed and piqued at Achilles's slowness to welcome her back
from Agamemnon. The other messages are in varying tones of remon-
strance with false lovers. Phyllis has the pathetic note of innocence
betrayed; Oenone, Ariadne, Dido express the bitterness of desertion;
Deianira upbraids her truant lord, until in the course of the letter, she is
interrupted by the news of his death; Hypsipyle and Medea show fierce
anger against Jason—Hypsipyle ominously threatening to prove 'a
Medea to Medea' (*Medeae Medea forem*), and Medea harbouring
thoughts of vengeance which must follow the dictates of wrath:

> *Quo fert ira sequar; facti fortasse pigebit.*

The letter-form is a mere literary device. Ovid did not imply that
Penelope knew her husband's address, or that there was a postal service
from Naxos for Ariadne's use. Unrealities or anachronisms inherent in
the framework are of trivial moment. All frameworks in literature are
more or less unnatural. But it is worth noting that Ovid has not cared
to aim at heroic simplicity in his portrayal. His psychology is usually
vivid; but it is the psychology of a civilised age. As a rule, the ultimate
naïveté of passion is missing. The traits are those of sophisticated
Roman ladies.[1] Very seldom can one truly imagine oneself listening to
the words of dames and damozels of the olden times. Oenone, for
example, has not always the touching artlessness of her closing reminder
to Paris:

> I'm thine; in childhood's years I played with thee;
> Thine for the rest of time I pray to be.[2]

Usually, it is a rhetoric clever but tending towards monotony, which
expresses weariness, expostulations, jealousy, or ineffectual cravings to
undo the past. How can one feel for Dido if she addresses an artificial
conceit to Venus as her mother-in-law, requesting that 'brother Cupid
embrace his cruel brother,' Aeneas, and press him into the service of
Love?[3] This is mythical fancy, not human suffering. Take Phaedra. The

---

[1] In this, as in other things, the author of the suspected half-dozen *Heroides*
is Ovidian. Helen replying to the impudent gallantry of Paris's overtures is a
society dame who makes a parade of virtue while she contrives to encourage her
admirer.

[2] *Her.*, v. 157:
> 'Sed tua sum tecumque fui puerilibus annis,
>   Et tua, quod superest temporis, esse precor.'

[3] *Her.*, vii. 31–32.

slave of overmastering desire, she can yet argue rhetorically and antithetically. She proves that if her husband Theseus is to be wronged, he
deserves scant respect. She advocates the ignoring of conventional
names which superstition might give to her passion for a stepson. Yet
though we constantly light upon the half prosaic trail of the *suasoria*, the
Heroides merit their popularity. They deserve to be read, as they have
been, pre-eminently for their psychological and picturesque merits in
handling a perennially engrossing subject—the way of a woman with
a man. The *Sappho*, whether by Ovid or not, exhibits, of all the *Heroides*,
the most distinct traces of passion, with its memories and visions of
love's transports:

> Phaon, thou fill'st my thoughts; I dream alway
> Of thee, in dreams more fair than beauteous day.[1]

The truest pathos in the collection lies perhaps in Canace's grief over
her new-born babe, doomed for her sin. But there are copious illustrations of Ovid's success in realising the workings of a woman's mind.
They impress one most when lit up by his picturesque manner. So we
remember Phyllis's anxious vigils on the sands for her unreturning
lover:

> Oft did I mark
> The gusty south bring home some white-sailed barque:[2]

we remember Ariadne by the seashore, the ground glittering with
morning frost, the moon still up, and the birds just beginning to sing, as
she makes the discovery that she is marooned on Naxos;[3] we think of
the one merciful Danaid, Hypermnestra, recalling the ghastly night of
the treacherous nuptials when warring motives ended in her failure to
slay her bridegroom;[4] and we cannot forget Medea's account of the
dawn of her love for Jason.[5]

The *Art of Love* embraces two books of instructions for men and one
for women. It was with a daring cynicism that the author adapted the
elegiac metre to the didactics of seduction. This *Vade-mecum* in wanton-
ness is not a product of youth: and Ovid assures readers that his inspiration comes from experience.[6] The atmosphere is that of a reckless pursuit of the voluptuous in a society amid which the *demi-monde* reached a
pitch of polished luxury unsurpassed in history. In Ovid's eyes Rome

---

[1] *Her.*, xv. 123:
> 'Tu mihi cura, Phaon; te somnia nostra reducunt,
> Somnia formoso candidiora die.'
Cf. 125–30 and 43–50.
[2] *Her.*, ii. 125–30 and 11–12:
> 'Saepe notaui
> Alba procellosos uela referre notos.'
[3] *Her.*, x. 7–44.
[4] *Her.*, xiv. 33–70.
[5] *Her.*, xii. 31–38.
[6] *A.A.*, i. 29:
> 'Vsus opus mouet hoc: uati parete perito.'

is a hunting-ground of desire.[1] Theatre, circus, and banquets are so
many fields on which conquests may be made. The precepts, Ovid
claims, do not concern the wooing of chaste matrons.[2] This pretence at
restricting the audience must have seemed to Augustus but a slight
mitigation of the poison. Such pornography was at war with virtue and
frankness; and Ovid, as the apostle of refined deception, was preaching
doctrine calculated to undermine the social fabric. It was the more
pernicious because of its attractive form. An old French madrigal,
imitated by Prior, has recommended it as a pleasant guide to destruction:

> Suivez les pas d'Ovide:
> C'est le plus agréable guide,
> Qu'on peut choisir pour s'égarer.

Statesmanship could pass no favourable judgement upon it. But criticism is bound to point out different qualities. In its profusion of genius,
in its astonishing medley of flippancy, sensuousness, and poetry, the
Ars Amatoria presents the closest parallel in ancient literature to
Byron's *Don Juan*. It lacks the advantage of the continued story of
Juan's fortunes. It also lacks Byron's cosmopolitan variety and cannot
rival his best things; but it is equally surprising in its facility and boldness. Ovid is undisturbed by qualms of conscience, patriotism, or
religion. His attitude towards divine things is that they are a serviceable convention:

> It pays there should be gods; so let us hold;
> Let wine and incense grace our altars old.[3]

His worldly wisdom dictates much effective advice—on love begetting
love (*ut ameris amabilis esto*), on the trick of provoking a little jealousy,
on tactful euphemisms in gallantry, on the inadvisability of asking a
lady's age. Everywhere appears evidence that he has studied the fair
sex from the secrets of the heart to the fondness for attracting notice in
public places:

> *Spectatum ueniunt, ueniunt spectentur ut ipsae.*

The ladies are particularly recommended[4] to consult his *Medicamina*,
where, as we can see, they may learn the effect of character on facial
expression, or find a recipe for a morning cosmetic or a cure for freckles.

---

[1] *A.A.*, i. 59:
  'Quot caelum stellas, tot habet tua Roma puellas.'

[2] *A.A.*, i. 31:
  'Este procul, uittae tenues, insigne pudoris,
      Quaeque tegis medios instita longa pedes.'

Cf. ii. 600.

[3] *A.A.*, i. 637:
  'Expedit esse deos: et, ut expedit, esse putemus,
      Dentur in antiquos tura merumque focos.'

[4] *A.A.*, iii. 205.

The impulsive voluptuaries for whom Ovid wrote, and their mistresses as well, were possessed of very considerable intellectual refinement. Ovid congratulates himself on belonging to a highly civilised age.[1] It is natural, then, that in addition to his prescribed devices, not always over-scrupulous, and in addition to the advantages of good looks, he should lay stress on the attraction exercised by mental qualities in the man[2] and by literary tastes in the woman.[3] His list of the best books for a lady of fashion throws interesting light on the feminine culture of the day. Besides Greek poets like Callimachus, Philetas, Anacreon, and Sappho, he recommends Propertius, Gallus, Tibullus, Varro, Virgil, with his own *Amores* and *Heroides*.

The *Remedia Amoris*, in carrying out its offer of relief from passion,[4] is a work of less genius and no more virtue. Its cold-blooded enumeration of the modes of stifling love is as devoid of morality as of romance.

In the marvellous stories of *The Changeling Shapes* (*Metamorphoses*) Ovid bequeathed a work which has profoundly moulded many generations of poets and painters. The fifteen books are not lightly to be read through: they have rather been a treasury to draw upon from time to time. In Ovid's view this was his *magnum opus*. In bulk it makes about one-third of his extant writings. It was to be his title to fame:

> A work which neither wrath of Jove nor fire
> Nor sword nor tooth of Time can e'er destroy.[5]

Ovid's opening words explain his title and aim.[6] The design was to tell of forms miraculously altered (*mutatas formas*) into new bodies. The range was to be from the origin of the world to Ovid's own day. In fact, he does begin with Chaos and the Elements, and through wonderfully varied tales of transformations into tree, rock, bird, beast, water, or heavenly body, leads up to the elevation of Julius Caesar into a star. The legends are mainly Greek. But in Book XIII, by inserting the voyage of Aeneas, Ovid opens an avenue for Roman themes. Book XIV then digresses over Virgilian episodes scarcely germane to his main theme, except in the turning of the Trojan fleet into sea-nymphs. The deifications of Aeneas and of Romulus follow. In the closing book King

---

[1] *A.A.*, iii. 121:
> 'Prisca iuuent alios: ego me nunc denique natum
> Gratulor: haec aetas moribus apta meis.'

[2] *A.A.*, ii. 111:
> 'Vt dominam teneas nec te mirere relictum,
> Ingenii dotes corporis adde bonis.'

[3] *A.A.*, iii. 329–46.

[4] *Rem.*, 16.

[5] *Met.*, xv. 871:
> 'Iamque opus exegi quod nec Iouis ira nec ignis
> Nec poterit ferrum nec edax abolere uetustas.'
Cf. 875–879.

[6] *Met.*, i. 1–4.

Numa's name heralds the details of the Pythagorean system, among which Ovid's interesting account of vegetarianism does not bear so closely on his subject as do the transmigration of souls and Egeria's vanishing into a fountain. In fact, his old skill in interweaving legends seems to have deserted Ovid: the impression left by the closing books is that he has tired of his task and would fain reach his conclusion. Contemporary history appears only in connexion with praises of the imperial house. It is the greatest glory of Julius to be 'father' of Augustus.[1] Julius's assassination is linked with mythology: Venus foresees and thinks of preventing it. Fate, however, permits no more than premonitory portents and Caesar's assumption into heaven. In compliment to Augustus, his deified predecessor is said to recognise the greater achievements of his adopted son.[2] Through such eulogistic patchwork Ovid comes to utter his *Vive l'empereur*:

> Far be the hour, delayed beyond our times,
> When great Augustus leaves the world he rules
> For heaven, to be a god and answer prayer.[3]

In itself the continuity of supernatural themes can hardly be said to cohere very adroitly with the idea promulgated of Caesar's apotheosis. Only remotely, then, in contradistinction to the *Aeneid*, does the work sound an imperial note.

In other respects the poem had scant bearing on the Rome of reality. Its domain, as contrasted with the real world of Ovid's loves, was an imaginary one into which he had made previous excursions in the *Heroides*. Ovid did not keep strictly to transformations; otherwise we should not have had such good stories as those on the Rape of Proserpina, the rending of Pentheus by the Bacchanals, and the death of Achilles. Many of the best legends, however, came naturally within his scheme. Passing through the bright idealism of Greek lyric, through the manifold analysis of Athenian drama, through the sophisticated erudition of Alexandria, the Hellenic mythology descended to find fresh treatment in the *Metamorphoses*. In the lost tragedies of Rome the myths had served serious and moral ends; but it was Ovid who galvanised them into a sensuous vitality which coloured deeply the letters and art of the European Renaissance. Lucretius himself would not have considered the Ovidian treatment of the gods to be superstitious. Fancy, not faith, is the secret endowment which recreates the old myths. Full of gods, Ovid's work is empty of reverence. It is a realm where capricious passions determine conduct for god and man. There is no deep analysis—no critical reflections on the gods. Nor is there deep feeling. When Ovid relates horrible cruelty, as he can, with realistic detail,[4] he

---

[1] *Met.*, xv. 750   [2] *Met.*, xv. 850.
[3] *Met.*, vi. 867.
[4] *E.g.*, when Philomela's tongue is barbarously cut out, it throbs like the tail of a serpent cut in two, vi. 559:

makes all clear but not pathetic. His faculty of limpid and rapid narration is nothing short of amazing. Now, this very ease ensnares him into
prolixity. He does not always know when to give over. On the other
hand, while not a few of his stories are too long, there is no greater
master of neatness in line and phrase. Take Apollo's answer to Phaethon's request for proof that it is in reality his sire who dreads to entrust
the youth with the sun-chariot:

> True pledge thou seek'st? true pledge is in my fear.[1]

Byblis is all confusion on the verge of revealing her passion:

> Begins and halts: writes, then destroys the note:
> Makes words and blots them: alters, frowns, approves.[2]

Hercules utters his sovereign disdain for the River-god's attempt to
confront him in snake-form:

> It is my cradle-task to strangle snakes.[3]

Ovid is particularly successful in neatly representing mental processes
at a crisis, such as Medea's conflict of emotions:

> *uideo meliora proboque,*
> *Deteriora sequor,*

or Procris's hope to have her suspicions falsified:

> *speratque miserrima falli,*

or the nervous apprehensions which beset love:

> *sed cuncta timemus amantes.*

Yet with brevity sometimes goes his craving for pointed antithesis
which ends in affectation. It is grotesquely unnatural for an alarmed
father to beseech Phaethon:

> Take my counsel, not my car.[4]

This smart artificiality characterises his line on Envy grieved to find
Athens prosperous:

> Seeing naught tearful, scarce restrains her tears
> (*Vixque tenet lacrimas quia nil lacrimabile cernit*).

'Vtque salire solet mutilatae cauda colubrae
Palpitat,'
or, again, note the realism of likening the spurting blood of Pyramus to the jet
of water from a burst leaden pipe, iv. 122-4.

[1] *Met.*, ii. 91:
'Pignora certa petis? do pignora certa timendo.'
[2] *Met.*, ix. 524:
'Incipit et dubitat, scribit damnatque tabellas,
Et notat et delet, mutat culpatque probatque.'
[3] *Met.*, ix. 67:
'Cunarum labor est angues superare mearum.'
[4] *Met.*, ii. 146:
'Consiliis, non curribus, utere nostris.'

It is the same with his paradoxes (*oxymora*) like *ne sit scelerata facit scelus* or *impietate pia est*. The elder Seneca[1] comments on Ovid's perverse partiality for the very blemishes of his style and on his lack, not of self-criticism, but of the will to prune extravagant conceits. Seneca has a saying and an anecdote in illustration. The saying was this of Ovid's — that a face was the comelier for having a mole on it (*decentiorem faciem esse in qua aliquis naeuos fuisset*). The anecdote ran that some friends once asked Ovid if he would allow them to specify in writing three lines of his poetry which should be cancelled. He consented on condition that he should independently specify in writing three lines to be exempted from criticism. When the notes on both sides were opened they were found to contain the same lines! Two of the three Albinovanus Pedo preserved:

> A semibovine man, a semihuman ox
> (*Semibouemque uirum semiuirumque bouem*)

and

> The chilly North-Wind and unchilly South
> (*Et gelidum Borean egelidumque Notum*).

For most purposes the *Metamorphoses* can be best represented, as it has often been, by an anthology. An anthology must be largely a matter of personal choice; but it would be difficult to omit stories or descriptions so good as the following: the Four Ages (i. 89 *sqq.*), the Palace of the Sun and Phaethon's Charioting (ii. 1–328), Echo and Narcissus (iii. 346–510), the Trysting of Pyramus and Thisbe (iv. 53–166), the Rescue of Andromeda (iv. 663–739), the Rape of Proserpina (v. 385–437), Arethusa (v. 577 *sqq.*), Medea's Soliloquy —to love or not to love (vii. 11–73), the Plague at Athens (vii. 518 *sqq.*), Cephalus and Procris (vii. 661–865), Daedalus and Icarus (viii. 152 *sqq.*), Baucis and Philemon (viii. 626 *sqq.*), Orpheus and Eurydice (x. 11 *sqq.*), Venus and Adonis (x. 525 *sqq.*), the Cave of Sleep (xi. 592 *sqq.*), the House of Fame (xii. 39 *sqq.*), the Contest between Ajax and Ulixes (xiii. 1 *sqq.*), Galatea's Giant Wooer (xiii. 750 *sqq.*), the Philosophy of Pythagoras (xv. 60 *sqq.*). Among such it is hard to particularise; but perhaps nowhere is Ovid's skill as a story-teller better shown than in the description of Echo's voice in the woods, the charmingly idyllic hospitality of Baucis and Philemon, and the tragic tale of Pyramus and Thisbe —the Romeo and Juliet of ancient legend. This latter is unquestionably one of the best told and most romantic stories in Ovid. The Giant's wooing of Galatea is related with a quality rare in Ovid —humour. When Polyphemus combs his hair with a rake, mows his beard with a scythe, parodies love-ditties to win Galatea, argues that his face (which he has seen mirrored in a stream) is presentable to look upon, and when he takes pride in his size and in his one eye, he cuts a transcendently ridiculous figure. The stories

[1] *Contr.*, II. x. 12.

are too long to illustrate by translation here; but the picturesque in Ovid's descriptions may be exemplified from the Golden Age:

> First sprang the Golden Age, which of its will,
> Without revenge or law, kept faith and right. . . .
> Spring reigned eternal; soft with genial breeze
> The zephyrs fanned the flowers of seedless birth.
> Soon, too, unploughed the earth bore crops: and land,
> Unfallowed, yet grew white with heavy corn.[1]

The blend of the picturesque with allegory was, after Ovid, never so well managed in literature till we reach the medieval *Romaunts*. This characteristic has been already noted in Love's Triumph and in the Grove where Elegy and Tragedy contended.[2] It is well seen in the symbolism of the Cave of Sleep:[3]

> Hard by the Mirk-folk is a hollow cave —
> Deep hollow home and lair of lazy Sleep.
> No beam of morn or noon or sundown e'er
> Can enter it. Earth breathes out, blent with dark,
> Her mists and gloaming of uncertain light.
> No sentry chaunticleer with crested head
> Crows for the Dawn; no restless dog, nor goose
> Yet shrewder, breaks the silence with a sound.
> Wild beasts, nor cattle, nor the wind-tost bough,
> Nor tongue of men a-quarrelling is heard.
> Dumb Quiet houseth here. Below the crag
> Wells Lethe's water in a murmuring rill,
> Whose slumbrous pebble-music woos to rest.
> Before the cave-mouth plenteous poppies bloom
> And countless herbs whose juice dank Night extracts —
> A draught to sprinkle dusky earth withal.
> In the whole House there is no door to creak
> On turning hinge; the threshold hath no guard.
> Towers in the midst a couch of ebony,
> Downy, self-coloured, draped with sable quilt.
> There lies the God, his limbs in languor lapped:
> And round him, aping divers shapes, recline
> Vain Dreams as many as the harvest-ears
> Or forest-leaves or sands upon the shore.

Ovid's subject of transformations had been a favourite with Greek poets — especially with Alexandrians. Such was the theme in Nicander's

[1] *Met.*, i. 89–90; 107–110:
> 'Aurea prima sata est aetas, quae uindice nullo,
> Sponte sua, sine lege fidem rectumque colebat. . . .
> Ver erat aeternum, placidique tepentibus auris
> Mulcebant zephyri natos sine semine flores.
> Mox etiam fruges tellus inarata ferebat,
> Nec renouatus ager grauidis canebat aristis.'

[2] *Am.*, I. ii. 23; III. i. *Cf.* p. 431.   [3] *Met.*, xi. 592.

'Ετεροιούμενα, in the Nicaean Parthenius's Μεταμορφώσεις, in Anti-
gonus's 'Αλλοιώσεις, in Boeus's 'Ορνιθογονία, and in works by
Theodorus and Didymarchus. In the absence of these, it is impossible
to estimate Ovid's obligations nicely or even to say whether he used
them all. One piece of ancient evidence is supplied by Probus,[1] to wit,
that Ovid drew from Nicander and Theodorus. Through a Greek work
by Antoninus Liberalis in the second century upon *Metamorphoses*, the
fact of Nicander's influence is confirmed. It is no hazardous conjecture
that Ovid handled his originals freely, interweaving material from
Homer, the Greek tragedians, and the Alexandrians.[2] Possibly he consulted mythological collections now lost. His extraordinary memory
accounts for the extent to which in the *Metamorphoses*, as in all his
works, he is verbally indebted to the chief Roman poets who preceded
him.[3]

The six books of the *Fasti* form a calendar for half the year. Its
record of festivals and anniversaries embraces matter drawn from history, legend, folk-lore, religion, and astronomy. The design, as set forth
by the poet, is to study ritual in the light of ancient records (*annalibus
eruta priscis*), and to commemorate great events on appropriate dates.[4]
The original impulse towards the undertaking may have been given by
Propertius's later poems on Roman legends. Ovid's opening promise to
sing *tempora cum causis* suggests that he had the Αἴτια of Callimachus
in view. His astronomical portions — containing several blunders — may
be inferred to have come from Greeks like Eratosthenes. But the bulk
of his material was to hand in Latin. The *Fasti* of Verrius Flaccus had
appeared. From him and Varro in matters antiquarian, from old annals
and probably from Livy in history, and from Clodius Tuscus in
astronomy, Ovid could derive needed information.

Consciously devoting the elegiac measure to a novel use, Ovid
associates the heightening of its tone expressly with the theme of sacred
observances.[5] He now regards the elegiac as concerned with something
loftier than love:

Nunc primum uelis, elegi, maioribus itis.

In sundry addresses to Germanicus, in eulogies upon the dead emperor,
in recording Augustus's titles,[6] and in such passages of imperial tone as

---

[1] In annotating Virg., *Georg.*, p. 44, Keil.
[2] *E.g.*, Näke has shown that, in Baucis and Philemon, Ovid drew directly
from Callimachus's *Hekale*, on the nature of which additional light is thrown by
the account written by R. Ellis in *Jrnl. Phil.*, xxiv, No. 47, 1895, on the fragments then recently discovered (for text, *C.R.*, vii, pp. 429–30). But whatever
his obligations, Ovid succeeds here in making the material indisputably his own.
[3] For illustrations, see Zingerle, *op. cit.*
[4] *Fast.*, i. 7–10.
[5] *Fast.*, ii. 3–8.
[6] *E.g.*, 'Augustus,' i. 587–616; 'Pater Patriae,' ii. 119–34; 'Pontifex Maximus,' iii. 419 *sqq.*; 'Imperator,' iv. 673–676.

that upon the *Ara Pacis* at the close of the first book, Ovid becomes intensely national. It is, however, not so much national and historical elements that lend interest to the *Fasti* as the wide field of social and religious custom traversed. The work, in treating the meaning and origin of Roman festivals and family gatherings, makes excursions into the province of inquiry which renders Plutarch's *Roman Questions* entertaining. The reader is at once arrested when the poet answers queries such as why New Year's Day should not be a complete holiday; why people wish one another 'A Happy New Year' and exchange gifts; why different sacrifices are suitable for different deities; why the Luperci run naked; how a spirit should be exorcised; why marriages are unlucky in May;[1] or why straw effigies are thrown into the Tiber.

As usual, Ovid tells a story, whether mythical or historical, with unsurpassable vividness. The Rape of Lucrece and the Rape of Proserpina (the latter common to *Fasti* and *Metamorphoses*) are fair specimens.[2] The unlucky midnight adventure of Faunus[3]—who, as Chaucer might have put it, found that he had 'foule yspedde'—presents similarity enough in situation, and directness enough in quality, to recall irresistibly *The Reves Tale* among the Canterbury pilgrims. Quite typical, too, are the luminous lines rehearsing the influence of Venus and the bond between Rome and the goddess.[4] Yet the clearness and grace lack the fervour and opulence of the famous Lucretian invocation. So Ovid's facile lucidity seems always to rob his style of a certain distinction. Book after book gives the impression of ease rather than of greatness.

The *Tristia* and *Epistulae ex Ponto* are collections of elegiac letters, monotonous because of their paramount concern with Ovid's miseries in banishment. Little difference can be detected between the two collections, except that the *Epistulae* are, unlike the *Tristia*, out of chronological order, and that, in the earlier collection, the names of the individuals addressed are withheld to avoid incurring imperial displeasure.[5] The five books of the *Tristia* were published at Rome volume by volume, each with a prologue and epilogue. Of the *Pontic Epistles*, Book IV, the last and longest, was issued posthumously. The pathetic effect of both sets of poems is immeasurably lessened by inordinate prolixity. There can be no doubt that the *Sorrows* came from a tortured soul, and that Ovid has sometimes the power to touch the heart, as in the musical melancholy with which he summons to the sessions of thought his last hours in Rome:

> Cum subit illius tristissima noctis imago
> Qua mihi supremum tempus in urbe fuit,
> Cum repeto noctem qua tot mihi cara reliqui,
> Labitur ex oculis nunc quoque gutta meis.

[1] *Fast.*, v. 490: 'Mense malum Maio nubere uulgus ait' *v.l.*, 'malas.'
[2] *Fast.*, ii. 791 *sqq.*; iv. 417 *sqq.*
[3] *Fast.*, ii. 331 *sqq.*
[4] *Fast.*, iv. 91 *sqq.* and 117 *sqq.*
[5] *Tr.*, III. iv. 65–70.

But upon the same kind of suffering, and especially upon self, it is impossible illimitably to ring skilful changes in verse without producing satiety. While, therefore, these nine books of *Tristia* and *Epistulae* together are a wonderful monument to Ovid's technical skill, much in them is superfluous. Much, however, we could not afford to lose. We gain from the *Tristia* the invaluable autobiographic sketch of IV. x, and from the *Pontic Letters* important knowledge of Ovid's friends. Book II of the *Tristia* is an interesting departure from the series of elegies in the other books: here Ovid devotes 289 couplets to his own defence. This *Apologia pro Arte sua* is a study of the amorous, particularly in Roman literature. His special pleading is blissfully unconscious of the depravity which made his own *Art of Love* more dangerous than anything by those whom he would have the emperor regard as fellow-offenders. In the main, one feels that the really impressive things have been said by Ovid when he has recorded his wistful longings for Rome (I. i), the eve of his farewell (I. iii), his gratitude for his wife's devotion (I. vi), his reflections on adversity as the test of friendship (I. ix), his voyage (I. x), loneliness and hardships at Tomis (III. iii and x, IV. i), plans for intercession with the emperor (V. ii), and the beguiling of solitude by composition and linguistic studies (V. vii, x, xii). One wishes that in Pontus, where 'three years were as ten,'[1] Ovid could have turned his abilities from the subject of self. But exile had broken him.

Facility has been already noted as the great characteristic of this 'idle singer of an empty day.' His ready dexterity was the offspring of genius tutored by rhetorical practice. Rhetoric is responsible for a large proportion of Ovid's weaknesses—for the tedious profusion of paraphrase and antithesis and *communes loci* with which he serves up a single thought, and for his straining after point, which fosters artificial *concetti*. His psychology presents no incisive introspection; his narrative no soaring imagination. Throughout, clever workmanship is more to him than a great subject—*materiam superabat opus*. In pursuit of effect, he luxuriates in rhetorical devices and witty turns with a self-will that led Seneca to censure his *pueriles ineptias* and Quintilian to style him *nimium amator ingeni sui*.[2] Further, the elegiac couplet, so suitable for neat epigrammatic phrases in poems of limited length, wearies on the scale to which it extends in Ovid: it wearies none the less because of the regular close of sense with the couplet and the close of the pentameter on a disyllable. Clearly, however, Ovid deserves more handsome commendation than Quintilian's, which is the exact counterpart of the fabled curate's remark on an unsatisfactory egg—*laudandus tamen in partibus*. To have gained the ear of the world, as Ovid has done, argues positive merits. Readiness and ingenuity are in themselves attractions. They seldom desert him; and, when he can resist the besetting tempta-

[1] *Tr.*, V. x. 1–4.
[2] Sen., *Q.N.*, III. xxvii. 12; Quint., *Inst. Or.*, X. i. 88.

tion to juggle with words, they evoke admiration. Both language and metre testify to extraordinary fluency. Unmistakable skill in composition goes to construct the mosaic of a verse like

Si quis, qui quid agam forte requirat, erit.

There is in him also, though less pervadingly, a great deal of beauty. The smoothness and transparency which Ovid added to the technique of his well-turned hexameters and masterly elegiacs were qualities eminently calculated to subserve the purposes of narrative. No one would rank Ovid as equal to Tibullus or Propertius in sincerity of feeling. He is shallow and repeatedly flippant. Yet it is the truth that Ovid's influence upon literature at large has, beyond all reckoning, outrun theirs. He abides as a testimony to the power of the narrator. The world always listens to a story well told.

It lay with Ovid rather to be a herald of romance than himself to be signally romantic. The potency of love is felt in some of his poems with a passionate realism that naturally wears a modern look. But there is no romance in his cynically practical handbook to sensuality. Romantic elements are rather to be found in the *Heroides* among his love poems, and in the *Metamorphoses* among his narratives. The appeal which the wonderful in past literature made to him largely explains the appeal which he in turn made to medieval writers. The strangest myths of shapes transformed and celestial lovers are seized on by him for the *Metamorphoses*. The love-*motif* in tragedy—the Euripidean sentimentality more than the Sophoclean restraint—appears in his eyes so all-important that he is lured into overstatement: 'Time would fail me, were I to recount the lovers' passions that are in tragedy,' and 'Tragedy, too, ever finds her subject in love.'[1] Some, then, of the more obvious elements of romance are in Ovid—the marvellous, strong contrasts, dashes of vivid colour; but of much that we nowadays associate with romance there is very slight intimation. There is little of the daring expression of personal feeling, apart from the narrow range of Ovid's own lusts and loneliness. There is, again, little of the vague suggestion of a sympathy between man and the external world. There is in his clear-cut descriptions no Virgilian sense of mystery. His fluent lucidity, therefore, was purchased by a forfeiture of glamour.

Ovid's authority in the rhetorical schools of the first century A.D. is shown by Quintilian's frequent citations. His mark on poetry was decided—Manilius, Seneca, Lucan, Silius, Statius, Martial, and the writers of *Priapea* borrow from him. It was not unnatural that, besides the *Nux* and *Consolatio*, many imitations in elegiacs should be spuriously foisted on his name. Equally significant of his wide popularity are lines scratched on the walls of houses at Pompeii. To Lactantius Placidus,

---

[1] *Tr.*, ii. 407:
'Tempore deficiar tragicos si persequar ignes,'
Tr., ii. 382:
'Haec quoque materiem semper amoris habet.'

about the seventh century, has been attributed a Latin prose abridgement of the *Metamorphoses*; and in the fourteenth, the erudite Planudes
turned *Metamorphoses* and *Heroides* into Greek prose. But there was no
lack of readers who went to Ovid's works direct. The large number of
MSS. bears witness to the vogue of the *Metamorphoses*, *Ars*, and
Heroides in medieval times.[1] Ovid became pre-eminently the Latin poet
of the Renaissance. Himself influenced by works of art in his day,[2] he
furnished ideas for painters of the Italian, French, and Flemish schools
—so that such a picture as Francesco Albani's in the Brera, of the Loves
dancing for joy at the seizure of Proserpina, seems to exhale the very
atmosphere of the *Metamorphoses*. In letters the stimulus was no less.
Tasso and Ariosto are good representatives of his influence in Italy;
Spenser, like Chaucer before him and Milton after him, in England.
Montaigne felt the spell of the *Metamorphoses* when a boy of eight.
Ovid's vogue in Elizabethan England—apart from the teaching in the
grammar schools—may be gauged from the fact that the version of the
Metamorphoses by Arthur Golding, of which four books appeared in
1565, and the completion in 1567, had run through half a dozen editions
by 1593. Turbervile's translation of the *Heroides* belongs to 1567. It was
Ovidian influence which Francis Meres primarily discerned in Shakespeare when he wrote the famous sentence:

'The sweete wittie soule of Ovid lives in mellifluous and hony-
tongued Shakespeare, witnes his *Venus and Adonis*, his *Lucrece*, his
sugred Sonnets among his private friends.'

Sandys's *Metamorphoses* of 1626 carried on the influence in the next
generation, while the translation by Dryden 'and other eminent hands'
appealed to a wide circle of English readers in the eighteenth century.

In Roman literature, elegy had the briefest summer of all literary
forms. It may be said to die with Ovid. When Statius wrote a lament on
man or bird, he turned to hexameters. Tibullus had written naturally and
feelingly on love, old age, and the country. But themes which had been
by him treated simply soon became fixed conventions. Ovid, despite his
clearness, contributed to the progress of artificiality. The loss of the true
Tibullian simplicity in theme and the loss of the true Ovidian ease in
movement are evident many generations before the elegies, at once sensuous and frigid, which were written by Maximianus in the sixth century.[3]

[1] These three had always been the favourites. The *Tristia*, as Zingerle has
shown, did affect subsequent poets; but the weaker influence of that work may be
inferred from R. Ehwald's sketch of its appreciation up to Petrarch and Mussato in
the fourteenth century (*Ad historiam carminum Ouidianorum recensionemque symbolae*, 1889). It appears that the *Tristia* are seldom quoted by grammarians —
never by Nonius, Macrobius, Isidorus, or such prose admirers of Ovid as the
Senecas.
[2] Ovid, in many descriptive passages, has works of art in his mind's eye.
See *Ovids Werke in ihr. Verhältn. z. antik. Kunst*, W. Wunderer, in *Acta
Seminarii Philol. Erlang.*, vol. v, 1891.
[3] See R. Ellis's notice, *C. Rev.*, xv, 368 *sqq.*, of Webster's ed. of *Elegies
of Maximianus*, 1900.

Chapter V

MINOR AUGUSTAN POETRY

Three patrons of literary circles, Pollio, Messalla, Maecenas –
Inter-action of influence – A Virgilian group of poets – A Horatian
group – The Messalla group – Friends and contemporaries of
Ovid – Grattius's *Cynegetica* – Manilius's *Astronomica* – His conception of the universe – Where Manilius is readable – Qualities of
style – The last of didactic poetry.

ONE reasonable mode of viewing Augustan poetry is to regard
it as emanating from a number of literary circles – not isolated,
but frequently intersecting. A trio of patrons stand out prominently – Pollio, Messalla, and Maecenas, all men of intellectual grasp and
literary tastes. Of these Pollio had served Antony and Messalla the
republic. C. Asinius Pollio, or Polio, (76 B.C. to A.D. 5) never entirely
forgot that the new *régime* had deprived him of a career in the state. He
compensated himself for his loss of a statesman's influence by drawing
round him a *coterie* of authors, and in trenchant literary criticism found
vent for an outspokenness no longer permissible in politics. His ability
had been best displayed in oratory – the very sphere most certain to suffer
restriction under empire. His *History of the Civil Wars* he closed with
Philippi, in discreet recognition of the wisdom of Horace's warning that
in such a task of risk and hazard, his march lay 'across fires smouldering
'neath treacherous cinder-crust.'[1] He was also a poet – the composer
of tragedies and erotic verse.[2] Such a circle as met under his auspices
filled the part of a literary *salon*. The interplay of genius was a whetstone for the wits. It afforded opportunities for readings from works
finished or in progress, and so set a standard of taste and criticism.
Pollio has the credit of having introduced the fashion of those *recitationes* by authors in the presence of trained writers. M. Valerius Messalla Corvinus (*circ.* 64 B.C.–A.D. 8), a statesman capable of coping
with Pollio in oratory and proud of his noble descent, became the patron
of the notable ring of poets associated with Tibullus. Linguistic niceties
had an attraction for him, and he composed bucolic poems in Greek.
But the most powerful circle was that around C. Cilnius Maecenas, the

[1] *Od.*, II. i. 7:
'Incedis per ignes
Suppositos cineri doloso.'
[2] Tac., *Dial.*, xxi.; Plin., *Epist.*, V. iii. 5.

knight of ancient Tuscan lineage who served the empire as much by his shrewd judgement of men as by sagacious counsel. While he in great measure controlled the world, he yet avoided publicity. He was fond of art, fond of the pleasures of life, fond of life on any terms —one of his little pieces prays for any torture in preference to death (*uita dum superest benest*). He found in the companionship of poets, and in the writing of verses himself,[1] a relaxation from the cares of state. Yet his aim was something beyond relaxation. To enlist talent in the service of the new order of things was with him a duty. Virgil was his *protégé* from 40 B.C., Horace from 38, and Propertius won his favour about twelve years later. It was inevitable that his circle should be that most definitely committed to one mode of thought on questions of state. All the poets of his following were in a sense court poets. It was impossible for Virgil or Horace to avoid the praises of Augustus as Tibullus, the member of a different circle, could do; for did not the emperor pleasantly remind Horace when he wrote too many *sermones* without mentioning his name?

The circles were doubtless permeated with varying intellectual sympathies and varying degrees of imperial enthusiasm. But if distinct, they were not independent. The interaction of all the spheres of influence is manifest. Virgil and Horace were indebted to the good offices of Pollio as well as of Maecenas. Propertius united in himself the influence of more groups than one; the patronage of Maecenas reinforced the Virgilian influence upon him, and the spirit of Messalla's circle works on him through Tibullus. Ovid is a typical link between the circles through his close relations with the palace and with the Messalla society. He is, too, a link in time between the earlier and the later Augustans. He lived early enough to see Virgil. The amorous elegy inaugurated by Virgil's friend, Gallus, practically dies with Ovid as last in a trio of successors; and, again, it is in Ovid's pages that we meet the names of the poetic mediocrities in which the Augustan age closed.

Nearly all the minor Augustan poets can be somehow related with the names of Virgil, Horace, Tibullus, or Ovid. Most are on friendly terms with the great poets; a few are their critics or butts, like Virgil's Bavius or Horace's Pupius. Those who are classed as friends of Virgil or Horace may be regarded as within, or at least in contact with, the circle of Maecenas. With Virgil may be joined several poets besides Gallus, already discussed. L. Varius Rufus (*circ.* 74–14 B.C.) was the *doyen* of Augustan poets. A friend of Virgil and Horace, he left some impress on their works. Both copied him,[2] and he lived to edit the *Aeneid*. His own poetry comprised epics on Caesar's murder (*De Morte Caesaris*) and on Augustus's greatness, also elegies, and the tragedy *Thyestes*, which

---

[1] For the remains of Maecenas, see Bährens, *Frag. Poet. Rom.*, 1886, pp. 338–9.
[2] Virg., *Aen.*, vi. 621–2, and (acc. to Acro) Hor., *Epist.*, I. xvi. 27–9, are quotations from Varius. For his fragments, Bährens, *F.P.R.*, 1886, p. 337.

Quintilian thought comparable with any Greek play.[1] The didactic poet Aemilius Macer of Verona (d. 16 B.C.) was the 'Mopsus' of the fifth eclogue. His chief model was Nicander. Ovid as a youth knew him, and refers to his *Ornithogonia*, on birds, *Theriaca*, on serpents, and perhaps to a separate *De Herbis*, on plants.[2] Codrus, mentioned several times in the *Eclogues*,[3] is perhaps a pseudonym for Cordus; as a poet he was highly esteemed by Valgius. The chief thing known about Bavius and Mevius (or Maevius) is that they were poetasters hostile to Virgil and disliked by him. Mevius incurred the wrath of Horace also, who wished him at the bottom of the sea.[4] That the erotic poet Anser was unfriendly to Virgil is not proved.[5] He was an adherent of Antony, and won a grant of land for verses in his honour.

Horace had more of the disposition which makes friends than Virgil had, and his poems admit of more references to them. C. Valgius Rufus, *consul suffectus* in 12 B.C., was a writer of considerable versatility, and belonged to the circle of Maecenas. Horace addresses an ode[6] urging him to forget a grief which had played a great part in his elegies. His activity included epigrams, a translation of the rhetorical system (τέχνη) of Apollodorus of Pergamum, and epistles on grammatical points. It is one of many instances exemplifying the interrelation of Augustan literary societies that the author of the eulogy on Messalla praises Valgius's epic gift as something Homeric.[7] M. Aristius Fuscus, who played on Horace the practical joke of leaving him in the clutches of the bore, and to whom he indited an ode and an epistle,[8] was a poet and grammarian. The brothers Visci, whom Horace mentions, are recorded to have combined excellence in poetry and criticism.[9] C. Fundanius[10] was a writer of comedies in an age which sometimes revived the old masters, but on the whole preferred mime and pantomime. Servius Sulpicius wrote love-poems.[11] Among junior friends of Horace whom we meet in his *Epistles*, Julius Florus[12] wrote satire; Titius,[13] Pindaric odes and tragedies; and Albinovanus Celsus[14] poems

[1] *Inst. Or.*, X. i. 98, 'Varii *Thyestes* cuilibet Graecarum comparari potest.'
[2] *Trist.*, IV. x. 43–4:
'Saepe suas uolucres legit mihi grandior aeuo
    Quaeque nocet serpens, quae iuuat herba, Macer.'
[3] *Ecl.*, v. ii; vii. 22 and 26.
[4] Hor., *Epod.*, x; *cf.* Virg., *Ecl.*, iii. 90. Mevius is the better spelling.
[5] Ovid, *Trist.*, ii. 435, 'Cinnaque procacior Anser.' It is unlikely that there is an allusion to him in *Ecl.*, ix. 36, 'argutos inter strepere anser olores.'
[6] *Od.*, II. ix; *cf. Sat.*, I. x. 82.
[7] Pseudo-Tibull., III. vii. (IV. i.) 179–80:
'Est tibi qui possit magnis se adcingere rebus,
    Valgius; aeterno propior non alter Homero.'
[8] *Od.*, I. xxii; *Epist.*, I. x. Cf. Porphyr. ad *Sat.*, I. ix. 61.
[9] Comm. Cruq. ad *Sat.*, I. x. 83, 'fuerunt optimi poetae et iudices critici.'
[10] Porphyr. ad *Sat.*, I. x. 40.
[11] Hor., *Sat.*, I. x. 86; Ovid, *Trist.*, ii. 441.
[12] Hor., *Epist.*, I. iii.; II. ii.
[13] Hor., *Epist.*, I. iii. 9–14.
[14] Hor., *Epist.*, I. 15–17; I. viii. 1.

which, to judge by Horace's hints, betrayed an inordinate tendency to plagiarise. Iullus Antonius, Mark Antony's son, wrote an epic on Diomede, and he wrote prose too.[1] Horace must also have known Domitius Marsus, who belonged to Augustus's literary set. He made another link between it and the Messalla set by lamenting in an epigram that the death of Tibullus had followed hard upon that of Virgil. Besides prose, he wrote amorous *Elegiae*, an epic *Amazonis*, *Fabellae*, and pungent epigrams in his collection called *Cicuta*—epigrams to which Martial makes repeated allusion. Melissus, a freedman of Maecenas, endeavoured to strike out a new line in light drama by his invention of the *trabeata*, or comedy representing the equestrian class.[2] What Horace's opinion on this was we do not know; but the too melodramatic tragedies of Pupius he dismisses as *lacrimosa poemata*, and sarcastically imagines the advice to make a fortune that would ensure seeing his plays to advantage from the knights' seats.[3]

The group around Messalla is best represented in the (already considered) poems by Tibullus or collected in the MSS. of Tibullus. The circle included Tibullus, Lygdamus, Sulpicia and the author who worked up part of her love-story, besides the author of the panegyric on Messalla himself. The author of the *Ciris* avowedly addressed the same patron. Propertius and Ovid are also to some extent in touch with the Messalla circle. With Propertius, on the evidence of his poems, one groups his friend Lynceus, whom he recommended to drop his Aeschylean tragedies in favour of love-poetry, and others like Ponticus,[4] who reappears in what we may call an Ovidian group.

Among friends of Ovid are included the epic poet Ponticus just mentioned; Tuticanus, a polished adapter of such Homeric subjects as the story of Nausicaa; the younger Macer, whom Ovid called *Iliacus* for his interest in legends anterior to the Trojan War; Sabinus, who wrote answers to Ovid's heroic epistles and modelled a work on his *Fasti*; Cornelius Severus, who discovered material for an epic in the Sicilian War against Sextus Pompey; and Albinovanus Pedo, who wrote a *Theseis* among other things, and whose epithet *sidereus* in Ovid is not to be taken to signify that he wrote of the stars.[5] Ovid furnishes a list of epic writers who chose mythological themes.[6] It may suffice, without naming them, to note that they drew some from Alexandrine, others from Homeric and Cyclic sources. Rabirius, whom Ovid thought 'mighty-mouthed' and Velleius coupled with Virgil as one of the preeminent intellects of his day, wrote epic poetry on contemporary his-

[1] Schol. ad Hor., *Od.*, IV. ii. 2.
[2] Suet., *Gramm.*, 21.
[3] Hor., *Epist.*, I. i. 67.
[4] Prop., II. xxxiv.
[5] *Ex Pont.*, IV. xvi. 6:
      'Iliacusque Macer sidereusque Pedo.'
[6] *Ex Pont.*, IV. xvi. 17 *sqq.*

Q

tory.[1] So did Sextilius Ena, a Spaniard from Corduba. The Augustan
poetry closes in mediocrity. The erotic poets Proculus and Alfius
Flavus, Ovid's friend Bassus the iambographer; Rufus, 'minstrel of the
Pindaric lyre';[2] and the tragic dramatists, Turranius and Gracchus, are
but names to us. Gleams of humour, and therefore of life, flash through
the eighty *Priapea*[3] in hendecasyllabics, distichs, and choliambics, collected partly from literature, but mainly from the walls of the shrines of
Priapus. They are the naughty but clever and well-written products of
leisured dilettantism among Augustan aristocrats.

Life is exactly the quality most lacking in two didactic poets who call
for fuller notice. About Grattius and Manilius (if that is his name) we
know too little personally to connect them with their contemporaries.
Ovid makes undoubted reference to Grattius's poem.[4] Regarding
Manilius, it is just possible that the whole of his work belongs to the
time of Tiberius, unless Robinson Ellis is right in finding an allusion to
it also in Ovid.[5] Grattius[6] has had unwarrantably conferred on him the
cognomen *Faliscus*. His own phrase *nostris Faliscis*[7] proves neither that
he came from Falerii nor even convincingly that he was an Italian. Such
conclusions are guesswork, as much as Wernsdorf's that he was a slave
and gained his knowledge of hunting from his duties. What we do know
is that, drawing material from Xenophon and from observation, and
being learned enough to imitate Lucretius and Virgil, he wrote a dull
book on the chase. So little permanent impress did his work leave that
successors on similar lines, Oppian, the Greek poet of the second century, and—more significant still—Nemesianus, the author of another
Latin *Cynegetica* in the third, do not so much as mention him. Of
Grattius's *Cynegetica* 536 complete hexameters are left. Metrically correct, they are monotonous. Grattius has a certain turn for condensed
expression, but he is obscure and digressive. His platitudes, for example,
on the sad results of human luxury, make but an awkward pendant to his
advice about the simple feeding of hounds. If there had been poetry in
his soul, it might have come out in the invocation to his silvan patroness,
Diana. When he takes up the subject of nets, springes, nooses, hunting-
spears, breeds of dogs and horses, there may be some instruction, but
there is no pleasure.

Subsequent to the *Georgics* there is no Latin didactic poem so con-

---

[1] *Ex Pont.*, IV. xvi. 5, 'magnique Rabirius oris'; Vell., II. xxxvi. 3.
[2] *Ex Pont.*, IV. xvi. 28:
        'Pindaricae fidicen tu quoque, Rufe, lyrae.'
[3] F. Bücheler, ed. min. of Petronius, 1882, ed. 4, 1904; E. Bährens, *Poet.
Lat. Min.*, i. 58.
[4] *Ex Pont.*, IV. xvi. 34:
        'Aptaque uenanti Grattius arma daret.'
[5] *Trist.*, II. 485–6.
[6] Text: Postgate's *C.P.L.*, vol. ii, ed. J. P. Postgate.
[7] Gratt., 40.

siderable as the *Astronomica* of Manilius.[1] Its five books—there may have been six originally—amount to nearly twice the length of Virgil's four. No ancient authority names Manilius; no grammarian quotes him; no MS. of his work is earlier than the eleventh century; no personal details occur in his poem. We are thus left with scant evidence in several problems concerning him. His name is generally conceded to have been Manilius,[2] though MSS. also furnish M. Mallius and Manlius. Misled by similarity of subject, one copyist ascribed his *Astronomica* to Aratus and another to Boethius,[3] the renowned author of the *De Consolatione Philosophiae*, who is known to have written about the stars. Bentley's surmise that Manilius was an Asiatic Greek is negatived by the reference to Greek as an *externa lingua* and by the absence of Grecisms. Manilius is apologetic when his subject demands Greek technicalities.[4] The clear allusion[5] to the annihilation in Germany of the three legions under Varus in A.D. 9 places the first book after that date. The passage proceeds as if the civil wars were not very far past, and would suit the close of Augustus's reign slightly better than the beginning of Tiberius's reign. The reference in the fourth book[6] to Rhodes as 'sheltering the future ruler of the world' would in itself suit any date after the recognition of Tiberius as heir to the succession. If Ovid has Manilius in view when he refers to descriptions of ball-throwing and swimming, then even Manilius's fifth book must have been written in the time of Augustus.[7] But the question of date as between the two reigns cannot be taken for settled.

The prevailing treatment of the heavenly bodies in the *Astronomica* is astrological. Manilius feels a superstitious hankering after the horoscope which deprives his work of the scientific spirit animating Lucretius. From the outset his avowed concern is with 'Fate's accomplice

---

[1] Text: M. Bechert in Postgate's *C.P.L.*, vol. ii; Th. Breiter, 2 vols. (i text, ii comm.), 1907–8 [Scaliger's ed. appeared at Paris, 1579; Bentley's at London, 1739; Jacob's at Berlin, 1846]. Textual criticism: J. P. Postgate, *Silua Maniliana*, 1897; R. Ellis, *Noctes Manilianae* (acc. coniect. in Germanici *Aratea*), 1891.

[2] See R. Ellis, *Noct. Manil.*, pp. 217–33, 'On the name of Manilius.'

[3] From this mistaken *Boeti* in a MS. heading probably came another accretion to Manilius's name, *Boeni*, and from that again *Poeni*, on which a hypothesis of his African origin was built.

[4] II. 693 *sqq.*, 830, 897; III. 40–1.

[5] I. 898 *sqq.*

[6] IV. 764.

[7] Compare Ovid, *Trist.*, ii. 485:
'Ecce canit formas alius iactusque pilarum,
Hic artem nandi praecipit, ille trochi,'
with Manilius V. 165–71 and 420–31. The double parallelism between the opening of *Astron.* Book II and 'Longinus' Περὶ ὕψους chap. xiii is important in view of the disputed date of the treatise *On the Sublime*. R. Ellis in a note, *C.R.*, xiii., 294, argues that the poet was the borrower. This would accord with Rhys Roberts's view and G. Kaibel's (*Herm.*, xxxiv, 107) that the book *On the Sublime* was written in the first century A.D. If it actually preceded Manilius, whose work must belong either to the end of Augustus's or beginning of Tiberius's reign, then the Περὶ ὕψους existed quite early in our era.

stars that chequer the sundered lots of man.'[1] It is by dint of this astrological handling that he makes good his claim to be the first Roman in his particular field.[2] Yet he is interested in the riddle of the universe as such. In his first book he glances at the various theories of its origin — chaotic, atomic, igneous, or aqueous. His attitude is diametrically opposed to the Lucretian. Again and again he emphasises the signs of providence which he claims to find in the world; all is 'the work of heavenly reason' (*caelestis rationis opus*); all is regulated by a divine world-spirit;[3] all supports his arguments from design.[4] It is a Stoic, not an Epicurean position, and naturally he is a fatalist.[5] One can imagine the scorn with which Lucretius might have withered the contention in the tedious queries whether without fate the flames would have shunned Aeneas, or the she-wolf suckled the twins, or Horatius kept the bridge, or Roman commanders outwitted Hannibal, or Marius achieved what he did.[6]

The readers of Manilius are few. They would be fewer if he had kept resolutely to astronomy or even astrology. He is careful not to raise expectations:

> Be not thy quest for dulcet strains;
> The very theme denieth ornament,
> Content if it be taught.[7]

It is not in his exposition of constellations, zodiac, or hemispheres that we are interested, but in his digressions. There, at any rate, if we do not find poetry, we discover a pleasant rhetoric; for already the stamp of the Silver Age is visible. Ingenuity has replaced the Lucretian fervour. We are never once stirred by Manilius, but we are occasionally attracted and entertained. The most readable pieces are the exordia to each of the books, where, for example, he expresses disdain for the beaten track of epic poetry,[8] or discourses eloquently on the majesty of human reason,[9] or moralises upon greed.[10] Very readable also are passages where he

[1] I. 1:
> 'Carmine diuinas artes et conscia fati
> Sidera diuersos hominum uariantia casus,
> Caelestis rationis opus, deducere mundo
> Aggredior.'
[2] I. 4–5.
[3] I. 111:
> 'Omniaque ad numen mundi faciemque moueri.'
[4] I. 476–503.
[5] *E.g.*, IV. 14:
> 'Fata regunt orbem, certa stant omnia lege.'
[6] IV. 20–49, ending in a summary of his position:
> 'Hoc, nisi fata darent, numquam fortuna tulisset.'
[7] III. 38:
> 'Nec dulcia carmina quaeras:
> Ornari res ipsa negat, contenta doceri.'
[8] III. *ad init.*
[9] II. 106 *sqq.*
[10] IV. *ad init.*

throws system to the winds, such as his attempt, in Virgilian manner, to treat comets as presagers of the future,[1] or his deviation from the constellation Andromeda into the legend of Andromeda's rescue by Perseus.[2] This episode, as a whole, has a charm which outweighs its several frigidities. It just escapes being ruined by artificialities like

> On virgin cross the maiden hung to die[3]

(where the 'virgin cross' is the rock to which she is chained), and by cheap scraps of the 'pathetic fallacy,' such as the paralysing of the sea and the weeping accents of the breeze.[4] The best piece, though it is not free of conceits, is the description of how Perseus falls in love at first sight:

> When, at the rock, he saw a maid fast-bound,
> His countenance fell, ne'er yet abashed by foe —
> Scarce could he grasp his spoil; Medusa's match
> Was outmatched in Andromeda; and now
> In envy of the very crags he sighs
> That those be happy chains to circle her.
> From her own lips he learned why she was doomed,
> And vowed to win a bride by war at sea,[5]
> Undaunted should a second Gorgon come.[6]

The Manilian hexameter shows considerable ease of movement, and due regard to elision. Manilius likes alliteration, not only in Lucretian echoes such as *moenia mundi*, but in such efforts of his own as

> *Saepe domi culpa est: nescimus credere caelo —*
> *Ciuilis etiam motus cognataque bella*
> *Significant,*

or

> *Perque patris pater Augustus uestigia uicit.*[7]

Certain uses of prepositions and moods, a remarkable scarcity of par-

---

[1] The concluding section of *Astronomica* I is obviously modelled on the close of *Georgics* I.

[2] V. 538 *sqq.*

[3] V. 553:
> 'Et cruce uirginea moritura puella pependit.'

[4] V. 566:
> 'Ipsa leui flatu refouens pendentia membra
> Aura per extremas resonauit flebile rupes.'

[5] Or does Manilius mean:
> 'And vowed to carry war to ocean's depths'?

[6] V. 570:
> 'Isque ubi pendentem uidit de rupe puellam,
> Deriguit facie, quam non stupefecerat hostis,
> Vixque manu spolium tenuit, uictorque Medusae
> Victus in Andromedast. Iam cautibus inuidet ipsis
> Felicisque uocat teneant quae membra catenas.
> Et postquam poenae causam cognouit ab ipsa,
> Destinat in thalamos per bellum uadere ponti,
> Altera si Gorgo ueniat, non territus ire.'

[7] I. 905 *sqq.* and 913.

ticles, and a fondness for pronouns like *is*, amount to idiosyncrasy but not to proof of foreign origin. At his best he is elegant. At his worst he is dull — for dulness is worse even than overdone conceits. One of his besetting sins is to run to death the habit of pointed balance. It is wearisome to meet scores of these carefully turned antitheses:

> *Et male conceptos partus peiusque necatos,*

or

> *uictam quia uicerat urbem,*

or of Andromeda's exposure to the monster

> *Virginis et uiuae rapitur sine funere funus.*

In endless repetition of such tricks classic simplicity is lost.

With Manilius the Virgilian tradition in didactic poetry approaches its close. *Aetna* has been already discussed. Of those works which fall beyond our period, Columella's tenth book, owing to subject, has most affinities with the *Georgics*. The fragments of Germanicus and the *Phaenomena* of Avienus have naturally, because of their relations to Aratus, the closest affinities with Manilius. In his *Cynegetica*, Nemesianus displays fuller command of poetic imagery than Grattius does; but the rhetorical colour has become more ingrained since Manilius wrote. In works like the *De Medicina Praecepta* by Serenus Sammonicus about Caracalla's time, or the *Carmen de Ponderibus et Mensuris* alleged to be Priscian's, one reaches the uttermost distortion and abasement of the didactic spirit. No rhetorical flourishes can make such work other than a badly disguised *memoria technica*. The Virgilian essence has irrevocably evaporated. Only the form has survived in the hexameter — like a useless rudimentary organ.

Chapter VI

AUGUSTAN PROSE AND LIVY

Predominance of matter over style – Oratory – Rhetoric – Philosophy – Law – Grammar and Scholarship – The lexicon of Verrius Flaccus – Special sciences and Vitruvius's *Architecture* – Its date and style – History – Pompeius Trogus.
Livy and Patavium – Livy in the capital – Divisions and summaries of the *Ab urbe condita libri* – Scale of treatment – Sources – Livy and Polybius – Science of the historian: (*a*) Credibility – (*b*) Faulty methods and prejudice – (*c*) Shortcomings if judged by modern standards – (*d*) Livy's conscious aim – (*e*) His ideal truth to Roman temperament – (*f*) Concept of the providential guidance of Rome – Art of the historian: (*a*) A survey of telling situations – (*b*) Speeches and character-drawing – (*c*) Descriptive power – (*d*) Dignity and poetic colour – (*e*) His style midway between Ciceronian and Silver Latinity – Livy's fame.

AUGUSTAN prose cannot show triumphs to match those of poetry. In history alone is there a really great name. The truth is that the monarchy cramped free development in both history and oratory, the two fields where Latin prose had been greatest during the preceding period. In such other fields as rhetoric, philosophy, law, grammar, antiquities, writers care more for their subject than its presentation: so matter throttles style.

The fate of oratory under the Roman empire is foreshadowed by the careers of the two chief speakers who lived on from the last years of the republic. Pollio and Messalla found their old occupation gone. Neither senate nor forum was the same arena as before. It was significant of something more than private animosity that Antony had Cicero put to death. The public environment of eloquence was undergoing radical change. Ciceronian oratory was impossible under Augustus. There continue to be orators,[1] like the group including Furnius, Atratinus, L. Arruntius, and the aged and remarkably ready speaker,[2] Q. Haterius, or a junior group including Messalla's sons, Messallinus and Aurelius Cotta. But the trend is towards artificial declamation. Cotta is typical of

---

[1] See Teuffel, *op. cit.*, § 267.
[2] Hieron., *Euseb. Chron.*, ann. Abr. 2040 (*i.e.*, A.D. 24): 'Q. Haterius promptus et popularis orator usque ad xc prope annum cum summo honore consenescit.' Tac., *Ann.*, IV. lxi, 'impetu magis quam cura uigebat.' Sen., *Contr.*, iv, *praef.* 6–11, '. . . tanta erat illi uelocitas orationis ut uitium fieret.'

the young speaker of the empire. He combined with the reputation of a voluptuary a name for smart sayings, facility in verse, and capacity as a pleader before the centumviral court. Ovid, at his place of banishment, read a copy of one such speech which had been circulated.[1] When speakers became as outspoken as T. Labienus and Cassius Severus, they brought trouble on their heads. Labienus earned the nickname of *Rabienus*. Both had their books burned by orders of the senate, and Cassius was exiled.[2]

Of the practice and theory of rhetoric the exponents were well-nigh numberless. For the names of the rhetoricians who taught Latin eloquence in the Augustan age, and of the considerable band of Greeks who taught in their own language, the invaluable authority is the elder Seneca. It was during his later years, in the time of Tiberius therefore, that he composed his *Oratorum et Rhetorum Sententiae, Diuisiones, Colores*,[3] an exhaustive survey of the ordinary themes in the rhetorical schools. It forms not only a history of rhetoric in his own times, but furnishes full criticism on the style of different rhetoricians, with plentiful specimens of their declamations. A few names may be selected. The improved status of professors of rhetoric can be gathered from the appearance of the knight Rubellius Blandus in the field. A more famous teacher was M. Porcius Latro, a man of high natural endowments and powerful voice, who never wholly unlearned his native Spanish ruggedness.[4] Among his pupils were Ovid and a certain Florus.[5] He had a way of compelling imitation: some of his students went the length of making themselves artificially pale to resemble their master![6] Arellius Fuscus was Asiatic by birth and manner. Cestius Pius was also foreign—from Smyrna. C. Albucius Silus of Novara was, on the evidence of Seneca's remarks, a speaker and writer possessed of varied gifts of style.[7] Rapidity, splendour, copiousness are among the qualities set to his credit. Essentially a declaimer, he did not achieve success in legal pleading. We may close, though we do not exhaust the list, by mentioning the Passieni, father and son; Junius Gallio, Seneca's friend, whose declamations retained a vogue in Jerome's time alongside of Cicero and Quintilian; Junius Otho, the author of four books of *Colores*; and Alfius Flavus, the poet.

Interest in philosophy of course continued. Epicureanism habitually ensured for natural science, as well as for ethics, a modicum of attention. Great writers like Virgil and Horace felt genuinely drawn to philoso-

---

[1] *Ex Pont.*, III. v. 7–8.
[2] Sen., *Contr.*, x, *praef.* 4 *sqq.*; Suet., *Calig.*, xvi; Tac., *Ann.* I. lxxii; IV. xxi.
[3] Text: A. Kiessling, 1872; H. J. Müller, 1887; H. Bornecque, two vols. (w. French trans.), ed. 2, 1932.
[4] Sen., *Contr.*, *praef.* 13–18, 20–4.
[5] Sen., *Contr.*, ix. 25, § 23–24. Probably not the satirist of p. 448.
[6] Plin., *Nat. Hist.*, xx. 160.
[7] Sen., *Contr.*, vii, *praef.*; Suet., *De Rhett.*, 6.

phical inquiry. Vitruvius considered philosophy, in its moral and natural branches, an essential for the sound training of an architect.[1] Augustus and Livy went as far as authorship. Yet the age was one of philosophical dilettantism rather than of systematic speculation. Some books on Stoicism were written by Fabius Maximus, an ex-Pompeian knight; Crispinus and Stertinius handled Stoicism in verse, the latter composing, if we could only believe Acro, 220 books.[2] The most important philosophical name of the period is that of Sextius senior, who 'philosophised in Greek words but with a Roman character.'[3] His strict guidance of his own conduct according to his theories commanded wide veneration. The younger Sextius continued his father's labours and influence, which widened through a succession of distinguished pupils. Papirius Fabianus, for example, combined his studies in oratory under Blandus and Arellius with a philosophical training under Sextius. He became in turn a public lecturer on philosophy, and numbered among his pupils the younger Seneca.

Jurisprudence came virtually to depend on imperial licence.[4] The right to give valid legal advice (*responsa*) was henceforth regulated by the consent of the *princeps*. Sanction involved restriction. This was intentional; for not all jurists approved the transformed constitution. The chief of the irreconcilables was M. Antistius Labeo (*circ.* 54 B.C.– A.D. 17), who maintained towards the illegality of Caesarism the same uncompromising attitude as his senior Cascellius. Labeo's wide erudition embraced philosophy and linguistics.[5] His works numbered four hundred volumes. Inferior to Labeo in scientific attainments and in literary production, but favoured by Augustus for his deferential attitude towards monarchical principles, C. Ateius Capito (34 B.C.– A.D. 22) was the head of the opposing school of lawyers. From the feud between the leaders sprang the two legal sects of the Sabinians and the Proculians.

In the investigations of Sinnius Capito the influence of Varro is traceable. He dealt with grammar and literary history. The freedman and librarian of Augustus, C. Julius Hyginus[6] (*circ.* 64 B.C.–*circ.* A.D. 17), a Spaniard like some of the rhetoricians, also received from Varro an impulse in the national direction of his studies. He resembled many contemporary scholars in presenting an antiquarian as well as a literary side. He wrote commentaries on a poem by Cinna and on Virgil. His *De Situ Vrbium Italicarum* and his works on theology, agriculture, bees, and on great figures in Roman history, show him under other aspects.

[1] Vitr., *De Archit.*, I. i. 7.
[2] Acro, ad Hor. *Epist.* I. xii. 20.
[3] Sen., *Ep.*, lix. 7, 'Graecis uerbis Romanis moribus philosophantem.'
[4] Pompon., *Dig.*, I. ii. 2, 49, 'primus diuus Augustus, ut maior iuris auctoritas haberetur, constituit ut ex auctoritate eius responderent.'
[5] Gell., *N.A.*, XIII. x and xii; Tac., *Ann.*, III. lxxv.
[6] Suet., *De Gramm.*, 20.

The general opinion is that a much later Hyginus was the author of the so-called *Fabulae* and the *De Astrologia*. Cloatius Verus investigated the debt of the Latin language to Greek in *Libri Verborum a Graecis Tractorum*. Atticus's freedman, Q. Caecilius Epirota, was the first lecturer on Virgil and on the modern school of poets;[1] and Domitius Marsus alludes to his literary influence in his line *Epirota tenellorum nutricula uatum*. L. Crassicius, another teacher, after making a stir by his commentary on the obscurities of Cinna's *Zmyrna*, took to philosophy under Sextius. Scribonius Aphrodisius, once a slave under the tuition of Horace's master Orbilius, worked on orthography. His severe criticisms on Verrius Flaccus, both as scholar and as man,[2] perhaps have no deeper ground than a quarrel with the views in his *De Orthographia*. Pedants turn their differences into feuds.

To Verrius Flaccus[3] belongs the credit of compiling the first encyclopaedic lexicon in Latin on alphabetical lines. An outline of his life is furnished by Suetonius.[4] He was a freedman, and an educationist of stimulating methods. His pupils were encouraged to compete for some beautiful or scarce copy of an ancient author. After the emperor appointed him tutor to his grandchildren, Verrius was required to give up all other teaching. Housed on the Palatine, and guaranteed a salary of about £1,000 a year (*centena sestertia in annum*), he found himself in a leisured environment specially favourable to a scholar's pursuits. He died in advanced age during Tiberius's reign. His lost works include *Fasti*, which Ovid used; a study *De Obscuris Catonis*; one on Etruscan antiquities; and one entitled *Saturnus*.[5] The massive *De Verborum Significatu* is also lost. Yet not absolutely, for much may be inferred from the mutilated half of the abridgement made by Festus at the end of the second century, and from the epitome of Festus made in turn by Paulus Diaconus at the time of the Carolingian revival. Moreover, traces of the influence of Verrius, direct or indirect, upon scholars during the first five centuries of the Christian era, supply data indiscoverable from his two epitomators alone. Remnants of Verrius are embedded in Quintilian, Pliny, Gellius, Nonius, Macrobius, Placidus, and others. It is even practicable to reconstruct portions of Verrius's glosses from a comparison of notes on an identical word in Nonius and Placidus with the corresponding entry in Festus and Paulus. All the evidence shows

[1] Suet., *De Gramm.*, 16.
[2] Suet., *ibid.*, 19.
[3] Text: *Pauli Diaconi Excerpta et Sext. Pompei Festi Fragmenta* in Lindemann's *Corp. Gramm. Lat. Veterum*, tom. ii, 1832; K. O. Müller, 1839, new ed. 1880. The foundations of modern criticism upon Verrius were laid in Jos. Scaliger's *Castigationes*, first issued in 1565, and included with a variety of other notes in the Paris ed. of Festus, 1584. On the sources, scope, arrangement, and influence of Verrius's lexicon, H. Nettleship, *Lects. and Essays*, 1885, pp. 201–47.
[4] Suet., *De Gramm.*, 17.
[5] Suet., *loc. cit.*; Gell., *N.A.*, XVII. vi. 2; Schol. Veron. ad *Aen.* X. 183 and 200; Macrob., I. iv. 7.

that Verrius's work was in every sense a greater one than that of his Antonine epitomiser, or that of Festus's Carolingian excerptor. This *magnum opus* was far more than a dictionary. It was a treasury of old Roman literature, custom and myth—an encyclopaedia of language, of grammar, but also of antiquities, religious, legal, and political. The arrangement was alphabetical, at least so far as the initial letter of a word was concerned. This made it handier for reference than Varro's books were. Several books might be assigned to a single letter: A had at least four: P had at least five.[1] Verrius had copious sources to draw from. There were commentaries and glossaries to many of the older writers, like the Plautine studies by Opilius, or annotations of different scholars on Lucilius. Verrius named Opilius more than once, and he was fond of citing Lucilius. From Festus we can prove that Verrius borrowed from Aelius Stilo, Santra, and from contemporaries like Valgius Rufus, Sinnius Capito, Ateius Capito, and Antistius Labeo. Varro he quotes mostly as an antiquary; yet it is scarcely safe to conclude with Müller that Verrius never read the *De Lingua Latina*. It is true the two scholars took opposite sides in etymology; for Verrius—as the briefest glance at Paulus's epitome will prove—was inordinately keen on Greek derivations for Latin words. A natural inference from certain features of arrangement is that it was part of Verrius's method to collect material from one author at a time, then to group the material alphabetically according to a leading word, and so finally to make his treatment of any one letter largely an aggregate of these separate series of extracts. The total achievement, however, was not simply a compilation. Verrius had conducted independent researches on Cato, and on orthography. We may assume that he incorporated some of his results in his encyclopaedia.[2] Other points we can leave only in interrogative form. Were his notes on Catullus, Lucretius, and Cicero due entirely to his own reading in these authors or to lost index-makers? Were his notes on Virgil his own? In other words, is Verrius the first of the long line of Virgilian scholars? The call for an epitome of Verrius two centuries after his date was in itself a testimony to the usefulness of his lexicon. When Festus went to work on Verrius, his aim was twofold. He desired to omit the obsolete, and greatly to condense the treatment.[3] The very spirit of the age, however, must have saved him from doing his worst in the way of curtailment. Had there not been enthusiasm for old Latin in the days of the Antonines, it may be guessed that Verrius would have suffered even

[1] Gell., *N.A.*, V. xvii. 2 and xviii. 2, on 'atros dies' and 'annales' respectively; Festus, p. 436 (Lindsay); 326 (Müller).

[2] *E.g.*, the frequent references to Cato in Paulus's epitome towards the end of the book on the letter 'V' suggest that this portion has been taken over from the other work.

[3] 218 (Müller) ' . . . cum propositum habeam ex tanto librorum eius numero intermortua iam et sepulta uerba atque ipso saepe confitente nullius usus aut auctoritatis praeterire, et reliqua quam breuissime redigere in libros admodum paucos.' (=Lindsay, p. 242).

460 THE LITERATURE OF THE GOLDEN AGE

more than he did through excision. From the ruins of this monumental work in the epitomised epitome by Paulus we can still gauge the proportions of the original. The illustrations range from the oldest Latin of the *Carmina Saliorum* down to contemporary poets like Virgil and Ovid, and to contemporary scholars and jurists. The wealth of quotation proves what a valuable index to Latin literature we have lost.

There were exponents of special sciences other than law, language, and antiquities. Pompeius Trogus, better known as a historian, wrote on zoology and botany, using Aristotle and Theophrastus as models. Clodius Tuscus composed an astronomical calendar which was translated into Greek. The medical writings once ascribed to the Augustan physician, Antonius Musa, belong to a later period. On architecture a treatise was produced, devoid of meritorious style, but with signal value as a document reflecting an epoch which transformed Rome from a city of brick into a city of marble. This is the *De Architectura* of Vitruvius Pollio (or Polio).[1] His cognomen is known from the epitome of Cetius Faventinus, which was used by Palladius in the first half of the fourth century A.D. Vitruvius refers to his military service under Julius Caesar; to his duties as officer of engineers under Augustus; and to an allowance from the emperor, on his sister Octavia's recommendation, which protected him against apprehensions of want.[2] His needs were not elaborate, for he expresses his contempt of money-making. He wrote his work when enfeebled by age.[3] He intended it to be of service to Augustus in his building schemes. It was in ten books. Some of its matter would not now be handled under architecture. The first seven books are chiefly concerned with building—the nature of architecture and the importance of situation; materials; temples, especially Ionic; temples Doric and Corinthian; secular edifices, fora, basilicae, theatres, and baths; dwelling-houses; decoration. Then follow three on water supply, the science of dials, machinery, respectively. The basic ideas underlying the greatness of the ancients in building can be traced in it—the desire to rest the art on its ultimate philosophy and its past history, and to insist upon a breadth of training at which the less enlightened modern would stand aghast. Even for the occasional workaday colour which the author's language takes on from the common speech (probably of his labourers) the work has its importance. It is unique, too—the one Roman treatise on architecture. For the works of the few Latin predecessors whom he names,[4] Fuficius, Varro, and P.

---

[1] Vitruuii *De Architectura Libri X*, V. Rose and H. Müller-Strübing, 1867; ed. 2, V. Rose, 1899 (includes Faventinus's extracts).
[2] VIII. iii. 25, 'C. Iulius Masinissae filius . . . cum patre Caesare militauit: is hospitio meo est usus: ita cotidiano conuictu necesse fuerat de philologia disputare.' I, *praef.* 2, '. . . Ad apparationem ballistarum et scorpionum reliquorumque tormentorum refectionem fui praesto . . . cum ergo eo beneficio essem obligatus ut ad exitum uitae non haberem inopiae timorem, haec tibi scribere coepi quod animaduerti multa te aedificauisse et nunc aedificare. . . .'
[3] II, *praef.* 4, 'faciem deformauit aetas, ualetudo detraxit uires.'
[4] VII, *praef.* 14.

Septimius, have perished. His garrulous prefaces are, on the whole, pleasantly discursive. They flit from point to point. Some give personal details—his gentlemanly etiquette in the avoidance of canvassing for orders or his gratitude to his parents for having had him taught his art. Others contain semi-philosophic reflections, notes on the past of architecture, or apologetic explanations to the *imperator*, the title by which he directly addresses the *princeps*, though he knows the more majestic one of *Augustus*. One preface contains his praise of great thinkers.[1] Another[2] acknowledges his obligations to Greek technical writers in a formidable list, which does not imply that he ransacked all of them, but does imply that his knowledge was not wholly derived at second-hand from a single Latin treatise such as Varro's. Elsewhere, he pauses to indicate his reading on the subject of different waters,[3] or with greater irrelevance, but also greater charm, he arrests one by genuine enthusiasm for some of the noble names in Roman literature—Ennius, Accius, Lucretius, Cicero, and Varro.[4] He is never weary—however much his reader is—of careful recapitulations of the subject-matter treated in the various books. Though a great deal is of necessity technical—he points this out himself—there is a great deal that is attractive. The sketch of the origin of building among primitive tribes, the points to be observed in laying out a town of the time, or in constructing temples, the scheme of rooms in a house, the greater regard for appearance in exalted homes, the use of painting interiors, the absurdities of fashionable house decoration, the obtaining of colours, the management of stucco, and half a hundred other details, vitally assist the imagination to reconstruct Roman civilisation. If the work fails to be literature in a strict sense, it at least makes the Augustan era and its literature more vivid and concrete, besides throwing light on the architectural remains of antiquity. It was natural that on its first appearance in print towards the close of the fifteenth century, in the hey-day of Renaissance architecture, it should have seemed to be a venerable voice of the past full of instruction for the new age.

The date of the work may be put about 14 B.C. It is later than the building of the Temple of Quirinus in 16:[5] it is earlier than the building of the theatre of Balbus in the year 13, for the author speaks of a single stone theatre in Rome.[6] His apologetic dedication to the emperor reads uncommonly like an expanded paraphrase of Horace's neat opening to the second book of his *Epistles*. But on the grounds of imperfections in the matter it has been declared that the author is not what he claims to be, a working architect; and on the ground of imperfections in style, the Augustan composition of the *De Architectura* has been denied. It is

---

[1] IX, *praef.*   [2] VII, *praef.*   [3] VIII. iv.
[4] IX, *praef.* 16, 'Itaque qui litterarum iucunditatibus intinctas habent mentes non possunt non in suis pectoribus dedicatum habere sicuti deorum sic Enni poetae simulacrum.'
[5] III. i. 7.   [6] III. ii. 2.

urged that his mistakes and omissions are those of an impostor, and that the debased style is typical of a stage nearer to the Romance languages which arose out of later Latin.[1] It is a hypothesis *prima facie* difficult of credence that an unknown closet-philosopher, who was no architect, should have been capable of forging a work on a subject necessarily foreign to his real tastes, that he should have posed as a practical man who had constructed the basilica at Fanum,[2] and that he should have been capable of supplying the work with the diagram[3] which once illustrated it. Such a clever *savant* would not need to apologise for his weakness in grammar, on the plea that he wrote merely 'as an architect';[4] he would scarcely have been likely to blunder into naming one 'Eucrates' among the comic dramatists of Greece.[5] It may be said in general that there is nothing in his inferior Latinity, or in his anticipations of decadent usage,[6] that may not be due to the influence of the vulgar Latin in the times of Augustus. Vitruvius's employment of prepositions, for example, is no more peculiar than that observable in Manilius. His faulty use of moods, just as much as his parade of earlier names in architecture, is more consistent with his account of his own standing than with the theory of imposture which also alleges against the author much shallow ignorance.

History afforded a fairer field for literary achievement than technical subjects. Here Augustan prose reached its highest quality. Yet undoubtedly history laboured under the same disadvantages as oratory. The opening of the period witnessed many eulogies on great men of the closing years of the republic. Volumnius and Bibulus wrote on M. Brutus, Tiro on Cicero, Q. Dellius on Mark Antony. Memoirs on their own political careers were composed by Agrippa and M. Messalla. But autobiography was safest when indulged in by the emperor himself. Asinius Pollio made the discovery that the candid narration of events so fresh as those during the Civil War would cause heartburnings. And, in general, the imperial embargo on the publication of proceedings in the senate limited the material for contemporary records. The muzzling of history, so noticeable during the first century A.D., had begun. The desire to avoid ruffling susceptibilities was largely accountable for the

---

[1] J. L. Ussing's *Observations on Vitruv. De Archit.* (trans. from Danish), 1898, attempts to support the contentions of the posthumous work of C. F. L. Schultz, *Untersuchungen über d. Zeitalter des röm. Kriegsbaumeisters M. Vitruvius*, 1856. Professor Ussing held that 'Vitruvius' translated freely from Athenaeus Περὶ μηχανημάτων, that Athenaeus was not Alexandrine but of the third century A.D., and therefore that the *De Architectura* was composed still later by a forger who fathered his work upon the Augustan name of Vitruvius.
[2] V. i. 6.
[3] I. vi. 12, '. . . in extremo uolumine formas siue uti Graeci σχήματα dicunt.'
[4] I. i. 17, '. . . ut si quid parum ad regulam artis grammaticae fuerit explicatum ignoscatur.'
[5] VI, *praef.* 3. Is 'Eucrates' a cross between 'Eupolis' and 'Crates'?
[6] For examples, see Ussing, *op. cit.*

choice of subjects, remote in time or locality, which characterises
Fenestella, Arruntius, Trogus, and Livy himself. It partly explains,
too, the antiquarian interest already observed in Hyginus and Verrius.
Another significant fact is that some of the best historical work of the
age was done by Greeks, whose national detachment and faculty for
adaptation saved them from political prejudice. Of the Roman historians, L. Arruntius fell back on the Punic Wars for subject and on
Sallust for style. Fenestella, who died, according to Jerome, in A.D.
19 at the age of seventy, composed *Annales*, and made a name for
knowledge of ancient manners, ritual, and constitutional history.

Pompeius Trogus[1] traced his descent from the Vocontii, a Gallic
tribe. His grandfather got the Roman franchise from Pompey. His father
was an officer high in the confidence of Julius Caesar.[2] As Verrius
designed a comprehensive lexicon, so Trogus designed a comprehensive
history in forty-four books. The latest clear allusion in the work is to the
recovery of the standards from Parthia in 20 B.C.[3] It was to embrace the
nations of the world, excluding Rome except in her relations with other
peoples as conqueror and apart from a sketch of her regal origins in the
last book but one. The work is entitled in the MSS. *Historiae Philippicae
et totius mundi origines et terrae situs*. Its central theme is Macedonian
history. The earlier books are introductory on Asia and Greece. The
work is based on Greek sources, conjecturally Timagenes in the main.
Our impressions of Trogus must be formed from an abridgement of the
Antonine age by Justinus. Justinus expresses admiration for the 'man
of old-fashioned eloquence' (*uir priscae eloquentiae*) who displayed
Herculean hardihood in thus essaying a chronicle of the world.[4] There
is a direct and workmanlike tone in Justinus; but an epitome is never a
fair test of the style of an original. Justinus is no more a term con-
vertible with Trogus, than Festus is with Verrius. It was Justinus's aim
to retain the number of books, and, by free omission of what he considered neither entertaining nor profitable, to make a brief anthology.[5]
We are most likely to have Trogus's actual words preserved in the
reported remarks which enliven the history. One of the rare instances
in which we are left a considerable passage of Trogus *verbatim* is the
address of Mithradates to his soldiers.[6] These chapters have the value of
illustrating Trogus's insistence on *oratio obliqua* as the right historical
form for reporting speeches. The direct speech seemed to him a pre-

[1] Text: *Iustinus: Trogi Pompei Hist. Philippicarum Epitoma*, J. Jeep, 1859;
F. Rühl, 1886.
[2] Iustin., XLIII. v.
[3] XLI. v.
[4] Iustin., *praef.*, 'Nonne nobis Pompeius Herculea audacia orbem terrarum adgressus uideri debet, cuius libris omnium saeculorum, regum, nationum
populorumque res gestae continentur?'
[5] *Praef.*, 'Omissis quae nec cognoscendi uoluptate iucunda nec exemplo
erant necessaria, breue ueluti florum corpusculum feci.'
[6] XXXVIII. iv–vii.

tentious departure from reality, and he regarded this rhetorical element as a blemish in Sallust and Livy.[1] The passage also illustrates Trogus's qualities of clearness and vigour. This is especially marked where Mithradates caps his indictment of the Romans with his sarcastic allusions to their traditional reverence for 'their founders nurtured at the she-wolf's teats: so has that whole people wolves' hearts, insatiate of blood and rule, and hungrily covetous of wealth.'[2]

No Augustan prose-writer is for a moment comparable with Livy. His prose-epic is own sister to the *Aeneid*. Not even in Virgil has the greatness of the Roman character found a more dignified or more lasting monument than in the colossal ruins of Livy's history. Titus Livius[3] (59 B.C.–A.D. 17) came, like Catullus and Virgil, from northern Italy. We derive the dates of his birth and death from Jerome's additions to Eusebius.[4] That Livy was a native of Patavium (the modern Padua) is authenticated by the epithet *Patauinus* applied to him, and by allusions in Martial and Statius.[5] Patavium left its impress on Livy. It was a city of note and of prosperity.[6] Like Rome itself, the district claimed a legendary connexion with Troy. It had withstood Etruscan and Gallic marauders; and Livy must have felt proud of his own romantic town when he recorded how its ancient prowess against Greek buccaneers was commemorated every year in a naval combat on the reaches of its river.[7] There is some justification for thinking that when Caesar's quarrel with the senate came to a head, and Livy was a boy of ten, Patavium took the anti-Caesarian side.[8] Certain it is that later the town was for the senate and against Antony.[9] It is hardly fanciful to see in

[1] XXXVIII. iii.

[2] XXXVIII. vi, '. . . conditores suos lupae uberibus altos: sic omnem illum populum luporum animos, inexplebiles sanguinis atque imperii, diuitiarumque auidos ac ieiunos habere.'

[3] Text: *T. Liui ab urbe condita libri*, erkl. von W. Weissenborn, 10 vols., 1860, neu bearbeitet v. H. J. Müller, ed. 8, 1885, etc.; J. N. Madvig and J. L. Ussing, 4 vols. (app. crit.), ed. 4, 1886 *sqq.* Select books: I, J. R. Seeley, 1871, ed. 2, 1874 (with valuable historical examination of Livy); II, R. S. Conway, 1905; II–III, H. M. Stephenson, 1886; IV, do., 1890; V, W. C. Laming, 1900; V–VII, A. R. Cluer and P. E. Matheson, new ed., 1889 (serviceable excursus on Livy's Latin); VII–VIII, F. Luterbacher, 1890; IX, H. M. Stephenson, 1901; XXI–XXII, Fabri and Heerwagen, 1852; XXI, M. T. Tatham, 1889; XXII, do., 1888; XXI, M. S. Dimsdale, 1894; XXII., do., 1896; XXVI, R. M. Henry, 1905; XXIX–XXX, F. Luterbacher, 1893. Literary qualities, etc.: H. Taine, *Essai sur Tite Live* (ouvrage couronné par l'Académie française, 1856), ed. 2, 1860; O. Riemann, *Études sur la langue et grammaire de T. L.*, 1879, ed. 2, 1885.

[4] In the Armenian version, however, the date of birth, Ol. 180, 4, corresponds to 57 B.C.

[5] Martial's allusion (I. lxi. 3), 'Censetur Apona Liuio suo tellus,' is to a spring 'Aponi fons' near Patavium. Statius (*Sil.*, IV. vii. 55) refers to Livy as 'Timaui alumnus.'

[6] Its wealth is indicated in Strabo's mention of its 500 citizens registered as possessing equestrian income (V. i. 7: *cf.* III. v. 3).

[7] X. ii.

[8] Weissenborn thinks so: Seeley demurs (Introd. to ed. of Livy I).

[9] Cic., *Phil.*, XII. iv. 10.

such local traditions the origin of the historian's romantic and political
bias; while from that decorous puritanism which was to make Patavium
still a pattern of morality a century after Livy,[1] he may have imbibed his
distaste for contemporary luxury and his enthusiasm for old-time simplicity. It may be too much, like Niebuhr, to detect beneath Livy's rich
colour the same local causes as underlay the Venetian school of painting, or, like Pichon, to consider him a Gaul who already possessed
the best qualities of the French genius. Yet undoubtedly the influences
of his home-land had time to sink deep into his spirit. There is no reason
to believe that he settled in Rome much before he was thirty: and the
note of provincialism implied in Asinius Pollio's charge of *Patauinitas*
had probably some firmer basis than either acrid criticism or mere dislike of Livy's divergence from the austerer prose-manner of the past. It
is true that Quintilian, in both passages where he records the accusation,
implies by his tone a want of sympathy with Pollio's attitude. But
Quintilian's assertion that he regards everything Italian as Roman does
in itself lend colour to the allegation that in Livy's style were discoverable words, notes, and idioms foreign to the best urban usage.[2]

At Rome, Livy's taste for philosophy and rhetoric produced sundry
minor works. For example, dialogues semi-philosophical and semi-
historical are mentioned by L. Seneca.[3] Again, it is likely enough that a
brief manual of rhetoric was contained in the letter addressed to his son,
in which Livy declared Demosthenes and Cicero, with such writers as
resembled them, to be the best models for study.[4] Citations by M.
Seneca and Quintilian, from literary counsels or preferences expressed
by Livy, support the view that he was a professor of rhetoric.[5] Of his
domestic life we know only that he had at least two children: the son to
whom he addressed the letter above-mentioned, and a daughter, inasmuch as we read of a son-in-law, Magius, who 'declaimed'[6]—perhaps a
pupil of his own. Soon after 27 B.C. it is clear that he was engaged on the
great work of his life—the narration of the history of Rome from
the beginning to his own times. In the first book, the use of the title
'Augustus' (conferred in 27) and the mention of one closing of the
Temple of Janus (in 29), but not of the later closing (in 25), yield

---

[1] Pliny, *Ep.*, I. xiv.; Martial, XI. xvi. 8.
[2] *Inst. Or.*, I. v. 56, '. . . Pollio deprehendit in Liuio Patauinitatem, licet
omnia Italica pro Romanis habeam.' (It is noticeable that Quintilian is discussing 'uerba aut Latina aut peregrina.') *Cf.* VIII. i. 3, 'In Tito Liuio, mirae
facundiae uiro, putat inesse Pollio Asinius quandam Patauinitatem.' Pollio, it
should be remembered, depreciated Cicero too, *Inst. Or.*, XII. i. 22.
[3] Sen., *Ep.*, C. 9 [XVI. v. 9].
[4] Quint., *Inst. Or.*, X. i. 39, '. . . legendos Demosthenem atque Ciceronem,
tum ita, ut quisque esset Demostheni et Ciceroni simillimus.'
[5] *E.g.*, Sen., *Contr.*, IX. ii. 26; IX. i. 14, on Livy's dislike for Sallust's style;
Quint., *Inst. Or.*, VIII. ii. 18, on Livy's mention of the preceptor who delighted
to hold up before his students obscurity as the ideal of style – 'Graeco uerbo
utens σκότισον.'
[6] Sen., *Contr.*, X, *praef.* 2.

definite indications of date.[1] The work was given to the world—like Gibbon's—in instalments, and brought Livy wide renown. Once he pauses to make the naïve acknowledgement that he has done enough for fame, but that the habit of writing has grown too strong to resist.[2] The younger Pliny[3] tells of a man from Cadiz who travelled to Rome expressly to see Livy, and having seen him, went straight back—the mighty capital contained nothing else so wonderful. Livy long enjoyed the emperor's intimacy. Quite early in his work[4] he quotes the gist of an inscription which Augustus told him he had read. Much later, when he reached the Civil Wars, his sympathetic treatment of Caesar's opponents won for him from Augustus the playful nickname of 'Pompeyite.'[5] The pro-senatorial leanings so marked in Livy's handling of the heroes of the early republic did not desert him in writing of his own generation. 'He nowhere calls Brutus and Cassius cut-throats and traitors—the usual epithets at the present day,' Tacitus makes Cremutius Cordus remark; 'he repeatedly designates them as heroes of distinction.'[6] Livy held it a moot question whether Caesar's birth had been a boon to Rome or not.[7] This attitude did not alienate the emperor. Indeed, Augustus never thought it desirable to dissociate himself too manifestly from the senate. Besides, much in Livy's work, like its constant homage to the grandeur and piety of the past, must have enlisted Augustus's favour just as the *Aeneid* did; and sentimental affection for the old republic was compatible with serene loyalty to the new constitution as a political necessity. So Livy need never have felt uncomfortable at court. He even fostered learning there; for it was at his instigation that Claudius—the future emperor—took to historical composition.[8]

The traditional title *Ab urbe condita libri* adequately embraces the general aim expressed in the preface.[9] Of the work—originally consisting of 142 books—about one quarter has survived the Middle Ages. Its massive proportions and an early, though not original, division into decads (or sets of ten books) militated against preservation intact. We possess Books I–X and XXI–XLV, or thirty-five books in all, of which XLI and XLIII are imperfect. But for all, except CXXXVI and CXXXVII, summaries (*periochae*) have come down. These synopses, unenlivened by any gleam of style, are yet precious as indexes to the scheme and proportion observed in the treatment of events. They were

[1] Livy. I. xix. 4.   [2] Plin., *N.H.*, *praef.* 16.
[3] *Ep.*, II. iii. 8.   [4] IV. xx.
[5] Tac., *Ann.*, IV. xxxiv, 'T. Liuius, eloquentiae ac fidei praeclarus in primis, Gnaeum Pompeium tantis laudibus tulit ut Pompeianum eum Augustus appellaret: neque id amicitiae eorum offecit.'
[6] *Ibid.*, '. . . hunc ipsum Cassium, hunc Brutum nusquam latrones et parricidas, quae nunc uocabula imponuntur, saepe ut insignes uiros nominat.'
[7] Sen., *Nat. Quaest.*, V. xviii. 4.   [8] Suet., *Claud.*, xli. 1.
[9] *Praef.* i, 'Facturusne operae pretium sim, si a primordio urbis res populi Romani perscripserim, nec satis scio,' etc.

not drawn directly from the original, but based, perhaps in the fourth century, on an abridgement then in existence. It is significant that as early as Martial's time some such condensation was available:

> In vellum small huge Livy now is dressed:
> My bookshelves could not hold him uncompressed.[1]

The division into books is the author's.[2] The arrangement by decads was known in the fifth century, but it is arbitrary, and is less true to natural breaks in subject-matter than groups of fifteen books with subdivisions into half decads. Thus, broadly, the first fifteen books treat Rome before the conflict with Carthage; the second fifteen, the Punic Wars; and the next fifteen, the Macedonian and other Eastern entanglements. At turning-points Livy inserted brief prefaces to mark fresh instalments—the introduction to Book VI marks the new historical era after the destruction of Rome by the Gauls in 390; and the opening of Book XXI heralds the struggle in the Second Punic War. Separate portions seem to have borne sub-titles; for example, to judge by the best MS. of the epitomes, CIX–CXVI were *Belli Ciuilis Libri Octo*.

The scale of treatment was not uniform. Fuller detail was introduced as the narrative approached the historian's own times. Thus, the first book extends over the regal period—roughly, about one-third of the whole time covered in the history. The next nine books (II–X) treat more than two centuries—down to 293 B.C. The lost second decad represents a chasm of about seventy-five years. The rest of the extant books (XXI–XLV) stretch from 218 to 167 B.C.—one of the most momentous half-centuries in Roman development. Then nearly a hundred missing books dealt with rather more than a century and a half. The gigantic undertaking was accomplished only by assiduous labour. Livy began, as stated, about 27 B.C. He had gone as far as Book IX before 20 B.C.[3] The Civil War in which Pompey figured began with Book CIX and must have been described considerably before the death of Augustus in A.D. 14 to admit of the emperor's criticism. Forty years of writing brought Livy to Book CXX and the events of 43 B.C. This portion was published about the end of Augustus's reign; for from the *Codex Nazarianus* we learn that CXXI appeared after the emperor's death. The author had then passed seventy, and the last three years of his life added twenty-two books. The epitome proves that the closing book, CXLII, carried the record to the death of Drusus in 9 B.C. Beyond a predilection for round numbers, and unless one could believe in some miraculous prescience on Livy's part, there is little to defend

[1] Mart., XIV, cxc:
> 'Pellibus exiguis artatur Liuius ingens
> Quem mea non totum bibliotheca capit.'

[2] Livy, VI. i. 1, 'Quae ab condita urbe Roma ad captam eandem urbem . . . quinque libris exposui.'

[3] When he wrote IX. xviii. 9, the recovery of the standards from the Parthians in 20 B.C. was not known to him.

the assertion often made that his scheme committed him to write 150 books and to include the death of Augustus.

Inquiry into Livy's sources has produced a mass of books and tractates.[1] Plausible conjectures have been made. Here a Valerian exploit may be guessed to come from Valerius Antias; there a Fabian, from Fabius Pictor; there, again, a version of facts singularly favourable to the Carthaginians may point to Caelius Antipater and his Greek source, Silenus, who was a kind of historiographer to Hannibal. But there must be wide uncertainty about a literary pedigree where so many of the originals have perished, and where the author so frequently omits all acknowledgement of borrowing, or leaves his authorities veiled under vague expressions like *inuenio apud quosdam*; *satis constat*; *qui huius pugnae auctores sunt tradunt*, followed by *apud alios inueni*. At times Livy is satisfied with tradition. *Traditur, dicitur, fertur, fama est* are vouchers for much of his record. Of public documents such as the *Annales maximi, libri lintei*, laws, treaties, and inscriptions, he certainly made less use than he might have made. It is even doubtful how far he troubled regularly to go back to the oldest among the chroniclers available. But even if his half-dozen references to Fabius Pictor do not involve in each case first-hand acquaintance, there is no question that directly or indirectly he drew from him. He was indebted to other Romans who wrote in Greek, L. Cincius Alimentus—Livy apparently cites the other Cincius as well—C. Acilius Glabrio, and A. Postumius Albinus, a writer of the second century. M. Porcius Cato might have been found useful for the history of the kings; but it is information about Cato's own career and attitude rather than details about the *Origines* of Italy that Livy appears to have chiefly selected from him. In an age when it was usual—as it is always easiest—to pillage one's immediate predecessors, Livy was certain to borrow most freely from later annalists. It may be safely said that he owes less to authors of the second century like Cassius Hemina, Calpurnius Piso, and Sempronius Tuditanus, than to writers of the age of Sulla, like Licinius Macer, Claudius Quadrigarius, and Aelius Tubero. It is natural to see Varro's influence in the well-known passage on the introduction of *ludi scenici* into Rome.[2] What surprises one is that it should not be traceable in many other places. His contemporary, Dionysius of Halicarnassus, neither influenced Livy nor was influenced by him: both seem to have had recourse independently to the same sources.

---

[1] *E.g.*, F. Lachmann, *De fontibus historiarum T. L.*, 1821; C. Peter, *Das Verh. d. Liuius u. Dionys. Halik. zu einander u. zu d. älteren Annalisten*, 1853; H. Peter, *Hist. Rom. Rell.*, I. ed. 2, 1914, lxxxviii, clxxix, ccxxv, cccxxiv, ccclx; F. Luterbacher, *De fontt. ll. xxi et xxii*, 1875; W. Soltau, *Zur Chronologie der hispanischen Feldzüge 212–206 v. Chr.* ('Ein Beitrag zur Quellenkritik des Liuius') in *Herm.*, xxvi. 408 *sqq.* (1891) and *Die griechischen Quellen in Liuius, xxiii–xxx*, in *Philologus*, liii. 588 *sqq.* (1894).

[2] The point is argued by J. Orendi, *M. T. Varro die Quelle zu Liuius VII. ii*, Progr., 1891.

To one of his forerunners Livy has obligations which assume a perfectly distinct kind of importance. It is only in the case of Polybius that we are able to compare an original with Livy himself. It is probable that these obligations were greater in the fourth and fifth decads, recounting Rome's eastward expansion, than in the third decad, recounting the Hannibalian campaigns.[1] What disappoints one most is Livy's inability to appreciate Polybius's excellence. No doubt the excellence was of a type alien to Livy's genius. Polybius is deliberate and cold: Livy impetuous and rhetorical—so that a crossing of the Alps is with him no unexciting thing, but a daring adventure which stirs the blood with its glowing incident and rhetoric. No doubt, then, Livy supplies a passion and beauty absent from Polybius. Yet when one remembers how sagaciously Polybius unified his inquiries by selecting a well-defined subject—the acquisition of universal dominion by Rome within a couple of generations—and when one remembers his handling of this subject with a conscious austerity, eschewing oratorical embellishment, emphasising the causal nexus among events, carefully weighing authorities and attaining a lofty standard of impartiality, one is astounded to meet in his Roman follower the chilly pronouncement that he is 'an authority in no wise to be despised.'[2]

In any estimate of Livy as historian considerations of his method and his credibility must arise. These are inevitable questions, though we shall find others equally important appertaining to his literary fame. In other words, one must ask not merely 'Had Livy a philosophy of history?' or 'What criteria did he apply in investigation?' but also 'Is he essentially true to the Roman character?'—'Does he suggest the very qualities which made Rome a world-power?'—'Has he composed a narrative which it is impressive and entertaining to read?'; in fine, 'Do we condone his defective science for his excellent art?' At first, it might look as if Livy's reputation had been seriously impaired by the changes wrought in modern times upon the attitude of scholars towards early Roman traditions. Unquestioning acceptance of the traditions had been challenged in France by Pouilly and De Beaufort before the middle of the eighteenth century; but it was Niebuhr, at the beginning of the nineteenth, who first subjected Livy's narrative to rigorous scrutiny. The extreme point of scepticism was touched by Sir G. C. Lewis, who, writing on *The Credibility of Early Roman History* in 1855, declined to

---

[1] Views differ regarding the extent to which Livy followed Polybius: *e.g.*, Hesselbarth, *Historisch-Kritische Untersuch. z. dritt. Dekade des Liuius*, 1889, concludes that Livy has in general borrowed from Polybius; A. v. Breska, *Quellenuntersuch. im 21 bis 23 Buche des L.*, Progr., 1889, argues that Livy does not take Polybius generally as his authority, but rather Caelius, the contention being that similarities between Livy and Polybius are traceable to the Carthaginian source, Silenus, used by Polybius and Caelius. *Cf.* H. A. Sanders *Die Quellencontamination im 21 u. 22 Buche des L.*, 1898.

[2] Livy, XXX. xlv. 5, 'haudquaquam spernendus auctor.' He becomes more appreciative in XXXIII. x. 10, 'Polybium secuti sumus, non incertum auctorem cum omnium Romanarum rerum, tum praecipue in Graecia gestarum.'

accept anything as trustworthy before 280 B.C. —that is, before the war
with Pyrrhus. This is now almost universally deemed too sweeping.
It is true that the destruction of records by the Gauls in 390 left practically no contemporary evidence for the regal period or for a century
after its close; it is true that Livy's oldest authority, Fabius Pictor, was
separated by over five centuries from the reputed date of the foundation
of the city; and it is true that in Livy's stories there is much of the incredible and no little of the inconsistent. Yet all this and more cannot
amount to proving the whole of the early history to be baseless. It may
be admitted that there is shaky ground in Livy subsequent to 390. We
shall immediately realise this when we note the defects in his method,
or rather want of method, when using authorities. Coming down later
than the legendary period to the fourth century B.C., we there find that
Livy's inaccuracies and confusions, due to negligence, or misdirected
patriotism, or reliance on biased authorities, have been fully discussed
by Niebuhr, Mommsen, and Ihne, and are undeniable. His account of
the Samnite Wars contains much that, on close analysis and on comparison with Diodorus, is seen to be intended to cover Roman defeat
and minimise Samnite successes. The narrative of the Caudine disaster
in Book IX is a brilliant piece of writing which bears inaccuracy on its
face. The exploits of Fabius in the war illustrate the common failing of
family chronicles. To take a still later period, his description of the
Punic Wars is by no means immaculate. Yet essential error grows far
less common as the work reaches a period where evidence could be
drawn from Roman, Greek, and even ultimately Carthaginian sources.
It is not unnatural, then, that Ihne, without being blind to Livy's
shortcomings, should particularly regret the loss of his guidance between
292 and 218 owing to the break in the history at Book X.

Nothing is simpler than to make out an apparently damaging case
against Livy. There are grave defects in method and knowledge. That
he was often content with second-hand information when first-hand
sources were available, that he gleaned the harvest of annalists rather
than grubbed among dusty archives himself, that he was slack in veri-
fication, indifferent to topography within his reach —these and other
sins of omission may be fairly laid to his charge. If one thinks of him
beside the historian of *The Decline and Fall*, Livy notably lacks Gibbon's power of sifting evidence or valuing authorities or tracing a causal
connexion —one even misses in him a military training parallel to that
which gave Gibbon reason to declare that the captain of the Hampshire
Grenadiers had 'not been useless to the historian of the Roman Empire.'
When Livy cites a conflict in accounts, his feebleness is most evident.
In the process of evaluation he has no fixed principles. Sometimes he
shirks all solution: then it is for the reader to choose. Sometimes the
author sides with the largest number of his authorities, sometimes with
what he thinks the likeliest story, sometimes —where figures are at

issue—with the most moderate, and at other times with the most Roman. His implicit reliance on second-hand evidence leads him astray till the truth is forced on him. For example, his slothful overtrust in Valerius Antias—whom he so freely used in the first decad—is rudely shaken by the tardy discovery of his exaggerations in numbers and his determination at all costs to glorify the *gens Valeria*. Livy therefore rounds on him, chagrined to realise too late that he has incorporated and published in good faith many of Valerius's mendacities.[1] Again, to ignore patent inconsistencies is a far greater blot than the intrusion of the incredible; and most will allow that to make Romulus's mother a Vestal virgin generations before Numa had, according to Livy's own account,[2] instituted the sisterhood at Rome, is worse history than a circumstantial report of the mysterious passing of the first king.[3] To modern ideas, one of the most provoking things in Livy is his failure to realise the true historical colour and value to be obtained by citing the exact terms of an old document. It is with a gasp of disappointment that one receives his decision not to quote the hymn to Juno by Livius Andronicus, as being too unpolished for Augustan taste.[4] There is, further, the bias of a cramping patriotism that renders him ungenerous towards his country's enemies—Samnites, Carthaginians, and others. There is the taint of partisan bias manifestly favourable to the senate, manifestly prejudiced against tribunician agitations and against the plebeians. The latter, in Livy's view, are not the whole commons of the city fighting for rights, but a rabble bent on clogging the wheels of public policy. Yet the bias does not entirely blind him to patrician faults, just as deference to imperial susceptibilities did not keep him, as we have seen, from doing justice to Pompey or from doubting whether Caesar's birth had been a benefit to Rome. It may be objected also that an imperfect historic sense has tempted him to over-idealise the past. Filled with the spirit of the declining republic, Livy does not divine the unsophisticated rudeness of primitive times any more than Virgil and Ovid do. What one gains poetically hereby, one loses historically. Under one aspect the long pageant which Livy presents is more immobile than it need have been; for while his professed theme is the development of Rome, yet he misses the full conception of her evolution from the simple into the complex.

All this and more may be substantiated. But, in fairness, other considerations have to be reckoned with. It is unreasonable to judge Livy by standards of modern research. It is imperative to take his own aim into account; his work in any case must be appraised as literature no

[1] *E.g.*, XXXIII. x, 'Si Valerio quis credat omnium rerum immodice numerum augenti.'
[2] *Cf.* I. iii. 11 and I. xx. 3.
[3] I. xvi.
[4] XXVII. xxxvii, 'illa tempestate forsitan laudabile rudibus ingeniis, nunc abhorrens et inconditum si referatur.'

less than as history; and he has a right to credit for his positive merits. In the whole question it is absolutely fundamental to grasp the object which the historian set before him in his preface. Livy conceived a colossal scheme. It was no less than an account of the life, customs, men, and training in peace and war, that had made Rome mistress of the world.[1] Such a conception was sufficiently wide to admit of treatment the most philosophic and scientific. But Livy remains wide rather than deep. His interest was avowedly not so much in critical inquiry as in lessons to be drawn from the past for the benefit of private citizens and of politicians.[2] He allots little direct attention to domestic manners. He has no authoritative grasp of the Roman constitution. He assigns no very scientific or romantic reason for the study of antiquity when he commends it as a means of taking one's mind off problems of contemporary deterioration.[3] He is not gifted with penetration into general tendencies; he is, in truth, overmuch in bondage to annalistic arrangement—witness his scrupulous rehearsal of annual prodigies—and neglectful of the extent to which the order of mighty movements must always be confused by strict adherence to the order of the years. In this respect even Sallust might have taught him something. Nor does Livy probe events resolutely to their causes. In this respect he cannot match the reasoning powers which Thucydides brought to bear upon politics and morals. Here Polybius might have taught him as well. Livy does not discover laws of change, or deep-seated motives for actions. His general attitude, consequently, towards historic truth falls far short of standards applicable to modern historians. His realisation of the absence of contemporary records for five centuries does not debar him from entering upon elaborately picturesque accounts of the kings and the early republic.

This brings us to the kernel of the matter. If as historian he sins, he sins wittingly. His is not 'the lie of the soul.' He consciously embellishes history with well-told fables. He is not altogether destitute of critical sagacity. We have seen that he was aware of the deficiency of evidence for the early period owing to the destruction of records by the Gauls.[4] He recognised the supernatural element in Roman origins, but argued that Roman prowess commanded world-wide respect for the appro-

---

[1] *Praef.* 9, 'Ad illa mihi pro se quisque acriter intendat animum, quae uita, qui mores fuerint, per quos uiros quibusque artibus domi militiaeque et partum et auctum imperium sit.'

[2] *Praef.* 10, 'Hoc illud est praecipue in cognitione rerum salubre ac frugiferum, omnis te exempli documenta in inlustri posita monumento intueri: inde tibi tuaeque rei publicae quod imitere capias, inde foedum inceptu, foedum exitu, quod uites.'

[3] *Praef.* 5, 'Ego contra hoc quoque laboris praemium petam, ut me a conspectu malorum quae nostra tot per annos uidit aetas, tantisper certe, dum prisca illa tota mente repeto, auertam.'

[4] VI. i. 10: *cf.* the difficulty felt when his oldest authorities fail him, *e.g.*, III. xxiii, *sub fin.*

priateness of the fabled connexion with Mars.[1] He was not deceived by falsifications in funeral *laudationes* and on the *tituli* of family busts.[2] His proclaimed attitude to the myths is 'neither to affirm nor to refute.'[3] The tale concerning the surprise of Veii by Romans bursting from a mine upon the king in the act of sacrifice is most justifiably ruled melo-dramatic by Livy; but, declining to reject it, he institutes the test of the plausible — 'In matters so ancient I should be content if what resembles truth be taken for true.'[4] He has, in short, the carelessness of the artistic temperament, but he does not wilfully falsify. He projected and achieved the composition of a narrative unfolding the whole course of Roman history in a manner so luminous and picturesque that readers might derive delight and benefit from the record of ancestral fortunes and misfortunes.

This does more than explain his attitude to the distant past. It gives to that attitude an ideal value. To this extent even the fabulous in his history contains truth — it indicates the belief of Augustan Rome about the Roman past. If Livy, prodigy-like, could have anticipated the methods of modern investigation, he would have been proportionately less representative of his age. It must always be allowed that he remains artist rather than historian, valuing the effective more highly than the scientific. However weak the foundations of a great deal in him, his literary charm stands untouched and untouchable by subsequent researches. His stories may be fabulous but they fascinate. And it must be remembered that his very art attains a truth of its own. He possessed gifts of real historical worth — the gift of reverence for the majesty of Rome; the gift of enthusiasm for olden times, olden heroes, olden virtues; the gift of imagination through sympathy which feels, even if imperfectly, the spirit of the past.[5] It will not do to leave as the final conviction one which Taine's essay inclines to suggest — that Livy was a rhetorician turned historian, who never shook off rhetorical faults. The record is copiously blended with the rhetorical, the poetic, and the incredible. But the question remains — does the total impression possess verisimilitude? Broadly it does. Apart from permanent value as enshrin-ing the view of the past prevalent in the Augustan age, Livy's history, fictions notwithstanding, is unsurpassed in its fidelity to the national

[1] *Praef.* 7, 'Datur haec uenia antiquitati ut miscendo humana diuinis primordia urbium augustiora faciat,' etc.
[2] VIII. xl, 'Vitiatam memoriam funebribus laudibus reor, falsisque imaginum titulis, dum familiae ad se quaeque famam rerum gestarum honor-umque fallente mendacio trahunt.'
[3] *Praef.* 6, 'Quae ante conditam condendamue urbem poeticis magis decora fabulis quam incorruptis rerum gestarum monumentis traduntur, ea nec adfirmare nec refellere in animo est.'
[4] V. xxi. 9, 'Sed in rebus tam antiquis si quae similia ueri sint pro ueris accipiantur, satis habeam: haec ad ostentationem scenae gaudentis miraculis aptiora quam ad fidem neque adfirmare neque refellere operae pretium est.'
[5] XLIII. xiii. 2, 'Ceterum et mihi, uetustas res scribenti, nescio quo pacto antiquus fit animus.'

character. If after perusal one feels admiration for Roman constancy, discipline, and wisdom, one has implicitly divined the secret of Roman success. The cause is conveyed and understood without being formulated.

If Livy lacks scientific method, he at least entertains certain concepts which impart an aspect of unity to his work. To be so keenly alert in marking (even with a degree of idealising overstatement) the prominent traits in the Roman character, such as the manliness, piety, and honour which contributed towards the building up of national greatness, implied a synthetic principle. Another synthetic conception was that of the development of a people under divine dispensation. The idea is comparable with Virgil's of the mission of Rome among the nations — though Livy's view is narrowed by his conviction of Rome's decadence. It is not always clear how definite Livy's belief was in a guiding and unifying power of Fate or Providence behind the procession of his facts. In general terms, it is the case that he held the partly Stoic, partly patriotic theory of the providential ordering of Roman affairs. This is illustrated by frequent reference to soothsaying and the Sibylline books. Presumably a mind so essentially religious[1] as Livy's sympathised with Camillus's creed touching the divine hand in Roman history.[2] But that he ever worked out the relation of the human agent to the controlling power is not to be imagined. Man seems to have now more, now less freedom. At one time human action plays an appreciable part —'gods and men' combined to save Rome from the last disgrace of living on as a people ransomed from the Gauls;[3] and, again, the best laid schemes of men are those which go least agley, because luck generally attends them.[4] On the other hand, when human aid fails, a Delphic oracle may be needed to throw light on Fate;[5] it is apparently inevitable Destiny pressing hard on Rome which prompts the Fabii to forget international usage and embroil their country with the Gauls;[6] and it is Fortune who blinds Rome so utterly that she fails to adopt against her new Gallic foe such measures as she had adopted against the less dangerous Veientines.[7]

[1] It was once thought needful to clear Livy from the charge of superstition: see *Adeisidaemon, sive Titus Livius a superstitione vindicatus: in qua Dissertatione probatur Livium Historicum in Sacris, Prodigiis, et Ostentis Romanorum enarrandis, haudquaquam fuisse credulum aut superstitiosum . . . autore J. Tolando*, 1709.
[2] V. li. 5, '. . . inuenietis omnia prospera euenisse sequentibus deos, aduersa spernentibus.'
[3] V. xlix. 1, 'Sed dique et homines prohibuere redemptos uiuere Romanos.'
[4] V. xix. 8, 'Omnia ibi summa ratione consilioque acta fortuna etiam, ut fit, secuta est.'
[5] V. xvi. 8, 'Iamque Romani, desperata ope humana, fata et deos spectabant,' etc.
[6] V. xxxvi. 6, 'Ibi, iam urgentibus Romanam urbem fatis, legati contra ius gentium arma capiunt.'
[7] V. xxxvii. 1, 'Cum tanta moles mali instaret (adeo obcaecat animos fortuna . . .),' etc.

It is in the art rather than in the science of history that Livy's mastery is best assured. Here the striking features are his power of graphic description, his dramatic contrivances, his management of orations, his attention to character, and his noble language. The most cursory glance along the procession of his events reveals a crowd of impressive situations and figures, so that the very recalling of them is a pleasure. There are books that stand out beyond others, as in the opening decad the first and the fifth do; but not one of the first ten books lacks its thrilling moments, and, at the risk of seeming merely to catalogue, one is tempted into passing some of them rapidly through the mind. In Book I it is almost impossible to particularise; but one thinks instinctively of the rescue of the divine twins from the river, the seizure of the Sabine women, the coming of Lucumo from Etruria to try his fortune in Rome, the exhibition of thought-reading by the augur Attus Navius before the king, the triple conflict between the Curiatii and Horatii, and many other deeds of wonder, or guile, or violence. No reader of Book II could forget the dread execution of the sons of the consul Brutus under their father's superintendence; or 'how Horatius kept the bridge'; or the parable whereby Menenius Agrippa reasoned with the commons on strike; or the interview between Coriolanus and his mother in his camp near Rome; or the tumultuous enthusiasm attendant upon the march of the Fabian clan out of Rome. In Book III the story of the deputies who are sent to announce the conferring of the dictatorship upon Cincinnatus and who find him working in the fields, is a story which loses no whit of its vividness through being told as a lesson for those who lay excessive store on riches. The arrogance and downfall of the decemvirs is then coupled with the nefarious design upon Virginia. Book IV presents such vivid spectacles as the summary slaying of Spurius Maelius and the single combat by which Cossus won the *spolia opima*. Book V sparkles with incident none the less telling because fable-encrusted: the conclusion of the siege of Veii—the Trojan War of Roman history; the bickerings between the classes; the heroism, but also the unpopularity, of Camillus; and the exciting doings of the Gauls in Rome. Book VI would be memorable even if it contained nothing more than the execution of M. Manlius. That he should be identified with the saviour of the Capitol and thrown from the Tarpeian Rock—within sight of his valiant exploit—are details which contribute to the dramatic effect what they subtract from historic truth. But there are other excellent things, such as the thrilling tale about the dawning of a sister's jealousy which had momentous political issues in the Licinian rogations.[1] 'No greater Roman good is there than arms and valour,' says M. Curtius in Book VII, as he devotes himself for his country by plunging on horseback into the yawning abyss at the forum. Then Livy pleasantly reminds us of the secret of half his charm: 'now when length

[1] VI. xxxiv.

of time precludes all certainty of evidence, we must stand by the rumour of tradition. It is not that pains would be grudged (*cura non deesset*),' he adds, 'only, such pains would be useless for investigating the truth of things so remote.' So the pageant of story proceeds. In Book VIII he is at his best in relating how T. Manlius, who had slain a Latin in a duel, was executed under the consular sentence of his father for fighting against orders. The situation recalls an earlier one; but it is characteristic of Livy to handle similar scenes without monotony. In the same book the well-nigh unrelenting anger of Papirius Cursor, as a stickler for military discipline against his insubordinate but successful Master of Horse, is handled with marvellous vigour. Book IX presents as perhaps its best remembered thing the disaster to the Roman arms at the Caudine Forks; but it is also vastly interesting to note how, in the comparison drawn between the mightiest of conquerors and Papirius, national bias blinds Livy to the real greatness of Alexander the Great, as it blinds him afterwards to the real greatness of Hannibal. After Book X, from which the battle of Sentinum is a typical passage, the first gap in the history occurs. When we resume our reading in Book XXI, Rome is within an ace of grappling with Hannibal. It would be futile to attempt a selection of all the powerful things in books so familiar as the Hannibalian; but the dramatic management of the prelude to declared hostilities calls for special note. The sworn hatred cherished by Hannibal against Rome, the sketch of his character, the attack on Saguntum, and the thrilling choice of war in the Carthaginian senate, together form a worthy prologue to scenes such as the crossing of the Alps, the battle at the Trasimene Lake, the appalling storm that blocked Hannibal when making for the Apennines, the disastrous field of Cannae, and the turning-point of this particular drama in Maharbal's famous rebuke to his commander — *Vincere scis, Hannibal: uictoria uti nescis.*[1] So through a chequered record of panic and cool-headedness, repeated failures, and dogged resistance, the Roman actors play their part and tire out the invader. The Roman capture of Syracuse is the memorable feature of Book XXV, and Scipio's continence of Book XXVI. After the third decad the interest is less intense. Perhaps the falling off is in the subject-matter; for one feels that neither the personalities nor the issues are so great as in the contest between Rome and Carthage. Yet, needless to say, there is most graphic writing: for instance, in the conference between Philip and Quinctius Flamininus attended by his Hellenic allies;[2] in the defeat of Macedon at Cynoscephalae,[3] as later in the victory over Perseus at Pydna;[4] in the magnanimity with which Flamininus during the hour of victory over Macedon remembered the imperial principle *parcere subiectis*;[5] in the excited '*encore*' which welcomed the Roman proclamation of Greek freedom at the Isthmian Games;[6] in Scipio's

[1] XXII. li.   [2] XXXII. xxxii–xxxvi.   [3] XXXIII. vii–x.
[4] XLIV. xl–xlii.   [5] XXXIII. xii.   [6] XXXIII. xxxii.

interview with Hannibal at Ephesus and their discussion concerning famous commanders;[1] in Hannibal's advice to King Antiochus;[2] in the sensational detection and punishment of the secret Bacchanalian enormities, related in connexion with the threatened ruin from which a devoted freedwoman saves her lover; and in the noble portraiture of the many-sided abilities and sterling worth of the great plebeian censor, Cato.[3]

Quintilian credited Livy with 'indescribable eloquence' in his speeches.[4] Delivered on home politics, on international diplomacy, or by a general to his troops, they vividly mark a crisis or illumine a character.[5] Here Livy found freest scope for his rhetoric. They are undisguisedly anachronistic. The utterances of Romulus or the impressive speech on the lips of Lucretia about to die can deceive no one. All the same, speeches contribute enormously to Livy's elucidation of character—for example, of Camillus piously horrified at the agitation to abandon Rome for Veii; of Papirius Cursor, theatrically incensed at his officer's successful defiance of orders; of Scipio, an egotist semi-puritan and semi-romantic; of Cato, austere and scathing in his denunciation of the 'monstrous regiment of women' and the social depravity foreshadowed by proposed repeal of the Oppian law.[6] What imparts exceptional animation to senatorial debates or tribunician harangues in Livy is his excellent ability to state both sides of a question. Similarly, if he refrains from censuring in so many words the quibbles wherewith the Romans repudiated the agreement concluded at the Caudine Forks, it is because he has made the retorts of the injured Samnites sufficiently eloquent to present their case.[7] The more direct description of character may be illustrated by his sketch of Hannibal:[8]

> When Hannibal was sent to Spain, his arrival immediately drew the whole army's attention. Veterans fancied that Hamilcar, in his youth, was restored to them; they observed the old strength in the look, the old fire in the eyes, the old cast of features in the face. Soon he contrived that to be his father's son was least among many factors in winning popularity. Never was temperament better fitted

[1] XXXV. xiv.

[2] XXXVI. vii sqq.

[3] XXXIX. viii sqq. and xl.

[4] Inst. Or., X. i. 101, '... cum in narrando mirae iucunditatis clarissimique candoris, tum in contionibus supra quam enarrari potest eloquentem.'

[5] The use of speeches in Livy and others is classified and illustrated in W. Soltau's art. on 'Der geschichtliche Wert der Reden bei den alten Historikern,' in Neue Jahrbr. f. d. kl. Altert., vol. vii. 10, 1901.

[6] For these several instances see V. li–liv; VIII. xxx–xxxv; XXVI. xli and l; XXXIV. ii–iv.

[7] The offended dignity of Pontius culminates in his refusal to detain the Roman prisoners or to release the Roman state from its obligation: 'haec ludibria religionum non pudere in lucem proferre, et uix pueris dignas ambages senes ac consulares fallendae fidei exquirere! i, lictor, deme uincla Romanis; moratus sit nemo quo minus ubi uisum fuerit abeant.' IX. xi. 12.

[8] XXI. iv. 1–9. Another typical piece is the character of Cato, XXXIX. xl.

for the most widely different duties of obedience and command. Thus one could not easily have decided whether he was higher favourite with general or with troops—Hasdrubal liked to appoint no one else when occasion called for gallant and energetic action; the soldiers never displayed more confidence or pluck under any other leader. To the acme of fearlessness in undertaking risks, he added the acme of resourcefulness in the thick of them. No toil could weary his body or subdue his spirit. Heat and cold he stood equally well: his allowance of food and drink was limited by natural desire, not by pleasure: his hours of wakefulness and sleep were not regulated by daytime or night. What remained after completing work was given to rest. It was a rest wooed by no soft bed or quiet surroundings. Many a man caught sight of him wrapped in his military cloak, stretched on the ground amidst the sentries and outposts of the soldiers. In dress there was nothing to mark him from his comrades: but his arms and horses were conspicuous. He was at once far the best soldier whether on horseback or on foot. First to advance to the charge, he was last to retire from an engagement. To counterbalance all those high qualities, he was a man who had gigantic faults—inhuman cruelty, treachery more than Punic, no truth, no reverence, no fear of the gods, no regard for an oath, no scruples whatsoever.

All round, Livy is not just to Hannibal. Yet in the last words which he puts into the exile's mouth there perhaps lurks the historian's condemnation of the unchivalrous persecution whereby the Romans hounded him to suicide:

> Let us free the Roman people from their protracted anxiety, since they deem it too long to wait for an old man's death. It will not be a great, not a memorable victory that Flamininus will win over one who is unarmed and betrayed. How much the character of the Roman people has altered, this very day will furnish proof. Their fathers gave timely warning to King Pyrrhus, their armed foe, who had his army in Italy—to beware of poison. The Romans of to-day have sent an ambassador of consular rank to suggest to Prusias a villainous murder of his guest.[1]

Livy's battle-pieces are those of an artist, not of a soldier. They entertain rather than instruct. In this way they present a most striking contrast in method and effect to those narrated by a straightforward military historian like Caesar. The vivid qualities of which Livy had such mastery are particularly visible in his descriptions of violent action, of panic, or sack. It would be difficult to mention any finer

---

[1] XXXIX. li: ' "Liberemus," inquit, "diuturna cura populum Romanum, quando mortem senis exspectare longum censent. Nec magnam nec memorabilem ex inermi proditoque Flamininus uictoriam feret. Mores quidem populi Romani quantum mutauerint, uel hic dies argumento erit. Horum patres Pyrrho regi, hosti armato, exercitum in Italia habenti, ut a ueneno caueret, praedixerunt: hi legatum consularem, qui auctor esset Prusiae per scelus occidendi hospitis, miserunt.' "

examples of his picturesque power than the four chapters[1] of Book V
on the arrival of the Gauls. It is a momentous crisis worthily described
in sentences typical of his best manner. The picture is largely psychological as well as physical. It contains the Gallic hesitancy in entering
Rome; the grief and consternation among the inhabitants; the prolonged
agony of waiting for the deferred attack; the resolve of the younger
Romans to hold the citadel; the commending to their valour 'of the last
remaining fortunes of a city for three hundred and sixty years victorious
in every war'; the flight of the common folk; the hasty saving of the holy
things; the amazement of the Gauls when they enter a city such as they
had never seen before; their nervous dread of a possible snare in the
silent streets and houses; the hunt for plunder; the half-respectful gaze
of the barbarians at the seniors sitting in their homes fully robed 'and
wearing, in addition to decorations and apparel of more than human
dignity, the semblance of gods in the majesty betokened by their
solemn faces and looks.' It was at this point that curiosity tempted a Gaul
to stroke the beard of one of these reverend ex-magistrates; an angry
blow of retaliation from the ivory staff followed; the massacre began.

After the butchery of the notables, not a man was spared: houses
were plundered, and fire set to them when they had been ransacked.[2]

Where Livy best sustains the pitch of his dignity and energy is in the
Hannibalic wars. Passages of extreme beauty prove the pains bestowed
on the composition. The indications of the fragments are too slight to
form a satisfactory basis of comparison, but ancient opinion suggests
that his later books were somewhat marred by a degenerate prolixity.
However regrettable, from the standpoint of historical matter, may be
the loss of the later decads—for which Livy could have employed a
notable accession of first-hand evidence—it may be questioned whether,
from the standpoint of style, it is not the very best of him which has

---

[1] V. xxxix–xlii.
[2] The Latin may be given from V. xli. 4: 'Galli, et quia interposita nocte a
contentione pugnae remiserant animos et quod nec in acie ancipiti usquam
certauerant proelio nec tum impetu aut ui capiebant urbem, sine ira, sine
ardore animorum ingressi postero die urbem patente Collina porta in forum
perueniunt, circumferentes oculos ad templa deum arcemque solam belli
speciem tenentem. Inde modico relicto praesidio, nequis in dissipatos ex arce
aut Capitolio impetus fieret, dilapsi ad praedam uacuis occursu hominum uiis
pars in proxima quaeque tectorum agmine ruunt, pars ultima, uelut ea demum
intacta et referta praeda, petunt. Inde rursus ipsa solitudine absterriti, ne qua
fraus hostilis uagos exciperet, in forum ac propinqua foro loca conglobati
redibant; ubi eos, plebis aedificiis obseratis, patentibus atriis principum, maior
prope cunctatio tenebat aperta quam clausa inuadendi: adeo haud secus quam
uenerabundi intuebantur in aedium uestibulis sedentes uiros, praeter ornatum
habitumque humano augustiorem, maiestate etiam quam uultus grauitasque oris
prae se ferebat, simillimos dis. Ad eos uelut simulacra uersi cum starent, M. Papirius unus ex iis dicitur Gallo barbam suam, ut tum omnibus promissa erat, per-
mulcenti scipione eburneo in caput incusso iram mouisse; atque ab eo initium
caedis ortum, ceteros in sedibus suis trucidatos. Post principum caedem nulli
deinde mortalium parci diripi tecta, exhaustis inici ignes.'

survived. His genius was of a kind to which distance in time must have yielded freer play. It was essentially poetic. His strength lies in using rich and luminous phrases to recompose a drama long since past and to reanimate its actors. The resultant life in his narrative has a poetic truth. Because Livy was poetic he was inestimably wiser and truer than Dionysius, whose early history is surcharged with details which prove their own falsity. Livy produced a much more real impression by avoiding the boredom of pedantic *minutiae*. His poetic outlook upon things is reflected in his language. Like the *Annals* of Tacitus, the preface opens with a metrical movement (*Facturusne operae pretium sim*), sounding, as it were, a note in unison with that poetic ring in the earliest legends which gives to the first book a permanent attraction. In other places, by bits of hexameter verse,[1] by alliterations,[2] by the use of poetic and sometimes distinctly Virgilian words,[3] Livy illustrates the hold which *poeticus color* was now obtaining upon Latin prose.

Livy marks the culmination of the periodic style in history. He holds in the evolution of prose a place analogous to that held by Virgil in the evolution of poetry. Livy's master in prose was Cicero. His general preference was for the flowing style—the Isocratean rather than the Thucydidean. Thus, although he varies his stately periods with short, lively sentences—especially in describing character—he avoids the abruptness of Thucydides's Greek and Sallust's Latin. It is a rich style meriting Quintilian's ascription of *lactea ubertas*. Quintilian,[4] too, where he compares Sallust with Thucydides, seems to find in Livy a Herodotean transparency. But the *clarissimus candor* of Livy is different from the *clarissimus candor* of Herodotus. Livy has not Herodotus's simplicity. Nor is he so clear and straightforward as the great Roman speaker whom he followed. Cicero had to be plain to hearers. Livy wrote for erudite readers. His sentences are often full of subordinate clauses wonderfully dovetailed together. Not infrequently they are too involved for an auditor to follow. Elaborate intricacy sometimes results in a curious subordination of the main idea. When we pass from the build of the sentence to language,[5] we find in Livy distinct traces of the

---

[1] *E.g.*, XXII. l. 10, 'Haec ubi dicta dedit stringit gladium cuneoque facto per medios.'

[2] *E.g.*, V. li. 10, 'foedus ac fidem fefellerunt'; VI. xxii. 7, 'uegetum ingenium in uiuido pectore uigebat, uirebatque integris sensibus'; VII. vi. 11, 'potuisse patres plebiscito pelli.'

[3] *E.g.*, phrases like 'ingruente fato,' V. xxxii. 7; 'urgente fato,' XXII. xliii. 9 (*cf. Aen.*, ii. 653, 'fatoque urgenti incumbere'); 'omnis culpae exsortem,' XXII. xliv. 7 (*cf. Aen.*, vi. 428, 'dulcis uitae exsortes'); XXII. xxxix. 17, 'una salutis est uia' (*cf. Aen.*, vi. 96, 'uia prima salutis'); and such poetic words as *fatiloquus, fatalis, sospitare, numen, cognominis*, adj. (V. xxxiv, 9, *cf. Aen.*, vi. 383), *prosecuisset* (in ritual, V. xxi. 8), *sata* ('crops'), *fides* ('proof'). Other instances are given in Cluer and Matheson's ed. of v-vii. in excursus on Livy's Latin.

[4] *Inst. Or.*, X. i. 101.

[5] See O. Riemann, *op. cit.*; L. Kühnast, *Hauptpunkte d. Livian. Syntax*, ed. 2, 1872.

changes in syntax, idiom, and vocabulary which had set in since Cicero wrote. This was no mere 'Patavinity,' such as Pollio detected in him, and which, in any case, was no longer obvious in Quintilian's day, when the Latin of the capital was virtually that of all educated Italy. There was less than half a century between the birth of Cicero and that of Livy: there was more than a century between the birth of Livy and that of Tacitus. Livy, as an index to the changes coming over prose, stands appropriately, both in time and manner, between the republican and the 'Silver' Latinity. On the one hand, there is much to recall Cicero in Livy's sonorous dignity and fulness almost to redundancy, his wealth of colour, his gift of pictorial vision, and his plethora of rhetorical exclamations and apostrophes. On the other hand, there is much that heralds the Latin of Tacitus. In fondness for striking and artificial turns of expression, and in his quest after variety in preference to symmetry, Livy marks the departure from Ciceronian uniformity. These are unmistakable signs of approximation towards the Silver Age. The poetic element in Livy already illustrated proves that the strict delimitation of the provinces of prose and poetry was no longer observed. The exact and logical distinctions between indicative and subjunctive moods become blurred—another sure sign of later Latin. Further, his literary prose borrows words and constructions from the popular speech[1] which Cicero and Caesar, except when writing informal notes, would have avoided. The old annalists whom he consulted contribute their tale of archaisms[2] to his diction: and this reintroduction of old words was accompanied by an opposite tendency— the discovery of fresh meanings for accepted words[3] and the invention of words entirely new.[4] All these phenomena are indicative of a process of gradual alteration; and some of them contain the seeds of decay. Livy's style is the work of a scholar who is partly influenced by the inevitable development of the language owing to circumstances and persons independent of him, and who is partly able to leave upon it his own individual impress as an artist.

The fame which Livy won in his own day was increased by the admiration of his immediate successors. The 'fairest appraiser of all great talents,' as the elder Seneca called him, was sure to find enthusiastic readers.[5] His eloquence is what the younger Seneca emphasised:

[1] E.g., *quaerere si* for *quaerere num*; *forsan* for *forsitan*; *oppido* for *maxime*, etc.

[2] E.g., *supplicia* for *supplicationes*; *tempestas* for *tempus*; *occipere* for *coepisse*, etc.

[3] Such old words with fresh meanings are *fauor*, 'popularity'; *titulus*, 'pretext'; *celeber*, 'famous' (applied to a person); *durare*, to endure.

[4] At least there are words which we do not find in Latin before Livy. He appears to like creating abstract nouns in -*us*, agent nouns in -*tor*, adjectives in -*bundus* and -*osus*, adverbs in -*im*, and frequentative verbs (see J. Brown, Introd. to Livy I).

[5] In reference to Livy's high estimate of Cicero, Sen., *Suas.*, vi. 22: 'ut est natura candidissimus omnium magnorum ingeniorum aestimator T. Liuius, plenissimum Ciceroni testimonium reddidit.'

R

and in one of two passages where Tacitus alludes to the same quality he adds signal honesty.[1] Quintilian, besides the tributes already mentioned, remarks on his psychological power.[2] It was a popularity with readers, rivalled only by Virgil's, that roused Caligula's insane desire to exclude both Livy and Virgil from all libraries.[3] In Domitian's reign one of the counts in the indictment against Mettius Pompusianus was that he carried with him the speeches of kings and generals excerpted from Livy.[4] Rhetoricians took such speeches as models. Latin historians like Valerius Maximus and Florus, and military experts like Frontinus, quarried in him. So did writers in Greek—Plutarch in his *Lives* went back to Polybius and Livy; Dio Cassius to Caelius and Livy. Poets like Lucan and Silius used him for their historical epics. Even the call for a compendium proved interest. It was a condensed Livy from which later writers like Julius Obsequens, Cassiodorius, and Eutropius drew. Yet the complete work, now divided into decads, lived on through the age of compendia and extracts. Priscian in the sixth century still quotes from the text direct. Thereafter Livy vanishes from sight till he reappears in John of Salisbury in the twelfth century. From that point onwards—in Dante, among the scholars of the Renaissance, and in more modern times—Livy's place has been secure.[5] He still represents, as he represented in his own day, the empire of the past over the present. Pessimistic regarding contemporary society and less prophetic than Virgil of the imperial destiny, Livy had given his heart to earlier times. At the threshold of empire it was he who set the very imprint of Rome upon his prose-epic of the republic.

[1] Sen., *De Ira*, I. xx. 6, 'apud disertissimum uirum, Liuium'; Tac., *Agric.*, x, 'Liuius ueterum, Fabius Rusticus recentium eloquentissimi auctores'; *Ann.*, IV. xxxiv, 'T. Liuius eloquentiae ac fidei praeclarus in primis.'

[2] *Inst. Or.*, X. i. 101.

[3] Suet., *Calig.*, xxxiv.

[4] Suet., *Domit.*, x, '. . . contionesque regum ac ducum ex Tito Liuio circumferret.'

[5] On the interest in Livy at the Renaissance, and on the gradual recovery of the extant books, see Schanz, *Röm. Lit.*, § 327.

Chapter VII

EPILOGUE

The evolution of Rome – Literature and the national life – Augustan cosmopolitanism and Dionysius of Halicarnassus – Other foreign authors: Timagenes, Juba, Nicolaus, Strabo – The actual achievement reached before the close of the Golden Age – The field left for Silver Latin – Distinction and continuity of periods.

THE course of Roman literature admirably illustrates the onward march of the national life. The evolution of Rome is among the most marvellous chapters in human civilisation. With great appropriateness it is the actual subject of Livy's history, in which Augustan prose culminates. What had once been the forest clearings and hill settlements of peasants, and then for centuries merely one of many city-states in Italy, had become the headquarters of a world-power. The early altars to tribal deities had long since given place to elaborate temples, and the native religion was now contaminated with strange imported worships. Primeval simplicity had in the process of conquest changed into the luxury that alarmed Horace and Livy. It was the outcome of contact with the East. One portion of the price paid for sovereign sway and for the heightening of intellectual and aesthetic standards was a frequent abandonment of the old plain virtues in favour of undermining vices. The evolution which the community underwent in power, religion, and morals is strictly parallel to its evolution in thought, language, art, and letters. The expansion which set Rome as arbiter of destiny over all the countries around the Mediterranean is no more amazing than the development from the uncouth stiffness of archaic Latin to the magical beauty in Virgil or the verbal agility displayed by Ovid.

The product, in the main, of writers belonging to or patronised by an aristocratic minority, this literature at the same time forms a surprisingly full index to the total life and growth of the social organism. However aristocratic, however remote from a popular audience the literature at some periods might be, it was yet subject to the same general conditions as acted upon the common people. The national *ethos*, though graded and differentiated, was one, just as the language, though graded and differentiated, was one. Certainly all the most important

483

aspects of Rome appear in the works of her poets, orators, and historians. The literature might be comparatively seldom in direct touch with humble folk; still, it runs in the full current of the national life. This largely accounts for its masculine vigour. It is rarely a mere bookish product. There are exceptions, but in great part it is written by men of affairs or by men interested in affairs. Hence, although some portions of Roman literature owe much to Alexandria, Alexandrinism could never have been characteristic of it as a whole. History in the making, and society in its relations and needs, stimulate the writers of Rome more vitally than history and society in books. This is broadly true from Naevius and Ennius onwards. So, then, one of the least illuminating modes of approaching Virgil and Horace is to overstress their opposition to Alexandrinism. No deliberate recoil on their part was required. Virgil had for *Georgics* and *Aeneid* themes based on actuality which called for no frippery or conceits. With all the idealism that is in him he was yet a keen observer of the new empire, and the supremely national significance of the *Aeneid* is due to his cognisance of a great present and future worthily united to a heroic past. Horace could decline official employment, but he was intensely interested in his surroundings. His common sense and alert outlook yielded him subjects unbeholden to Alexandrian *réchauffés*. The love of polish, wherein he resembles the Alexandrians, induced his under-estimation of the old Latin literature; but Horace is strongly national whenever he considers the social phenomena of his day and the imperial attitude thereto.

One of the outstanding features of Augustan Rome —testifying at once to its complex life and to its imperial eminence —was its cosmopolitanism. A babel of tongues and a medley of religions came with crowds of men of different nationalities —Greek from Europe and Asia, Thracian, Gaul, Spaniard, Moor, Egyptian, Chaldean, Jew, and Syrian. As Juvenal said later, the Orontes was already a tributary of the Tiber. The cosmopolitan atmosphere of the imperial city has no clearer illustration than the number of foreign scholars who made a home in it. The history, philosophy, and rhetoric of the Augustan age were, of course, not confined to works in Latin. There were many learned aliens who, as visitors to Rome, or at least as subjects of the empire, felt the stimulus of the times and contributed to literature. It was but the continuation of a phenomenon noted in the preceding century. Foreign lecturers and thinkers, especially from Greek lands, had been steadily on the increase. A few leading names will serve as examples. Following Diodorus the Sicilian, author of a *Universal History*, who stands on the threshold of the Augustan age, we have the representative name of Dionysius from Halicarnassus. Coming to the capital not long after Actium, he remained there till his death sometime after 7 B.C., enjoying the intimacy of distinguished men like Q. Aelius Tubero and the rhetorician Caecilius. An admiring student of Roman history, he wrote his

works in Greek. Of twenty books of his *Roman Archaeology*, about half
survive. Like Polybius, he rears a monument to Roman greatness, but
in a very different manner. Dionysius is in history uncritical and ver-
bose. He lavishes elaborate colour upon a legend or an imaginary
speech. He enjoys illustrating the mythological origins of a people
whom his own compatriots had unfairly considered 'barbarians.'
Enough survives to prove that he was really much more effective as a
literary critic than as an historian. His literary treatises included an *Art
of Rhetoric*, *On the Composition of Words*, *Criticism of the Ancients*
(largely on Greek poets and historians), *Comments on Ancient Orators*,
and *On Thucydides*.

Rhetoric and history were often combined. Timagenes, the rhetorician, was induced to write upon Augustus's exploits. Juba, king of
Mauretania, thanks to the development of his ability by his early
training at Rome, composed treatises in Greek on a wide range of subjects. These included, besides works on grammar and botany, *A History
of Africa*, *A History of Rome*, *A History of Arabia*, *A History of the
Theatre*, and *A History of Painting*. Nicolaus of Damascus, once tutor
to the children of Antony and Cleopatra, was another prolific author –
on philosophy as well as rhetoric and history. King Herod, who found
him a useful adviser in his Hellenising policy, encouraged Nicolaus to
compose a massive *Universal History*, now lost. Of its hundred and
forty-four books a few fragments remain. We have, however, considerable portions of his autobiography and his declamatory panegyric
upon Augustus. He enjoyed a large measure of the emperor's respect.
The probability that the treatise *On the Sublime*, ascribed to Longinus,
may belong to the Augustan age has been already mentioned. In Strabo
the age produced one of the great geographers of antiquity. While his
history, in continuation of Polybius, has perished, the seventeen books
of his *Geographica* have come down nearly complete as a valuable
account of the Roman world of his day, and as an indication of the widespread blessings of a systematised administration. Strabo was a highly
educated Cappadocian who had travelled extensively in Asia Minor and
Egypt. During a stay of some duration in Rome he doubtless acquired
information about countries, like Spain, which he had not visited. His
design was to attract a cultured class of readers, especially those engaged
in the civil service. His method is, in consequence, to avoid dry lists of
geographical names, and to enrich his description of the physical
characteristics of a country with sketches of noteworthy figures and
events in its history. After two introductory books on questions of
general physical geography, such as the shape and size of the earth,
Strabo devotes eight books to European lands, six to Asia, and the last
book to Egypt and Libya.

A conspectus of the Golden Age affords fair opportunity for surveying rapidly what so far was the actual achievement in Roman literature. In some departments the highest mark had been reached before the first century B.C. This is true of the drama, comic and tragic. The literary comedy came to be outbidden in popular favour by vulgar spectacles: tragedy died perhaps in part from an excessive quest after wholesomeness in preference to breadth and beauty. In the Augustan age neither Fundanius could revive the one nor Varius and Ovid the other. But it was in the Golden Age that most forms attained their zenith. Roman literature had never again such triumphs to show as those won by Cicero in oratory, by Lucretius in didactic, by Virgil in epic, by Catullus and Horace in lyric, by Tibullus, Propertius, and Ovid in elegy, and by Livy in historical prose of the periodic style. In realms of knowledge the Augustan age showed particular capacity for summing up the results obtained by previous generations. This is true of criticism, philology, and law, and it is illustrated in the works of Hyginus, Fenestella, and Verrius.

Yet there was a large field left open for subsequent writers under the empire. Under verse it is mainly in satire and epigram, under prose it is mainly in rhetoric, history, philosophy, and various special branches of learning, that the Silver Age can claim to produce work comparable to what had preceded. Nothing can eclipse Juvenal for energy or Pliny's letters for social bearing. With the decay of chastened form there was often a decided gain in human interest. This is illustrated by the vigorous freshness of those tales of adventure whereby Petronius and Apuleius anticipated the picaresque romance. In many ways the changing environment must be taken into reckoning. The prose of Seneca, or the latest prose of Tacitus, original in piquancy, as it is with both, must be judged by standards inapplicable to the Ciceronian prose. Like a great proportion of the Silver Latin, it is related to the educational system of the times. The training in rhetoric brought faults in its train; but it had the signal merit of creating such a capacity for the effective use of language in speeches and in writings as probably no official class other than the Roman has ever attained all round. Further, the repressive measures adopted by many of the emperors have to be remembered among the factors which hampered the free growth of literature by limiting the choice and treatment of themes. This perforce generated a tone different from that which characterised the best literature of the republic.

That portion of Latin literature which culminated in the Golden Age deserves separate study, such as this work has attempted, not because it is organically separate from what followed, but because it exemplifies all that is greatest in Roman character and Roman power of expression. The literature of the Silver Age, whether investigated to the times of the Antonines or carried on to include Ausonius, is the same with differences. The same language too persists—amid changes due to new environment — whether it is the vehicle of patristic theology or of scholastic learning. It is the task of the historian of literature to observe and, if possible, explain the manifold and undeniable differences which exist between the periods, but not to suggest that the differences brought Latin literature to an end in the second century or the fourth, or even much later. So, if one proceeds to examine Roman literature and intellectual movements from the Augustan *régime* to the days of Marcus Aurelius, one does not imply that there was a scientific and absolute break at the age of the Antonines. But there was an apparent break. This apparent break may be said to justify a separate study of the Latin literature of the first two centuries A.D., just as a previous natural break justifies a separate study of the literature up to the close of the reign of Augustus. The natural break towards the end of the second century A.D. is due to the entrance of new movements in thought and belief; and, in art, to the appearance of new factors, Eastern and Western, which deeply modified Latin and adapted it to fresh needs. After Marcus Aurelius there are still the last though not the least of the pagan poets — this suggests continuity; but it is also true that after Marcus Aurelius the study of Latin letters must take into account the writings of the Christian Fathers — and this suggests change. A period like the Silver Age deserves separate study for its intensely interesting features — the play of the Virgilian tradition and of rhetorical expertness upon literature, and the fluctuations in taste between standards old and new. Still, distinctions marking off one period from another do not constitute isolation. All the periods may be studied in detail with varying degrees of profit; but this should not obscure the fact that through the literature of the Republic, of the Golden Age, of the Silver Age, through the works of Christian Fathers, and of medieval schoolmen, there is continuity. This ought to appear a truism; yet it is a reassertion needful at intervals, because the restrictions of purists have not infrequently conveyed the impression that Latin is negligible after a certain more or less limited period called the 'classical age.' The incontestable superiority of the Golden Age does not justify stamping all that followed as base metal. 'Decadence' does not sum up the whole truth about the later Roman literature, and there are fresh categories under which some of that later work must be placed. So one is to realise that Latin prose runs on from Cicero to Lactantius, Jerome and Augustine, to Thomas Aquinas, Erasmus, Bacon, and Grotius; and that Latin poetry runs on from Virgil to Ausonius and Claudian, and from Catullus to Prudentius and Boethius, and so on to the Neo-Latin poets. Herein there is nothing derogatory to the dignity of the best work of the best period.

Supplementary Bibliography

THE following bibliography does not claim to be exhaustive. It owes a great deal to J. A. Nairn's *Classical Handlist* (Blackwell, Oxford), edition 2, 1939 and edition 3, 1953; to N. I. Herescu, *Bibliographie de la littérature latine*, Paris, 1943; and to J. Marouzeau, *Dix années de bibliographie classique* (covering 1914-24) and *L'année philologique* (covering 1924 onwards). The paginal reference to the left of subject or author indicates the place where the subject or author is introduced in the text. In general, works already mentioned in the appropriate bibliographical footnotes to the text are omitted here, but reference is made to such notes immediately after the naming of author or subject in this bibliography, so that this and the original bibliographies may be consulted together. Readers are reminded that many of the footnotes not specifically bibliographical nevertheless contain bibliographical matter. Occasionally, where I have thought it necessary, works cited in such notes are repeated in the following lists. In the longer sections the order of editions, commentaries and translations is (within the various subdivisions) chronological, while that of other works is alphabetical, except that references to Schanz-Hosius, Teuffel, Herescu, and collections of fragments, are usually placed either at the beginning or the end of each section. Place of publication is omitted, except in some cases where the country of origin is not obvious.

ABBREVIATIONS
The most obvious are omitted

A.J.P.	American Journal of Philology, 1880–
B.L.L.	N. I. Herescu, Bibliographie de la littérature latine, 1942
Budé	Collection des Univ. de France, publiée sous le patronage de l'Assoc. Guillaume Budé.
C.	Commentary
C.A.H.	Cambridge Ancient History, 1923–39
C.J.	Classical Journal, 1905–
Conc.	Concordance

C.P.   Classical Philology, 1906–
C.R.F.   Comicorum Romanorum Fragmenta, being Vol. II of O.
           Ribbeck, Scaenicae Romanorum Poesis Fragmenta, ed. 3,
           (Teub.), 1898
F.P.L.   Fragmenta Poetarum Latinorum epicorum et lyricorum
           praeter Ennium et Lucilium. Post E. Baehrens ed. W.
           Morel, 1927
G.R.F.   H. Funaioli, Grammaticae Romanae Fragmenta (Teub.),
           Vol. I alone published, 1907
H.R.R.   H. Peter, Historicorum Romanorum Reliquiae, 1906–14
J.R.S.   Journal of Roman Studies, 1911–
Loeb   Loeb Classical Library
O.C.D.   Oxford Classical Dictionary, 1949
O.C.T.   Oxford Classical Texts
O.L.T.   Oxford Library of Translations
O.R.F.   H. Malcovati, Oratorum Romanorum Fragmenta (Paravia),
           1930; ed. 2, 1955
O.W.   Other Works
Paravia   Corpus Scriptorum Latinorum Paravianum (Turin)
P.L.M.   Poetae Latini Minores: ed. E. Baehrens, 5 vols. 1879–83,
           rev. by F. Vollmer (I, II, V alone completed), 1911–35
P.R.V.R.   Poetarum Romanorum Veterum Reliquiae, sel. E. Diehl,
           1911
P.W.   A. Pauly, G. Wissowa, W. Kroll, Real-Encyclopädie d.
           Klassischen Altertumswissenschaft, 1893–
Rh.M.   Rheinisches Museum für Philologie, 1827– ; Neue Folge,
           1842–
Riv. Fil. Rivista di Filologia, 1873–
R.O.L.   E. H. Warmington, Remains of Old Latin (Loeb), 1935–40
S.H.   M. Schanz, Geschichte d. römischen Literatur (I. von
           Müller's Handbuch der Altertumswissenschaft, Abt.
           VIII). Vol. I, ed. 4, 1927, Vol. II, ed. 4, 1935, both by
           C. Hosius (Later volumes do not concern us)
T.   Text
Teub.   Bibliotheca Scriptorum Graecorum et Romanorum Teub-
           neriana, 1849–
Tfl.   W. S. Teuffel, Geschichte d. römischen Literatur, 3 vols.,
           ed. 6 (Vol. II ed. 7), by W. Kroll and F. Skutsch, 1913–20.
           Eng. Tr. by G. C. Warr of L. Schwabe's revision (=5th
           Germ. ed.), 2 vols. 1900
Tr.   Translation
T.R.F.   Tragicorum Romanorum Fragmenta, being Vol. I of O.
           Ribbeck, Scaenicae Romanorum Poesis Fragmenta, ed. 3
           (Teub.), 1898

GENERAL WORKS

H. Bardon, La litt. lat. inconnue: vol. i, L'époque republ., 1952, vol. ii, L'époque imp., 1956

J. Bayet, Littérature latine (Histoire: pages choisies traduites et commentées), ed. 6, 1953

W. Beare, The Roman Stage. A short History of Latin Drama in the time of the Republic, ed. 2, 1955

G. Becatti, Arte e gusto negli scrittori latini, 1951

E. Bickel, Lehrbuch der Gesch. der röm. Literatur, 1937

E. Bignone, Storia della letteratura latina, 1942– (vol. iii–1950–concludes republican period)

K. Büchner, Röm. Literaturgeschichte: Ihre Grundzüge in interpretierender Darstellung, 1958

K. Büchner and J. B. Hofmann, Latein. Literatur u. Sprache in der Forschung seit 1937 (Bern), 1951

A. Cartault, La Poésie latine, 1921

L. Castiglioni, Poesia lirica in Roma nel primo sec. a. C., 2 vols., 1953–4

C. Cichorius, Römische Studien, 1922

M. L. Clarke, Rhetoric at Rome, 1953

M. L. Clarke, The Roman Mind, 1956

C. T. Cruttwell, Hist. of Roman Lit. to death of M. Aurelius, ed. 7, 1910

M. S. Dimsdale, Hist. of Lat. Literature, 1915

G. E. Duckworth, The Nature of Roman Comedy (U.S.A.), 1952

P. J. Enk, Latijnsche Letterkunde, ed. 2, 1935

'Entretiens sur l'antiquité classique,' tome ii: L'Influence grecque sur la poésie lat. de Catulle à Ovide, by J. Bayet and others, Geneva and Paris, 1956

H. N. Fowler, Hist. of Roman Literature (U.S.A.), ed. 2, 1923

T. Frank, Life and Literature in the Roman Republic (U.S.A.), 1930

M. Grant, Roman Literature, 1954

M. Hadas, A History of Latin Literature (U.S.A.), 1952

G. Highet, Poets in a Landscape (U.S.A.), 1957

A. Klotz, Gesch. d. röm. Literatur, 1930

W. Kroll, Studien zum Verständnis der röm. Literatur, 1924

W. A. Laidlaw, Latin Literature, 1951

J. W. Mackail, Latin Literature, 1895 (rep. 1927)

C. Marchesi, Storia della letteratura latina, ed. 5, 1940

E. Norden, Röm. Literatur, ed. 5, 1954

E. Norden, Die antike Kunstprosa, 1898 (rp. w. supplements, 1909)

E. Paratore, Storia della letteratura latina, 1950

E. Paratore, Storia del teatro latino, 1957

H. J. G. Patin, Études sur la poésie latine, 1868–9 (rp. 1914)

M. Platnauer, Fifty Years of Classical Scholarship, 1954
F. Plessis, La Poésie latine, 1909
R. Pichon, Hist. de la litt. latine, ed. 5, 1912
B. Riposati, Il teatro romano, vol. i, Dalle origini a Plauto, 1956
E. Rolando, Storia della lett. lat., ed. 6, 1954
H. J. Rose, Handbook of Latin Literature, 1936
A. Rostagni, La letteratura di Roma repubblicana ed augustea (being Vol. XXIV of 'Storia di Roma' a cura dell' Istituto di Studi Romani), 1938
A. Rostagni, Storia della letteratura latina, 2 vols., ed. 2, 1954
M. Schanz, Gesch. d. röm. Lit. See S.H., in list of abbrevns.
E. E. Sikes, Roman Poetry, 1923
W. S. Teuffel, Gesch. d. röm. Lit. See Tfl., in list of abbrevns.
V. Ussani, Storia d. lett. lat. nelle etá rep. e aug., ed. 2, 1950
F. Villeneuve, Études de litt. lat., 1947
J. Whatmough, Poetic Scientific and other forms of discourse. A new approach to Greek and Latin Literature, Sather Class. Lect. (U.S.A.), 1956
A number of other general works I have found it convenient to place under the authors or subjects they specially illuminate.

INTRODUCTION

Chapter II

5. ORIGINS 6 n. 2; 11 nn. 1, 3, 6

C.A.H., II (1926), xxi; IV (1926), xii, xiii (Bibliographies are given for all these chapters. See also bibl. in Vol. VII (1928), p. 912)
O.C.D., s.v. Italy (bibl.)

Chapter III

14. LATIN LANGUAGE 15 nn. 1, 3; 16 n. 7; 20 n. 1

C.A.H., VIII (1930), xiii (bibl. on p. 765)
O.C.D., s.v. Latin Language (bibl.)
F. Altheim, Gesch. der latein. Sprache v.d. Anfängen bis zum Beginn der Literatur, 1951
C. Battisti, Alle fonti del latino, 1945
K. Buechner and J. B. Hofmann, Latein. Lit. u. Sprache in der Forschung seit 1937 (Bern), 1951
J. Cousin, Bibliog. de la langue latine, 1951 (covering 1880–1948)
J. Cousin, Évolution et structure de la langue latine, 1945
G. Devoto, Storia della lingua di Roma (being vol. xxiii of 'Storia d. Roma' a cura dell' Istituto di Studi Romani), 1940
A. Ernout, Morphologie du latin, ed. 3, 1953
R. G. Kent, The Forms of Latin (U.S.A.), 1946
J. Marouzeau, Quelques aspects de la formation du latin littéraire, 1949
L. R. Palmer, The Latin Language, 1954
V. Pisani, Grammatica latina storica e comparativa, 1948

V. Pisani, Le lingue dell' Italia antica oltre il latino, 1953
F. Sommer, Handbuch der latein. Laut- u. Formenlehre (rp. of ed. 2 and 3) (Heidelberg), 1948
L. Spitzer, Linguistics and Literary History (U.S.A.), 1948
E. Vetter, Handbuch der Ital. Dialekte, vol. i (Texte, mit Erkl., Glossen, Wörterverzeichnis), 1953

Chapter IV

29. ROMAN CHARACTER

A. Grenier, Le génie romain dans la religion, la pensée et l'art, 1925 (Eng. tr., 1926)
H. Grose-Hodge, Roman Panorama, 1944, ch. 12 (for schools and general reader)
G. Michaut, Le génie latin, 1900
Tfl. § 1 (convenient collection of passages fr. ancient authors illustrating Roman character)
O. Weise, Language and Character of the Roman People (tr. fr. Germ. by H. A. Strong and A. Y. Campbell), 1909
See also infra, re p. 48, Originality of Roman literature

38. ROMAN RELIGION

F. Altheim, Röm. Religiongesch. 1931–4 (Eng. tr. by H. Mattingly, 1938); ed. 2, 1951–3
C. Bailey, Phases in the Religion of Ancient Rome, 1932
C. Clemen, Die Religion d. Etrusker, 1935
A. Grenier, Les religions étrusque et romaine (pt. of vol. ii. 3 of Introd. à l'histoire des religions – Collection Mana) (Paris), 1948
A. K. Michels, Early Roman Religion 1945–1952 (bibl.), Cl. Wkly., 1954–5, 25 f. and 41 f.
M. Renard, Initiation a l'étruscologie (Brussels), 1943
H. J. Rose, Ancient Roman Religion, 1948
W. Warde Fowler, The Religious Experience of the Roman People, 1911
W. Warde Fowler, Roman Ideas of Deity, 1914
G. Wissowa, Religion u. Cultus d. Römer (I. von Müller's Handbuch), ed. 2, 1912

PART I: THE EARLIER LITERATURE OF THE REPUBLIC

GENERAL

Besides relevant portions of general works cited above, see:

E. Cocchia, La lett. lat. anteriore all' influenza ellenica, 1924–5
P. J. Enk, Handboek des Latijnsche Letterkuude van de oudste tijden tot het optreden van Cicero (only vols. i and ii publd. i (1928) Voor den invloed van het Hellenisme; ii (1937) Livius Andronicus, Naevius en Plautus).
P. Lejay, Histoire de la litt. lat. des origines à Plaute, 1923
F. Leo, Gesch. d. röm. Lit.: Vol. I (only one published) – Die archaische Lit., 1913
F. Marx, Röm. Volkslieder (Rh. M., 1929, pp. 348–426)
H. de la Ville de Mirmont, Études sur l'anc. poésie lat., 1903
C. Pascal, Feste e poesie antiche, 1926
G. Pasquali, Preistoria della poesia latina, 1936

Chapter I

48. ORIGINALITY OF ROMAN LITERATURE
W. Warde Fowler, The Imagination of the Romans (*Procgs. Class. Assoc.*, 1920)
E. Fraenkel, Rome and Greek Culture (Oxford), 1935
F. Leo, Die Originalität in d. röm. Litteratur, 1904
A. Rostagni, Genio greco e genio romano nella poesia (*Riv. fil.*, 1929, pp. 305 ff.)
See also *supra*, re p. 29, Roman character

49. LEGES REGIAE, IVS PAPIRIANVM
A. Ernout, Recueil de textes latins archaïques, 1916, pp. 112–13.
S.H., § 16
Tfl., § 70–1

50. TWELVE TABLES 50 n. 1
A. Ernout, Recueil de textes lat. arch., 1916, pp. 114–21
R.O.L., iii (Introd. and Bibl.: Text and Trans. of fragm. and ancient citations, pp. 424–515)
R. P. Coleman-Norton, The Twelve Tables (U.S.A.), 1948
B.L.L., § 5
O.C.D., s.v. *Twelve Tables* (bibl.)

50. ARCHAIC INSCRIPTIONS
A. Ernout, Rec. d. textes lat. arch., 1916, pt. i.
R.O.L., iv
  (Praenestine *fibula*: Rec. 3–4; R.O.L. 196–7
  Inscr. fr. forum: Rec. 4–7; R.O.L. 242–5
  Duenos bowl: Rec. 7–9; R.O.L. 54–7
  M. Fourio, etc.: Rec. 25–6; R.O.L. 72–3
  Scipionum epitt. Rec. 12–21; R.O.L. 2–9
  Inscr. on *Col. Rostr.*, Rec. 109–11; R.O.L. 128–31)
See also for Duenos Bowl: T. Bolelli, Per l'iscrizione di Duenos (*Studi ital. d. filol. class.*, 1946, pp. 117–23)

54. SATURNIAN VERSE 55 nn. 2, 4; 56 nn. 1, 3
O.C.D., s.v. *Saturnian Metre* (Bibl.)

57. CARMINA SALIARIA 57 n. 3
T. (reconstructed): B. Maurenbrecher, Carm. Sal. Rel. (*Fleckeis. Jahrb.*, Suppl., 1894)
O.W., A. Kappelmacher, Die Axamenta der Salier (*Wiener Studien*, 1924–5, pp. 224 ff.)
A. Reichardt, Die Lieder der Salier und das Lied der Arvalbrüder, 1916

57. CARMEN ARVALE 58 n. 1
T.C., A. Ernout, Rec. d. textes lat. arch., 1916, pp. 107–9
T. Tr., R.O.L., iv, pp. 250–3
O.W., M. Nacinovich, Carmen Arvale (Rome), 1933
E. Norden, Aus altröm. Priesterbüchern (*Acta Reg. Soc. Hum. Litt. Lundensis*, no. 29), 1939, p. 178
A. Reichardt, Die Lieder der Salier u. d. Lied d. Arvalbrüder, 1916

58. FOLK POESY
F. Marx, Römische Volkslieder (*Rh. M.*, 1929, pp. 348–426)

494   SUPPLEMENTARY BIBLIOGRAPHY

59. FUNERAL DIRGES
W. Kroll in P.W., s.v. *Nenia*
H. de la Ville de Mirmont, Études sur l'anc. poés. lat., 1903, pp. 359 ff.

59. VERSVS FESCENNINI
E. Hoffmann, Die Fescenninen (*Rh. M.*, 1896, pp. 320–5)
G. Wissowa in P.W., s.v. *Fescennini*

60. SATVRA   60 n. 5
W. S. Anderson, Recent Work in Roman Satire (1937–1955), *Cl. Wkly.*,
    1956–7, pp. 33–48
P. Boyancé, A propos de la satura dramatique (*Rev. des études anciennes*, 1932,
    pp. 11 ff.)
J. W. Duff, Roman Satire (U.S.A.), 1936, ch. 1
G. C. Fiske, Lucilius and Horace (U.S.A.), 1920
G. L. Hendrickson, Dramatic Satura and the Old Comedy at Rome (*A.J.P.*,
    1894, pp. 1 ff.)
G. L. Hendrickson, A Prevarronian Chapter of Rom. Lit. Hist. (*A.J.P.*, 1898,
    pp. 285 ff.)
G. L. Hendrickson, Satura – the Genesis of a Literary Form (*C.P.*, 1911,
    pp. 129 ff.)
U. Knoche, Die röm. Satire, ed. 2, 1957
W. Kroll in P.W. s.v. *Satura*
A. Maisack, Das dialogische Element in der röm. Satire, 1949
F. Marx, Lucilii Reliquiae i, 1904 (Introd.)
F. Müller, Zur Gesch. der röm. Satire (*Philologus*, 1923, pp. 230–80)
N. Terzaghi, Per la storia della satira, 1944
B. L. Ullman, Satura and Satire (*C.P.*, 1913, pp. 172–94)
B. L. Ullman, Dramatic Satura (*C.P.*, 1914, pp. 17–23)
B. L. Ullman, The Present Status of the Satura Question (*Univ. of N. Carolina
    Studies in Philol.*, 1920, pp. 379–401)
O. Weinreich, Röm. Satiren (Zurich) 1949 (Introd.)

61. FABVLA ATELLANA   62 n. 2
P. Frassinetti, Fabula Atellana. Saggio sul teatro popolare latino, 1953
J. J. Hartman, De Atell. fab. (*Mnemosyne*, 1922, pp. 225 ff.)
F. Marx in P.W., s.v. *Atellanae Fabulae*
A. Nicoll, Masks, Mimes and Miracles, 1931
K. Sittl, J personaggi dell' Atellana (*Riv. di stor. ant.*, 1895, pp. 27 ff.)

63. PRIESTLY AND CIVIC LITERATURE
S.H., i, § 13–14. Tfl., § 73–9
P.W., s.vv. *Annales, Commentarii, Fasti*
G. De Sanctis, Storia dei Romani, vol. i, 1907, ch. 1
E. Kornemann, Die älteste Form der Pontificalannalen (*Klio*, 1911)
G. Rohde, Die Kultsatzungen der röm. Pontifices ('Religions-geschichtliche
    Versuche u. Vorarbeiten' – ed. A. Dietrich, etc. – xxv, 1936)
W. Rowoldt, Librorum Pontif. Rom. de caerimoniis sacrificiorum rel., Halle,
    1906
B.L.L., § 6

64. TITVLI, LAVDATIONES FVNEBRES
F. Vollmer in P.W., s.v. *Laudatio funebris*
S.H., § 19 and 19a. Tfl., § 81. B.L.L., § 6

64. TWELVE TABLES. See *supra, re* p. 50

65. IVS FLAVIANVM
S.H., § 17.   Tfl., § 88.   P.W., s.vv. *Flavius* (15) and *Ius Flavianum*

66. APP. CLAUDIUS CAECUS
O.R.F., i.   F.P.L.   S.H., § 20.   Tfl., § 90
P.W., s.v. *Claudius* (91).   B.L.L., § 7
P. Lejay, App. Claud. Caecus (*Rev. de Philol.*, 1920, pp. 92–141)

Chapter II

68. INVASION OF HELLENISM
G. Colin, Rome et la Grèce de 200 à 146, 1905
G. De Sanctis, Der Hellenismus und Rom, in 'Propylaen-Weltgeschichte' (ed. W. Goetz), vol. II, 1931, pp. 241 ff.
M. Lenchantin de Gubernatis, Appunti sull' ellenismo nella poesia arcaica latina, 1912
S. Lo Cascio, L'influenza ellenica nell' origine della poesia lat. (*Riv. fil.*, 1892, pp. 41 ff.)
C. Pascal, Graecia capta (Florence), 1905
G. Pasquali, Preistoria della poesia romana, 1936

Chapter III

88. LIVIUS ANDRONICUS   88 n. 2
T. (Epic Fragm.), F.P.L.
T.C. (Epic Fragm.), S. Mariotti (see *infra*)
T. Tr., R.O.L. ii.
O.W., W. Beare, The Roman Stage, ed. 2, 1955
   E. Fraenkel in P.W. (suppl. V), s.v. *Livius Andronicus*
   F. Kunz, Die älteste röm. Epik in ihrem Verhältnis zu Homer, 1890
   S. Mariotti, L.A. e la traduzione artistica. Saggio critico ed ediz. dei frammenti dell' *Odyssea*, 1952
   E. M. Sanford, The Tragedies of L.A. (*C.J.*, 1923, pp. 274–85)
   J. Tolkiehn, Homer u.d. röm. Poesie, 1900

93. CARMEN NELEI   93 n. 1
H. de la V. de Mirmont, Études sur l'anc. poés. lat., 1903, pp. 203 ff.
S.H., § 25a.

93. NAEVIUS   93 n. 3
T. (*Bell. Pun.*), F.P.L.
T.C., E. V. Marmorale, ed. 2 (Florence) 1950; (*B.P.*) S. Mariotti (see *infra*)
T. Tr., R.O.L., ii.
O.W., W. Beare, The Roman Stage, ed. 2, 1955
   F. Boehmer, N. und Fabius Pictor (*Symb. Osl.*, 1952, pp. 34–53)
   E. Fraenkel in P.W. supplbd. vi, s.v. *Naevius* 2
   Th. B. De Graff, Naevian Studies (U.S.A.), 1931
   S. Mariotti, Il *Bellum Punicum* e l'arte di N. Saggio con ediz. dei framm. del *B.P.*, 1955
   H. T. Rowell, The original form of N.'s *Bell. Pun.* (*A.J.P.*, 1947, pp. 21–46)
   R. Sabbadini, Poeti Latini: Nevio, 1935

L. Strzelecki, De Naeviano carmine quaest. selectae (Krakow), 1935

N.B. The usual arrangement of the fragments of the *Bell. Pun.* assigns some of them to books other than those to which ancient authorities assigned them. Strzelecki and Rowell in their rearrangement have restored the original assignments. They are followed by Marmorale and Mariotti. According to this reconstruction bk. I takes the first Punic war to the fall of Agrigentum in 262 and starts the digression on the legendary period, which is continued in bks. II and III; then Naevius returns to history, and bks. IV–VII cover the rest of the war, 262–241 B.C. The historical part of bk. I is a plunge *in medias res*.

100. ENNIUS 100 n. 1

T., J. Vahlen, Ennianae Poesis Reliquiae, ed. 2, 1903 (rp. 1928). (Sel.) E. Diehl, P.R.V.R., 1911
T.C. (*Annales*), E. M. Steuart, The Annals of Q. Ennius, 1925
T. Tr., R.O.L., i.   (Ital.) R. Argenio, 1951
O.W., W. Aly, Livius und Ennius, 1936
  W. Beare, The Roman Stage, ed. 2, 1955
  A. Cordier, Les débuts de l'hexamètre latin: Ennius, 1947
  E. S. Duckett, Studies in E. (U.S.A.), 1915
  M. Lenchantin de Gubernatis, Ennio: saggio critico (Turin), 1915
  E. Norden, E. und Vergilius, 1915
  W. Röser, Ennius, Euripides und Homer, 1939
  E. Skard, E. und Sallustius (Oslo), 1933
  F. Skutsch in P.W., s.v. *Ennius* 3
  O. Skutsch, The *Annals* of Q. Ennius (Inaug. lect.) (London), 1951
  N. Terzaghi, La technica tragica di E. (*Studi Ital. di filol. class.*, 1928, pp. 175–96)

Chapter IV

115. ROMAN THEATRE 115 n. 1

J. T. Allen, Stage Antiquities of the Greeks and Romans and their Influence (U.S.A.), 1927
W. Beare, The Roman Stage, ed. 2, 1955
M. Bieber, Hist. of the Greek and Roman Theater (U.S.A.), 1939
S.H., § 54

117. PLAUTUS 119 n. 1; 140 n. 2; 145 n. 6

T., W. M. Lindsay (O.C.T.), ed. 2, 1910
T.C. (Sep. plays – in alphabetical order of editors)
  J. Brix and M. Niemeyer: *Capt.*, ed. 7 by O. Köhler, 1930; *Men.*, ed. 6 by F. Conrad, 1929; *Mil. Gl.*, ed. 4 by O. Köhler, 1916; *Trinummus*, ed. 6 by F. Conrad, 1931
  G. E. Duckworth: *Epidicus* (U.S.A.), 1940
  P. J. Enk: *Mercator* (Leiden), 1932; *Truc.* (Leiden), 1953
  A. Ernout: *Bacchides* (without text), 1935
  J. H. Gray: *Asin.*, 1894; *Epid.*, 1893; *Trin.*, 1897
  L. Havet: *Amph.*, 1895; (and A. Freté) *Asin.*, 1925
  P. T. Jones, *Menaechmi*, 1918
  W. M. Lindsay: *Capt.*, ed. 2, 1924
  F. Marx: *Rudens*, 1928
  N. Moseley and M. Hammond: *Men.* (U.S.A.), 1933
  A. Palmer: *Amph.*, 1890
  E. A. Sonnenschein: *Most.*, ed. 2, 1907; *Rud.*, 1891
  E. H. Sturtevant: *Pseud.* (U.S.A.), 1932

R. Y. Tyrrell: *Mil. Gl.*, ed. 3, 1889
T.C. Tr. (Ital.), *Mil. Gl.* and *Aul.*, I. Ripamonti (Milan), 1953
T. Tr., P. Nixon (Loeb), 1916–38
A. Ernout (Budé), 1932–40
Tr., In G. E. Duckworth, *Complete Roman Drama* (U.S.A.), 1942
Lexicon: A. Lodge, 2 vols., 1904–33
O.W. (For Prosody, see *infra*, *re* p. 143)
K. Abel, Die Plautusprologe, 1955
F. Arnaldi, Da P. a Terenzio, 1946–7
W. Beare, The Roman Stage, ed. 2, 1955
W. Beare, *Contaminatio* in P. and Terence (*Rev. Philol.*, 1940, pp. 28–42)
C. H. Buck, A Chronology of the Plays of P. (U.S.A.), 1940
F. della Corte, Da Sarsina a Roma. Ricerche plautine, 1952
E. Fraenkel, Plautinisches im P., 1922
A. Freté, Essai sur la structure dramatique des comédies de P., 1930
G. Jachmann, Plautinisches u. Attisches, 1931
C. W. Leffingwell, Social and Priv. Life in the Time of P. and Terence (U.S.A.), 1918
P. E. Legrand, Daos: tableau de la comédie grecque, 1910 (Eng. tr.: J. Loeb, The New Greek Comedy (U.S.A.), 1917)
P. Lejay, Plaute, 1925
F. Leo, Plautinische Forschungen z. Kritik u. Gesch. d. Komödie, ed. 2, 1912
W. M. Lindsay, Syntax of Plautus, 1907 (rp. 1936)
A. de Lorenzi, I precedenti greci della commedia romana, 1946
G. Michaut, Plaute, 1920
G. Norwood, Plautus and Terence, 1932
R. Perna, L'originalità di P., 1955
K. H. E. Schutter, Quibus annis comoediae Plautinae primum actae sint quaeritur (Groningen), 1952
Sonnenburg in P.W., s.v. *Maccius*
B. A. Taladoire, Essai sur le comique de P. (Imprim. Nat. de Monaco), 1956
K. M. Westaway, The Original Element in P., 1917

121. MENANDER   122 n. 1
(Representative of New Greek Comedy)

T., A. Koerte, ed. 3 (Teub.), vol. i, papyrus fragm., 1938; vol. ii, old fragm., 1953
T.C. (extant portions of four plays), O. E. Capps (U.S.A. and London), 1910 (papyrus fragm. of four plays), J. van Leeuwen, ed. 3, 1919 (Latin comm.) (selections), W. G. Waddell, 1927
T. Tr. (*Epitrepontes*), M. Croiset, 'L' Arbitrage' (Paris), 1908 ('Principal fragm.' – in fact, most of Menander up to 1921), F. G. Allinson (Loeb), 1921, rp. 1930, (w. ample bibliog.)
(*Dyscolos* – newly discovered – the only complete play), V. Martin (Geneva), 1958 (Greek text and French trans.; Eng. and Germ. trans. added)
Tr. (*Periceiromene*), G. Murray, 1942 (with gaps conjecturally filled in)
(*Epitrep.*), G. Murray, 1945 (with gaps conjecturally filled in)
O.W., A. W. Gomme, Essays in Greek History and Literature, 1937
A. Koerte, in P.W., s.v. *Menandros*
P. E. Legrand, *op. cit.*, under Plautus, *re* p. 117
G. Murray, Aristophanes, 1933
G. Norwood, Greek Comedy, 1931
T. B. L. Webster, Studies in Menander, 1950

143. PLAUTINE PROSODY   143 n. 5
H. Drexler, Plautinische Akzentstudien, 1932–3

E. Fraenkel, Iktus u. Akzent, 1928
W. M. Lindsay, Early Latin Verse, 1922
C. F. W. Müller, Plautinische Prosodie, 1869–71

146. CAECILIUS STATIUS
T., C.R.F. (Sel.) E. Diehl, P.R.V.R.
T. Tr., R.O.L., i.
O.W., W. Beare, The Roman Stage, ed. 2, 1955
P. Faider, Le poète comique Cécilius, sa vie et son œuvre (Musée Belge, 1908,
    pp. 269–341; and 1909, pp. 5–35)
I. Negro, Studio su Cecilio Stazio, 1919
C. Pascal, Feste e poesie antiche, 1926 (pp. 149–82)

147. TRABEA, etc.   147 n. 8
S.H., § 46.   Tfl., § 107

148. TERENCE   149 n. 4
Ancient Commentary: Aeli Donati quod fertur commentum Terenti; acced.
    Eugraphi comm. et scholia Bembina, P. Wessner (Teub.), 3 vols., 1902–8
T., R. Kauer and W. M. Lindsay (O.C.T.), 1926
T.C., S. G. Ashmore (U.S.A.), 1908
G. Coppola (Turin), 1927
(Sep. plays) Adelphi: A. Sloman, ed. 2, 1892; K. Dziatzko (Leipzig), ed. 2,
    1903 (rp. 1921); S. G. Ashmore, 1926
Andria: A. Spengel, ed. 2, 1888 (Germ. C.); C. E. Freeman and A. Sloman,
    ed. 3, 1912; G. P. Shipp, 1938
Eunuchus: P. Fabia (Paris), 1895; B. G. Bonino (Ital.), 1910; F. Arnaldi (Ital.)
    1947 (w. relevant portion of Donatus's comm.)
Heaut.: J. H. Gray, 1902; F. G. Ballentine (U.S.A.), 1910
Hecyra: P. Thomas (Paris), 1887 (Fr. C.); S. Stella (Ital.), 1936
Phormio: A. Sloman, ed. 2, 1890; K. Dziatzko (Leipzig), ed. 4, 1913
T. Tr., J. Sargeaunt (Loeb), 1914
W. Ritchie, 1927
J. Marouzeau (Budé), 1942–50
(Ital.), A. Pratesi, vol. ii (Ph. Hec. Ad.), 1952; vol. i in prep.
Tr., F. Perry, 1929
In G. E. Duckworth, 'Complete Roman Drama' (U.S.A.), 1942
Index, E. B. Jenkins, 1932
O.W. (for Prosody see infra, re p. 158)
J. T. Allardyce, The Syntax of T., 1929
F. Arnaldi, Da Plauto a Terenzio, 1946–7
A. Barbieri, La vis comica in T. (Arona), 1951
W. Beare, Contaminatio in Plautus and T. (Rev. Philol., 1940, pp. 28–42)
W. Beare, The Roman Stage, ed. 2, 1955
L. Castiglioni, T. e Virgilio, 1955
P. J. Enk, T. as an Adapter of Greek Comedies (Mnemosyne, 1947, pp. 81–93)
R. C. Flickinger, A Study of T.'s Prologues (Philol. Quarterly, 1927, pp.
    235–69)
G. Jachmann in P.W., s.v. Terentius 36
I. Lana, T. e il movimento filellenico in Roma (Riv. filol. class., 1947, pp. 44–
    80 and 155–75)
C. W. Leffingwell, Social and Priv. Life in the Time of Plautus and T.
    (U.S.A.), 1918
A. de Lorenzi, I precedenti greci della commedia romana, 1946

G. Norwood, The Art of T., 1923
G. Norwood, Plautus and T., 1932
E. Reitzenstein, Terenz als Dichter (Amsterdam), 1940
W. Schmid, T. als Menander Latinus (*Rh. M.*, 1952, pp. 229 ff.)
J. D. Straus, T. und Menander. Beitrag zu einer Stilvergleichung (Zürich), 1955
N. Terzaghi, Prolegomena a Terenzio, 1931

158. TERENTIAN PROSODY 158 n. 6
W. A. Laidlaw, The Prosody of Terence, 1938
See also bibl. for Plautine prosody

159. JUVENTIUS, etc., and TURPILIUS 159 n. 7
S.H., § 46. Tfl., § 113–14

160. TOGATAE, TABERNARIAE, LATER ATELLANAE, MIMI
T., C.R.F. (*Atell.*) P. Frassinetti (Paravia), 1955
O.W., W. Beare, The Roman Stage, ed. 2, 1955
E. Courbaud, De Comœdia Togata (Paris), 1899
P. Frassinetti, Fabula Atellana. Saggio sul teatro popolare latino, 1953
H. J. G. Patin, Études sur la poésie latine, 1868–9 (rp. 1914), ii, pp. 302 ff.
H. Reich, Der Mimus, 1903
See also *supra, re* p. 61, *Fabula Atellana*

Chapter V
163. PACUVIUS
T., T.R.F. (Sel.) E. Diehl, P.R.V.R.
T. Tr., R.O.L., ii.
Tr., see C. Faggiano, *infra*.
O.W., W. Beare, The Roman Stage, ed. 2, 1955
C. Faggiano, Pacuvius: Ricostruzione dei drammi e trad. dei frammenti, 1930
R. Helm in P.W., s.v. *Pacuvius*
I. Lana, P. e i modelli greci (*Atti Accad. Torino*, lxxxi (1947), pp. 26–62)
L. Müller, De Pac. fabulis disputatio, 1889
M. Valsa, Marcus Pacuvius poète tragique (Paris), 1957

165. ACCIUS
T. (dram. fragm.), T.R.F.
(other fragm.), F.P.L.
(sel.), E. Diehl, P.R.V.R.
T. Tr., R.O.L., ii
O.W., W. Beare, The Roman Stage, ed. 2, 1955
F. Marx in P.W., s.v. *Accius*
L. Müller, De Acci fabulis disputatio, 1890

168. FABVLA PRAETEXTA
S.H., § 52. Tfl., § 14. T.R.F.

169. MINOR TRAGEDIANS
S.H., § 51. Tfl., § 13. T.R.F.

Chapter VI
171. LUCILIUS 172 n. 2
T., N. Terzaghi, C. Lucilii Sat. Rel. (Florence), 1934, ed. 2, 1944
T. C. Tr., E. Bolisani, L. ed i suoi frammenti, 1932

T. Tr., R.O.L., iii.
C., N. Terzaghi, Lucilio (Turin), 1934
O.W., W. S. Anderson, Recent Work in Roman Satire, 1937–55 (*Cl. Wkly.*,
   1956–7, pp. 33–40)
J. W. H. Atkins, Lit. Criticism in Antiquity, vol. ii, 1934 (rp. 1952)
C. Cichorius, Untersuchungen zu L., 1908
G. Coppola, Gaio Lucilio, cavaliere e poeta, 1941
J. F. D'Alton, Roman Literary Theory and Criticism, 1931
J. W. Duff, Roman Satire (U.S.A.), 1936, ch. 3
G. C. Fiske, L. and Horace (U.S.A.), 1920
A. Kappelmacher, in P.W., s.v. *Lucilius*
U. Knoche, *op. cit. re* p. 60, *Satura*
M. P. Piwonka, Lucilius und Kallimachus, 1949
H. Stewart, The Date of L.'s Birth (rp. fr. *Procgs. of Leeds Philos. Soc.*, Lit.
   and Hist. Section, vol. I, pt. vi, 1928, pp. 285–91)
N. Terzaghi, Per la storia della satira, 1944
See also *supra, re* p. 60, *Satura*

178. POST-ENNIAN MINOR POETRY (Epic; Didactic; Elegiac epigram)
F.P.L.
P.W., s.vv. *Elegie, Epigramm, Laevius*
L. Alfonsi, Poetae Novi: storia di un movimento poetico, 1945
H. Bardon, Q. Lutat. Catulus et son cercle littéraire (*Études Classiques* (Namur)
   1950, pp. 145 ff.)
A. A. Day, Origins of Latin Love-Elegy, 1938
L. Illuminati, L'elegia romana in relaz. all' eleg. greca, 1946
F. Jacoby, Zur Entstehung der röm. Elegie (*Rh. M.*, 1905, pp. 38–105)
H. de la V. de Mirmont, Études sur l'anc. poésie lat., 1903, pp. 221–345 (Le
   poète Laevius)
M. Pinto, Il circolo letterario di Q. Lutazio Catulo (*Giorn. Ital. Fil.* (Naples),
   1956, pp. 210 ff.)
A. L. Wheeler, Catullus and the Traditions of Ancient Poetry (U.S.A.), 1934

Chapter VII

182. HISTORIANS (Fabius Pictor to Lucullus) 182 n. 1
H.R.R., i. S.H., § 64–73, 112–14. B.L.L., § 69–71
M. L. W. Laistner, The Greater Roman Historians (U.S.A.), 1947, ch. 2
For Cato, see *infra, re* p. 191

186. ORATORS (Pre-Ciceronian)   186 n. 3
O.R.F., i and ii. S.H., § 19, 74, 75, 75a
A. Berger, Hist. de l'éloquence latine . . . jusqu'à Cicéron, ed. 3, by V. Cucheval,
   1892
A. Cima, L'eloquenza latina prima di Cicerone, 1903
L. Illuminati, L'eloquenza romana prima di Cicerone, vol. ii, 1948

190. RHETORICA AD HERENNIVM
T., F. Marx (Teub.), ed. 2, 1923 (good introd.)
T. Tr., H. Bornecque (Paris), 1932
   H. Caplan (Loeb), 1954
O.W., see B.L.L., § 115

191. LEARNING (Pre-Varronian)
G.R.F., i. S.H., § 76–7 and 81–2)

191. CATO

De Agri Cultura
T., H. Keil, ed. 2 by G. Goetz (Teub.), 1922
T. C., H. Keil 1882–94 (Lat. Comm.)
E. Bréhaut, Cato the Censor on Farming, 1933
T. Tr., W. D. Hooper and H. B. Ash (Loeb), 1934 (w. Varro, *De R.R.*)
Tr. (Ital.): G. Curcio, La primitiva civiltà lat. agricola ed il libro dell' agricoltura di M.P.C., 1930 (w. introductory essays)
All remains other than *De Ag. C.* Text: H. Jordan (Leipzig), 1860 (w. proleg.). Fragm. of *Origines*, H.R.R. i; of speeches; O.R.F. i; Kienast (*infra*)
O.W., G. Cortese, De M. Porcii Catonis vita operibus et lingua, 1883
M. Gelzer and R. Helm in P.W., s.v. *Porcius*, 9
M. Gerosa, La prima enciclopedia romana (Pavia), 1911
J. Hörle, Catos Hausbücher, 1929
O. Jaeger, M. Porcius Cato, 1892
B. Janzer, Hist. Unters. zu d. Redensfragmenten des M.P.C., 1937
D. Kienast, Cato der Zensor. Seine Personlichkeit (w. rhet. fragm.), 1954
E. V. Marmorale, Cato Maior, ed. 2, 1949
A. Mazzarino, Introd. al *De Agri Cultura* di C., 1952
M. Sargenti, Il *De Agri Cultura* di C. e le origini dell' ipoteca romana (*St. et Doc. Hist. et Iuris* (Rome), xxii (1956), pp. 158 ff.)
R. Till, Die Sprache Catos (*Philologus*, suppl. xxviii, 1935)
U. Zuccarelli, Rassegna bibliografica di studi e pubblicazioni su Catone, 1940–1950 (*Paideia*, 1952, pp. 213–17)
See also *re* p. 186, Orators (pre-Ciceronian)

193. JURISTS
S.H., § 78–80. F. Bremer, Iurispr. Antehadr. (Teub.), 1896–1901

PARTS II AND III
THE LITERATURE OF THE GOLDEN AGE
PART II: THE CICERONIAN PERIOD

Chapter I

202. LUCRETIUS 202 n. 1
T., C. Bailey (O.C.T.), ed. 2, 1921
J. Martin (Teub.), ed. 3, 1957
T.C. Tr., H. A. J. Munro, 1886, 3 vols. (Vol. II – comm. – rp. w. essay by E. N. da C. Andrade, 1928)
C. Bailey, 1947
T.C., C. Giussani, 1896–8
W. A. Merrill (U.S.A.), 1907
W. E. Leonard and S. B. Smith (U.S.A.), 1942 (w. quotns. fr. Gk. authors in trans.)
(Sep. bks.) i, iii, v, J. D. Duff, 1923–30; iii, R. Heinze 1897 (Germ. C.); iv, A. Ernout, 1915 (Fr. C.)
C., A. Ernout and L. Robin, 1925–8
T. Tr., H. Diels (Berlin), 1923–4
W. H. D. Rouse (Loeb), 1924
A. Ernout (Budé), ed. 8 and 7, 1948
Tr., C. Bailey, ed. 2, 1936

R. C. Trevelyan, 1937
W. H. Brown (U.S.A.), 1950
R. E. Latham (Penguin), 1951
(Fr.) R. Waltz, 1954
(Eng. V.) A. D. Winspear (U.S.A.), 1955
Index, J. Paulson, ed. 2, 1926
O.W., G. Barra, Struttura e composizione del De r. nat. di L., 1952
J. Bayet, Études lucrétiennes I and II (*Cahiers du collège philosophique Grenoble*, 1948, pp. 57–138)
J. Bayet, L. devant la pensée grecque (*Museum Helv.*, 1954, pp. 89 f.)
K. Büchner, Beobachtungen über Vers u. Gedankengang bei L., 1936
G. Della Valle, Tito Lucrezio Caro e l'epicureismo campano, 1932
G. Della Valle, Marco Tullio Cicerone editore e critico del poema di L. (*Mem. Accad. d'Italia, Cl. di Sc. Mor. e Stor.*, VII, i. 3, pp. 307–416, Rome, 1941)
R. E. Deutsch, The Pattern of Sound in L. (U.S.A.), 1939
A. Ernout, Lucrèce (Brussels), 1947
L. Ferrero, Poetica nuova in L., 1949
P. Friedländer, Pattern of Sound and Atomistic Theory in L. (*A.J.P.*, 1941, pp. 16 ff.)
P. Giuffrida, L'epicureismo nella lett. lat. nel primo sec. a. C., Vol. II, 1950
C. Giussani, Studi Lucreziani, 1906
G. D. Hadzsits, L. and his Influence (U.S.A.), 1935
H. Klepl, L. und Vergil in ihren Lehrgedichten, 1940
D. Logré, L'Anxiété de L., 1946
J. Mewaldt in P.W., s.v. *Lucretius* 17
V. P. Naughtin, Metrical Patterns in L.'s Hexameters (*Class. Quarterly*, 1952, pp. 152 ff.)
O. Regenbogen, Lukrez: s. Gestalt in s. Gedicht, 1932
M. Rozelaar, Lukrez: Versuch einer Deutung (Amsterdam), 1943
G. Santayana, Three Philosophical Poets: Lucretius, Dante, Goethe (U.S.A.), 1953
E. E. Sikes, Lucretius, Poet and Philosopher, 1936
A. P. Sinker, Introd. to L., 1937
G. Soleri, Lucrezio, 1945
O. Tescari, Lucretiana, 1935; Lucrezio, 1939
A. Traglia, Sulla formazione spirituale di L., 1948
P. Vallette, La doctrine de l'âme chez L., 1934
R. Waltz, Lucrèce dans Lucrèce (*Bull. Assoc. Budé*, 1953, 4, pp. 43–63)

Chapter II

225. 'ALEXANDRIAN' CONTEMPORARIES OF CATULLUS   225 n. 4
F.P.L. S.H., § 97–101 and 107–9
L. Alfonsi, Poetae novi: storia di un movimento poetico, 1945
E. Castorina, Licinio Calvo, 1946
M. M. Crump, The Epyllion fr. Theocritus to Ovid, 1931, ch. 6
A. Gandiglio, Cantores Euphorionis, 1904
L. Hermann, Trois poèmes de P. Valerius Cato (*Latomus*, 1949, pp. 111–44)
C. Pascal, Poeti e personaggi Catulliani, 1916 (chs. 1 and 2 for Calvus and Cinna)
F. Plessis, Essai sur Calvus (*Ann. Fac. Lett. Caen*, 1885). Cf. *infra*, re p. 289
A. Rostagni, Partenio di Nicea, Elvio Cinna ed i 'poetae novi' (*Atti Accad. Torino*, 1932–3, pp. 497–545)
V. Sirago, La scuola neoterica: saggio con edizione dei frammenti, 1947
B.L.L., § 86

227. CATULLUS   227 n. 8; 233 n. 3

T., M. Schuster (Teub.), ed. 2, 1954
  E. Cazzaniga (Paravia), ed. 3, 1956
T.C., E. T. Merrill (U.S.A.), 1893, rp. 1951
  G. Friedrich, 1908 (Germ. C.)
  W. Kroll, ed. 2, 1929 (Germ. C.)
  M. Lenchantin de Gubernatis (Turin), ed. 3, 1947
T. Tr., F. W. Cornish (Loeb), 1913
  G. Mazzoni (Bologna), 1939
  E. d'Arbela, 1947
  G. Lafaye (Budé), ed. 3, 1949
Tr., Sir W. Marris, 1924
  H. Macnaghten, 1925
  F. A. Wright, 1926
  Various hands, ed. W. A. Aiken (U.S.A.), 1950
Index, M. N. Wetmore (U.S.A.), 1912
O.W., R. Avallone, C. e i suoi modelli romani, I, 1944
  R. Avallone, Catullo poeta triste (Antiquitas, 1951–2, pp. 37 ff.)
  R. Avallone, Catullo poeta della natura (Antiquitas, 1951–2, pp. 72 ff.)
  R. Avallone, C. e Apollonio Rodio (Antiquitas, 1953, pp. 8–75)
  H. Bardon, L'Art de la composition chez C., 1943
  H. Bardon, C. et ses modèles poétiques de langue latine (Latomus, 1957, pp. 614–27)
  D. Braga, C. e i poeti greci, 1950
  F. della Corte, Due studi Catulliani, 1951
  M. M. Crump, The Epyllion fr. Theocritus to Ovid, 1931, ch. 6
  L. Ferrero, Un' Introd. a C., 1955
  L. Ferrero, Interpretazione di C., 1955
  T. Frank, C. and Horace: Two poets in their Environment, 1928
  S. Gaetani, La poesia di C., 1934
  P. Giuffrida op. cit. re p. 202, Lucretius
  E. A. Havelock, The Lyric Genius of C., 1939
  N. I. Herescu, Catullo (Rome), 1943
  H. Heusch, Das Archaische in der Sprache Catulls, 1954
  O. Hezel, C. u. d. griech. Epigramm, 1932
  P. Maas, Chronology of the Poems of C. (C.Q., 1942, pp. 79 ff.)
  E. V. Marmorale, L'ultimo Catullo, 1952
  J. A. S. McPeek, C. in Strange and Distant Britain (U.S.A.), 1939
  C. Pascal, Poeti e personaggi Catulliani, 1916
  A. Ronconi, Studi catulliani, 1953
  I. Schnelle, Untersuchungen zu Cs. dichterischer Form, 1933
  M. Schuster in P.W., s.v. Valerius, 123
  V. Sirago, Catullo, poeta della giovinezza, 1947
  M. Soles, Studies in colloquial Language in the Poems of C. (U.S.A.), 1954
  J. Svennung, Cs. Bildersprache (Upsala), 1945
  G. Vaccaro, Introd. allo studio della lingua dell' uso in C. (Giorn. Ital. Fil., 1951, pp. 33 f.)
  O. Weinreich, Die Distichen d. C., 1926
  A. L. Wheeler, C. and the Traditions of Anc. Poetry, 1934

Chapter III

241. VARRO   241 n. 1

T. (L.L.), F. Schoell and G. Goetz (Teub.), 1910
  (Menipp.) in F. Bücheler, Petronius, ed. 6 by W. Heraeus, 1922

(*R.R.*), H. Keil (Teub.), ed. 2 by G. Goetz, 1929
(*Gramm. fragm.*), G. Funaioli, G.R.F. i.
(*Logist. and Imag.*) C. Chappuis, Fragm. des ouvrages de V. . . . (Paris), 1868
T.C. (*Menipp.*), F. della Corte (Ital. C.), 1953
T.C. Tr. (*L.L.* v), J. Collart (Fr. Tr. and C.), 1954
  (*L.L.*, x), A. Traglia (Ital. Tr. and C.), 1956
C. (*L.L.*, viii), H. Dahlmann, 1940
T. Tr. (*L.L.*), R. G. Kent (Loeb), 1938
(*R.R.*) W. D. Hooper and H. B. Ash (Loeb), 1934 (w. Cato, *De Agri Cultura*)
O.W. (general), F. della Corte, Varrone il terzo gran lume romano, 1954
H. Dahlmann in P.W., s.v. *Terentius*, 84
(*L.L.*), J. Collart, Varron grammairien latin, 1954
H. Dahlmann, V. u. d. hellenistische Sprachtheorie, 1932
D. Fehling, V. u. d. grammatische Lehre von der Analogie u. d. Flexion
  (*Glotta*, 1957, pp. 48 ff.)
(*Menipp.*), L. Alfonsi, Intorno alle Menippee di V. (*Riv. Fil.*, 1952, pp. 1–37)
W. S. Anderson, Recent Work in Roman Satire, 1937–1955 (*Cl. Wkly.*,
  1956–7, pp. 33–40)
F. della Corte, La poesia di V. ricostruita (*Mem. Accad. Torino*, 1937–8)
J. W. Duff, Roman Satire (U.S.A.), 1936, ch. 5
L. Riccomagno, Studio sulle Sat. Men. di V., 1931
See also B.L.L., § 289–92

253. NIGIDIUS FIGULUS and other scholars
W. Kroll in P.W., s.v. *Nigidius Figulus*
L. Legrand, P. Nig. Fig. philosophe pythagoricien orphique, 1931
A. Swoboda, P. Nig. Fig. operum reliquiae, 1889
G.R.F., i. H.R.R., i. S.H., § 97, 116, 181, 195–6, 197a

254. SULPICIUS RUFUS and other jurists 254 n. 1
O.R.F., iii. G.R.F., i. S.H., 198–9
F. Bremer, Jurisp. Antehad. (Teub.), 1896–1901
R. L. James, Cicero and Sulpicius, 1933 (ed. of Cic. *Phil.* ix and the corre-
  spondence bet. C. and S. - including the two extant letters of S.)
P. Meloni, Ser. Sulp. Rufo e i suoi tempi (Cagliari), 1946

Chapter IV

255. CICERO   255 n. 1
Ancient Commentator (Orations): Asconius: A. C. Clark (O.C.T.), 1907 (comm.
  on five speeches extant)
T. (*op. omn.*), C. Atzert, A. Klotz, O. Plasberg, H. Sjögren and others (Teub.),
  1914–
  (orations) A. C. Clark and W. Peterson (O.C.T.), 1905–18
  (letters) L. C. Purser (O.C.T.), 1901–3; U. Moricca and A. Moricca Caputo
  (Paravia), 1950–5
  (rhet. wks.) A. S. Wilkins (O.C.T.), 1903
  (*De Fin.*) J. N. Madvig, ed. 3 (Copenhagen), 1876 (Lat. textual notes)
  (poetry) see next section
T.C. (orations)
  (*Rosc. Am.*) St. George Stock, 1890
  (comm. only) G. Landgraf, ed. 2, 1914
  (*In Caec.* and *In Verr.* I) J. R. King, 1912
  (*In Verr.* II, Bk. V) R. G. C. Levens, 1946

(*Pro Caecina*) C. A. Jordan (Leipzig), 1847
(*Lege Man.*) J. R. King, 1917
(*Pro Clu.*) W. Y. Fausset, ed. 4 (London), 1910
(*Cael.*) R. G. Austin, 1933; ed. 2, 1952
(*Mur.*) W. E. Heitland, 1875
(*Pro Fl.*) A. du Mesnil (Leipzig), 1883 (Germ. C.); T. B. L. Webster, 1933
(*De Domo*) R. G. Nisbet, 1939
(*Marc., Lig., Rege D.*) W. Y. Fausset, ed. 2, 1906
(*Phil.* i, ii) J. D. Denniston, 1926
(letters)
R. Y. Tyrrell and L. C. Purser, edd. 2 and 3, 1904–33
(sel. letters) W. W. How and A. C. Clark, 1925–6
(rhetorical works)
(*Brutus*) O. Jahn, ed. 5 by W. Kroll, 1908
(*Orator*) W. Kroll, 1913 (Germ. C.)
(philosophical works)
(*De Amic.*) M. Seyffert–C. F. W. Mueller, ed. 2 (Leipzig), 1876 (Germ. C.)
(*De Divin.*) A. S. Pease (U.S.A.), 1920–3
(*De Fin.*) W. M. L. Hutchinson, 1909; (i, ii) J. S. Reid, 1925
(*De Legg.*) A. du Mesnil (Leipzig), 1897 (Germ. C.)
(*De Nat. D.*, I) A. S. Pease (U.S.A.), 1955
(*Paradoxa Stoicorum*) A. G. Lee, 1953
(*De Rp.*) G. H. Sabine and S. B. Smith (U.S.A.) 1929 (without text but with
  trans.); L. Ferrero (Florence) 1950; C. Appuhn (Paris), 1935 (w. *De Legibus*)
(*De Sen.*) L. Huxley, ed. 2, 1925
(*Tusc. Disp.*) T. W. Dougan and R. M. Henry, 1905–34
(*Tusc. D.* i, ii) M. Pohlenz (Leipzig), 1912 (Germ. C.)
T. Tr., Most of Cicero's works are by now covered by the Budé and Loeb
  collections
Tr. (Select Speeches: *Catil., Mur., Mil., Phil. II*) H.E.D. Blakiston, 1894
(*Academica*) J. S. Reid, 1885
(*Brutus, N.D., Div., Off.*) H. M. Poteat (U.S.A.), 1950
(*De Nat. Deorum*) F. Brooks, 1896
(*De Off.*) G. B. Gardiner, 1899
(Sel. Letters) L. P. Wilkinson: Cicero's Letters: a new Selection in Trans-
  lation, 1949
Conc. (to letters) W. A. Oldfather, H. V. Canter, K. M. Abbott: Index Ver-
  borum Cic. Epp. (U.S.A.), 1938
Lexica, H. Merguet: (speeches) 4 vols., 1877–84; (philos. wks.) 3 vols.,
  1887–94; (Handlexicon zu Cicero) 1905
O.W., W. Allen, A Survey of selected Ciceronian Bibliography, 1939–1953
  (*Cl. Wkly.*, 1953–4, pp. 129–39)
W. Ax, Cicero Mensch u. Politiker, 1953
F. Arnaldi, Cicerone, ed. 2, 1948
J. W. H. Atkins, Lit. Criticism in Antiquity, vol. II 1934 (rp. 1952),
H. Bornecque, *Les Catilinaires* de C., 1938
H. D. Broadhead, Latin Prose Rhythm, 1928
M. van d. Bruwaene, La théologie de C., 1938
C.A.H., ix (1932), chs. 11–12 and 15–19: x (1934), ch. 1
J. Carcopino, Les secrets de la corresp. de C., 1947 (Eng. tr. by E. O. Lorimer,
  1951)
E. Castorina, L'Atticismo nell' evoluzione del pensiero di C., 1952
I. Cazzaniga, Il *Brutus* di C., 1947
E. Ciaceri, C. ed i suoi tempi, 1926–30
E. Costa, Cicerone giureconsulto, 1927

J. F. D'Alton, Roman Literary Theory and Criticism, 1931
H. Eulenberg, Cicero Redner Denker Staatsmann, 1949
H. Frisch, C's. Fight for the Republic (Copenhagen), 1946
G. Galbiati, De fontibus Ciceronis librorum de r.p. et de legg. quaestiones, 1916
M. Gelzer and others, in P.W., s.v. Tullius, 29
H. J. Haskell, This was Cicero: Mod. Politics in a Roman Toga (U.S.A.), 1942
A. Haury, L'ironie et l'humour chez C. (Leiden), 1954
R. Hirzel, Untersuchungen zu Cs. philos. Schriften, 1877–83
J. Humbert, Les plaidoyers écrits et les plaidoiries réelles de C., 1925
H. A. K. Hunt, The Humanism of Cicéro (Melbourne), 1954
J. Klass, C. und Caesar, 1939
L. Labowsky, Die Ethik des Panaitios, 1934
L. Laurand, Cicéron: (vie et œuvres, etc.), ed. 2, 1935
L. Laurand, Cicéron: vol. complémentaire (questions diverses, bibliographie, tables détaillées), ed. 2, 1938
L. Laurand, Études sur le style des discours de C., ed. 3 and 4, 1931–8
L. Laurand, Cicéron est intéressant, 1937
J. Lebreton, Études sur la langue et la grammaire de C., 1901
J. Lengle, Röm. Strafrecht bei. C. u. d. Historikern, 1934
E. Lepore, Il princeps Ciceroniano e gli ideali politici della tarda repub., 1954
M. D. Liscu, Étude sur la langue de la phil. morale chez C., 1930
M. Maffii, C. ed il suo dramma politico, 1933
P. Parzinger, Beiträge zur Kenntnis der Entwickelung des Ciceronischen Stils, 1910
T. Petersson, Cicero: A Biography (U.S.A.), 1920
O. Plasberg, C. in s. Werken u. Briefen, ed. by W. Ax, 1926
M. Pohlenz, Antikes Führertum: C. de Officiis u. d. Lebensideal d. Panaitios, 1934
R. Poncelet, Cicéron traducteur de Platon: L'expression de la pensée complexe en latin classique (Paris), 1957
V. Pöschl, Röm. Staat u. griech. Staatsdenken bei C.: Untersg. z. Cs. Schrift de R.P., 1936
M. Rambaud, Cicéron et l'histoire rom., 1953
G. C. Richards, Cicero, 1935
G. Righi and A. Lanza, Il pensiero di C., 1947
B. Riposati, Studi sui Topica di C., 1947
J. C. Rolfe, Cicero and his Influence (U.S.A.), 1923
V. Salmon, La culture supérieure à Rome d'après C. (Brussels), 1950
M. Schäfer, Ein frühmittelstoisches System d. Ethik bei C., 1934
O. E. Schmidt, Der Briefwechsel d. C. v. s. Prokonsulat in Cilicien bis zu Caesars Ermordung, 1893
O. Seel, Cicero. Wort, Staat, Welt, 1953
E. G. Sihler, Cicero of Arpinum (U.S.A.), 1914
S. E. Smethurst, C.'s Rhet. and Philos. Works: A Bibliographical Survey (1939–1956), Cl. World, LI (1957–8), pp. 1–4, 24, 32–41
E. E. Sprott, C.'s Theory of Prose Style (Philol. Quarterly (Iowa), 1955, pp. 1–17)
J. L. Strachan-Davidson, Cicero and the Fall of the Roman Republic, ed. 2, 1925
W. Suess, Die dramat. Kunst in den philos. Dialogen Cs. (Hermes, 1952, pp. 419 ff.)
M. Valente, L'éthique stoicienne chez C., 1957
G. della Valle, op. cit. re p. 202: Lucretius
J. Vogt, Ciceros Glaube an Rom, 1935

F. Wiesthaler, Die Orat. obl. als künstlerliches Stilsmittel in den Reden
Ciceros (Innsbruck), 1956
R. N. Wilkin, Eternal Lawyer: A legal biography of C. (U.S.A.), 1947
Th. Zielinski, C. im Wandel d. Jahrhunderte, ed. 4, 1929
Th. Zielinski, Das Clauselgesetz in Cs. Reden, 1904
Th. Zielinski, Der constructive Rhythmus in Cs. Reden, 1914

269. CICERO'S POETRY   255 n. 1 and 269 n. 3

T., A. Traglia, 2 vols. (Rome), 1950-2
(exc. *Aratea*), F.P.L.
(*Aratea*) E. Baehrens P.L.M., 1879-83, vol. I
T.C., W. W. Ewbank, Poems of Cicero, 1933
T.C. Tr. (*Aratea*), V. Buescu (Paris), 1941
Index verborum, J. W. Spaeth (U.S.A.), 1955
O.W., M. Guendel, De Ciceronis poetae arte (Leipzig), 1907
E. Koch, Ciceronis carmina historica restituta atque enarrata, 1922
E. Malcovati, Cicerone e la poesia, 1943
A. Traglia, La lingua di C. poeta, 1950
B.L.L., § 282-5

288. HORTENSIUS

O.R.F., iii.   H.R.R., ii.   S.H., § 136-7
L. Illuminati, L'eloquenza romana prima di Cicerone, vol. II, 1948

289. ORATORS OF CICERO'S DAY   289 n. 5

O.R.F., iii.   S.H., § 136-9
Cicero, *Brutus*
G. Curcio, De Ciceronis et Calvi reliquorumque atticorum arte dicendi quaestiones, 1899
F. Plessis, Calvus: étude biogr. et litt. (combined with J. Poirot, Le polémique de Cicéron et des Attiques, 1896)

Chapter V

291. CAESAR   291 n. 1

T., A. Klotz (Teub.); *B.G.*, ed. 4, 1952; *B.C.*, ed. 2, 1950; *B. Alex.*, etc., 1927. (orat. fragm.), O.R.F., iii
T.C. (*B.G.*) C. F. Kraner and W. Dittenberger, ed. 17 by H. Meusel, 1913-20
T. Rice Holmes, 1914
H. van Looy (Antwerp), 1952
(*B.C.*) C. F. Kraner and F. Hofmann, ed. 11 by H. Meusel, 1906
(*B.C.* I.) A. G. Peskett, 1896
T.C. Tr. (*B.G.*), M. Rat (Paris), 1955
C. (*B. Hisp.*), A. Klotz, 1927
T. Tr. (*B.G.*), H. J. Edwards (Loeb), 1917; L. A. Constans (Budé), ed. 4, 1947
(*B.C.*), A. G. Peskett (Loeb), 1928; P. Fabre (Budé), ed. 3, 1947
(*B. Afr.*), A. Bouvet (Budé), 1949
(*B. Al.*), J. Andrieu (Budé), 1953
(*Bb. Al. Afr. Hisp.*), A. G. Way (Loeb), 1955
Tr. (*B.G.*), T. Rice Holmes, 1908; F. P. Long, 1911; F. Arnaldi, 1939 (w. comm.); E. T. Burdock (U.S.A.), 1940
Lexicon, H. Merguet (Jena), 1884 f.
O.W., F. E. Adcock, Caesar as a Man of Letters, 1956
K. Barwick, Caesars *B. Civ.* (Tendenz, Abfassungszeit u. Stil), 1951

K. Barwick, Cs. Comm. u.d. Corpus Caesarianum (*Philologus*, Suppl. xxxi, 2 (1938))

F. Beckmann, Geographie u. Ethnogr. in Cs. *B.G.*, 1930

J. H. Collins, Propaganda, Ethics and Psychol. Assumptions in C.'s Writings (diss.) (Frankfurt-a.-M.), 1952

P. Huber, Die Glaubwürdigkeit Caesars i.s. Bericht über d. gallischen Krieg, ed. 2, 1931

E. C. Kennedy, Roman Poetry and Prose. Caesar, Virgil, Livy, Ovid, 1956

M. L. W. Laistner, The Greater Roman Historians (U.S.A.), 1947

E. Longi, Giulio Cesare scrittore: la guerra gallica, 1939

O. Matthies, Entstehungzeit u. Abfassungsart von Cs. *B.G.*, 1955

D. Nisard, Les quatre grands historiens latins, 1874

H. Oppermann, Caesar d. Schriftsteller u.s. Werk, 1933

A. la Penna, Tendenze e arte del *B.G.* di C. (*Maia*, 1952, pp. 191 ff.)

M. Rambaud, L'art de la déformation historique dans les Comm. de C., 1953

C. E. Stevens, The *B.G.* as a work of propaganda (*Latomus*, 1952, pp. 3–18 and 165–79)

On the continuators see S.H., § 121; K. Barwick, *op. cit.* (Cs. Comm., etc.), and O. Seel, Hirtius: Untersgn. über ps.–Caesar. *Bella* u.d. Balbusbrief, 1935

On Caesar's life and times, see bibl. in O.C.D., s.v. *Caesar*

302. SALLUST 303 n. 1

T. (*Cat.* and *Iug.*) A. W. Ahlberg (*collectio Upsaliensis*), 1911–15 (w. parallel passages fr. other authors)

(*Cat. Iug.* and *Hist.* frag.) A. W. Ahlberg (Teub.), 1919 (ed. maior); 1932 (ed. min.); ed. 3, by A. Kurfess (Teub.), 1957

(*Epist. ad Caes.*) A. Kurfess (Teub.), ed. 4, 1955

(*Invect.*) A. Kurfess (Teub.), ed. 3, 1957

T.C. (*Cat.* and *Iug.*) R. Jacobs, ed. 11 by H. Wirz and A. Kurfess, 1922 (Germ. C.)

E. Malcovati (*Cat.*) ed. 3, 1956; (*Iug.*) ed. 3, 1956 (Ital. C.)

(*Hist.* – new fragments) John Rylands Papyrus, 473 (ed. C. H. Roberts, 1938)

(*Epist. ad Caes.* and *Invect.*) D. Romano, Palermo, 1948

T.C. Tr. (Ital.), V. Paladini (*Epp. ad Caes.*), 1952; (*Oratt. et Epp. ex Hist. excerptae*), 1956

T. Tr., J. C. Rolfe (Loeb), 1920 (without *Epp. ad C.* and *Invect.*)

A. Ernout (Budé), 1941

(Germ.), W. Schoene and W. Eisenhut, 1950; (Ital.) G. Lipparini, 1955

O.W., A. W. Ahlberg, Proleg. in Sallustium, 1911

E. Bolaffi, Le style et la langue de S. (*Phoibos*, 1952–3, pp. 57–96)

K. Buechner, Der Aufbau von Sallusts B. *Iug.*, 1954

E. Cesareo, Sallustio, 1932

L. S. Fighiera, La lingua e la grammatica di S., 1900

Funaioli in P.W., s.v. *Sallustius*, 10

M. L. W. Laistner, The Greater Roman Historians (U.S.A.), 1947

G. Lanzani, Sallustio, 1929

K. Latte, Sallust, 1935

A. D. Leeman, A Systematical Bibliog. of S. (1879–1950) (Leiden), 1952

D. Nisard, Les quatre grands historiens latins, 1874

L. Olivieri Sangiacomo, Sallustio, 1954

V. Paladini, Sallustio, 1948

V. Paladini, Le epistulae ad Caesarem. Prolegomena I (L'autore, l'uomo, il politico) (Bari), 1956

P. Perrochat, S. et Thucydide (*Rev. des études lat.*, 1947, pp. 90–121)

SUPPLEMENTARY BIBLIOGRAPHY 509

P. Perrochat, Les modèles grecs de S. (*Coll. Ét. lat.*, Sér. scientif., xxiii, Paris), 1949

V. Pöschl, Grundwerte röm. Staatsgesinnung in d. Geschichtswerken des S., 1940

W. Schur, Sallust als Historiker, 1934

O. Seel, Sallust v. d. Briefen ad Caes. zur Coniur. Cat., 1930

E. Skard, Ennius und Sallustius, 1933

E. Skard, S. u. s. Vorgänger: Eine sprachliche Untersuchung (*Symb. Osl.* fasc. suppl. xv, 1956)

R. Ullmann, La technique des discours dans S., Tite-Live et Tacite (Oslo), 1927

K. Vretska, Studien zu Sallusts B. Iug. (*Sitzb. Akad. Wiss. Wien*, ccxxix, 4, 1955)

R. Zimmermann, Der Sallusttext in Altertum, 1929

309. NEPOS   309 n. 4

T., H. Malcovati, 1934

T.C., K. Nipperdey, ed. 11 by K. Witte, 1913
(six biogr. only) L. Voit (Munich), 1949

T. Tr., A. M. Guillemin (Budé), 1923

J. C. Rolfe (Loeb) 1929 (w. Florus by E. S. Forster)

O.W., F. Leo, Griech.–Röm. Biographie, 1901 (ch. 10)

A. Levi, La grammatica di C. N. (*Studi Ital. di Filol. Class.*, 1915, pp. 338–466)

B. Lupus, Der Sprachgebrauch d. C. N., 1876

D. R. Stuart, Epochs of Greek and Roman Biography (U.S.A.), 1928

312. LABERIUS   314 n. 2

W. Kroll in P.W., s.v. *Laberius* 3

G. Malagoli, Cavaliere e mimo (*Atene e Roma*, 1905, pp. 188–197)

314. PUBLILIUS SYRUS   314 n. 7

T. Tr. (*Sententiae*), J. W. and A. M. Duff, Minor Latin Poets (Loeb), ed. 2, 1935

PART III: THE AUGUSTAN PERIOD

Chapter I

317. IMPERIAL PATRONAGE

H. Bardon, Les empereurs et les lettres latines, 1940 (for Augustus, chs. 1 and 2)

C. O. Reure, Les gens de lettres et leurs protecteurs à Rome, 1891

D. M. Schullian, External Stimuli to Lit. Production in Rome, 90–27 B.C. (U.S.A.), 1932

S.H., § 208–11. See also *infra*, re p. 446

318. VIRGIL   318 n. 1

Ancient Commentaries and Biographies:

Ti. Claudius Donatus: *Interpretationes Vergilianae*, H. Georgii (Teub.), 1905–6

Servius: *In V. carmina commentarii*, G. Thilo and H. Hagen (Teub.), 1881–1902 (rp. 1922–7) – Includes the appendix Serviana

Servius: E. K. Rand and others (Harvard edition), 5 vols.; only vol. II (on *Aen.*, i and ii) as yet published, 1946
N. Marinone, Elio Donato, Macrobio e Servio, commentatori di V., 1946
A. Santoro, Esegeti virgiliani antichi (Donato, Macrobio, Servio), 1946
Vitae Vergilianae, J. Brummer (Teub.), 1933
Vitae Verg. antiquae (suppl. in reissue by C. Hardie of R. Ellis's *App. Verg.*, O.C.T., 1954)

T., G. Janell (Teub.), ed. 2, 1930; R. Sabbadini, 1930
(*Ecl.*) C. Hosius (Bonn), 1915 (cum auctoribus et imitatoribus)
T.C., A. Forbiger, ed. 4, 1872–5 (Lat. C.)
  T. E. Page, 1894–1900; A. Sidgwick, 1890
(*Aeneid*) J. W. Mackail, 1930
(*do.* sep. bks.) i, R. S. Conway, 1935; A. Salvatore, 1947
  iv, C. Buscaroli (w. Ital. tr.), 1932; A. S. Pease (U.S.A.), 1935; E. Paratore, 1947; R. G. Austin, 1955
  vi, H. E. Butler, 1920; E. Norden, ed. 3, 1926 (w. Germ. verse tr.), rep. 1957
  xii W. S. Maguiness, 1953
(*Ecl.*) F. Della Corte, 1939
  O. Tescari (w. Ital. tr.), 1947
(*G.* i and ii) E. Paratore (Milan), ed. 3, 1952
T. Tr., H. R. Fairclough (Loeb), vol. I, 1916; vol. II, ed. 2, 1934
(*Ecl.*) E. de Saint Denis (Budé), ed. 2, 1949
F. Giancotti (Rome), 1952 (Ital. tr.)
(*Georg.*) H. Goelzer (Budé), ed. 5, 1947; E. de Saint Denis (Budé), 1956
(*Aen.*) H. Goelzer and A. Bellessort (Budé), ed. 6, 1948
Tr., J. Jackson, ed. 2, 1930
(*Ecl.*) E. V. Rieu, Virgil: the Pastoral Poems (Penguin), 1949
(*Ecl. and Georg.* – Verse) R. C. Trevelyan, 1944
(*Georg.*) L. A. S. Jermyn, The Singing Farmer, 1947
C. D. Lewis (U.S.A.), ed. 6, 1948
S. P. Bovie (Chicago and London), 1957
(*Aen.*) C. J. Billson, ed. 2, 1923
J. W. Mackail, rp. 1953
C. D. Lewis (U.S.A.), 1956
W. F. J. Knight (Penguin), 1956
Index, M. N. Wetmore, ed. 2, 1930
Lexicon, H. Merguet (Leipzig), 1912
O.W., G. d'Anna, Il problema della composizione dell' *Eneide*, 1957
F. Arnaldi, Studi Virgiliani, 1948
C. Bailey, Religion in V., 1935
A. Bellessort, Virgile, son œuvre et son temps, ed. 2, 1949
R. Billiard, L'agriculture dans l'antiq. d'après les *Geo.* de V., 1928
H. Boas, Aeneas's arrival in Latium (Amst.), 1933
F. Boemer, Vergil und Augustus (*Gymnasium*, lviii, 1951, pp. 26 ff.)
C. M. Bowra, From V. to Milton, 1945
P. Boyancé, Le sens cosmique de V. (*Rev. Ét. Lat.*, 1954, pp. 220 ff.)
K. Buechner and E. Mehl in P.W., s.v. *Vergilius*, 7
J. Carcopino, V. et les origines d'Ostie, 1919
J. Carcopino, V. et le mystère de la IVe églogue, 1930
A. Cartault, L'art de V. dans l'Énéide, 1926
D. Comparetti, V. nel medio evo (rp. a cura di G. Pasquali of 1937 and 1941 ed.) (Florence), 1955
L. A. Constans, L'Énéide de V., 1938
A. Cordier, Études sur le vocab. épique dans l'Énéide, 1939

SUPPLEMENTARY BIBLIOGRAPHY 511

A. Cordier, L'allitération latine: le procédé dans l'Énéide, 1939
M. M. Crump, The Growth of the Aeneid, 1920
M. M. Crump, The Epyllion fr. Theocritus to Ovid, 1931 (ch. 9)
R. W. Cruttwell, V.'s Mind at Work, 1946
P. J. Enk, La tragédie de Didon (*Latomus*, 1957, pp. 628 ff.)
J. B. Evenhuis, De V. *ecl.* sexta commentatio (Groningen), 1955
T. Fiore, La poesia di V., 1930
W. Warde Fowler, V.'s Gathering of the Clans, ed. 2, 1918
W. Warde Fowler, Aeneas at the Site of Rome, ed. 2, 1918
W. Warde Fowler, The Death of Turnus, 1919
T. Frank, Vergil: A Biography, 1927
A. M. Guillemin, L'originalité de V., 1931
A. M. Guillemin, V. poète, artiste et penseur, 1951
T. J. Haarhoff, V. the Universal, 1949
R. Heinze, Virgils epische Technik, ed. 3, 1915 (rep. 1928 and 1957)
J. Hubaux, Le réalisme dans les Bucol. de V., 1927
M. Hügi, Vs. *Aeneis* u.d. hellenistische Dichtung (Bern), 1952
E. C. Kennedy, *op. cit. re* p. 291, Caesar
H. Klepl, Lukrez u. V. in ihren Lehrgedichten, 1940
W. F. J. Knight, Vergil's Troy (Essays on *Aen.* ii), 1932
W. F. J. Knight, Roman Vergil, 1944
W. Kuehn, Ruestungsszenen bei Homer u. V. (*Gymnasium*, 1957, pp. 28 ff.)
F. J. H. Letters, Virgil, 1946 (popular)
G. Lipparini, Virgilio: l'uomo, l'opera, i tempi, 1930
J. W. Mackail, V. and his Meaning to the World of To-day, 1923
G. Mambelli, Gli studi virgiliani nel secolo xx, 1940
J. B. Mayor, R. S. Conway, W. W. Fowler, V.'s Messianic Eclogue, 1907
F. Mehmel, V. and Apollonius Rhodius, 1940
C. W. Mendell, The Influence of the Epyllion on the Aeneid (*Yale Cl. St.*, xii, 1951, pp. 203 ff.)
G. Monaco, Il libro dei ludi (*Aen.* v) (Palermo), 1957
B. Nardi, The Youth of V. (tr. fr. Ital. by B. P. Rand, U.S.A., 1930)
E. Norden, Ennius und V., 1915
E. Norden, Orpheus u. Eurydice (Berlin), 1934
E. Paratore, Introd. alle Georgiche, 1938; Virgilio, ed. 2, 1954
F. Peeters, A Bibliography of Virgil (U.S.A.), 1933
J. Perret, V. l'homme et l'œuvre, 1952
V. Pöschl, Die Dichtkunst Virgils (Vienna), 1950
G. Radke, Fachbericht über Vergil (*Gymnasium*, 1957, pp. 101–92)
E. K. Rand, The Magical Art of V. (U.S.A.), 1931
P. Richard, Virgile auteur gai, 1951
H. J. Rose, The Eclogues of V. (U.S.A.), 1942
T. F. Royds, Beasts, Birds and Bees of V., ed. 3, 1930
J. Sargeaunt, Trees, Shrubs and Plants of V., 1920
C. Saunders, V.'s Primitive Italy, 1930
F. Skutsch, Aus Vs. Frühzeit, 1901; Gallus und V., 1906
J. Sparrow, Half-lines and Repetitions in V., 1931
T. W. Stadler, Vs. Aeneis: eine poetische Betrachtung (Einsiedeln), 194
B. Tilly, V.'s Latium, 1947
E. Turolla, La poesia delle Georgiche e la sua evoluzione, 1955
J. H. Whitfield, Dante and Virgil, 1949

Chapter II

353. MINOR POEMS ATTRIBUTED TO VIRGIL (*Appendix Vergiliana*)
    353 n. 1; 355 n. 4

T., F. Vollmer, P.L.M. (Teub.), Vol. I, 1927
  (without *Aetna*) R. Ellis, O.C.T., 1907, reissued with *Vitae Verg. antiquae* by
    C. Hardie, O.C.T., 1954
  (*Ciris* and *Culex*) A. Salvatore (Paravia), 1957
T.C. (*Catalepton*) Th. Birt, Jugendverse und Heimatpoesie Vergils, 1910; E.
    Galletier, 1920; R. E. H. Westendorp Boerma, vol. i, covering *Cat.* i–viii
    (Groningen), 1949
  (*Ciris*) M. Lenchantin de Gubernatis (Turin), 1930; R. Helm, 1937; H.
    Hielkema (w. Dutch trans.), 1941
  (*Culex*) C. Plésent, 1910
  (*Dirae*) C. van der Graaf (w. trans.; comm. and tr. in Engl.) (Leiden), 1945
  (*Maec.*) M. C. Miller (U.S.A.), 1941 (w. trans.)
T. Tr. (without *Aetna* and *Maec.*), H. R. Fairclough, Virgil (Loeb) vol. II.
    ed. 2, 1934
  (*Aetna* and *Maec.*) in J. W. and A. M. Duff, Minor Latin Poets (Loeb) ed. 2,
    1935
  (*Aetna*) J. Vessereau (Budé) 1923
O.W., K. Buechner in P.W., s.v. *Vergilius* 7 (Section on 'Jugendwerke', cols.
    1061–1180)
A. Rostagni, Virgilio minore, 1933
  (*Aetna*) J. H. Waszink, De Aetnae carminis auctore (*Mnemosyne*, 1949, pp.
    224 ff.)
  (*Catalepton*) R. S. Radford, The Language of the Pseudo-Vergilian Catalep-
    ton, w. spec. ref. to its Ovidian characteristics (*Transact. Amer. Philol.
    Assoc.*, 1923, pp. 168–86)
  (*Ciris*) M. M. Crump, Epyllion fr. Theocritus to Ovid, 1931 (ch. 8)
A. Haury, La Ciris poème attrib. à V. (Bordeaux), 1957
R. Helm, Ein Epilog zur Cirisfrage (*Hermes*, 1937, pp. 78 ff.)
F. Munari, Studi sulla Ciris (*Atti Accad. d. Italia, Memorie, Cl. di Sc. morali e
    stor.* VII, 4, 9, Florence, 1944)
F. Skutsch, Aus Vs. Frühzeit, 1901; Gallus und Vergil, 1906
  (*Culex*) M. M. Crump, op. cit., ch. 7
D. L. Drew, Culex, 1925
R. Helm, Beiträge zum Culex (*Hermes*, 1953, pp. 49 ff.)
W. Holtschmidt, De Culicis sermone et tempore, 1913
S. E. Jackson, Authorship of Culex (*C.Q.*, 1911, pp. 163 ff.)
C. Plésent, Le Culex: étude sur l'alexandrinisme latin, 1910
F. Skutsch, Aus Vs. Frühzeit, 1901 (pp. 125–35)
  (*Dirae*) C. van der Graaf's edn. See *supra*
  (*Maec.*) Th. Copray, Consolatio ad Liviam, Elegiae in Maec., I (Nijmegen),
    1940
T. H. Schumacher, Elegiae in Maec.: Consol. ad Liviam: Stilkritische Unter-
    suchungen, etc., 1946
R. B. Steele, The Nux, Maec., and Consol. ad Liviam (U.S.A.), 1933
  (*Moretum*) W. Kroll in P.W., s.v. *Moretum*

Fuller bibl. in B.L.L., § 315–17

Chapter III

363. HORACE 363 n. 1

T., E. C. Wickham, rev. H. W. Garrod (O.C.T.), ed. 2, 1912
O. Keller and A. Holder, ed. 2, 1899–1925
F. Vollmer (Teub.), ed. maior 2, 1912; ed. minor 5, 1931
F. Klingner (Teub.), ed. 2, 1950
(*Od.* and *Epod.*) M. Lenchantin de Gubernatis (Paravia), 1945
T.C., A. Kiessling, rev. R. Heinze, 3 vols., edd. 8, 6, 5, 1955–7
I. Bond, rev. A. Rostagni, Turin, 1948
(*Od.* and *Epod.*) F. Plessis, 1924; O. Tescari, 1936; A. Y. Campbell, ed. 2, 1953
(*Epodes*) C. Giarratano, 1930
(*Sat.*) P. Lejay, 1911 (masterly introd.)
(*Epist.* I) O. A. W. Dilke (London), 1954
(*A.P.*) A. Rostagni, 1930
T.C. Tr. (*Od.* and *Epodes*) M. L. de Gubernatis and D. Bo (Ital. C. and Tr.), 1950
(*A.P.*) L. Herrmann (Brussels), 1951 (Fr. C. and Tr.)
C. (*A.P.*), O. Immisch, 1932
T. Tr., F. Villeneuve (Budé), 1927–34
(*Od.* and *Epod.*) C. E. Bennett (Loeb), 1914
(*Sat. Ep. A.P.*) H. R. Fairclough (Loeb), 1926
Tr., E. C. Wickham, H. for English Readers, 1903
U. Moricca, 1941 (Ital. verse)
(*Od.*) W. S. Marris, 1912 (verse); H. Macnaghten, 1926 (verse)
A. S. Way, 1936 (verse); Sir E. Marsh, 1941 (verse)
(*Sat.*) H. H. Chamberlin, 'Horace talks' (U.S.A.), 1940
Conc., L. Cooper, A Concordance of the Works of Horace (U.S.A.), 1916
O.W., V. Andersen, Horaz (Vol. i, Antiken; Vol. II, fra Middelalder til Nytid) (Copenhagen), 1939–40
W. S. Anderson, Recent Work in Roman Satire, 1937–1955 (*Cl. Wkly.*, 1956–7, pp. 33–40)
J. W. H. Atkins, Lit. Criticism in Antiquity, ii, 1934 (rp. 1952), pp. 47–104
N. A. Bonavia-Hunt, Horace the Minstrel, 1954
P. Boyancé, Grandeur d'Horace (*Bull. Assoc. Budé*, 1955, 4, pp. 48–64)
A. Y. Campbell, Horace: A New Interpretation, 1924
V. Capocci, Difesa di Orazio, 1951
F. Cupaiuolo, L'epistola di Orazio ai Pisoni, 1941
J. F. D'Alton, H. and his Age, 1917
J. F. D'Alton, Roman Literary Theory and Criticism, 1931
H. Drexler, Horaz: Lebenswirklichkeit u. ethische Theorie, 1953
J. W. Duff, Roman Satire (U.S.A.), 1936 (ch. 4)
E. Fraenkel, Horace (Oxford), 1957
T. Frank, Catullus and H.: Two Poets in their Environment (U.S.A.), 1928
R. J. Getty, Recent Work on Horace, 1945–1957 (*Class. World*, March 1959, pp. 167 ff.)
H. Hommel, Horaz, der Mensch u. d. Werk, 1950
F. Klingner, Horazens Brief an d. Pisonen, 1937
U. Knoche, *op. cit. re* p. 60, *Satura*
U. Mancuso, Orazio poeta civile. Dalle odi romane alle ode cesaree, 1953
A. Noyes, Horace, a Portrait (U.S.A.), 1947; Portrait of Horace, 1947
C. Pascal, La critica dei poeti romani in Orazio, 1920
G. Pasquali, Orazio lirico, 1920
G. Pavano, Introd. all' A. P. di Orazio, 1944
E. K. Rand, H. and the Spirit of Comedy (U.S.A.), 1937

S

A. Rostagni, Orazio, 1937
H. D. Sedgwick, Horace: a Biography (U.S.A.), 1947
N. Terzaghi, Per la storia della satira, 1944
W. Wili, H. u. d. augusteische Kultur (Basle), 1948
L. P. Wilkinson, H. and his Lyric Poetry, 1945; ed. 2, 1951
Th. Zielinski, H. et la société romaine du temps d'Auguste, 1938

Chapter IV

400. EARLY LATIN ELEGY
See *re* p. 178, Post-Ennian Minor Poetry

402. CORNELIUS GALLUS
W. Morel, F.P.L. S.H., § 270–2
L. Alfonsi, L'elegia di Gallo (*Riv. fil.*, 1944, pp. 46 ff.)
H. Bardon, Les élégies de Cornelius Gallus (*Latomus*, 1949, pp. 217 ff.)
E. Bréguet, Les élégies de G. d'après la X*e*. bucolique de Virgile (*Rev. des études lat.*, 1948, pp. 204–14)
F. Skutsch, Aus Vergils Frühzeit, 1901; Gallus und Vergil, 1906
B.L.L., § 342

403. TIBULLUS   403 n. 1
T., J. P. Postgate (O.C.T.), ed. 2, 1914; F. W. Lenz (Teub.), 1937
T.C., K. F. Smith (U.S.A.), 1913 (Comm. confined to I, II and IV, ii–xiv)
E. Cesareo, 1938
(Sel.) J. P. Postgate, ed. 2, 1910
T.C. Tr., O. Tescari (Ital. C. and Tr.), 1951
(III, 1–6) H. de la Ville de Mirmont, 'Le poète Lygdamus', 1904 (w. crit. study)
T. Tr., J. P. Postgate (Loeb), 1913 (w. Catullus by F. W. Cornish and *Pervig. Ven.* by J. W. Mackail)
M. Ponchont (Budé), ed. 3, 1950
(IV, ii–xii) E. Bréguet, 'Le roman de Sulpicia,' Geneva, 1946 (w. crit. study)
O.W., L. Alfonsi, Albio T. e gli autori del Corp. Tib., 1946; new ed. 1956
L. Alfonsi, Sulla datazione del Paneg. di Mess. (*Epigraphica*, 1946, pp. 3–10)
E. Burck, Röm. Wesenzüge der augusteischen Liebeselegie (*Hermes*, 1952, pp. 163 ff.)
A. Cartault, A propos du Corp. Tib., 1906
A. Cartault, T. et les auteurs du Corp. Tib., 1909
A. Cartault, Le distique élégiaque chez T., Sulpicia, Lygdamus, 1911
S. Ehrengruber, De carmine paneg. Mess. pseudo-Tibulliano, 1889–99
J. Hammer, Proleg. to an Edition of the Paneg. Mess. (U.S.A.), 1925
R. Hanslik, Der Dichterkreis des Messala (*Anz. Akad. Wiss. Wien*, lxxxix, 1952, pp. 22–38)
L. Pepe, Tibullo minore, 1948
M. Platnauer, Latin Elegiac Verse: A study of the metrical usages of Tib., Propertius and Ovid, 1951
B. Riposati, Introd. allo studio di T., 1945
N. Salanitro, Tibullo, 1938
A. Salvatore, Tecnica e motivi tibulliani nel Paneg. di Mess. (*La parola del passato*, 1948, no. 7, pp. 48–63)
M. Schuster, Tibull-studien, 1930
R. Verdière, L'auteur du *Paneg. Mess.* tibullien (*Latomus*, 1954, pp. 56–64)
K. Witte, Gesch. d. röm. Elegie: I, Tibullus, 1924

P. W. s.vv. *Albius, Lygdamus, Sulpicia*

410. PROPERTIUS   410 n. 1

T., J. S. Phillimore (O.C.T.), ed. 2, 1907; O. L. Richmond, 1928; C. Hosius
    (Teub.), ed. 3, 1932; E. A. Barber (O.C.T.), 1953; M. Schuster, ed. by
    F. Dornseiff (Teub.), 1954
T.C., M. Rothstein, ed. 2, 1920–4; H. E. Butler and E. A. Barber, 1933;
    (Bk. I) P. J. Enk (Leiden) 1946
T.C. Tr., S. J. Tremenheere, ed. 2, 1933; O. Tescari (Turin), 1956
T. Tr., H. E. Butler (Loeb), 1912; M. Paganelli (Budé), 1947 (rp.)
Tr., J. S. Phillimore (O.L.T.), 1906
    (Eng. Verse), E. H. W. Meyerstein, 1935
Index, J. S. Phillimore, 1906
O.W., L. Alfonsi, L'elegia di P., 1945
    D. R. Shackleton Bailey, Echoes of Propertius (*Mnem.*, 1952, pp. 307 ff.)
    D. R. Shackleton Bailey, Propertiana, 1956
    J. Benda, Properce ou les amants de Tibur, ed. 3, 1928
    E. Burck, *op. cit. re* p. 403, Tibullus
    A. Carbonetto, Properzio: saggio critico, 1936
    P. W. Damon and W. C. Helmbold, The Structure of P's Book ii (*Univ. Calif.
        Publ. in Cl. Philol.*, xiv, 6, 1952, pp. 215–54)
    P. J. Enk, Ad P. carmina commentarius criticus (Zutphen), 1911
    R. Helm in P.W. s.v. Propertius 2
    A. la Penna, P. e i poeti latini dell' età aurea (*Maia*, 1950, pp. 209 ff., and 1951,
        pp. 43 ff.)
    A. la Penna, Properzio: saggio critico seguito da due ricerche filol., 1951
    V. Mogni, Umorismo e mimo in P. (*Giorn. ital. filol.*, 1950, pp. 238–67)
    M. Platnauer, *op. cit.*, under Tibullus
    L. Ramaglia, P. e le elegie romane (*Riv. Stud. Class.*, Turin, ii, 1954, pp. 191 ff.)
    E. Reitzenstein, Wirklichkeitsbild u. Gefühlsentwickelung bei P., 1936

422. OVID   422 n. 1; 426 n. 2; 432 nn. 1, 2, 3, 7

T., R. Merkel, R. Ehwald, F. W. Lenz (Teub.), edd. 1 and 2, 1888–1932
    (*Fasti*) L. Castiglioni, ed. 2, by C. Landi (Paravia), 1950
    (*Metam.*) H. Magnus (Berlin), 1914
    (*Tristia, Ib., Ex P., Hal., Fragm.*) S. G. Owen (O.C.T.), 1915
    F. W. Lenz (Paravia) (*ex P.*), 1938; (*Ibis*), ed. 2, 1956; (*Hal., Fr., Nux, Cons.
        ad L.*), ed. 2, 1956
    (*Nux, Consol. ad Liviam* – pseudo-Ovidian) F. Vollmer, P.L.M. (Teub.), II,
        ii, 1923
T.C. (*Amores*) G. Némethy (Buda-Pest), 1907 (Lat. C.); suppl. 1922
    P. Brandt, 1911 (Germ. C.)
    (*Met.*) M. Haupt and O. Korn, rev. R. Ehwald, edd. 9 and 4, 1915–16 (Germ. C.)
    D. E. Bosselaar and B. A. Proosdig (Leiden), 1951 (Lat. C.)
    (*Met.* i) A. G. Lee, 1953 (Eng. C.)
    (*Rem. Am.*) G. Némethy (Buda-Pest), 1921
    (*Tristia*) S. G. Owen, sep. bks.: i, ed. 3, 1902; ii (w. trans.), 1924; iii, ed. 2,
        1893; T. J. de Jonge (Bk. iv) (Groningen), 1951 (Lat. C.); J. T. Bakker
        (Bk. v) (Groningen), 1946 (Lat. C.)
    (*Ex P.* i) A. Scholte (Groningen), 1933 (Lat. C.)
    (*Ibis*) A. la Penna, 1957 (Ital. C.)
    (Ps.-Ovid. *Cons. ad Liv.*) A. Witlox (Maestricht), 1934 (Lat. C.)
    (Ps.-Ovid. *Nux*) S. Wartena (Groningen), 1928 (Lat. C.)
T.C. Tr. (*Amores*) F. Munari (Florence), ed. 2, 1955
    (*Fasti*) Sir J. G. Frazer, 1929; F. Boemer (Heidelberg), 1957–8

C. (*Ex P.*) G. Némethy (Buda-Pest), 1915 (Lat. C.); suppl., 1922
    (*Tristia*) G. Némethy (Buda-Pest), 1913 (Lat. C.); suppl., 1922
T. Tr. (Loeb), G. Showerman, *Her.* and *Amores*, 1914
    J. H. Mozley, *A.A.*, *Rem. Am.*, *Ib.*, *Cons.*, *Nux*, 1929
    A. L. Wheeler, *Trist.*, *Ex Ponto*, 1924
    F. J. Miller, *Metam*, 1916
    Sir J. G. Frazer, *Fasti*, 1931
    (Budé) H. Bornecque, G. Lafaye, M. Prévost, 1924 ff.
    (*Ars Amat.*) B. P. Moore, 1935 (verse)
Tr. (*Met.*) A. E. Watts (w. etchings of P. Picasso) (U.S.A. and London), 1955
    M. M. Innes (Penguin), 1955
Conc., R. J. Deferrari, M. I. Barry, M. R. P. McGuire (U.S.A.), 1939
O.W., J. C. Arens, De Godenschildering in O.'s Metamorphosen (Nijmegen)
    1946
    E. Bickel, De Cons. ad Liv. pro Claudio . . . scripta (*Rh. M.*, 1950, pp. 193 ff.)
    W. Brewer, O.'s *Metam.* in European Culture, 1933
    E. Burck, *op. cit. re* p. 403, Tibullus
    Th. Copray, Consolatio ad Liviam, Elegiae in Maec., I (Nijmegen), 1940
    M. M. Crump, Epyllion fr. Theocritus to O., 1931, chs. 10–11
    H. Fraenkel, Ovid, a Poet between two Worlds (U.S.A.), 1945
    R. Heinze, Ovids elegische Erzählung, 1919
    E. C. Kennedy, *op. cit. re* p. 291, Caesar
    W. Kraus in P.W., s.v. *Ovidius* 3
    G. Lafaye, Les *Metam.* d'O. et leurs modèles grecs, 1904
    E. Martini, Einleitung zu O., 1933
    F. Peeters, Les *Fastes* d'Ovide (hist. du texte) (Brussels), 1939
    M. Platnauer, *op. cit.* under Tibullus
    E. K. Rand, O. and his Influence, 1925
    E. Ripert, Ovide, poète de l'amour, des dieux, et de l'exil, 1921
    T. H. Schumacher, Eleg. in Maec.: Consol. ad Liviam, 1946
    R. B. Steele, The Nux, Maec., and Consol. ad Liviam (U.S.A.), 1933
    W. Vollgraff, Nikander u. Ovid, I (Diss. Groningen), 1909
    L. P. Wilkinson, Ovid Recalled, 1955

Chapter V

446. POLLIO, MESSALLA AND MAECENAS   447 n. 1

O.R.F., iii.   H.R.R., ii.   F.P.L.   S.H., § 212–17
J. André, La vie et l'œuvre d'Asinius Pollion, 1949
R. Avallone, I frammenti di Mec., 1945
H. Bardon, Trois écrivains du temps d'Auguste (*Rev. Ét Lat.*, 1949, pp. 163 ff.)
    i.e., Maecenas, Aemilius Macer, Domitius Marsus
A. Dalzell, C. Asinius Pollio and the early hist. of public recitation at Rome
    (*Hermathena*, lxxxvi, 1955, pp. 20–28)
A. Dalzell, Maecenas and the Poets (*Phoenix*, X, 1956, pp. 151 ff.)
A. Fougnies, Mécène ministre d'Auguste protecteur des lettres (Brussels), 1947
R. Hanslik, *op. cit.* under Tibullus
P. Lunderstedt, De C. Maecenatis fragmentis, 1911
E. Pierce, A Roman Man of Letters: C. Asinius Pollio (U.S.A.), 1922
See also *re* p. 317, Imperial Patronage

447. VARIUS RUFUS   447 n. 2

F.P.L.   S.H., § 267.   Tfl., § 223.   B.L.L., § 344
E. Bickel, Varii carmen epicum . . . (*Symbolae Osloenses*, 1950, pp. 17 ff.)

448. AEMILIUS MACER

F.P.L. S.H., § 268. Tfl., § 223. B.L.L., § 383
H. Bardon, *op. cit. re* p. 446

448. MISCELLANEOUS AUGUSTAN POETS

F.P.L. S.H., § 273–7 and 315–20. Tfl., § 233, 241–4, 252, 254
H. Bardon, *op. cit. re* p. 446

450. PRIAPEA 450 n. 3

F. Vollmer, P.L.M. (Teub.) II. ii, 1923. S.H., § 319
C. Pascal, Carmina Ludicra Romanorum (Turin), 1931
R. S. Radford, The Priapea and the Vergilian Appendix (*Transact. Amer. Philol.*
    Assoc., 1921), pp. 148–77
R. F. Thomason, The Priapea and Ovid: A Study of the Language of the Poems
    (U.S.A.), 1931
B.L.L., § 319–20

450. GRATTIUS 450 n. 6

T., F. Vollmer, P.L.M. (Teub.), II. i, 1911; P. J. Enk (Zutphen), 1918 (w. Lat.
    comm.)
T. Tr., J. W. and A. M. Duff, Minor Lat. Poets (Loeb), ed. 2, 1935
O.W., P. J. Enk, De Grattio et Nemesiano, *Mnemos.*, 1917, pp. 56–68
    M. Fiegl, Des Gratt. Fal. *Cyneg.*, seine Vorgänger u.s. Nachfolger, 1890

450. MANILIUS 451 n. 1

T., J. van Wageningen (Teub.), 1915; A. E. Housman, ed. 2, 1937
C. (Lat.), J. van Wageningen (Amsterdam), 1921
T.C. Tr. (Bk. II), H. W. Garrod, 1911
O.W., G. Vallauri, Gli *Astr.* di M. e le fonti ermetiche (*Riv. Fil.*, 1954, pp. 133 ff.)
    J. van Wageningen in P.W., s.v. *Manilius* 6

Chapter VI

455. ORATORS (AUGUSTAN) 455 n. 1

Tfl., § 267; for T. Labienus, see also H. Peter, H.R.R., ii

456. SENECA THE ELDER 456 n. 3

T. Tr., H. Bornecque, ed. 2, 1932
T.C. Tr. (*Suasoriae*) W. A. Edward, 1928
O.W., S. F. Bonner, Roman Declamation in the late Republic and early Empire,
    1949
    J. W. Duff, Lit. Hist. of Rome in the Silver Age, 1927, pp. 42 ff. (bibl. p. 42,
    n. 1, is brought up to date in the new ed. 1960)

456. RHETORICIANS

Tfl., § 268. S.H., § 334–7. B.L.L., § 406–7
S. F. Bonner, *op. cit.* in preceding section

456. PHILOSOPHERS

Tfl., § 266. S.H., § 338–9

457. ANTISTIUS LABEO and ATEIUS CAPITO

Tfl., § 265. S.H., § 354. G.R.F., i
G. Baviera, Le due scuole dei giureconsulti romani, 1898

F. P. Bremer, Jurisprud. Antehadr. (Teub.), 1896–1901
A. Pernice, M. Antistius Labeo (Halle), vol. 1, 1873
B.L.L., § 412–3

457. HYGINUS
(Gramm. frag.) G.R.F., i
(Hist. frag.) H.R.R., ii
(Agric. frag.) R. Reitzenstein, De scriptorum rei rusticae libris deperditis,
1884, p. 53
S.H., § 347–50. Tfl., § 262. B.L.L., § 405

457. SINNIUS CAPITO and other GRAMMARIANS
G. Funaioli, G.R.F., i. S.H., § 341a and 351–3. Tfl., § 260, 263

458. VERRIUS FLACCUS 458 n. 3
(De Verb. Signif.) See W. M. Lindsay, Sex. Pompei Festi De Verborum Significatu quae supersunt cum Pauli epitome (Teub.), 1913
(other fragm.) G.R.F. I
S.H., § 340–1. Tfl., § 261. B.L.L., § 411

460. POMPEIUS TROGUS
See re p. 463

460. CLODIUS TUSCUS
S.H., § 353. Tfl., § 263

460. VITRUVIUS 460 n. 1
T., F. Krohn (Teub.), 1912
T.C. Tr., A. Choisy, 1909
T. Tr., F. Granger (Loeb), 1931–4
Tr., M. H. Morgan, 1914; E. Storzenacher (Germ.), 1938; C. Perrault (Fr.),
1945
O.W., H. Koch, Vom Nachleben Vitruvs, 1951
F. Pellati, Vitruvio, 1938
W. Sackur, Vitruv, Technik u. Literatur, 1925

462. HISTORIANS
H.R.R., ii. S.H., § 331. Tfl., § 255, 259

463. POMPEIUS TROGUS 463 n. 1
T., Justinus, Tr. Pomp. Hist. Phil. Epit., F. Rühl, rev. by O. Seel (Teub.), 1935
O.W., M. Rambaud, Salluste et Trogue-Pompée (Rev. des études lat., 1948,
pp. 171–89)
E. Schneider, De Trogi historiarum consilio et arte, 1913
S.H., § 328–30. Tfl., § 258

464. LIVY 464 n. 3
T., W. Weissenborn and M. Müller, rev. by W. Heraeus (Teub.), 1930–3
(includes periochae, fragm., index)
(i–x, xxi–xxx) R. S. Conway, C. F. Walters, S. K. Johnson (O.C.T.), 1914–35
T.C., W. Weissenborn, H. J. Müller, O. Rossbach, edd. 2–10, 1880–1924
T. Tr., B. O. Foster and others (Loeb – in progress), 1922–
J. Bayet and G. Baillet (Budé – in progress), 1940–

Tr., W. M. Roberts (Everyman), 1912–24
O.W., for sources see *infra, re* p. 468
W. Aly, Livius und Ennius, 1936
H. Bornecque, Tite-Live, 1933
E. Burck, Die Erzählungskunst d. T. Livius, 1934
E. Burck, Einführung in die dritte Dekade des L., 1950
F. Calderaro, Nuovi discorsi sulla prima deca di T.L.; Studio filosofico storico politico, 1952
G. M. Columba, etc., Studi Liviani, 1934
G. Còsta, Tito Livio, 1943
G. De Sanctis, La légende historique des prem. siècles de Rome (*J. des Savants*, 1909, pp. 126 ff. and pp. 205 ff.)
G. De Sanctis, Livio e la storia della storiografia romana (*Pegaso*, 1931, pp. 278 ff. – rp. in 'Problemi di storia antica,' 1932)
C. Giarratano, Tito Livio, 1937
K. Gries, Constancy in Livy's Latinity (U.S.A.), 1949
K. Gries, L.'s Use of Dramatic Speech (*A.J.P.*, 1949, pp. 118 ff.)
F. Hellmann, Livius-Interpretationen, 1939
E. C. Kennedy, *op. cit. re* p. 291, Caesar
A. Klotz in P.W., s.v. *Livius* 9
A. Klotz, Livius u. s. Vorgänger, 1940
A. Kolar, De orationum Liviano operi insertarum numerositate (*Mnem.*, 1953, pp. 116 ff.)
M. L. W. Laistner, The Greater Roman Historians (U.S.A.), 1947
A. Lambert, Die indirecte Rede als künstlerisches Stilmittel des L. (Zürich), 1946
M. A. Levi, Tito Livio e gli ideali augustei (*La parola del passato*, no. 10, 1949, pp. 15–28)
D. Nisard, Les quatre grands historiens latins, 1874
E. Pais, Storia di Roma, 1926–8 (for bks. i–x)
R. B. Steele, The Historical Attitude of L. (*A.J.P.*, 1904, pp. 15 ff.)
G. Stübler, Die Religiosität des L., 1941
R. Ullmann, La technique des discours dans Salluste, Tite-Live et Tacite (Oslo), 1927
R. Ullmann, Étude sur le style des discours de T.-L. (Oslo), 1929
P. G. Walsh, The Literary Techniques of Livy (*Rh. M.*, 1954, pp. 97 ff.)
P. G. Walsh, L.'s Preface and the Distortion of History (*A.J.P.*, 1955, pp. 369 ff.)
P. Zancan, Tito Livio: saggio storico (Milan), 1940

468. LIVY'S SOURCES   468 n. 1; 469 n. 1

A. Klotz, Livius u. s. Vorgänger, 1940
Detailed bibliography to 1939 in B.L.L., § 398 c

INDEX

The letter *n* after a number means a footnote on the page indicated. For the main subjects treated under leading authors, readers are referred to the summary prefixed to each chapter. The index includes modern authorities cited in the footnotes, where such names definitely represent a literary theory or a literary illustration.

Sévigné, Mme de, 278

Sextius junior 457

Sextius senior 457

Shakespeare, 17, 126, 129, 131, 132, 141-2, 151, 239, 297, 298n, 335, 445

Shelley, 229, 239

Sheridan, 297

Shuckburgh, E. S., 204n

Sibylline books, 43, 249, 405, 474

Sidonius Apollinaris, 429

Silentiarius, 422

Silenus, 184n, 310, 468, 469n

Silius Italicus, 100, 108, 113, 350, 351, 444, 482

Simonides, 233

Simulans, 161

Siro (Epicurean), 319, 321, 322

Sisenna (commentator), 185

Sisenna (historian), 84, 185, 304, 307, 308

Sisyphus (Atellan), 62

Sittl, K., 17, 20n, 21n

Situ Vrbium, De, 457

Skutsch, F., 100n, 145, 355

Solon, 64, 399

Soltau, W., 468n, 477n

Somnium Scipionis, 279, 280

Sonnenschein, E. A., 143n, 144n

Sophocles, 85, 92, 93, 104n, 148, 163, 164, 166, 169, 222, 271, 282, 389, 432, 444

Sosilus, 310

Sota, 107

Sotadean verse, 143

Sotades, 107

Spenser, Edmund, 218, 353n, 356, 445

Staberius Eros, 253

Stampini, E., 203n

Statius, Caecilius. *See* Caecilius

Statius, P. Papinius, 221, 350, 352, 359, 397, 422, 444, 445, 464

Stertinius, 457

Stesichorus, 380

Stichus, 117n, 120, 124, 133, 134, 135

Stoicism, 81-2, 83, 85-6, 190-1, 198, 200, 209, 215, 245n, 249, 253, 257, 258, 261, 267, 281, 284-7, 328, 334, 338, 362, 375, 379, 386, 387, 452, 457, 474

Strabo, 16, 252, 485

Strachan-Davidson, J. L., 266n

Strong, Eugenie, 30n

Suasoria, 423, 434

Sueius, 179

Suetonius, 59, 62, 80, 88, 100, 148, 149, 203, 252, 291n, 318, 359, 367, 403, 458

Sulla, 70, 75, 185-6, 198, 206n., 258, 293, 302, 307

Sulla, Pro, 263

Sulpicia, 199, 402, 405, 407, 449

Sulpicius Apollinaris, 120, 150

Sulpicius Blitho, 310

Sulpicius Galba, Ser., 188

Sulpicius Rufus, P., 190

Sulpicius Rufus, Ser. (jurist), 254, 277, 282

Sulpicius, Ser. (poet, possibly son or grandson of the jurist), 400, 448

Swift, 282n

Swinburne, 239

T

Tabernaria. See Fabula

Tabula Bantina (Oscan), 10, 15

Tacitus, 9, 10, 95, 271n, 423; his style, 28, 197, 300, 486; strictures on cranks, 66; opinion of Lucilius, 176; his greatness as a historian, 201; student of Sallust's style, 309; Virgil's influence on, 350; comparison with Livy, 480, 481; allusion to Livy, 482

Taine, 29, 53, 473

Tarentilla, 96

Tasso, 445

Telamo, 104

Telephus (Ennius), 104

Temporibus Meis, De, 270

Tennyson, 142n, 200n, 203, 215, 238

Terence, 8, 115, 121, 175, 271, 298, 308; his polish, 21, 73, 84, 85, 123, 147, 156-8; dress in his plays, 116; division into scenes, 143; career, 148-9; his plays, 148-59; chronology of his plays, 149-51; sources of, 151; compared with Plautus, 151, 154-6; his characters, 154-5, 252; homespun

Printed in Great Britain by
Lowe and Brydone (Printers) Limited, London, N.W.10